THE
CONSERVATIVE
SENSIBILITY

The Pursuit of Happiness and Other Sobering Thoughts

The Pursuit of Virtue and Other Tory Notions

Statecraft as Soulcraft: What Government Does

The Morning After: American Success and Excesses, 1981–1986

The New Season: A Spectator's Guide to the 1988 Election

Men at Work: The Craft of Baseball

Suddenly: The American Idea Abroad and at Home

Restoration: Congress, Term Limits and the Recovery of Deliberative Democracy

The Leveling Wind: Politics, the Culture and Other News, 1990–1994

The Woven Figure: Conservatism and America's Fabric: 1994–1997

Bunts: Curt Flood, Camden Yards, Pete Rose, and Other Reflections on Baseball

With a Happy Eye But…America and the World, 1997–2002

One Man's America: The Pleasures and Provocations of Our Singular Nation

A Nice Little Place on the North Side: Wrigley Field at One Hundred

THE
Conservative
Sensibility

George F. Will

NEW YORK BOSTON

Hachette Books
Hachette Book Group
1290 Avenue of the Americas, New York, NY 10104
hachettebooks.com
twitter.com/hachettebooks

First Edition: June 2019

Excerpt from "For C." from MAYFLIES: New Poems and Translations by Richard Wilbur. Copyright © 2000 by Richard Wilbur. Reprinted by permission of Houghton Mifflin Harcourt Publishing Company. All rights reserved.

Hachette Books is an imprint of Perseus Books, LLC, a subsidiary of Hachette Book Group, Inc. The Hachette Books name and logo are trademarks of Hachette Book Group, Inc.

The publisher is not responsible for websites (or their content) that are not owned by the publisher.

Library of Congress Cataloging-in-Publication Data

Names: Will, George F., author.
Title: The conservative sensibility / George F. Will.
Description: First edition. | New York, NY : Hachette Books, 2019. | Includes bibliographical references and index.
Identifiers: LCCN 2018048055| ISBN 9780316480932 (hardcover) | ISBN 9781549195235 (audio download) | ISBN 9781549148682 (audio book) | ISBN 9780316480918 (ebook)
Subjects: LCSH: Conservatism—United States—History. | United States—Politics and government.
Classification: LCC JC573.2.U6 W54 2019 | DDC 320.520973—dc23
LC record available at https://lccn.loc.gov/2018048055

ISBNs: 978-0-316-48093-2 (hardcover), 978-0-316-48091-8 (ebook), 978-0-316-53488-8 (BN signed hardcover)

Printed in the United States of America

LSC-C

10 9 8 7 6 5 4 3 2 1

To the memory of Barry Goldwater.

He was the "cheerful malcontent" who
showed that it is possible to wed
that adjective and that noun.

CONTENTS

I do not mean to say, that the scenes of the revolution *are now* or *ever will be* entirely forgotten; but that like every thing else, they must fade upon the memory of the world, and grow more and more dim by the lapse of time…At the close of that struggle, nearly every adult male had been a participator in some of its scenes. The consequence was, that of those scenes, in the form of a husband, a father, a son or a brother, a *living history was* to be found in every family…But *those* histories are gone. They *can* be read no more forever. They *were* a fortress of strength; but, what invading foemen could *never do*, the silent artillery of time *has done*; the leveling of its walls.

Abraham Lincoln
Address Before the Young Men's Lyceum of
Springfield, Illinois
January 27, 1838[1]

PREFACE

John A. Wheeler (1911–2008) a theoretical physicist at Princeton University, was fond of this aphorism: "Time is Nature's way of stopping things happening all at once." When he shared this with Martin Rees, Astronomer Royal of Great Britain, Rees responded with an aphorism of his own: "God invented space so that not everything had to happen in Princeton."[1] Some interesting things do have Princeton pedigrees, and they continue to reverberate in America's political arguments.

INTRODUCTION

Princeton, 1777

I t did not have to turn out as it did. The antecedent of the pronoun could be almost anything, but in this case it was a battle that is an exhilarating illustration of contingency in history.

In the American Revolutionary War, the fate of a continent, and of an idea, was at stake in a protracted conflict involving military forces that were, compared to those of the Napoleonic wars in Europe less than a generation later, astonishingly small. The war was won, in large measure, through the skillful maneuvering, which often meant retreating, by George Washington, who lost most of the not very numerous battles in which he directly engaged British forces. One of the battles he won might, if he had lost it, have ended the war and the Revolution.

The Battle of Princeton is often, but mistakenly, considered a mere lagging episode—a minor echo—of the Battle of Trenton. It was more than this, and for the purpose of this book it is a suitable subject with which to begin because the subsequent chapters are, among other things, an argument against the temptation of historicism—the belief that the unfolding of events is an autonomous process with its own laws and logic. The Battle of Princeton is an invigorating illustration of the history-making role of individual agency. It occurred less than two miles from Princeton University's Nassau Hall. You can stroll across the battlefield in fewer than half the number of minutes—

forty-five—that the fight is estimated to have lasted. As a historic site, it is shamefully neglected. As a historic event, the January 3, 1777, Battle of Princeton is astonishingly underestimated. It was one of the most consequential battles in world history because of what did not happen but easily could have. In it, the American Revolution, and the hope for a republic based on natural rights that limit government, survived a near-death experience.

The Battle of Princeton was a small skirmish in an eight-year war in which only 25,000 Americans died. This was, however, 1 percent of the new nation's population, making the Revolutionary War second only to the Civil War in its lethality. In December 1776 the revolution was failing. Britain had dispatched to America 36,000 troops—at that point, the largest European expeditionary force ever—hoping to crush the rebellion quickly and forestall a French intervention on behalf of the Americans. General George Washington had been driven from Brooklyn Heights, then from Manhattan, then out of New York. The nation, whose independent existence had been proclaimed just five months earlier, barely existed as he retreated across New Jersey and into Pennsylvania. From there, however, on Christmas night, he crossed the Delaware River ice floes for a successful forty-five-minute battle with Britain's Hessian mercenaries at Trenton. This was Washington's first victory; he had not been at Lexington, Concord, or Bunker Hill. Trenton would, however, have been an evanescent triumph, were it not for what happened ten days later.

On January 2, 1777, British General Charles Cornwallis began marching 5,500 troops from Princeton to attack Washington's slightly outnumbered forces, which Cornwallis hoped to pin down with their backs to the Delaware. Washington, leaving a few hundred soldiers to tend fires that tricked Cornwallis into thinking that the entire patriot army was encamped, made a stealthy fourteen-mile night march to attack three British regiments remaining at Princeton. The opposing forces collided shortly after dawn.

The most lethal weapons in this war were bayonets. The British had them; few Americans did. The Americans beat a panicked retreat from the advancing steel. By the example of his personal bravery, Washington reversed the retreat and led a charge that saved a nation. Serving Washington there was a fellow Virginian, a future Washington biographer and chief justice of the Supreme Court, John Marshall. So, in that small contested field that day were the two men most important in making the infant republic into a nation. When the redcoats ran, the British aura of invincibility and the strategy of "securing territory and handing out pardons" were shattered.[1] And the drift of American opinion toward defeatism was halted. The patriots' blood that puddled on frozen ground that twenty-degree morning bought the birth of American freedom. The British historian George M. Trevelyan wrote of Trenton: "It may be doubted whether so small a number of men ever employed so short a space of time with greater and more lasting effects upon the history of the world."[2] But this would not have been the judgment of any historian if Washington had not prevailed at Princeton.

The British retreated into Princeton, where some took refuge in Nassau Hall. Of the three cannonballs that American soldiers fired at Nassau Hall, one missed, one bounced off the south wall, leaving a pockmark that is still visible, and the third supposedly sailed through a window and neatly removed the head from a portrait of King George III. It is said that the artillery was commanded by a Washington aide named Alexander Hamilton. It is altogether appropriate that Nassau Hall, which at the time was the largest building in New Jersey and the largest academic building in the nation, was, so to speak, present at this moment in the nation's creation. In that building James Madison, who was to become the nation's fourth president, had lived and studied, and Woodrow Wilson, who was to become the twenty-eighth president, would begin his ascent to national prominence from his Nassau Hall office as president of Princeton University.

This book is about American political thought, which today is, to a remarkable extent, an argument between Madisonians and

Wilsonians. My subject is American conservatism. My conviction is that, properly understood, conservatism is the Madisonian persuasion. And my melancholy belief is that Woodrow Wilson was the most important single figure in the largely successful campaign to convince the nation that the Madisonian persuasion is an anachronism. This book is not an exercise in exegesis. It is not a systematic study of the origins and development of either man's thought. There are many such studies, many of them excellent. Rather, my purpose is to show how the nature and stakes of today's political arguments can best be understood by placing the arguments in the context of a debate now more than a century old. It is reassuring as well as clarifying to trace the pedigree of today's arguments to long-standing American disagreements between large figures of impressive learning. We can dignify our present disputes among small persons of little learning by connecting them with great debates about fundamental things.

Princeton, 1964

There is a braided relationship between a person's political philosophy and his or her sensibility, meaning a proclivity for seeing and experiencing the passage of time and the tumult of events in a particular way. Which comes first? Perhaps, in most cases, neither; they evolve entwined and are mutually reinforcing. A sensibility is more than an attitude but less than an agenda, less than a pragmatic response to the challenge of comprehensively reforming society in general. The conservative sensibility, especially, is best defined by its reasoning about concrete matters in particular societies. The American conservative sensibility, as explained in this volume, is a perpetually unfolding response to real situations that require statesmanship— the application of general principles to untidy realities. Conservatism does not float above all times and places. The conservative sensibility is relevant to all times and places, but it is lived and revealed locally, in the conversation of a specific polity. The American conservative sensibility is situated here; it is a national expression of reasoning, revealed in practices.

Charles de Gaulle began his war memoirs with a justly famous sentence whose power derives from its simplicity: "All my life I have thought of France in a certain way."[3] The way people think about their country can be difficult to distill into sentences. But Americans' feelings are, to some degree, and often at a subliminal level, connected to ideas that were present at the country's creation. This book is an explanation of how I think about America. And the book is about why I think doing so is conducive to national flourishing and personal happiness, the pursuit of which is, after all, the point of American politics.

This book's primary purpose is not to tell readers what to think about this or that particular problem or policy. Rather, the purpose is to suggest how to think about the enduring questions concerning the proper scope and actual competence of government. This book is an exercise in intellectual archeology, an excavation to reveal the Republic's foundations, intellectual and institutional, which have been buried beneath different assumptions and policies. My belief is that by this retrieval something quite beautiful can be revealed and put to practical use. Apologetics are writings that offer reasons, particularly to nonbelievers, for believing what the writer does. This book is my unapologetic presentation to unbelievers, who are a majority of contemporary Americans, of reasons why they should recur to the wisdom of the nation's founding.

Conservatism is about the conservation of that wisdom, or it is nothing of much lasting significance. The proper question for conservatives is: What do you seek to conserve? The proper answer is concise but deceptively simple: We seek to conserve the American Founding. What, however, does it mean to conserve an event—or, more precisely, a congeries of events—that occurred almost 250 years ago? This book is my attempt to answer that question by showing the continuing pertinence of the Founding principles, and by tracing many of our myriad discontents to departures from those principles.

I have been thinking about this since arriving at Princeton University's Graduate School in 1964 to begin earning a doctoral degree in political philosophy. The Graduate School is located on a small hill a fifteen-minute walk from Nassau Hall. The fact that the school is there is a matter of historic importance.

The university counts James Madison as its first graduate student because, although he graduated with the class of 1771, he remained there for a year to study Hebrew with the university's president, John Witherspoon. The school was formally established in 1900, but its permanent location had not yet been decided upon when Woodrow Wilson became the university's president in 1902. His restless, reforming spirit did much to propel the university to greatness—and to irritate portions of the university's faculty, trustees, and alumni. Many of the changes he drove forward, changes concerning academics and student life, were more important than the question of where to locate the Graduate School. But this matter, coming after a long train of acrimonious skirmishes, became decisive. Wilson wanted the Graduate School integrated into the main campus. He was given to investing his preoccupations with immense significance, so he said: "Will America tolerate the seclusion of graduate students? Will America tolerate the idea of having graduate students set apart?"[4] Actually, America was not all that fascinated by this campus dust-up. Perhaps it should have been.

Wilson's nemesis was Andrew Fleming West, the dean of the Graduate School from 1901 to 1928. West's statue graces the school where it now is, where West wanted it to be. Defeat provoked Wilson to resign in 1910. He immediately entered politics and was elected governor of New Jersey that November. We Madisonians rarely regret the defeats that Wilson suffered. We do, however, wonder whether subsequent American history might have been different, and better, if he had got his way concerning the location of the Graduate School and hence had remained in the president's rooms in Nassau Hall, instead of rapidly rising to the nation's capital.

From June until November 1783, the town of Princeton was the capital of the United States. The national government, such as it feebly was, had decamped from Philadelphia to seek refuge from restive American soldiers who were unhappy about the government, which, unable to levy taxes, was unable to pay them. The Continental Congress met in Nassau Hall, where it received General George Washington after the British surrender at Yorktown. It is therefore satisfying that Nassau Hall can be considered the symbolic epicenter of American political philosophy. In the era of revolutionary ferment, the building was, among other things, a dormitory housing James Madison, who would be the most creative participant in the process that produced the Constitution that produced a national government without the infirmities that drove the previous government to shelter in Princeton. By 1902, Nassau Hall contained the university's administrative offices, including those of the new president, Woodrow Wilson, who would become the first president of the United States to criticize Madison's constitutional architecture. The sixteenth president would vindicate this architecture while saving it from destruction.

I was born and raised in central Illinois, and although I have not lived in the state since leaving for college in 1958, four months after my seventeenth birthday, I remain a Midwesterner, marinated in the spirit and lore of Abraham Lincoln. It was at Princeton's Graduate School that I began the thinking that has culminated in the writing of this book, which in a sense began with my doctoral dissertation, half a century ago.

"BEYOND THE REACH OF MAJORITIES"

My home was in Champaign, which is cheek-by-jowl with Urbana, where sits Champaign County's red sandstone courthouse, built in 1849. When Abraham Lincoln was a circuit-riding lawyer from Springfield, he had cases that brought him to Urbana, and he was, according to local lore, in the courthouse when he learned of the passage of the Kansas-Nebraska Act. Lincoln's rise to greatness began with his recoil against this act that, by repealing the Missouri Compromise of 1820, lit the fuse that led to the Civil War. The Compromise had forbidden slavery in the Louisiana Territory north of a line that included the Kansas and Nebraska territories. The Kansas-Nebraska Act, introduced by Illinois senator Stephen A. Douglas, empowered the residents of those two territories to decide whether or not to have the institution of slavery. The act's premise was that the principle of "popular sovereignty" is the distilled essence of democracy, and that therefore giving maximum scope to the principle of majority rule is the essential point of the American project. Lincoln disagreed.

He responded to the act with a controlled, canny, patient but implacable vehemence. So, the most luminous career in the history of American democracy, the most morally edifying career in the history of world politics, took its bearings from the principle that there is more to the American purpose, and more to justice, than majorities having their way. If justice is what Thrasymachus said it was in his debate with Socrates in Book I of Plato's *Republic*—if justice is the interest of the strong—then two conclusions follow. One is that Douglas was right in arguing that justice regarding slavery in the territories was whatever pleased the strongest faction—a majority— in the territories. The other conclusion is that in a democracy, the crucial machinery of justice is the adding machine—that justice is known, simply and decisively, when votes are tabulated. Lincoln knew better.

Fifty years ago I submitted to the politics department of Princeton University a doctoral dissertation titled "Beyond the Reach of Majorities: Closed Questions in an Open Society." The title came from the Supreme Court's 1943 opinion in *West Virginia v. Barnette*, the second of the flag salute cases involving public school children who were Jehovah's Witnesses. As told by Noah Feldman, the two cases, which culminated in one of the most striking reversals by the court in its history, began on an October morning in 1935 in Minersville, Pennsylvania, when William Gobitas (the Supreme Court misspelled the family's name as Gobitis), a ten-year-old fifth grader, refused to salute the flag during the Pledge of Allegiance. "The teacher," Feldman writes, "tried to force his arm up, but William held on to his pocket and successfully resisted." The next day his sister Lillian, eleven, a seventh grader, also refused to salute the flag, explaining to her teacher, "The Bible says at Exodus chapter 20 that we can't have any other gods before Jehovah God."[5]

At that time, Feldman explains, the flag salute, as Americans gave it, "closely resembled the straight-arm Nazi salute, except that the palm was to be turned upward, not down."[6] A national leader of the Jehovah's Witnesses had recently given a speech denouncing the Nazi salute, and several Witnesses' children around the country had come to the same conclusion that Lillian explained to her teacher: Saluting the flag was idolatry. Lillian and William were shunned at school, the Gobitas family grocery store was threatened with violence and boycotted, the school district changed saluting the flag from a custom to a legal duty, and the Gobitas children were expelled from school.

Their case wended its way to the Supreme Court as war clouds lowered over the world, a context, Feldman notes, that was not favorable to the Witnesses. They were pacifists, had opposed US participation in World War I and were opposing any US involvement in any war in Europe. In June 1940, just days after Nazi troops marched into Paris, the court ruled 8–1 that the school district had the power to make saluting the flag mandatory. The opinion for the court was written by Justice Felix Frankfurter, a former member of the national committee of the American Civil Liberties Union. He was Jewish and had been born in Austria, which the Nazis had occupied in 1938. As a Jew, he was anxious to avoid practices that allowed schoolchildren to be treated differently because of their religion. The case *Minersville v. Gobitis* dealt, he said, "with an interest inferior to none in the hierarchy of legal values. National unity is the basis of national security."[7] He said his personal opinion was that the school board should allow the Witnesses' children their dissent. He was, however, as most political progressives had been for many decades, an advocate of judicial restraint, and he thought the court should acknowledge that the elected school board had made a defensible, meaning reasonable, choice expressing the will of a majority of its constituents. To put the point in judicial language that would become familiar in subsequent decades, the school board's policy passed the "rational basis" test.

The eight members of the court's majority had all been nominated by President Franklin Roosevelt, whose anger with the court's refusal to be deferential toward Congress' enactment of New Deal legislation led to his ill-fated attempt to "pack" the court. The lone dissenter in *Gobitis* was Harlan Fiske Stone, who had been appointed by President Calvin Coolidge. Minersville's flag salute law, wrote Stone, was "unique in the history of Anglo-American legislation" because it forced the children "to express a sentiment which, as they interpret it, they do not entertain, and which violates their deepest religious convictions." So, deference to the school board's legislative judgment amounted to "the surrender of the constitutional protection of the liberty of small minorities to the popular will."[8] As Feldman says, "In 1940, the idea that the Court should protect minorities from the majority was not the commonplace it would later become. Stone had first introduced it in 1937, burying it in a footnote."[9] Indeed, this became the most famous and consequential footnote in the court's history, one we shall consider in Chapter 4.

Taking their cue from the court's decision, many communities made flag saluting mandatory. There was an upsurge of violence against Witnesses, including that by a mob of 2,500 who burned down the Witnesses' Kingdom Hall in Kennebunk, Maine. In 1943, however, with a world war raging, the court agreed to hear another flag salute case concerning Jehovah's Witnesses, for the purpose of overturning the decision it had reached just thirty-six months earlier. Writing for the majority in a 6–3 decision, Justice Robert Jackson, who had not been on the court when *Gobitis* was decided, said: "The very purpose of a Bill of Rights was to withdraw certain subjects from the vicissitudes of political controversy, to place them beyond the reach of majorities and officials, and to establish them as legal principles to be applied by the courts....Fundamental rights may not be submitted to vote; they depend on the outcome of no elections."[10]

First as a graduate student, then briefly as a professor of political philosophy, and now for five decades as a Washington observer of American politics and governance, I have been thinking about the many vexing issues implicated in these two flag salute cases. The issues include the source of American rights, the nature of the Constitution and the role of the Supreme Court in construing it, and what fidelity to democracy does and does not require regarding the rights of majorities. There is, I believe a coherent philosophy that provides intellectually satisfying and politically prudent answers to these and other questions. It is American conservatism, rightly understood.

Such American conservatism takes its bearings from the American Founding, properly understood. William James called philosophy "a peculiarly stubborn effort to think clearly."[11] My effort is to explain three things: the Founders' philosophy, the philosophy that the progressives formulated explicitly as a refutation of the Founders, and the superiority of the former. An explanation of terminology is helpful here. Although it distresses some American conservatives to be told this, American conservatism has little in common with European conservatism, which is descended from, and often is still tainted by, throne-and-altar, blood-and-soil nostalgia, irrationality, and tribalism. American conservatism has a clear mission: It is to conserve, by articulating and demonstrating the continuing pertinence of, the Founders' thinking. The price of accuracy might by confusion, but this point must be made: American conservatives are the custodians of the classical liberal tradition.

In the Anglophone world, this tradition began with Thomas Hobbes and John Locke, in the context of authoritarian governments that ruled confessional states, those with established churches. Liberalism acquired its name, and became conscious of itself, in the eighteenth and nineteenth centuries, when liberty was threatened by the forces of order—by institutions and instruments of the state, often operating in conjunction with ecclesiastical authorities. Liberalism championed individualism and the rights of the individual against those forces of enforced order. The label "liberal" was minted to identify those whose primary concern was not the protection of community solidarity or traditional hierarchies, but rather was the expansion and protection of individual liberty. Liberals were then those who considered the state the primary threat to this. Liberals espoused the exercise of natural rights within a spacious zone of personal sovereignty guaranteed by governments instituted to serve as guarantors of those rights. Today, when the French describe—disparage, really—Margaret Thatcher's kind of free market doctrines as "neo-liberalism" their terminology is not mistaken. For many years now, American conservatism has been the strongest contemporary echo of this liberalism in the trans-Atlantic world.

American progressivism developed as an intended corrective to traditional liberalism. Progressives aimed to redress what they perceived as a dangerous imbalance. Their goal was to strengthen the powers of order—of the state—which had supposedly become anemic relative to the surging powers of entities and autonomous forces in America's industrial society—banks, corporations, railroads, trusts, business cycles. In Europe today, the too few people who think the way American conservatives do are commonly called liberals, and people who think as American progressives do are called social democrats. In America today, there are a few intellectually fastidious people who think as eighteenth- and nineteenth-century liberals did, but who are reluctant—perhaps for what they consider reasons of historical accuracy—to call themselves conservatives, so instead call themselves classical liberals.

In recent decades, many Americans who were comfortable identifying themselves as liberals, and who prospered politically by doing so, have come to refer to themselves as progressives rather than liberals. They have done this for tactical reasons: The label "liberal" was devalued by association with various governance disappointments. Progressives are, however, terminologically accurate. Progressivism represents the overthrow of the Founders' classical liberalism.

The progressives' indictment is that the Founders' politics is cramped and uninspiring because it neither aspires to, nor allows for, the integration of the individual's spiritual needs and yearnings with the individual's political identity and activities. To this indictment the American conservative's proper response is a cheerful, proud plea of guilty. The world has suffered much, and still suffers, from politics freighted with the grand ambition of unifying the individual's social and moral lives. Such politics inevitably aims to fuse individuals into an organic community, with little social space in civil society for institutions—civic, religious, commercial—that can respond to human needs with politics largely left out.

One lesson of the twentieth century is that the comprehensive politics of the integrated state promises fulfillment but delivers suffocation. In contrast, American patriotism is "an intricate latticework of ideals, sentiments and overlapping loyalties" that involves politics but is not primarily about politics.[12]

Conservatism's celebration and protection of individual autonomy does not, as many critics now charge, condemn the individual to a desiccated life of shriveled social attachments or to the joyless pursuit of material enjoyments. Conservatism neither advocates nor causes individuals to be severed from familial, communal, or religious affiliations. Rather, it demarcates a large zone of individual sovereignty in which such affiliations can be nurtured. By pruning the state's pretentions and functions, conservatism prevents the emergence of an enveloping state, in the shade of which other institutions cannot thrive, and often wither. In a political setting that insists upon the reality of individual autonomy and the morality of self-reliance, some find solace in an omnipresent and omniprovident state. Conservative governance should minimize opportunities for indulging this temptation.

Conservatism's great gift is preservation of the social space for the personal pursuit of higher aspirations. If people fail to use this space well, that is their failure, not conservatism's.

THE ADJECTIVE

In the phrase "American conservatism," the adjective carries a lot of weight. Conservatism became conscious of itself as a political philosophy through the writings of Edmund Burke. Subtle and profound, his works are rich in prudential lessons that remain germane. Nevertheless, his thinking is in the European tradition of throne-and-altar conservatism. America has no throne, and most Americans want altars kept apart from the state's business. Burke's conservatism was, in large measure, produced by British premises and French events. European conservatism has generally sought to conserve institutions and practices, such as social hierarchies and established churches, that were produced by the slow working of historical processes spanning many centuries. American conservatism seeks, as Alexander Hamilton did in the Republic's infancy, to conserve or establish institutions and practices conducive to a social dynamism that dissolves impediments to social mobility and fluidity. So American conservatism is not only different from, it is at bottom antagonistic to British and continental

European conservatism. The latter emphasizes the traditional and dutiful, with duties defined by obligations to a settled collectivity, the community. Because American conservatism is about individual liberty, it cultivates spontaneous social order and hence encourages novelty.

In the stream of Western political thought, American conservatism is exceptional in a way that is related to the theory of "American exceptionalism." The multifaceted postulate of American "exceptionalism" includes one or more of these ideas: Americans were born exceptionally free from a feudal past, and hence free from an established church and an entrenched aristocracy. This made them exceptionally receptive to intellectual pluralism and exceptionally able to achieve social mobility. America had an exceptional revolution, one that did not attempt to define and deliver happiness, but one that set people free to define and pursue it as they please. Americans codified their Founding doctrines as a natural rights republic in an exceptional Constitution, one that does not say what government must do for them but what government may not do to them. And because the Founding experience was the result of, and affirmed the potency of, human agency, Americans are exceptionally impervious to bleak modern anxieties about human destiny being decisively shaped by vast impersonal forces. America's central government is exceptionally constructed to limit the discretion of those in power by balancing rival centers of power.

All of these ideas are related to the doctrine of natural rights. It supposedly guarantees a substantial zone of individual autonomy by guaranteeing limited government. But suppose it does not do that?

Everything, including this or that aspect of America's supposed exceptionalism, is perishable. The modern world has learned that there are more forms of social entrenchment, more impediments to social mobility, than those that descended from feudalism. By now, America's government has long been involved in defining and delivering happiness, understood as material well-being and freedom of self-expression. For at least half a century, it has been impossible to believe that the Constitution created a government that remains limited by the mere enumeration of its powers. Trying to restrain the modern executive, which is the motor of the administrative state, by depending on the Madisonian architecture of checks and balances seems increasingly akin to lassoing a locomotive with a cobweb. Furthermore, and most important, Americans' sense of their exceptionalism is increasingly attenuated because of their absorption of important aspects of European social thought since the Amcrican Founding. The doctrine of natural rights is the most solid foundation—perhaps the only firm foundation—for the idea of the political equality of all self-directing individuals. But what happens when people begin to wonder to what extent individuals actually are self-directing? Such wondering is prompted when the very concept of the self seems to have become problematic. As we shall see, consciousness has become a political problem and a political project.

"It has been our fate as a nation," the historian Richard Hofstadter said, "not to have ideologies but to be one."[13] This sentence sacrificed accuracy for felicity. Writing in the middle of the twentieth century, Hofstadter surely understood that the United States had long since ceased to be a nation embodying one ideology. Since early in that century, and especially since the New Deal, there have been two political philosophies contending for supremacy. The original one, the Founders' natural rights philosophy, began losing ground to progressivism more than a century ago and today is seeking to regain lost ground. What progressives aimed for, and largely achieved, was a second American Founding, this one taking its bearings not from unchanging nature but rather from history, which is a river of change.

As Margaret Thatcher said, European nations were made by history, the United States was made by philosophy. Unique among all nations, the United States knows precisely when and exactly why it was founded. American conservatism is an ongoing meditation on America's Founding, which means on the Declaration of

Independence and on the Constitution, which should be construed in the bright light cast by the Declaration's affirmation of natural rights. The American project, distilled to its essence, was, and the conservative project is, to demonstrate that a government constructed on the assumptions of natural rights must be limited government. The natural rights theory is that individuals in the state of nature possess rights that pre-exist government; that government is created for the limited purpose of securing those rights; and that the individual surrenders some sovereignty to government on the basis of a rational calculation that government secures more sovereignty than it requires to be surrendered.

One cannot do political philosophy without engaging in intellectual history. "The safest general characterization of the European philosophical tradition," said Alfred North Whitehead, "is that it consists of a series of footnotes to Plato."[14] The American tradition of political philosophy, which flowered during the ferment of the American Revolution and the framing of the Constitution, was consciously trans-Atlantic. It drew particularly heavily from John Locke, who knew he was arguing with, among others, Hobbes, who in turn was arguing with various contributors to an argument running back to, of course, Plato. If America can be said to have a national political philosophy, it comes from a political philosopher from another nation. Locke, whom we shall meet again in Chapter 1, reasoned that all persons are naturally free, meaning free in a state of nature, and would surrender portions of their freedom to a government of their creation in order to prevent injuries or inconveniences. And in order to achieve positive goals that can be achieved best, or only, collectively, through political action. Because individuals are equal in possession of freedom, government's fundamental purpose is to provide them equal protection in the exercise of their freedom to pursue happiness.

Sensibility as well as philosophy, and more frequently than philosophy, shapes the contours of a nation's political practices. People embrace a conservative or liberal agenda or ideology largely because of something basic to their nature and nurturing, meaning their temperament as shaped by education and other experiences. Broadly speaking, there are conservative and progressive conceptions of human nature, conservative and progressive assumptions about how history unfolds, and conservative and progressive expectations about how the world works. Few people have systems of ideas that can be properly called political philosophies. Most people have political sensibilities, meaning sensibilities with political relevance and consequences. All human beings, however, have feelings, and human beings are the only animals capable of feeling melancholy because only they can compare what is with what might have been. Among the nations, the United States is especially susceptible to national melancholia because it was begun with such glittering aspirations for what it should become. The fact that it has been and remains, on balance, a tremendous success does not immunize Americans from recurring bouts of uneasiness. We are experiencing one such now.

At the risk of depressing readers prematurely, I want to advise them that what follows does not contain a comprehensive agenda for political reform and social improvement. Although some recommendations for action are explicit and others are implicit in the analysis, one lesson of conservatism is that many problems are more or less intractable, for reasons relating to an abundance of politics or a paucity of knowledge. Consider three matters. First, the nation's most destructive social problem, which is discussed in Chapter 6, is family disintegration. No one understands what opaque tangle of factors has caused this, which is one reason no one knows what public policies might ameliorate it. Second, the nation's most ominous governance problem is the unsustainable trajectory of the entitlement state because of the unfunded promises that have been made regarding pensions and medical care. Everyone understands what must be done: a mixture of increases of taxes and reductions of promised benefits. Everyone also knows that there is insufficient political will for either part of this remedy. Third, the fundamental cause of the public perception—which is not mistaken—of a corrupt national political culture is the fact that the federal government has promiscuously involved itself in every aspect of American life. As this government has become ever more important in the allocation of wealth and opportunity, it has become an ever more enticing target of rent-seeking factions, which are incited by the government's interventionist behavior. The necessary, and probably sufficient, cause of this misuse of government was the death of the doctrine of enumerated powers. Its principle was that, as Madison said in Federalist 45, the powers delegated by the Constitution to the federal government are "few and defined." That principle is dead as a doornail. The powers have turned out to be, effectively, undefined and for that reason too numerous to be enumerated.

These somewhat bleak judgments are, however, not sterile. Understanding the limits of the possible is a prerequisite for avoiding misplaced confidence, of which there has been an abundance in the last half century of governance. Such confidence sends people careening off on tangents that make matters worse. And by understanding the price we have paid, and continue to pay, for abandoning certain political principles and practices, we can slow the pace of mistakes and minimize disappointments. And perhaps even make some improvements that do not make matters worse. That many supposed improvements do make matters worse is a truth that is not, alas, self-evident.

Before long, the nation will be a quarter of a millennium old; soon thereafter, its Constitution will be. This is, therefore, a good time to appraise the American project as it is, as it might have been, and as it might become. In 1948, when postwar politics were in ferment and conservatism was beginning to stir as more than a particular flavor of cultural criticism, one of its texts was Richard Weaver's *Ideas Have Consequences*. Weaver, a professor of English at the University of Chicago, could actually have said that *only* ideas have large and lasting consequences. There then were, however, those who considered "conservative ideas" an oxymoron. "In the United States at this time," wrote Lionel Trilling in 1950, "liberalism is not only the dominant but even the sole intellectual tradition. For it is the plain fact that nowadays there are no conservative or reactionary ideas in general circulation." Trilling worried that "it is not conducive to the real strength of liberalism that it should occupy the intellectual field alone."[15] That is one worry that liberalism has been subsequently spared. In the past sixty or so years, conservatism has grown from a small homogeneous fighting faction in an unconverted country into a persuasion with sufficient political muscle and intellectual firepower to contest progressivism's ascendency. Conservatism's growth as a force in electoral politics accelerated ten years after Trilling wrote what he did.

The unlikely accelerant was a politician who never pretended to be, or aspired to be, an original thinker. Arriving near the end of, and hastening the end of, the hegemony of New Deal progressivism, he was gifted at distilling, and unapologetically espousing, sentiments that were then more widely shared than they were frequently expressed in political discourses. He did not have a finely articulated program, but he did have a broad judgment about how conservatism could contribute to the good life. So, let us here take a brief stroll down memory lane to meet this person, for whom I cast my first presidential vote and to whom this book is dedicated. The stroll will illustrate the persistence of the vocabulary of limited government in American politics.

"ALL RIGHT, DAMN IT, I'LL DO IT"

It is commonly but wrongly said that the 1960s was a decade of dissent begun on campuses and on the left, with the first spark struck in 1964 with the Free Speech Movement in Sproul Plaza on the campus of the University of California, Berkeley. Actually, a more consequential dissent began in July 1960 in Chicago, when Arizona's junior senator strode to the podium of the Republican National Convention. Seething with the ancient (by American standards) and accumulated grievances of the American West against the American East, Barry Goldwater growled to the convention, "Let's grow up, conservatives. Let's, if we want to take this party back—and I think we can some day. Let's get to work."[16]

"All right, damn it, I'll do it" were, three years later, the reluctant Goldwater's words of surrender to those in the conservative movement who had been importuning him to seek the Republican Party's 1964 presidential nomination.[17] He understood that the November 22, 1963, assassination of President John Kennedy reduced the value of this nomination: Americans, he knew, would not choose to have three presidents in fourteen months. Goldwater, however, knew the campaign could still serve a long-term purpose. He would use it to breathe new life into an old political vocabulary, one that had been neglected during the long ascendency of New Deal premises. Doing so, he would reinvigorate a political tradition that had become dormant and inarticulate. In this sense, Goldwater won in 1964—it just took sixteen years to count the votes. This book, written at a moment when conservatism is again a persuasion without a party, is, in part, an attempt to do what Goldwater attempted—to revive a worthy tradition.

Or perhaps one might say a worthy persuasion. Six decades ago, the historian Marvin Meyers published a seminal book, *The Jacksonian Persuasion*, about how the Jacksonians thought and spoke in the rough-and-tumble of politics and policy-making. Meyers' subject was, he said, "not a consistent doctrine, not a finely articulated program but a persuasion: a broad judgment of public affairs informed by common sentiments and beliefs about the good life in America."[18] Meyers was writing more than intellectual history, he was distilling a political philosophy from its intimations in political practices. My portrait of American conservatism as I think it should understand itself deals with some doctrines and programs. It is, however, especially concerned with sentiments about how the world actually works. And with beliefs about how America would work if it avoided making matters worse while trying to make the good life more attractive and accessible.

In 1964, the Goldwater persuasion carried only six states but enabled conservatism to capture the levers and pulleys of the Republican Party's machinery. This sealed conservatism's Republican victory in an internecine struggle that had simmered and sometimes raged since 1912, when a former Republican president, Theodore Roosevelt, challenged an incumbent Republican president, William Howard Taft, for the party's nomination. TR represented progressives, Taft represented conservatives. In 1980, Ronald Reagan, who became a national political force by giving a nationally televised speech for Goldwater in October 1964, was elected president. The conservatism of both Goldwater and Reagan was colored by the libertarianism of the American West of wide-open spaces.

When I visited Goldwater at his home in Phoenix a few years before his death in 1998, he said he had built his house on a hill to which, when he was young, he would ride his horse and sleep under the stars. When he was a boy, about 100,000 people lived in the Valley of the Sun. When Goldwater died, the population of one *suburb* of Phoenix—Mesa—was larger than St. Louis. Today, the population of the Phoenix metropolitan area, the nation's sixth largest, is approximately 4.7 million. So, you must remember this: Goldwater was a conservative from, and was formed by, a place with precious little past to conserve, and with an unlimited impatience with the idea of limits.

Westerners have no inclination to go through life with a crick in their necks from looking backward. When Goldwater became the embodiment of American conservatism—partly by his own efforts and partly because he was conscripted by others for the role—this guaranteed that the mainstream of American conservatism would be utterly *American*. The growing conservative intelligentsia would savor many flavors of conservatism, from Edmund Burke's to T. S. Eliot's, including conservatisms grounded on religious reverence, nostalgia, and resistance to the permanent revolution of conditions in a capitalist, market society. But such conservatisms would have been unintelligible, even repellent, to Goldwater, if he had had time or inclination to notice them. Goldwater was a man of many parts—politician and jet pilot, ham radio operator and accomplished photographer—but no one ever called him bookish. And if anyone ever had, Goldwater, a man of action and of the West, might have said—echoing the protagonist of the novel that invented the Western, Owen Wister's *The Virginian* (1902)—"When you call me that, *smile!*"[19] Then Goldwater would have smiled, because although he could be gruff, he could not stay out of sorts. He was well described (by the *New Yorker's* Richard Rovere) as "the cheerful malcontent."[20]

As America approaches the quarter-millennium mark it is neither cheerful nor content. Its discontents arise, in part, from the fact that for a century progressivism has been ascendant in the nation's political thought and practices. Many of the nation's disappointments and difficulties stem from the resulting repudiation of the principles of the nation's Founding. Many thoughtful progressives have articulated what they consider the necessity of this repudiation, which they say is grounded in improved understanding of modern social conditions and in fresh understanding of the human condition. The progressives' premise is that whatever is fixed in human nature is and ought to be less determinative in the construction of social arrangements than the possibility that social forces can shape new forms of human material. This is so, they think, because the most important characteristic of the human material is its plasticity. This progressive premise means that Americans, whether they know it or not, and regardless of whether they want it or not, are engaged in a new episode of an old debate.

It is a debate that has dominated Western political philosophy for many centuries. It is a debate about whether, or to what extent, nature contains standards, or whether it is mere material to be subject to human willfulness. The stakes could hardly be higher. If our rights are natural, they are discernible by reason, which is constitutive of human nature. Such rights also are natural because they pre-exist acts of collective human will and cannot be nullified by such acts. If rights are natural, so, too, is limited government. If rights are natural, government's legitimating function is, in the most neglected word in the Declaration of Independence, to "secure" these rights.

The Founders believed, as did almost every political philosopher before them, that there is a permanent human nature and that the task of statesmanship is to devise a political system that is conducive to human flourishing because the system accords with certain permanent human capacities, aspirations, passions, and tendencies. These are not all manifested at all times, but they are always part of the raw material of politics and must enter the calculations of statesmen who design regimes and wield power. Progressivism, which began as a forthright rejection of the Founders' philosophy, embraced and brought into political thinking the modern sense that *everything* is in flux, always and everywhere. Progressives argue that there may be, in a sense, various human natures at various historical moments, and in particular social contexts. Human nature, however, is always in a state of becoming. If it is the nature of human beings to have no fixed nature, then a political project inevitably flows from this fact. If what is called human nature is characterized by its historicity, if it is merely the consciousness derived from the shaping forces that produced it, then the jurisdiction of politics will inevitably include mastering and comprehensively directing those forces. If human nature is malleable under the pressure of the social context, then the content of that context can be, indeed must be, a political choice. The politics of consciousness is a European import into, and discordant with, the original civic discourse of our nation, which was born in battles fought to secure the founding of a nation with premises unique among the nations.

On July 4, 1776, the United States contained less than 2.8 million persons, 80 percent of whom lived within twenty miles—a day's ride—of Atlantic tidewater. Today the nation has 330 million residents and extends from the Atlantic to a state that reaches to within fifty-five miles of Russia. Another state is 700 miles closer to the capital of Japan than to the capital of the United States. Yet considering the pace and scale of American change, there is, as Michael Barone says, an astonishing continuity in our politics.[21] We have been holding congressional and presidential elections for almost 250 years, a process not interrupted even by the Civil War. The Democratic Party emerged as a vehicle for mass mobilization in the 1830s, the Republican Party exploded into existence in 1854 in reaction against the Kansas-Nebraska Act, and these two parties have organized American politics ever since. By the time of the election of 1800, the United States had political parties, which just thirteen years earlier the Framers of the Constitution had neither anticipated nor desired. Ratification in 1804 of the Twelfth Amendment, bringing the presidential election process into line with the existence of parties, attested to the swift and irrevocable acceptance of government by parties.

Today, however, the conflict between conservatives and progressives reflects the most durable and consequential *discontinuity* in American politics. The conflict is between the Founders' vision and the progressives' explicit repudiation of this, a conflict that is now a century old and showing no signs of abating. Indeed, it is intensifying as both sides, their convictions honed in debate, acquire sharpened understandings of how fundamental their differences are. It is an exhilarating time to be engaged in America's civic discourse because engagement immerses participants in the unmatched drama of this nation's history. The argument begins as the nation did, with some truths that were then considered self-evident.

CHAPTER 1

The Founders'
Epistemological Assertion

THEY KNEW WHAT CAN BE KNOWN

The sacred rights of mankind are not to be
rummaged for among old parchments or musty
records. They are written, as with a sunbeam, in
the whole *volume* of human nature…

Alexander Hamilton[1]

On February 22, 1842, the 110th anniversary of George
Washington's birthday, Abraham Lincoln, then thirty-three,
addressed the Washington Temperance Society of Springfield,
Illinois. He criticized attempts to reform the intemperate by
addressing them "in the thundering tones of anathema and denunciation." To expect this to be efficacious was, Lincoln said, "to
expect a reversal of human nature, which is God's decree, and never
can be reversed."[2] With those words, which were a rhetorical flourish not intended to say anything novel, the man who would become
the nation's sixteenth president expressed a foundational assumption of the first president and the rest of the nation's Founders.
Today, it is conventional wisdom that there is no knowledge, only
opinion, about moral questions, and that this is so because human
beings have no nature other than their capacity to acquire culture.
They supposedly acquire it much as soft wax passively acquires the

1

marks of whatever substance presses upon it. The thirtieth president did not think so.

On July 5, 1926, President Calvin Coolidge, who was born on the Fourth of July, 1872, spoke in Philadelphia to commemorate the 150th anniversary of the Declaration of Independence. Coolidge was more learned than his cultured despisers know and more learned than most of them are. He translated Dante's *Inferno* as a wedding gift for his wife, he read Cicero in Latin, and there is no extant evidence that he ever said "the business of America is business." That day in Philadelphia he spoke "to reaffirm and reestablish those old theories and principles which time and the unerring logic of events have demonstrated to be sound." The founding of the United States, he said, represented a "new civilization...a new spirit...more developed in its regard for the rights of the individual" than any in Europe. Coolidge said "life in a new and open country" had given rise to "aspirations which could not be realized in any subordinate position." These aspirations, "decreed by the very laws of human nature," testified to the fact that "man everywhere has an unconquerable desire to be the master of his own destiny." The Declaration's "great truths were in the air" Americans then breathed.[3]

As evidence of this, Coolidge cited Virginia's Declaration of Rights which George Mason presented to that state's general assembly on May 27, 1776: "All men are created equally free and independent."[4] Coolidge could also have cited Alexander Hamilton's anonymous 1775 pamphlet "The Farmer Refuted," in which Hamilton rejected the "absurd and impious doctrine" that he ascribed to Thomas Hobbes, the idea that all moral obligation "is derived from the introduction of civil society; and there is no virtue, but what is purely artificial, the mere contrivance of politicians, for the maintenance of social intercourse." Against this, Hamilton argued that humanity is endowed with "rational faculties" to discern the natural rights necessary for "preserving and beatifying" existence. Even in the state of nature no one "had any *moral* power to deprive another of" those rights. So, "the origin of all civil government, justly established, must be a voluntary compact, between the rulers and the ruled; and must be liable to such limitations, as are necessary for the security of the *absolute rights* of the latter."[5]

As further evidence that the Declaration's truths were "in the very air" of eighteenth-century America, Coolidge could have cited the slave petition for freedom submitted to the Massachusetts legislature on January 13, 1777, which read: "The petition of A Great Number of Blackes detained in a State of slavery in the Bowels of a free & Christian Country Humbly shuwith that your Petitioners apprehend that thay have in Common with all other men a Natural and Unaliable Right to that freedom which the Grat Parent of the Unavers hath Bestowed equalley on all menkind and which they have Never forfuted by any Compact or agreement whatever...."[6] Coolidge could have cited the 1778 Essex Result, a set of town resolutions intended to influence the drafting of the Massachusetts constitution: "All men are born equally free. The rights they possess at their births are equal, and of the same kind." The Result continued that some resolutions affirm "the true principles of government." They affirmed that "reason" and "the experience of all ages" confirm that "the benefits resulting to individuals from a free government, conduce much more to their happiness, than the retaining of all their natural rights in a state of nature." Because "much happiness cannot be enjoyed" in a state of nature, men enter into political society to "remove the inconveniences" of that state.[7] The mild word "inconveniences" signals a Lockean belief in some inherent sociability: Because of man's natural reason and sociability, life in the state of nature is not, as Hobbes said, characterized solely by "continual fear and danger of violent death" and therefore departing this state by entering political society is not so urgently necessary that it justifies a sweeping sacrifice of rights that are natural and pre-exist government.[8] The *limited* curtailment of *some* rights is justified in order to rectify those aspects of life that are inconvenient. The convention that between September 1, 1779, and

March 2, 1780, wrote the constitution for "the State of Massachusetts Bay" declared in its preamble that the purpose of government is "to secure the existence of the body-politic; to protect it; and to furnish the individuals who compose it with the power of enjoying, in safety and tranquility, their natural rights, and the blessings of life."[9]

This vocabulary of natural rights was, in part, a response to Americans' physical situation. In a 1670 sermon, a Massachusetts cleric spoke of the Puritans having undertaken an "errand into the wilderness."[10] In the next century's imperial crisis, the idea of Americans as intrepid tamers of a wilderness was drained of its theological content and filled with political gunpowder. By 1770, more and more Americans were arguing that their rights derived not from the common law of placid, settled England but rather were natural rights that existed in the essentially pre-political conditions of the American wilderness. So, when John Adams asked, "how do we New Englandmen derive our laws?" he answered, "not from Parliament, not from common law, but from the law of nature" in an America that was "not a conquered but a discovered country." America "was not granted of the king by his grace, but was dearly, very dearly earned by the planters, in the labor, blood, and treasure which they expended to subdue it by cultivation."[11] Americans had not brought their rights with them by ship from England. Rather, they had, as it were, found them in the wilderness.

This, then, is the full importance of Adams' famous formulation in his August 24, 1815, letter to Thomas Jefferson, with whom he was by then reconciled. Circumstances—the physical setting—had decisively conditioned the minds of Americans: "What do we mean by the Revolution? The War? That was no part of the Revolution; it was only an *effect* and *consequence* of it. The Revolution was in the minds of the people, and this was effected, from 1760 to 1775, in the course of fifteen years before a drop of blood was shed at Lexington."[12] The Revolution was also, however, a consequence of intellectual waves radiating from two English philosophers.

Hobbes is usually quoted as declaring that in the state of nature life is "nasty, brutish and short," but his description actually begins with two other adjectives: "solitary, poor, nasty, brutish and short."[13] The first adjective is crucial. Because individuals in the state of nature are solitary, they are vulnerable to the force of everyone else situated in similar insecurity. Locke, however, postulated that individuals in the state of nature are not so solitary. Rather, they have a certain natural sociability. What Locke surmised, many modern biologists, anthropologists, and sociologists believe they have confirmed. They think they have identified natural inclinations for fairness, understood as reciprocity, and for duty. For Locke, this propensity for sociability meant that people did not need to cede so much of their natural freedom to a sovereign power. Mankind's rudimentary sociability is not sufficient to obviate the need for a government to maintain order and administer justice. There is, however, enough natural sociability to limit the amount of power that must be entrusted to government. Lockean government must mediate and ameliorate, but unlike Hobbesian government, it need not dominate. So, the germ of the idea of limited government is in Locke's tempering of Hobbes' insistence on the "solitary" condition of the individual in the state of nature.

Hobbes thought that the great and universal motivator for human action was fear—of insecurity and especially of violent death. Locke thought the universal incentive was happiness: Ancient philosophers "did in vain enquire, whether Summum bonum consisted in Riches, or bodily Delights, or Virtue or Contemplation." This inquiry was as futile as arguing about whether "the best Relish were to be found in Apples, Plumbs or Nuts." "Cheese or lobsters" are "delicious" to some but "to others extremely nauseous and offensive." It depends, Locke said, on the "particular Palate." So Hobbes and Locke differed— but not about the important point, which is that there is no single *Summum bonum*. There are as many as there are palates. It is a matter of taste. This is, in two senses, the beginning of the political philosophy of modernity, the dawn of the modern enterprise. The challenge of modernity is to argue that a broad spectrum of tastes exists, and many tastes should be accommodated, even though not all tastes are equally admirable or socially beneficial. Regarding the ultimate good, Locke said "men may chuse different things, and yet all chuse right." This proposition was the point of embarkation for what would become what now is called classical liberalism.[14]

Locke put Western political philosophy on a path toward pluralism, toward accommodating the variety of goods that people pursue as they define for themselves the worthy life. Hobbes, however, began a wonderful benefaction for humanity—the great demotion of politics from an activity invested with semi-sacerdotal grandeur to something matter-of-factly utilitarian: Government exists to keep the peace so that people can get on with their private lives in a zone of personal sovereignty protected by government. And before Hobbes wrote, Niccolò Machiavelli disturbed the Western mind as an early and vivid example of modern masterless man, obedient to no god and only to rules he wrote. But as has been well said, Machiavelli is no more "the father of power politics" than William Harvey was "the father of the circulation of the blood."[15] With astonishing matter-of-factness, Machiavelli said that vice is needed in politics if virtue is to stand a chance. And the purpose of politics is not to make men virtuous, but to make the state (he more than anyone else gave this word currency) safe. In him was the embryo of modern politics, the individualism of self-interested strivers: every man a prince.

The fact of human diversity—of different ways of life both arising from, and producing, varieties of human characters—is not a discovery of modern anthropology, or even of pre-modern travels and explorations. The ancient political philosophers grounded their thinking in the observable fact that politics has the highest possible stakes precisely because different polities' laws and practices are conducive to different human characteristics. But this in no way contradicted their confidence in a constant human nature. Rather, it was by reflection about this constancy, and about human flourishing as the achievement of human nature's highest potentialities, that they reasoned to conclusions about the nature of the best regime. The early modern philosophers whose thinking gave rise to liberal government—rights-based limited regimes—discerned unity beneath diversity in this way: Reason is often the servant of the passions, which are universal; the principal passion is the desire for security from violent death; when this security is achieved, political reasoning advances to the achievement of higher goals important for human flourishing.

In the imagined state of nature, human beings are, Locke said, of the same "species and rank" and have "all the same advantages of nature," meaning the same "faculties," and therefore should "be equal one amongst another without subordination." Elsewhere, in his *Conduct of the Understanding*, Locke acknowledged that there is "great variety in men's understandings" and "amongst men of equal education there is great inequality of parts." This inequality arises from the fact that as regards understanding, "there is a greater distance between some men and others...than between some men and some beasts." All persons have the "seeds" of rationality, but many are "of low and mean education" and are never mentally elevated "above the spade and the plow." So, "[i]n his own subdued way, Locke is as much of an 'elitist' as Plato or Aristotle." But his way was subdued because it allowed for education to enable everyone to reach the threshold of rationality requisite for participation as equals in society's governance.[16]

Jefferson thought that the average American of his time had reached that threshold. He acknowledged that his object in writing the Declaration of Independence was "not to find out new principles, or new arguments, never before thought of, not merely to say things which had never been said before; but to place before mankind the common sense of the subject, in terms so plain and firm as to command their assent." James Parton, described by historian Gordon Wood as "America's first professional biographer," wrote in 1874: "If

Jefferson was wrong, America is wrong. If America is right, Jefferson was right."[17]

Politics originates in nature, in the constancy of human nature, which impels people to associate in society to avoid violent death and other inconveniences, and then to gain other, positive advantages. If, however, there is no universal human nature, there can be no universal principles of political organization and action. If what we call human nature is but the distillation of a particular people's traditions and experiences, then nature, at bottom, has no bottom. It is merely the most durable aspect of something that is ultimately not durable— the sediment of history from transitory cultures. If so, this deals a devastating blow against America's distinctive patriotism, which is inextricably linked to belief in the universality of certain self-evident truths, including the "proposition" to which the nation is "dedicated," that all are created equal in their possession of certain inalienable rights. The case for limited government is grounded in the empirical evidence that human beings have something in common—human nature—but are nevertheless incorrigibly different in capacities and aspirations. From this it follows, not logically but practically, that government cannot hope to provide happiness to all. Rather, the most it can reasonably expect to provide are the conditions under which happiness, as each defines it, can be pursued, as each is equipped, by nature or nurture, to do.

Individuals do not inherently possess rights in the empirically demonstrable way that they possess appendixes. But the concept of rights has come to be considered necessary for the moral vocabulary used in reasoning about the political demands of human dignity. The concept of rights does not require us to begin our political reasoning with a concept of the solitary individual shorn of all culturally acquired attributes. Rather, individuals' natural rights are standards by which the conventions of a political culture are judged: Are the conventions suitable for creatures of our nature? Do the conventions facilitate human flourishing? All human beings are partially shaped

8

by, they are even somewhat composed of, complicated social factors. The words "partially" and "somewhat" contain modernity's dissent from the ancients' conception of politics.

The ancients' conception, most powerfully presented in Plato's *Republic*, was of the community as an all-enveloping, unending school for affirming, and instructing citizens in, a particular understanding of the worthy life. For the ancients, politics was a homogenizing process for a closed society. For moderns, politics is the art of accommodating differences in societies open to disagreements about the proper ends of a worthy life. For the ancients, life in the polity was an encompassing determinant of moral outlook. For moderns, life in society requires rights *against* the polity, rights that protect a zone of individual sovereignty in which the inherent dignity of the individual is expressed in the free exercise of agency. These rights include the right of voluntary membership in the non-state institutions of civil society. Each of us is, as Hegel said, "a child of his time," but none of us is, or at least none of us needs to be, only this.[18] Each of us is a child of our parents, but as every parent learns, every child is much more than the sum of the parenting he or she experiences.

Man, said Hamilton, is endowed "with rational faculties, by the help of which, to discern and pursue such things, as were consistent with his duty and interest, and invested him with an inviolable right to personal liberty, and personal safety." Because "in a state of nature, no man had any *moral* power to deprive another of his life, limbs, property or liberty," any justly established government "must be a voluntary compact, between the rulers and the ruled; and must be liable to such limitations, as are necessary for the security of the *absolute rights* of the latter." Said Hamilton, "*Civil liberty is only natural liberty, modified and secured by the sanctions of civil society*. It is not a thing, in its own nature, precarious and dependent on human will and caprice."[19]

When Hamilton said of the Constitution (in Federalist 84),

"Here, in strictness, the people surrender nothing," he was echoing what James Wilson said at the Constitutional Convention, that the document did not invent any new rights.[20] The Founders were not disciples of Hobbes, who depicted the state of nature as anarchic and barbaric because there were, he insisted, no rights antecedent to government, and there was no morality antecedent to civil society, that cannot exist antecedent to government. The American Founding is unintelligible other than as a decisive rejection of Hobbes' doctrine. A limited government—a government whose powers are limited because they are enumerated—presupposes a reservoir of rights that pre-exist government. And Thomas Paine's axiom that "society is produced by our wants and government by our wickedness" assumes, as Locke did with his more benign view of the state of nature, that some sociability and arrangements of cooperation precede government.[21]

Theories of natural law explain the necessary and sufficient elements of individual flourishing and of communities conducive to social fulfillment. Because the idea of natural law is about what constitutes worthy living for beings of our nature, natural law is inextricably connected to the idea of a constant and knowable human nature. The problem for natural law theorists is to square that idea with the fact that people—including honorable, intelligent, and educated people of good will—differ about what constitutes human flourishing.

We are individual animals with passions and appetites, over the promptings of which we are only intermittently and imperfectly sovereign. If, or when, reason is, as David Hume said, "the slave of the passions," then we, too, are slaves, lacking the dignity of beings capable of meaningful ethical behavior.[22] Reason is not always autonomous; it is sometimes subservient to our animal imperatives. But reason must be capable of autonomy, even if only imperfectly and intermittently. If reason cannot be, in this sense, free, then our choices cannot be products of reflection, and the idea of an ethical life is meaningless. When, before Hume, Hobbes said that our "thoughts" serve our "desires" as "scouts and spies" that "range abroad" to "find the way to the things desired," he, like Hume, made problematic the idea of a human capacity for real agency. The concept of natural law attempts to solve this problem.[23]

We are social animals, dependent for our physical survival and mental well-being on some degree of sociability. To speak of natural rights is to bring the theoretical into the service of the practical: Are there things we must do, and must not do, in order to improve the probability of commodious and worthy living for creatures with our natures? Are there claims—natural rights—that, in a good society, people should be able to effectively assert in order to protect such ways of living? At no point does one need to feel bound to postulate that natural law, in the sense described here, requires a transcendent lawgiver. One can believe in moral knowledge teased from reflection on human nature and historic experience without believing that this is related to God's revealed intentions.

If there is a God, and if God has intentions regarding us, presumably He caused them to be incorporated into nature. This is the optional theological foundation of natural rights doctrine. It is not a necessary foundation. A secular basis for natural rights reasoning is that rights are natural in the sense that they are discovered by something that is natural: reason. But the enjoyment of natural rights requires something that is not natural, that does not arise spontaneously and amply from nature's processes. For rights to be established and defended in a social context requires certain virtues; so does the worthy use of those rights. The language of natural law, which can supplement the natural rights vocabulary, need not presuppose a divine lawgiver. Rather, this language is merely a way of talking about the appropriate ends and efficient means for human flourishing. Natural law discourse is like scientific discourse in that it is empirical: If, as experience and philosophical reasoning suggests, X is a desirable end, then experience also suggests that Y is conducive to that end.

JEFFERSON'S EQUIVOCATION

Hence the meaning, and unimportance, of what C. Bradley Thompson calls "Jefferson's equivocation" in the Declaration's first paragraph when he referred to "the Laws of Nature and of Nature's God." Jefferson, Adams, and others were, Thompson argues, firmly in a tradition "which said that the moral laws of nature would still be valid and operational even if, in the words of Grotius, 'there is no God, or that he has no Care of human affairs.'"[24] Some Americans thought their rights derived from history; others thought their rights could be read in the book of nature. This was a distinction without much, if any, difference. Both sets of Americans were, without quite knowing it, rule utilitarians. That is, they were saying that certain behaviors, practices, and conventions are, as a general rule, conducive to happiness and flourishing.

Among the Founders the ideas of natural law and natural rights were severed from any necessary connection with religion and transcendence. Nature, including human nature, can be known by reason unassisted by revelation. So, therefore, can the rules of ethics and politics that are pertinent to human flourishing. They are learned, as most things are, by trial and error, through which humanity learns what is and is not conducive to flourishing. It is therefore difficult, and perhaps pointless, to distinguish between, on the one hand, natural law and natural rights reasoning and, on the other hand, the reasoning of rule utilitarianism. Both those who reason in the vocabulary of natural law and natural rights and those who reason as rule utilitarians are recommending behaviors and arrangements they consider, as a general rule, most useful to creatures with our natures. This is what Thompson calls "an *if-given-then*' conditional imperative."[25] *If* you want to achieve a particular outcome, *given* the facts about human beings, *then* the following rules are apposite.

In the epigraph that begins this chapter, Alexander Hamilton speaks of natural rights as written "in the whole volume of human nature." Nature is, like a book, a volume that can be read by anyone with basic literacy about the human condition. Hamilton's sentence went on to say that the rights are written "by the hand of the divinity itself."[26] That, however, was almost a verbal tic among eighteenth century writers, lacking theological meaning.

How can we say that convictions about natural rights were important to the statesmen who framed the Constitution that accommodated slavery? Here is how: The Framers were statesmen. "There is," wrote Leo Strauss, "a universally valid hierarchy of ends, but there are no universally valid rules of action." Steven Hayward, a student of Straussians who shares their belief that statesmanship is a *philosophically* serious subject, improves upon Strauss' formulation by writing: "The prudence of the statesman may be described as the combination of attachment to principle along with a profound under-standing of the circumstances." Two archetypal instances of prudence in American statecraft concern slavery. Had the Constitution's Fram-ers not accommodated the existence of slavery, the document would not have been written, and the nation would have been stillborn. As Harry Jaffa, a student of Lincoln's statesmanship, put the point, "If [the Founders] had attempted to secure *all* the rights of *all* men they would have ended in *no* rights secured for *any* men." And had Lincoln not been willing to accept the continuation of slavery where it was— while attempting to confine it there, and thereby put it "in the course of ultimate extinction"—he could not have won the presidential office from which he steered the nation through the war that saved the Union. As Jaffa wrote, "Negroes have voting rights and serve on juries today owing in large measure to the fact that Lincoln in the 1850s disavowed any intention to make them voters or jurors."[27]

How does a society decide what the natural rights are? The answer is: It argues. The argument can never be concluded because it has a large empirical dimension, the ongoing accumulation, from history and contemporary life, of evidence pertinent to what Randy Barnett, very like C. Bradley Thompson, calls "given-if-then" reasoning: *Given* the constancy and regularities of human nature, *if* our aim is the flourishing of creatures of this nature living in close proximity to one another, *then* the following institutional arrangements are requisite for securing the rights deemed, on the basis of a constantly enriched body of evidence, necessary, or at least powerfully conducive to, such flourishing.[28] Any political regime is necessarily, unavoidably built in a way that encourages and discourages certain habits. Indeed, regimes are defined by the moral dispositions they nurture, intentionally or otherwise. A regime may eschew the enforcement, or even the promotion, of the good life, but it cannot be indifferent to the prevention or discouragement of certain gross evils. Or to the encouragement of an array of attitudes and aptitudes deemed conducive to human flourishing. So public policy must be informed by political philosophy.

Politics *can* be what Aristotle called the "master science" because government, having a monopoly on legal authority and the legitimate force to impose it, *can* undertake to control the education and other sources of norms by which society is regulated.[29] Limiting such uses of political power is a political choice, one that does much to define the liberal democratic political order. The empirical case for limited government is that although human beings have something in common—human nature—they are different in capacities and aspirations. From this it follows, not logically but practically, that government cannot hope to provide happiness to all. The most it can reasonably expect to provide are the conditions under which happiness, as each defines it, can be pursued.

So, let the argument—actually, the interlocking arguments—boil on: What do we mean by human nature? How do we sort the natural attributes—those constitutive of human nature—from those acquired from nurturing and from culture? By what criteria should we measure human flourishing? What do history and current practices reveal about how institutions—of civil society and government; political and economic and cultural institutions—contribute to this?

Intelligent, learned, public-spirited people will differ, often strenuously, about all of these matters. Of course they will. This is what makes politics in an open society—a society based on persuasion—so demanding and so exhilarating. But differences debated can converge, reaching, if not consensus, at least clarity about disputes and a narrowing of differences. What is important is to reorient American debate about these questions and by so doing to insinuate the Founders' natural rights vocabulary back into our political discourse. This will buttress that which the Founders created for the purpose of securing natural rights: limited government. We shall see the direct pertinence of the reorientation in subsequent chapters dealing with, among many other things, the role of the judiciary in the supervision of democracy and with the relationship of the government to the economy.

The reorientation I recommend is radical relative to current political practices. It reverts to the radicalism of the American Revolution, as explained by historian Gordon Wood. This radicalism consisted in its overturning a society of deference. The social conditions normally considered precursors of revolutions—gross poverty and severe political oppression—were not present. "In fact," Wood writes, "the colonists knew they were freer, more equal, more prosperous, and less burdened with cumbersome feudal and monarchical restraints than any other part of mankind in the eighteenth century." Nevertheless, says Wood, it is wrong to say that the revolution was merely an intellectual event, the culmination of a constitutional argument about American rights, a dispute that had nothing to do with social conditions. These are elements of the argument that ours was a conservative revolution, an argument that Wood emphatically rejects. He insists that the American Revolution "was as radical and as revolutionary as any in history," but was "radical and social in a very special eighteenth-century sense."[30] It severed the conception of society from the conception of government. Hitherto, the assumption was that the state precedes and sustains society; America's revolutionary idea was to reverse that formulation. What made the colonists restive, and then revolutionary, was, Wood writes, their acute sense that government was the root cause of their social grievances:

> Social honors, social distinctions, perquisites of office, business contracts, privileges and monopolies, even excessive property and wealth of various sorts—all social evils and social deprivations—in fact seemed to flow from connections to [...] monarchical authority. So that when Anglo-American radicals talked in what seems to be only political terms—purifying a corrupt constitution, eliminating courtiers, fighting off crown power, and, most important, becoming republicans—they nevertheless had a decidedly social message.... [I]n destroying monarchy and establishing republics they were changing their society as well as their governments, and they knew it.[31]

The colonists lived, Wood argues, in a society that was "traditional in its basic social relationships and in its cultural consciousness. All aspects of life were intertwined" in that authority and liberty depended on personal relationships. The colonists "thought of themselves as connected vertically rather than horizontally, and were more apt to be conscious of those immediately above and below them than they were of those alongside them." Gazing down, those at the top saw those below them as almost a different species. They were "the grazing multitude," in the words of one member of the elite, a Virginia planter named George Washington. Indeed, paternalism and patriarchy "may even have been stronger in America than in England precisely because of the weakness in the colonies of other institutions." Counting not only slaves but also others who were indentured or otherwise bound in legal dependency, "at any one moment as much as one-half of colonial society was legally unfree." The sense of "personal clientage and dependency" was reinforced by the fact that provincial governments were small crumbs from the upper crust: "The combined membership of the New York colonial assembly and council was even smaller than a committee in today's House of Representatives."[32]

Yet in spite of all this, Americans were, in Edmund Burke's phrase, quick to "snuff tyranny in every tainted breeze." America was, Wood says, "primed for republicanism" because "it had no oppressive established church, no titled nobility, no great distinctions of wealth, and no generality of people sunk in indolence and poverty." Furthermore, colonial America's defining surplus—land to the west—powerfully beckoned as a ladder up from dependency and thus it worked as a solvent of "the ligaments of patronage and kinship."[33]

Burke considered it a signal virtue of the English political tradition that its constitutional order emerged slowly, organically from the nation's organic history rather than being "formed upon a regular plan or with any unity of design."[34] A conservative sensibility does indeed dispose people against attempting the rearrangement of the state in accordance with a preconceived design. This, however, is essentially what America's Founders did. Nations are made in two ways, by the slow working of history or the galvanic force of ideas, or by both. Most nations are made mostly the former way, emerging slowly from the mist of the past, gradually coalescing within concentric circles of shared sympathies, with an accretion of consensual institutions. One nation, however, was formed and defined by the citizens' assent to a shared philosophy. The United States was from its beginning a nation of immigrants whose social diversities are subsumed beneath a shared dedication to a creed.

Before there could be this creedal nation, this extensive republic "dedicated" to certain self-evident truths, the American Revolution had to be followed quickly by Madison's revolution in democratic theory. Prior to him there had been a pessimistic consensus among political philosophers: If democracy were to be possible, this would be only in small societies akin to Pericles' Athens or Rousseau's Geneva—"face-to-face" societies sufficiently small and homogeneous to avoid the supposed great threat to freedom: "factions." In turning this notion upside down—this is what a revolution does—Madison taught the world a new catechism of popular government:

What is the worst result of politics? Tyranny. To what form of tyranny is democracy prey? Tyranny of the majority. How can that be avoided? By preventing the existence of majorities that are homogeneous, and therefore stable, durable, and potentially tyrannical. How can that be prevented? By *cultivating factions*, so that majorities will be unstable because they are short-lived coalitions of minorities.

The cultivation of factions is what an "extensive" republic does by its sheer scale. This was Madison's sociology of freedom, which he explained in his contributions to the most penetrating and influential newspaper columns ever penned—the Federalist Papers, to which Alexander Hamilton and John Jay also contributed. In Federalist 10, Madison wrote that "the extent" of the nation would help provide "a republican remedy for the diseases most incident to republican government." He said: "Extend the sphere, and you take in a greater variety of parties and interests; you make it less probable that a majority of the whole will have a common motive to invade the rights of other citizens." Because "the most common and durable source of factions" is "the various and unequal distribution of property," the "first object of government" is the "protection of different and unequal faculties of acquiring property." The maelstrom of self-interested behavior that is characteristic of Madisonian democracy often is not pretty. However, Madison knew better than to judge politics by aesthetic standards. He saw reality steadily and saw it whole, and in Federalist 51 he said people could trace "through the whole system of human affairs" the "policy of supplying, by opposite and rival interests, the defect of better motives."[35]

The Founders' philosophy began with accommodation of, not cures for, human defectiveness. Harvey C. Mansfield rightly says of the Founders, "It is true that they distrusted democracy, but not because they loved aristocracy. They distrusted democracy for the same reason they rejected aristocracy—because they distrusted human nature."[36]

The importance of politics is that because of human nature, the world is an unfriendly place when it is without government. It is, however, often equally or more unfriendly when bad governments are unlimited and unleashed to work their wills upon subjects who are subject to whatever their government wills. Conservatism's foundational premise is that the world is an inherently dangerous place and politics is necessary to mitigate its dangers.

But politics itself also is dangerous. It can be the ultimate danger because it can organize violence. In the interest of social peace, modern politics have pushed the higher aspirations of the ancients to the margins of social life. To modern political philosophers, those aspirations were at best unrealistic and at worst dangerous. Henceforth, politics would not be a sphere in which human nature is perfected; the political project would not include prodding people to their highest potentials. Instead, modern politics would be based on the assumption that people will express, and act upon, the strong impulses of their flawed natures. People will be self-interested. The ancients had asked, What is the highest attainment of which mankind is capable and how can we pursue this? Hobbes and subsequent moderns asked, What is the worst that can happen and how can we avoid it?

In 1762, fourteen years before America's Founders launched the first modern nation, Jean-Jacques Rousseau wrote in *The Social Contract*: "Those who dare to undertake the institution of a people must feel themselves capable, as it were, of changing human nature, of transforming each individual [...] into a part of a much greater whole, [...] of altering the constitution of a man for the purpose of strengthening it."[37] Here we have the beginning of the great divide in modern political thinking, and a germ of American progressives' collectivist tendency. America's Founders believed that in creating a polity, statesmen must take their bearings from unchanging human nature. They did not aspire to a political system so cleverly constructed that no one needs to be public-spirited: They did, however, want a system that did not presuppose an abundant and constant supply of public-spiritedness.

For the Founders, law existed mostly for mundane purposes. The word "mundane" has come to mean dull or boring, but its primary meaning is "of this world." The law's primary purposes are to keep the peace and facilitate quotidian transactions—to resolve disputes and regularize behaviors and expectations. The law is not supposed to be salvific; it is not written to perfect either the individual or the community. When government undertakes, by methodical policy, to improve and fix the citizenry's consciousness, the citizenry ceases to be composed of citizens, properly understood. When government presumes to adjust the attitudes of the people, it vitiates the concept of consent, from which the just powers of government arise.

Consent is the primal act of a republican citizenry; the right to consent to government is the right to insist on the recognition of other rights. The right to consent presupposes the right to be persuaded. This presupposes in the citizenry a certain threshold of rationality, hence a durable claim to respect. A government that is required by the ethos of republicanism to persuade is a government inherently secondary to that which must be persuaded, a society composed of self-determining individuals. Such a government need not be uninterested in improving the souls of its citizens, but it must do so by respecting their reasonableness and thereby encouraging them to subordinate passions to reason. When Aristotle defined human beings as political animals and as language-using animals he was making a single argument for democracy, meaning government by the consent of the governed. Human beings can speak to one another, and to their leaders, who can speak back. Human communities feature constant talk about alternative arrangements for living together. The reasons for preferring some arrangements over others require us to speak about justice. Which is why, in America's constitutional order, the First Amendment comes first.

America's Founders, and particularly the wisest and most subtle of them, James Madison, insinuated their unsentimental view of self-interested human beings into the Constitution's separation of powers. In Federalist 51, Madison said: "Ambition must be made to counteract ambition." The self-interests of rival institutions will check one another. Madison continued: "It may be a reflection on human nature, that such devices should be necessary to control the abuses of government. But what is government itself, but the greatest of all reflections on human nature? If men were angels, no government would be necessary. If angels were to govern men, neither external nor internal controls on government would be necessary." So, said Madison, we must have a policy of "supplying, by opposite and rival interests, the defect of better motives."[38] But neither Madison nor the other Founders meant that we should presuppose that America could prosper without anyone having any good motives. Such motives are manifestations of good character, and America's Founders did not suppose that freedom can thrive, or even survive, without appropriate education and other nourishments of character. They meant education, broadly understood to include not just education by schools but also by all the institutions of civil society that explain freedom and equip citizens with the virtues freedom requires. These virtues include industriousness, self-control, moderation, and responsibility, virtues that reinforce the rationality essential to human happiness.

When Madison, like the Founders generally, spoke of human nature, he was not speaking, as modern progressives do, of something malleable, inconstant, fluid, and evolving, something constantly formed and re-formed by changing social and other historical forces that can and should be controlled and manipulated by government. When people today speak of nature, they generally speak of flora and fauna—of trees and animals and other things not human. But the Founders spoke of nature as a guide to, and measure of, human action. They thought of nature not as something to be molded for human convenience but rather as a source of norms to be discovered. They understood that natural rights could not be asserted, celebrated, and defended unless nature, including human nature, was regarded as a normative rather than a merely contingent fact. This was a view partially derived from and buttressed by the teaching of Biblical religion: Nature is not chaos but rather is the replacement of chaos by an order reflecting the mind and will of the Creator. This is the Creator who endows us with natural rights that are inalienable and universal—and hence the foundation of democratic equality. And these rights are the foundation of limited government—government defined by the limited goal of securing those rights so that individuals may flourish in their free and responsible exercise of those rights.

A government thus limited is not in the business of imposing its opinions about what happiness the citizens should choose to pursue. Having such opinions is the business of other institutions—private and voluntary ones, including religious ones, that nourish the conditions for liberty. The Founders did not consider natural rights reasonable because religion affirmed them; rather, the Founders considered religion reasonable because it secured those rights. There may, however, be a cultural contradiction in modernity. The contradiction is that although religion can sustain liberty, liberty does not necessarily sustain religion or the other preconditions for its own security. This is of paramount importance because of the seminal significance of the Declaration of Independence's second paragraph:

> We hold these truths to be self-evident, that all men are created equal, that they are endowed by their Creator with certain unalienable Rights, that among these are Life, Liberty and the pursuit of Happiness.—That to secure these rights, Governments are instituted among Men, deriving their just powers from the consent of the governed,—That whenever any Form of Government becomes destructive of these ends, it is the Right of the People to alter or to abolish it, and to institute new Government,

laying its foundation on such principles and organizing its powers in such form, as to them shall seem most likely to effect their Safety and Happiness.

America was born with an epistemological assertion: The important political truths are not merely knowable, they are known. They are self-evident in that they are obvious to any mind not clouded by ignorance or superstition. It is, the Declaration says, self-evidently true that "all men are created equal" not only in their access to the important political truths, but also in being endowed with certain unalienable rights, including the rights to life, liberty, and the pursuit of happiness. Perhaps the most important word in the Declaration is the word "secure": "[T]o secure these rights, governments are instituted among men." Government's primary purpose is to secure pre-existing rights. Government does not create rights; it does not dispense them. This assumption, the bedrock premise of American political thought, has hardly been uncontroversial in our time. It has been at the center of the controversy that has shaped our political debate for more than a century. Since the rise of progressivism, the debate has been between adherents of the Founders' thought and progressives who have confidently advocated leaving that thought behind.

In his first inaugural address, addressing himself to "my dissatisfied fellow countrymen," Abraham Lincoln expressed "a patient confidence in the ultimate justice of the people."[39] Note his cagey nuances. Confidence must be patient because the justice of the people can be counted on only ultimately. He was delicately stepping onto contested ground where Jefferson had preceded him. In 1801, in Jefferson's first inaugural address, he said, "Though the will of the majority is in all cases to prevail, that will to be rightful must be reasonable; that the minority possess their equal rights, which equal law must protect, and to violate would be oppression."[40] Jefferson's formulation is not altogether clear. When he said the majority "is" to prevail in all cases, was he merely making a neutral prediction? Or was he enunciating an ethical norm? Did he mean that the majority inevitably will prevail, or that it ought to? If he meant either, he was soon to be shown to be wrong.

Two years later, in *Marbury v. Madison*, Chief Justice John Marshall, the cousin whom Jefferson detested, established judicial review. This would temper the dubious assumption and dangerous practice that under America's written Constitution the majority, understood as the voice of a representative, majoritarian process, must and should have its way. In many cases, majorities have a right to have their way even when they are unreasonable. Majorities have vigorously exercised this right throughout American history. Jefferson said majorities have no right to violate minority rights, but he did not say why majorities do not have this right. If he meant that no majority has a right to violate the natural rights of any person or group of persons, then the will of the majority should not only not prevail in all cases, it should not prevail in many cases. We shall recur to this subject in Chapter 4, where we examine the justification for, and the increasingly urgent need for, judicial supervision of democracy.

This supervision is one answer to the question that fascinated Alexis de Tocqueville. He understood that this nation would be the great laboratory in which mankind might discover whether "democratic liberty" can flourish without giving way to "democratic tyranny." Martin Diamond, who masterfully placed the Founders in the stream of Western political thought, noted the philosophic pedigree of an interesting fact about the writing of the Declaration of Independence. In Jefferson's original draft he wrote that all men "are created equal and independent." The word "independent," Diamond said, "refers to the condition of men in the state of nature, to their utter nonsubordination, in the state of nature, to each other or any common political sovereign."[41] Democracy would be the mechanism of political subordination. But it would be democracy limited, tempered and refined by institutional architecture intended to guarantee that limited subordination through democracy would be instrumental to the enjoyment of liberty. And the regime of liberty would mean all persons having equal rights to become unequal.

The Declaration, said Diamond, was, in Lincoln's language, "conceived in liberty," meaning that "the deepest stratum of American political life"—"the very foundation of American political existence"—*is* the liberty in which the Declaration was conceived. All individuals are "created equally entitled to that liberty."[42] The nation that began four score and seven years before 1863—that began with the Declaration—had, congenitally, meaning from birth, the single defining goal of equal political liberty. The Declaration did not stipulate a form of government. It was silent on that subject as it declared that "these united colonies are, and of right ought to be, free and independent states." There was a war for independence to be won, and the Articles of Confederation to be improvised among the "united colonies," which would lead to the constitutional convention. All this occurred in just eleven tumultuous years that culminated in the nation committing itself in the Constitution to a democratic form of government to secure equal liberty for themselves and subsequent generations. It was, however, as Diamond wrote, "a sober and cautious commitment."[43]

The constitutional architecture was created by men sobered by deep reading about earlier republics, and made cautious by hard experience during what historians have termed the "critical period" of American history under the Articles. The Constitution's Framers created, Diamond said, "a democratic government carefully safeguarded and structured so as to enhance the excellences of democracy while guarding against its dangers and defects." The fact that the Framers spoke often about those dangers and defects has led many, following the lead of the progressive historians of the first half of the twentieth century, to portray the Framers as reluctant democrats, or even as anti-democratic. However, they spoke insistently about the difficulties of democracy (e.g., Edmund Randolph on its "turbulence and follies") because they had no intention of creating any other form of government. This explains the Declaration's silence, or what Diamond calls its neutrality, about the proper form of government. The silence reflected not uncertainty but consensus about the basic matter: America's government would be based on mechanisms for securing the regularly recurring consent of the governed. But as Diamond said, the Declaration's silence also underscored this: "[D]emocracy is made, not the *end* of government, but merely the governmental *means* for the securing of the true end, namely, the people's equal liberties."[44]

So, the Constitution follows logically from the Declaration; the Constitution is entailed, Diamond argued, by the Declaration's implicit "subordination of democracy to liberty." By its very silence about the proper form of government, the Declaration proclaims that all forms of government are to be judged by how instrumental they are to the project of securing inalienable rights. Thus, wrote Diamond, "the Declaration teaches Americans to view even their own democratic self-rule coolly" because any form of government is to be judged against a standard higher than itself. The Constitution, with its separation of powers and other provisions for refining and elevating public opinion, reflected what Diamond called "the American people's sensible self-doubt."[45] The fact that they had decided that democracy was the best instrument for securing equal liberty did not mean that it was not risky. The Founders understood, from their study of history and their personal experiences, that democracy is susceptible to degeneracy, folly, and oppression. Nevertheless, the Founders' unsentimental embrace of democracy was a firm embrace. They were modern men who, armed with what they considered a new science of politics, consciously turned their backs on the ancients. Diamond understood the rupture between ancients and moderns:

The ancients saw man as capable of reaching nearly to the divine and took their bearings from the highest possibilities of human nature. While the ancients had no illusions about the capacity of *most* men, they thought that every resource of the political art should be employed to draw out and up the potential of the exceptional few. Their very idea of human nature led classical thinkers to make the preeminent political task the bringing toward completeness or perfection the relative few who were naturally capable of fulfilling their humanness. The classical idea of human nature is, as it were, aristocratic: all men are human but some are more so, and that is the crucial political fact. The modern idea of human nature is democratic: no difference among us can reach so far as to alter our naturally equal humanness, and *that* is the crucial fact.[46]

For the ancients, the art of politics was "strenuous and demanding." And, America's Founders thought, it was utopian, aiming at the unattainable. The Founders' political science would strive "to achieve, not the delusive heights at which the ancients aimed, but solid human decencies." They would rely on the low but solid and— this was, after all, *political* science—predictable constants of "human passions and interests."[47] As Diamond shrewdly saw, from this flinty realism about human nature and possibilities came a powerful new argument for democracy. The Founders' realism did more to deflate the pretensions of the few than to disparage the capacities of the many. The new science of politics, by taking its bearing not from the radical inequality among people but from capacities concerning which people are most equal, denies the *political* relevance of human inequalities. No inequality confers an entitlement to elevated political status.

Again, Diamond: "In the old view, the 'common good' was understood to include certain virtues or excellences which could be nurtured and made preeminent only by the rule of those who peculiarly and unequally possessed those excellences. Now the common good came to mean the protection of what all had in common [...] an equal interest in securing their inalienable rights." In the process of putting the ancients in their place, the Founders also made the case against a characteristic of contemporary progressivism, what Diamond called "sanguine egalitarianism": "[The Founders] did not expect that the mass of mankind could ever rise to such levels of mind and character as would warrant the untrammeled rule of the majority. They did not believe that such a transformation of human nature could be effected by any means, not by education, leisure, greater affluence, the experience of political participation, the benevolent influence of collective social arrangements, or any of the strategies upon which egalitarianism is obliged to pin its hopes."[48]

Woodrow Wilson would explicitly argue that although the separation of powers had once been required to restrain overbearing factions, American society in its temperate maturity had reached such a point of consensus about social progress that the power of majorities was no longer frightening. Particularly when guided by the strong leadership of an enlightened president, factions would no longer pose a menace and so should be untrammeled. The Founders neither saw nor anticipated any such conditions. For them, inequality in social outcomes was inevitable and by no means inherently deplorable. The voluntary interactions of individuals in what we now call the private sector, and what in the Founders' era was called society, aka almost all of life, would *naturally* produce inequalities. Individuals who are naturally unequal in endowments, desires, and exertions would, in a context of political liberty, experience different social results. "In the Founders' understanding," Diamond wrote, "whoever says equality of liberty thereby says inequality of outcomes; whoever says equality of outcomes thereby says inequality of liberty, because only the unequal handicapping of the superior will prevent their capacities from manifesting themselves."[49]

The Founders were not indifferent to virtue, but they were not going to wager the nation's future on an ample supply of it in government officials. Rather, they would implement what Madison called "auxiliary precautions."[50] The Founders thought that America should reap the benefits of virtue not by granting it political entitlement but rather by allowing it scope to manifest itself in the spontaneous order of a lightly governed society. Jefferson's anticipation of, and celebration of, a "natural aristocracy" expressed his confidence that when privileges conferred by custom or buttressed by law are eliminated, natural excellence will well up and should prevail.[51]

More than anyone else's among history's most creative political thinkers, Madison's life exemplified the unity of theory and practice, with each of those influencing the other. If philosophy is impractical, meaning not useful as a guide to political action, it is a sterile exercise. Madison's political philosophy has been singularly applicable, informing the republic's formation, and its understanding of itself. To the distressingly limited extent that it informs American politics today, it is as a disposition or inclination—less a political agenda than a braiding of prudential wariness with a foundation in the doctrine of natural rights. Although Jefferson called Madison "the greatest man in the world," all that many Americans know of Madison is that his wife was a pistol.[52] But he, more than any other Founder, clearly understood and unsparingly articulated the nation's premises and their institutional implications. If we really believed the pen is mightier than, or even more dignified than, the sword, the nation's capital would be named not for the soldier who wielded the revolutionary sword, but for the thinker who was ablest with a pen. It would be Madison, D.C.

Madison was, in the words of a colleague, "no bigger than half a piece of soap," which might be one reason why there is no monument to him in Washington.[53] There is a tall, austere monument to the tall, austere man for whom the city is named, a man of Roman virtues and eloquent reticence. There is a Greek-revival memorial to Madison's boon companion, the tall, elegant, eloquent Jefferson, who is to subsequent generations the most charismatic of the Founders. But there is no monument to the smallest (five feet four inches) but subtlest of the Founders, without whose mind Jefferson's Declaration and Washington's generalship could not have resulted in this republic. Until 1981, there was not even a government building named for

Madison. Then, however, the Library of Congress, which began with Jefferson's donation of his library, needed a new building and named it after the most supple intellect among the Founders—the James Madison Memorial Building.

Madison's rival Alexander Hamilton possessed the conviction, and the brassy indifference to delicacy, to write (in Federalist 6) that "the uniform course of human events" and "the accumulated experience of ages" demonstrate that men are "ambitious, vindictive and rapacious." Madison was, characteristically, more measured. He was less provocative than Hamilton without being less wary when he wrote (in Federalist 55), "As there is a degree of depravity in mankind which requires a certain degree of circumspection and distrust, so there are other qualities in human nature which justify a certain portion of esteem and confidence."[54] A portion that requires institutional precautions. And as will be argued in Chapter 4, today these precautions must involve, more than Madison could have comfortably accepted, the judiciary.

Political philosophy begins with an assertion of the natural—with, that is, a delineation of what is given, meaning permanent, about human nature, and hence the human condition. Or perhaps we should say that political reflection begins with a decision: Should we assume that *anything* is permanent because it is natural? If so, political philosophy begins with human beings prior to society—before society makes its marks upon them. Human beings are social creatures because, as Thomas Paine wrote, their needs, material and immaterial, "impel the whole of them into society, as naturally as gravitation acts to a center." Paine's recourse to the Newtonian vocabulary, which was natural to the eighteenth century, made the point that sociability and society are not optional, not choices. So when he said "we have it in our power to begin the world over again," he was saying we can restart the world of politics and government, but not society.[55] A century on, progressivism's project would be to subordinate society to politics and government.

In 1955, at the high tide of the academic consensus about "consensus" being the central theme of America's political development, political scientist Louis Hartz wrote, "Locke dominates American political thought, as no thinker anywhere dominates the political thought of a nation. He is a massive national cliché."[56] To which conservatives now say: If only that were true. As William James said, we live forward but understand backward. So, if we are to understand the arguments that are shaping America's unfolding future, it is essential that we understand the past from which comes the Founders' vocabulary of our politics. The fact that this vocabulary is increasingly anachronistic and decreasingly controlling is a measure of the steady, more than a century-long ascent of progressivism. To that we now turn, tracing the path of progressivism to Franklin Delano Roosevelt's 1934 speech to San Francisco's Commonwealth Club. Exactly thirty years after which, in "The Speech," as conservatives came to call it, the nationally televised one that Ronald Reagan gave in October 1964 in support of Barry Goldwater's presidential candidacy, Reagan was not wrong when he said: "Our natural, inalienable rights are now considered to be a dispensation of government."[57]

CHAPTER 2

THE PROGRESSIVES' REVISION

AN EMANCIPATION (FROM NATURAL RIGHTS) PROCLAMATION

> What we have to undertake is to systematize the foundations of the house, then to thread all the old parts of the structure with the steel which will be laced together in modern fashion, accommodated to all the modern knowledge of structural strength and elasticity, and then slowly change the partitions, relay the walls, let in the light through new apertures, improve the ventilation; until finally, a generation or two from now, the scaffolding will be taken away, and there will be the family in a great building whose noble architecture will at last be disclosed, where men can live as a single community, co-operative as in a perfected, coordinated beehive....
>
> Woodrow Wilson
> *The New Freedom* (1912)[1]

In 1911, a fire in the Triangle Shirtwaist factory in Manhattan resulted in the deaths by suffocation or jumping of 146 workers. The building had only one fire escape, and many doors were locked, supposedly to prevent pilfering of materials by employees. Watching in horror from the streets was a young social worker, Frances Perkins, who twenty-two years later would become, as President Franklin Roosevelt's secretary of labor, the first woman in a president's cabinet. She served on the commission that studied the Triangle disaster and advocated many of the health and safety laws that defined an emerging kind of liberalism that wielded government to regulate enterprise and shape society's allocation of wealth, opportunity, and security.[2]

American politics can be considered a tale of three liberalisms,[3] the first of which, classical liberalism, teaches that the creative arena of human affairs is society, as distinct from government. Government's proper function is to protect the conditions of life and liberty, primarily for the individual's private pursuit of happiness. This is now called conservatism. Until the New Deal, however, it was the Jeffersonian spirit of most of the Democratic Party. FDR's New Deal liberalism was significantly more ambitious. He said that until the emergence of the modern industrial economy, "government had merely been called upon to produce the conditions within which people could live happily, labor peacefully and rest secure."[4] Now it would be called upon to play a grander role. It would not just provide conditions in which happiness, understood as material well-being, could be pursued. Rather, it would become a deliverer of happiness itself. Government, FDR said, has "final responsibility" for it.[5] This "middle liberalism" of the New Deal supplemented political rights with economic rights. The New Deal, the modern state it created, and the class of people for whom that state provided employment led to the third liberalism, that of the 1960s and beyond. This "managerial liberalism" celebrates the role of intellectuals and other policy elites in rationalizing society from above, wielding the federal government and the "science" of public administration, meaning bureaucracy. This liberalism promises that government's mastery of economic management will end business cycles, thereby guaranteeing a steady flow of revenues for building more than a merely good society, but a Great Society.

The path liberalism has taken to the present began with Woodrow Wilson, passed through the presidency of the man who first came to Washington as Wilson's assistant secretary of the navy, and culminated with the first president to have spent most of his adult life in Washington: Lyndon Johnson, who in 1935, at age twenty-six, began his long climb up the ladder of American politics when he was named by FDR to head the National Youth Administration in Texas. Thirty years later he was president and able to pursue a grandiose agenda because the 1964 election—the landslide defeat of Barry Goldwater—produced in Congress the first liberal legislative majority since the coalition of Republicans and conservative Democrats emerged after voters in the 1938 elections reproved FDR for his plan to "pack" the Supreme Court by enlarging it. Harry McPherson, one of Johnson's senior aides, described how LBJ envisioned the nation as a patient whose pathologies were to receive presidential ministrations: "People were [seen to be] suffering from a sense of alienation from one another, of anomie, of powerlessness. This affected the well-to-do as much as it did the poor. Middle-class women, bored and friendless in the suburban afternoons; fathers, working at 'meaningless' jobs, or slumped before the television set; sons and daughters desperate for 'relevance'—all were in need of community, beauty, and purpose, all were guilty because so many others were deprived while they, rich beyond their ancestors' dreams, were depressed. What would change all this was a creative public effort."[6] It is a wonder America did not wind up with a Department of Meaningful Labor, a "war on anomie," and an Agency for Stimulating and Friendly Suburban Afternoons.

LBJ promised a Great Society "where the city of man serves not only the needs of the body and the demands of commerce but the desire for beauty and the hunger for community."[7] The progressive impulses unleashed after the 1964 election were in their infancy fifty years earlier. In 1914, when Walter Lippmann was helping to launch *The New Republic* magazine, his and its progressivism was of crystalline purity. He wrote: "We can no longer treat life as something that has trickled down to us. We have to deal with it deliberatively, devise its social organization, alter its tools, formulate its method, educate and control it. In endless ways we put intention where custom has reigned." We can, he said, "break up routines" because "the great triumph of modern psychology is its growing capacity for penetrating to the desires that govern our thought."[8] Lippmann was wrong to suppose that hitherto no generation had considered dealing "deliberatively" with life. And it was not unprecedented for reformers to aim to break what Walter Bagehot called "the cake of custom."[9] What was, however, distinctive to American progressives early in the twentieth century was the sweep of their serene confidence that science, including and especially political science, now enabled the benevolent control of "life"—all of it.

If, however, life were to be submitted to progressives' intentions "in endless ways," one impediment had to be removed. Human life could not be made sufficiently malleable until human beings were disabused of the idea of human nature. The philosophy of natural right, which was the Founders' philosophy and the Republic's foundation, rests on one premise: There is a universal human nature. From that fact, by way of philosophic reasoning, come some normative judgments: Certain social arrangements—particularly government by consent attained by persuasion in a society that accepts pluralism—are right for creatures of this nature. Hence the doctrine of *natural* right and the idea of a nation "dedicated," as Lincoln said, to the "proposition" that all men are created equal. Progressivism rests on a historic and, in its way, heroic negative.

It rests on a refusal to accept that nature sets limits to the malleability of human material. The vehemence of political progressives' recoil from the Founders' philosophy is explained by the progressives' investment in the idea that human beings are essentially blank slates on which pretty much anything can be written if the writers know the techniques for doing so. To the question "What most determines the trajectories of individuals, nature or nurture?" the progressives' answer is that nature is negligible, or can be rendered so. Nurturing can be sovereign if it is sufficiently ingenious and determined. The theory that a properly organized and governed society can write progress on humanity's blank slate radically raises the stakes of politics. It also increases the grandeur of government's role, and the importance of governing elites, who are the progressive vanguards of a steadily perfected humanity. Because progressives invest history with a logic and lessons crucial to progress, historians are given special standing. One such, Richard Hofstadter, an intellectual luminary of the post–World War II era, boldly asserted that "no man who is as well abreast of modern science as the Fathers were of eighteenth-century science believes any longer in an unchanging human nature."[10] Hofstadter did not, however, explain what evidence modern science has provided for this conclusion. Indeed, it is difficult to imagine what such evidence would be.

At the turn of the twentieth century, academicians in the burgeon-ing new field of political science presented as a scientific necessity the repudiation of the Founders' natural rights tradition. In 1903, the year the American Political Science Association was founded, the University of Chicago's Charles Edward Merriam published *A History of American Political Theories*, which is still in print. His chapter on "Recent Tenden-cies" celebrated the turn, in the second half of the nineteenth century, toward a method of understanding politics that was "more systematic and scientific" than "the individualistic philosophy of the early years of the century."[11] American academics, going abroad in search of advanced degrees not yet widely available in their country, found in Germany in the second half of the nineteenth century a bureaucracy that they thought of as what Hegel, in the century's first half, had celebrated as the "universal class." Because the bureaucracy's mission was to apply experts' knowledge, the bureaucracy was considered uniquely disinter-ested, and hence was not a class at all.[12] American political scientists, "many of whom were trained in German schools," had, Merriam wrote, "acquired a scientific method of discussing political phenomena." This method discredited the concept of a "social contract" by which the sole source of government and political obligation is "a contract between independent individuals" that creates political society *ex nihilo*.[13] The "state of nature," from which mankind supposedly emerged by means of the social contract, is a fiction. So, therefore, are natural rights that pre-exist government and are independent of it. John Dewey, America's most eminent philosopher in the first half of the twentieth century, wrote that natural rights "exist only in the kingdom of mythological social zoology."[14]

To this, America's Founders might have replied: The purpose of postulating a particular kind of natural state in humanity's distant past was to achieve a particular kind of not-so-distant future for humanity. Those flinty realists' contention was not that the state of nature was a clear historical antecedent—an anthropological condition of which we have evidence. Nor was their contention that a social contract was signed at a spontaneous conclave in some meadow in the state of nature. Rather, the social contract was for the Founders a heuristic concept to illustrate two things. The first was man's natural capacity—and need—for sociability, which is the basis of Aristotle's definition of man as a political animal. Second, the concept illustrated the idea that certain rights are so natural, so essential to human flourishing, that governments are instituted to "secure," not to bestow, them. This, of course, is the language of the most important paragraph in humanity's political history, the second paragraph of the Declaration of Independence.

The "present tendency," wrote Merriam complacently, is to believe that all rights "have their source not in nature, but in law." And government, which is the source of law, is not "the result of a deliberate agreement among men" but is "the result of historical development, instinctive rather than conscious."[15] To which the Founders might have replied by emphasizing that when they talked about the state of nature they were doing philosophy, not anthropology. They also might have directed Merriam's attention to the first paragraph of the first of the Federalist Papers, in which Alexander Hamilton wrote that "it seems to have been reserved to the people of this country, by their conduct and example, to decide the important question, whether societies of men are really capable or not, of establishing good government from reflection and choice, or whether they are forever destined to depend, for their political constitutions, on accident and force."[16]

What Merriam called "the modern school" had formulated "a new idea of liberty, widely different from that" of the Founders. The crux of the difference was that rights "have their source not in nature, but in law," and that laws creating rights do not take their bearings from nature. The state is the "creator" of liberty because it makes liberty possible; the state is not only the "source" of liberty, it guarantees and protects it. Therefore, the state is entitled to determine liberty's limits. Stripped of its status as a natural right, liberty is understood as obtained "only through the organization of political institutions." There is an "inseparable connection between political liberty and political capacity." The "'protection theory' of government"—that government exists to protect life, liberty, and property—is to be "broadened out" to encompass government doing for people what they cannot, or should not, or will not do alone. Hence "the only limitations on governmental action are those dictated by experience or the needs of the time." Which were not really limitations, if Professor Woodrow Wilson was correct that society, and hence government, exists for the unlimited purpose of supplying "mutual aid to self-development." Summing up the consensus of "modern thinkers," Merriam said: "It is not admitted that there are no limits to the action of the state, but on the other hand it is fully conceded that there are no 'natural rights' which bar the way. The question is now one of expediency rather than of principle." So, there being no limiting principle, government is "limited" only by its own assessment of its own expediency.[17]

If human beings are essentially historical, if they are merely creatures capable of adapting to cultural promptings, then the concept of human nature is erased. If so, all that can be known, and all that can be pertinent to politics, is the nature of human beings in a particular social context at a particular moment. If there is no sense in which there is an eternal human nature, there cannot be eternal principles—certainly no self-evident truths—of political organization and action. Because progressivism sought to supplant nature with history as a source of standards for judging political arrangements, it was fitting that a history book became one of progressivism's defining texts. Because progressivism held that new economic forces had rendered America's political arrangements anachronistic, it was appropriate this history text would be written by a Columbia University professor who began in the history department but moved to a position teaching politics and government. And because the advancement of progressivism required disparagement of the Founders who had put in place the political system that progressivism aimed to discredit, it was understandable that this text would teach that economic motives—basically, venality—explain the Founders' political behavior. Hence Charles Beard's *An Economic Interpretation of the Constitution of the United States*, published in 1913, the year a Princeton professor became president of the United States.

A century later, it is difficult to appreciate this book's canonical status for a generation of progressive historians. The Constitution, Beard explained, is a "delicate instrument" designed by the Founders—"we cannot help marveling at their skill"—for the purpose of rendering the popular will impotent by shattering it. Madison, Beard noted, had seen danger in "an interested and over-bearing majority." The purpose of progressivism, Beard thought, was to emancipate majorities and enable them to succeed in their attack on entrenched wealth and power. The Founders' "leading idea was to break up the attacking forces at the starting point: the source of political authority for the several branches of the government." The separation of powers guaranteed the "disintegration of positive action." And in Beard's judgment, the most sinister of the powers was that of the judiciary, which used "the sanctity and mystery of the law as a foil to democratic attacks." He thought "the keystone of the whole structure" is "judicial control," which he called "the most unique contribution to the science of government which has been made by American political genius." The power of judges nominated by presidents and confirmed by the Senate, and the fact that the two political branches of government have different constituencies and electoral rhythms, means, Beard lamented, that "a complete renewal of the government at one stroke is impossible."[18]

The philosopher John Dewey was a pioneer of pragmatism, and it was understandable that progressivism in politics emerged simultaneously with pragmatism in philosophy. Pragmatism, as Harvey C. Mansfield says, "seeks a science of the emergent, the evolving, the developing."[19] It is result-oriented, although it has difficulty saying exactly why whatever emerges constitutes improvement. It simply says that by emerging from whatever was, it represents, by definition, advancement. At the time, advancement meant moving up from individualism. In the first decades of the twentieth century, progressives based their attack on individual rights on a rejection of the concept of individualism. Dewey argued that "the individual is society concentrated," and government should be "as comprehensive as society." In 1918, after the invigorating experience of social solidarity and comprehensive government during World War I, Mary Follett, a philosopher and student of organizational theory and behavior, said that Dewey's vision posed no threat to liberty. Once we are emancipated from the idea of "the particularist individual," and hence from the idea of natural rights belonging thereto, we can reach "a true definition of liberty": "We see that to obey the group which we have helped to make and of which we are an integral part is to be free because we are then obeying ourself [sic].... The state must be no external authority which restrains and regulates me, but it must be myself acting as the state in every smallest detail of life."[20]

Breaking an unruly society and unregenerate individuals to the saddle of the state was the mission of Herbert Croly, a diligent scold whose severities earned him the reputation as "Crolier than thou." Few American books first published in 1909 are still in print; one of them has never since then been out of print, and its influence on American governance goes marching on. Herbert Croly's *The Promise of American Life*, a manifesto for the progressive movement, was perhaps the twentieth century's most influential book on American politics. Teddy Roosevelt adopted Croly's phrase "new Nationalism" and adopted Croly as an adviser after reading the book (it was given to him by Louis Brandeis) during an African safari. It was, however, the Democratic administrations of Woodrow Wilson (whom Croly endorsed in 1916), Franklin Roosevelt, and Lyndon Johnson that were animated by Croly's belief that "national cohesion" required the emancipation of Americans from "traditional illusions," especially the Jeffersonian tradition of "individualist and provincial democracy." Croly spoke for a growing class of progressive intellectuals and politicians for whom progress meant movement away from local institutions and attachments, which they regarded as retrograde. Progress meant conscripting the people into a national consciousness and collective undertakings. This must include, Croly said, "increasing control over property in the public interest." He believed that "human nature"—human nature, not just behavior—"can be raised to a higher level by an improvement in institutions and laws."[21] If that is so, however, there really is no human nature, only malleable human material taking whatever shape that institutions, and the elites that command them, choose.

In 1909, progressives were full of faith in modernity, meaning, among other things, experts applying science to society. This would be done for the improvement of what Croly called "unregenerate citizens," by whom he meant most citizens. He was candid where later, more circumspect progressives would be cryptic. He said "the average American individual is morally and intellectually inadequate to a serious and consistent conception of his responsibilities as a democrat." So national life should be a "school": "The exigencies of such schooling frequently demand severe coercive measures, but what schooling does not?" And "a people are saved many costly perversions" if "the official schoolmasters are wise, and the pupils neither truant nor insubordinate."[22] Croly's book was a blueprint for a twentieth-century progressive aspiration—the state as schoolmarm.

Croly was forthright about his desire to "emancipate American democracy from its Jeffersonian bondage," the bondage to the doctrine of natural rights. Croly called for "a new Declaration of Independence" that would affirm that Americans are "free to organize their political, economic, and social life in the service of a comprehensive, a lofty, and far-reaching democratic purpose." To achieve this, Americans must be cured of the "superstitious awe" with which they regard what he called, dismissively, the "existing" Constitution. "There comes a time in the history of every nation," he wrote, "when its independence of spirit vanishes, unless it emancipates itself in some measure from its traditional illusions."[23] And what is the American illusion that must be shed? The belief—the superstition, Croly thought—that the Constitution, and the limited government it erects for the protection of natural rights (another superstition), is adequate to the exigencies of modern America.

In 1914, five years after *The Promise of American Life*, Croly published *Progressive Democracy*, in which he made explicit his belief that such democracy is properly contrasted with constitutional democracy. Progressive democracy aims for "the emancipation of democracy from the bondage to the Law," partly by making it much easier to amend the fundamental law. He thought progress would be served by making the Constitution amendable "according to the dictates of a preponderant prevailing public opinion." To that end, amendments should be submitted for approval by a mere majority of both houses of Congress, or by just one-fourth of the states, and amendments should be approved by referendums—by a majority of votes in a majority of states. This would virtually eliminate the distinction between the Constitution and ordinary law, so the popular will would no longer be thwarted by constitutional obstacles. Transcending what Croly disparaged as "passive constitutionalism" would enable the government to get on with a bold agenda of "positive economic and social functions." "Republicanism"—by which Croly meant, primarily, Theodore Roosevelt—had "been prophetic of progressivism" but could not go sufficiently far in that direction because of "the limitations of its underlying traditions," meaning the natural rights tradition that had been emphatically reaffirmed by the first Republican president.[24]

Croly had the progressive's distaste for political parties, whose partisanship was incompatible with progressivism's aspiration for government by disinterested experts served by and implementing social science: "American parties had been organized to work with the Constitution, and to supply the deficiencies of that document as an instrument of democratic policy.... The emancipation of the government from the Law brings with it the emancipation of the democracy from its bondage to partisan organization. The government itself, rather than the parties, is to be responsible for the realization of the popular will." Croly spoke of the nation "trying to pull itself together for a new attack upon the problems of its life" and attempting to "release its collective life from the bondage to bad habits." He included among those bad habits Americans' excessive regard for the Constitution and for the natural rights tradition it presupposes. "American nationality," he said, "was associated at its birth with the attempt to create a righteous political and social system." However, "this ideal of social righteousness has been gradually disentangled from the specific formulation in which lawyers and political thinkers embodied it at the end of the eighteenth century." Continuing his theme of bondage, a term still heavily freighted in Croly's day with association with slavery, he said: "The bondage of the national will has been due, not to the existence of the ideal, adhesion to which would always be binding and liberating, but to the sacredness attached to a particular method of applying the ideal, which was the result of a genuine and valuable but limited and, in part, superseded phase of political and social experience." The constitutional system of limited government had been fine long ago, but had become a system of enslavement that must be "superseded."[25]

With a nod to the strength of the superstition he was trying to cure, Croly still referred to the authors of modern America's misfortune reverently as "the Fathers." But he said that they committed a cardinal sin in the eyes of those who, like progressives, had come to see the world, including the social world, through Darwin's eyes. The Fathers, Croly said, made the mistake of believing in permanency. They "believed they could guarantee the righteous expression of the popular will by a permanent definition of the fundamental principles of right, by incorporating these specific principles in the fundamental law and by imposing obedience to these principles on the organs of government whereby the popular will was expressed." Twentieth-century America, Croly exulted, differed from the Fathers regarding fundamentals. America had "abandoned the innocent yet pedantic rationalism of the eighteenth century" and developed "a different conception of the nature of political sovereignty." The people remain sovereign, but the people are, at last, to be properly educated and led in ways commensurate with the new century's enlightenment: "The value of the social structure is commensurate with the value of the accompanying educational discipline and enlightenment. A better society may be built up, but only in so far as better men and women are called forth by the work. Human beings are at once the designers of the house, its artisans, its materials, and its fruits."[26]

The Constitution's separation of powers is, Croly said, "desirable," but then he retracted that concession. He said progressivism's constitutional project is to "graft on the Constitution some regular method of giving back to the government sufficient integrity of organization and action." This "must be derived not from constitutionalism, but from the ability of the people to achieve some underlying unity of purpose."[27] Manufactured unity could be produced by war or various moral equivalents of war. On March 4, 1933, the nation would hear

Croly-like language from its new president, who would say that to have the "power to wage war against the emergency" of the Depression, "we must move as a trained and loyal army" wielding "broad executive power" that should be "as great as the power that would be given to me if we were in fact invaded by a foreign foe."[28]

Croly saw nothing incongruous or paradoxical about urging that national power be brought to bear on the project of promoting "the increase of American individuality."[29] He was untroubled by the possibility that government programs for the advancement of individuality would result in the promotion of what government considers a wholesome sameness—individuality purged of what government, reflecting majority opinion, regards as retrograde elements. However, the development of the modern sciences, which mesmerized progressives, posed two threats to mankind: the danger of hubris and the danger of demoralization—literally, de-moralization. There was the temptation to believe that, armed with the scientific method, anything in nature or society could be subdued and manipulated by human intentions. Recall Lippmann's aspiration to "put intention where custom has reigned."[30] One implication of the new social science was that human beings, far from being masters, are themselves thoroughly mastered because they are imbedded in natural causation. These ideas were embraced by the leading jurist of the era.

Oliver Wendell Holmes, wounded many times from Ball's Bluff to Antietam during the Civil War, was fifty-four in 1895 when, in a Memorial Day oration, he wished for more war: "In this snug, over-safe corner of the world we need it, that we may realize that our comfortable routine is no eternal necessity of things, but merely a little space of calm in the midst of the tempestuous untamed streaming of the world, and in order that we may be ready for danger." We need war, Holmes said, "in this time of individualist negations" when people were "denying that anything is worthy of reverence." His longing for reverence was hardly congruent with his jurisprudence, the premise of which was that society, like the universe, is merely a field of forces, the strongest of which deserves to prevail. His Memorial Day prayer "not for comfort, but for combat" did, however, express his view that it is wrong and, worse, pointless for law to try to tame, stymie or deflect social forces, which should be free to work themselves out.[31]

Holmes enjoyed using rhetoric that would *épater les bourgeois*, as when he said that "a law should be called good if it reflects the will of the dominant forces of the community even if it will take us to hell."[32] But a significant portion of the American bourgeoisie—the progressive portion, whose approbation gratified Holmes—was not at all shocked by his truculent majoritarianism. Unleashing majorities was a progressive objective. "With your belief in some apriorities like equality," Holmes wrote in a letter to the English political theorist Harold Laski, "you may have difficulties. I who believe in force (mitigated by politeness) have no trouble—and if I were sincere and were asked certain *whys* by a woman should reply, 'Because Ma'am I am the bull.'"[33] Holmes delighted in saying "that we have not the kind of cosmic importance that the parsons and philosophers teach. I doubt if a shudder would go through the spheres if the whole ant heap were kerosened."[34] Sometimes Holmes likened human beings not to insects but to canines. He said that behind many legal rights there is not a pre-existing right, but only a "fighting will" to maintain the rights: "A dog will fight for his bone."[35] Sometimes the determinism Holmes invoked was not biological but social: "[M]an is like all other growing things and when he has grown up in a certain crevice for say twenty years you can't straighten him out without attacking his life."[36] This jurist, who likened human beings to ants, dogs, and plants, saw society merely as a field of forces and thought of law as, inevitably and properly, an accommodation of those forces.

In 1910, Mark Twain, who in that last year of his life lapsed into a nihilism similar to Holmes', wrote: "I see no great difference between a man and a watch, except that the man is conscious and the watch isn't, and the man *tries* to plan things and the watch doesn't. The watch doesn't wind itself and doesn't regulate itself—these things are done exteriorly. Outside influences, outside circumstances, wind the *man* and regulate him."[37] In a similar spirit, Holmes in 1897 had argued for capital punishment because human agency is a fiction when an individual's "structural reaction" explains his actions: "If the typical criminal is a degenerate, bound to swindle or to murder by as deep-seated an organic necessity as that which makes the rattlesnake bite, it is idle to talk of deterring him by the classical method of imprisonment. He must be got rid of; he cannot be improved, or frightened out of his structural reaction."[38]

In 1924, Clarence Darrow, a famed defense attorney and leading progressive, argued that capital punishment would be inappropriate for his clients Nathan Leopold and Richard Loeb. These University of Chicago undergraduates were nineteen and eighteen respectively when they read Nietzsche and decided to show disdain for conventional morality by committing what nowadays is called a "transgressive" act. They committed a random murder, driving a chisel into the skull of a fourteen-year-old boy and dumping his body in a drainage ditch. Darrow argued to the judge that a death sentence would be unjust because "something" had made his clients victims: "Why did they kill Bobby Franks? Not for money, not for spite, not for hate. They killed him as they might kill a spider or a fly, for the experience. They killed him because they were made that way. Because somewhere in the infinite processes that go to the making up of a boy or the man something slipped, and these unfortunate lads sit here, hated, despised, outcasts with the community shouting." What Holmes explained as a "structural reaction" for which the death penalty was appropriate, Darrow explained as some sort of mental slippage that occurred because of the way his clients were "made" by "infinite processes" that made a death sentence inappropriate. The judge, who opposed capital punishment, sentenced them to life in prison.[39]

Holmes and Darrow, however, agreed that the human condition, properly understood in the light of modern science, left little room for the concept of human agency. It did, however, leave a lot of room for manipulating the human material. Remember the youthful Walter Lippmann's enthusiasm for dealing "deliberately" with "life" itself, in all its complexity, guided by modern science. This facet of progressivism put it on a straight path to eugenics, the science of straightening out the crooked timber of humanity.

Progressivism, in its initial semi-utopian confidence, held that history follows a path of improvement, generally toward enlarged liberty, as progressives understood this. Although the theory of ineluctable improvement was considered a social analogue of Darwinism, it was crucially different. Darwin's fundamental insight was that species do change by natural selection but do not change on a predictable trajectory or toward a predetermined end. Rather, they change over time in response to the promptings of local conditions, which themselves can change over time. Progressives held that by using government power to change social conditions, predetermined social ends could be attained. It was a short step from here to the project of not just reforming social conditions but directly modifying the human stock. Progressivism in politics not only developed in tandem with, but also shared intellectual sources with, the late nineteenth-century and early twentieth-century interest in eugenics.

The term "eugenics," the root of which is the Greek word for "well born," was coined by a cousin of Charles Darwin. Darwinism had quickened interest in racial and ethnic differences, and in the possibility of racial evolution or degeneration. Woodrow Wilson, in his first book, *The State* (1889), said his interest was in the government of the "Aryan races," which included the English colonists who in America had let their "race habits and instincts have natural play." Richard T. Ely was a progressive economist who spent most of his career at the University of Wisconsin but who also taught at Johns Hopkins, where Woodrow Wilson was one of his students. Ely and Charles Van Hise, the president of the University of Wisconsin, were exemplars of what early in the twentieth century was called the Wisconsin Idea. Under Governor Robert La Follette, a Republican progressive, the University of Wisconsin became a source of expertise for America's first "administrative state," at the state level. "By 1908," Thomas C. Leonard says, "all the economists and one-sixth of the University's entire faculty held appointments on Wisconsin government commissions." Ely was thirty-one when, in 1885, he cofounded the American Economic Association, which he envisioned as an instrument for advancing the social gospel, the agenda of liberal Protestantism that included social regeneration through applied science. "God," he said, "works through the state." And in doing God's work the state must not be squeamish. Leonard, an economist and historian of the tangle of race, eugenics, and economics in the Progressive era, writes that the duties of the state "would regularly require overriding individuals' rights in the name of the economic common good." This was especially so regarding those whom Van Hise called "human defectives." His confidence was striking: "We know enough about eugenics so that if that knowledge were applied, the defective classes would disappear within a generation."[40]

The problem of the social costs of mentally inferior people became a preoccupation of reformers. Robert Yerkes was president of the American Psychological Association, which had been founded in 1892 as part of the proliferation of professional academic associations. At Yerkes' urging, the US Army did intelligence testing of draftees during World War I and concluded that 47 percent of white and 89 percent of black conscripts were "morons," defined as mental defectives who were sufficiently high-functioning to pass as normal. This posed a problem for persons hoping to improve the nation's human resources. Ely praised the army testing for enabling the nation to inventory its human stock just as it does its livestock. Plato in the *Republic* wondered why cattle were bred but humans were not. Eugenicists also wondered. Eugenics was not a fully developed science but, Ely said, "we have got far enough to recognize that there are certain human beings who are absolutely unfit, and should be prevented from a continuation of their kind." Progress depended on this.[41]

After the war, when Congress set about restricting immigration, the army's test results influenced the setting of national quotas. In 1902, the final volume of Woodrow Wilson's widely read *History of the American People* contrasted "the sturdy stocks of the north of Europe," who arrived before 1880, with southern and eastern Europeans who had "neither skill nor energy nor any initiative of quick intelligence." Carl Brigham, a Princeton psychologist, said the army's data demonstrated "the intellectual superiority of our Nordic group over the Mediterranean, Alpine and Negro groups." Severe immigration restrictions, which excluded immigrants from an "Asiatic Barred Zone," were legislated in 1924.[42]

In 1907, Indiana became the first of thirty states to enact a forcible sterilization law. In 1911, Governor Woodrow Wilson signed New Jersey's, which applied to "the hopelessly defective and criminal classes." In 1927, in *Buck v. Bell*, the US Supreme Court upheld a Virginia sterilization law, saying that a state's police power that extended to compulsory vaccination was "broad enough to cover cutting the Fallopian tubes." Justice Holmes, whose jurisprudence of restraint pleased progressives by removing judicial impediments to the force of majorities, famously wrote in his opinion for the court that "three generations of imbeciles is enough." In a letter to Harold Laski, a leading light of Britain's Fabian socialists—a group also tempted by eugenics—Holmes wrote that in affirming the law requiring the sterilization of imbeciles he "was getting nearer to the first principle of real reform."[43]

Progressives believed that science, which is cumulative expertise, should hold the reins of society, determining the "human hierarchy," ranking groups from those with the most aptitudes to those with the least.[44] There was, of course, a contradiction in this. Progressives dismissed the idea of deriving natural rights from the facts of a fixed human nature, yet they were confident that racial groups had fixed natures that were pertinent to the formulation of various public policies. Progressives resolved this contradiction when they, like most of the rest of society, abandoned racialism, the belief that race determines human traits and capacities, a belief often associated with polygenism, the faux science that purported to prove that the human races are tidily distinct, that each race was created independent of all the others, and hence that each race is a separate species.

In his book *The Winning of the West*, Roosevelt wrote that the vanquishing of Native Americans had proven the continuing vitality of the Anglo-Saxon stock that traced its valor back to battles in Europe's forests: "Its true significance will be lost unless we grasp, however roughly, the past race-history of the nations who took part therein."[45] At the turn of the twentieth century, progressivism's racial doctrines intersected with, and influenced, US foreign policy. In a Senate speech in 1900, Senator Albert Beveridge of Indiana, who twelve years later would be the keynote speaker at the Progressive Party convention that nominated Theodore Roosevelt for president, argued that an American withdrawal from the Philippines would "renounce our part in the mission of our race, trustee under God, of the civilization of the world." C. Vann Woodward wrote that among the strangest aspects of "the strange career of Jim Crow" was the permeation of foreign policy under President William McKinley by "Southern attitudes on the subject of race." This was noted at the time by the *Boston Evening Transcript*, which on January 14, 1899, acerbically wrote that Southern racial policy was "now the policy of the Administration of the very party which carried the country into and through a civil war to free the slave."[46] America's first significant legislation restricting immigration was passed to exclude Chinese. Theodore Roosevelt supported this, in part because he thought Chinese immigrants would depress American wages, but also because he believed that they would be "ruinous to the white race."[47]

Eugenics was one manifestation of progressivism's repudiation of the Founders' individualism, which asserted the natural equality of human beings in their capacity to reason and their right to choose and pursue their interests. Progressives preached a different, and they thought richer, understanding of freedom as each person's realization of his or her potential through immersion in collectivities. That is, freedom is not something individuals are born into, it is something individuals must attain by diluting or shedding their individualism. Eugenics entered the picture through progressives' belief that science was demonstrating that different races had different inherent capacities. For that reason, and for cultural reasons, different races were collectively becoming free—fulfilling their potentials—in different degrees and on different schedules. Therefore "rights granted at law must vary in relation to the relative development of the group in question." And "whereas those deemed more advanced could be allowed to exercise a higher measure of control over their own most immediate concerns, as well as public decision-making, those groups lagging furthest behind could not." So it is not astonishing that the Jim Crow regime in the South "was not only catalyzed, in important part, by Progressive academics, but was also explicitly championed by Southern Progressives."[48]

PROGRESSIVISM'S WEDGE

Progressives would quickly and thoroughly disentangle themselves from racialism and eugenics, so progressivism should not be judged by this dark detour. But this walk on the wild side by progressivism should be contemplated for what it says about the peril of severing political philosophy, and hence political practices, from the concept of a fixed human nature that was the Founders' anchor. Remember Calvin Coolidge's summation of their vision and sensibility on the 150th anniversary of the Declaration of Independence: It was in opposition to the ideas that Coolidge espoused that John Dewey spoke eight years later in "The Future of Liberalism," his December 1934 address to the American Philosophical Association. Dewey consigned to history's dustbin the liberalism that he described as emphasizing "individuality and liberty." It had, he said, rendered "valiant service" but the "fundamental defect was lack of perception of historic relativity." This lack was "expressed in the conception of the individual as something given, complete in itself, and of liberty as a ready-made possession of the individual, only needing the removal of external restrictions in order to manifest itself." Dewey said that the fatal flaw of this liberalism, which had "degenerated," was its "absolutism," meaning its "denial of temporal relativity." A more enlightened liberalism would, he said, recognize that "an individual is nothing fixed, given ready-made." Rather, an individual is something "achieved not in isolation, but with the aid and support of conditions, cultural and physical."[49]

Read one way, this is anodyne, even banal. Read another way, it is the thin end of a wedge of the most dangerous radicalism, a wedge enormous enough to chisel away the Founders' intellectual legacy and to unleash totalitarian aspirations. The banal reading is that people are to some extent marked, shaped, socialized, conditioned—pick your verb—by their circumstances. Who denies, or ever has denied, this? Certainly not Plato, whose *Republic* has been well described as a book about education and its powerful potential for countering the influence of malign social factors. Jefferson certainly agreed that "conditions, cultural and physical," have shaping effects on individuals. This is why he lauded rural yeomen and deplored cities. He thought the sturdy—because it was based on ownership of land—self-sufficiency of farmers nurtured the habits, mores, customs, and dispositions requisite for self-government. And he thought cities and factories bred a dependency inimical to the democratic spirit. Jefferson's great rival, Alexander Hamilton, was Jefferson's intellectual companion in stressing the moral effects of physical conditions and the cultural milieus that are shaped by physical conditions. Hamilton, however, praised the effects of conditions that Jefferson deplored. Jefferson, a slaveholding son of the Virginia gentry, desired the social stasis of an agricultural society. Hamilton, an upstart immigrant doing well in bustling Manhattan, welcomed the churning of capitalism as a solvent of social hierarchies that blocked the ascent of strivers like him. But regarding philosophic fundamentals, Jefferson and Hamilton were more than just compatible. Both spoke the language that progressives like Dewey wanted to retire, the language of natural rights. Dewey's real aim was not merely to insist what no one disputed—that an individual's social context has consequences. Rather, his radical aim was to assert the limitless plasticity of personhood under the prompting of properly calibrated and manipulated social conditions. His intellectual project had a European pedigree.

In 1883, delivering the eulogy at Karl Marx's grave in London's Highgate Cemetery, Friedrich Engels said: "Charles Darwin discovered the law of the development of organic nature upon our planet. Marx is the discoverer of the fundamental law according to which human history moves and develops itself, a law so simple and self-evident that its simple enunciation is almost sufficient to secure assent."[50] In his preface to *Das Kapital*, Marx wrote that his "standpoint, from which the evolution of the economic formation of society is viewed as a process of natural history, can less than any other make the individual responsible for relations whose creature he socially remains, however much he may subjectively raise himself above them."[51] Marx, the archetypal modern radical, was, in his fascination with laws of history, not altogether unlike a great conservative. "We must all obey the great law of change," according to Edmund Burke.[52] If, however, we must obey it, human agency is circumscribed, if not nullified. Much, therefore, depends on how much of the life of society is thought to be under the sway of this or that "great law." The nineteenth century was to be the arena of competing historicisms, of Hegel and Marx and others who postulated dialectics and other ways by which laws of change worked *their* wills. Burke, fortunately, stopped short of erecting such an ambitious intellectual architecture. For him, as Yuval Levin correctly reads him, "nature offers not a source of principles and axioms, but a living model of change."[53] It is a model functioning as an admonition; a model of how change ought to occur, not how it must occur. So Burke was an eighteenth-century man, but one decisively unlike America's Founders, who did distill principles and axioms from nature, including human nature.

Dewey and likeminded progressives rejected, root and branch, the constriction of politics implicit in the Founders' principles. "Liberalism," Dewey said, referring to the new and supposedly improved liberalism he was outlining, "knows that social conditions may restrict, distort, and almost prevent the development of individuality." It follows that better social conditions can foster an individual's undistorted development. Liberated from the Founders' "absolutism" about nature and natural rights, and embracing historical relativity and what Dewey called "experimentalism," progressives could get on with a politics muscular enough to nurture a better humanity. The Founders, Dewey said, "assumed that history, like time in the Newtonian scheme, means only modification of external relations; that it is quantitative, not equalitative and internal." The business of Dewey's "thorough-going social liberalism" would be to superintend and shape the whole person and the entire society. This liberalism is committed to experimental processes, and hence to the "continuous reconstruction of the ideas of individuality and of liberty in intimate connection with changes in social relations."[54]

The continuous reconstruction of basic categories of political thought means a constant revision of political practices and social life. This cannot be, to use Coolidge's language, restful. But, then, progressive politics is exhilarating to its practitioners precisely because it has dismissed the confinement of any finalities. A progressive's work is never done because *everything* is progressivism's business. This is partly because, in political philosophy, epistemology is destiny. "Let us then," wrote Locke, "suppose the Mind to be, as we say, white Paper, devoid of all Characters, without any *Ideas*; How comes it to be furnished?"[55] How indeed. Locke's epistemology suggested an unavoidable political project and a dangerous temptation. Government can hardly be altogether indifferent to the processes by which the white paper is written upon. Neither, however, can it be entrusted with comprehensive supervision of these processes.

Suppose someone construes *very* broadly the extent to which people are shaped by their situations. Suppose someone subscribes to an especially severe form of Lockean sensationalism—more severe than did Locke, who postulated a certain sociability that presupposes some innate, and hence universal, human qualities. Suppose, that is, that someone believes individuals are almost entirely blank slates on which the external world writes what it will—that the world writes with the pen of external stimuli that are recorded by, and that act upon, the senses. Even such a person does not need to deny any fixity to human nature and need not postulate limitless human malleability. There still remains room for constancy in the human makeup, some universality in the mental mechanism by which people process the world's promptings. Dewey, however, was staking out quite different and more exotic intellectual terrain. It was terrain on which Rousseau had first trod.

An important pivot in modern political thought occurred when Rousseau argued that in the formation of human beings, human nature was supplanted by culture, which gives human beings a second nature, for better or worse. Politics thereby acquired the enormously important and deeply dangerous task of trying to fine-tune culture in order to tune the citizens' second nature. If you wish to know precisely what the Founders and Framers did *not* intend, read Rousseau: "He who dares to undertake the making of a people's institutions ought to feel himself capable, so to speak, of changing human nature, of transforming each individual...into part of a greater whole from which he in a manner receives his life and being; of altering man's constitution for the purpose of strengthening it.... He must, in a word, take away from man his own resources and give him instead new ones alien to him, and incapable of being made use of without the help of other men. The more completely these natural resources are annihilated, the greater and the more lasting are those which he acquires."[56] There you have, with remarkable concision, the germ of the European radicalisms, of the left and the right, that would become twentieth-century totalitarianisms. The politics of consciousness exuded the confidence that inherited traits can be scrubbed away by a determined government and replaced by more desirable ones. The crux of modern radicalism is that human nature has no constancy, that it is merely an unstable imprint of the fluctuating social atmosphere. This fallacy emboldens political actors to adopt agendas of ambitious social engineering.

It is not a mere coincidence that modernism in literature and art grew as the speed of transportation and communication accelerated. This bombardment of the senses by new stimuli—this blitzkrieg by the social environment—left many people feeling that the sense of one's self was becoming derivative, attenuated, and brittle. Neither is it a coincidence that the politics of consciousness has engulfed America's college campuses, where progressivism uses its hegemony to control speech, lest unprogressive social promptings impede the engineering of better consciousnesses. All of this is, in a sense, a lingering reverberation of what moved Dewey. He had imbibed the core scientific proposition of the first half of the twentieth century, the proposition that the essence of life is matter in motion. Hence any idea of fixity, including a fixed human nature, was considered scientifically retrograde and, potentially at least, politically reactionary.[57] The entire progressive edifice depends on denying fixity—the stubborn fact of a human nature that is not malleable.

Fixity circumscribes the potency of politics, draining politics of some of its excitement. On the other hand, the larger the sphere of things considered to be mere "social constructs," the more majestic is the jurisdiction of politics, and the greater is the dignity attaching to its practitioners. It is, therefore, understandable that the leakage of postmodernism's assumptions and vocabulary into society has been welcomed by progressives, for whom politics, the supposed driver of progress, is supremely important.

Because progressivism had such high hopes for power, and because progressives had an urgent desire to free power from institutional circumscriptions, this desire translated into impatience with the constitutional architecture through which Founders codified their prudence about power and human nature. With remarkable thoroughness, this impatience produced the enormous political achievement that would be a necessary precondition for all other progressive achievements. The achievement was the creation of the modern presidency—and the constitutional disequilibrium that this has produced. The causes and consequences of this are still unfolding.

THEODORE ROOSEVELT: HEGEL ON HORSEBACK

The twentieth century began for America with a bang, that of the assassin's bullet that in 1901 put the boisterous Theodore Roosevelt, just forty-two, in the presidential chair that had been occupied by a notably sedentary man, William McKinley, who in 1896 had campaigned seated on his front porch in Canton, Ohio. Roosevelt was, as a contemporary said, "a steam engine in trousers." This Harvard-educated patrician cowboy from Manhattan galloped into the Dakota Badlands wearing spurs and a pearl-handled revolver from Tiffany, and charged up San Juan Hill in a uniform from Brooks Brothers. He was the first president born in a big city, and the first known to the nation as an intimate—by his initials. A toothy grin crinkled his entire face as he lived life as "one long campaign."[58] Author of thirty-six books and 100,000 letters, the most intellectual president since John Quincy Adams sometimes read two books a day—some in Italian, Portuguese, Latin, Greek, or other languages he knew, and he could recite the entire "Song of Roland." Just as he transformed himself from a frail asthmatic child too starved for breath to blow out his bedside candle, he transformed the presidency.

When, in *The Strenuous Life*, Theodore Roosevelt wrote about men capable of "feeling the mighty lift that thrills 'stern men with empires in their brains,'" he was quoting a James Russell Lowell poem from 1862, a grim year when the nation needed many stern men.[59] Lowell's trope was echoed in bumptious post–Civil War America by Sam Walter Foss' poem "The Coming American," written in 1894, when Roosevelt was very much a coming man:

Bring me men to match my mountains;
Bring me men to match my plains,—
Men with empires in their purpose,
And new eras in their brains.

Roosevelt vibrated like a tuning fork to Foss' call for "men whose thought shall pave a highway up to ampler destinies."[60] Roosevelt, who then was just four years away from his charge up Cuba's San Juan Hill and to the pinnacle of American politics, had thoughts that were grounded in progressive premises and that would justify an imperial destiny. With his progressive penchant for seeing in the sweep of history an ascent to higher stages, Roosevelt's thinking echoed a letter Jefferson wrote in 1824:

Let a philosophic observer commence a journey from the savages of the Rocky Mountains, eastwardly towards our sea-coast. These he would observe in the earliest stage of association living under no law but that of nature, subscribing and covering themselves with the flesh and skins of wild beasts. He would next find those on our frontiers in the pastoral state, raising domestic animals to supply the defects of hunting. Then succeed our own semi-barbarous citizens, the pioneers of the advance of civilization, and so in his progress he would meet the gradual shades of improving man until he would reach his, as yet, most improved state in our seaport towns. This, in fact, is equivalent to a survey, in time of the progress of man from the infancy of creation to the present day.[61]

The crucible of Franklin Roosevelt's post-polio agony, physical and psychological, made him into one of the four presidents who were larger than the government into which they entered as officials. Washington established the central government's authority. Lincoln preserved that authority. TR fueled executive supremacy. FDR settled the central government's supremacy and the sufficiency of its powers for national purposes. Something, however, was missing in FDR. What he lacked, however, made him great. He lacked the capacity even to imagine that things might turn out badly. He had a Christian's faith that the universe is well constituted and an American's faith that history is a rising road. In this, FDR was very like his cousin Teddy. TR contrasted what he called people with a disreputable appetite for "milk-and-water cosmopolitanism" with the hardier types of "great expanding peoples" who eat "roast beef" and can "make their blows felt in the world."[62] Woodrow Wilson, the professor in politics, had a persona that would, in time, set Teddy Roosevelt's gleaming teeth on edge.

In 1890, the US Census Bureau declared the American frontier closed. In 1893, Frederick Jackson Turner cast a retrospective glance in one of the most influential essays in American historiography, "The Significance of the Frontier in American History." Later that year, he looked ahead. With remarkable prescience, he suggested that the nation's growth need not end when the frontier did: The "energies of expansion" hitherto invested in taming the continent could find new outlets if a "popular hero" directed them into foreign policy goals such as "an interoceanic canal" and "revival of our power upon the seas." Turner had imagined the essence of the agenda of the man who would be president eight years later.[63]

To the question "Who among all the presidents would you most like to be seated next to at a dinner party?" the answer is surely

Theodore Roosevelt. He had an infectious talent for happiness, he overflowed with enthusiasms, and he was a Roman candle of ideas. However, what he did not have, and this lack was related to his boundless energy, was a constitutional temperament. In September 1895, when he was thirty-seven, Roosevelt exhorted a Buffalo audience to "Read *The Federalist*—it is one of the greatest—I hardly know whether it would not be right to say that it is on the whole the greatest book dealing with applied politics there has ever been."[64] Six years later, as president, he began an era of executive exuberance that expressed his ever-intensifying exasperation with the constitutional architecture that *The Federalist* essays were written to justify. And by the time he campaigned in 1912 for a return to the presidency, he was full cry against the political philosophy that produced this architecture. There were three reasons for this.

First, it is an old axiom that where you stand often depends on where you sit. When Roosevelt sat at the presidential desk, he naturally thought, as even less egocentric presidents have thought, that the president should be the sun in the constitutional solar system. Roosevelt took to heart what Madison said in Federalist 51: "The interest of the man must be connected with the constitutional rights of the place."[65] Roosevelt's interest was in maximizing presidential powers. Second, in politics, even more than in life generally, temperament is telling. Henry Adams called Roosevelt "pure act." He would have filled any office he occupied with overflowing energy. The third and most interesting reason for Roosevelt's presidential and post-presidency impatience with the Founders' handiwork is an idea, or a constellation of closely related ideas, concerning the basic mechanics of social development. As Jean M. Yarbrough writes, "Roosevelt was far more interested in the growth and expansion of America than in its 'founding.'" For the authors of the Federalist Papers, nature supplied what Yarbrough calls "the moral ground against which political action must be judged."[66] For Roosevelt, history supplied that ground.

Of the foreign languages that Roosevelt mastered, the most important was German, the subject in which he received his best grades as a Harvard undergraduate. His interest in things German was congruent with a strong inclination of the American intelligentsia in the fourth quarter of the nineteenth century. It was German philosophy, and particularly a philosophy of history, that seized the imaginations of many American intellectuals. This philosophy implied an understanding of progress that was, as Yarbrough says, "at odds with the political principles the Exposition was at least nominally celebrating." Roosevelt's intellectually formative years coincided with what Yarbrough calls "the Hegelian moment in American politics." Before the Civil War, Europe had been a beacon to Southerners seeking intellectual armament against the natural rights philosophy that pitted the American creed against their region's distinguishing institution. After the war, Northerner intellectuals looked to Germany for inspiration. Yarbrough says that Hegel, who taught "the progressive unfolding of freedom in history," and who presented the state as "the embodiment of the ethical life of the nation," spoke powerfully to a generation of scholars seeking to find meaning in the Civil War trauma that their nation had endured.[67] Many of them found in Hegel two other things. One was the idealization of the bureaucratic state administered by supposedly disinterested experts. Second, this ideal justified the conclusion that the separation of powers was an anachronism, no longer necessary or even tolerable.

The recent cobbling together of a great German nation from a congeries of rival principalities had made unity in the regime a supreme value. The doctrine of the separation of powers, Hegel wrote, implies that government cannot be "a living unity."[68] Once a nation has progressed to be such a living unity, it can be administered by a disinterested state. Then the doctrine of separation of powers becomes pointless. This doctrine's premise is that institutions necessarily have their own institutional interests, appetites, and constituencies that arise from, and reflect, society's pluralism of factions, interests, and ideologies. But because progress—the ascent to an ever richer and broader consensus—brings social homogenization, the separation of powers serves only to impede the efficiency of the modern state. Applied to the United States, this theory justified a greatly enlarged presidency, to which TR felt suited.

Paradoxically, the fact that the Constitution vests the presidency with few explicit powers—the powers to veto legislation, to make appointments (including those contingent on Senate approval), to make treaties with Senate approval, and to command such armed forces as Congress creates—has actually helped to make the office especially powerful. The Constitution's silence about other presidential powers has encouraged the belief—the Rooseveltian belief—that whatever presidents are not forbidden to do they can do with a tranquil constitutional conscience. About half of Article II's little more than 1,000 words pertain to the selection, compensation, and means of removing presidents. The very parsimony of Article II's language about presidential power has facilitated the growth of that power. Political nature abhors a vacuum, and into Article II's vacuum came an elementary force of nature named Roosevelt, with his "stewardship" theory of the presidency. Writing eleven years after, and regarding, his 1902 threat to seize Pennsylvania coal mines during a miners' strike, Roosevelt wrote that "a genuine democracy of desire to serve the plain people" explained and justified his "theory that the executive power was limited only by specific restrictions and prohibitions appearing in the Constitution or imposed by the Congress under its Constitutional powers."[69] His "democracy of desire" demanded, and deserved, vast scope:

My view was that every executive officer, and above all every executive officer in high position, was a steward of the people bound actively and affirmatively to do all he could for the people, and not to content himself with the negative merit of keeping his talents undamaged in a napkin. I declined to adopt the view that what was imperatively necessary for the Nation could not be done by the President unless he could find some specific authorization to do it. My belief was that it was not only his right but his duty to do anything that the needs of the Nation demanded unless such action was forbidden by the Constitution or by the laws.... I did not usurp power, but I did greatly broaden the use of executive power.[70]

In his 1910 speech unveiling the "New Nationalism," former (and, he hoped, future) president Roosevelt took aim at "special interests" who "twist the methods of free government into machinery for defeating the popular will." His proposed solution was "a policy of far more active governmental interference with social and economic conditions in this country than we have yet had." Large combinations of wealth were here to stay but could be tamed by "completely controlling them in the interest of the public welfare." This was sensible if one believed, as he did, that "the danger to American democracy lies not in the least in the concentration of administrative power in responsible and accountable hands. It lies in having the power insufficiently concentrated, so that no one can be held responsible to the people for its use."[71]

More than a century later, having had abundant experience with the administrative state, Americans should be skeptical that concentrating ever more power in this state is a recipe for accountability and responsibility. Roosevelt, however, began America's long march to the present. America now has what Yale law professor Alexander Bickel termed "a Gaullist presidency...needing no excuse for aggregating power to itself besides the excuse that it could do more effectively what other institutions, particularly Congress, did not do very rapidly or very well, or under particular political circumstances would not do at all."[72]

TR, who a critic said "keeps a pulpit concealed on his person,"[73] was an individualist who considered the individualism of others an impediment to the social unity he thought was a prerequisite for national greatness. He advocated what one scholar has called "warrior republicanism."[74] TR saw virtue emerging from struggle, especially violent struggle, between nations, with human nature evolving toward improvement through conflict. The dark vision of potentially unlimited progress through unending strife caused him to advocate the concentration of power in the federal government as an efficient instrument of his vision. His agenda was radically more ambitious than the Founders' project of limited government maintaining order, protecting property, and otherwise staying largely out of the way of individual striving. TR welcomed "an age of combination," meaning vast interlocking economic entities.[75] Big was, he thought, beautiful and, besides, it was inevitable. So government, and especially the presidency, must become commensurate to the task of breaking American individualism to the saddle of collective purposes. He wanted the state to rescue America from the danger, as he saw it, that a commercial republic breeds effeminacy. Government as moral tutor must pull chaotic individualists up from private preoccupations and put these elevated people in harness for redemptive collective action. The purest such action was, TR thought, war.

TR's Harvard teacher William James spoke of a "moral equivalent of war." TR's idea was: Accept no substitutes. TR wanted the body politic to really be one body, with the president as the head. He gave short shrift to civil society—the institutions that mediate between individuals and the state, insulating them from dependence and coercion. He had a Rousseauian notion that the individual could only attain real freedom through immersion in the collective. Above all, he was a great precursor, a man whose career was a prerequisite for that of the man he came to loathe, Woodrow Wilson.

WOODROW WILSON: THE PROFESSOR IN POLITICS

There was something in the social atmosphere of the early twentieth century that made some people who were intelligent enough to know better have extravagant thoughts. "On or about December 1910," Virginia Woolf said in a 1924 essay, "human character changed." (She was referring to a Postimpressionist art exhibit. Really.)[76] In 1912, Woodrow Wilson, campaigning for the presidency, had been similarly excited: "We are in the presence of a new organization of society." He added: "A new social age, a new era of human relationships, a new stage-setting for the drama of life." Hence it was time to put away childish things, such as the political formulations of the Founders, from "the old-fashioned days when life was very simple." As Princeton's president, Wilson had endeavored "to make the young gentlemen of the rising generation as unlike their fathers as possible." It is not surprising that their fathers, who Wilson said "were out of sympathy with the creative, formative and progressive forces of society," were emphatically out of sympathy with Wilson and glad to see him gone from Princeton.[77] Nevertheless, Wilson correctly thought that the advent of mechanical transportation and communication changed the nature of the nation. Before such transportation, no one had moved faster than Julius Caesar had. Before the telegraph, no one had communicated over a distance greater than a human voice can carry or without physically transporting something tangible from here to there. New modes of transportation and communication—and energy and manufacturing—made many changes in the nation. The pertinent question, however, was and is: How did these changes alter the relevance and meaning of what the Founders had wrought?

Wilson began from the jejune premise that there was "no historical foundation" for the supposition that government arose from a social compact among consenting individuals.[78] Sounding a Burkean theme, Wilson said that far from being "a matter of contract and deliberate arrangement," government "is an institute of habit, bound together by innumerable threads of association, scarcely one of which has been deliberately placed." Hence, as Michael Zuckert writes, progressives believed that "individuals and individualism are the result, not the cause of government."[79] They said that history and anthropology support this contention that individuals and individualism are not natural, pre-political facts, they are social and political achievements. This does not, however, alter the wisdom of the social contract schema for understanding the proper relation of the citizen to the state. If the individual and individualism appear not at the beginning of social and political life but as late achievements, then perhaps they deserve special admiration and deference. Wilson, however, did not think this way.

He had the briefest career in public service of anyone ever elected president before 2016. His life in academia had not prepared him for the transactional nature of politics, with its bargaining and splitting of differences. In 1912, he likened constructing his "New Freedom" to erecting a "great building" in which "men can live as a single community, cooperative as in a perfected, coordinated beehive."[80] Human beings as bees? God wants this because, as Wilson also said to an associate in 1912, "God ordained that I should be the next president of the United States."[81] God or History. This was a distinction without much difference when a Presbyterian's sense of the providential was melded with a progressive's belief in teleological history.

Wilson thought that a national government competent for the challenges of the modern age could not exist without "wresting the Constitution to strange and as yet unimagined uses." He chose an interesting word: To wrest something is to jerk it with some violence. "If I saw my way to it as a practical politician," Wilson said, "I should be willing to go farther and superintend every man's use of his chance."[82] Yet during the 1912 campaign, Wilson said, "No man that I know and trust, no man that I will consent to consort with, is trying to change anything fundamental in America."[83] Traveling in Jacksonian America, Alexis de Tocqueville said that "what most strikes the European who travels through the United States is the absence of what is called among us government or administration."[84] He marveled that "the hand directing the social machine constantly slips from notice."[85] Wilson set out to make this hand much more visible.

Wilson, and those thinkers and political practitioners who today are the legatees of his thought and policies, are, for conservatives, formidable adversaries whose arguments are serious and touch the largest themes in Western political thinking. Wilson was not the nation's most intellectually gifted president; in originality and subtlety, he ranks behind Jefferson, Lincoln, John Quincy Adams, Theodore Roosevelt, and especially Madison. Wilson was, however, an intellectual; he was keenly interested in ideas, and he earned his living in the academic study of them. He was an energetic and gifted synthesizer of ideas advanced by more original thinkers. He was almost present at the creation of political science as an academic discipline—Professor Wilson of the Johns Hopkins University was the first president of the American Political Science Association—and he contributed much to the creation of the study of public administration. He came of age as a thinker in an era of intellectual turbulence involving the intersection of political philosophy and science. Wilson was the first president to criticize the American founding, which he did with a root-and-branch thoroughness. Few people nowadays recognize the radicalism of the Wilsonian and progressive repudiation of the Founders' project. For progressives then as now, moving up from the Founders' cramped, premodern, and unscientific vision of political possibilities is central to the very definition of progress.

It is common, and not wrong, to emphasize a split among the Founders, the rivalry between Alexander Hamilton and Thomas Jefferson, a rivalry that quickly produced America's infant party system, with the Hamiltonian Federalists competing with the Jeffersonian Republicans. These two factions did indeed have important disagreements about what the nation's regime should be, about the proper role of the central government, about the appropriate "energy in the executive" (Hamilton's phrase), and much more.[86] These disagreements were, however, less profound than Wilson's disagreement with both, who shared the defect, as he saw it, of claiming universality for their most basic (and mostly shared) principles. Both subscribed to the principles Jefferson affirmed in the second paragraph of the Declaration of Independence: There are universal political truths, some of which are self-evident; one is that all men are created equal in that they are equally endowed with certain inalienable rights; governments that are just are instituted to secure these rights, and derive their powers from the consent of the governed, and when a government becomes destructive of these rights, the people have the residual right to alter or abolish it. And so on. Wilson did not so much disagree with this or that provision of this American creed as he did with what he considered the static, "transhistorical" (Ronald J. Pestritto's term) nature of the entire creed—the belief that these "abstract" truths, as Lincoln called them, were, as Lincoln believed, "applicable to all men and all times."[87]

The Founders' conviction was characteristic of the Enlightenment and was crucial to their confidence in launching the Revolution. The purpose of politics, the Founders thought, is to cope with the problems inherent in unchanging human nature. A perennial problem of politics is how to cope with the disunity and conflict caused by factions. "The latent causes of factions," said Madison in Federalist 10, are "sown in the nature of man."[88] This premise is, strictly speaking, anti-progressive, for two reasons. One is that it stipulates limits to the conditions beyond which humanity can progress. The second reason is that a just and durable regime will respect the rights of factions while limiting the toll they take on social harmony and the public's welfare.

The worst cost of factions comes when they capture the state for rent-seeking—for the purpose of directing the state's power for the benefit of themselves, and for the exploitation and even the oppression of others. But because this problem is "sown" in human nature, which is permanent, so, too, is the problem. Hence there can be no end—no *conceivable* end—to the need to limit government by circumscribing its powers that can be captured by factions. This is true even—actually, especially—when the power of the state is wielded in response to a majority faction.

Wilson recognized that the Founders' understanding of human nature—an understanding he thought was defective because it was unhistorical—was an impediment to a more open, unconstrained vision of government with a vast jurisdiction and grand uses. Hence the need to dilute—to refute, really—the Founders' bedrock assumption of an unchanging human nature. If human nature itself could be, as it were, put into play—if it could become plastic to the touch of government—the stakes of politics could become exponentially greater. This is why as late as 1911, the year before he was elected president, when his convictions were no longer of merely academic interest but were of intense practicality, he said that "the rhetorical introduction of the Declaration of Independence"—that second paragraph—"is the least part of it." To drive his point home he added: "If you want to understand the real Declaration of Independence, do not read the preface." Or read it as an interesting artifact, an archaic shard of a transcended past: "Every Fourth of July should be a time for examining our standards, our purposes, for determining afresh what principles, what forms of power we think most likely to effect our safety and happiness. That and that alone is the obligation the Declaration lays upon us."[89] That alone.

It was, Wilson thought, a reason for rejoicing that in his day "grave, thoughtful, perspicacious, and trusted men all around us agree in deriding those 'Fourth of July sentiments.'" Retrograde people who cling to those sentiments were the sort whose "bosoms swell against George III, but they have no consciousness of the war for freedom that is going on today."[90] This was, for Wilson, a war to emancipate the nation from its enthrallment to the Founders' fetish (as Wilson regarded it) about individual rights and the Founders' anachronistic worries about majorities. So, once a year Americans should consider "afresh," without reference to, let alone reverence for, the Founders' philosophic patrimony, the principles they should adopt and by which they should live, at least until the next Fourth of July. Those truths that seemed self-evident in the eighteenth century should be deemed to have passed away with that century. The natural rights tradition must be scrubbed out of American history. To do so, Wilson had to radically reinterpret America's greatest political thinker since the Founding: Lincoln.

With an audacity that ignores Abraham Lincoln's well-known words and deeds, Wilson celebrated Lincoln as a statesman whose greatness was related to his indifference to abstractions, such as natural rights theory: "What commends Mr. Lincoln's studiousness to me is that the result of it was he did not have any theories at all...Lincoln was one of those delightful students who do not seek to tie you up in the meshes of any theory."[91] Wilson's brazenness was breathtaking. He was draining Lincoln's career of what makes it intelligible and noble. Lincoln's greatness was commensurate with that of the Founders because his overarching purpose was to reconnect the nation with the Founders, and particularly with their vigorous affirmation of the natural rights tradition. By the 1850s, slavery had become an existential crisis for the nation because it had become a temptation to apostasy from the tradition that defined a nation dedicated to the Declaration's great proposition. Remember Lincoln in Philadelphia at Independence Hall on February 22, 1861: "I have never had a feeling politically that did not spring from the sentiments embodied in the Declaration of Independence."[92] Someone defending Wilson's eccentric understanding of Lincoln could perhaps try to make much of Lincoln's use of the words "feeling" and "sentiments" to buttress the contention that Lincoln lacked political "theories." But surely many of Lincoln's other words slam the door on such an argument.

There are his words spoken in November 1863 at the dedication of a military cemetery 110 miles west of Independence Hall. But four years before that, in an 1859 letter declining an invitation to speak at a Boston celebration of Jefferson's birthday, Lincoln had said: "All honor to Jefferson—to the man who, in the concrete pressure of a struggle for national independence by a single people, had the coolness, forecast, and capacity to introduce into a merely revolutionary document, an abstract truth, applicable to all men and all times, and so embalm it there, that today, and in all coming days, it shall be a rebuke and a stumbling-block to the very harbingers of re-appearing tyranny and oppression."[93] These are the words of a statesman "who did not have any theories at all"? Wilson, who surely was familiar with this well-known letter, was rebuked by it. Or he would have been, but for his implacable determination to recast America's political premises. He would allow no facts to interfere with this enterprise. Lincoln was an enormous stumbling block for Wilson, one too large to be conjured away by ignoring Lincoln's statements.

Wilson was, of course, correct that Lincoln's greatness as a statesman was inextricably entwined with the virtue of prudence. But Pestritto rightly says that prudence, as the ancient philosophers understood it, involves adherence to a universal idea of the good while applying it, however incompletely and imperfectly, in a particular historical situation. Wilson makes the ancient idea of prudence—fidelity to principles that transcend the moment, in the constraining context of the moment—almost disappear. He does so by arguing that the historical situation supplies its own principles. As Pestritto says, "the main tenets of Wilson's thought" all required the "assertion of historical contingency over the permanent principles of American constitutionalism" and the "coupling of historical contingency with a faith in progress."[94] That faith was, at bottom, faith in history. The most portentous development in political philosophy in the nineteenth century—the century after the Founding and the century of Wilson's intellectually formative years—was that history became History, a proper noun. In the hands of Karl Marx, this became a fighting faith with world-shaking consequences. But it was to one of Marx's precursors, Hegel, that Wilson was intellectually indebted, for reasons similar to those Theodore Roosevelt was.

Wilson understood that the task of refuting the Founders' politics of limited government required him to postulate a social harmony that would drain politics of its dangers. If the basic political problem is factions, and if fractiousness arises from a permanent facet of human nature, then the solution is to postulate a historical process that will remove the roughness from human nature, or refute the idea of human nature. Wilson, amending Immanuel Kant, believed that from the crooked timber of humanity something straight enough can be made that we can put aside the fears that caused the Founders to favor a government of limited powers and limited objectives.

A century after Wilson entered politics, "diversity" is, ostensibly, a progressive value. For Wilson and the progressive project, however, the diversity of interests in society was a problem—in a sense, *the* problem to be surmounted. Happily, or so progressives thought, history—aka History, aka progress—would take care of that. But first it had to refute Madison, whose mistake, as Wilson saw it, was in assuming that the problem of factions is a hardy perennial because human nature is an unchanging constant. History, Wilson thought, would produce unity in the public mind. Progress would pull the fractious public up from rival particularities, to a harmony that Madison, who was wedded to a static understanding of human nature, could not fathom. When mankind steps onto Wilson's sunny upland of (in Pestritto's words) a "unity of national sentiment," mankind will have pretty much left politics behind and entered what Wilson serenely anticipated as the age of administration.[95]

Here Wilson was resuscitating an old dream, that of Friedrich Engels who, echoing St. Simon and the Enlightenment rationalists, foresaw the "government of persons" being supplanted by "the administration of things."[96] In the epoch of unity—actually, a future of perpetual unity—that Wilson foresaw, the individual would no longer need to feel trepidation about the state. This ancient fear, from which modern liberalism arose, would be transcended. When the will of the people is unified, there will be no need to limit a government responsive to that will. Rather, the modern problem will become the opposite of the one that preoccupied the Founders. They aimed to limit government by means of an institutional architecture of separated and rival powers in order to keep government on a short constitutional leash. The modern problem, Wilson thought, was to unleash government so that it could be a properly efficient servant of the will of a harmonious people. It is telling that what Wilson hoped for in a government was "wieldiness."[97] Who is to wield it? Experts, as we shall see.

The fatal failing of Madison, and of the Founders generally, was, Wilson thought, the ahistorical perspective that gave them misplaced confidence in their ability to enunciate timeless, universal principles. Wilson thought, with considerable justification, that he could affect a revolution in American political thought by convincing the country to put away the childish things the Founders thought and instead embrace this idea: All political propositions are products of a historical context, and their truth is no more permanent or universal than this perishable context. Would, however, this self-consciously modern moment itself be perishable?

Wilson was an early exponent of an "end of history."[98] In the extraordinary year 1989, the two hundredth anniversary of the outbreak of the French Revolution, the Berlin Wall came down, the Cold War ended, and so did, some people thought, history. They did not, of course, believe that there would never again be big events. They did, however, believe that events would not turn on big differences about big ideas. Humanity had, they thought, truly reached the end of ideology. The last of the fighting faiths, socialism, was a spent force. Market societies were to be the last "wave of the future" because the future had arrived in the form of consensus about the broad parameters of sensibly organized societies. Wilson had arrived at a similar conclusion almost a century earlier. He thought: If history had shaped America into a harmonious whole, and henceforth the people and the state were fused in common understandings and purposes, what could put asunder this happy marriage? History? Surely not. That would be a retreat from progress, an unintelligible possibility. Progress *meant* an ascension to unity. History's unfolding *is* progress.

In 1883, Wilson began his graduate education at Johns Hopkins University where, Pestritto writes, he had teachers who were "all educated in Germany and in the tradition of German state theory and philosophy of history." These teachers were steeped in Hegelian modes of thought, the essence of which was Hegel's disavowal of any attempt to "construct a state as it ought to be." Comprehension—or perhaps interpretation, a word we shall encounter again in Wilson's thoughts about presidential leadership—is, if not everything, at least sufficient: "To comprehend what is, this is the task of philosophy, because what is, is reason. Whatever happens, every individual is a child of his time; so philosophy too is its own time apprehended in thoughts. It is just as absurd to fancy that a philosophy can transcend its contemporary world as it is to fancy that any individual can overleap his own age."[99]

To a historicist like Hegel, the idea of willful individuals changing the world in a premeditated manner is mistaken, even ludicrous. Hence America's elemental understanding of itself as a nation consciously created at a Founding is not merely wrong, it is intellectually childish. The world changes, but history sees to that. People may think they are propelling the process, but Hegel knew better than to emphasize the idea—the fiction—of human agency. The world that people live in supplies the furniture of their minds; it gives them the categories by which they think. The rare "world-historical individuals" can perhaps accelerate history's progress, but they do so only because they embody, in especially vivid and concentrated form, the spirits of their ages.[100]

Wilson basically agreed, and probably thought of himself as such a history-accelerating individual. "Human choice," he said, "has in all stages of the great world processes of politics had its part in the shaping of institutions," but those great "processes" are so powerful, so autonomous, that human choice "has been confined to adaptation." It is "altogether shut out from raw invention."[101] Wilson's belief was that individuals can choose to adapt to what history's unfolding produces, or they can be consigned by history to oblivion. As another historicist, Leon Trotsky, said when he denounced the Mensheviks who walked out of the Second Congress of Soviets on October 25, 1917, "Go where you belong from now on—into the dustbin of history."[102]

There was nothing novel about Americans acknowledging the power of events to circumscribe the efficacy of human choices. "Things are in the saddle, and ride mankind," wrote Emerson in 1846, during the tumult surrounding the war with Mexico.[103] During a later, larger war, Abraham Lincoln said: "I claim not to have controlled events, but confess plainly that events have controlled me."[104] Another president, William McKinley, wrote that "the march of events rules and overrules human action."[105] But American history is replete with instances of people putting saddles—and bridles and snaffles—on events. And when Wilson had to come to terms with the undeniable example of an individual who certainly seemed to have wrenched history from its predetermined path and put it on a new path, Wilson's historicism turned murky, which is to say theological. George Washington, Wilson wrote, "was neither an accident nor a miracle." In his next sentence, however, Wilson turned Washington into something very like a miracle: "Neither chance nor a special Providence need be assumed to account for him. It was God, indeed, who gave him to us; but God had been preparing him ever since English constitutional history began."[106] For a historicist, the ways of God only seem very odd to the untutored eye. A large event, such as the appearance of a George Washington on the stage of history, may seem random and hence astonishing. But when we have a historicist such as Wilson to act as our docent in the museum of history, we learn that ripeness is all: Washington came about because history had summoned him as the man to suit the moment. Theology was brought in to rescue Wilson's historicism from the awkward fact of what seemed to have been a history-making individual.

Wilson melded theology with a kind of racialism that was then common among intellectuals. The fact that America had progressed so far, and had done so with a decentralized and unwieldy government and without reliance on potent executive leadership, was proof of Providence's kindly attention: "Unquestionably we believe in a guardian destiny! No other race could have accomplished so much with such a system." With, that is, a defective system that was retrograde in its reliance on a limited government. Fortunately, "the battle of life progresses and the army of Saints ever gains ground under divine generalship."[107] Such rhetoric blurs, to the point of erasure, the distinction between history and God. Wilson's tendency to associate God with his, Wilson's, hopes and policies would eventually infuse him, as president, with an unbending righteousness that wrecked his greatest dream, American membership in the League of Nations.

Wilson thought that societies could shrug off obsolete social norms and institutions, and that the advanced societies of his time had done so, thereby escaping "inexorable custom." Except Wilson did not think it was inexorable after all.[108] No individual can, however, stand outside his age and criticize the state because the state *is*, and what *is* embodies reason. Hence it is odd, even unintelligible, to want to do what America's Founders did—place limits on the state. The Founders' emphasis on the separation of the government's powers expressed a nonsensical suspicion of the state. The logic of Wilson's progressivism was that the spirit of the age is in the saddle, riding humanity. Historicism, with its strong flavor of determinism and inevitability, blurs, even annihilates, the distinction between public and private. It does this because it thoroughly embeds the individual in the "age"—in a social context that no individual can "overleap."

In 1891, when Wilson was a professor at Princeton, he drew

up a list of books he deemed essential for students of politics. The list included works by Edmund Burke, Walter Bagehot, James Bryce, and two of his own, *Congressional Government* and *The State*. While writing the latter, he said, he "wore out a German dictionary."[109] The list included no works from the founding era, such as *The Federalist*. Burke was hostile to the natural rights thinking that fueled the American Revolution, with which Burke sympathized. But this sympathy was negligible compared to his antipathy for the French Revolution. He thought natural rights theory begat the social compact theory of the origins of governments, and that this theory begat, as America's Founders thought, the idea of a right to revolution. This was an affront to Burke's evolutionary conservatism, which stressed that political institutions are akin to organic entities growing in response to stimuli in their particular social environments. What seems to have most offended Wilson about the social compact theory of the origins of government is that it presupposes this: The natural, meaning the original, condition of life is individual autonomy. To begin political theory with an emphasis on this autonomy, and on the exercise of autonomy in conjuring the state into existence, gives rise to what Wilson considered a fundamentally misguided belief in the efficacy of human choice.

Wilson's evolutionary progressivism asserted that the evolution of society involves the domestication of passions, which henceforth would pose a steadily diminishing threat to the social order. A society formerly driven by conflicting passions had evolved into one with a "common consciousness": "Our life has undergone radical changes since 1787, and almost every change has operated to draw the nation together, to give it the common consciousness, the common interests, the common standards of conduct, the habit of concerted action, which will eventually impart to it in many more respects the character of a single community."[110] Wilson was evidently unimpressed by the 1886 Haymarket riot, the Pullman strike of 1894, and myriad other signs that the rapidly industrializing nation was not quite drawn together into a common consciousness. Wilson was, however, correct in identifying a foundational tenet of modern politics: Consciousness is in play, and shaping it is the primary purpose of politics. Suddenly the stakes of politics could hardly be higher.

Wilson was not against passionate politics in the service of this consciousness-raising objective. The "national consciousness" had been "cried wide awake by the voices of battle" in the Civil War. The "sweep of that stupendous storm" had swept away the last remnants of the world the Framers knew. The purpose of the Constitution they drafted in 1787 was no longer the protection of individual rights; rather, its new purpose was to empower "the passionate beliefs of the efficient majority of the nation."[111] A jurist whose thinking was forged in the fires of the Civil War would become a hero of progressivism by his emphatic majoritarianism. Explaining his disposition to defer to the legislative branch when considering challenges to the constitutionality of its acts, he said he did not weigh the wisdom or, in any meaningful sense, the constitutionality of those acts: "If my fellow citizens want to go to hell I will help them. It's my job."[112] So said Justice Oliver Wendell Holmes in 1920, the last full year of President Wilson's administration.

As early as 1889, Wilson identified the era in which he lived as "this modern time of history's high noon when nations stand forth full-grown and self-governed." For a historicist, this language was awkward. At high noon, the sun is directly above. But it does not stay there. And for things that are full-grown—Wilson considered government a living, organic thing—the future holds decline, even decrepitude. Governments that are living beings must be created and regulated by living constitutions. "Constitutions are not mere legal documents: they are the skeleton frame of a living organism."[113] But as shall be argued in Chapter 4, it is unclear how a "living" constitution, which derives its life from the spirit of the age, can, in any meaningful way, *constitute* a polity.

That, however, did not deter or detain Wilson, whose aim was to remove impediments to the freedom of majorities to work their will. This aim is, strictly speaking, anti-constitutional, in two senses. It rejects the very idea of a constitutional democracy, which must have *something* to do with limiting, inhibiting, and tempering the *demos*. And it rejects the American Framers' goal of protecting individual rights—a spacious sphere of individual autonomy—from infringement by overbearing majorities. To this end, the Framers applied the principle of the separation of powers. To Wilson, this was not merely unwise, it was absurd because, as Pestritto paraphrases Wilson, "a living thing cannot have its own organs offset one another." In the modern age of history-produced harmony, Wilson thought, majorities could be trusted to wield power vigorously. And given this harmony, the liberty of individuals should be understood as their free participation in a government controlled by majorities. Majority-made law is the will of the state made manifest, "the external organism of human freedom." The collectivism implicit in Wilson's thought became unpleasantly explicit in *The New Freedom* (1913), a collection of pronouncements from the 1912 presidential campaign that included his vision of the end of history "where men can live as a single community, co-operative as in a perfected, coordinated beehive."[114]

It would be wise for politicians to eschew insect metaphors when explaining the role of the people in the paradise the politicians envision. Analogies between the body politic and the human body also are problematic. "Justly revered as our great Constitution is," Wilson wrote, "it could be stripped off and thrown aside like a garment, and the nation would still stand forth clothed in the living vestment of flesh and sinew, warm with the heart-blood of one people, ready to recreate constitutions and laws." If so, why is the Constitution "justly revered"? If constitutions are so readily replaceable, why would any one of them stand forth as "great"? Wilson seemed to think that epochs come and go with great speed, and therefore constitutions, or at least their meanings, should, too. In the presidential campaign of 1912, he said: "The life of America is not the life that it was twenty years ago; it is not the life that it was ten years ago. We have changed our economic conditions, absolutely, from top to bottom; and, with our economic society, the organization of our life." It was perhaps understandable that someone alert to the advances of applied science at the time—Marconi, Edison, Ford, the Wright brothers, et al.— would have an exaggerated sense of the velocity of events and their supposed constitutional consequences. Still, if constitutions must be plastic under what Wilson called "the sheer pressure of life," the question about constitutions becomes: Why bother?[115]

Today, wise people, remembering a European nation galvanized by the slogan "*Ein Volk, ein Reich, ein Führer*" flinch from Wilson's trope about "the heart-blood of one people." It is one thing to postulate that history will produce ever increasing social harmony; it is another and ominous thing to speak of society as "one people" in an organic sense. If society is *supposed* to be an organic unity because the laws of history's unfolding say so, and if society is, as a matter of morality, *supposed* to be as united as the human body, then behold: Disagreements and factionalism become symptoms of bodily diseases. Such language greases society's skids toward virulent intolerance of dissent, the sort of intolerance that gripped America during World War I and tarnished Wilson's second presidential term. Wilson was, however, so thoroughly wedded to the conception of society as a single organism, his thinking could not accommodate even a flicker of the Founders' anxieties about government being *inherently* dangerous, *especially* governments wielded by majorities. Such anxieties, which were present at the creation of classical liberalism in the seventeenth and eighteenth centuries, seemed to Wilson not merely misplaced but illogical. As early as 1879, Wilson ridiculed those who denounce "the tyranny of partisan majorities" yet praise "true representative government." Such people "do not dream that they are laughably inconsistent." Ten years later, he reasoned similarly: "If society itself be not an evil, neither surely is government an evil, for government is the indispensable organ of society."[116]

Society can, however, pose problems without being "evil"; and government, without being "evil," can be simultaneously indispensable and susceptible to becoming a threat to the happiness of the governed. Wilson envisioned for government a stupendous mission, so he could not countenance the Founders' wariness regarding power. As we have seen, in 1885 he said the new role for the national government would require "wresting the Constitution to strange and as yet unimagined uses." By 1908, the idea of "wresting" it had been softened to "a nice adjustment": "As the life of the nation changes so must the interpretation of the document which contains it change, by a nice adjustment, determined, not by the original intention of those who drew the paper, but by the exigencies and the new aspects of life itself." "The State," Wilson said, "is an instrumentality for quickening in every suitable way…both collective and individual development."[117]

Well, then, who or what is to determine what ways might not be "suitable"? The answer must be the state itself, because it is the historically determined and "indispensable" expression of the social organism. In his 1887 essay "Socialism and Democracy," he wrote that the latter "proposes that all idea of a limitation of public authority by individual rights be put out of view" and "that no line can be drawn between private and public affairs which the State may not cross at will." Erasing such a line, however, means the annihilation of the inviolable zone of individual sovereignty that is indispensable to—indeed, *is*—freedom. So, one might assume that Wilson was, as it were, clearing his throat for a robust denunciation of socialism. But he was not. Instead, he insisted that "the difference between democracy and socialism is not an essential difference, but only a practical difference": "In fundamental theory socialism and democracy are almost if not quite one and the same. They both rest at bottom on the absolute right of the community to determine its own destiny and that of its members. Limits to the wisdom and convenience to the public control there may be: limits of principle there are, upon strict analysis, none." Note well: the community's right is "absolute."[118]

The Founders' republicanism was based on individual rights; Wilson's democratic theory made those rights subordinate to collective rights, the rights of the community. The rights, that is, of majorities, those potentially oppressive collectivities that the Constitution's Framers tried to improve, tame, leash, and circumscribe. To underscore his point that differences between democracy and socialism are only matters of practicality, a character in his essay called the "democrat" who speaks for Wilson says to the "socialist": "You know it is my principle, no less than yours, that every man shall have an equal chance with every other man: if I saw my way to it as a practical politician, I should be willing to go farther and superintend every man's use of his chance. But the means? The question with me is not whether the community has power to act as it may please in these matters, but how it can act with practical advantage—a question of *policy*." And by "policy" Wilson meant administration. Were he convinced that the community *could* "superintend" every person's life as minutely as necessary to serve progress, there would be no reason not to, no reason of political philosophy or constitutional propriety. If sufficient administrative expertise could be brought to bear, this should be done. No scruples rooted in anachronistic individualism should inhibit it. Wilson admired socialist government as a "revolt from selfish, misguided individualism," an attempt "to bring the individual with his special interests, personal to himself, into complete harmony with society with its general interests."[119] Yes, *complete* harmony was Wilson's goal.

Wilson's grand conception of the role of government was not grander than the role he envisioned for scholars such as himself. On December 28, 1898, he wrote in his personal journal, "Why may not the present age write, through me, its political *autobiography*?" To do so, the age would have to come to terms with the "radical defect in our federal system [which is] that it parcels out power and confuses responsibility as it does." He was referring to the "mischievous" theory of the system of checks and balances. "It is quite safe to say," he wrote in *Congressional Government*, "that were it possible to call together again the members of the wonderful Convention to view the work of their hands in the light of the century that has tested it, they would be the first to admit that the only fruit of dividing power had been to make it irresponsible." But what made the Constitutional Convention so "wonderful" if the following century proved that its work was radically defective? This praise of the Framers was a perfunctory nod by Wilson to what he considered the regrettably obligatory pieties that he dismissed as "Fourth of July sentiments."[120]

Wilson regretted Article I, Section 6 of the Constitution, which prohibits sitting members of Congress from serving in the executive branch. At one time he favored having the president's cabinet composed of members of the majority party in Congress—even if the president and that majority were of opposite parties. He correctly understood that his notion of government efficiency required dismantling the wall of separation between legislative and executive functions, the better to perform government's primary function as, in Pestritto's words, "a coordinated extension of the organic will of the people." Which brings us to a central oddity of Wilson's thought.

As a conscientious democrat, he wanted government to allow, and in some sense to embody, the clear and, contrary to the Founders' preference, direct expression of public opinion. But being a progressive, he did not want to sacrifice on the altar of public opinion the government's efficiency, its "wieldiness" in performance of its obligation to "superintend" the lives of citizens. After all, if public opinion is presumed to be enlightened concerning the intricacies of modern society, administration of society by progressives would not be so urgently needed. The defining dichotomy of Wilson's thinking was his distinction between politics and administration. The fact that Congress could not cope with its myriad tasks in the twentieth century "is its misfortune, not its fault." That this might be the fault of progressives, with their ambitions for the regulatory, administrative state, did not occur to Wilson, or if it did, it did not trouble him. "There is," he said, "scarcely a single duty of government which was once simple which is not now complex; government once had but a few masters; now it has scores of masters." These masters are majorities that, with what Wilson considered impertinence, are constantly intruding on government and presuming to direct it: "Majorities formerly only underwent government; they now conduct government. Where government once might follow the whims of a court, it must now follow the views of a nation. And those views are steadily widening to new conceptions of state duty; so that, at the same time that the functions of government are every day becoming more complex and difficult, they are also vastly multiplying in number."[121]

Note a contradiction in progressivism that has become steadily more severe in the century since Wilson wrote. Progressivism has no objection to the steady enlargement of the "conceptions of state duty." Quite the contrary, such enlargement *is* the progressive agenda—the expansion of the central government's supervision of society's complexities. But as solicitous government permeates society with its superintending, society responds in an inconvenient way. As government's interests multiply, so do interest groups. As government seeks to supplement and even supplant market forces in the allocation of wealth and opportunity, there is a corresponding and commensurate multiplication of factions determined to influence the actions of activist government.

In the second decade of the twenty-first century, after a full century of progressivism's extensions of the reach of the regulatory state, progressives are dismayed by the predictable result of these extensions. At least they were predictable to Madisonians, with their clear-sighted understanding of the interestedness that is sown in human nature and with their rejection of sentimentalism about history imposing harmony on the welter of self-interestedness. People will pursue their interests, and like-minded people will join together to pursue their shared interests. And the more things government touches, the more people will have interests in touching, and wheedling, government. Progressives purport to be scandalized by modern Washington, which is indeed an unlovely maelstrom of interest groups maneuvering to maximize their rent-seeking. This is, however, the Washington that progressives should have known they were making. But they only could have known this if they had a keen Madisonian sense of political sociology. And if progressives had had this, they would have had to reconsider their premises.

Instead, progressives, who are scandalized by the clamorousness of modern politics, have recently responded not by pruning the government's interventions in the disposition of money, but by trying to regulate the spending of money to influence elections that determine the composition of government. It is, however, an iron law: The more government does to influence the flow of money, the more money will be spent to influence elections. Talk about treating symptoms: Progressives advocate using campaign finance regulations to limit political spending, thereby supposedly somehow reducing the amount of rent-seeking. Unfortunately for progressives, the Supreme Court has noted the obvious: Almost all campaign spending is for the dissemination of political advocacy. The court has come to the obvious conclusion that many limits on such spending violate First Amendment protections of free speech.

Wilson cannot fairly be faulted for not foreseeing how fast and how far the administrative state would metastasize and how unlovely would be the political culture that this metastasizing would produce. And if some particularly farseeing contemporary had warned Wilson about this, he might well have replied that he could forestall the emergence of such unseemly politics. He would do so by making politics more democratic but simultaneously diminishing the importance of politics. Wilson believed that democracy is history's destination, but it should be democracy of an attenuated sort. His two instruments for accomplishing this attenuation would be presidential leadership and the science of public administration.

As Pestritto notes, Wilson's fascination with the presidency was apparent in the earliest of Wilson's political writings, from his undergraduate years, which advocated making training in rhetoric an important part of Princeton's curriculum. Arthur Link, the Princeton historian who was Wilson's biographer and editor of Wilson's collected writings, thought that Theodore Roosevelt's "revivification of the presidency" influenced Wilson's turn toward an emphasis on the presidency as the representative of what Wilson called the nation's "oneness of personality." Because only the president "represents the people as a whole, exercising national choice," he is the "spokesman for the real sentiment and purpose of the country." In 1897, Wilson wrote an essay on the presidency of Grover Cleveland, who had retired in Princeton after leaving the White House in 1897, and who died there in 1908. (The Gothic tower over the Graduate School is Cleveland Tower.) Today, it might seem strange that Wilson was fascinated by the personality of Cleveland, whom contemporaries would not have called charismatic, had that term then been in use. Wilson nevertheless insisted that Cleveland's personality restored the presidency to its proper centrality in American politics. It was, Wilson thought, a progressive development that, under Cleveland, American politics began "waiting for [the president's] initiative, and how the air at Washington filled with murmurs against the domineering and usurping temper and practice of the Executive. Power had somehow gone the length of [Pennsylvania] avenue and seemed lodged in one man."[122]

Wilson's celebration of the "popularization" of the presidency as the nation's voice was related to his animus against federalism as a subtraction from the nation's unity. His apotheosis of the presidency also came at the expense of Congress, which he disparaged as not really part of "the government." The essential business of governing was done by the presidency wielding the new science of public administration. The president could speak *for* the nation by speaking *to* the nation, infusing it with its latent spirit by articulating that spirit.

This is the meaning of Wilson's cryptic proposition that "leadership, for the statesman, is *interpretation*." As a president uses transformative rhetoric, he will eclipse and marginalize Congress, so the real business of government can proceed through a new class of nonpartisan, apolitical administrators. In 1878, when he was still one of them, he said that "if the thirty thousand young men who are pursuing studies at the different colleges of this country" would "throw off the party spirit" and form opinions "intelligently and independently," America's future could be entrusted to them.[123]

A properly rhetorical presidency, combined with a disinterested class of administrators, could overcome what Wilson considered (in Pestritto's words) "the forced fragmentation of the founders' constitutionalism." A Wilsonian president could "instruct and persuade a multitudinous monarch called public opinion." Allowing himself to be carried away by the thought of rhetoric powerful enough to carry men away, Wilson said: "Men are as clay in the hands of the consummate leader." Steeped in historicism, Wilson fell easily into the language of teleological history: A leader sees the "road" society is on and discerns the "direction" a nation is heading. His job is not to pave new roads or choose new directions; rather it is to "discern and strengthen the tendencies" history has imposed. "Where all minds are awake," he said, "some minds will be wide awake." The latter, including the minds of the 30,000 collegians, are the minds of leaders alert to history's "tendencies."[124]

Wilson became murky, in a Hegelian manner, when he insisted that it is not the leader's "business to judge *for* the nation, but to judge *through* the nation as its spokesman and voice." But the implication of Wilson's mystical voice of presidential and other leadership is clear enough. Wilson, like the leaders he envisions, is history's handmaiden. When a real leader takes the field, "Resistance is left to the minority, and such as will not be convinced are crushed." Hegel, too, had said that a leader must "crush to pieces many an object in its path." Pestritto emphasizes that "for both Wilson and Hegel, leadership is ultimately connected to history, which is an irresistible force of progress." Pestritto says the "crucial difference" between Hegel and Wilson is that whereas "Hegel's World-Historical Individual is more of an unconscious tool of world history," Wilson's leader "has to some degree a vision of where history is going." Notice, however, the hedging—"more of" and "to some degree"—that Pestritto, a judicious scholar, finds necessary. But he might be making a distinction without much difference. Both Hegel and Wilson consigned leaders, and the led, to the tides of history; neither believed that tides could be resisted or deflected for long.[125]

The words "leader" or "leaders" appear thirteen times in *The Federalist*, once with reference to those who led the Revolution and twelve times in a context of disparagement. The Founders, apprehensive about the people's potential for irrational passions, were wary of leaders who would seek to ascend to power on waves of such passions. Wilson, surveying America from the pinnacle of progress where history had placed him, was untroubled by the threat of demagoguery. "Great passions," he said equably, "when they run through a whole population, inevitably find a great spokesman." Both the passions and the spokesmen are churned up by history. With presidential leaders speaking to, through, and for—all those prepositions apply—the nation, Congress, in Wilson's analysis (and aspiration), is marginalized and reduced to giving only the most general directives to the real government. It consists of the class of educated, disinterested, apolitical experts recruited from those 30,000 young men Wilson hoped to summon from campuses to public service to practice the new science of public administration. As Hegel wrote in *The Philosophy of Right*, conferring on a civil servant a secure place in a bureaucracy would purge from that individual the temptation of self-interestedness. For Wilson, the eclipse of Congress was desirable; progressivism, which produced the administrative state, made the eclipse inevitable.[126]

The Constitution's Framers *planned* for conflict between the branches, which are *supposed* to be jealous rivals. Today this no longer is, if it ever was, a fair fight. They are not equal in the competition for control of the modern state. The playing field tilts more and more against the legislative branch. In notes made for some Princeton lectures in the 1890s, Wilson wrote: "Administration cannot wait upon legislation, but must be given leave, or take it, to proceed without specific warrant in giving effect to the characteristic life of the state." Note well: "or take it." That makes the idea of the rule of law blurry, and the actual rule of law attenuated. "In the case of the Historically Normal Government," Wilson wrote, "we may say that, in the absence of specific legal developments to the contrary, the presumption is in favor of the principle, that the sphere of administrative authority is as wide as the sphere in which it may move without infringing the laws."[127] Now, *there* was an interesting twist on Hobbes' idea that freedom depends on "the silence of the law."[128] The administrative state is free to do whatever the legislature, through legislation, has not proscribed. This was Wilson's extension of Theodore Roosevelt's idea of presidential "stewardship": The administration of things supplants meaningful governance, or even supervision, by elected representatives.

In his "Study of Administration," which did much to launch the academic field of public administration, Wilson argued that the development of a mature bureaucracy would cause the public to abandon its anxieties about almost-autonomous administrators wielding extraordinary power and exercising vast discretion—much of it, but by no means all of it, expressly delegated to it by Congress. By consigning Congress to the chore of expressing public sentiments and leaving to professional administrators the codification of these sentiments in regulations—the flesh on the skeleton of sentiments— the problem of modern democracy would be solved. Remember Wilson saying, "The problem is to make public opinion efficient without suffering it to be meddlesome." Wilson granted that there are instances in Europe where bureaucracy had become utterly severed from democratic control and put to oppressive uses. America, however, could emulate the virtues while avoiding the vices: "If I see a murderous fellow sharpening a knife cleverly, I can borrow his way of sharpening the knife without borrowing his probable intention to commit murder with it; and so, if I see a monarchist dyed in the wool managing a public bureau well, I can learn his business methods without changing one of my republican spots." Or as he said more pithily: "We borrowed rice, but we do not eat it with chopsticks."[129] Would that things were so simple.

The constantly multiplying tasks of government, and government's constantly thickening layers, are, in Wilson's telling, rather like strata of geological sediments, the product of ineluctable processes proceeding without much regard to conscious planning. Government's new tasks, he said, are those "the State has had laid upon it by reason of history, through Law, which is the product of history."[130] His use of the capital letter is supposed to confer a certain status, but the nature of that status is unclear, as is the reason why he capitalized the L in law. Having done so, why did he not capitalize the H in history?

One interpretation of Wilson's thinking is that before becoming president he was a Southern Jeffersonian who opposed the more robust Hamiltonianism of his principal opponent in the 1912 presidential race, Theodore Roosevelt. But the pressures of events during Wilson's presidency drove his New Freedom in a direction similar to the unapologetic centralization of Roosevelt's New Nationalism. Pestritto's interpretation of the evolution of Wilson's thought is that it did not evolve very much. He argues that "what united Wilson and Roosevelt was far more substantial than what divided them." The exigencies of winning the Democrats' 1912 presidential nomination compelled Wilson to try to differentiate his thinking from Roosevelt's. Wilson was nominated on the forty-sixth ballot of the Democratic convention in Baltimore, where he won by winning the support of the party's three-time nominee, William Jennings Bryan. "Central to Bryan's populism," Pestritto writes, "was a fear of national executive power and a deep distrust of business interests in the Northeast." Whatever Jeffersonian tone Wilson gave to his 1912 campaign was, as Pestritto says, a politically driven "anomaly." Once elected, Wilson quickly and emphatically reverted to his long-held and clearly stated principles of centralization.[131]

FROM WILSON'S STRADDLE TO FDR'S CONTRACT

Even before the election he was in an ideological straddle. During the 1912 campaign, in a speech to the New York Press Club, Wilson declared that "the history of liberty is the history of the limitation of governmental power." That is liberty's history. But what of its future? Two weeks later Wilson said: "While we are followers of Jefferson, there is one principle of Jefferson's which no longer can obtain in the practical politics of America. You know that it was Jefferson who said that the best government is that which does as little governing as possible.... But that time is passed. America is not now and cannot in the future be a place for unrestricted individual enterprise."[132] This is rather like someone saying: "I am a Marxist, except for the foolishness about the class struggle being the motor that drives history."

Wilson was a follower of Jefferson, except for the essence of Jeffersonianism. His reason was that "life is so complicated that we are not dealing with the old conditions." But Wilson's rejection of Jefferson's thinking was actually more radical than that: "It is his speculative philosophy that is exotic, and that runs like a false and artificial note through all his thought. It was un-American in being abstract, sentimental, and rationalistic, rather than practical. That he held it sincerely need not be doubted; but the more sincerely he accepted it so much the more thoroughly was he un-American." Of Wilson's four derogatory adjectives, the most telling is "speculative." He was referring to natural rights theory. Hence he is judging Jefferson's, and America's, Declaration of Independence "un-American."[133]

More than a century after Wilson said this, the degradation of American government is writ large in a semantic shift. The Declaration says government is instituted to "secure" rights that pre-exist government. But more and more of what government does consists of transferring wealth to members of groups that the government has decided are entitled to transfers. And the word "rights" is coming to be used interchangeably with "entitlements." Hence the unspoken but unmistakable supposition is that the more entitlements people enjoy, the more rights they have—and that rights, like entitlements, trickle down from government.

The Founders hoped that some potentially disruptive passions might be tamed by being diverted from factional politics into commerce. They hoped that dangerous energies would be sublimated in wealth-creation and acquisition. But what was to prevent acquisitive people from coming to regard government as just another arena in which they could strive for material well-being? Nothing was to prevent that, because the nation was to abandon the Constitution's underlying ideas and because some new ideas were to encourage actively the conception of government as deliverer of material well-being.

In October 1932, the Democratic Party's presidential nominee said, "I have…described the spirit of my program as a 'new deal,' which is plain English for a changed concept of the duty and responsibility of Government toward economic life."[134] By the time of his 1938 State of the Union Address Franklin Roosevelt would say, "Government has a final responsibility for the well-being of its citizenship."[135] Thus was the final responsibility for much of life removed from private life to the public sector—and to the banks of the Potomac. And thus was the "well-being" of the citizen defined with reference to material conditions and without reference to the citizen's character or virtues or responsibilities. In his January 1944 State of the Union message, President Roosevelt proclaimed a government "duty" to establish "an American standard of living higher than ever before known," and he said: "We cannot be content, no matter how high that general standard of living may be, if some fraction of our people—whether it be one-third or one-fifth or one-tenth—is ill-fed, ill-clothed, ill-housed, and insecure." This was a summons to permanent discontent on the part of citizens and government. This bestowed on government a roving commission to define civic health solely in terms of the material standard of living, yet also to add to the growing list of citizens' entitlements an entitlement to a mental state: a sense of security. Roosevelt said political rights would no longer suffice to insure "equality in the pursuit of happiness," so there must be a "second Bill of Rights." It would include rights to "a useful and remunerative job," "adequate" food and clothing and recreation, "good" education, "decent" homes, a "decent" living for farmers, "adequate" medical care, and a right to freedom from "unfair competition" and from "the economic fears of old age, sickness, accident, and unemployment."[136]

All these rights, and myriad others that would be enumerated as the years rolled by, were necessary, Roosevelt said, because "necessitous men are not free men."[137] Therefore, government's new task would be nothing less than the conquest of necessity. And so, twenty years later, in 1964, at the Democratic convention, the presidential nomination was accepted by a man who had been in Washington since Roosevelt was president and who planned to complete Roosevelt's project—the elimination of necessity from Americans' lives. Lyndon Johnson said to the 1964 convention: "This Nation—this generation—in this hour, has man's first chance to build the Great Society—a place where the meaning of man's life matches the marvels of man's labor."[138] It was going to be hard to top that entitlement—the entitlement to meaningfulness. And twenty years after that, the Democratic Party gave its presidential nomination to Walter Mondale, perhaps the last nominee to adhere to New Deal liberalism, or at least the last not to disguise his adherence. In his concession statement after losing forty-nine states, Mondale said his thoughts were with all those in need of caring government, including "the poor, the unemployed, the elderly, the handicapped, the helpless, and the sad."[139] Sadness, too, like necessity, qualified as a public concern.

How did it happen that liberalism annihilated all sense of limits on government's responsibilities and competence? In President Johnson's 1965 speech at Howard University, which adumbrated the rationale for what has come to be called affirmative action, he said "men are shaped by their world." That is certainly true. Johnson also said people are shaped by "a hundred unseen forces."[140] That also is true. But what was new was the idea that government could and should master those forces, the unseen and the seen, and, for that matter, should master "the world." The planted axiom was that, because government frames society, government is complicit in, and hence morally responsible for, all social outcomes and should make them come out right.

This, however, erases the distinction on which classical liberalism—the liberalism of Locke and the American Revolution—was founded and which today's conservative sensibility cherishes. It is the distinction between the public and the private spheres of life. On this distinction, freedom depends. About this, progressivism says: Never mind. Government should undertake to "level the playing field." This recurring phrase is revealing: Playing fields are leveled by bulldozers, which are not nice emblems of government. The result of government's equalizing aspirations is a paradox—power wielded by elites claiming expertise in the manufacture of equality. In its attempt to equalize "well-being," progressivism came to exalt one virtue: compassion. Which is a passion. And compassion is a capacious concept. It can mean the prevention or amelioration of pain, of discomfort, of insecurity, or even of sadness. However, the frustration of desires is uncomfortable and can make people sad. So compassionate government must toil for the satisfaction of all desires. If a desire unfulfilled is painful, or even discomforting, fulfilling that desire is a duty of compassionate government. Such government believes that the pain of unfulfilled desires makes fulfilling the desires necessary. So the desires are upgraded to necessities. People suffering disappointed desires are therefore necessitous people, and, according to Franklin Roosevelt, they are not free.

What moderation, what temperance, what restraint can there be in government animated by the idea that freedom, understood as emancipation from necessity, is the gift of comprehensively compassionate government? Such government has metastasized recklessly, and one of conservatism's missions is to temper such government's hubris and overreaching. This can be accomplished only by shifting the winds of public opinion. So the central political problem for conservatives is to get the public to consent to government that refuses to fulfill many of their desires. But in order for popular government to be strong enough to say "no" to popular desires, it must be respected. And if our constitutional government is to be respected, the Constitution must be regarded as something more, something grander, than a mere framework for competing forms of willfulness. The conservative agenda of governmental restraint depends on government having the strength that comes from respect, which is never accorded to the servile.

Franklin Roosevelt's most famous speech was his first as president, his inaugural address reassuring an anxious nation that it had nothing to fear but fear itself. But his most nuanced, revealing, and portentous speech was delivered forty-six days before he was elected, on September 23, 1932, at San Francisco's Commonwealth Club. It was more radical than his more vituperative speeches of the 1936 campaign (about "economic royalists" and so on), and it foreshadowed, and explains, a less-remembered portion of Roosevelt's first inaugural address. In San Francisco, he approached his startling philosophical point obliquely, by taking sides in a defining American rivalry. He associated himself with Jefferson, apostle of American individualism, rather than Hamilton, the first powerful advocate of an energetic central government in the service of organized financial power. Roosevelt delivered a barbed compliment, calling Hamilton "the most brilliant, honest and able exponent" of the belief that "popular government was essentially dangerous and essentially unworkable."[141] This was a meretricious description of the author of fifty-one of the eighty-five Federalist papers, and of his argument that the Constitution, properly understood and faithfully adhered to, would make popular government safe and functional. But Roosevelt's presentation of Hamilton served Roosevelt's purpose of reminding his listeners that the nation had much experience with Hamiltonian measures, and with what might be called Hamiltonian men, the embodiments of commercial dynamism.

In a trenchant argument intended to discomfit his largely business audience, Roosevelt correctly noted, "It has been traditional, particularly in Republican administrations, for business urgently to ask the government to put at private disposal all kinds of government assistance." Tariffs were imposed first for the ostensible purpose of protecting so-called infant industries, and then were retained because vested interests had become comfortable relying on them. Also, "railroads were subsidized" with money and grants of land that included some of the nation's most valuable oil lands.[142] The merchant marine was subsidized with direct monetary grants and with mail subsidies. Roosevelt did not enumerate these entanglements of government with willing business interests merely in order to tweak the commercial class for its situational ethics regarding laissez-faire. Rather, he did so to set up his larger point about how the sweep of history had brought humanity to an inevitable and potentially wholesome dependence on a strong state.

"We are," he said, "likely to forget how hard people have worked to win the privilege of government." Europeans developed strong central governments in order to "impose peace upon ruling barons." Strong government became in Europe "a haven of refuge to the individual," and it could and should become such a haven in America, where the likes of European barons existed in the form of what Roosevelt, quoting his cousin Theodore, called "malefactors of great wealth." Society had decided to give wide latitude to these men of "tremendous will and tremendous ambition" as long as America's population "was growing by leaps and bounds," and as long as the nation had an abundance of free land as a "safety valve" for those who needed a second chance after losing out in the turbulent scramble of our congested cities. However, "Our task now is not discovery or exploitation of natural resources, or necessarily producing more goods. It is the soberer, less dramatic business of administering resources and plants already in hand."[143]

In seeing administration as the essence of governing, Franklin Roosevelt placed himself firmly in the Wilsonian tradition. Said Roosevelt, "The day of enlightened administration has come." He saw a future of scarcity requiring a strong state to regulate the allocation of scarce things. "We are not able," Roosevelt said, "to invite the immigration from Europe to share our endless plenty. We are now providing a drab living for our own people." This, and the supposed fact that "some six hundred odd corporations" controlled two-thirds of the nation's industry, set the agenda of strong government. And this required a new understanding of the American contract.[144] Herewith Roosevelt's real revolution, which he mildly called "a re-appraisal of values":

> The Declaration of Independence discusses the problem of government in terms of a contract. Government is a relation of give and take, a contract, perforce, if we would follow the thinking out of which it grew. Under such a contract rulers were accorded power, and the people consented to that power on consideration that they be accorded certain rights. The task of statesmanship has always been the re-definition of these rights in terms of a changing and growing social order.[145]

The radically revised role that Roosevelt sketched in San Francisco for the central government became explicit 102 days later when, standing on the East Front of the US Capitol, the new president called for "engaging on a national scale in a redistribution" of population to rectify "the overbalance of population in our industrial centers." For this and other enormous undertakings "we must move as a trained and loyal army willing to sacrifice for the good of a common discipline." He spoke of "a sacred obligation" to embrace "a unity of duty hitherto evoked only in time of armed strife." Action on the scale he envisioned is "feasible" under the Constitution, which is "so simple and practical that it is possible always to meet extraordinary needs by changes in emphasis and arrangement without loss of essential form." Then, however, he warned that this time "the normal balance of public procedure," aka the Constitution, might not suffice: "But it may be that an unprecedented demand and need for undelayed action may call for temporary departure from that normal balance of public procedure.... I shall ask the Congress for...broad executive power to wage a war against the emergency, as great as the power that would be given to me if we were in fact invaded by a foreign foe."[146] The military imagery—another moral equivalent of war—signaled, and served, the eclipse of individualism, the supremacy of the collectivity in a transformed America.

Invocations of martial solidarity should grate on free people. In Muriel Spark's 1963 novel *Girls of Slender Means*, the membership of a women's club goes to Buckingham Palace to celebrate V-E day on May 8, 1945. They joined in "the huge organic murmur of the crowd," in which "many strange arms were twined round strange bodies" and "many liaisons, some permanent, were formed." Then tomorrow arrived. "The next day everyone began to consider where they personally stood in the new order of things. Many citizens felt the urge, which some began to indulge, to insult each other, in order to prove something or to test their ground."[147] Yes, where did they *personally* stand when the collective strenuousness of war subsided? Individualism must occasionally, in exigent circumstances, yield to solidarity fused by danger, as the New Deal faced. But such solidarity should not be a norm aspired to.

The New Deal made, and was made possible by, something novel in American history: a sanguine estimation of the competence and trustworthiness of the central government. The New Deal frame of mind was presaged by this change: Eleven of the Constitution's first twelve amendments added more restrictions to the federal government than those written into the document in Philadelphia in 1787. Six of the next seven amendments, however, enlarged federal powers. Still, from the Founding until the 1930s, the American premise was itself a formidable inhibition of the central government. That premise was that the function of government is to provide the conditions—ordered liberty—in which happiness can be pursued, but not to provide happiness itself. Since the New Deal, the government has become steadily more ambitious. Americans have not, however, become more content with their government.

Historians have rightly seen significance in the fact that many of the leading lights of progressivism around the turn of the twentieth century—Woodrow Wilson, for example—were children of Protestant clergymen. The premise of Christian theology is that we are fallen creatures who either do not know what we want or want the wrong things (e.g., golden calves), and hence need to be governed by moral auditors. Robert Fogel, economist and Nobel laureate, argues that three religious "awakenings"[148]—changes in and intensifications of religious sensibilities—have shaped American history. The first, which began around 1730, presaged the American Revolution by fomenting skepticism about traditional forms of authority. The second, after 1800, stressed personal perfection and America's mission to pursue social perfection. This fueled anti-slavery passions. The third awakening began around 1890, during urbanization, immigration, industrialization, labor unrest, and the ascent of the Reverend Joseph Ruggles Wilson's son, Thomas Woodrow. It preached that unreformed society, not inherent sinfulness, is the source of moral corruption. This encouraged a modernist or progressive agenda of material amelioration, culminating in the entitlement state. What began as an exercise of redemptive politics has, however, reached a point of civic sourness, and a sense that sprawling, interventionist government, by encouraging dependency and enabling rent-seeking, is making matters worse.

The epigraph of this chapter, taken from Woodrow Wilson's 1912 presidential campaign, uses an extended architectural analogy to explain his vision for a comprehensively remodeled America. More than a century later, the nation's constitutional architecture has become ramshackle, incoherent, and incapable of protecting representative government, the rule of law, and liberty. This trifecta of failure is writ large in the subject of the next chapter: the swollen presidency atop the administrative state.

CHAPTER 3

PROGRESSIVISM'S INSTITUTIONAL CONSEQUENCES

THE PRESIDENCY TRIUMPHANT, THE ADMINISTRATIVE STATE RAMPANT, CONGRESS DORMANT

If you have ever been to a formal dinner…in England, you will recall that after dessert and coffee, and before it is permitted to light a cigarette, a toast is customarily presented: "Ladies and gentlemen, the Queen." And if you have ever been to a diplomatic function involving participants from England and the United States, you will recall that it is custom to reply to that toast with a toast "To the president of the United States." Every time I hear that progression it strikes me that the comparison does not really work. The president is, to be sure, both our chief executive and our head of state, our prime minister and queen combined. But if one wishes to evoke the deep and enduring symbol of our nationhood and our unity as a people, it seems to me the toast ought to be 'Ladies and gentlemen, the Constitution of the United States.' For that is…not only the token but indeed the substance of what continues to bind us together as a people.

Antonin Scalia, April 1991[1]

There is a paradoxical aspect of the American Founding. The foundational document, the Constitution, was written to provide institutional arrangements that could function and endure without the regular occurrence of exceptional leaders. The arrangements presuppose that, as Madison wrote with notable understatement in Federalist 10, "enlightened statesmen will not always be at the helm."[2] Machiavelli earned a bad reputation by severing the assessment of a politician's job performance from the assessment of his moral qualities. Less radical thinkers—temperate Machiavellians—know that a morally exemplary leader is an occasional bonus in political life, and occasionally is imperative, but is not necessary for the normal functioning of a well-founded regime. But if George Washington had not been, as it were, waiting in the wings to assume the presidency, the Constitution's authors might not have so boldly swept away the Articles of Confederation. And the office of president, of which the Articles had no analogue, might not have been created, at least not in the form it was given by the Constitutional Convention.[3] Except it barely had a form. It was soft wax that would take the shape given it by occupants, especially the first one. And if Virginia's ratifying convention had rejected the Constitution, as it might have done (the Constitution passed eighty-nine to seventy-nine; Richard Henry Lee, an ardent and potent opponent of ratification, was too ill to attend), Washington would not have been a resident of the United States and so could not have become president. Charles de Gaulle once mordantly said that the graveyards are full of indispensable men. Washington, however, truly was such a man.

In the immediate aftermath of his election as the first president, Washington was unlike any subsequent American political figure. There was no significant public faction opposed to him as he traveled to New York City "in a large coach with six matching cream-colored horses, four servants, and two gentlemen on horseback." But a few prescient observers fretted about presidential magnificence. Benjamin Rush, the Philadelphia physician who was a member of the Continental Congress and a signer of the Declaration of Independence, worried that Washington's unanimous election was symptomatic of an "idolatrous and exclusive attachment," and he warned, "Monarchy is natural to Americans."[4] George Washington chose to be inaugurated in a suit made in America from what was called "homespun" broadcloth, but it had gilt buttons that went nicely with the diamond buckles on his shoes.[5]

Samuel Adams, who lived through the apotheosis of George Washington, said, "[L]et us beware of continental and state great men." Adams' republican reflex was shared by others. During President Washington's first term, there occurred what Madison called "a small circumstance…worthy of notice": The federal government proposed to issue its first coin—featuring Washington's profile. The House of Representatives, sniffing the odor of monarchy, amended the relevant bill to substitute lady liberty for the first president, but the Senate rejected this amendment. So the House passed it again, by an increased margin, and the Senate relented.[6] Actually, this was not a small matter: If it had become normal to honor sitting presidents on the common currency, every occupant of the office would have been given a vague but unmistakable imprimatur as somehow elevated above partisanship. Responding to Vice President John Adams' belief that "neither dignity, nor authority can be supported in human minds, collected into nations…without a splendor and majesty,"[7] the Senate spun a grandiloquent title for President Washington: "His Highness the President of the United State of America, and the Protector of their Liberties."[8] Such pomposity did not last, in part because Washington's austere manner was sufficient to guarantee a republican form of dignity.

Although Washington was as revered throughout the new nation as his unanimous election suggested, his relations with Congress began to fray almost immediately. In 1789, Thomas Jefferson, wishing to make a temporary return to the United States, requested an official leave of absence from Paris, where he was serving as US minister to

France. Washington duly instructed John Jay, who was conducting foreign affairs, to grant it. Several senators objected that Washington had "transgressed his Powers" because he had not consulted with the Senate. One senator saw a danger "that some points may be conceded to him from a sense of his virtue & a confidence that he will never make an improper use of his power." Only a few months into this first presidency, some senators bridled at the idea that their constitutional power to advise and consent to presidential appointments did not extend to the power to consent to the removal of executive branch officers. One senator warned that Washington's "virtues will depart with him, but the powers which you give him will remain." When the question of removal came to a vote, the Senate was evenly divided, so the man who would be Washington's successor, John Adams, cast the deciding vote, affirming Washington's power unilaterally to remove unsatisfactory subordinates. This was the first such exercise of this vice presidential tie-breaking power, and Adams wielded it to augment presidential power.[9]

Since then, presidential power has been multiplied many times and manifested in myriad ways that would have amazed Adams. The ever-expanding powers and pretenses of the presidency have become a menace to America's Madisonian balance of separated powers. The powers and pretensions of presidents should long since have become an embarrassment to the public. Upon what meat doth this our Caesar feed, That he is grown so great? The presidential office has fattened on the exigencies of a sprawling, intrusive government and on the (somewhat consequent) childishness of the citizenry.

PRESIDENTIAL ALCHEMY

Alchemy, which was the dream that chemistry could turn base metals into gold, is properly derided as a medieval superstition. Many contemporary Americans, however, have faith in political alchemy: The faith is that 270 electoral votes can do more than turn a person into a president, they can turn a lout into a gentleman, a mediocrity into a savant, a master of electoral politics into a moral tutor and embodiment of the national spirit. The modern presidency is a pernicious conflation of the function of a government executive with that of a semi-sacerdotal official catering to the spiritual care of people who seek from politics some excitements, satisfactions, and consolations that politics should not try to supply. Granted, an extensive republic is especially in need of an energetic executive, regardless of what Hamilton in Federalist 67 called the "aversion of the people to monarchy,"[10] and regardless of the fear that, as Edmund Randolph said, any single executive is "the foetus of monarchy."[11] The anti-Federalist who wrote as the Federal Farmer conceded that in any populous polity "there must be a visible point serving as a common centre in the government, toward which to draw their eyes and attachments."[12] This was long before graphic journalism began to draw eyes to the one institution suited to be such a focal point, the presidency. Then came such journalism, and modern technologies enable presidents to communicate to the public without mediating journalists.

William Allen White, the nationally prominent Kansas newspaper editor, told in his autobiography a story of President William McKinley at his home in Canton, Ohio, in the summer of 1901. When a photographer approached to take the president's picture, McKinley laid aside his cigar, saying, "We must not let the young men of this country see their president smoking!" The camera was a harbinger of the graphic revolution in communication that would help enlarge the place of the presidency, the most photogenic piece of America's government, in the nation's consciousness. McKinley was a transitional figure. He had presided over America's passage into imperialism in the war with Spain, and his assassination late in the summer of 1901 produced the first modern president, who proclaimed his office a "bully pulpit" to be used for shaping the public's mind and morals. McKinley's discarded cigar was evidence that presidents were acquiring the extra-constitutional role as role model. Eleven decades later, this seems as unhealthy as McKinley's cigar now seems.

No newspaper had posted a reporter at the White House in the nineteenth century. President Grover Cleveland underwent cancer surgery on board a yacht in New York Harbor without the press knowing anything about it. But presidential ascendancy was well advanced by the time one of William McKinley's secretaries began briefing the press at ten o'clock each evening. McKinley's successor, the first president filmed by a movie camera, was the first charismatic president. Twenty-five years later, Teddy Roosevelt's cousin would master a medium—radio—that reached over the heads of Congress and journalists, directly to the electorate. Twentieth-century American history was to a significant extent a story of the economic consequences of war and the political consequences of mass communication. Radio made FDR America's first "intimate" public figure, one insinuating himself into everyone's living room. FDR had none of Churchill's eloquence, but he had a flair as a phrasemaker: "rendezvous with destiny," "day that will live in infamy," "economic royalists." No wonder he once said that if he had not gone into politics he might have gone into a profession that burgeoned when he was restless in the 1920s: advertising.

Modern communications technologies have changed governance to the advantage of the executive. In the middle of the twentieth century, for the first time since the city-states of ancient Greece, a national leader could be "seen and heard in real time by most eligible citizens."[13] The first presidential news conference was March 15, 1913, conducted by the president who, nine months later, would become the first president since Jefferson to deliver his State of the Union report in person, as an address to Congress rather than in a written report. The nation was nearing the end of the tradition that most presidential communication was primarily written, not spoken, and was directed to the legislative branch, not the public. Unmediated presidential communication crossed another frontier at 8:38 a.m. on

May 15, 2015: "Hello, Twitter! It's Barack. Really!" First name? Two exclamation marks? Really?

The ubiquity of presidents in American life is both cause and effect of what Gene Healy calls "the cult of the presidency," which he thinks reveals an American hunger for "redemption through presidential politics." Progressives and conservatives basically "agree on the boundless nature of presidential responsibility." Progressives agree for reasons of progressivism: They think boundless government is beneficent and that presidents claiming a unique stature as embodiments of the nation can arouse public support to bend Congress into compliance, thereby vitiating the Founders' blunder, the great impediment to energetic government acting with dispatch, the separation of powers. Conservatives—actually, faux conservatives—agree on the boundless nature of presidential responsibility because they have forgotten their raison d'être. They practice situational constitutionalism, favoring what Healy calls "Caesaropapism" as long as the Caesar-cum-pope wields his limitless powers in the service of things they favor.[14]

The archived copy of President Franklin Roosevelt's first fireside chat with a national radio audience does not contain the words with which he began the broadcast: "My friends." Americans are now so used to the spurious intimacy of omnipresent presidents that they do not pause to wonder: Do we really want presidents pretending to be our friends? What does this chumminess reveal about them? And about us? "Tell me your troubles," said Roosevelt in another fireside chat with a radio audience.[15] Try to imagine George Washington—or any president prior to FDR—talking like that.

In 1960, the nation elected a president concerning whom the word "charisma"—a term drawn from Christianity—came into common use. That year an eminent political scientist described the presidency as "the incarnation of the American people in a sacrament resembling that in which the wafer and the wine are seen to be the body and blood of Christ." Good grief. In 1992, Governor Bill Clinton promised a "New Covenant" between government and the governed. That, Healy notes, was "a metaphor that had the state stepping in for Yahweh." Hillary Clinton, stepping in for Sigmund Freud, diagnosed America as in need of presidential ministrations for "a sleeping sickness of the soul" because Americans do not know "who we are as human beings in this postmodern age."[16] The idea of presidents dogpaddling around in such shallow philosophical waters in order to answer existential questions no longer strikes people as ludicrous. Neither were there wholesome guffaws when, in 2008, Michelle Obama said that her husband "will never allow you to go back to your lives as usual, uninvolved, uninformed."[17] Leave aside the insult—how did she know Americans were uninvolved and uninformed? But do Americans really elect politicians to yank them out of their usual lives?

Americans are mistakenly said to be political cynics. Actually, they are besotted presidential romantics. When, during the 1992 campaign, Bill Clinton, President George H. W. Bush, and Ross Perot appeared in a town hall–style debate, a member of the audience asked them this question: "How can we, as symbolically the children of the future president, expect…you to meet our needs, the needs in housing and in crime and you name it?" If you can name it, presidents are responsible for it. Politicians understand the infantilization of the public. "The average American," said President Richard Nixon, "is just like the child in the family—you give him some responsibility and he is going to amount to something." So, personal responsibility is dispensed to individuals from on high, by presidents. Government, said Vice President Al Gore, should act like "grandparents in the sense that grandparents perform a nurturing role."[18] "I think," wrote the poet Randall Jarrell, "that George Washington would be extremely afraid of the traffic on the Merritt Parkway, but I think that we would be afraid of George Washington."[19] Indeed, his remote, austere demeanor would be not merely off-putting but would seem to be a reproach.

Washington was acutely aware that he was fated to improvise a presidential manner congruent with republican simplicity. He avoided what has now encrusted the presidency—a vulgar grandiosity, which is a modern accretion. President James Monroe was faulted for excessive formality because he complained that diplomats constantly dropped in on him uninvited and expected tea. President John Quincy Adams regularly swam naked in the Potomac, accompanied only by a servant in a canoe. All day long citizens wandered into his White House to pester him for loans, jobs, or other favors. A British visitor shrank from the "brutal familiarity" with which President-elect Andrew Jackson was treated when traveling from Tennessee to Washington. It was not as brutal as the treatment White House furniture got from the crush at Jackson's inaugural blast, which was an open house. President John Tyler founded Washington's metropolitan police essentially to guard the White House, but President Franklin Pierce in 1853 became the first president to have a personal guard (an old army buddy). Enemy cannon were across the river and spies infested the city, but almost anyone at any time could wander into Lincoln's White House. Through the late nineteenth century presidents regularly received the public each day in the East Room. President Ulysses Grant had a staff of three. President Grover Cleveland answered the White House doorbell himself.[20] Until FDR, there was a New Year's Day receiving line for anyone who joined the queue out on the street. Security became serious during World War I, but then until Dec. 7, 1941, the White House lawn was again a public park. Portions of the mansion's first floor were open to everyone. You could even park on the narrow street between the White House and what is now the Executive Office Building. Harry Truman was the last president to live approximately as his countrymen did and do: He strolled across Pennsylvania Avenue to do his banking. His normality had something to do with the fact that he was the last president before television turned America into a wired nation and made presidents constant presences in the nation's living rooms: In his only presidential campaign, that of 1948, he appeared on television once, for three minutes, urging people to vote.

Presidential grandiosity manifests itself in many ways. When a young military officer directed Lyndon Johnson toward his helicopter, the president responded, "Son, they're all my helicopters." This confusion between himself and the office he temporarily occupied, and his equating the office with the assets at its disposal, involved a kind of derangement that probably had something to do with Johnson's Great Society and Vietnam overreaching. Be that as it may, one source of the modern presidency's grandiosity, its rhetorical dimension, has great potential for good and for mischief.

Ronald Reagan said that he sometimes wondered how presidents who had *not* been actors had been able to function. He was on to something. Two of this century's greatest leaders of democracies, Churchill and de Gaulle, had highly developed senses of the theatrical element in politics. FDR did, too. So, however, have evil leaders in what Churchill called this age of "mass effects." Hitler, Mussolini, and Castro all mastered ceremonies of mass intoxication. A political actor, be he good or evil, does not deal in unreality. Rather, he creates realities that matter—perceptions, emotions, affiliations. An actor not only projects, he causes his audience to project certain qualities— admiration, fear, hatred, love, patriotism, empathy. In some nations the actor's role has been assigned to a constitutional monarch. The role is not necessarily incompatible with republican values, but it is inherently problematic.

Rhetoric has a tainted reputation in our time, for several reasons. One is the carnage produced by murderous demagogues. Another is the public's uneasiness about modern means of mass manipulation, including propaganda and advertising. But rhetoric is indispensable to good politics and can be ennobling. Ancient political philosophers, such as Aristotle and Cicero, and the best modern politicians, such as Lincoln and Churchill, understood that rhetoric that is systematic eloquence can direct the free will of the community to the good. At its best, rhetoric does not induce irrationality, it leavens reasoning, fusing passion to persuasion. Some people, said Michael Oakeshott, the British political philosopher, consider government "an instrument of passion; the art of politics is to inflame and direct desire." On the other hand, a person with a conservative sensibility "understands it to be the business of government not to inflame passion and give it new objects to feed upon, but to inject into the activities of already too passionate men an ingredient of moderation; to restrain, to deflate."[21]

Today the rhetorical presidency is an instrument incessantly used to incite and inflate. The Founders would be appalled. They believed presidential appeals to, and manipulation of, public opinion would be an anti-constitutional preemption of deliberate processes. Thus there was, until this century, a "rhetorical common law."[22] Presidents spoke infrequently and about little. Washington averaged just three popular speeches a year; Adams, one; Jefferson, five. Madison, president during a war that burned his house, gave none. The twenty-four presidents prior to Theodore Roosevelt gave about one thousand speeches, but more than half of these were by three presidents (Hayes, Harrison, McKinley). Until the twentieth century, presidents communicated primarily with the legislative branch, not "the people," and communicated in written messages suitable for deliberative reasoning. Then modern technologies of transportation and communication gave presidents new capacities, and Woodrow Wilson supplied a theory for using them.

Presidents, Wilson said, should engage in "interpretation," meaning the discovery of what is in the hearts of the masses—or would be there if the masses were sensible. Soon presidents were everywhere, moving about, by railroad and then airplane. They were on the air by radio, then television. America was on its way to today's notion of the president as tribune of the people, constant auditor of the nation's psyche, molder of the public mind. Logically—not that logic has much sway in such matters—this is odd. Logically, executive power is secondary, having as its primary duty the execution of the result of the primary power, that of the legislature. The US

Constitution is remarkably—given what the presidency has become since 1787—reticent about presidential duties, the essence of which is in the Take Care Clause: The president shall "take care that the laws be faithfully executed." The idea of direct election of the president received short shrift from the Constitutional Convention, which more seriously considered but also rejected election of the president by Congress, upon which the president would then have been dependent and to which the president would have been subordinate. With this rejection, the die was cast: Political dynamics would trump logic, and the presidency would eventually eclipse Congress. When Hamilton, in Federalist 68, foresaw a "constant probability" of the presidency being occupied by "characters preeminent for ability and virtue,"[23] he was, as Harvey Mansfield says, assuming that the people would have "the virtue to appreciate virtue."[24] Hamilton, who wrote this before the emergence of political parties, could not have anticipated the sequence of presidential methods of selecting the parties' presidential candidates, methods that are not overly focused on virtue.

American politics, always a form of entertainment and always entertaining, used to be far from president-centric. Once upon a time, Americans' zest for politics at more local levels astonished the world. In Jules Verne's *Around the World in Eighty Days* (1873), the Englishman Phileas Fogg, passing through San Francisco, gets swept up in a tremendous election hullabaloo. Fogg asks if the awesome commotion is for "the election of a general-in-chief, no doubt?" He is told, "No, sir; of a justice of the peace." In 1858, the first of seven Lincoln-Douglas debates, in Ottawa, Illinois, a city of about 7,000, was witnessed—you cannot say heard—by about 20,000, none of whom, in those days before direct election of senators, could vote for either candidate. At that time, American politics was the best entertainment money did not have to buy, and it was entering its era of maximum popular participation. Soon, however, "progressive" high-mindedness would help to put a stop to that.

Michael Schudson argues that politics from the colonial period through the Revolution was a "politics of assent." Elections were acts of deference, ratifying rule by the gentry, which regarded political office as an obligation connected with social standing. But urbanization produced heterogeneous populations. The spectacular growth of newspapers, fueled by cheap newsprint and mass literacy, stimulated argumentativeness in a society where immigration was producing fierce rivalries among ethnic communities. Soon mass-based parties replaced the politics of deference with the "politics of affiliation." Between Lincoln and Theodore Roosevelt, writes Schudson, no president captured the public's imagination, yet "these were the years of the highest voter turnout in our entire history. Americans of that era enjoyed politics." It was not elevated politics, it was a sport of rival social groups organized into teams (parties) around "ethnocultural" issues—immigration, church schools, temperance—that were at least as bitterly divisive as today's social issues.[25]

In the late nineteenth century in the North, 70 percent or more of those eligible usually voted in presidential elections. This was partly a tribute to political machines: Pennsylvania's Republican organization had 20,000 wage-earning workers—more employees than most of the state's railroads. And Schudson says that during the Gilded Age as many as 20 percent of New York City voters may have been paid in some form or other as Election Day workers. Then righteous reformers and caring government took much of the fun, and many of the voters, out of politics. Reformers wanted fewer parades and more pamphlets—voting should be not an act of group solidarity but an individual act of informed competence. Parties, said well-bred reformers, should not just rally committed followers, who often were, well, not the sort of folks who knew which fork to use with the fish course. Rather, parties should persuade the uncommitted. The progressive aspiration, says Schudson, was a "citizenship of intelligence rather than passionate intensity." The coming of solicitous government gave people rights to things they once received for services rendered to the party. In the nineteenth century, Schudson says, people could "smell and taste the material benefits in politics," such as turkeys at Christmas.[26] Under the twentieth century's sanitized, omnipresent, and omniprovident government, services became less connected with elected officials than with bureaucracies.

The nationalization of governance made presidential politics the sun around which America's political solar system orbits. Because of the swollen place the presidency now occupies in the nation's consciousness, we are never not preoccupied with presidential campaigning. The Constitution's Framers would be mystified and dismayed. The nation reveres the Framers but long ago abandoned the presidential selection process that, James Ceaser says, they considered so important that they made it one of the four national institutions created by the Constitution.[27] Three are the Congress, the Supreme Court, the presidency; the fourth is the presidential selection system based on the Electoral College. This system, wherein the selection of candidates and election of a president by each state's electors occurred simultaneously—they were the same deliberation—soon disappeared. Since the emergence of the party system in the 1790s, and the ratification of the Twelfth Amendment in 1804, candidates have been selected by several different processes: First by their party's congressional caucuses. Then by nominating conventions controlled by the party's organizations. Then by conventions influenced by primaries and caucuses. (Vice President Hubert Humphrey won the 1968 Democratic nomination without entering any primaries.) And since 1972, entirely by primaries and caucuses that have made conventions merely ratifying, not deliberative, bodies.

So many things, including the evolved party system and the myriad functions of the federal government, have made the modern presidency that it is possible to lose sight of one more thing: war. In 1918, Randolph Bourne, whose pacifism cost him much of his journalistic career, many of his friends, and, hence, perhaps his health, became, on December 22, one of the more than 600,000 Americans killed by the influenza unleashed by the war that he strenuously opposed. An unpublished manuscript, rescued from his wastebasket after his death, contained his most famous words: "War is the health of the State." And of the executive.

Madison had said as much, less pithily but more informatively, 123 years earlier: "Of all the enemies to public liberty war is, perhaps, the most to be dreaded, because it comprises and develops the germ of every other. War is the parent of armies; from these proceed debts and taxes; and armies, and debts, and taxes are the known instruments for bringing the many under the domination of the few. In war, too, the discretionary power of the Executive is extended; its influence in dealing out offices, honors, and emoluments is multiplied; and all the means of seducing the minds, are added to those of subduing the force, of the people."[28] The colonies' pre-Revolutionary experience with the costs and other inconveniences of the British army's presence in North America had given rise to some of the complaints recorded in the Declaration of Independence. Hence the most interesting, because most resonantly modern, aspect of Madison's warning about war is his reference to executive aggrandizement.

It is, however, in domestic policy that a disproportionate presidency is most alarming, because there it disrupts Madison's intended equilibrium between the three branches. Today's disequilibrium results from Congress' forfeiture of its natural advantages, its inherent supremacy. As Madison wrote in the Pacificus-Helvidius debates with Hamilton, "All [the president's] acts, therefore, properly executive, must presuppose the existence of the laws to be executed."[29] There are other acts that are not so strictly executive, such as those taken in his capacity as commander-in-chief of the military. Madison's sound point, however, is that the president's core function is to execute the will of others, the legislators.

Back in the day, not many people were eager to come to Congress, and fewer were willing to linger there. In the first half of the nineteenth century, Washington was difficult to get to, its climate was insalubrious, and living accommodations were uncongenial. This helps explain why "between 1800 and 1830, two-thirds of congressmen served two terms or less, two-thirds of senators lasted for one term or less. More than half of the 242 members of the Twenty-fourth Congress (1835–37) were not around in the Twenty-fifth." And during the next three decades "the average congressman served for only four years. The senatorial average was a bit over five, less than a full term."[30]

Today, Congress has more permanence—too much of it; read on—but is swamped by the growth of government that Congress itself mandates and funds. The First Congress had more senators (twenty-six) and representatives (sixty-five) than there were members of the entire federal bureaucracy. For many decades, until civil service reform in the second half of the nineteenth century, the bureaucracy was not the formidable presence that it has become. In 1861, when the first Republican president took office, what we today refer to as "the permanent government"—the bureaucracy—was not only small but was highly impermanent. After the 1860 election, all but 300 of the 1,500 most important officeholders resigned or were fired by Lincoln or his appointees.[31] For more than a century now, Congress has been living in the deepening shadow cast by the rest of the federal government.

As far back as Woodrow Wilson's presidency there were already almost as many members of the national legislature—531—as there are today. Since the admission to statehood of Hawaii and Alaska in 1959, there have been 535. It is difficult to precisely quantify the increase in the business—and the busy-ness—of Congress since then. It is, however, reasonable to assume that the increase is at least fifty-fold. The federal budget has increased much more than that. Congress has been a participant in the government's growth, but Congress also has been a victim of it, although often a willing, accommodating victim. This is so because the expansion of the regulatory, administrative state necessarily means the marginalization of the legislative branch. As a symptom and symbol of this, consider the consequential matter of working space.

In Congress' early years, the senators' offices were their desks. By the 1830s these were inadequate to the exigencies of the growing federal agenda, so mahogany writing boxes, three inches high, were added to the desks. To be precise, they were added to all the desks but one. New Hampshire's Daniel Webster said that his predecessors had managed without this superfluity and so could he. To this day, Webster's desk, which always is assigned to New Hampshire's senior senator, remains unblemished by a writing box. However, the Iron Law of Emulation soon was at work. Daniel Patrick Moynihan named that law, drawing upon the work of his former Harvard colleague James Q. Wilson. Wilson studied the dynamics and cultures of bureaucracy and concluded that organizations in conflict with one another come to resemble one another. Moynihan applied this insight to government: "Whenever any branch of the government acquires a new technique which enhances its power in relation to the other branches, that technique will soon be adopted by those other branches as well."[32]

It is not surprising that, regarding working space, the first move was made on behalf of the presidency, and by Theodore Roosevelt, who gave Woodrow Wilson ideas. Until the turn of the twentieth century, presidents had done much of their work in the living quarters of the White House, which must have been inconvenient, not to mention annoying, to their wives. So in 1902, TR built the West Wing, where the Oval Office is. As Moynihan noted, "Of a sudden, the President was an executive. He no longer worked in his living room, but had an office building in the manner of the business leaders of the age. (Here one observes the federal government as a whole adopting the techniques of the business world with which it was then increasingly in conflict.)" So, in 1903, the House of Representatives voted to construct an office building, which is now called the Cannon Building. In 1904, the Senate, emulating the

House, voted for what now is the Russell Building. What Moynihan called "the migration of technique from the executive to the legislative" had begun.[33] The House opened the Longworth and Rayburn buildings in 1933 and 1965, respectively; the Senate opened the Dirksen and Hart buildings in 1958 and 1982, respectively. The judicial branch was watching when the legislature's building spree began. Chief Justice of the Supreme Court William Howard Taft, who had been president, and who did not cotton to being housed in Congress' space, in the Capitol, saw to the building of a temple across the street. It opened in 1935.

Until 1906, no president had left the country while in office. That year, TR—yes, him again—went to Panama. In 1909, TR's successor, Taft, went there, too. Taft's successor, Woodrow Wilson, went to Paris. Congress took note. In 1954, it began to provide ample and easily accessible resources to make foreign travel routine for its members. In 1921, the executive branch created the Bureau of the Budget (which became the Office of Management and Budget in 1971); in 1975, after Congress' conflict with a Watergate-weakened President Richard Nixon over presidential impoundment of appropriated funds, Congress created the Congressional Budget Office. In 1962, there came a new appendage of the presidency, the Office of Science and Technology, successor to a 1957 creation, the President's Science Advisory Committee. In 1974, Congress created its Office of Technology Assessment. And so it goes, still.

This is not to disparage any of these developments; each may have been wise and necessary. But Congress does seem to be reactive and emulative. And it cannot keep up. In an intragovernmental arms race, for space or expertise, the legislative branch will always lose. One measure of how much ground it has already lost is apparent in the limited, but less limited than it used to be, presidential participation, through the conditional veto, in the making of laws. In the beginning, presidents cast vetoes primarily, or only, when they deemed the legislation in question to be unconstitutional. Presidents have, however, long since adopted the practice of vetoing bills for purely policy reasons, thereby asserting for themselves at least parity with Congress in setting the national agenda. Franklin Roosevelt was president for 4,422 days, during every one of which his party controlled both houses of Congress, yet he still vetoed 635 bills.

All of America's era-defining national agendas—Theodore Roosevelt's New Nationalism, Woodrow Wilson's New Freedom, Franklin Roosevelt's New Deal, Harry Truman's Fair Deal, John Kennedy's New Frontier, Lyndon Johnson's Great Society, the Reagan Revolution—have been summations of presidents' agendas. This helps to explain why, James Ceaser notes, there is no Mount Rushmore celebrating congressional stalwarts. And it is interesting that the four men celebrated on Mount Rushmore together had just one congressional term—Lincoln's two years in the House. This is acknowledgment in stone of what Andrew Jackson claimed.

Until the late 1820s, presidential elections were doubly indirect. Presidents were elected by electors chosen not by voters but by state legislatures. But after Jackson's election in 1828, he became the first president to argue that presidents, the only officials elected by national votes, necessarily acquire mandates that put them at least on a par with Congress, which is a conglomeration of representatives of lesser constituencies. Prior to Jackson and for most of the nineteenth century after him, the prevailing doctrine was that Congress is the principal representative of the people. Jefferson's first message to Congress was couched in language of a nonpartisan executive: "Nothing shall be wanting on my part to inform, as far as in my power, the legislative judgment, nor to carry that judgment into faithful execution." According to Edward S. Corwin, the constitutional historian, "The tone of [Jefferson's] messages is uniformly deferential to Congress."[34] So totally did Monroe subscribe to the doctrine of congressional supremacy, he was utterly silent on the burning issue of the day, the admission of Missouri to statehood and the status of slavery in Louisiana Territory.

In the second half of the twentieth century, Republicans fully embraced the presidential supremacy that had so irritated them during the New Deal. Between 1952 and 1988, Republicans controlled both houses of Congress for only two years (1953–54) but won six of ten presidential elections. Between 1968 and 1988, Republicans won five of six presidential elections, while controlling the Senate for just six years (1981–86). Republicans held the presidency for all but twelve of the forty years prior to 1992. As a result, conservatives became fixated on the presidency and opportunistically adopted the vocabulary of president-centrism, arguing that social progress is a measure of, because it is a consequence of, presidential aptitudes. The unconservative premise of this—its pedigree traces to turn-of-the-century Progressives—is that government, particularly the executive branch of the federal government, is the most important creative agency in society.

Never mind that the Constitution's Take Care Clause makes the president responsive to what Congress does. And regarding only one matter, the president's conditional veto, does the Constitution make the president's will superior to simple majorities in both houses of Congress. Yet the will of the president, although far from dispositive in setting public policy, is now superior. This is so largely because presidents have the means to arouse public passions, and no longer does a "common law of presidential behavior" restrain them from doing so. The controlling and regulating of the public's passions are not supposed to be done by government officials acting as Platonic guardians. Rather, the controlling and regulating are to be done by the government's architecture, by the tension between, and the mutual wariness of, its competing institutions. These should temper public passions by channeling them through countervailing institutions that compel the passions to be felt only indirectly by those making policy. So, when Madison said the government is the controller and regulator of the passions, he meant that the Constitution itself is. And for quite a while it was.

For about 150 years after the Founding, many political controversies at the federal level were apt to begin with debate about constitutional principle: Did the federal government's enumerated powers entitle it to act on a particular subject? Only after this debate came the policy discussion. Today, almost nobody in either the legislative or executive branch believes that there is any subject, any sphere, from which the federal government is constitutionally excluded. The eclipse of that idea does not, however, mean that prudence should not do what constitutional principle once did: restrain the federal government's itch to be active everywhere. This itch is discrediting the federal government and making a mockery of federalism by reducing the states to administrators of federal undertakings.

James Q. Wilson noted that from the Founding until the Civil War the defining problem was that of firmly grounding the federal government's legitimacy.[35] From the Civil War until the New Deal the defining problem was power: Under what limits did the federal government operate? From the New Deal until recently, the defining problem was representation: Were all groups appropriately involved in Washington's increasing importance? Today, Wilson said, the defining problem concerns collective choice: Can a federal government that acknowledges no limits to its scope, and that responds promiscuously to the multiplying appetites of proliferating factions, make choices that serve the society's long-term interests? The answer, based on the avalanche of evidence from current governance, is an emphatic "no."[36] The evidence is in the rise of the administrative state and the fall of fiscal responsibility.

FDR'S "TEMPORARY DEPARTURE"

It has been eight decades since President Franklin Roosevelt, in his first inaugural address, called for a "temporary departure from the normal balance" between "executive and legislative authority." Since 1933, the departure has become permanent. It is the new normal. Running for president in 2008, Barack Obama said, "The biggest problems that we're facing right now have to do with George Bush trying to bring more and more power into the executive branch and not go through Congress at all. And that's what I intend to reverse when I'm president."[37] Hardly. As president, he said that although it would be "nice" for Congress to "help" him, he would not wait for it.

Increasingly, such promulgating and revising are done by or through regulatory agencies of the administrative state. Concerning which Madison was, as usual, unusually farsighted. Writing in 1791 in anxious response to Hamilton's plans for national direction of economic development, Madison foresaw this practice taking a toll first on federalism and then on the federal government's separation of powers. As the federal government began to exercise powers and claim responsibilities properly belonging to state and local governments, the federal legislature would find itself inundated by multiplying new tasks, and this would "force a transfer of many of" these functions from the legislative branch "to the executive department." Thus did Madison discern the administrative state in embryo.[38] In 1887, Congress created the Interstate Commerce Commission, which was the fetus of the administrative state. That state was a muscular and still-growing creature in 2016, when Congress passed 2,966 pages of laws and federal agencies churned out thirty-two times more pages— 97,110—of new regulations.

Calvin Coolidge, the longest-serving president in the decade before the administrative state was put firmly in place, already sensed that the transformation of the federal government was far advanced: "This is not the government which was put into form by Washington and Hamilton, and popularized by Jefferson. Some of the stabilizing safeguards which they had provided have been weakened."[39] Notice Coolidge's sly way of saying something that is correct but also is discordant with American sentiment: Washington and Hamilton did the most to create a constitutional order that Jefferson merely "popularized." Coolidge, however, could not have had any inkling of how the administrative state would evolve. Gary Lawson has provided a justly famous description of the working of one molecule of the administrative state, the Federal Trade Commission:

> The [Federal Trade] Commission promulgates substantive rules of conduct. The Commission then considers whether to authorize investigations into whether the Commission's rules have been violated. If the Commission authorizes an investigation, the investigation is conducted by the Commission, which reports its findings to the Commission. If the Commission thinks that the Commission's findings warrant an enforcement action, the Commission issues a complaint. The Commission's complaint that a Commission rule has been violated is then prosecuted by the Commission and adjudicated by the Commission. The Commission adjudication can either take place before the full Commission or before a semi-autonomous Commission administrative law judge. If the Commission chooses to adjudicate before an administrative law judge rather than before the Commission and the decision is adverse to the Commission, the Commission can appeal to the Commission.[40]

A quarter of a century on, the workings of the administrative state have become much more opaque, recondite, and untethered from accountability. This has now been underway for almost a century and has had distinguished advocates. Two of the leading intellectual lights of the New Deal were James Landis and Felix Frankfurter, both of whom came to Washington from Harvard Law School. They dismissed as a "jejune abstraction" the idea that Congress cannot delegate legislative powers to executive agencies. They were rejecting an idea that had a distinguished pedigree: John Locke argued that a legislature "cannot transfer the power of making laws to any other hands, for it being but a delegated power from the people, they who have it cannot pass it over to others." Perhaps they should not, but they certainly can and regularly do. Modern government operates on the assumption that Landis and Frankfurter were correct in asserting "the inadequacy of a simply tripartite form of government to deal with modern problems."[41]

The various agencies that are in various ways emanations of the executive branch have become so numerous, so collectively enormous, and so central to governance that they almost constitute a fourth branch of government. Philip Hamburger says that "administrative law found a place in American government when it still could be believed that administrative regulations and adjudications would merely be exceptions within the traditional constitutional structure." By now, however, "the exception has swallowed the rule." Administrative law has "dwarfed statutory law and has become the federal government's pervasive mode of dealing with the public." Federal agencies' regulations filled 18,000 pages of the Code of Federal Regulations in 1938 and 175,000 by 2014. The Consumer Financial Protection Bureau, which did not exist until 2010, in 2014 churned out 1,099 pages of regulations and explanatory material pertaining to just one of the CFPB's concerns, mortgage lending.[42]

Although Madison could hardly have imagined, let alone anticipated, this traducing of the separation of powers, it fits the warning he issued in Federalist 47: "The accumulation of all powers, legislative, executive, and judiciary, in the same hands, whether of one, a few, or many, and whether hereditary, self appointed, or elective, may justly be pronounced the very definition of tyranny."[43] Candid progressives confess, or used to, that this "accumulation" is not a merely ancillary or unintended consequence of the administrative state. Today, progressives believe that this is the point of the administrative state, which was conceived as a cure for the great defect of the Founding, the separation of powers. In 1803, in *Marbury v. Madison*, in which judicial review was firmly planted in American political practices, Chief Justice John Marshall said that it is "emphatically the province and duty of the Judicial Department to say what the law is."[44] So, if Marshall could have imagined today's administrative state, he would not have considered much of what this state now does compatible with the rule of law.

Senator Mike Lee, a Utah Republican, has a didactic disposition, as visitors to his office discover when they see there two stacks of papers. One, a few inches high and containing about 800 pages, is all the laws passed in a recent session of Congress. The other stack, about eleven feet tall and containing about 80,000 pages, is all the regulations proposed and adopted in one year by executive agencies. The lesson that Lee wants visitors to his office to learn, and to be dismayed about, is that Congress is no longer the primary institution of American's self-government. So the lesson is that Lee's primary job, that of legislator, has been moved to the margins of American governance. The evidence of this is everywhere and overwhelming. For example, the 2010 Dodd-Frank Act reforming financial regulations was less important for what it explicitly did than for what it directed others to do: It mandated almost 400 rule-making decisions.

Lee gives two especially striking examples of the attenuation of representative government by the transfer by Congress of its legislative power to executive agencies. During the Depression, Congress authorized the Department of Agriculture to aid some farmers (and to injure many more consumers) by increasing the price of certain agricultural products. The department did this by setting quotas that would limit the sale of these products, which included oranges.[45] So, from 1933 until 1992, when the Depression was a fading memory, the government prevented a third of navel oranges from being sold in the American market. The Department of Agriculture created a Navel Orange Administrative Committee, and a private agribusiness, Sunkist, was empowered to nominate five of the committee's eleven members. A direct phone line connected the committee with Sunkist, and the committee staff was covered by Sunkist's pension plan. So legislative power had been ceded by Congress to an executive department that in turn ceded some of it to a private interest. The involvement of the American people's elected representatives in this policy was vanishingly small.

With the Clean Air Act, Congress empowered the Environmental Protection Agency to put whatever limits it wanted on whatever pollutants the limiting of which it considered "requisite to protect the public health." Soon the EPA construed this grant of power over pollutants as allowing it to mandate tolls on some New York City bridges in order to raise funds to support mass transit, thereby reducing air pollution from automobiles.[46] In response to angry constituents, some members of Congress representing the city—members who had voted for this capacious grant of policy-making power to the EPA—led a march to protest what they had done in delegating their policy-making responsibilities.

Today, the number of *criminally* enforceable federal regulations might—no one can say with certainty—exceed 300,000.[47] Most of these are made by executive agencies. They, or other agencies, decide how violations should be punished. In this era of institutional derangements, Lee notes, "a single statute empowering the Food and Drug Administration to make rules for 'medical devices' had led to the FDA's regulation of weight-lifting equipment, mouthwash, sunglasses, and television remote controls."[48] Many members of Congress were incensed when President Barack Obama declared, "If Congress won't act, I will" and proceeded to push the limits of—or to demonstrate that there are few limits to—unilateral presidential powers.[49] But he did this in a context conditioned by decades of Congressional sloth and carelessness in forfeiting policy-making powers. Congress' renunciation of its responsibilities has contributed to a condition far worse than Madison could have imagined when he wrote in Federalist 62: "It will be of little avail to the people that the laws are made by men of their own choice, if the laws be so voluminous that they cannot be read, or so incoherent that they cannot be understood; if they be repealed or revised before they are promulgated, or undergo such incessant changes that no man who knows what the law is today, can guess what it will be tomorrow. Law is defined to be a rule of action; but how can that be a rule, which is little known and less fixed?"[50] This is why the rule of law is the ultimate casualty of Congress' dereliction of duty that makes the administrative state rampant. As Ocie and Carey Mills learned, and Senator Lee laments.

Congress stipulated in the Clean Waters Act that landowners are required to obtain a permit before discharging materials into "the waters of the United States." But Congress neglected to define what it meant by such waters. So the EPA and the Army Corps of Engineers did the defining. They said that the "waters" in question include "areas that are inundated or saturated by surface or ground water at a frequency and duration sufficient to support, and that under normal circumstances do support, a prevalence of vegetation typically adapted for life in saturated soil conditions." Ocie Mills and his son, Carey, built a house near Florida's Escambia Bay, on wooded land that contained a small patch of marsh grass. They were prosecuted for discharging a "pollutant"—dry sand they used in constructing their house—into "navigable waters" because their plot of land contained, although not where they built their house, marsh grass. The judge at the Millses' jury trial declared that a "layman" would not reasonably expect the term "waters" to apply to "land that appears to be dry, but which may have some saturated-soil vegetation, as is the situation here." But he had to sentence the father and son to thirty-three months in prison in obedience to a rule made by an executive agency because Congress decided "to abdicate its power to define the elements of a criminal offense."[51]

Progressives hoped that as governance became more presidential, the public would increasingly acquiesce in the power and auton-omy of administrative agencies. The progressive's hope was that by making a popular, even charismatic president the focus of the nation's political consciousness, the public could be content to be governed by supposedly detached, disinterested experts who are cloaked with democratic legitimacy because they are formally obedient to the will of a president enjoying a national mandate. And in fact, the public is remarkably docile about government micromanaging life.

Today the federal government regulates the kind of light bulbs we can use and the amount of water that can flow from our showerheads and through our toilets. The pell-mell proliferation of laws has profound implication for the criminal justice system. As Ilya Somin says, ignorance of the law is a) not a valid excuse for breaking the law, and b) inevitable. Hence the title of a book by Harvey Silverglate, a civil liberties lawyer: *Three Felonies a Day*. That is Silverglate's somewhat puckish but essentially serious estimate of the number of felonies an American commits on a given day. He recounts that young prosecutors in a particular office used to play a game in which someone would pick a famous person—say, Mother Teresa or William Faulkner—and the rest would search for some law the person could be indicted for breaking.[52] As Lavrentiy Beria, the head of Stalin's secret police, said and, during the 1930s purge trials and the Great Terror, demonstrated, "Show me the man and I'll show you the crime." This is not to say that the glut of laws is making the United States ripe for such state-administered domestic repression. It is, however, to say that a surfeit of laws provides, in the nooks and crannies of the sprawling government, rich opportunities for prosecutorial and other abuses. When in 1780 John Adams wrote into the constitution of the state of Massachusetts the commitment to a "government of laws, not of men," he perhaps assumed that the rule of law meant the rule of laws, no matter how many of them there might be.[53] He could not have imagined his country today.

Charles Evans Hughes was governor of New York (1907–10), then Supreme Court justice (1910–16), and then almost became president: A switch of 1,711 votes in California would have given the 1916 election to him rather than Woodrow Wilson. Next, Hughes was secretary of state (1921–25). This man of vast experience called the Constitution "the greatest instrument ever designed to prevent things from being done." Well, yes, to this extent: By its explicit language it forbids the doing of some specific things—abridging freedom of speech, establishing religion, conducting unreasonable searches and seizures, etc. But by its structure it stipulates how the general business of government shall get done. It does not prevent things from being done, it just makes the process—assembling concurrent majorities: House, Senate, and presidential—somewhat difficult. During the Obama administration, however, when the impatience of a progressive president was at its peak, and (hence) so were academic and media lamentations about "gridlock," Congress passed the most sweeping social policy legislation since the enactment of Medicare and Medicaid in 1965 (the Patient Protection and Affordable Care Act, aka Obamacare) and the most ambitious regulation of the nation's financial system since the New Deal (the Dodd-Frank legislation).

Still, today's government, like Gulliver among the Lilliputians, is almost tangled in its thousands of threads of commitments. This presents a striking contrast with the nimbleness of government at the dawn of modern liberalism. On day two of FDR's famous first hundred days he ordered a national bank holiday. On day five Congress passed his banking bill almost unanimously. On day seven, in spite of a revolt by ninety Democrats, the House passed his bill cutting veterans' benefits and federal employees' pay. On day twelve he submitted a farm bill that presaged many of the subsequent follies of federal agriculture programs. The House passed it on day eighteen. On day seventeen, FDR proposed the Civilian Conservation Corps; it became law three weeks later. On day thirty-six he proposed the Tennessee Valley Authority; he signed it into law on day seventy-six. On November 2, 1933, he was given the proposal for a Civil Works Administration to employ people on such public works as street repair and digging sewers. By November 23, 800,000 people were employed; five weeks later, 4.25 million—8 percent of the nation's labor force. Today it would take many months just to prepare the environment impact statements for such a program.

The governmental activism of the 1930s, Ronald Reagan's formative years, may or may not have been, on balance, wise, but at least the activism was driven by something dire—the Depression. Imagine: One day in May 1934 a dust storm, stretching from Texas to Canada and soaring 15,000 feet, blew east. Dust settled on FDR's desk and on ships hundreds of miles out on the Atlantic. By December, two of every five South Dakotans were on relief—the nation's highest percentage. In July 1935, the grasshoppers returned. The government activism of the 1960s, the years of Ronald Reagan's political ascent in opposition to that activism, was driven by the self-interest and hubris of the government. By then, government itself—the governing class—had become the largest interest group, lobbying itself for the enlargement of itself. Other than the Civil Rights Acts of 1964 and 1965, the creations of governmental activism of the 1960s, unlike those of the 1930s, had few glittering consequences because they were not produced by the sort of broad, powerful political forces that produced, say, Social Security and unemployment insurance. What, then, produced much of the activism of the 1960s? A class of professional reformers whose mission was to change the parameters of politics.

In the 1960s there began the explosive growth in the number of subjects considered political and suited to government attention. Perhaps this had something to do with Lyndon Johnson being the first president to have spent almost his entire adult life in Washington. Be that as it may, by the end of the 1960s, Daniel Patrick Moynihan was worrying about the increasing introduction into politics and government of ideas originating in the social sciences, ideas that promised to bring about social change through manipulation of society's most basic processes. This was, he said, part of a transformation of politics: "Not long ago it could be agreed that politics was the business of who gets what, when, where, how. It is now more than that. It has become a process that also deliberately seeks to effect such outcomes as who *thinks* what, who *acts* when, who *lives* where, who *feels* how."[54] This is why, as James Q. Wilson said, there emerged in the 1960s "a true national state within the confines of a constitutional system designed to ensure that no such state would be created."[55]

The administrative state inevitably means executive government and the derogation of the legislative branch, both of which produce exploding government debt. In explaining these perverse effects of progressivism, Christopher DeMuth explains contemporary government's cascading and reinforcing failures. Executive growth fuels borrowing growth because of the relationship between what DeMuth calls "regulatory insouciance and freewheeling finance." Government power is increasingly concentrated in Washington, Washington power is increasingly concentrated in the executive branch, and executive branch power is increasingly concentrated in agencies that are unconstrained by legislative control. Debt and regulation are, DeMuth says, "political kin": Both are legitimate government functions, but both are now perverted to evade democratic accountability, which is a nuisance, and transparent taxation, which is politically dangerous.[56]

Today's government uses regulation to achieve policy goals by imposing on the private sector burdens less obvious than forthright taxation would be, burdens that become visible only indirectly, in slower economic growth and higher prices. Often the goals that government pursues surreptitiously are goals that could not win legislative majorities—e.g., the Environmental Protection Agency's regulation of greenhouse gases following Congress' refusal to approve such policies. And deficit spending—borrowing—is, DeMuth says, "a complementary means of taxation evasion." It enables the political class to provide today's voters with significantly more government benefits than current taxes can finance, leaving the difference to be paid by voters too young to vote or not yet born.[57]

Two developments demonstrate, DeMuth says, how "delegation and debt have become coordinate mechanisms of legislative abnegation." One is Congress' anti-constitutional delegation of taxing authority to executive branch regulatory agencies funded substantially or entirely by taxes the agencies levy, rather than by congressional appropriations. For example, DeMuth says, the Federal Communications Commission's $347 million operating expenses "are funded by payments from the firms it regulates," and its $9 billion program subsidizing certain Internet companies is funded by its own unilateral tax on telecommunication firms. The Consumer Financial Protection Bureau, another freebooting agency not tethered to the appropriations process, requests and receives a share of the profits of the Federal Reserve banks. A second development is "the integration of regulation and debt-financed consumption."[58] Recently, a 2013 *Washington Post* headline announced: "Obama administration pushes banks to make home loans to people with weaker credit."[59] This illustrates DeMuth's point about how unfettered executive government uses debt-financed consumption and "regulatory conscription of private markets" to force spending "vastly beyond what Congress could have appropriated in the light of day."[60]

High affluence and new technologies have, DeMuth believes, "led to unhealthy political practices." Until recently, the three basic resources required for effective political action—discretionary time, the ability to acquire and communicate information, and persuasion skills—were scarce and possessed only by elites. But in our wealthy and educated society, interest groups can pressure government without being filtered by congressional hierarchies. Legislative leaders—particularly committee chairs—have lost power as Congress has become more porous and responsive to importuning factions using new media. Congress, responding to the increased difficulty of legislating, has delegated much lawmaking to specialized agencies that have fewer internal conflicts. Congress' role has waned as that of autonomous executive agencies has waxed. The executive has driven the expansion of the consumption of benefits that are paid for by automatic entitlement transfer payments, by government-mandated private expenditures, and by off-budget and non-transparent taxation imposed by executive agencies.[61]

Government used to spend primarily on the production of things—roads, dams, bridges, military forces. There can be only so many of such goods. Now, DeMuth says, government spends primarily for consumption: "The possibilities for increasing the kind, level, quality and availability of benefits are practically unlimited. That is the ultimate source of today's debt predicament. More borrowing for more consumption has no natural stopping point short of implosion."[62] Funding the welfare state by vast borrowing and regulatory taxation hides the costs from the public. Hence its political potency. Until the implosion.

THE RULE OF "VELLEITIES" VERSUS THE RULE OF LAW

DeMuth notes that Congress often contents itself with enacting "velleities" such as the wish, found in the 900-page Dodd-Frank financial reform act, that "all consumers have access to markets for consumer financial products and services…[that are] fair, transparent, and competitive." How many legislators voting for the bill even read this language? And how many who did read it understood that they were authorizing federal rule makers to micromanage, for example, overdraft fees? In Dodd-Frank, Obamacare, and much else, the essential lawmaking is done off Capitol Hill, by unaccountable bureaucratic rule-making. Fish gotta swim, birds gotta fly, and regulators, too, have a metabolic urge to do what they were created to do. Hence, DeMuth says, they often pursue their missions beyond the point of diminishing marginal returns, using health, safety, environmental, and other standards "with costs exceeding any plausible measure of their benefits." Regulatory power is executive power, which can be checked and balanced only by the other two branches. But, DeMuth notes, although courts can, under the Administrative Procedure Act, block regulations that are "arbitrary," "capricious," or "an abuse of discretion," courts usually defer to regulators, partly because courts are usually without requisite scientific or other expertise.[63]

The problem of excessive judicial deference is the subject of the next chapter. Here, however, note this: As the administrative state distorts the United States' constitutional architecture, Supreme Court Justice Clarence Thomas becomes America's indispensable constitutionalist, urging the judicial branch to limit the legislative branch's practice of delegating its power to the executive branch. In four opinions issued in 112 days between March 9 and June 29, 2015, Thomas indicted the increasing incoherence of the court's separation of powers jurisprudence, a subject that is central to today's argument between constitutionalists and progressives. The former favor and the latter oppose holding Congress to its responsibilities, restricting both delegations of legislative powers and executive discretion.

"The Constitution," Thomas noted, "does not vest the Federal Government with an undifferentiated 'governmental power.'" It vests three distinguishable types of power in three different branches. The court, Thomas said, has the "judicial duty" to enforce the vesting clauses as absolute and exclusive by policing the branches' boundaries. Particularly, it should prevent Congress from delegating to executive agencies the essentially legislative power of formulating "generally applicable rules of private conduct." Such delegation, Thomas says, erases the distinction between "the making of law, and putting it into effect." This occurs when Congress—hyperactive, overextended, and too busy for specificity—delegates "policy determinations" that "effectively permit the President to define some or all of the content" of a rule of conduct. Today, if Congress provides only "a minimal degree of specificity" in the instructions it gives to the executive, a deferential court, Thomas says, abandons "all pretense of enforcing a qualitative distinction between legislative and executive power." As a result, the court has "overseen and sanctioned the growth of an administrative system that concentrates the power to make laws and the power to enforce them in the hands of a vast and unaccountable administrative apparatus that finds no comfortable home in our constitutional structure."[64]

The administrative state, so inimical to conservatism's aspiration for government limited by a constitutional structure of rival branches, depends on something conservatives too frequently and reflexively praise. It depends on judicial deference to the majoritarian institution of Congress, even when Congress delegates its legislative powers to unaccountable agencies. In an 1887 essay, then-professor Woodrow Wilson of Bryn Mawr College said that the complexities of modern life demand government by expert administrators with "large powers and unhampered discretion."[65] When, during the New Deal, the court became permissive about Congress delegating essentially legislative powers, there was, Charles J. Cooper says, "an implicit bargain: The Court would permit Congress to delegate—and the administrative state to exercise—legislative, executive, and judicial power, but it would review administrative exercises of such power to prevent lawlessness and abuse." However, three decades ago the court "reneged on the deal," adopting the principle (called "Chevron deference," more about which anon) that it lacks the competence to be other than deferential.[66]

The court said, in a Wilsonian spirit, "judges are not experts."[67] Today, we are governed by Wilson's clerisy, but it does not deliver what is supposed to justify the overthrow of James Madison's constitutional system: efficient, admirable government. Evidence that Congress may, however, be rediscovering its institutional conscience was the maiden speech delivered in 2015 by Republican Nebraska senator Ben Sasse, a Yale University PhD (in history) and former college president. He rose from his desk—the one he requested, the one that formerly was used by another academic in politics, Moynihan—and asked: "Would anything be lost if the Senate didn't exist?" He said: "The growth of the administrative state, the fourth branch of government, is increasingly hollowing out the Article I branch, the legislature—and many in Congress have been complicit in this."[68]

If Congress is to regain the role that sensible conservatives favor as the First Branch of government, or if Congress is even to be an effective check on, and auditor of, the executive branch, it must do something that might irritate some conservatives: It must spend more on itself, on larger and more knowledgeable staff. If the separation of powers is to function anything like a true balance of powers, Congress must, at a minimum, "know what the executive branch is doing." This was not an insurmountable burden until the twentieth century. In 1900, there were eight federal departments (seven new Cabinet departments have been created since 1953) with 230,000 employees, 135,000 of them working for the Post Office. "Congress could roughly apprehend the rudiments of the whole of the federal government." Since then, there have developed severe "information asymmetries." Such asymmetries actually were intensified as an unintended consequence of civil service reform. The Pendleton Act of 1883, essentially ending federal patronage, "expanded the knowledge gap between legislators and executive agencies."[69] Executive bureaucrats are specialists; legislators are generalists. They are harried generalists who spend about one-third of their time on policy-making and oversight, devoting the rest of their energies to constituent services, messaging interest groups, traveling in their constituencies, and preparing for the next election (fund-raising). Congress is in Washington Tuesdays through Thursdays about one-third of the year. The government grinds on 365 days a year.

The Senate has crippled itself with rules that are sanctified neither by long tradition nor the logic of the Senate's purposes. So Senate rules should be changed to rectify a mistake made half a century ago. There was no limit on Senate debate until adoption of the cloture rule empowering two-thirds of senators present and voting to limit debate. This occurred on March 8, 1917—twenty-nine days before Congress declared war on Germany—after a filibuster prevented a vote on a momentous matter, the Armed Ship Bill, which would have authorized President Woodrow Wilson to arm American merchant ships. (Of course he armed them anyway.) In 1975, imposing cloture was made easier by requiring a vote of three-fifths of the entire Senate, a change the importance of which derived from what Majority Leader Mike Mansfield (Democrat of Montana), the longest-serving majority leader in history, had done five years earlier: He created the "two-track" system whereby the Senate, by unanimous consent or the consent of the minority leader, can set aside a filibustered bill and move on to other matters. Hitherto, filibustering senators had to hold the floor, testing their stamina and inconveniencing everyone else to encourage the majority to compromise. In the fifty-two years after 1917, there were only fifty-eight cloture motions filed; in the almost fifty years since 1970, there have been almost 2,000.

A minority should be able to extend debate in order to compel debate and, perhaps, compromise. Post-1970 filibusters, however, are used to prevent debate. As Representative Tom McClintock of California says, "The mere threat of a filibuster suffices to kill a bill as the Senate shrugs and goes on to other business." McClintock urges the Senate to make a "motion to proceed" to consideration of a bill undebatable and hence immune to filibustering. "Great debates should be had on great matters—but not great debates on whether to debate." And he says the Senate should abandon the two-track system. This would prevent the Senate from conducting other business during a filibuster but would require filibusterers to hold the floor. It was this mutual inconvenience that, between 1917 and 1970, made filibusters rare and produced pressure for compromise to resolve the impasse. As a result of today's Senate paralysis, McClintock says, "the atrophy of the legislative branch drives a corresponding hypertrophy of the executive branch." The promiscuous use of faux filibusters—requiring sixty votes to proceed with consideration of, or votes on, ordinary legislation—blurs the implicit constitutional principle that extraordinary majorities are required only for extraordinary matters, such as proposing constitutional amendments, overriding vetoes, and ratifying treaties.[70]

The trivialization of filibusters—no longer requiring them to be strenuous and disruptive events—has deprived them of dignity. Restoring them to what they once were would affirm the principle that mere majoritarianism—simply counting numbers; government by adding machine—should be tempered by a reformed filibuster as a mechanism for measuring the intensity of a minority's opposition to a majority position. The Constitution affirms the power of each house of Congress to "determine the rules of its proceedings," so any Senate procedures are compatible with the Constitution's text. But the practices made possible by the post-1970 rules have contributed to institutional disequilibrium, destabilizing the Constitution's design by inciting a dangerous expansion of presidential power. Hence Georgetown Law professor Randy Barnett and Jay Cost of the American Enterprise Institute urge forbidding filibusters of appropriations bills: "Democrats have discovered that if they block individual appropriations bills, the entire operation of government will inevitably be rolled into an omnibus appropriations bill, and the majority must either accept it in toto or face a partial shutdown of the government. This maneuver has largely eliminated Congress' ability to discipline the executive via line-item spending cuts."[71]

The filibuster is suited to a non-majoritarian institution in which fewer than 600,000 Wyomingites have as much representation as do almost 40 million Californians. Besides, filibusters delay but do not defeat political processes: Can anyone name anything that a majority of Americans have desired, strongly and protractedly, that has been denied to them because of a filibuster? Furthermore, some of what government does it has no constitutional warrant to do, and much of what government tries to do it does not know how to do. So the cause of good government, or at least of minimizing bad government, involves stopping things. On the other hand, when there is promiscuous rather than prudent recourse to procedures protecting the rights of legislative minorities, the resulting legislative paralysis makes elections seem of minor importance. This diverts political energies away from persuasion, sullenness permeates civic life, and politics become nasty, brutish, and interminable. When the Senate is dysfunctional, the House of Representatives might as well be, because the measures it sends to the Senate die there, not from amendments or rejection but from languishing in the limbo of senatorial unwillingness to proceed with what should be the regular order of a deliberative body.

It might seem whimsical, and it certainly is futile, to argue that instituting direct election of senators was a mistake. However, it was. The Framers were right to have senators chosen by state legislature. The House, directly elected and with two-year terms, was designed for responsiveness. The Senate, indirectly elected and with six-year terms, was designed to be more deliberative and less responsive. Furthermore, grounding the Senate in state legislatures strengthened the structure of federalism. Giving the states an important role in determining the composition of the federal government gave the states power to resist what has happened since the Seventeenth Amendment was ratified in 1913—the progressive (in two senses) reduction of the states to administrative extensions of the federal government. Severing senators from state legislatures, which could monitor and even instruct senators, made senators more susceptible to influence by nationally organized interest groups based in Washington. Many of those groups, who preferred one-stop shopping in Washington to being persuasive in all the state capitals, campaigned for the Seventeenth Amendment. So did urban political machines, which were organizing an uninformed electorate swollen by immigrants. Alliances between such interests and senators led to the lengthening of the senators' tenures. The Framers gave the three political components of the federal government (the House, Senate, and presidency) different electors (the people, the state legislatures, and the Electoral College as originally intended) to reinforce the principle of separation of powers, by which government is checked and balanced.

While we are recommending the inconceivable, another wholesome reform would be term limits for members of Congress—six consecutive terms for members of the House of Representatives, two consecutive terms for members of the Senate. Yes, this would deprive Congress of much institutional memory, thereby perhaps exacerbating the information and experience gap between the executive and legislative branches. So, term limits would further strengthen the case for larger, more professional congressional staffs. Of course, Congress will never send to the states for ratification a constitutional amendment limiting their careers. (In 1995, the Supreme Court ruled, 5–4, that term limits alter the qualifications for office in Congress and hence can only be imposed by an amendment.) So members of Congress will never put their careers at risk by making the decisions (e.g., pruning, or raising taxes sufficient to pay for, promises made in entitlement programs) necessary to put the nation's fiscal policy on a sustainable path. Careerism contributes to carnivorous politics because for people who enter politics young and plan to stay forever, electoral defeat means not just the inconvenience of a career change but the terror of professional annihilation. So, absent term limits, campaigning becomes even more constant and desperate. Because of the presence of TV cameras in both chambers, the House and Senate floors have become stages for year-round campaigning. Televising Congress has had one effect predicted by those who opposed it: Floor speeches are used to generate an unending stream of pungent sound bites for the evening news. This has a deleterious effect on the deliberative nature of Congress' proceedings.

What is conceivable, and increasingly urgent, is a constitutional amendment to compel Congress to deliberate by compelling it to make choices. John F. Kennedy said in his 1962 State of the Union Address, "The Constitution makes us not rivals for power, but partners for progress."[72] Such boring boilerplate serves the interests of presidents, who use it to assuage public and congressional anxieties about the growth of presidential power. This growth results both from presidential aggression and congressional supineness. To say that "Congress has been complicit in its own diminution" is to be too kind to Congress; its complicity amounts to almost complete responsibility.[73] Congress has either willingly vested vast discretion in presidents and executive agencies or it has refused to use its ample and adequate powers, the most efficacious of which is the power of the purse, to bring the executive branch to heel. Incapable of performing the most basic act of governance, the writing of a budget, Congress lurches from one "continuing resolution" or gigantic spending package to another, with members faced with the choice of accepting a pork-stuffed package in its entirety or shutting down the government. So the growth of government is the only alternative to chaos. Congress can at least partially rescue itself from itself, and by doing so serve the country and the Constitution its members are sworn to defend, by binding itself to another alternative.

For many decades, conservatives subscribed, or said they did, to the "starve the beast" strategy for fiscal responsibility. Their theory was that if the government's revenues were cut sufficiently, spending cuts would soon follow. As Milton Friedman wrote in 2003, "How can we ever cut government down to size? I believe there is one and only one way: the way parents control spendthrift children, cutting their allowance." What fun this promised to be: Republicans could have the immediate pleasure of cutting taxes, and the disagreeable business of cutting spending would be put off until tomorrow. But tomorrow is always a day away. William A. Niskanen, a member of President Ronald Reagan's Council of Economic Advisors, who probably wished that this would work, knew it would not: "It is most implausible that reducing the current tax burden of federal spending would *reduce* the amount of federal services that voters demand." Actually, it is apt to *increase* that amount because it reduces the current cost—the cost to recipients—of those services. There is, Niskanen wrote in 2006, "no significant evidence that a recent high deficit ever had an effect similar to that of reducing a child's allowance; the difference is that the federal government has a credit card with no effective debit limit. Federal spending is better described as buying government services at a discount equal to the deficit, the costs of which will be borne by someone sometime in the future."[74]

Today's political discord is less durable and dangerous than an obvious consensus, one that unites the political class more than ideology divides it. The consensus is that, year in and year out, in good times and bad, Americans should be given substantially more government goods and services than they should be asked to pay for. Lamentations about the paucity of bipartisanship ignore the permanent, powerful, bipartisan incentive that the parties share and indulge to run enormous deficits, thereby making big government cheaper, for the moment. Government borrows part of its costs; the burden of the borrowing falls on future generations. This is a form of expropriation—taxation without representation of the unborn. No one knows at what percentage of gross domestic product the debt's deleterious effect on economic growth becomes severe; no sensible person doubts that there is such a point. We will discover that point the hard way, unless Congress promptly sends to the states for prompt ratification a constitutional amendment requiring balanced budgets.

The amendment proposed by R. Glenn Hubbard, dean of Columbia University's business school, and Tim Kane, economist at the Hoover Institution at Stanford University, would limit each year's total spending to the median annual revenue of the previous seven years, allowing temporary deficits to be authorized in emergencies by congressional supermajorities. Because reverence for the Constitution is imperiled by tinkering with it, and because the supply of ideas for improving Madison's document always exceeds society's supply of Madisonian wisdom, the document should be amended rarely and reluctantly. Today, however, a balanced-budget amendment is required to counter two developments: the abandonment of the original understanding of the Constitution and the death of the political morality that expressed that understanding. For approximately 140 years, the government was restrained by the Constitution's enumeration of its powers, which supposedly were "few and defined."[75]

Before Congress acted, it considered what James Q. Wilson called the "legitimacy barrier": Did the Constitution empower the government to do this or that? As late as the 1950s, Congress at least feigned fealty to constitutional limits: When it wanted to build the interstate highway system or subsidize college students, it referred, if perfunctorily, to the enumerated responsibility for defense. Hence the names of the National Interstate and Defense Highways Act (1956) and the National Defense Education Act (1958). Wilson thought the legitimacy barrier's collapse was complete in 1965 when Congress intruded into the quintessentially state and local responsibility with the Elementary and Secondary Education Act.

Democracy generally, and especially legislative bargaining, is inherently additive: Majorities are assembled by attracting components with particularized benefits. Christopher DeMuth notes that from the Founding to the 1930s–1960s New Deal–Great Society era, this natural tendency of government to grow was inhibited by the bipartisan political ethic: Deficits were neither prudent nor seemly except when "borrowing was limited to wars, other emergencies, and investments such as territorial expansion and transportation; and incurred debts were paid down diligently." This tradition of borrowing for the future dissipated as government began routinely borrowing *from* the future in order to finance current consumption of government goods and services. DeMuth argues that a balanced-budget amendment is required because of the transformation of government from a provider of public goods (defense, infrastructure) to a provider of benefits (money and services) directly to individuals.[76]

A constitutional amendment imposing congressional term limits would not obviate, but would lessen, the need for a balanced-budget amendment by diminishing the incentive to think of the next election rather than the next generation. Unfortunately, the careerism that makes term limits advisable means that Congress will also never vote for Warren Buffett's instant fix for deficits: When, absent a war or other emergency, the budget is not balanced, all congressional incumbents are ineligible for re-election. Critics of a balanced-budget amendment warn that Congress will evade it by means of creative bookkeeping, stealthy spending through unfunded mandates on state governments and the private sector, the promiscuous declarations of spurious "emergencies," and other subterfuges. Such critics inadvertently make the case for the amendment by assuming, not unreasonably, that the political class is untrustworthy. And that the people's representatives really are, unfortunately, representative of the increasingly irresponsible people.

The institutional reforms just discussed would help. But what Washington really needs are two things that the people who are represented there generally consider disreputable: ambition and pride. Neither is, however, a sin, in its proper place. Washington is at all times awash in ambition. Too much of it, however, is personal ambition, unleavened by institutional pride. At least two things are required to correct the current constitutional disequilibrium of presidents untethered from a sensible conception of their responsibilities and the administrative state unsupervised. One requirement is more institutional ambition in Congress. The other is more diligence from the judiciary in performing its indispensable duty to referee skirmishes along the borders of the separation of powers.

This crux of America's constitutional architecture works only when the possessors of the separated powers are jealous of their turf and prerogatives: "Ambition," as Madison famously wrote in Federalist 51, "must be made to counteract ambition. The interests of the man must be connected with the constitutional rights of the place."[77] Unlike many of America's social problems (e.g., family disintegration), the causes of which are unclear and the solutions to which are unknown, the causes of, and the correctives for, the imbalance among the federal government's branches are, we might say, self-evident. The way for Congress to stop off-loading its powers onto the executive branch is to stop. To stop passing faux laws that merely express Congress' sentiments (e.g., for this or that educational or environmental outcome), leaving to executive agencies the actual lawmaking task of saying what behaviors are prescribed and proscribed. And Congress can claw back some abandoned powers by, for example, requiring congressional approval of all new "major" regulations—those with at least a $100 million impact on the economy. These measures would require an end to slovenly lawmaking by a Congress too lazy, or risk averse, or both, to be precise in making intellectually difficult and politically dangerous policy choices. Doing so would, by minimizing ambiguities, obviate the Supreme Court mistake known as "Chevron deference." It is named for the 1984 case in which the court propounded this principle: Courts are required to defer to administrative agencies' interpretations of "ambiguous" laws when the interpretations are "reasonable." This is an incentive for slapdash legislating by Congress, especially when a congressional majority thinks of itself, in an un-Madisonian way, not as custodian of a rival institution but as a supportive teammate of the president currently commanding the executive branch.

Finally, if Congress so lacks institutional assertiveness that it sloughs off its Article I powers onto Article II entities, then the Article III courts, and especially the Supreme Court, should revive and enforce the non-delegation doctrine. It is that Congress cannot constitutionally delegate legislative powers to government agencies or private entities. Such delegation, which has fueled, and been justified by, the growth of the administrative state, is convenient for Congress, which thereby outsources some of its responsibilities. But such delegation is incompatible with the separation of powers and those first fourteen words of the Constitution that follow the Preamble: "All legislative powers herein granted shall be vested in a Congress of the United States."

Like Chevron deference, which Justice Neil Gorsuch calls "a judge-made doctrine for the abdication of the judicial duty," non-enforcement of the non-delegation doctrine is a judicial temptation that courts have dealt with as Oscar Wilde recommended dealing with temptation: by succumbing to it.[78] Courts are understandably wary of the intellectual challenges and political risks involved in defining what degree of discretion that Congress grants to agencies amounts to an unconstitutional grant of legislative power. But if the courts will not police this practice, it will proceed and, unpoliced, will accelerate. It will because it serves the aggrandizement of the executive and the flight from responsibility by the legislature. This perverse convergence of the disreputable interests of the two political branches of the federal government is one reason, but only one, the next chapter will argue, that the judicial branch must become more energetic and engaged in defense of the separation of powers that the separation is supposed to serve: Liberty.

CHAPTER 4

THE JUDICIAL SUPERVISION OF DEMOCRACY

DIFFICULTIES WITH THE "COUNTER-MAJORITARIAN DIFFICULTY"

> There is no such thing as an achieved liberty; like electricity, there can be no substantial storage and it must be generated as it is enjoyed, or the lights go out.
>
> Justice Robert H. Jackson[1]

Symbols can resonate like well-struck cymbals. There is profound constitutional importance in the symbolic fact that the Constitutional Convention met in the room in which the Declaration of Independence was debated and endorsed. By replacing the Articles of Confederation, the convention effected a course correction, but not a rupture with the nation's fundamental purpose and destiny. The Constitution continues what the Declaration began. Lincoln did not begin the first of the Gettysburg Address' ten sentences with the words "Three score and fifteen years ago..." That would have meant that "our fathers" had "brought forth" a new nation in 1787, with the writing of the Constitution. The Constitution created a new regime. The nation, however, was born with the Declaration of Independence. Lincoln's career, indeed his life, was devoted to strengthening the cords of understanding by which citizens are bound to the republic. This required imbedding the Founding and the doctrine of natural rights at the center of national identity. And as the philosopher Leon Kass says, the Declaration was not a specifically "democratic" document in that "it did not by itself specify any particular form of government."[2] Any government is legitimate if it secures natural rights and rules by the recurrently expressed consent of the governed. So, of the three prepositions in Lincoln's formulation—government of, by, and for the people—it is the third that is dispositive. It is most probable that government will function for the people—will, that is, do what is most important, secure their rights—if it is government of and by the people. So the Declaration is a contingently, implicitly democratic document; it implies that democracy is the form of government with the highest probability of being government truly for the people.

Connecticut's Roger Sherman said that the central argument in the Constitutional Convention, of which he was an especially influential member, was "not what rights naturally belong to man, but how they may be most effectually guarded in society."[3] Justice William Brennan, the Supreme Court's most consequential liberal in the second half of the twentieth century, said, "Our Constitution was not intended to preserve a preexisting society but to make a new one, to put in place new principles that the prior political community had not sufficiently recognized."[4] One can quarrel with Brennan's choice of the word "society," which encompasses much more than what the Constitution addresses, which is the structure and procedures of one of America's many governments. Society, particularly American society, is characterized by fluidity and dynamism—a constant churning leading we know not where. Still, conservatives can agree with Brennan—if, but only if, by the Constitution putting "in place" new principles he means putting into institutional arrangements and processes the principles of the Declaration.

The essential drama of democracy derives from the inherent tension between the natural rights of the individual and the constructed right of the community to make such laws as the majority deems necessary and proper. Natural rights are affirmed by the Declaration of Independence; majority rule, circumscribed and modulated, is constructed by the Constitution. The Declaration is not just chronologically prior to the Constitution, it is logically prior. As Timothy Sandefur writes, the Declaration "sets the framework for reading" the Constitution, so it is the Constitution's "conscience": By the terms with which the Declaration articulates the Constitution's purpose—the purpose is to "secure" unalienable rights—the Declaration intimates the standards by which one can distinguish the proper from the improper exercises of majority rule. "Freedom is the starting point of politics; government's powers are secondary and derivative, and therefore limited.... Liberty is the goal at which democracy aims, not the other way around."[5]

The progressive project, now in its second century, has been to reverse this, giving majority rule priority over liberty when they conflict, as they do, inevitably and frequently. This reflects the progressive belief that rights are the result of government; they are "spaces of privacy" that government "has chosen to carve out and protect." This doctrine amounts to, and was intended as, the overthrow of the Founders' vision, to which James Madison adhered throughout his life. In December 1835, at age eighty-four, eighteen years after he left the presidency, and seven months before his death, Madison wrote an "Essay on Sovereignty" in which he argued that "the sovereignty of the society" is "vested in and exercisable by the majority," which "may do any thing that could be *rightfully* done." However, "the reserved rights of individuals (of conscience, for example)" are "beyond the legitimate reach of sovereignty."[6] Or as the Supreme Court would hold, in that 1943 case about the rights of conscience, certain things are "beyond the reach of majorities."[7]

THE THIRD-MOST IMPORTANT AMERICAN

The two most important Americans were presidents. Without George Washington, there would have been no country. Without Lincoln, a shattered nation would never have been reconnected with the Founders' premises. The third-most important American, however, was one of fifteen siblings raised in a two-room log cabin, and a self-taught lawyer—he had one year of formal education and a six-week apprenticeship with a legal instructor. In his thirty-four years as chief justice of the US Supreme Court, John Marshall embedded constitutional reasoning at the core of American governance. When in 1792 Marshall, a rival (and cousin) who Jefferson detested, was contemplating seeking a seat in the House of Representatives, Jefferson hit upon the idea of putting this person where Jefferson thought he could do less harm. Writing to Madison, Jefferson said, "I think nothing better could be done than to make him a judge."[8] Thus was Marshall put on the path to establishing judicial review and making the judicial branch important to the supervision of democracy. But the path was long and winding before Marshall completed it.

In 1215, in the Magna Carta, "John, by the grace of God King of England," said that "to all free men of our kingdom" we have granted "all the liberties written out below, to have and to keep for them and their heirs, of us and our heirs."[9] This expansion of liberty by an act of the sovereign's grace was progress and was followed by other incremental gains extracted from various sovereigns. Then, however, came 1776. Writing in 1792, James Madison said, "In Europe, charters of liberty have been granted by power. America has set the example...of power granted by liberty."[10] The change was from top down to bottom up: Rather than rights being granted by government to set people increasingly at liberty, people who are born free to exercise their freedom create a government for their convenience, and particularly to secure their natural rights that pre-exist government.

George Washington underscored this on September 17, 1787, the final day of the Constitutional Convention, of which he was president. In his letter transmitting the document to Congress, Washington put in two sentences the distilled essence of natural rights theory, and of the unending debate about rights, unenumerated yet retained: "Individuals entering into society, must give up a share of liberty to preserve the rest.... It is at all times difficult to draw with precision the line between those rights which must be surrendered, and those which may be reserved."[11] Drawing that line is the fundamental and unending task of the judicial branch. This suggests how one should think about Article III of the Constitution: It is tertiary in order but not in level of importance. It is the constitutional culmination: The legislative branch writes laws, the head of the executive branch takes care that the laws are faithfully executed, at which point the judiciary is perpetually poised to scrutinize the content and application of the laws. Which makes the judiciary the epicenter of constitutional government.

In the months before the September 1786 Annapolis convention that was called to consider remedies for the inadequacies of the Articles of Confederation, Madison read from the two trunks of books that he had asked Jefferson to send from Europe. They were books about ancient and modern confederations of states, and the lessons to be learned from their experiences. He noted that the articles of union for the Dutch confederacy stipulated that "everything done contrary to them [is] to be null and void." This, says Noah Feldman, was "Madison's first reference to the principle of constitutional supremacy."[12] In the American context, that principle would soon— seventeen years later, in the Supreme Court's 1803 *Marbury v. Madison* decision—entail judicial review. This was, however, foreshadowed before 1786.

One of Marshall's recent biographers, Joel Richard Paul, notes that during the early 1780s Marshall served on Virginia's Council of State, which had the power to disallow any action by the state's governor. The governor was authorized by statute to remove justices of the peace, which Governor John Randolph did when Justice of the Peace John Price Posey misappropriated assets of an estate he was responsible for overseeing. Marshall persuaded his colleagues on the council that the statute giving the governor this power violated the spirit of the state's constitution, which represented the "supreme permanent will of the people" (Paul's words) and so must be superior to any state statute. Thus was intimated the principle of judicial review, which Chief Justice Marshall would establish two decades later.[13]

Of all the unanticipated, or only dimly foreseen, American political developments since 1787—the emergence of political parties, presidential dominance of even the legislative process, the direct election of senators, the gradual but complete abandonment of the theory that the federal government's powers are "few and defined"—none has been more consequential than the acceptance of judicial review.[14] Nowhere in Articles I or III is there a constitutionally stipulated requirement that Congress acquiesce in any Supreme Court judgment or in the reasoning by which the court reaches it. Deference to the court's decisions is a tradition, a practice hallowed by reiteration. Paradoxically, the tradition was strengthened by the prestige that accrued to the court as a result of the 1954 *Brown v. Board of Education of Topeka* school desegregation decision, which was far in advance of public opinion, not just in the South but nationally. The prestige came *because* the court acted without reference to public sentiments, and by doing so addressed an injustice with which majoritarian institutions could not then cope.

Only fifty-five of the seventy-four men chosen to attend the Constitutional Convention actually did so, and some of them were absent much of the time. Although they were young—more than a third of the delegates were in their thirties—they were remarkably seasoned: Thirty-nine had had congressional experience. They did not, however, confront this indisputable truth: If Congress is the sovereign arbiter of the parameters of its own power, then there is no institutional buttress for limited government. Therefore judicial review is not just implied by, it is required by the government's constitutional structure. It is unlikely that the convention's veterans of legislative cultures anticipated the coming role of the judiciary through judicial review of legislative acts. This practice was, however, implicit in, among other things, the Constitution's Preamble.

In the Constitutional Convention, Gouverneur Morris of New York was, historian Joseph J. Ellis notes, "the only delegate to speak more frequently than Madison," and he spoke for those delegates who favored, as Madison did, a more national understanding of what they were drafting, as opposed to a state-centered confederation. Morris was the most important member of the Committee on Style and Arrangements, and in that role he accomplished a convergence of style and substance when he undertook to revise the preamble written by the Committee on Detail. The Committee's preamble had begun, "We the people of the states of New Hampshire, Massachusetts, Rhode Island..." and on through the thirteen states. Morris replaced that with seven words: "We the people of the United States..." By this, which Ellis calls "probably the most consequential editorial act in American history," Morris "smuggled the national agenda into the preamble." This embedded "a crucial and clear presumption that the rest of the document was designed to finesse: namely, that the newly created government operated directly on the whole American citizenry, not indirectly through the states."[15]

The Supreme Court has defined citizenship as "the right to have rights."[16] It might better have said "the right to have one's natural rights recognized and their exercise protected." Until the second half of the twentieth century, personal rights were not emphasized as the bulwark of liberty. Rather, the structure of the regime—the allocation of powers among the three branches of the federal government and between the federal and state governments—was the bulwark. The word "bulwark" was a favorite of some important Founders. In Federalist 78, published on May 28, 1788, Alexander Hamilton said that a "strong argument for the permanent tenure of judicial offices" is that courts are to function as "bulwarks of a limited Constitution against legislative encroachments."[17] A year later, on June 8, 1789, James Madison, arguing in the House of Representatives for adoption of the Bill of Rights, said "independent tribunals of justice will consider themselves in a peculiar manner the guardians of those rights; they will be an impenetrable bulwark against every assumption of power in the legislative or executive."[18] A bulwark is a defensive measure that deflects, contains, halts various forces of man or nature. The structure of the government as devised at Philadelphia in 1787, and supplemented by the Bill of Rights in 1791, is supposed to channel, contain, and sometimes frustrate the force of public opinion, including and sometimes especially the opinion of a majority.

The idea that the federal judiciary wielding judicial review is an anomaly, grafted onto popular government, is mistaken. Such a judiciary is a republican institution in that it is connected to the people, but indirectly. Its members are nominated by the president and confirmed by the Senate. As Madison wrote in Federalist 39: "We may define a republic to be…a government which derives all its powers directly *or indirectly* from the great body of the people; and is administered by persons holding their offices during pleasure, for a limited period, or during good behavior….It is sufficient for such a government, that the persons administering it be appointed, either directly *or indirectly*, by the people."[19] (emphasis added) Therefore it is natural and proper that the judiciary always has been, and is now more than ever, somewhat reflective of political concerns, aspirations, and passions.

AN AMERICAN PARADOX

It is paradoxical that in a nation where skepticism about government is at the core of the political philosophy bequeathed by the Founders, the elaboration and application of this political philosophy has been done largely by or through a government institution, the Supreme Court. There is a profound truth about the American polity and its history that is sometimes missed by even the most accomplished students of American history. It is often said that ours is a nation indifferent to, even averse to, political philosophy. And it is said that this disposition is a virtue and a sign of national health. The theory is that only unhappy nations are constantly engaged in arguing about fundamental things and that the paucity—actually, it is merely a postulated paucity—of American political philosophy is evidence of a contented consensus about our polity's basic premises. For example, Daniel J. Boorstin, then a University of Chicago historian and later Librarian of Congress, published a slender volume, *The Genius of American Politics*, that appeared in 1953, during America's postwar introspection about the nature and meaning of our nation's sudden global preeminence. Boorstin's argument, made with his characteristic verve and erudition, aimed to explain why our success was related to "our antipathy to political theory." The genius of our democracy, said Boorstin, comes not from any geniuses of political thought comparable to Plato and Aristotle or Hobbes and Locke. Rather, it comes "from the unprecedented opportunities of this continent and from a peculiar and unrepeatable combination of historical circumstances." This explains "our inability to make a 'philosophy' of them" and why our nation has never produced a political philosopher of the stature of, say, Hobbes and Locke, or "a systematic theoretical work to rank with theirs."[20]

Well. Leave aside the fact that James Madison was a political philosopher of such stature. He was such *because* he was also a practicing politician. And leave aside the fact, which it surely is, that *The Federalist Papers*, although a compendium of newspaper columns written in haste in response to a practical problem (to secure ratification of the Constitution), is a theoretical work that ranks with Hobbes' *Leviathan* and Locke's *The Second Treatise on Civil Government*. Considered in the second decade of the twenty-first century, as we stand on the dark and bloody ground of today's political contentions, Boorstin's book remains interesting, but primarily as a period piece. It is a shard of America's now shattered consensus. Or, more precisely, it is a document from the calm before the storm of the conservative counterattack against progressives' complacent assumption that their ascendancy was secure.

The American argument about philosophic fundamentals is not only ongoing, it is thoroughly woven into the fabric of our public life. Far from being rare and of marginal importance, political philosophy is more central to our public life than in that of any other nation. It is implicated in almost all American policy debates of any consequence. Indeed, it is, like Edgar Allan Poe's purloined letter, hidden in plain sight. All American political arguments involve, at bottom, interpretations of the Declaration of Independence and of the Constitution that was written to provide institutional architecture for governance according to the Declaration's precepts. So, constitutional lawyers are America's practitioners of political philosophy. One such, Randy Barnett, calls the Constitution "the law that governs those who govern us." It is, he argues, properly read through the lens of the great document that preceded it, the Declaration of Independence. The Constitution was written to provide the practices requisite for a national life lived in accordance with fifty-five words: "We hold these truths to be self-evident, that all men are created equal, that they are endowed by their Creator with certain unalienable Rights, that among these are Life, Liberty and the pursuit of Happiness. That to secure these rights, Governments are instituted among Men, deriving their just powers from the consent of the governed."[21]

Those words are so familiar that the importance of two of them, a verb and an adjective, is insufficiently understood. Governments can derive many powers from the consent of the majority, but not all exercises of those powers are, simply because they flow from a majority, "just." And governments are instituted to "secure" our pre-existing rights, not to bestow them. As Barnett insists, the great divide in

America today is between those who believe, as the Founders did, that "first come rights and then comes government" and those who believe, as progressives do, that "first comes government and then come rights." The former, he says, are adherents of the Republican Constitution. The latter have given us the Democratic Constitution.[22]

The debate between these cohorts is, Barnett believes, "about the meaning of the first three words of the Constitution: 'We the People.' Those who favor the Democratic Constitution view We the People as a group, as a body, as a collective entity. Those who favor the Republican Constitution view We the People as individuals." The choice between these two understandings has enormous consequences, especially concerning the proper meaning of popular sovereignty. A Republican Constitution is a device for limiting government, including government's translation of majority desires into laws and policies when those conflict with the government's primary task of securing the natural rights of individuals. A Democratic Constitution is a device for giving priority to the will of a collective, the majority. This Constitution expresses the desires of a majority of the people, allowing the majority's will to prevail. Hence, any principle or practice, such as judicial review, that impedes the will of the majority is, say advocates of a Democratic Constitution, presumptively illegitimate until proven otherwise. And "the only individual rights that are legally enforceable are a product of majoritarian will."[23]

Barnett believes that, for decades now, American Lockeans have been losing ground to Hobbesians. Those who take their bearings from John Locke are "those for whom individual liberty is their first principle of social ordering." Those who are Thomas Hobbes' intellectual children "give priority to the need for government power to provide social order and pursue social ends," even if the rights of individuals must be abridged in order to do so. Not all Hobbesians are progressives, but all progressives are Hobbesians because they say America is dedicated to a *process*—to majoritarian decision-making that legitimates the exercises of government power that majorities endorse. Not all Lockeans are libertarians, but all libertarians are Lockeans because they say America is dedicated to a *condition*: liberty. Hobbesians say the core American principle is the right of the majority to have its way. Lockeans stress rigorous judicial protection of individual rights, especially those of private property and the freedom of contract, that define and protect the zone of sovereignty within which people are free to act as they please.[24]

The 1896 *Plessy v. Ferguson* decision, in which the Supreme Court deferred to the right of the majority to codify racial segregation under the rubric of "separate but equal," was, Barnett argues, an example of the Democratic Constitution's majoritarianism. He says the 1954 *Brown v. Board of Education* decision, affirming the individual rights of individual schoolchildren against a majority's preference for segregated schools, represented long overdue fidelity to the Republican Constitution. Barnett has become a leader of those who are reasserting the natural rights tradition that was overthrown during progressivism's long success in defining the nature of the Democratic Constitution and the judiciary's permissive role in construing the government's powers under it. But Barnett's challenge to progressives is also, and perhaps primarily, a challenge to conservatives. He is summoning them to reexamine the philosophic premises that have impelled them to celebrate judicial modesty, understood as deference to majoritarian institutions. Hence Barnett disturbs the dogmatic slumbers of people who occupy various positions along the political spectrum.[25]

As the ancients understood it, liberty was a weight to be shouldered, a burden of constant immersion in civic obligations. These obligations were not thought to impinge upon the private sphere of life because there was no clear distinction between the public and private spheres. The business of liberty was comprehensive; it took time and leisure, which often were provided by slavery. Modernity's gift has been the ability and determination to sharply delineate private and public spheres, with the private being the zone of individual sovereignty. It is the realm of the household, the family, and the work that sustains both. This is the basis of the proposition that the Constitution of the first consciously modern nation, the United States, protects the sovereignty of private individuals, not the sovereignty of a public collective, "the majority."

THE FRAME OF SILVER FOR THE APPLE OF GOLD

Natural rights are affirmed by the Declaration. Majority rule, circumscribed and modulated, is constructed by the Constitution. And a properly engaged judiciary is duty-bound to declare majority acts invalid when they abridge natural rights. This tension was illustrated in Elena Kagan's confirmation hearing to be a justice, when she was asked if she believes there are natural rights that are not among the rights the Constitution enumerates. She replied: "I don't have a view of what are natural rights, independent of the Constitution." She added: "I'm not saying I do not believe that there are rights preexisting the Constitution and the laws, but my job as a justice is to enforce the Constitution and the laws." And: "I think that the question of what I believe as to what people's rights are outside the Constitution and the laws, that you should not want me to act in any way on the basis of such a belief."[26] Actually, we do want that. Natural rights, which are grounded in nature, are thus "independent of" the Constitution. They are not, however, "outside" of it because its paramount purpose is the protection of those rights.

Madison and others originally resisted the idea of adding a Bill of Rights to the Constitution as it would emerge from the convention, for two reasons. They thought a Bill of Rights would be superfluous because the structure of the government itself—the separation of powers; powers dispersed among rival institutions—would suffice to guarantee the safety of the citizens from abusive government. And they thought a Bill of Rights would be potentially dangerous: By enumerating certain rights, others not enumerated might be disparaged. Madison and like-minded Framers relented, promising a Bill of Rights in order to facilitate ratification of the Constitution by the various state conventions, where anti-Federalists were demanding an enumeration of rights. When, after ratification, the First Congress began consideration of a draft of the Bill of Rights, Representative Theodore Sedgwick, who had sat in the Continental Congress, responded to a colleague who questioned why those who had prepared the draft had enumerated only certain rights. Sedgwick said: "They might have gone into a very lengthy enumeration of rights; they might have declared that a man should have a right to wear his hat if he pleased, that he might get up when he pleased, and go to bed when he thought proper; but [I] would ask the gentleman whether he thought it necessary to enter these trifles in a declaration of rights, under a government where none of them were intended to be infringed."[27] Sedgwick had a point: When you start enumerating rights, where do you stop? And why? And what are the consequences of stopping? This had been Madison's point. The attempt to solve, or at least finesse, this problem is the Ninth Amendment: "The enumeration in the Constitution, of certain rights, shall not be construed to deny or disparage others retained by the people." If you believe, as Robert Bork did, that this amendment is a meaningless "inkblot," you must believe that the Framers were slapdash draftsmen about this, and only this, provision.

The Constitution is America's fundamental law but not its first law. The Declaration appears on page one of volume one of the US Statutes at Large, and it is at the head of the United States Code under the caption "The Organic Laws of the United States." Since the 1864 admission of Nevada to statehood, every state's admission has been conditioned on adoption of a constitution consistent with the US Constitution—and the Declaration.[28]

"The Constitution," said Justice Clarence Thomas in a 1996 speech, "means not what the Court says it does but what the delegates at Philadelphia and at the state ratifying conventions understood it to mean.... We as a nation adopted a written Constitution precisely because it has a fixed meaning that does not change."[29] The meaning, however, is not fixed only by how the delegates and the conventions understood the immediate applications of what they were doing. If they understood their handiwork as providing institutional means to the Declaration's ends, then the fixed meaning of the Constitution is to be found in its mission to protect natural rights and liberty in changing—unfixed—circumstances. Fidelity to the text requires fidelity to some things that were, in a sense, prior to the text—the political and social principles and goals for which the text was written. It was written in order to be instrumental to goals served by the principles.

With an asperity born of exasperation, Antonin Scalia once wrote, "If you want aspirations, you can read the Declaration of Independence," but "there is no such philosophizing in our Constitution," which is "a practical and pragmatic charter of government." Oh? Are we to conclude that philosophy is impractical and unpragmatic? There is no philosophizing in the Constitution—until we put it there by construing it as a charter of government for a nation that is, in Lincoln's formulation, dedicated to a proposition that Scalia dismisses as "philosophizing," the proposition that all men are created equal in possession of natural rights. In the words of constitutional scholar Walter Berns, the Constitution is related to the Declaration "as effect is related to cause."[30] Or as Lincoln said, the Declaration of Independence is the "apple of gold" that is "framed" by something "silver": the Constitution. Silver is valuable and frames serve an important function, but gold is more valuable and frames are of subsidiary importance to what they frame.[31] Today, the apple nourishes those of us who believe that the judiciary has been too accommodating to legislatures that are too responsive to majorities.

In an 1810 case, *Fletcher v. Peck*, Justice John Marshall gave scant comfort to those of us who think the judiciary should be more amenable than it usually is to the principle that much of what Congress does should be presumed to be constitutionally dubious. And Marshall then did not give encouragement to those who think the judiciary should be energetic in finding unenumerated rights to protect. He said judicial review must be wielded with "much delicacy," and laws should be declared unconstitutional "seldom, if ever...in a doubtful case."[32] But why, when an act of Congress is constitutionally doubtful, should the doubts be disregarded? Or why should Congress be given the benefit of the doubt about its exercise of its powers? If the judicial ethic is that the judiciary should defer to even constitutionally dubious acts of Congress, why is that ethical? Such an ethic subordinates fidelity to the Constitution to the celebration of one part of that document: Article I. And this implies a suspension of judgment in order to pledge allegiance to majoritarianism. It is hardly hard-core libertarianism to hold that the freedom of individuals to enter into voluntary exchanges and other transactions, contractual or otherwise, is presumptively important and owed respect by the government, and therefore that government bears the burden of proving that an interference with this freedom is necessary for achieving a compelling public interest.

The principle of judicial restraint, distilled to its essence, is that an act of the government should be presumed constitutional, and that the party disputing the act's constitutionality bears the heavy burden of demonstrating unconstitutionality beyond a reasonable doubt. The contrary principle, the principle of judicial engagement, is that the judiciary's primary duty is to defend liberty, and that the government, when challenged, bears the burden of demonstrating that its action is in conformity with the Constitution's architecture, the purpose of which is to protect liberty. The government dispatches this burden by demonstrating that its action is both necessary and proper *for the exercise of an enumerated power*. A state or local government dispatches the burden by demonstrating that its act is within the constitutionally proscribed limits of its police power.

But are there any longer such limits? There were in 1905. That there no longer are is suggested by the widespread—and mistaken—disdain for a Supreme Court decision made that year. For a century there has been a broad and durable consensus among progressive scholars of constitutional law that the court decided the 1905 *Lochner* case improperly. And there is a comparable consensus among progressive historians that the case defined an entire era of constitutional law and social policy. Sensible conservatives believe the case was correctly decided. And David E. Bernstein's study of the Supreme Court's record, and of the record of state courts, concerning states' exercises of their police power regarding social legislation, refutes the theory that there was a "Lochner era," meaning a prolonged period in which almost all social legislation was overturned by judicial rulings that imposed an unreasonably cramped interpretation of the states' police powers.

The Lochner episode began May 2, 1895, when the New York legislature enacted a law that began this way: "No employee shall be required or permitted to work in a biscuit, bread or cake bakery or confectionary establishment more than 60 hours in any one week, or more than 10 hours in any one day…"[33] Little did the legislators know that they were providing fodder for the US Supreme Court, which in turn would fuel among progressives an indignation industry that is still manufacturing disapproval of the court's decision. Ostensibly, New York's legislature limited the permissible work hours of bakery employees in order to protect the workers' health and safety. That is what the legislature said. If you believe that legislatures should be taken at their word, if you assume that they can be assumed to be candid about their motives, then the subsequent Supreme Court ruling was, indeed, as its critics say, an indefensible exercise of judicial power—an essentially legislative act. If, however, you have a less sentimental and more empirical approach to evaluating political behavior, and if you think courts should be similarly unenthralled when judging the work of legislatures, then *Lochner v. New York* richly repays reconsideration.

Joseph Lochner, the immigrant from Bavaria who successfully challenged the law's Constitutionality, was fined fifty dollars for violating the limits it placed on the employees of his Utica bakery. He argued that he and his employees had a right, absent a compelling government interest, to voluntarily contract for longer working days and weeks. Lochner did this with Aman Schmitter, who lived with his family above Lochner's bakery. Lochner and Schmitter together exercised a right they said was not only rooted in the Anglo-American tradition but was antecedent to positive law and discoverable by reason. It was, in a word, natural and unalienable.[34]

The political antecedents and legislative history of New York's law demonstrate beyond peradventure that the law was an exercise in rent-seeking by large, unionized bakeries and the unions that represented those bakeries' employees. Rent-seeking is an unfortunately opaque name that has come to be attached to an even more unfortunate practice. Adam Smith distinguished between three kinds of income: profits, wages, and rents. Rents are captured when a third party, most often a government, confers a benefit on one party by depriving a second party of access to opportunity. Tariffs, for example, confer rents on manufacturers of protected goods by depriving consumers of the ability to purchase competing imported goods without paying the price of the tariff. Occupational licensing restrictions, by limiting the entry of new competitors into professions, confer rents on those who are already established in the professions: The rents are the economic value of the government-imposed exemption from competition. Regulations can confer rents that handicap some participants in a market at the behest of rival interests, interests that succeed in what is called the "regulatory capture" of the regulating agency. The permutations of rent-seeking are as many as the administrative state is vast. Rent-seeking is the activity of attempting to increase one's income without increasing the quantity or quality of the goods or services offered to customers. It is the attempt to manipulate public power for private advantage—to get government to improve your economic circumstances by conferring a benefit on you or a handicap on your competitors.

The law that Lochner violated was enacted—this is not disputed—at the behest of the large unionized bakeries and the unions with which they dealt. In these bakeries, overtime work was rare. The purpose of the law was to burden small, family-owned, non-unionized competitors that depended on flexible work schedules. Lochner's challenge to the law was, Bernstein notes, funded "almost entirely with donations from small retail bakers." The fact that Schmitter swore in an affidavit that he had happily exceeded the sixty-hour work week in Lochner's establishment in order to learn cake baking did not stay the hand of the state. New York filed a criminal complaint against Lochner. When the case reached the US Supreme Court, New York state's remarkably short (nineteen pages) brief asserted that the maximum hours law was simply a health law, an exercise of the police power to protect the health of the public and of bakery workers. Progressives at the time were concerned about the influx of immigrants, and the state's brief acknowledged that the law targeted immigrants' bakeries because "there have come to [New York] great numbers of foreigners with habits which must be changed."[35]

The Supreme Court ruled, 5–4, for Lochner. It said that the production of "clean and wholesome bread" does not depend on limiting the hours of workers, who are "in no sense wards of the state." And there was, the court held, no evidence that baking is an especially unhealthy profession. Hence the law was an unconstitutional "interference" with the liberty of contract.[36] This is an unenumerated right, meaning one not specifically mentioned in the Constitution. But the Constitution affirms the existence of unenumerated rights. The Ninth Amendment says: "The enumeration in the Constitution, of certain rights, shall not be construed to deny or disparage others retained by the people."

The main dissent offered by the Supreme Court's minority radiated the statism that was the natural product of progressive paternalism. It was, this dissent said, legitimate for New York's state government to exercise its police power to forbid workers, including willing workers, from working hours that might damage their "physical and mental capacity to serve the State, and to provide for those dependent upon them." In another dissent, which became famous and influential, Justice Oliver Wendell Holmes asserted an almost unlimited government police power flowing from "the right of a majority to embody their opinions in law." Notice that Holmes' majoritarianism led him to assert an essentially unlimited right. It is the majority's right to embody not just its opinions about proper protections of the public's health or workers' safety, but its opinions, period. Hence Holmes thought the right of an individual to liberty of contract should not be interpreted "to prevent the natural outcome of a dominant opinion."[37] Implicitly, Holmes was accepting the idea that any law enacted by a democratically elected legislature represents the will of a majority. In this regard, Holmes, who fancied himself a flinty realist immune to sentimentality, was adhering to an abstract and sentimental theory of democratic practice, a theory remarkably uninformed by empirical evidence available to anyone who even casually observes legislative practices, then or now.

Progressives celebrated Holmes' assertion that government should be able to exercise almost untrammeled police powers as long as government asserts what would come to be called a "rational basis" for exercises of this power. And a mere assertion should suffice. Courts, Holmes said, should defer to economic regulations because the Constitution does not "embody a particular economic theory, whether of paternalism and the organic relation of the citizen to the State or of *laissez faire*."[38] This was the beginning of progressives' distortion of the *Lochner* decision as expressing nothing more dignified than the court's commitment to an economic doctrine that then was supposedly enjoying untrammeled sway over political practices. Because Holmes held the preposterous view that the Constitution was written to govern persons of "fundamentally" different views, he rejected the idea that the Lochner case turned not on an economic theory but on the political philosophy that is fundamental American doctrine. It holds that among the unalienable rights every individual possesses is a right to liberty of contract, which includes the right to freely contract to sell one's labor or to purchase the labor of others. And this right cannot be legislated out of existence for casual or, as in the Lochner episode, disreputable reasons, even when legislatures cloak their reasons in the language of social betterment. Hence progressivism's disapproval of "individualism" that allows individual rights, particularly those of property and contract, to impede the administrative state's regulation of society for collectivist ends, unimpeded by judicial review.

Often before and after *Lochner*, liberty of contract was invoked—sometimes successfully but usually not—against progressives' legislation that falsely purported to be disinterested instruments for purely humane and altruistic purposes. For example, many maximum-hours and minimum-wage laws were written to apply only to women. To be sure, these were often written to give effect to the era's conventional wisdom that "the natural and proper timidity and delicacy which belongs to the female sex evidently unfits it for many of the occupations of civil life" and "the paramount destiny and mission of woman are to fulfill the noble and benign offices of wife and mother." So wrote three of the dissenting justices in the *Slaughter-House Cases* of 1873. In 1895, the Illinois state supreme court, reasoning as the US Supreme Court would in *Lochner* ten years later, admirably struck down a state law imposing maximum-hour limits on women's work weeks, a law that had been advocated by many groups that would come to be called progressive. The Illinois court, like the Supreme Court in *Lochner*, cited liberty of contract, saying women "are entitled to the same rights under the Constitution to make contracts with reference to their labor as are secured thereby to men."[39]

Bernstein notes that supposedly protective legislation for women was supported by progressives of different stripes. There were paternalists who worried about women's health. There were maternalists who thought that women working outside the home, regardless of hours and wages, subverted women's natural role as homemakers. There were moralists who thought long hours or low wages would tempt women into prostitution. And there were eugenicists who thought that women who worked outside the home weakened the race. Eugenics attracted progressives because, Bernstein notes, it was congenial to persons committed to "anti-individualism, efficiency, scientific expertise, and technocracy."[40]

The various reasons then given for using the states' police powers to protect women now seem anachronistic and offensive, but they were not always cynical reasons for limiting liberty of contract. However, guess what entrenched economic faction worked successfully, in the name of motherhood and other non-economic values, for state laws prohibiting women from being lawyers: Male lawyers favored such laws in order to limit competition for legal services. And as late as 1948 the US Supreme Court, fully committed to anti-*Lochner* jurisprudence, upheld a Michigan law forbidding, ostensibly for moral reasons, women to work as bartenders. The court chose to treat as irrelevant the fact that the most forceful advocates of the law were labor unions representing mostly male bartenders in Michigan, where women were allowed to work as cocktail waitresses.

Progressives' hostility to inhibiting government's police power also made progressives hostile to early attempts to wield the liberty of contract against racial segregation. Advocates of integration argued that the right of property and liberty of contract guaranteed by the Fourteenth Amendment should trump laws enforcing residential segregation. Progressives, however, were eager to vindicate the power of government to regulate for the collective good unimpeded by assertions of individual rights. And progressives were committed to the principle of broad deference to a government's definition of the collective good. Enforcement of restrictive real estate covenants written to maintain segregated neighborhoods was justified as necessary for reducing racial friction, reducing the spread of communicable diseases, and protecting property values. Even progressives who found this practice repugnant were deferential to government enforcement in order to serve the higher good of enlarging government's scope. In Kentucky, a Louisville ordinance forbade "any colored person to move into and occupy as a residence…any house upon any block upon which a greater number of houses are occupied…by white people than are occupied…by colored people." Progressives inclined to resist this found themselves disarmed when Kentucky's Court of Appeals adopted their vocabulary in affirming the ordinance. It said "the advance of civilization…has resulted in a gradual lessening of the dominions of the individual over private property and a corresponding strengthening of the relative power of the state in respect thereof."[41]

Progressives occasionally were stymied when courts recognized, in the name of individual rights, limits on states' police powers. After World War I, some progressives, remembering Randolph Bourne's axiom that "war is the health of the State," were delighted by the war's centralizing and homogenizing effects on government and culture. So they advocated banning private schools, or at least making them subordinate to the regulatory state, in order to fuse a nationalized citizenry into greater acceptance of government power. In 1925, however, the US Supreme Court overturned an Oregon law, enacted by referendum, that required all children between ages eight and sixteen to attend public schools. In affirming the right of parents to control their children's education, the court disregarded Oregon's claimed police power to mandate public schools. The state's purpose was to keep America's melting pot hot by eliminating parochial schools.

The explicit reasoning of the *Lochner* case was put to some honorable uses, as when, in 1926, Georgia's Supreme Court held that liberty of contract justified striking down a law that forbade black barbers to cut the hair of white children. The Georgia court did not defer to Woodrow Wilson's principle that the purpose of government is "to bring the active, planning will of each part of the government into accord with the prevailing popular thought and need." And the court did not defer to the "dominant opinion" to which Oliver Wendell Holmes deferred and which in Georgia in 1926 did not favor the right of black barbers to cut white children's hair.[42]

Ninety-eight years after *Lochner* was decided, the recoil against it made a cameo appearance in a Supreme Court dissent. In 2005, in *Lawrence v. Texas*, the court invalidated, as a violation of the Fourteenth Amendment's guarantee of equal protection of the law, a Texas statute criminalizing sexual intimacy by same-sex couples. Dissenting, Justice Antonin Scalia demonstrated a deep division in American conservatism when he said the Constitution no more protects the right to engage in such intimacy than it protects the right to work "more than 60 hours per week in a bakery." Scalia, consistent in his majoritarianism, was as wrong about *Lawrence* as he was about *Lochner*.[43]

In his *Lochner* dissent, Holmes said, the "Fourteenth Amendment does not enact Mr. Herbert Spencer's *Social Statics*." Here the epigrammatic Holmes was, characteristically, memorable and mistaken. He was referring to the British philosopher and sociologist of the Victorian era who defended libertarian economic policies— government largely confining itself to creating and refereeing free markets, and defending property rights. Granted, the Constitution does not "enact" this or that fiscal or monetary policy. It does, however, erect a structure designed to protect a large sphere of individual liberty. And it provides no textual or other justification for treating economic liberty as a somehow inferior form of liberty, entitled only to lackadaisical protection. The Constitution is John Locke's political philosophy translated into institutional architecture. It is from Locke that Jefferson and other Founders derived their understandings of the natural rights to life, liberty, and property. They understood that the right to property could not be severed from an implied corollary right: the liberty to contract to create arrangements important to the acquisition and disposition of property. Therefore, because liberty is the crux of the Constitution's purpose, the document does, in a sense, "enact" powerful protections for a libertarian society not unlike that praised in Spencer's *Social Statics*.[44]

Among judges and the law professoriate, Robert Bork was perhaps the most forthright and rigorous majoritarian since Holmes. "In his 1905 *Lochner* opinion," Bork wrote, "Justice Peckham, defending liberty from what he conceived to be 'a mere meddlesome interference,' asked rhetorically, '[A]re we all...at the mercy of legislative majorities?' The correct answer, where the Constitution is silent, must be 'yes.'"[45] But how does the Constitution "speak"? Does it speak in only one manner about the legislative powers? Does it say that legislative majorities may do what they want to unless and until they bump up against a right that the Constitution explicitly singles out for immunity from regulation or other abridgement by a majority? Or does the Constitution mean what it says in taking cognizance of unenumerated rights?

For several generations, progressivism was complacently committed to majoritarian politics. This commitment of convenience justified—actually, it mandated—judicial restraint, and thereby emancipated legislatures, and especially Congress, to exercise virtually unlimited police powers in regulating the economy. The predicate for progressives' partial retreat from judicial restraint was placed in 1938, in the most famous footnote in Supreme Court history, footnote 4 in *United States v. Carolene Products*. Written by Justice Harlan Fiske Stone, it said that special judicial scrutiny and energy should be devoted to the defense of "discrete and insular" minorities that are denied effective access to the political process. Where political change is blocked, the court can legitimately be an active agent of change.

The thrust of footnote 4, however, was to create a bifurcated regime of constitutional protections. Government acts that are injurious to "discrete and insular" minorities, such as blacks in the South, would receive heightened judicial scrutiny and diminished judicial deference.

But government measures that are injurious to minorities are acceptable if those who are injured by outcomes of the political process have access to that process, and if the measures pass the extremely permissive "rational basis" test. If, that is, the legislature could be said to have had *any* non-capricious, non-arbitrary reason for enacting the measures. Henceforth, if a "discrete and insular" minority were injured by being excluded from the majoritarian political process, the court would ride to the rescue. If, however, the interests of a minority with formal access to the political process were trampled by the majority, then judicial deference would remain appropriate.

This is pernicious. Instead, the court should forthrightly enunciate this principle: The Due Process Clause, properly construed, prohibits arbitrary government actions, particularly actions that unjustifiably restrict individuals' liberties. That is, the Due Process Clause is not purely about process. As Timothy Sandefur writes, what distinguishes *due* process is an outcome that is not arbitrary. Granted, the Constitution's text does not explicitly infuse the concept of due process with substance. There are, however, implicit limits on government power, limits inherent in the idea of law. As Sandefur says, a legislative act that fails the tests of generality, regularity, fairness, and rationality (being a cost-efficient means to a legitimate end) is not a law, so enforcing it cannot be due process *of law*.[46]

When the Constitution is read as what it actually is—as the implementation of the principles of the Declaration of Independence—the Constitution guarantees government that secures individual rights by establishing lawful, meaning non-arbitrary, rule. So, in determining whether there has been due process, a court must examine not just the form of a statute or the procedural formalities that produced it, but also its substance. This is because, as Sandefur writes, the Constitution gives priority to liberty, not just to the democratic processes that produce government acts. Again, the Constitution does not require just *any* process but *due* process. Were "due" simply a synonym for "democratic," the due process guarantee would guarantee nothing.

THE ACTIVITY OF JUDGING

If a Constitution is to truly *constitute* a polity, its language must be construed by enunciated principles that serve continuity by providing applicable standards that do not change as circumstances change. Ongoing attempts to distill such standards from constitutional practices, especially from the corpus of Supreme Court decisions construing the document's text, have produced a literature rich in insights—and intelligent disagreements. There is, however, agreement about this: We must begin with the language chosen by the Constitution's Framers. This agreement, however, leaves abundant scope for disagreement about the *activity* of construing the language. Some say that sound constitutional reasoning begins, and very nearly ends, with intellectual archeology—by excavating the original normal public meaning of the constitutional language at the time the Framers used it. But the Eighth Amendment, which forbids "cruel and unusual" punishments, provides a lesson in the limits of this kind of originalism and points toward a more supple and balanced approach to construing the Constitution's text.

Regarding punishment of criminals, America's standards of decency began to change significantly at the time of the Revolution, and because of ideas integral to the revolutionary ferment, particularly the idea that all men are created equal. Historian Gordon Wood argues that the colonial authorities, steeped in British class prejudices, believed that crime was generally caused by unchecked passions and that the lower orders were characterized by what today is called weak impulse control. Hence the lower orders should be regarded warily as prone to criminality, a tendency that could be checked only by "fear or force." Therefore "pillorying, whipping, and mutilating of the criminals' bodies had been standard punishments in the colonies," and these lurid displays of community disapproval were performed in public for the purpose of "overawing and deterring the spectators." Many spectators regarded such public punishments as neither cruel nor unusual but rather as entertainments: "Men and women in eighteenth-century Boston were taken from the huge cage that had brought them from the prison, tied bareback to a post on State Street, and lashed thirty or forty times" while the screams of the punished mingled with the roar of the mobs. The stocks were moved about within the community as a moveable feast of scorn for the miscreants and for the education of the public. Permanent shaming was achieved by mutilations, such as branded foreheads and cropped ears, that left criminals forever exposed to the contempt of their communities. In the colonial era, the idea of rehabilitation of lawbreakers was rarely advocated, and when it was it was dismissed as fanciful and sentimental. Hence Pennsylvania had twenty capital crimes, and Virginia had twenty-seven. In the colonial era, "capital punishment had been common not only for murder but for robbery, forgery, housebreaking, and counterfeiting as well."[47]

Then came the Revolution, and halting, tentative attempts to follow the logic of equality wherever it might lead. Americans should remember, said the Philadelphia physician Benjamin Rush, that criminals, too, "possess souls and bodies composed of the same materials as those of our friends and relatives." What revolutionary doctrine encouraged, empirical evidence reinforced: An upsurge in crime in the 1780s suggested that savage punishments were ineffective deterrents. "Sheriffs began refusing to cut off the limbs of criminals and to draw and quarter the bodies of those hanged." The American intelligentsia, influenced by Lockean epistemology, began to wonder: If the mind takes its impressions from data supplied by the senses, might it also be the case that the sources of criminal behavior are also located, at least in part, in the promptings from the social environment? If so, society must entertain the thought that criminals might be only partially responsible for their behavior. So a New Hampshire minister could say in 1796: "We all must plead guilty before the bar of conscience as having had some share in corrupting the morals of the community, and leveling the highway to the gallows."[48]

When in a 1958 case Chief Justice Earl Warren said that the Eighth Amendment "must draw its meaning from the evolving standards of decency that mark the progress of a maturing society," he referred to a fact: Standards of decency do evolve. Which is not to say that they invariably become better; "evolving" is not a synonym for "improving."[49] Still, it would be peculiar to insist that a conscientious originalist in the twenty-first century must construe the Eighth Amendment's proscription of "cruel" punishments with reference to the eighteenth century's public understanding of cruelty. Surely an originalist analysis should say: The Eighth Amendment's *meaning* is that the Framers *intended* a society in which government would not practice cruelty, and it falls to every generation to guarantee that its practices conform to this original intent.

Here there is something useful to be gleaned from an unlikely source. Linguistic philosophy, the high tide of which coincided with this author's two years at Oxford, was often arid, and sterile regarding social and political questions. It had and has, however, something to say about today's skirmishing on the contested ground concerning originalism, textualism, and other rivalrous schools of thought about how the Constitution should be construed. A leading practitioner of linguistic philosophy, Oxford's J. L. Austin, stressed the concept of "speech acts" and argued that any speech act—including, of course, written speech—is part of a performative activity: It involves persuading, promising, requesting, warning, exhorting, and so on.[50] The *meaning* of a speech act depends on the speaker's *intention*, and on the nature of the audience with which the speaker is communicating. The relevance of this to constitutional reasoning is this: It is fallacious to think that the meaning of the document's text can be understood without examining the intentions of its authors. Some will say: Such an examination is difficult and problematic because it must descend into speculations. To which the proper rejoinder is: We have no choice because meaning and intention are braided.

Three things follow from this. One is that Aristotle's advice in the *Nicomachean Ethics* is particularly pertinent to construing the Constitution. He said that "precision is not to be sought for alike in all discussions, any more than in all the products of the crafts." And: "It is the mark of an educated man to look for precision in each class of things just so far as the nature of the subject admits."[51] The second implication of the inseparability of meaning and intention is the importance of the fact that the intention of the Constitution's Framers was to give institutional life to the premises and purposes of the Declaration of Independence. The third is that there is wisdom in Jack Balkin's idea of "living originalism," which is not, as some allege, an oxymoron.

Balkin calls for fidelity to the original meaning of the Constitution's text as this meaning is derived with reference to the rules, standards, and principles explicitly or implicitly in the text. The Constitution, he says, is basically "a plan for politics." Its practical initial purpose was to ignite American politics. Its long-term purpose was, and remains, to make politics safe, meaning not dangerous to liberty. Balkin does not recommend just this or that doctrine of constitutional construction. Rather, he recommends "using all of the various modalities of interpretation: arguments from history, structure, ethos, consequences, and precedent." Advocates of "originalism"—adhering to the original public meaning of the words of the text—should not simply favor what Balkin terms "the original expected application" of the text. Rather, they should discern and apply the Framers' original *intent* to contemporary circumstances. Balkin terms this idea "living originalism": "In every generation, We the People of the United States make the Constitution our own by calling upon its text and its principles and arguing about what they mean in our own time." It took time, meaning historical learning, for the nation to come, a century after ratification of the Fourteenth Amendment's affirmation of equal national citizenship, to the conclusion that this required equal rights for women. The flawed doctrine of "original expected applications" could not countenance this just outcome. The fact that the Framers adopted "general and abstract" concepts meant that subsequent generations would have no alternative to working out the scope and application of the abstractions to changing concrete circumstances. Hence, as Balkin says, the Constitution commits the country to "the tradition of continuous arguments."[52]

This guarantees the perpetual frustration of all those who hanker for a theory of constitutional construction that will deliver the serenity of finality. It also consigns all generations to endless arguing. The fact that ratification of the Constitution meant a contentious American future was, Balkin notes, immediately demonstrated by the heated argument that erupted—and provoked the emergence of political parties, which the Framers neither desired nor anticipated— about whether the Constitution's enumeration of Congress' powers authorized Congress to charter a national bank. In this argument, Alexander Hamilton and James Madison, who wrote eighty of the eighty-five Federalist Papers, were at daggers drawn. Americans who find perpetual arguing stressful or otherwise unsatisfying should consider finding another country. It is not quite right to say, as Justice Antonin Scalia did, that the Constitution's "whole purpose is to prevent change—to embed certain rights in such a manner that future generations cannot readily take them away."[53] Rather, the government's Madisonian architecture was designed to refine and elevate opinion so that future generations would not want to take away important rights. The desires that majorities have over time are probably going to be satisfied, so attention must be paid to the shaping and moderating of desires.

And sometimes majorities must be disregarded. Professor Alexander Bickel of the Yale Law School, who was a clerk for Justice Felix Frankfurter when the court was considering the *Brown* school desegregation case, later said that examination of the legislative process that produced the Fourteenth Amendment "easily leads" to the "obvious conclusion" that the amendment "as originally understood, was meant to apply neither to jury service, nor suffrage, nor anti-miscegenation statutes, nor [school] segregation." But Michael W. McConnell, former judge on the US Court of Appeals for the Tenth Circuit and currently professor at Stanford Law School, has made an especially sinewy argument for the proposition that the *Brown* decision was not merely compatible with, but was entailed by, the Fourteenth Amendment. McConnell undertakes to do what the Warren court "made no pretense" of doing, to demonstrate that *Brown* "was an authentic translation of what the Fourteenth Amendment meant to those who drafted and ratified it."[54] He acknowledges that "school desegregation was deeply unpopular among whites, in both North and South, and school segregation was very commonly practiced." And he concedes that "constitutional amendments generally reflect, rather than contradict, popular opinion." He, however, martials powerful evidence that the congressional authors who passed, and the state legislators who ratified, the amendment were acting in the immediate aftermath of the Civil War carnage and that a majority of them "considered entrenchment of their principles more important than pleasing constituents."[55]

So let us stipulate that learned people of goodwill can disagree about this. And let us try a thought experiment: Suppose Bickel was correct and McConnell was mistaken. Does this mean that in 1954 there was no way to responsibly find in the Constitution's text a legal (as distinct from policy) reason for finding school segregation unconstitutional? No, it means only this: Although originalism, as McConnell and most other self-described originalists practice it, is a useful and disciplining starting point when construing the Constitution, it is insufficient.

Many critics, representing many schools of thought about how the Constitution should be construed, conclude that the reasoning of *Brown* is weak and strained, which it is, and therefore that the result is dubious. This is, however, operating backward. At the risk of seeming cavalier, herewith a modest proposal: The threshold question when evaluating any particular mode of construing the Constitution is whether the mode would dictate declaring public school segregation unconstitutional. No acceptable theory for construing the Constitution can invalidate the court's *conclusion* in *Brown*; the conclusion invalidates any theory that rejects it. If a theory of constitutional interpretation cannot find in the document's text, when the text is construed to serve the document's purpose of framing a government that secures natural rights, grounds for striking down racial segregation in schools, a practice facially inimical to equal enjoyment of the blessings of liberty, then this theory must be discarded. The phrase "the blessings of liberty" is of course from the Constitution's Preamble. But the Preamble is not a mere decorative filigree on the Constitution. It is a statement of the objectives of all that follows.

What follows the Preamble, the Constitution, "read as a whole," requires acknowledging various values that are of equal constitutional dignity. Let former Supreme Court Justice David Souter explain this. In his 2010 commencement speech at Harvard, a year after retiring from the court, Souter offered a lucid and subtle argument for distinguishing in constitutional law between judicial activism and the activity of judging. He did so by demonstrating that construing the Constitution is rarely merely a matter of a "fair reading" of the document's text with reference to simple facts.[56]

To see what constitutional reasoning rarely is, Souter said, suppose one of the twenty-one-year-old graduates in his Harvard audience were to claim a place on the ballot for a US Senate seat being contested that year. The claim could be easily disposed of by confirming the claimant's age, noting the constitutional provision that a senator must be at least thirty years old, and interpreting this as disqualifying from ballot access someone who, if elected, would not be qualified to serve. Although the Constitution's provision stipulating the age requirement for senators says nothing about ballot access, no one would charge that the ruling involved judicial lawmaking.[57]

Of course a case such as this would not get to the Supreme Court precisely because it does not involve what Souter called the

Constitution's "good share" of "deliberately open-ended guarantees," such as the rights to due process of law, equal protection of the law, and freedom from unreasonable searches. Such provisions, Souter said, are unlike the age requirement for senators in that "they call for more elaborate reasoning to show why very general language applies in some specific cases but not in others, and over time the various examples turn into rules that the Constitution does not mention." These are judge-made rules but, Souter argues, rules that judges cannot help but make. They "turn into" rules over time, by the process of coping with cases. This slow creation of rules comes about for three reasons. First, the Constitution must have a lot of general language "in order to be useful over long stretches of time." Second, the Constitution "contains values that may well exist in tension with each other, not in harmony." The third and most complex reason is that the facts that determine whether a constitutional provision is pertinent may be quite unlike facts like a person's age. What Souter called "constitutional facts" often will require judges to decide "the meaning that the facts may bear." He illustrated this with reference to two cases, one from 1971, the other from 1954.[58]

The 1971 "Pentagon Papers" case illustrates, Souter said, that the Constitution is not a "simple contract" because "its language grants and guarantees many good things" that "compete with each other and can never all be realized, all together, all at once." With the Vietnam War raging and passions at a boil in the summer of 1971, the *New York Times* and the *Washington Post* obtained classified documents—the Pentagon Papers—prepared by government officials and pertaining to the past conduct of the war. The government sought a court order to prevent the newspapers from publishing the documents. The government made what Souter called "the most extreme claim known to the constitutional doctrines of freedom to speak and publish." It claimed the power to exercise "prior restraint"—the power not merely to punish unauthorized publication but to prevent publication. At issue were fourteen words of the First Amendment:

"Congress shall make no law…abridging the freedom of speech, or of the press." Representing the government was Solicitor General Erwin Griswold, who had been dean of Harvard Law School for twenty-one years. During oral argument in the Supreme Court, Griswold's most interesting interlocutor was Justice Hugo Black, who was not unreasonably called a "First Amendment absolutist." He believed that the amendment's words should be read literally: There can be no legitimate abridgement of the freedom of speech or press. "And in fairness to him," Souter said, "one must say that on their face the First Amendment clauses seem as clear as the requirement for 30-year old senators, and that no guarantee of the Bill of Rights is more absolute in form." But, Souter said, when construing the Constitution, its words are frequently freighted with meaning and importance that is not "on their face."[59]

Black told Griswold that permitting prior restraint of publication would make judges into censors. Griswold argued that publication of the purloined documents would threaten lives, jeopardize attempts to end the war through diplomacy, and complicate future attempts of the government to negotiate with foreign governments that would question America's ability to keep secrets. He said that there was no alternative to prior restraint. When Black said the First Amendment was the alternative, Griswold replied: "The problem in this case is the construction of the First Amendment. Now Mr. Justice, your construction of that is well-known, and I certainly respect it. You say that no law means no law, and that should be obvious. I can only say, Mr. Justice, that to me it is equally obvious that 'no law' does not mean 'no law,' and I would seek to persuade the Court that that is true. As Chief Justice Marshall said, so long ago, it is a Constitution we are interpreting."[60] A Constitution. All of it.

Souter correctly told his Harvard audience that although the government lost the case, and the Pentagon Papers were published, Griswold won his argument with Black. Griswold won because in its ruling the court took his point—and Marshall's—that when construing a portion of the Constitution, the totality of the Constitution can come into play and must be considered. Souter said that in addition to guaranteeing freedom of speech and the press against government abridgements, the Constitution also grants to the government authority and responsibility, *and hence the appropriate power*, to provide for the nation's security and to enable the president to conduct foreign policy and command the military. In its decision, the court did not say that the words "no law" allowed no exceptions. Rather, the court recognized that *in some circumstances* the exigencies of governing, such as those to which Griswold referred, could justify prior restraint. But the court held that the government had not performed the daunting task of demonstrating that the facts *in this case* justified prior restraint. As examples of such potential facts, members of the court mentioned prior restraint to prevent something like publication of the details of the D-Day invasion plans, or to block publication of something that might provoke a nuclear holocaust.

Souter stressed that even a constitutional provision as facially absolute as the First Amendment—"a right as paramount as any fundamental right can be"—still "does not quite get to the point of an absolute guarantee." This is so because "the Constitution has to be read as a whole, and when it is, other values crop up in potential conflict with an unfettered right to publish." The Constitution's most explicit terms "can create a conflict of approved values" and those terms "do not resolve that conflict when it arises." Judges do, by the activity of *judging*. Which means by choosing: "The guarantee of the right to publish is unconditional in its terms, and in its terms the power of the government to govern is plenary."[61]

The problem in this case did not arise from any vagueness of constitutional language. The problem, Souter said, arose from the fact that the Constitution embodies the desire of the American people to have two excellent things, security and liberty, that are not always clearly and cleanly compatible. These "paired desires," as Souter called them, can, and in this case did, clash. The court had to decide which desire had "the better claim, right here, right now." Why must *judges*—appointed and accountable to no constituency—do this? Who else could? Souter noted that choices like the one the court made in this case "make up much of what we call law." Does this mean that we have "judge-made law" and that judges are legislating? Not really, because the judges were largely confined and controlled, as legislators rarely if ever are, by their necessary focus on the Constitution's text, which severely circumscribes their deliberations. Souter concluded this example by asking: "Can it be an act beyond the judicial power when a choice must be made and the Constitution has not made it in advance in so many words? You know my answer. So much for the notion that all of constitutional law lies there in the Constitution waiting for a judge to read it fairly."[62]

The Pentagon Papers case illustrates what Souter called "the tensions within constitutional law." The second case he considered illustrates what he calls "the subtlety of constitutional facts."[63]

In 1954, in *Brown v. Board of Education of Topeka*, the Supreme Court held, unanimously, that racial segregation imposed by law on public schools violated the Constitution's guarantee of equal protection of the law. The *Brown* decision began the painfully protracted process of ending the doctrine that "separate but equal" provisions for the races could pass constitutional muster, a doctrine codified in 1896 in *Plessy v. Ferguson*, wherein the court found no violation in requiring the races to travel in separate but equal railroad cars.

In *Plessy*, the court heard and rejected the argument that placing blacks in separate cars carried a stigma of inferiority. The court said that the law was on its face race-neutral, so if blacks felt that it imposed a badge of inferiority, that was simply a result of their thinking and not constitutionally germane. So separate but equal facilities did not violate the guarantee of equal protection of the laws. Fifty-eight years later, the court found that separate facilities in primary and secondary education, even if truly equal facilities (which they never were), violate that guarantee. This, said Souter, must have seemed mystifying, or an act of raw judicial willfulness, to people who think that constitutional judging merely involves "fair reading of [constitutional] language applied to facts objectively viewed."[64] The constitutional language did not change between 1896 and 1954. What did? Souter said it was something to do with those two dates.

Members of the 1896 court remembered when slavery was established by law in many states. To those justices' generation, Souter said, "the formal equality of an identical railroad car meant progress." The justices sitting in 1954, however, "looked at enforced separation without the revolting background of slavery to make it look unexceptional by contrast." The consequence was that the 1954 court "found a meaning in segregating the races" that the *Plessy* majority did not: "That meaning is not captured by descriptions of physically identical schools or physically identical railroad cars. The meaning of facts arises elsewhere, and its judicial perception turns on the experience of the judges, and on their ability to think from a point of view different from their own. Meaning comes from the capacity to see what is not in some simple, objective sense there on the printed page. And when the judges in 1954 read the record of enforced segregation it carried only one possible meaning: It expressed a judgment of inherent inferiority on the part of the minority race."[65]

The judges in *Brown* stated a conclusion not written in the Constitution. But that fact does not entail the conclusion that they must have, in Souter's words, crossed "some limit of legitimacy" and entered into "law making." They were only guilty of impermissible "activism" if it really is the case that "the facts just lie there waiting for an objective judge to view them." But in constitutional adjudication, facts are not like that. "The Constitution," Souter said, "is a pantheon of values, and a lot of hard cases are hard because the Constitution gives no simple rule of decision for the cases in which one of the values is truly at odds with another." Judges must choose "not on the basis of measurement, but of meaning." The "tensions" that Souter said are "the stuff of judging in many hard constitutional cases" are "creatures of our aspirations," our conflicting aspirations that require "tenacity" if we are to "keep the constitutional promises the nation has made." The Constitution's Framers left such tensions "to be resolved another day; and another day after that, for our cases can give no answers that fit all conflicts, and no resolutions immune to rethinking when the significance of old facts may have changed in the changing world."[66]

There is, Souter said, an unavoidable, irreducible complexity to the Constitution and constitutional law, which means that the natural human hunger for simplicity and clarity is bound to be unsatisfied. "And who has not felt that same hunger? Is there any one of us who has not lived through moments, or years, of longing for a world without ambiguity, and for the stability of something unchangeable in human institutions? I don't forget my own longings for certainty, which heartily resisted the pronouncement of Justice Holmes, that certainty generally is illusion and repose is not our destiny."

THE SESQUICENTENNIAL REVOLUTION: 1937 AGAINST 1787

Liberty is commonly understood as the ability to do what you want to do. Virtue means choosing well what you want to do. The challenge for a free society is to preserve liberty while nurturing virtue. A religion tells its adherents things that they ought to do and ought not do. The US Constitution, which is replete with proscriptions, tells Americans a number of things they cannot do even if a majority of them wants them done. There is a recurring impulse to argue that courts should have a somewhat majoritarian mentality or that they should be directly subjected to majoritarian supervision. In his 1912 presidential campaign, Theodore Roosevelt argued that "when a judge decides a constitutional question, when he decides what the people as a whole can and cannot do, the people should have the right to recall the decision if they think it wrong."[67] In Hillary Clinton's 2016 presidential campaign she said, "The Supreme Court should represent all of us."[68] Actually, it should represent no one. Not if we understand representation to mean serving as a mirror to the public. "Reflecting" what, exactly? Or weighing "the people's" or a faction's "interests." Interests in what, exactly?

Abraham Lincoln spoke more judiciously about the sometimes ambiguous role of the Supreme Court in America's democracy. In his first inaugural address, he asserted that "the candid citizen must confess that if the policy of the Government upon vital questions affecting the whole people is to be irrevocably fixed by decisions of the Supreme Court...the people will have ceased to be their own rulers, having to that extent practically resigned their Government into the hands of that eminent tribunal."[69] This is true, but note the adverb "irrevocably." Lincoln understood as well as any politician before or since that in a democracy everything depends, ultimately, on public opinion, and public opinion is shiftable sand. The nation's preeminent tribunal can shift this sand; it did so in the twentieth century with its civil rights decisions, most notably with *Brown v. Board of Education*. This is judicial prudence as Alexander Bickel understood it. While Bickel believed the court should think of itself as a "pronouncer and guardian" of national principles, he thought judicial prudence required that such principles be clearly grounded in the nation's experience. Yet he also said, somewhat more permissively, that the court should "declare as law only such principles as will— in time, but in a rather immediate foreseeable future—gain general assent."[70] So the Court can affirm principles that are not yet generally assented to, but that the court calculates might become so, partly as a result of its affirmation of those principles, for better or for worse.

Worse arrived in 1937. In what has come to be known as "the constitutional revolution of 1937" the Supreme Court stepped out of the way of the New Deal's drive to expand the reach of federal power. The court essentially stopped enforcing limits to the Constitution's grant of power to Congress to "regulate commerce...among the several states." Almost any activity could be said to have "substantial effects" on interstate commerce, and so Congress could regulate almost any activity. This was, however, an invitation to, even an incitement to, constitutional sophistry. It threatened to rationalize the annihilation of the distinction between national and local problems, and between federal responsibilities and state and local responsibilities. Thus it went far toward making a mockery of the idea that the United States has a limited government, as Roscoe Filburn was to find out.

In 1941, Filburn was an Ohioan caught in the toils of federal agriculture policy. In 1933, Congress passed an anti-Depression measure called the Agricultural Adjustment Act, which sought to stabilize commodity prices by restricting production. In 1936—the last year of constitutional government, as some conservatives see it— the Supreme Court struck down that act on the ground that the federal government was prohibited from regulating production by the Tenth Amendment, which says: "The powers not delegated to the United States by the Constitution, nor prohibited by it to the states, are reserved to the states respectively, or to the people." And soon the court's composition changed. So there came to be another Agricultural Adjustment Act, which authorized the setting of production quotas not only for wheat sold into interstate commerce but also for wheat that was consumed on the farm as food, or as seed or feed for poultry and livestock. Filburn thought that this provision, as a putative exercise by the federal government of its power to regulate interstate commerce, was a travesty. So he produced 239 bushels of wheat in excess of his quota for use as chicken feed on his farm, and he refused to pay the stipulated penalty. The case reached the Supreme Court, which used it to further dismantle the constitutional doctrine (aka the Framers' intent) that the federal government is a government of limited and enumerated powers.[71]

The court upheld the act's provision, arguing that the cumulative effect of even minor and utterly local economic activities can have interstate consequences—rather like the butterfly in Brazil that by beating its wings has some indiscernible but supposedly real effect on

Boston's weather. The court said that even if wheat such as Filburn's 239 bushels never goes to market, "it supplies a need of the man who grew it which would otherwise be reflected by purchases in the open market. Home-grown wheat in this sense competes with wheat in commerce."[72] And if wheat prices rise, many farmers like Filburn might send their wheat grown for home use to market after all, upsetting the government's plans.

In 1995, however, there was a flicker of a pulse in the principle Filburn had tried to assert. The Supreme Court dusted off an idea that had not been in vogue since 1937, an idea that went out of fashion exactly 150 years after the Constitutional Convention of 1787 made it a bedrock principle of the Republic. The court reaffirmed the idea. "We start with first principles," said Chief Justice William Rehnquist, who enjoyed doing just that. "The Constitution creates a federal government of enumerated powers."[73] The case that occasioned Rehnquist's exercise in intellectual resurrection began in 1990 when Congress, seized by one of its frequent fits of grandstanding about crime, passed the Gun-Free School Zones Act, criminalizing possession of firearms in or near schools. Decreeing gun-free schools is a popular idea, which is why forty states already had such laws in 1995. Congress' largely redundant law was remarkable neither as a further step in its almost absentminded federalization of criminal law, nor as yet another careless assertion by Congress that there is no problem too local to be beyond its purview. Rather, Congress' 1990 law was remarkable because it aroused the slumbering court, provoking it to give a jerk on the leash that Congress was astonished to learn that it still wears.

In 1992 Alfonso Lopez, a San Antonio twelfth grader, was arrested under the Texas law banning guns in schools. Federal prosecutors elbowed aside Texas authorities, and Lopez responded with a question that seemed like a constitutional impertinence: Where does the federal government get the right to exercise what are essentially local police powers? The federal government gave the answer it had routinely, almost reflexively, given to many such questions since 1987: We get it from the commerce clause, so pipe down.

Chief Justice William Rehnquist spoke up for Lopez. Writing for the majority of a court divided 5–4, Rehnquist argued that a public school is not engaged in commerce, and possessing a gun is not an act of commerce, hence it is not an act that can have a "substantial effect" on commerce. In a muscular concurrence with Rehnquist's opinion, Justice Clarence Thomas minced no words: "Apart from its recent vintage and its corresponding lack of any grounding in the original understanding of the Constitution, the substantial effects test suffers from the further flaw that it appears to grant Congress a police power over the nation. When asked at oral argument if there were any limits to the Commerce Clause, the government was at a loss for words. Likewise, the principal dissent insists that there are limits, but it cannot muster even one example."[74]

The author of that dissent, Justice Stephen Breyer, essentially accepted the argument made by the government that schools can be considered to be engaged in commercial activities, and that therefore the possession of a gun by an individual near a school can be regulated by Congress because—take a deep breath—the gun might produce violence, which would affect the economy by spreading insurance costs throughout the population, and by reducing the willingness of individuals to travel, and by injuring the learning environment and thus resulting in a less productive citizenry. But as Rehnquist said, Breyer's rationale could classify child rearing as a commercial activity that Congress can regulate. Given Breyer's willingness to justify constitutional permissiveness because of the extended ripple effects that any activity can have on commerce, how could Breyer argue against a Commerce Clause rationalization for, say, a federal law requiring all students to eat their spinach and do their homework? Breyer said the court's opinion "threatens legal uncertainty" about Congress' reliance on the Commerce Clause as a justification for its activism.[75] The alternative, however, would allow Congress to be the arbiter of its own limits. Given Congress' promiscuous use of the Commerce Clause, there would then be no limits.

In 1937, under the pressure of public opinion and FDR's threat to "pack" the court by enlarging it, the court adjusted its jurisprudence to the dominant impulse of the 1930s here and abroad—the expansion of the state. "Beginning in 1937," writes historian William E. Leuchtenburg, "the Supreme Court upheld every New Deal statute that came before it" and "legitimated the arrival of the Leviathan State."[76] But sixty-three years after Filburn's defeat, and ten years after the San Antonio case, another case made it clear that the ruling regarding San Antonio was a false down, an evanescent moment of sound thinking.

Justice Clarence Thomas unfurled farmer Filburn's principles, again in a losing cause, again in a case involving a crop. It concerned two chronically ill Californians who grew their own marijuana to treat their pain. Medical marijuana was legal in California, but the federal government seized the two persons' six marijuana plants and charged the two with violating the federal Controlled Substances Act. The US Supreme Court deferred to the federal government, detonating a memorable Thomas dissent against this excessive deference. He said the Californians "use marijuana that has never been bought or sold, that has never crossed state lines, and that has had no demonstrable effect on the national market for marijuana. If Congress can regulate this under the Commerce Clause, then it can regulate virtually anything—and the Federal Government is no longer one of limited and enumerated powers." He added: "If the [Court's] majority is to be taken seriously, the Federal Government may now regulate quilting bees, clothes drives, and potluck suppers throughout the 50 states."[77] Indeed it can, and it was imprudent of Thomas to give the government these ideas. His fundamental point was, however, indisputable: Thanks to misguided judicial deference, for which conservatives bear considerable blame, and for as long as such deference persists, a limited federal government is a fiction.

In 1944, with the nation more at war abroad than ever before, and with the federal government permeating the nation's life more than ever before, Justice Felix Frankfurter, writing for the Court, recurred to Woodrow Wilson's theme of the effect of modern technology on federalism. Frankfurter insisted, "The interpenetrations of modern society have not wiped out state lines. It is not for us to make inroads upon our federal system, either by indifference to its maintenance or excessive regard for the unifying forces of modern technology. Scholastic reasoning may prove that no activity is isolated within the boundaries of a single State, but that cannot justify absorption of legislative power by the United States over every activity." Such reasoning might be, in Frankfurter's pejorative term, scholastic, and such "absorption" might be, as Frankfurter insisted, unjustified, but Frankfurter went immediately on to say that the court should do next to nothing about it. He said: "When the conduct of an enterprise affects commerce among the States is a matter of practical judgment.... The exercise of this practical judgment the Constitution entrusts primarily and very largely to the Congress, subject to the latter's control by the electorate."[78]

However, the lesson of 206 years of constitutional history is, alas, clear: If the federal government is to be limited, it will be limited not by congressional or presidential devotions to constitutional niceties, but only by properly engaged courts diligently construing the Constitution. Absent such judicial engagement, the Constitution will be merely a parchment barrier to enlargements of the federal government's sphere. Of course, limits on government must ultimately be grounded in the character of the people. But there can be this auxiliary precaution: a federal judiciary stocked with men and women committed to enforcing constitutional limits consonant with the Framers' intentions.

ABOUT MAJORITIES

Democracy and distrust usually are, and always should be, entwined. American constitutionalism, with its necessary component known as judicial review, amounts to institutionalized distrust. It is not true that, as Dr. Stockmann declares in Henrik Ibsen's *An Enemy of the People*, "the majority is always wrong." It is true, however, that the majority often is wrong and that the majority often has a right to work its mistaken will anyway. The challenge is to determine the borders of that right, and to have those borders policed by a non-majoritarian institution—the judiciary.

Alexander Hamilton said that because the judiciary "may truly be said to have neither force nor will, but merely judgment," it will always be the branch "least dangerous to the political rights of the Constitution."[79] But Alexander Bickel considered judicial review philosophically and morally problematic because it makes the Supreme Court a "deviant institution" in American democracy. The power to declare null and void laws enacted by elected representatives of the people poses what Bickel called the "counter-majoritarian difficulty."[80] This is, however, a grave difficulty only if the sole, or overriding, goal of the Constitution is simply to establish democracy, and if the distilled essence of democracy is that majorities shall rule in whatever sphere of life where majorities wish to rule. In which case the court is, indeed, a "deviant institution." But such a reductionist understanding of American constitutionalism is peculiar.

It is excessive to say, as often has been and still is said, that the Constitution is "undemocratic" or "anti-democratic" or "anti-majoritarian." It is, however, accurate to say that the Constitution regards majority rule as but one component of a system of liberty. The most important political office is filled not by simple majority rule expressed directly but by the Electoral College. Supreme Court justices and all other members of the federal judiciary are nominated by presidents but must be confirmed by the Senate, whose members were, under the unamended Constitution, elected indirectly, by state legislatures. Of the major institutions created by the Constitution—Congress, the presidency, the Supreme Court—only one half of one of them, the House of Representatives, was, in the Framers' original design, directly elected by the people. Furthermore, the Constitution has eleven supermajority provisions pertaining to amendments, ratification of treaties, impeachments, and other matters. All such supermajority requirements empower minorities.

One reason to empower minorities is that majority opinion often is not in any meaningful sense a judgment, meaning a conclusion arrived on the basis of information and reflection. The processes of democracy are supposed to refine and elevate public opinion, not merely reflect it. But woe betide the political candidate who suggests that the public's opinion needs to be refined and elevated, or even informed. When Supreme Court Justice Antonin Scalia died in February 2016, Senate Republicans argued that his successor should not be confirmed until "the people" had spoken in that year's presidential elections. It was, however, risible to assert that more than a negligible portion of the electorate had opinions about, say, constitutional originalism, or fidelity to stare decisis, or the proper scope of Congress' power to regulate interstate commerce. The problem is not that translating public opinion directly into public policy might be imprudent, although it certainly would be. Rather, the problem is that public opinion, in any meaningful sense, hardly exists about many, probably even most, public policies. Those whom Edmund Burke delicately called "the less inquiring" might be as large a portion of the population today as they were when Burke wrote in the late eighteenth century.[81] Then, very few could vote, so the many had small incentive to be inquiring about politics and government. Today, everyone can vote but no one can believe that his or her vote is apt to matter, and few have the time or incentive to become conversant with the complexities of the policies administered by the gargantuan and opaque administrative state. As Madison said in his analysis of ancient democracies, the larger the group engaged in determining the government's composition and behavior, the larger will be the portion who are "of limited information and of weak capacities."[82]

There are two reasons not to be greatly concerned about the counter-majoritarian difficulty. First, much of what majoritarian institutions do is done not to satisfy a demand or desire of a majority; the majority is completely oblivious of most of what today's government does. Most voters most of the time are ignorant—rationally so—of the government's processes and activities. The second reason to not lose sleep over the counter-majoritarian difficulty is that majority rule is not the point of the American project.

Sentimentalists about democracy generally insist that its defects result because voters' views are sensible but ignored. It is, however, at least as often the case that democracy produces unfortunate results because voters' views are foolish but honored. Often the problem is not that government is unresponsive but that it is too responsive. The political class is prudently reticent about the subject of the electorate's competence at rendering judgments, and democracies generate an ethos of contentment about their premises, so there rarely is heard a discouraging word about voters' political knowledge. It was, therefore, bracing, if naughty, for Winston Churchill to say—if he actually did so; sources differ—that "the best argument against democracy is a five-minute conversation with the average voter." Nevertheless, many voters' lack of information about politics and government is undeniable. And it raises awkward questions about concepts central to democratic theory, including consent, representation, public opinion, electoral mandates, and—this is perhaps the fundamental function of modern democracy—the ability of voters to hold elected officials accountable.

Ilya Somin of the libertarian Cato Institute argues that, in general, an individual's ignorance of public affairs is essentially rational because the likelihood of his or her vote being decisive in an election is vanishingly small. But if choosing to remain ignorant—to not invest the time and effort necessary to become knowledgeable—is rational individual behavior, this can and often does have destructive collective outcomes. The quantity of political ignorance matters because voting is not merely an act of individual choice. It also is the exercise of power over others. And "the reality that most voters are often ignorant of even very basic political information is one of the better-established findings of social science."[83]

In the Cold War year 1964, two years after the Cuban missile crisis, only 38 percent of Americans knew the Soviet Union was not a member of NATO. In 2003, about 70 percent were unaware of enactment of the prescription drug entitlement, then the largest welfare state expansion since Medicare arrived in 1965. In a 2006 Zogby poll, only 42 percent could name the three branches of the federal government. Such voters cannot hold officials responsible because they cannot know what the government is doing, or which parts of government are doing what. So political ignorance "is an obstacle to its own alleviation." Given that more than 20 percent of Americans (and Europeans) think the sun revolves around the Earth, it is unsurprising that only 30 percent can name their two senators, and even at the peak of a campaign a majority cannot name any congressional candidate in their district. According to a 2002 Columbia University study, 35 percent believed that Karl Marx's "From each according to his ability, to each according to his need" is in the US Constitution.[84]

Many people acquire political knowledge for the reason many people acquire sports knowledge—because it interests and entertains them, not because it will alter the outcome of any contest. And with "confirmation bias," many people seek political information in order to reinforce their pre-existing views. Committed partisans are generally the most knowledgeable voters, independents the least. And the more political knowledge people have, the more apt they are to discuss politics with people who agree with them. A normal citizen learns about the politics of the day in the same way that a child first learns a language—by a blend of observation and osmosis of the conversation of society going on around the child. The average American expends more time becoming informed about choosing a car or television than choosing a candidate. But, then, the consequences of the former choices are immediate and discernible; the consequences of choosing a candidate often are neither. "The single hardest thing for a practicing politician to understand," said an experienced and successful politician, Britain's Tony Blair, "is that most people, most of the time, don't give politics a first thought all day long. Or if they do, it is with a sigh."[85]

When this author's children were young in the mid-1980s and they would ask if they had my permission to do this or that, if my answer was "yes" I would say: "Go ahead, it's a free country—Mondale lost." I was being droll and no doubt unintelligible. The point I was trying and almost certainly failing to make was this: Ours is a constitutional republic, in which the basic elements of happiness and civic safety are not put at risk in routine elections. If former Vice President Walter Mondale had defeated Ronald Reagan in 1984, America would have remained as it was, a free country. The Will children were innocent of political knowledge. Their excuse was that they were children. Adults need a better excuse. Trying to ameliorate the problem of political ignorance by increasing voter knowledge is an unpromising undertaking. Demand for information, not the supply of it, is the major constraint on political knowledge. The arrival of broadcast television in the 1950s and 1960s did increase political knowledge among the segments of the population traditionally least informed. There is, however, evidence that cable television and the Internet may have produced, among those segments, a net subtraction from political knowledge by providing a rich menu of alternative distractions.[86]

New information technologies have served primarily to increase the knowledge of the already well-informed. This is, on balance, good, but it also increases the ability of some to engage in "rent-seeking" from the regulatory state, manipulating its power to transfer wealth to themselves. So political knowledge, which often is a function of social and educational inequality, exacerbates inequality. And if political knowledge is measured relative to government's expanding scope, ignorance is increasing rapidly: There is so much more about which to be uninformed. A better ameliorative strategy would be to reduce the risks of ignorance by reducing government's consequences—its size, complexity, and intrusiveness. Somin correctly notes that in the nineteenth century, voters' information burdens were much lighter because important federal issues—expansion of slavery, disposition of public lands, tariffs, banking, infrastructure investments—were much fewer.

Today, political ignorance strengthens the case for judicial power by weakening the supposed "counter-majoritarian difficulty" with judicial review. If much of the electorate is unaware of the substance or even existence of policies adopted by the sprawling regulatory state, the policies' democratic pedigrees are weak. Hence Somin's suggestion that the extension of government's reach "undercuts democracy more than it furthers it."[87] If an engaged judiciary would enforce anything like the Framers' idea of government's "few and defined" powers, more decisions would be made not by government but by markets and institutions of civil society. This would make the phrase "the will of the people" more meaningful regarding government actions because a less activist government would reduce the voters' knowledge burdens. In any case, facing the facts about the public's political knowledge usefully dilutes the sentimentality and romanticism about democracy that encourage government's pretensions and ambitions. And failures.

IS AMERICAN POLITICS ABOUT A CONDITION OR A PROCESS?

Americans frequently "pledge allegiance to the flag of the United States of America and to the Republic for which it stands." But what does the Republic stand for? Simply for, as Oliver Wendell Holmes thought, the right of "the dominant forces of the community" to dominate:[88] This is what one should expect from a jurist who delighted in saying such startling things as "Our tastes are finalities." And that ethical judgments are "more or less arbitrary.... Do you like sugar in your coffee or don't you?" And: "When men differ in taste"— that word again—"as to the kind of world they want the only thing to do is to go to work killing." And: "Deep-seated preferences cannot be argued about—you cannot argue a man into liking a glass of beer— and therefore, when differences are sufficiently far reaching, we try to kill the other man." Holmes, a full-throated majoritarian, was the linear intellectual descendent of Hobbes: "Good and evil are names that signify our appetites and aversions."[89] Hence Holmes' reduction of American political philosophy to mere majoritarianism: There is no possibility of objective evaluation by standards of reasonableness, so force must prevail, even if in the civility of democracy that means the power of the most numerous faction to have its way.

Because there is more to American political morality than sweeping aside impediments to unmediated majorities, courts matter in America more than in any other democracy. Unlike Britain's constitutional documents, which are political documents that it is Parliament's prerogative to construe, the US Constitution is a legal document construed by courts, not Congress. Whenever judicial supervision of our democracy seems tiresome, consider the alternatives. Who wants Congress exercising the final power to construe the Constitution that allocates enumerated powers to Congress? Worse still would be presidents being dispositive when they construe their explicit and, much more important, their implicit powers. The purpose served by the Constitution's allocation of powers is the protection of liberty. The allocation serves to protect the citizens from one another as they join in rivalrous factions and to protect citizens, by means of regular elections, from the government.

By including in the Constitution a provision for amending it, the Founders acknowledged that their handiwork might have been less than perfect as it emerged from the 1787 Convention, and that changes might be necessary to respond to unanticipated future exigencies. But the Founders also made the amendment process difficult. Only six proposed amendments have been sent by Congress to the states for ratification and then failed to achieve ratification. This is because the requirement of a congressional supermajority for proposed amendments is a high hurdle. Although constitutions are adopted in order to enable orderly social change, their primary purpose is to conserve what should not be changed, at least not quickly and easily. The primary purpose of the Constitution is also the primary purpose of American conservatism, conserving the principles of the Founding.

It is elementary that a majority can and will do some things that are unjust but legitimate in that they are done in accordance with the constitutional rules of the political game. It also is elementary that not all injustices are created equal, and those that violate important rights must, for that reason, be declared illegitimate. Declared by whom? By the non-majoritarian portion of government, the judiciary. Because America's judiciary is part of the fabric of popular government, the prudence appropriate for the judiciary may make it, in varying degrees, reluctant to provide aggrieved factions with a path around the political process. The judiciary's prudent hope often is that its reluctance will compel the aggrieved to attempt a majoritarian remedy—persuasion—for majoritarian mistakes. But this prudence must be limited by this principle: Rights should not be secure only for persuasive people.

The argument against the supervision of democracy by an engaged judiciary is that elections produce tolerably good government, and that when they produce deplorable government this is appropriate and instructive punishment for the electorate. Elections are, after all, not the only way to perform the necessary function of filling public offices. Selection by lot would suffice, if all that mattered was filling the offices. But as Harvey Mansfield has said, "an election as opposed to selection by lot is an essentially aristocratic device (because it presupposes that some people are better than others—a point to be learned from Aristotle)."[90] Hence it was reasonable for the most democratic of the Founders, Jefferson, to speak without a trace of irony or paradox about a "natural aristocracy" that is to be discovered and elevated by elections. Readers can judge for themselves how this is working in contemporary America, which has a population more than sixty-two times larger than the 5.3 million when, in 1801, after Jefferson and Aaron Burr received the same number of electoral votes, Jefferson was elevated to the presidency by the House of Representatives.

Is the natural aristocracy that is wielding Article I and Article II powers nowadays a sufficient protection of liberty and the rights of minorities? If not, it is time to remember Justice Robert Jackson's admonition that an "achieved liberty" is an illusion.[91] Liberties must be defended as they are exercised; indeed, exercising them *is* the defense of them. The regulatory itch of the administrative state, combined with the pandemic rent-seeking that the incessant interventions by this state in economic life invites, guarantees that liberties are always in danger of being nibbled away. The executive branch is the motor of the administrative state. The legislative branch can barely supervise an executive branch that has grown gargantuan with the legislative branch's complicity and because of the legislative branch's lassitude. So it falls to judicial supervision of democracy to help preserve the institutional equilibrium.

Robert Bork, before he was a judge, and before the unsuccessful 1987 nomination of him by President Ronald Reagan to the Supreme Court provoked one of the most bitter confirmation fights in the history of the court, was Alexander Bickel's colleague on the Yale Law School faculty. Bickel, said Bork, "identified, and attempted to resolve, the central problem of constitutional law: Our political ethos is majoritarian, but the Supreme Court, with the power to strike down laws democratically enacted, is counter-majoritarian."[92] It is, however, unsatisfactory to say that constitutional law's central problem is, or even derives from, an "ethos." The central premise and purpose of America's collective existence is not simply that majorities shall rule. When the court strikes down a law because of its incompatibility with the Constitution, the court is not being counter-majoritarian. Rather, the court is preferring a previous and privileged majority, that of the generation that framed and ratified the Constitution, to a current and secondary one.

The Constitution was written by remarkable men who are deservedly revered. And they are long gone. They believed that their handiwork, in order to be legitimately binding, had to be ratified—consented to—by conventions composed of, and selected by, interested people. Those people, too, are long gone. So why does the Constitution continue to deserve our adherence? The answer points to the basic political question of our day and to an answer to that question. The question is: Is the Constitution's primary purpose the creation of a governmental architecture that ensures, as much as possible, the protection of natural rights? Or is its primary purpose merely the creation of a government that facilitates effective majority rule?

If majority rule is the goal to which other goals are subordinate, then the Constitution's legitimate claim to our deference would indeed seem to be based only on the continuing, year-by-year consent of the polity's ever-changing majority. But how is this consent registered? Is it to be inferred from the implied consent of the people who voluntarily continue to live under the Constitution? And from the fact that they participate in the political process that the Constitution structures? And that they register their serious discontents not in violent disruptions but through the Constitution's provision for amendments? However, tacit consent, inferred from behaviors rather than registered by explicit consent, necessarily becomes more attenuated as government becomes bigger, more active, more complex, and less transparent. As there is an ever-widening disparity between what the government does and what a majority of the people knows that the government is doing, "tacit consent" becomes diluted to the point of disappearance.

Suppose, however, that the protection of natural rights, not the guarantee of majority rule, is the function that confers continuing validity on the Constitution. If so, the Framers' purpose was not merely to facilitate the politics of popular sovereignty but rather to facilitate a certain purpose of politics, and hence a particular kind of politics. This purpose dictates the general content of politics, a politics of a limited government securing rights that are natural and hence exist prior to government.

Justice Antonin Scalia held that "[t]he whole theory of democracy…is that the majority rules; that is the whole theory of it. You protect minorities only because the majority determines that there are certain minority positions that deserve protection.…[Y]ou either agree with democratic theory or you do not. But you cannot have democratic theory and then say, but what about the minority? The minority loses, except to the extent that the majority, in its document of government, has agreed to accord the minority rights."[93] If, however that is the "whole theory" of democracy, then democratic theory is not very interesting. What is interesting is what begins after this theory is recognized as thin intellectual gruel. What should begin is reflection on the institutional and cultural measures necessary to increase the likelihood that majorities will be temperate and reasonable.

In a 2006 interview, Supreme Court Justice Stephen Breyer said the Constitution is "basically about" one word—"democracy."[94] That word, however, appears in neither that document nor the Declaration of Independence. Democracy is America's way of allocating political power. The Constitution was adopted to confine that power. It is supposed to confine it in order to "secure the blessings of" that which simultaneously justifies, and justifies limits on, democratic government: natural liberty. The fundamental division in American politics is between those who take their bearings from the individual's right to a capacious realm of freedom and those whose fundamental value is the right of the majority to have its way in making rules about which specified liberties shall be respected, and to what extent. For the many Americans who are puzzled and dismayed by the heatedness of political argument today, Timothy Sandefur has a message: The temperature of today's politics is commensurate with the stakes of today's argument.

Progressives, who consider democracy the *source* of liberty, reverse the Founders' premise, which was: Liberty pre-exists governments, which, the Declaration says, are legitimate when "instituted" to "secure" natural rights. Progressives consider, for example, the rights to property and free speech as, in Sandefur's formulation, "spaces of privacy" that government chooses "to carve out and protect" to the extent that these rights serve democracy.[95] Conservatives believe that liberty, understood as a general absence of interference, and individual rights, which cannot be exhaustively listed, are natural and that governmental restrictions on them must be as few as possible and rigorously justified. Invoking the right of a majority to have its way is an insufficient justification.

With the Declaration, Americans ceased claiming the rights of aggrieved Englishmen and began asserting rights that are universal because they are natural, meaning necessary for the flourishing of creatures with our natures. The perennial conflict in American politics, Sandefur says, concerns "which takes precedence: the individual's right to freedom, or the power of the majority to govern." The purpose of the post–Civil War's Fourteenth Amendment protection of Americans' "privileges or immunities"—protections that were almost entirely vitiated by an absurdly narrow Supreme Court reading of that clause in 1873—was to assert, on behalf of emancipated blacks, national rights of citizens. National citizenship grounded on natural rights would thwart Southern states that were then asserting their power to acknowledge only such rights as they chose to dispense. Government, the Framers said, is instituted to improve upon the state of nature, in which the individual is at the mercy of the strong. But when democracy, meaning the process of majority rule, is the supreme value—when it is elevated to the status of what the Constitution is "basically about"—the individual is again at the mercy of the strong: the strength of mere numbers. Sandefur says progressivism "inverts America's constitutional foundations" by holding that the Constitution is "about" democracy, which rejects the Framers' premise that majority rule is legitimate "only within the boundaries" of the individual's natural rights. These include—indeed, these are mostly— unenumerated rights whose existence and importance are affirmed by the Ninth Amendment. Some conservatives will be discomfited by Sandefur's analysis, which entails this conclusion: Conservatives' indiscriminate denunciations of "judicial activism" serve progressivism.[96] The protection of rights, those constitutionally enumerated and others, requires a judiciary actively engaged in enforcing what the Constitution actually is "basically about," which is compelling majority power to respect individuals' rights.

In a book published in 2010, during his seventeenth year on the Supreme Court, Justice Breyer asked, "Why would people want to live under the 'dead hand' of an eighteenth-century constitution that preserved not enduring values but specific eighteenth-century thoughts about how those values then applied?"[97] Why, indeed, if the Constitution is connected to no "enduring values"? And how could it be connected, if there are no enduring values in a world in which the only constant is the perpetual emergence of new "values"? A world in which the past is always a "dead hand." One does, however, wonder what Breyer thinks his job is, given that he thinks that construing the Constitution consists in applying, or perhaps just pretending to apply, eighteenth-century "thoughts" in a twenty-first century that has its own "thoughts." It is, surely, momentous that a member of the Supreme Court assumes that the American people do not want to live under the Constitution. Anyway, all laws are impositions of "dead hands" upon the present because all laws are supposed to continue in force beyond the instant of enactment. This is especially true of constitutions, which are, purposefully, candidly instruments of "dead hands" in that they are laws about how subsequent and lesser laws are to be made and applied. In 2010, Judge Don Willett of the Texas Supreme Court cogently addressed, and largely dissolved, the supposed "dead hand" and counter-majoritarian difficulties.[98]

There are, he said, two different, but not equal, majorities involved. He began, as judicial review began, with *Marbury v. Madison*, in which Chief Justice John Marshall wrote: "The powers of the legislature are defined and limited; and that those limits may not be mistaken or forgotten, the Constitution is written."[99] In distinguishing between proper judicial deference to legislative majorities and the dereliction of the judicial duty to police the excesses of majorities, Willett said: In our democracy, the legislature's policymaking power "though unrivaled, is not unlimited." The Constitution is supreme. When a legislature says a certain law is desirable, "desirable" is not a synonym for "constitutional." Although "the political branches decide if laws pass," it is for courts to decide "if laws pass muster." So, "if judicial review means anything, it is that judicial restraint does not allow everything." To avoid a "constitutional tipping point" where "adjudication more resembles abdication," courts must not "extinguish constitutional liberties with nonchalance." This requires fidelity to the supermajority against which other majorities must be measured. "There must remain judicially enforceable constraints on legislative actions that are irreconcilable with constitutional commands."[100]

But why "must"? Because, Willett said, the Texas Constitution, like the US Constitution, is "irrefutably framed in proscription." It "declares an emphatic 'no' to myriad government undertakings," even if majorities desire them. Judicial review means preventing any contemporary majority from overturning yesterday's supermajority, the one that ratified the Constitution. Federal judges are accountable to no *current* constituency. But when construing the Constitution, they are duty-bound to be faithful to the constituency of those who framed and ratified it. This, Willett said, is the "profound difference between an activist judge and an *engaged* judge."[101] The former creates rights that are neither specified in nor implied by the Constitution. The latter defends rights the Framers actually placed there—and the unenumerated rights they acknowledged—and prevents the elected branches from usurping the judiciary's duty to declare what the Constitution means.

THE "RATIONAL BASIS" OF IRRATIONAL DEFERENCE

Madison was uncharacteristically too sanguine when he said in Federalist 51 that majorities will seldom form in an extended republic except on the basis of "justice and the general good."[102] What he did not anticipate, and could not have anticipated, was this phenomenon: As government has grown bigger in size, scope, and pretensions, it has become more attentive to small factions that do not claim to represent the will of the majority. The most that each faction claims is that a majority would favor what the faction favors if the majority were thinking clearly. Or that it knows better what is best for the majority. Or that it does not give a tinker's damn what other factions think. The main problem of contemporary American democracy is not that majorities cause the government to make unwise or unjust decisions. Rather, the problem is that so much of what modern government does pertains hardly at all to any majorities.

The Constitution creates institutions for the conduct of government business. It does not articulate principles about the proper goals of government. It does, however, intimate the broad contours of a general philosophy of government, with clear and powerful implications for government's purposes. The Constitution does this with the separation of powers, one implication of which is that governmental efficiency, understood as nimbleness in acting with dispatch, is less important than, and in tension with, the need for mechanisms that slow, and perhaps block more government action, thereby encouraging deliberation, compromise, and limitations. Also, the Constitution's Madisonian tapestry of separated powers, checks and balances, federalism, and guarantees of individual rights attests to what Professor Richard Epstein calls a "presumption of error."[103] The tapestry is designed to slow the political process because all government interventions in the processes of society's spontaneous order are presumptively of dubious legitimacy. This is so because the government is presumed to not be a disinterested umpire but rather to be responsive to factional interests. This is now more frequently true than ever, and it is certain to become even more often true as government becomes bigger, more intrusive, and more opaque.

This idea is anathema to those—today, probably an American majority—who believe that majority rule is the sovereign value that trumps all others. They believe that the degree of America's goodness is defined by the extent to which majorities are able to have their way. Such people are bound to believe that it is the job of the judicial branch to facilitate this by adopting a modest, deferential stance regarding what legislatures do. And regarding what executive branch officials and agencies do. Here, judicial deference is said to be dictated by the plebiscitary nature of the modern presidency: Because presidents alone are elected by a national constituency, they are unique embodiments of the national will, and hence should enjoy the maximum feasible untrammeled latitude to translate that will into policies.

The three-fold problem is that majorities can be abusive. And that some questions are not properly submitted to disposition by majority rule because there are some—actually, there are many— closed questions even in an open society. And that many things that majoritarian institutions do have nothing to do with the desires of majorities. So, we must ask: How aberrant—how frequent—are abusive majorities? A related but different question is: How often do legislatures act on behalf of minority factions? My belief, based on almost half a century observing Washington, the beating heart of American governance, is this:

As government becomes bigger and more hyperactive, as the regulatory, administrative state becomes more promiscuously intrusive in the dynamics of society and the lives of individuals, a steadily shrinking portion of what the government does is even remotely responsive to the will of a majority. Rather, the more that government decides that there are no legal or practical limits to its proper scope and actual competence, the more time and energy it devotes to serving the interests of minority—often very small minority—factions. So, paradoxically, as government becomes bigger, its actions become smaller. As it becomes more grandiose in its pretensions, its preoccupations become more minute. Consider a few examples from government below the federal level.

Ali Bokhari emigrated from Pakistan in 2000, settled in Nashville, became a taxi driver, and got a very American idea: He started a business to serve an unmet need. He bought a black Lincoln Town Car and began offering cut-rate rides to and from the airport, around downtown, and in neighborhoods not well served by taxis. After one year he had twelve cars. Soon he had twenty, and fifteen independent contractors with their own cars, and a website and lots of customers. Unfortunately, he also had some powerful enemies. The cartel of taxi companies had not been able to raise their rates since Bokhari came to town. Those companies, in collaboration with limo companies that resented Bokhari's competition, got the city government's regulators to require him to raise his prices and imposed many crippling regulations.[104]

Sandy Meadows was an African-American widow in Baton Rouge. She had little education and no resources, other than her talent for making lovely flower arrangements, which a local grocery store hired her to do. Then Louisiana's Horticulture Commission—there is such a body, for rent-seeking reasons—pounced. It threatened to close the store in order to punish it for hiring an unlicensed flower arranger. Meadows tried but failed to get a license, which would have required her to take a written test and to make four arrangements in four hours. The adequacy of the arrangements would have been judged by licensed florists who were acting as gatekeepers to their own profession, restricting the entry into it of competitors. Meadows, denied re-entry into the profession from which the government had expelled her, died in poverty. But the people of Louisiana were protected by their government from the menace of unlicensed flower arrangers.[105]

Elsewhere in Louisiana, the monks of St. Joseph Abbey also attracted government's disapproving squint. In 2005, Hurricane Katrina damaged the trees that for many years the monks had harvested to finance their religious life. Seeking a new source of revenue, they decided to make and market the kind of simple wooden caskets in which the abbey has long buried its dead. The monks were unwittingly embarking on a career in crime. Louisiana has a State Board of Embalmers and Funeral Directors. Its supposed purpose when created in 1914 was to combat diseases. It has, however, long since succumbed to "regulatory capture": It has been taken over by the funeral industry that it ostensibly regulates. At the time the monks began making and selling caskets, nine of the board's ten members were funeral directors. One of their principal sources of income is selling caskets. In the 1960s, Louisiana made it a crime to sell "funeral merchandise" without a funeral director's license. To get one, the monks would have had to stop being monks. They would have had to earn thirty hours of college credits and spend a year as apprentices at a licensed funeral home to acquire skills they had no intention of using. And their abbey would have been required to become a "funeral establishment" with a parlor able to accommodate thirty mourners, and they would have had to install an embalming facility, even though they only wanted to make rectangular boxes, not handle cadavers. The law requiring all this rigmarole served no health or sanitary purpose: Louisiana does not stipulate casket standards or even require that burials be done in caskets. Furthermore, Louisianans can buy caskets from out of state—from, for example, Amazon, which of course sells everything. Obviously, the law was brought to bear against the monks to protect the funeral directors' casket-selling cartel.[106]

The government action used to prevent a Pakistani immigrant from entering into his chosen profession of operating a transportation company, and the government action that blocked an aspiring flower arranger from exercising her skill, and the government action that blocked the monks from supporting themselves by making and selling wooden boxes, and thousands of government actions like these, from coast to coast, should be, but usually are not, considered unconstitutional. They should have been struck down even though they issued from formally majoritarian processes—from elected officials or from regulatory agencies created by elected officials. They should have been struck down as violations of a natural right, the right that Lincoln understood as the right to free labor, the right that was, of course, at the core of the slavery crisis. It is the unenumerated, but surely implied, constitutional right to economic liberty. But laws abridging that right survive and proliferate because, since the New Deal, courts have largely stopped doing their duty to defend this economic liberty against its rent-seeking enemies.

In a sense, the problem began in Louisiana sixteen years before the monks' monastery was founded in 1889. It began across Lake Pontchartrain from the monastery, in New Orleans. That city had awarded some rent-seeking butchers a lucrative benefit. The city had made them into a cartel by requiring that all slaughtering be done in their slaughterhouses. Some of the excluded butchers went to court, all the way to the US Supreme Court, challenging this law. They lost when, in the 1873 Slaughterhouse Cases, the court, in a 5–4 decision, upheld the law that created the cartel. In doing so, the court effectively expunged a clause from the Fourteenth Amendment. The clause says: "No state shall make or enforce any law which shall abridge the privileges or immunities of citizens of the United States." The court construed the phrase "privileges or immunities" so narrowly that it disappeared from constitutional law. This was a tragic fate for a phrase that was intended as shorthand for the full panoply of rights of national citizenship.

Since the New Deal, courts have abandoned the protection of economic rights, including the fundamental right to earn a living without arbitrary and irrational government hindrances. Instead, courts have adopted the extremely permissive "rational basis" test for judging whether government actions are permissible. Courts almost invariably hold that if a government stipulates a reason— any reason—for a law or regulation that burdens economic activity, or even if the court itself can imagine a reason for the law or regulations, then the court should defer to the elected legislature, elected city council, or other majoritarian institution that produced the law or regulation. In 2004, the Tenth Circuit upheld an Oklahoma law requiring online casket retailers to have funeral licenses. To obtain such licenses, applicants are required to take several years of course work, serve a one-year apprenticeship, embalm twenty-five bodies, and take two exams. Upholding this travesty, the court wrote, with breezy complacency, that "while baseball may be the national pastime of the citizenry, dishing out special economic benefits to certain in-state industries remains the favored pastime of state and local governments."[107] The court did not say, but it might as well have said: Majority rule requires that courts only reluctantly and rarely engage in the judicial supervision of democracy, because majority rule is the value that trumps all others. There are, however, two things wrong with this formulation.

First, it is simpleminded to think that there is majority support for, or majority interest in, or even majority awareness of, even a tiny fraction of what governments do in "dishing out" advantages to economic factions. Does anyone really think that when the Nashville city government dispenses favors for the taxi and limo cartel, it is acting on the will of a majority of the city's residents? Can anyone actually believe that a majority of Louisianans or Oklahomans give a hoot about who arranges flowers or sells caskets?

The second and more fundamental fallacy behind a passive judiciary deferring to majoritarian institutions is this: We know, because he said so, clearly and often, that Lincoln took his political bearings from the Declaration of Independence. We know that Lincoln believed, because the Declaration says so, that governments are instituted to *secure* our natural rights, which pre-exist government and include the unenumerated ones affirmed in the Constitution's Ninth Amendment. Yet for many years and for several reasons, too many conservatives have unreflectively and imprudently celebrated "judicial restraint." The reasons for this include an understandable disapproval of some of the more freewheeling constitutional improvisations of the Warren court. There also is the conservatives' understandable belief that most judges are not conservative: The law schools that train future judges, and the law reviews that influence current judges, are, on balance, not balanced: They give short shrift to conservatism. It is, however, time for conservatives to rethink what they should believe about the role of courts in the American regime. Many conservatives favor judicial deference and restraint because they succumb to the populist temptation. Conservatives are hardly immune to the temptation to pander, to preach that majorities are presumptively virtuous, and that the things legislatures do are necessarily right because they reflect the will of "the people."

The progressive project, now entering its second century, has been to give majority rule priority over liberty when the two conflict, as they inevitably and frequently do. This reflects the progressive belief that rights are the result of government; they are "spaces of privacy" that government "has chosen to carve out and protect." The progressives' principle of judicial restraint, distilled to its majoritarian essence, is that an act of the government should be presumed constitutional and that the party disputing the act's constitutionality bears the heavy burden of demonstrating the act's unconstitutionality beyond a reasonable doubt. The contrary principle of judicial engagement is that the judiciary's principal duty is the defense of liberty, and that the government, when challenged, bears the burden of demonstrating that its action is in conformity with the Constitution's architecture, the purpose of which is to protect liberty.

Arguments about the judicial supervision of democracy at all levels of American governance are as old as the Republic. Lemuel Shaw, who served for three decades (1830–1860) as chief justice of the Massachusetts Supreme Judicial Court, provided the controlling definition of states' police power. It is "the power vested in the legislature by the constitution, to make…all manner of wholesome and reasonable laws…as they shall judge to be for the good and welfare of the commonwealth."[108] But who, if anyone, was to have the right to contest the supposed wholesomeness and reasonableness of laws? After the Civil War and the application of the Bill of Rights to the states, courts would have the duty to provide opportunities for plucky people eager to contest state laws that unreasonably advance unwholesome interests. In a June 1928 letter, Justice Louis Brandeis foreshadowed the court's path, a decade later, to footnote 4. The letter was to his friend Felix Frankfurter, who was then a professor at Harvard Law School and who would join the court in 1939, the year Brandeis retired. Brandeis wrote: "In favor of property, the Constitution is liberally construed—in favor of liberty, strictly."[109] By "liberally" Brandeis meant permissively regarding government's desires to regulate. By "strictly" he meant wary about government power. He was reading the Constitution to say that it was less "in favor of" property than it is of liberty.

There is, however, nothing in the document's text that mentions or even intimates such a distinction, let alone recommends or mandates it. Furthermore, there is an overwhelming abundance of evidence from the thinking of the nation's Founders and the Constitution's Framers that they would have found this distinction not just objectionable but unintelligible. They thought that individuals have property in—ownership of—themselves which is necessary for the pursuit of happiness. And they understood that ownership of property provides the individual with a zone of sovereignty in which the individual is at liberty to use his resources for the pursuit of happiness. Conservatism has no more urgent task than that of convincing the country that judicial deference often is dereliction of duty, and that an energetically engaged judiciary is necessary lest, in Justice Robert Jackson's words, "the lights go out."[110]

CHAPTER 5

POLITICAL ECONOMY

RESCUING THE GREAT ENRICHMENT
FROM THE FATAL CONCEIT

> The curious task of economics is to demonstrate
> to men how little they really know about what
> they imagine they can design.
> Friedrich Hayek[1]

Kaskaskia, a town on the Mississippi River, was the first capital of
Illinois territory until 1818, when Illinois became a state. The
capital was then moved about eighty miles northeast to Vandalia,
partly because this town was in one of the most sparsely settled parts
of the state. The purpose of the move was to encourage people to
move there. The act of making Vandalia the capital was what then was
called an "internal improvement"—a government investment to promote social mobility and economic growth. Such measures were
much on the mind of the twenty-five-year-old state legislator who
came to Vandalia from his home in Springfield in November 1834.

Abraham Lincoln, his best friend Joshua Speed later recalled, said
that his highest ambition at that time "was to become the DeWitt
Clinton of Illinois."[2] Clinton, the sixth governor of New York,
was the driving force behind the first great American infrastructure
project, perhaps the most consequential until the Interstate Highway
System—the Erie Canal. Clinton saw this project as a means of

preventing states in the West from detaching themselves from the Union. The canal would "bind the union together by indissoluble ties" because the people would be "habituated to frequent intercourse and beneficial inter-communication," and all Americans would be "bound together by the golden ties of commerce and the adamantine chains of interest."[3] The canal also, and inadvertently, helped to bring down the old order in Europe. By bringing cheap wheat from America's Great Plains, the canal struck at the roots of Europe's landed aristocracy. Daniel Patrick Moynihan, a New York chauvinist, delighted in saying that the canal did more than Europe's socialist movements did to upend Europe's class structure. Such are the unanticipated caroms of economic forces when they are allowed the freedom to flow.

Two weeks after arriving in Vandalia, Lincoln proposed that the state build a toll bridge across a creek in Sangamon County. Next, he proposed a road from the Indiana border to Peoria and then to the Mississippi River on the border with Missouri. In his first term he proposed seven other road bills, to be paid for by a 20 percent premium to the states from the sale of federal lands. His most grandiose idea was for a canal connecting Lake Michigan with the Mississippi, via the Illinois River. When money from the sale of 236,000 acres of public land was quickly exhausted, Lincoln doubled down, proposing that Illinois establish a state bank to finance such projects. So it is not surprising that, long before disunion became an existential threat to the republic, Henry Clay's proposed "American System" of internal improvements for unifying the nation's sections appealed to Lincoln. Clay created the Whig Party, with which Lincoln identified when running for re-election to the state legislature in 1836.

Clay came as a young man to a Washington where rain often made Pennsylvania Avenue impassable. It was a Washington where President Thomas Jefferson reluctantly agreed to sign the bill authorizing federal construction of roads, but admonished Congress that the Constitution should be amended to authorize such activities, lest the doctrine of "implied powers" become a large loophole and the Constitution itself become mostly a loophole. Clay quickly became what the country became and still is: Rhetorically he was a Jeffersonian; actually he was a Hamiltonian, asserting for the federal government implied powers sufficient for his "American System." That system involved enactment of tariffs, building or subsidizing roads, canals and railroads, and other elements of the infrastructure of a unified commercial nation with an energetic central government that would be, in Hamilton's words, "adequate to the exigencies of the Union."[4]

Establishing sound public finance was the first challenge of the new nation, which is why the Treasury Department had forty employees when the State Department had only five. The sale of government bonds to banks was crucial to expanding the money supply, which ignited commerce, which, in time, united the regions. America's march to true nationhood was halting, in part because of economic rivalries among the nation's regions. Even Chief Justice John Marshall, the supreme nationalizer, used "nation" gingerly: "America has chosen to be, in many respects, and to many purposes, a nation."[5] Early in the nineteenth century, during debates on the building of the National Road, Senator William Smith of—where else?—South Carolina objected to this "insidious word" which was, he said, inimical to "the origins and theory of our government" as a confederation of sovereign states.[6] It took roads—and canals, railroads, the postal service, and, especially and finally, the New Deal's redistribution of wealth toward the South—to provide the economic prerequisite of national unity.

Defending the "national idea" in 1830, Daniel Webster cited the Delaware breakwater, an artificial harbor the federal government was building near the mouth of Delaware Bay. He argued that none of the neighboring states would have built it because it was not for the sole benefit of any one of them, so only the federal government could do it. Historian James McPherson writes that prior to 1815 most roads were rutted paths impassable in wet weather. Commerce depended on sailing ships and riverboats, and the cost of moving goods thirty miles inland equaled the cost of moving them across the Atlantic. Transatlantic trade exceeded inland commerce, and economic growth barely exceeded population growth. Then, however, came all-weather macadamized roads, and the Erie Canal ignited emulative construction: By 1850 there were 3,700 miles of canals. Next, railroads freed commerce from frozen canals in winter, cut travel time from New York to Chicago from three weeks to two days, and cut the price of shipping a ton of wheat from Buffalo to New York from one hundred dollars to ten dollars. The difference between the wholesale price of pork in Cincinnati and New York plummeted from $9.53 to $1.18. Suddenly urban workers had more disposable income to spend on manufactured goods.[7]

A poetic episode in our national history occurred July 4, 1826. On that fiftieth anniversary of the Declaration of Independence, the author of that founding document, Thomas Jefferson, died, as did John Adams, who had done as much as anyone to produce the occasion for Jefferson's document. Three days later, in Quincy, Massachusetts, after attending Adams' funeral, some dignitaries were taken to see a prosaic force that would shape what the two Founders had helped to found. They saw a railroad, one of the nation's first, and not much of one. It was built to carry granite a few miles from Quincy to Boston for the Bunker Hill Monument. As a harbinger, however, it was huge. Railroads soon would have constitutional consequences, and not just because, in the coming war against Southern insurrection, they would help the army of the central government settle a constitutional argument about the primacy of that government. Railroads also had constitutional consequences because they influenced Americans' thinking about the nature of their regime. Railroads, and the industrialism of which they were emblematic, filled our "extensive Republic" with energy. Our big country acquired a big economy, and a bigger government than it was used to.

But is government as big as today's government required or prudent? Today, conservatism is asking whether a big government is merely a contingent, or a necessary, outcome in a big country with a big economy. That this country was to be big was never in doubt. In the Revolutionary era, Americans, most of whom lived on the continent's Atlantic fringe, audaciously called their legislature the Continental Congress. They knew where they were headed— to California. They would get there by many means, including railroads. To promote construction of these steel sinews of national strength, the central government lent its considerable weight. By 1908, eight decades after the deaths of Adams and Jefferson, a professor of political science marveled at what industrialism had wrought: "The copper threads of the telegraph run unbroken to every nook and corner of the great continent, like the nerves of a single body.... Railways lie in every valley and stretch across every plain.... Industrial organization knows nothing of state lines, and commerce sweeps from state to state." So wrote Princeton's Professor Woodrow Wilson, five years before becoming president of the United States.[8]

As early as the 1850s, the roar of steam-powered steel wheels clattering over steel rails had been the sound of American society, whose economy was preparing to settle what politics and legislatures could not settle. The supposedly prosaic matter of "internal improvements" was crucial to the improvement of the nation's inner, meaning moral, life, and to the showdown over slavery. Railroads carrying conscripts, who were carrying weapons mass-produced from interchangeable parts, would be the North's decisive riposte to the South's constitutional arguments in favor of a right to secede. Railroads, and the steel mills and coal mines and immigrant labor behind them, closed this question that had been resistant to compromises.

John Steele Gordon, a historian of America's enterprise culture, has noted that seven of America's ten largest fortunes in 2014 were made possible by the microprocessor that Intel first marketed in 1971. In the intervening years, even the Walton family fortune, estimated at $130 billion in 2018, depended on Walmart's worldwide system of precise inventory controls and logistics that would be impossible without the microprocessor. There is, however, nothing new about vast fortunes resulting from the socially beneficial, and largely egalitarian, effects of new technologies. Gordon notes that before James Watt's rotary steam engine, which was patented in 1781, "only human and animal muscles, water mills and windmills could supply power." After Watt, low-cost energy that had been stored in coal but had been essentially useless for commerce suddenly revolutionized manufacturing (the factory system) and transportation (railroads). The Vanderbilt, Harriman and other vast fortunes were made in railroading, which made a national market. This made possible economies of scale that greatly benefited the masses.[9]

Simon Winchester has described the remarkable extent to which the United States, with its "convoluted" pedigree, has become united through two and a half centuries of material achievements deliberately created to foster unity. Once the homogeneous nature of America's early Puritan settlements had been diluted, America "became too much of a mongrel nation" to enjoy simple organic unity. Because America lacked "the communal simplicities" of nations such as Japan or Norway, "man has had to do the hard work in bringing America together." Winchester, British by birth and American by choice, brings an immigrant's sensibility to the task of answering this question: "What factors have ensured that, say, a Chinese migrant in rain-swept Seattle can find himself locked in some near-mystical concord with a Sephardic Jewish woman in Manhattan or a Cherokee student in Minnesota or a Latina stallholder in a market in Albuquerque—all of them being able to enjoy the same rights and aspirations, encapsulated in their shared ability to declare so simply, I am an American?" Winchester's answer is this: In addition to "the adhesive nature of the ideas on which the nation was founded," unity has been a product of "the physiology and the physics of the country, the strands of connective tissue that have allowed it to achieve all it has." These include the innumerable visible, tangible connections of roads, canals, railways, telephone lines, power grids and now, Winchester notes, "by submerged rivers of electrons."[10]

It is altogether fitting that Lincoln, the man most responsible for using the adhesive idea of equality to preserve the union, was also, and first, a railroad lawyer who was an early and ardent advocate of a transcontinental railroad. Five years after the war that saved the Union, the railroad industry was the nation's second-largest employer, a breathtakingly rapid emergence. As Winchester writes: "When Tennessee's Andrew Jackson was elected president in 1828, he traveled to the White House in a horse-drawn carriage; when he stepped down from his second term, just eight years later, he left for home aboard a steam train. Less than twenty miles of track had existed in the country when he took office; there were nearly three thousand when he left." A poet rhapsodized that "gliding cars, like shooting meteors run/The mighty shuttle binds States in one." And almost half the financing of early railroads was by government, truly a program of nation-building. While Winchester is hardly an uncritical celebrant of big government, he correctly insists: "Without an engaged and functioning federal government, the development of these various strands of the country's connective tissue would probably have been either delayed or never achieved at all."[11]

Daniel Patrick Moynihan thought so, too. He said: Behold California's Imperial Valley, unchanged since "the receding of the Ice Age."[12] Only God can make an artichoke, but government—specifically, the Bureau of Reclamation—made the valley a cornucopia. The historical record is clear: Governments, federal and state, have long been involved in stimulating and steering economic growth. But this, too, is clear: America has been, from the first, primarily a market society powered by incentives for individual striving.

This distinctively American frame of mind emerged early. In 1623, there was an episode that illustrated the toll that reality takes on ideology. It also illustrated the fecundity of individualism and enlightened self-interest. The first important book-length manuscript written in America was *Of Plymouth Plantation,* the journal of William Bradford, the colony's governor for nearly thirty-six years. In a section on private versus communal farming, Bradford wrote that in 1623, because of a corn shortage, the colonists "began to think how they might raise" more of it. After much debate, they abandoned a doctrine that they had brought with them on the *Mayflower*, the idea that all agriculture should be a collective, community undertaking. It was decided, Bradford wrote, that "they should set corn every man for his own particular, and in that regard trust to themselves." That is, they "assigned to every family a parcel of land," ending communal cultivation of that crop. "This," Bradford reported, "had very good success; for it made all hands very industrious, so as much more corn was planted than otherwise would have been by any means." Indeed, "the women now went willingly into the field, and took their little ones with them to set corn, which before would allege weakness and inability; whom to have compelled would have been thought great tyranny and oppression."[13] So began the American rejection of collectivism. Just three years after the settlers came ashore, they began their ascent to individualism. One hundred fifty-three years before Adam Smith's *The Wealth of Nations,* the earliest of Americans understood how to harness for the general good the fact that human beings are moved, usually and powerfully, by self-interest. So began the unleashing of American energies through freedom—voluntarism rather than coercion. So began America.

What the Pilgrims quickly understood in the seventeenth century the Russians and Chinese learned the slow and hard way with agricultural collectivization in the twentieth century. Francis Fukuyama notes: "By breaking the link between individual effort and reward, collectivization undermined incentives to work, leading to mass famines in Russia and China, and severely reducing agricultural productivity. In the former USSR, the 4 percent of land that remained privately owned accounted for almost one-quarter of total agricultural output. In China, once collective farms were disbanded in 1978 under the leadership of the reformer Deng Xiaoping, agriculture output doubled in the space of just four years."[14]

The system we praise as capitalism was named by its enemies, and especially by the German émigré who sat for so many hours in seat G7 in the reading room of the British Museum. The system that Karl Marx and other critics intended to disparage by labeling it "capitalism" is a system of private property regulated minimally by government interventions and mostly by market forces. And by the rule of law governing the making and adjudicating of voluntary contracts. Leon Trotsky once said that the problem with capitalist society is that every person thinks of himself and no one thinks of everyone. But beginning with the Soviet regime that Trotsky helped to found, the most hideous political oppressions have flowed from governments that have claimed to be able to, and to have a duty imposed by History to, think of everyone. About the basics, there is today little of the debate that raged in many countries well into the twentieth century. It is no longer controversial that the basic engine of social improvement is people using their private property to pursue personal profits through reasonably free markets.

To an age fascinated by physics and the "laws of motion" in planets and other bodies, Adam Smith announced that men, and hence the body politic, obey "laws of motion." He discovered orderliness beneath the turmoil of society—predictability based on the simplicity of man's unchanging desires and self-interestedness. The uncoerced cooperation of people pursuing their private interests produces, through the mechanism of free markets, social betterment. This result is unplanned; no one aims to better society's condition; each person aims to better only himself. It is, Smith said, as though a "hidden hand" guided the process whereby the public good, although unintended, results from the pursuit of private goals.

Before the modern age, of which Smith was a herald, political philosophers disagreed about what constituted the public good but agreed that the public good was to be discovered by reason—by the reasoning of the wisest. Modern political philosophy holds that the public good is rooted in, and produced by, the desires of the many—including desires (for wealth, acquisition, consumption) that are often considered by the high-minded to be low. The modern assumption is that the public good (defined by Smith and other moderns as increased consumption) is produced by the unfettered pursuit of private purposes. It is because of this system that almost all of us live in a way that would have been unimaginable to our not very distant ancestors.

Almost everyone now alive is directly descended from people who lived in grinding poverty. Until around 1800, this was the condition of almost everybody. What the economist and historian Deirdre N. McCloskey calls the Great Enrichment began in seventeenth-century Holland, gathered steam—literally—in eighteenth-century Britain and the American colonies. Although agriculture was invented about 11,000 years ago, it took 4,000 years for it to supplant hunting and gathering as mankind's main source of food. This made possible the rise of cities, which involved transactions that led to the development of writing about 5,000 years ago and mathematics about 4,000 years ago. But modernity means velocity. It took 4,000 years for mankind to adapt harnesses to the long necks of horses. But just sixty-six years after the Wright brothers' first flight, which covered a distance shorter than the wingspan of a Boeing 747, a man walked on the moon.

Modernity also means having a hard time fathoming how extraordinary modern conditions are. An earthquake once shook the Western mind by striking Lisbon on All Saints' Day, 1755, killing thousands in churches and thousands more who, fleeing to the seashore, were drowned by a tidal wave. It was as though nature, unamused by humanity's expanding sense of mastery, had muttered, "Oh, really? Says who?" The quake was an exclamation point arbitrarily inserted into the Age of Reason, raising doubts about the beneficence of the universe and about God's enthusiasm for the Enlightenment. In our increasingly secular age, when the phrase "acts of God" denotes only disasters, we still can learn from these events. One of the striking vignettes from television coverage of the aftermath of San Francisco's 1989 quake was a policeman exhorting citizens to "go home and prepare for 72 hours without services."[15] For perhaps three days they would have no electricity, no gas, no running water. Of course, it was not until very recently in the human story that anyone had any of these things.

Until the middle of the nineteenth century, one-fifth of the English population was too malnourished to perform regular work. Cities grew faster than did the understanding of urban public health problems, so between 1790 and 1850 life expectancy in America's northern states declined 25 percent. In the 1830s and 1840s, life expectancy at birth in New York City and Philadelphia was twenty-four years—six years less than for a Southern slave. Even in 1900, only half of those born in the same year were alive at age forty. Today, it is not until age eighty that only half of an age cohort survives.[16] In 1900, the American population spent twice as much on funerals as on medicine, fewer than 2 percent of Americans took vacations, and there were only two generally observed holidays, Christmas and Independence Day.[17] Calling the Great Enrichment "the most surprising secular event in history" (she is an Episcopalian), McCloskey notes that since 1800, the goods and services available to the average Swede or Taiwanese have risen "by a *factor* of 30 or 100. Not 100 percent, understand—a mere doubling—but in its highest estimate a factor of 100, nearly *10,000* percent, and at least a factor of 30, or 2,900 percent." McCloskey attributes this to "the great oomph of liberty and dignity." That is, the enrichment came about because society decided to allow ordinary people the liberty to strive, and to respect and honor them for achieving. "People in Holland and then England didn't suddenly start alertly attending to profit. They suddenly started admiring such alertness, and stopped calling it sinful greed."[18] So the Great Enrichment is both the cause and the consequence of a revolution in thinking about morals and behavior.

Some philosophers distinguish between virtues that are natural and those that are artificial—between, for example, a natural sense of justice and fellow feeling that is supposedly constitutive of human nature and the virtues of, say, cooperativeness and trustworthiness, which are acquired over time by habitual behaviors in conformity with social expectations. This might be, however, a distinction without a difference. The natural virtues, if such there are, can be worn away as individuals accommodate themselves to social settings where such virtues are disadvantages. And in settings where such virtues are inculcated in the socialization of children, the virtues are not natural, or not merely natural, for very long. They become compounds of natural inclinations and social reinforcements.

CAPITALISM AS SOULCRAFT

A third of a century ago, this author delivered Harvard University's Godkin lectures, which subsequently became a book read by dozens, *Statecraft as Soulcraft: What Government Does*. The subtitle underscored the book's theme, which is that soulcraft—shaping the morals and manners of its citizens—is not merely something that government can or should choose to do. Rather, it is something government cannot help but do. It may not be done competently or even consciously, but it is not optional. Legal regimes, and the commercial and educational systems that the laws create and sustain, have consequences on the thinking, behavior, expectations, desires, habits, and demands—cumulatively, on the souls—of the citizenry.

Another of the book's themes was quite wrong. It was that the American nation was "ill-founded" because too little attention was given to the explicit cultivation of the virtues requisite for the success of a republic. In fact, the nature of life in a commercial society under limited government is a daily instruction in the self-reliance and politeness—taken together, the civility—of a lightly governed open society. Capitalism requires, and therefore capitalism develops, a society in which economic dealings are lubricated by the disposition and ability to trust strangers. Walk into almost any American commercial establishment and you will receive the signature greeting of one stranger to another in a commercial society: "How may I help you?" Politeness is woven into the society's interactions, and over time, through endless iterations, it produces a fabric of civility. Virtues are not revealed by good habits; good habits *are* virtues. We call a person good because he or she characteristically—habitually—acts in certain ways: honestly, bravely, empathetically, compassionately. Therefore, a commercial republic—a market society—promotes the habits (virtues) of politeness and sociability.

It used to be said that an armed society is a polite society. The point was that if your interlocutor has a sword at his side or a Colt on his hip, you are apt to mind your manners. It might also be said that a commercial society will be sociable. Alfred Marshall, one of the founders of modern economics, wrote in 1890, "Man's character has been molded by his every-day work, and the material resources which he thereby procures, more than by any other influence unless it be that of his religious ideals; and the two great forming agencies of the world's history have been the religious and the economic."[19] Friedrich Hayek wrote that commerce, which requires trust, cooperation, and rules-constrained competition, "is as much a method for breeding certain types of mind as anything else." Or as Deidre McCloskey says, "The invisible hand gently pushes people out of their solipsistic cocoons to consider what is valued in trade by other people." Which Montesquieu knew: "Commerce polishes and sweetens barbarian ways."[20] William Blackstone, the eighteenth-century jurist so influential among America's Founders, described the English of his era as "a nation of freemen, a polite and commercial people."[21]

There was then a theory that commercial societies would subsume dangerous energies in economic competition, thereby making wars less likely. That theory has been slain by this fact: "History's most destructive wars have in fact occurred *since* the bourgeois revolution."[22] Nevertheless, commercial societies are apt to be, on balance, civilized because an economic system is an educational regime. When Oscar Wilde published in 1891 an essay titled "The Soul of Man Under Socialism" he got almost everything wrong about how the world works or can be made to work, but he was not wrong to think that the system by which we shape the material world around us, and the way we allocate its resources, shapes people's souls.

The phrase "elective affinity" was coined in the eighteenth century as a technical term to denote the behavior of certain chemical substances when brought together. So, when Max Weber said there was an "elective affinity" between Protestantism and capitalism he meant that aspects of each were shared by, or reinforced aspects of, the other. There is an elective affinity between capitalism and the individualism woven into the fiber of a society with a government limited by respect for pre-existing natural rights. Individualism was explicit in Adam Smith's description of the "system of natural liberty" as one in which "every man, as long as he does not violate the laws of justice, is left perfectly free to pursue his own interest his own way, and to bring both his industry and capital into competition with those of any other man, or order of men."[23] Smith's *The Theory of Moral Sentiments* is logically as well as chronologically (by seventeen years) prior to *The Wealth of Nations*. The former, beginning with its first line, affirms attributes of human nature that define the context for the practice of economic liberty: "How selfish soever man may be supposed, there are evidently some principles in his nature, which interest him in the fortune of others, and render their happiness necessary to him, though he derives nothing from it except the pleasure of seeing it."[24] John Stuart Mill, too, understood that "the creed and laws of a people act powerfully upon their economical condition; and this again, by its influence on their mental development and social relations, reacts upon their creed and laws."[25] This can be a virtuous feedback loop when people adapt to the trust and politeness of commerce and to social rewards being determined by impersonal market forces rather than by political connections.

At the founding of the American nation, Americans agreed that an economic system is a system of soulcraft, although they disagreed, strenuously, about which system to adopt. Political scientists Jeffrey K. Tulis and Nicole Mellow argue that the debate between the Federalists and the Anti-Federalists, the former favoring and the latter opposing ratification of the Constitution, was so intense because both sides agreed about the most important point. Both understood that "the new Constitution represented a plan for a new way of life, not just a new arrangement of power." The "agrarian ideal" was "implicit" in the Anti-Federalists' arguments because the Constitution "would replace a republican ideal of smaller, homogeneous communities in which commerce was wedded to agriculture, with a regime of continental dimension, a commercial republic in which agriculture would play a supporting role." So, "manners, mores, habits" would be "fundamentally altered" as the Constitution ushered in "a revolution in the design of the whole polity—new forms of living as well as new forms of governance." This fact is inconvenient for the progressive critique of the Constitution, which holds that because the document was written for a vanished society, it must be radically revised in order to suit today's unanticipated polity. Tulis and Mellow argue that today's commercial society of constant churning was not just anticipated, it was planned by the Framers and midwifed by the Constitution. As a result of what they call "our forward-looking Founding," America's political development from 1789 on has had "a constitutionally induced direction." So the Constitution "would not be a 'living document' whose meaning needed to be changed to accommodate unknown and unanticipated economic and social developments but rather would itself set in motion a polity that would generate such economic and social change as a necessary consequence of the basic choices the Constitution represented."[26]

The Founders were Aristotelians, not because they had studied his *Politics* and *Nicomachean Ethics*, although some of them had, but because they reasoned as Aristotle did about the human good. He asked what the "function" of a human being is: "[J]ust as for a flute-player, a sculptor, or any artist, and, in general, for all things that have a function or activity, the good is thought to reside in the function, so would it seem to be for man, if he has a function. Have the carpenter, then, and the tanner certain functions or activities, and has man none? Is he naturally functionless? Or as eye, hand, foot, and in general each of the parts evidently has a function, may one lay it down that man similarly has a function apart from all these?"[27]

It has been said that the United States is the only nation founded on a good idea—the pursuit of happiness. "The object of government," wrote Madison in Federalist 62, is "the happiness of the people."[28] He and his fellow Founders conceived of happiness as Aristotle did, as a steady, durable state of worthy satisfaction with life. To be worthy, satisfaction must flow from the vigorous employment of the faculties that make us human—individual reasoning and social participation. What man does distinctively, and other animals do not, is use his intelligence through reasoning. Happiness, which is not mere pleasure, is found in man's natural function, which is this *activity* on his own behalf. A restless individualism is inherent in the Founders' Aristotelian understanding of human nature.

For Locke, the category of "property" encompassed not just land and other material possessions but also one's self, meaning one's life and the liberty to make use of it. This is how he meant "government has no other end but the preservation of property."[29] So a draft of the Declaration of Independence said it is "self-evident" that "among" humanity's unalienable rights are those of "life, liberty and property." Some people consider this significantly different from, and inferior to, Jefferson's final formulation "life, liberty and the pursuit of happiness." Actually, it is neither, for two reasons. First, in eighteenth-century usage, individuals were said to have, as Locke believed, property in themselves—in their bodies. Second, this usage was and is sensible because when government protects private property it protects the property owner's zone of sovereignty. Possession is not a trivial thing, be it possession of a house that provides privacy, of a car that confers mobility, of clothes that express individuality, or of the ability to undertake travel that educates and entertains. And consumption is not peripheral, let alone inimical, to the personal fulfillment that is a goal of life and hence of politics. Property is the result of the individual's planning and aspiring, of his or her choices and exertions. As such, it is a signature of individuality expressed in the zone of sovereignty in which one is able to behave as one chooses. This is not restful; freedom in a market society does not just allow striving, it requires it. And the social churning that is a consequence of this dynamism can, and usually does, take a toll on security, and hence on serenity. Hence Tocqueville's contrast between American society and Europe's "calm and immobile" societies with their rigid hierarchies of classes.[30]

Modernity's decisive break from the ancients' understanding of politics, and modernity's great gift to the politics of liberty, is its idea of new possibilities for "individuality." It was modernity's insistence that the individual can be *and ought to be* pulled forward from his social background and should not be envisioned merely as clay comprehensively and passively shaped by immersion in social relationships and duties. Modernity gave birth to individualism by painting a picture of man that mankind then came to resemble, a picture of a restless, competitive, striving, and acquiring person. Rousseau overstated things when he declared that "no people could ever be anything but what the nature of its government made it."[31] It is, however, true that the nature of a regime, and the values the economic system necessarily embodies and encourages, shapes the people raised under the regime. What Adam Smith, Rousseau's contemporary, called "universal opulence," meaning wealth broadly dispersed, is the aim, and eventually the achievement, of a sensibly governed society.[32] And it is the aspiration of economic theory when melded with political philosophy, the former giving the latter a democratic inclination. Commerce always results in inequalities of outcome, and always should result in unequal rewards because different people have different abilities and desires to add value to the economy. It is, however, also true that commerce, which is based on contracts between equally consenting buyers and sellers, insinuates throughout society an egalitarian ethos that is subversive of aristocratic status.

When Washington Irving's Rip Van Winkle awoke from his twenty-year sleep that began before the Revolution, he was amazed: "The very character of the people seemed changed. There was a busy, bustling, disputatious tone about it, instead of the accustomed phlegm and drowsy tranquility." A society of deference, and the habits that both produced it and were reinforced by it, were being shucked off as the cake of custom crumbled under the assault of energies let loose in an increasingly market-driven commercial society where social hierarchies would, presumably, be based on merit.

One of contemporary conservatism's services to society has been to refocus attention on an elemental fact that the Founders understood: Society is a crucible of character formation, and a capitalist society does not merely make us better off, it makes us better. Human beings are political, meaning social, beings, fulfilled in and through voluntary associations. Government can damage associational life, and big government can do big damage. This nation's party system was born of an argument about the action of American society on itself and on the character of Americans. Hamiltonians wanted a society of high-velocity commercial energy and restless, striving individualism in order to produce national greatness. Jeffersonians aimed to promote other virtues, particularly simplicity and the serene independence of the self-sufficient yeoman. Such Americans would, Jefferson thought, avoid the degrading dependence of the urban manufacturing workers who, Jefferson said, must live "on oatmeal and potatoes" and "have no time to think."[33] Americans have never stopped worrying and arguing about national character and how the economic system affects it.

In his *Report on Manufactures*, Alexander Hamilton connected his vision of commercial dynamism with the encouragement of various human types. A commercial society, unlike the mostly agricultural society envisioned by his rival Jefferson, would provide "greater scope for the diversity of talents and dispositions which discriminate men from each other," thereby generating a distinctive mentality: "To cherish and stimulate the activity of the human mind, by multiplying the objects of enterprise, is not among the least considerable of the expedients, by which the wealth of a nation may be promoted..."[34] Hamilton is most remembered for his praise, in Federalist 70, of "energy in the executive."[35] His more fundamental and comprehensive objective, however, was energy in *everybody*.

His idea that public policy should incite the animal spirits of the wealthy investor class for the betterment of society as a whole has come to be called, with stigmatizing intent, "trickle-down economics." But there also is an American tradition of "trickle-up economics." William Jennings Bryan, the three-time Democratic presidential nominee, said, "The Democratic idea has been that if you legislate to make the masses prosperous, their prosperity will find its way up through every class which rests upon it."[36] The trickle-down and trickle-up hypotheses are more or less testable, even allowing for the inability to control the relevant variables in the laboratory of a modern society in a globalized world. To a considerable extent, however, trickle-down is not optional: The rich will always be with us, and their entrepreneurial talents will gather large reservoirs of financial resources, which they will have a steady incentive to put to productive use.

Not everybody read Hamilton that way. When Madison sought Henry Lee's opinion of Hamilton's *Report on Manufactures*, he received a blast of the economic sociology that then was commonplace thinking. Madison relished Lee's disapproval of what Hamilton, who was Madison's rival, advocated. Lee said that whereas good Jeffersonians, like him, favored an agrarian economy that would shape the archetypal American as "a stout, muscular ploughman full of health...with his eight or ten blooming children," Hamilton would populate the nation with "squat, bloated fellows all belly and no legs who can walk two miles in the hour and manufacture a little."[37]

In 1802, Hamilton, seething about President Jefferson's rejection of Hamilton's plans for a national highway system and other stimulants of economic dynamism, wrote acidly: "Mr. Jefferson is distressed at the codfish having latterly emigrated to the southern coast, lest the people there should be tempted to catch them; and commerce, of which we have already too much, receive an accession."[38] Jefferson, however, was not altogether hostile to the encouragement of social churning. He drafted Virginia's legislation abolishing primogeniture (the right of a firstborn son to inherit the parents' entire estate) and entail (the inheritance of property over a number of generations) in order to encourage conditions for social fluidity and the virtue of individual aspiration. But Jefferson's palliative measures were no match for the social inertia created by slavery, as Alexis de Tocqueville discerned.

Traveling down the Ohio River in the fourth decade of the nineteenth century, Tocqueville noted that a traveler in the middle of the river navigates between two economic systems that produce two mentalities—two kinds of people. From both the Ohio and Kentucky banks of the river stretched undulating soil that offered "inexhaustible treasures to the laborer." The two states differed only in that Kentucky had slaves and Ohio did not. On the river's left bank, where "the population is sparse," "society is asleep; man seems idle." On the right bank "rises a confused noise that proclaims from afar the presence of industry." On the left bank, "work is blended with the idea of slavery," hence it is "degraded." There "one cannot find workers belonging to the white race, [for] they would fear resembling slaves." So Kentucky men "have neither zeal nor enlightenment." On the right bank, "one would seek in vain for an idle man: the white extends his activity and his intelligence to all his works." Nature "has given man an enterprising and energetic character" on both banks of the Ohio, but two radically different economic systems result in radically different kinds of people.[39]

The Founders intended the Constitution to promote a way of life, and they understood that to promote a way of life is to promote a kind of person. Consider the words of the Constitution's first and greatest construer, John Marshall. In his biography of Washington he wrote: "[The] great and visible economic improvement occurring around 1790 [was in part due to] the influence of the Constitution on habits of thinking and acting, [which] though silent, was considerable. In depriving the states of the power to impair the obligations of contracts, or to make anything but gold and silver a tender in payment of debts, the conviction was impressed on that portion of society which had looked to the government for relief from embarrassment, that personal exertion alone could free them from difficulties; and an increased degree of industry and economy was the natural consequence of this opinion."[40] Marshall said the Constitution was designed to encourage particular habits of thinking and acting. From visible habits we make inferences as to invisible attributes of the soul. Therefore statecraft, as the Founders understood it, is soulcraft. Hence politics has a great and stately jurisdiction, and politics is an inherently dignified vocation, no matter how imperfectly practiced at any given time.

Marshall understood that acceptance of the Constitution was an act of self-denial in the name of self-government. The Constitution deprived the states of certain powers that they had used licentiously under the Articles of Confederation. The states had produced what Madison tartly called "a luxuriancy of legislation."[41] Because the Founders understood the contagion of faction, they did not believe that the best government is always that which is closest to the people. Being unsentimental about the people, the Founders were not sentimental about state and local governments. As Marshall saw, by depriving states of some of their powers, the Constitution helped to equip citizens for the dignity of life without degrading dependence on government.

The Anti-Federalists opposed the Constitution in the name of intimate government; the Founders framed the Constitution to provide effective government and to spare citizens the discomfort and dependence that comes from being too intimate with government. The Founders hoped that one effect of exalting the central government over other governments would be a diminution of the total amount of government—local, state, and national. This, the Founders thought, would encourage self-reliance in the pursuit of happiness, which was an important dimension of the argument for a strengthened central government. But this government was supposed to be strong within the strict limits of enumerated powers. We have not, however, had such a government for a long time. It can be argued that we never really did.

From its first year, the national government has asserted powers proportional to national needs, and from the first, it has defined national needs in ways that did not produce government precisely, or even notably, limited in sphere or methods. Of the thirty-nine members of the House of Representatives who were present when the First Congress took up its first order of business, sixteen were Framers—they had been at the Constitutional Convention. Yet their first order of business was the enactment of tariffs. And they regarded tariffs not merely as revenue-raising devices but as instruments of what today is called "industrial policy." Their aim was to pick winners and losers, to promote local or regional interests, and to purchase political advantage by protecting "infant industries."

The Louisiana Purchase, and restrictions on the expansion of slavery, were supposed to guarantee a vast inland empire of small farmers perpetually renewing the young Republic's yeoman virtues of independence and self-sufficiency. But the nature of nineteenth-century America—huge tracts of land to be cultivated and a scarcity of labor—spurred the mechanization of agriculture. This increased production, and price fluctuations, and debts, and defaults. Farmers saw their economic, political, and social standing decline. Their independence and self-sufficiency were, by other names, loneliness and vulnerability forced upon them by bad roads, bad communications, and cycles of overproduction, declining prices, failure, and foreclosure. This is why big, activist government was not only, or initially, a response to urban industrialism. Forty years before the New Deal, rural populism was America's first powerful political movement to insist that the federal government should acknowledge broad ameliorative responsibilities. Government responded with rural free delivery, rural electrification, paved roads (as late as the 1920s, most of South Dakota was impassable during rainy springs), regulation of railroads and grain elevators, and the then-radical policy of commodity price parity—an economic entitlement, a harbinger of the welfare state, which migrated to urban America from down on the farm.

So big government did not fall out of the sky, unbidden, like hail in Kansas. And it was not foisted on a reluctant public. It grew for many reasons. One use to which the Interstate Commerce Commission was put after its creation in 1887 was to keep certain east-west freight rates low in order to encourage commerce that would strengthen the national union. The federal Meat Inspection Act of 1906, which initiated federal inspection, did not come about simply because the nation's stomach was turned by Upton Sinclair's novel *The Jungle,* which depicted, with shocking accuracy, life in Chicago's meatpacking plants. The federal government began regulating that industry because the industry wanted it to be regulated: States' regulations were so unreliable that some European markets were being closed to American meat.

As Daniel Patrick Moynihan said, incantations praising minimalist government are part of the liturgy of America's "civic religion," avowed but not constraining. Government grows partly because of the ineluctable bargaining process among interest groups that favor government outlays that benefit them. And government grows because knowledge does, and knowledge often grows because of government. Knowledge, said Moynihan, is a form of capital, much of it formed by government investment in education. And knowledge begets government. Time was, hospitals were simple things. Then came technologies—diagnostic, therapeutic, pharmacological—that improved health, increased costs, and expanded government's involvement in the allocation of access to health care that was becoming increasingly valuable because medicine was increasingly competent. When I was born in 1941, the principal expense of most hospitals was clean linen. This was before MRIs, CAT scans, electron microscopes, laser surgery, and many other costly technologies.

THE FATAL CONCEIT

"Political economy" once was, and should still be, the name for the academic study of economics. To study economics is to study how the production and exchange of goods and services, domestically and among nations, is shaped by customs, mores, laws, and governments, and by social aspirations concerning equity. A mature capitalist economy is, inevitably, a government construct. A properly functioning free market system does not spring spontaneously from society's soil as dandelions spring from suburban lawns. Rather, it is a complex creation of laws and mores that guarantees, among much else, transparency, meaning a sufficient stream—a torrent, really—of reliable information about the condition of markets and the conduct of corporations. Karl Polanyi, the Austrian-born economic historian, famously pointed to a paradox when he said that "laissez-faire was planned."[42] Markets freed from government control are a creation of governments. Laws that shape, and are shaped by, social norms are necessary. Politics is not everything, and everything should not be politicized, but much of what makes life congenial and rewarding, from fulfilling work to stimulating culture, depends upon the functioning of a sound political order. And one of the most important attributes of such a political order is knowing what is not—what cannot be—known.

In the last quarter of the nineteenth century, as part of the rapid growth of American higher education, and especially of graduate schools and PhD programs, the academic discipline of economics acquired the confidence of a scientific profession. After the prodigies of industrial mobilization that produced victory in World War II, President John Kennedy exemplified the serene postwar confidence in the management of the economy. Addressing Yale's graduating class of 1962, Kennedy said, "What is at stake in our economic decisions today" is not a passionate clash of ideologies but just "the practical management of a modern economy," a "basic discussion of the sophisticated and technical questions involved in keeping a great economic machinery moving ahead." This, he said, "is basically an administrative or executive problem." Which meant, to Kennedy and his like-minded listeners, it was not much of a problem, and certainly not a political problem. America's economic challenges, Kennedy said, demanded "technical answers, not political answers."[43] In his 1969 inaugural address, Richard Nixon, as though announcing a universally understood truism, serenely said, "We have learned at last to manage a modern economy to assure its continued growth."[44] Thirty-one months later, he was sufficiently flummoxed about the problem of "managing" the economy that he ordered wage and price controls, the most aggressive peacetime expansion of government power over the economy in American history. Within fifteen years of Kennedy's Yale commencement address, the nation would be suffering from a phenomenon that economic theory said was impossible: stagflation, the simultaneous afflictions of stagnant growth and an inflation rate that reached 13 percent in 1979.

There was, however, a remarkable confluence of events in three years early in the fourth quarter of the twentieth century. In 1978, Deng Xiaoping began his market-oriented reforms of China. In 1979,

Margaret Thatcher became Britain's prime minister, vowing to revive the sclerotic economy of the island nation where the industrial revolution first gained traction. In 1980, Ronald Reagan was elected with a mandate to lighten the weight of government in order to enlarge the sweep of market forces. In the first quarter of the twenty-first century, however, after economists failed to anticipate the Great Recession of 2008, and found it difficult to prescribe policies that would produce steadily brisk economic growth, the confidence and prestige of economists was diminished, again. It is time to get back to basics.

The study of economics is, always and everywhere, first and foremost, the study of incentives. The study of economics, when it began in the eighteenth century, was called political economy and was first taught in America at the College of William and Mary. It is the study of production, distribution, and exchange as they are influenced by the laws and customs of particular nations or the international order. One reason the study of political economy came to be renamed "economics" was to suggest scientific rigor supplanting political calculations. But what is needed is scientific rigor *about* the alternative social contexts in which economic activity occurs. Economics is the science of efficiently allocating scarce resources for the achievement of myriad and competing ends. So economics can only take us so far. It is for the market to aggregate individuals' preferences in determining the hierarchy of ends. Politics intrudes in this process in order to accomplish things: Democracy aggregates the desires of majorities, or of intense and compact and politically deft minorities, for collective actions.

While allowing for enormous variations along the continuum from one economic model to the other, there are two basic economic models: voluntary market exchanges and exchanges administered by government commands and controls. The former, called capitalism, is what freedom looks like in economic affairs. It is the consensual pursuit of happiness between contracting or otherwise cooperating individuals or groups of them. The most elegant and enduring affirmation of this is almost a quarter of a millennium old, and its publication coincided with the birth of the nation in which capitalism would most spectacularly succeed.

In 1776, in *The Wealth of Nations*, Adam Smith argued that "the sovereign"—for our purposes, the government—has no "duty of superintending the industry of private people, and of directing it towards the employment most suitable to the interest of society." The government has no such duty because in attempting to perform such a duty it "must always be exposed to innumerable delusions, and for the proper performance of which [duty] no human wisdom or knowledge could ever be sufficient."[45] In the twentieth century, Friedrich Hayek explained why this is so.

In 1945, with World War II having been won by prodigious feats of industrial mobilization, the prestige of government was at an apogee, and so was the confidence of many intellectuals in the possibility and advisability of "economic planning." So, in the September issue of *The American Economic Review*, Hayek responded with "The Use of Knowledge in Society," his sobering thoughts about what he would come to call "the fatal conceit." The irremediable impediment to governments successfully constructing what Hayek calls "a rational economic order"—an economy organized and administered by central planning—is this: "The knowledge of the circumstances of which we must make use never exists in concentrated or integrated form, but solely as the dispersed bits of incomplete and frequently contradictory knowledge which all the separate individuals possess." His point was that markets are mechanisms for generating and collating information that only market processes can produce: "Fundamentally, in a system where the knowledge of the relevant facts is dispersed among many people, prices can act to coordinate the separate actions of different people in the same way as subjective values help the individual to coordinate the parts of his plan." He cited "the marvel" of the market's response to the scarcity of a raw material: Without any government directive being issued, without more than a few people knowing the cause of the scarcity or the response to it, innumerable thousands of people, who are unknown to each other and whose identities could not be discovered by exhaustive investigation, are caused to use the scarce material more sparingly.[46]

Hayek said he used the word "marvel" in order to "shock the reader out of the complacency with which we often take the working of this mechanism for granted." Unfortunately for the reputation of markets, their misfortune is that they are "not the product of human design." So "the people guided by it usually do not know why they are made to do what they do." That is, markets are denied the prestige that accrues to human designs, including those that accomplish less marvelous things than markets routinely accomplish in allocating scarce resources. Hayek approvingly quoted a contemporary philosopher, Alfred North Whitehead, expressing the conservative sensibility. "It is a profoundly erroneous truism, repeated by all copy-books and by eminent people when they are making speeches, that we should cultivate the habit of thinking [about] what we are doing. The precise opposite is the case. Civilization advances by extending the number of important operations which we can perform without thinking about them." Mankind, Hayek said, "stumbled upon" the price system, meaning the working of a free market, without understanding it.[47] This did not matter because the market will communicate information anyway, without market participants' understanding. At least it will when not afflicted by what Smith delightfully called "impertinent obstructions": "The natural effort of every individual to better his own condition, when suffered to exert itself with freedom and security, is so powerful a principle, that it is alone, and without any assistance, not only capable of carrying on the society to wealth and prosperity, but of surmounting a hundred impertinent obstructions with which the folly of human laws too often incumbers [sic] its operations."[48]

Hayek was enthusiastic about markets, but not because of utopian expectations. He was enthusiastic *because* markets comport with what he called the Tragic View of the human condition. Human beings are limited in what they can know about their situation, and governments composed of human beings are limited in their comprehension of society's complexities. The simple, indisputable truth is that everyone knows almost nothing about almost everything. Fortunately—yes, fortunately—this is getting more true by the day, the hour, the minute. As humanity's stock of knowledge grows, so, too, does the amount that, theoretically, can be known but that, practically, cannot be known. As Hayek wrote, "The more men know, the smaller the share of all that knowledge becomes that any one mind can absorb. The more civilized we become, the more relatively ignorant must each individual be of the facts on which the working of civilization depends."[49] So, in a sense, ignorance really is bliss because so many other people, who also are ignorant of almost everything, are knowledgeable about something, and we can make use of their knowledge. People who travel by air as routinely as earlier generations traveled by bus do not need to know anything about how planes are built or flown or, for that matter, why they fly. Advancing scientific and technological sophistication constantly multiplies the number of things we do not need to think about because others are doing this for us. This division of labor into ever more minute bits liberates us to get on with our lives.

Matt Ridley wonders why, "If life needs no intelligent designer, then why should the market need a central planner? Where Darwin defenestrated God, [Adam] Smith just as surely defenestrated Leviathan."[50] In a sense, the natural sciences begin where the social sciences should begin, with awed appreciation of the emergence of complex yet undesigned systems, be they animal organisms or markets based on voluntary exchange. In his 1974 lecture accepting the Nobel Prize in Economics, titled "The Pretence of Knowledge," Hayek noted that the general public had granted to economics "some of the dignity and prestige of the physical sciences." This, he thought, was a mistake because economics deals with "essentially complex phenomena," such as markets, "which depend on the actions of many individuals" whose circumstances "will hardly ever be fully known or measurable." Economics, like other social sciences, deals with "structures of *essential* complexity," involving "relatively large numbers of variables," which means that the observing scientists can never know "all the determinants" of the particular social order. "This means that to entrust to science—or to deliberate control according to scientific principles—more than scientific method can achieve may have deplorable effects."[51]

Hayek was warning against the "scientistic" frame of mind, which involves extravagant hopes for "a more scientific direction of all human activities and the desirability of replacing spontaneous processes by 'conscious human control.'" The public had been dazzled by advances in physical sciences where "explanation and prediction could be based on laws which accounted for the observed phenomena as functions of comparatively few variables." We need "a theory of essentially complex phenomena" to "safeguard the reputation of science" from injury done by importing into the social sciences procedures superficially similar to those in the physical sciences.[52]

Hayek illustrated "the inherent limitations of our numerical knowledge" by considering a sport played by "a few people of approximately equal skill." If we know not only the players' general abilities but also know precisely "their state of attention, their perceptions and the state of their hearts, lungs, muscles, etc. at each moment of the game," we should be able to know the outcome. But of course such comprehensive knowledge is impossible, and hence the game's outcome is "outside the range of the scientifically predictable."[53] Which, as the saying goes, is why they play the games. Hayek's point was that a society's relevant variables are immeasurably more numerous than those of a game between teams. The variables are numerous enough to defeat certitude in predictions. To pretend otherwise, to ignore the market's "efficient mechanism for digesting dispersed information," is to tread a path to "charlatanism and worse" in an attempt to subject not only our natural but also our social environment to our will:

To act on the belief that we possess the knowledge and the power which enable us to shape the processes of society entirely to our liking, knowledge which in fact we do *not* possess, is likely to make us do much harm. In the physical sciences there may be little objection to trying to do the impossible; one might even feel that one ought not to discourage the over-confident because their experiments may after all produce some new insights. But in the social field the erroneous belief that the exercise of some power would have beneficial consequences is likely to lead to a new power to coerce other men being conferred on some authority. Even if such power is not in itself bad, its exercise is likely to impede the functioning of those spontaneous ordering forces by which, without understanding them, man is in fact so largely assisted in the pursuit of his aims.[54]

The most succinct summation of Hayek's thinking is in two sentences from his last book, the title of which firmly embedded a phrase in our political lexicon: *The Fatal Conceit*. "The curious task of economics is to demonstrate to men how little they really know about what they imagine they can design. To the naïve mind that can conceive of order only as the product of deliberate arrangement, it may seem absurd that in complex conditions order, and adaptation to the unknown, can be achieved more effectively by decentralizing decisions, and that a division of authority will actually extend the possibility of overall order."[55] Adam Smith preceded Hayek in reaching the conclusion that Hayek came to concerning any government official who thinks he has mastery of society's variables: "He seems to imagine that he can arrange the different members of a great society with as much ease as the hand arranges the different pieces upon a chess-board. He does not consider that the pieces on a chess-board have no other principle of motion besides that which the hand impresses upon them; but that, in the great chess-board of human society, every single piece has a principle of motion of its own, altogether different from that which the legislature might choose to impress upon it."[56]

"We," said Benito Mussolini in 1929, "were the first to assert that the more complicated the forms assumed by civilization, the more restricted the freedom of the individual must become."[57] Leave aside the characteristic grandiosity and falsity of his boast: Woodrow Wilson and others had said similar things, although sometimes they purported to be modernizing the idea of freedom. What makes Mussolini's formulation interesting is that it is the opposite of an insight that Hayek would soon have: The more complex society becomes, the more government should defer to the spontaneous order generated by the voluntary cooperation of freely contracting individuals.

IT'S EASY TO RAISE SNAKES

The economist John Cochrane, who blogs as The Grumpy Economist, says economics is "perhaps best described as a collection of funny stories about unintended consequences." One such explains Cochrane's career choice: "I became an economist one day very young, reading a newspaper story about a program to get rid of poisonous snakes. The government had offered a bounty on each dead snake. Guess what happened. Hint: It's easy to raise snakes."[58] The law of unintended consequences is: In a complex society, the unintended effects of government interventions that are intended to tame and regulate processes are apt to be larger than, and opposite to, the intended effects. This is another reason for practicing what is called "Hayekian humility." Hayek's career was a long summons to epistemic humility, epistemology being the field of philosophy concerned with the nature and limits of human knowledge. A free market, which is a mechanism for generating knowledge by aggregating information, is a design— an artifact, a political construct, a choice. It is a deliberate arrangement by a central government to enable a policy of decentralizing decision-making. It is a social choice to have government facilitate social change by getting out of the way of the market. One of the great truths about society is that most of the cumulative results of conscious human choices are not the result of any human design. Most of what makes up society, and most of what is most important in society, is the result of choices too numerous to count, not the planned intention of any individual or group of individuals. Hence the law postulated by Robert Conquest, the historian and poet: Everyone is conservative about that which he or she knows the most about. This is so because when one knows something well, one knows its complex antecedents and evolution.

Hayekian humility in the face of social complexity contrasts with the statist hubris that doomed what Hayek devoted his life to opposing: socialism. The fundamental cause of the collapse of the Union of Soviet Socialist Republics was ignorance. That is socialism's systematic problem. Socialism, in which government planning supplants market signals, must be ignorant of almost everything, such as: how much bread should cost. Socialism cannot know, because it cannot know what flour and other ingredients should cost, or what labor, packaging, transportation, or advertising should cost. Markets are mechanisms for generating billions, even trillions of bits of information daily. Markets thereby produce reasonable allocations of wealth and opportunity. Make the market illegal in an industrialized society and what you get is what the Soviet Union was: "Upper Volta with ICBMs." That is, a Third World economy with pockets of modernity. Communism's prodigious achievement was to keep a potentially rich nation poor. The Soviet economy remained substantially a hunter-gatherer economy based on extraction industries—furs, oil, minerals, caviar (eggs extracted from fish).

Eventually, and too late, Communist Party officials, supposedly the vanguard of the proletariat, noticed that their nation was foundering in the wake not only of Western industrial societies, which had had a head start, but also of Taiwan, Singapore, and other Asian economies of the information age. To repeat: Markets produce many things secondarily, from shoes to trucks to novels, but primarily they produce information, in torrents that no government is intelligent enough to comprehend or nimble enough to respond to. Americans' intuitive understanding of this helps to explain why, even in extreme distress, they were impervious to economic statism: In 1932, three years into the shattering, terrifying experience of the Depression, the Socialist Party's presidential candidate, Norman Thomas, received fewer votes (884,885) than the 913,693 that Eugene Debs won in 1920, when, thanks to the wartime hysteria Woodrow Wilson fomented, Debs was in jail.

The American government, however, then succumbed to its incontinent desire to bring even small economic entities into obedience with its commands, as Jacob Maged discovered. In 1934, the tailoring and cleaning establishment at 138 Griffith Street in Jersey City, New Jersey, belonged to Maged, a Polish immigrant who was then forty-nine. With his responsibilities as a father of four, Maged should have shunned a life of crime. Instead, he advertised his criminal activity with a placard in his shop window, promising to press men's suits for thirty-five cents. This he did, even though President Franklin Roosevelt's New Dealers, who thought that they knew an amazing number of things—his economic aides were pleased to be called a "Brains Trust"—were sure that they knew the proper price for pressing a man's suit: forty cents. The National Recovery Administration said so. This, the first NRA, was the administrative mechanism for the National Industrial Recovery Act of 1933, which envisioned regulating the economy back to health by using, among other things, codes of "fair competition." The theory, involving a whopper of a non sequitur, was: In a depression prices fall; therefore the way to cure a depression is to force prices to rise. So, competition, which leads to price cutting, should be sharply curtailed by government edicts. The cartelization of labor should be promoted by encouraging unions, and the cartelization of industries should be promoted by codes that would inhibit competition. So prices would be propped up and prosperity would return.

Soon there were more than 500 NRA codes covering the manufacture of products from lightning rods to dog leashes to women's corsets. Businesses were asked to display flags and posters emblazoned with a blue eagle, an emblem signifying participation in the NRA. General Hugh "Iron Pants" Johnson, an admirer of Mussolini and head of the NRA, declared, "May God have mercy on the man or group of men who attempt to trifle with this bird."

On April 20, 1934, Maged was fined one hundred dollars—serious money when the average family income was about $1,500—and sentenced to thirty days in jail. *The New York Times* reported that Maged "was only vaguely aware of the existence of a code." Not that such ignorance was forgivable. It is every citizen's duty to stay up late at night, if necessary, reading the fine print about the government's multiplying mandates. "In court yesterday," the *Times* reported, "he stood as if in a trance when sentence was pronounced. He hoped that it was a joke."

Actually, Maged's sentence was a judicial jest. After he spent three days in jail, the judge canceled the rest of his sentence, remitted the fine, and, according to the *Times*, "gave him a little lecture on the importance of cooperation as opposed to individualism." Then, like a feudal lord granting a dispensation to a serf, the judge promised to have Maged "measure me for a new suit." Maged, suitably broken to obedience, removed from his shop window the placard advertising thirty-five-cent pressings and replaced it with a blue eagle. "Maged," reported the *Times*, "if not quite so ruggedly individualistic as formerly, was a free man once more." So *that* is freedom—embracing, under coercion, a government propaganda symbol.

Strangely—or perhaps not—as the quantity and velocity of information and change increased in the second half of the twentieth century, so, too, did government's delusions of mastery. Michael Barone notes that the Labor Department building, constructed in the

1960s, has two conference rooms adjacent to the secretary of labor's office, one for management and one for labor, so the secretary could shuttle between them. The three big units of American society would work together subduing turbulent reality. This serene confidence that the future would be a more or less harmonious allocation of abundance was an afterglow of America's preeminence at the middle of the twentieth century.

In 1951, when the average American ate 50 percent more than the average European, Americans controlled two-thirds of the world's productive capacity, owned 80 percent of the world's electrical goods, produced more than 40 percent of its electricity, 60 percent of its oil, and 66 percent of its steel. America's 5 percent of the world's population had more wealth than the other 95 percent, and Americans made almost all of what they consumed: 99.93 percent of new cars sold in America in 1954 were US brands. By the end of the fifties, GM was a bigger economic entity than Belgium, and Los Angeles had more cars than did Asia. Such pell-mell economic progress produced soaring expectations: This would be the new normal. In 1950, 40 percent of Americans had never seen a television program; by May 1953 Boston had more televisions than bathtubs.

Economist Robert Gordon, however, argues that an unprecedented and unrepeatable "special century" of life-changing inventions had a lingering echo in unrealistic expectations, so the future was bound to disappoint: "The economic revolution of 1870 to 1970 was unique.... No other era in human history, either before or since, combined so many elements in which the standard of living increased as quickly and in which the human condition was transformed so completely." Gordon says that for most Americans in 1870, the world was more medieval than modern. Three necessities—food, clothing, shelter—absorbed almost all consumer spending. Except that often there really was no consumer spending involved because often all three necessities were made within the family. Households were not wired for electricity. Flickering light came from candles and whale oil, manufacturing power came from steam engines, water wheels, and horses. Urban horses, alive and dead, were a constant urban sanitation problem, as was the fact that window screens were rare, so insects commuted to and fro between animal and human waste outdoors and dinner tables indoors. A typical North Carolina housewife in the 1880s carried water into her home eight to ten times daily, walking 148 miles a year to tote thirty-six tons of it. Few children were in school after age twelve.[59]

But on October 10, 1879, Thomas Edison found a cotton filament for the incandescent light bulb. Less than twelve weeks later, in Germany, Karl Benz demonstrated the first workable internal combustion engine. In the 1880s, refrigerated rail cars began to banish "spring sickness," the result of winters without green vegetables. Adult stature increased as mechanical refrigeration and Clarence Birdseye's Birds Eye frozen foods improved nutrition. By 1940, households were networked—electrified, with clean water flowing in and waste flowing out, radio flowing in and telephonic communications flowing both ways. Today's dwellings, Gordon notes, are much more like those of 1940 than 1940 dwellings were like those of 1900. By 1940, gone was the lack of privacy for people mostly living and generally bathing in the kitchen, which often had been the only room that was warm year-round. Since 1940, however, only air conditioning, television, and the Internet have dramatically changed everyday life, and these combined have not come close to matching the impact of pre-1940 changes. By the end of the twentieth century, the classic modernization trek from rural conditions into sanitized urban life, and the entry of women into the workforce, were vast but unrepeatable advances.

It would, however, be rash to assume that they were the last vast advances. "The uncivilized," said Calvin Coolidge, "make little progress because they have few desires. The inhabitants of our country are stimulated to new wants in all directions."[60] Often their wants are prompted by undemanded products. Consider one that has become ubiquitous in a historical blink.

In 1983, Motorola brought out a cell phone for which there was not much of a market. It was the size of a brick, weighed two pounds, and cost $3,995 (about $10,000 in today's dollars). Its charged battery lasted half an hour. Until the arrival of cell phones for the masses, hundreds of millions of Americans, and billions of others around the planet, were generally satisfied with their telephone service. Suddenly, however, cell phones caused a wholesome epidemic of dissatisfaction. Instead of calling a place and hoping that the person to whom you wished to speak was there, you called the person, who had a phone in his or her pocket or purse. People were pleased, until 2007. Then the smartphone arrived, letting loose a tsunami of impatience on the part of people who soon could hardly imagine how they had been content with anything as primitive as the phones that in 2006 they had considered wondrous instruments of emancipation. Ten years later, billions of people had in their pockets and purses high-quality cameras, instant access to more information than is contained in the Library of Congress, and more computing power than the NATO alliance had at its disposal in 1960. Has there ever been a more dramatic demonstration of Say's Law that supply can produce its own demand? The cell phone was not produced in response to an existing demand. Still less was the smartphone even imagined, let alone demanded, by the billions who soon snapped it up.

The iPad was perhaps an even more interesting illustration of a demand occurring in response to the creation of a new product. After all, the smartphone was just an improvement, albeit a dramatic one, of something familiar: a mobile phone. But baffled consumers at first wondered what an iPad, which was neither a phone nor a laptop, was for. Crowds had gathered to purchase the first smartphone and continued to gather in response to each new iteration of it. But in 2010 no crowds flocked to snap up the first iPads. Yet by the end of the iPad's first year, 7 million had been sold, and 11.55 million were sold in a single quarter of 2018.

WELCOMING WAYWARDNESS

The conservative sensibility delights in such waywardness, such surprises produced by the spontaneous order of an open, market society. The progressive sensibility yearns for predictability, for the sense that the future can be planned because the movement of society's variables can be anticipated and controlled. Consider an anxiety that affected progressives in the 1950s, when voters twice rejected their presidential candidate, Adlai Stevenson, in favor of Dwight Eisenhower, whose electoral successes elicited a new strain in progressivism—disdain for average Americans. Progressives dismissed the Eisenhower administration as "the bland leading the bland"; they said the New Dealers had been supplanted by car dealers. How could they explain the electorate's dereliction of taste? Here is how: The bovine masses had been manipulated, mostly by advertising, particularly on television, which in the 1950s became the masses' entertainment and the epicenter of American marketing. Intellectuals, that herd of independent minds, were, as usual, in lock step as they deplored "conformity." Fear of this had begun when the decade did, with David Riesman's *The Lonely Crowd* (1950), which was followed by C. Wright Mills' *White Collar* (1951), Sloan Wilson's novel *The Man in the Gray Flannel Suit* (1955), William Whyte's *The Organization Man* (1956), Vance Packard's *The Hidden Persuaders* (1957), and, most important, John Kenneth Galbraith's *The Affluent Society*, which expressed progressivism's inherent and growing inclination toward scolding and condescension.

Adlai Stevenson, the Democratic presidential nominee in 1952 and 1956, asked: "With the supermarket as our temple and the singing commercial as our litany, are we likely to fire the world with an irresistible vision of America's exalted purpose and inspiring way of life?"[61] His question radiated disdain of America's "consumer society." Today, however, thoughtful people have more appreciation of the complex prerequisites—social, political, and intellectual—of a society that produces abundance. Such a society is comfortable with, and honors, the emancipation of choice and desire that results in supermarkets, advertising, and other things that are woven inextricably into the fabric of a free society. Those mundane things actually are related to what exalts America and makes it inspiring. Unbounded imaginative desiring can be a problem for democratic governance, but it is both a cause and a consequence of a democratic culture.

Nevertheless, Galbraith brought to the progressive chorus a special verve in asserting that Americans are as manipulable as clay. Hence Americans were what modern progressives relish: victims, to be treated as wards of a government run by progressives. Advertising, Galbraith argued, was a leading cause of America's "private opulence and public squalor": Advertising inflamed Americans' consumerism, which produced their reluctance to surrender more of their income to taxation for government to spend wisely. If, however, advertising were as potent as Galbraith thought, the advent of television—a large dose of advertising, delivered to every living room—should have caused a sharp increase in consumption relative to savings. No such increase coincided with the arrival of television, but Galbraith, unwilling to allow empiricism to slow his flow of theory, was never a martyr to Daniel Patrick Moynihan's axiom that everyone is entitled to his own opinion but not to his own facts. Although Galbraith coined the phrase "conventional wisdom," and thought of himself as the scourge of groupthink, *The Affluent Society* was the distilled essence of the conventional wisdom in faculty clubs.[62]

In the 1960s, progressivism became a stance of disdain, describing Americans not only as Galbraith had, as vulgar, but also as sick, racist, sexist, imperialist, etc. Not amazingly, voters were not amused when told that their desires—for big cars, neighborhood schools, and other things—did not deserve respect. For progressives, however, that was precisely the beauty of Galbraith's theory. If advertising could manufacture demands for whatever corporations wanted to supply, there was no need to respect markets, which exist to bring supply and demand into equilibrium. *The Affluent Society* was the canonical text of modern progressivism's disparagement of the competence of the average American. Of course, if advertising really could manufacture consumer wants willy-nilly, few new products would fail. But many do. *The Affluent Society*, postulating the awesome power of manufacturers to manufacture whatever demand they might find it convenient to satisfy, was published nine months after Ford Motor Company put all of its marketing muscle behind a new product, the Edsel.

Ford was not the first automobile company to demonstrate how wrong it is possible to be concerning the wonderful waywardness of unplanned economic dynamism: In 1903, the Mercedes Corporation concluded that there never would be a world market for more than 1 million automobiles because there would never be more than 1 million people trainable as chauffeurs. Galbraith was particularly impressed by the invulnerability of General Motors to the competition of rivals or the fickleness of consumers. In 1978, when General Motors enjoyed a 46 percent share of the domestic auto market, Galbraith was sure that auto manufacturers would not seriously compete with one another because they had a mutual interest in preserving their power to raise prices. He was especially confident that none would be so rash as to challenge General Motors: "Everyone knows that the survivor of such a contest would not be the aggressor but General Motors."[63] By 2014, after General Motors had struggled through bankruptcy with the help of a federal bailout, its market share was 17 percent.

Instead of regretting such vanished supremacies, freedom-loving people should relish the way the future unfolds in spurts that defy anticipation. This is, after all, the story of the Great Enrichment. The primary technology of steam power—James Watt patented his rotary steam engine in 1781—produced the secondary technology of railroad steam locomotives, which produced a national market. The Internet, a primary technology, produced Amazon, which in 2015 dethroned Walmart as the nation's largest retailer. And so it goes with the unplannable ricochets of developments in technology and consumer tastes.

Galbraith was representative of the intellectuals who were, and are, impatient with people who are wary of government supplanting markets as the primary allocators of resources and opportunities. There were, however, other intellectuals on the way.

At Oxford University in 1962 and 1963, a small coterie of students, most of them American graduates of American universities, merrily rowed against the leftist political currents that then, as now, flowed among intellectuals. Some of these rowers had been at the University of Chicago. Others had come within the ambit of scholars from there, including Milton Friedman, whose *Capitalism and Freedom* was published in 1962. All members of the coterie were infused with the doctrines of laissez-faire political economy prevalent in Chicago's economics department, and in its Committee on Social Thought, where Friedrich Hayek had written *The Constitution of Liberty* (1960), which, like Friedman's book, was published by the University of Chicago Press. A conservative member of the British parliament agreed to meet with these free-market firebrands, and he began the conversation saying, "Well, presumably we agree that at least the roads should be owned by the government."[64] The group greeted with stony silence this deviation from the tenets of limited— very limited—government. In one of the group's favorite periodicals, *The New Individualist Review*, a quarterly published at Chicago, a theorist argued that government must own the lighthouses because no price mechanism could price the services that a lighthouse renders. This heresy provoked a spirited rebuttal: When the light sweeps the ocean's surface, it improves the surface. As John Locke explained, ownership can flow from improvements made to nature's materials, so the surface of the ocean becomes the property of the lighthouse owner, who can charge whatever price the market will bear for the right of ships to cross the illuminated surface. Case closed? Not quite. Does the property right lapse when fog prevents the beam of light from sweeping the ocean's surface? Hairs were split, then split again, as ideological purity hung in the balance.

These contumacious students, including this writer, were, as students frequently are, inebriated by ideas to the point of silliness. They were, however, early enlistees in a swelling army of people eager to provide an intellectual defense of capitalism as not merely efficient but also ethical, as singularly congruent with the political philosophy of an open society.

Marx, a Victorian intellectual, predicted that capitalism would be undone by its immiseration of the proletariat. Actually, capitalism has done more to jeopardize itself by annoying intellectuals. Many of them look down their upturned noses at the marketplace, and therefore at those who thrive in it. The intellectuals' disdain is a manifestation of resentment about the fact that markets generally function nicely without the supervision of intellectuals. Their disdain is, among other unattractive things, ingratitude. The vulgar (as the intellectuals see them) men and women of commerce who make markets productive also make the intellectual class possible. As George Stigler (University of Chicago; winner of the 1982 Nobel Prize in Economics) said, "Since intellectuals are not inexpensive, until the rise of the modern enterprise system, no society could afford many intellectuals." So "we professors are much more beholden to Henry Ford than to the foundation which bears his name and spreads his assets."[65] Intellectuals' disparagement of the system that supports them is a tangle of aesthetic and moral judgments: The profit motive encourages unlovely materialism by ratifying and rewarding it; commerce is comparable to poker in being a zero-sum transaction in which one person's gain must equal one or more persons' losses. Intellectuals also are disconcerted by the permanent unpredictability of things in a capitalist society, which defeats those who delight in discerning, and then planning, the future. Intellectuals are, as George Orwell wrote, in the business of discerning, or at least postulating, trends. They are, they think, visionaries whose farsightedness gives them privileged access to the future and a claim to the power to steer society toward its foreordained destination, aka progress. One problem, however, is that, as Orwell understood, intellectuals become invested in their prognostications. In 1963, when the Oxford University Press published the third and final volume of Isaac Deutscher's admiring biography of Leon Trotsky, Oxford's student Marxist club held a reception for Deutscher to celebrate the occasion. I was then a student at Oxford and attended this fete, where I heard Deutscher say: "Proof of Trotsky's farsightedness is that none of his predictions have come true yet." This was a glimpse into the mind of the true believer, a mind stocked with unfalsifiable propositions.

In 1914, the Bureau of Mines said US oil reserves would be exhausted by 1924. In 1939, the Interior Department said the world's petroleum reserves would last thirteen years. Oil subsequently fueled a global war and the postwar boom, and in 1951 Interior said the world had…thirteen years of proven reserves. In 1970, proven reserves were estimated at 612 billion barrels. By 2006, more than 767 billion barrels had been pumped—and proven reserves were 1.2 trillion. In 1977, President Jimmy Carter said mankind could "use up" all the world's proven reserves "by the end of the next decade."[66] Since then, the world has consumed three times more oil than was then in the proven reserves. Today, shale rock formations in Texas and Louisiana, Montana and North Dakota, and New York, Pennsylvania, and elsewhere may contain 2,000 trillion cubic feet of clean-burning natural gas.

Two generations ago, in 1972, humanity was warned (by computer models developed at MIT) that it was doomed. In fact, it was supposed to be pretty much extinct by now, or at least miserable. It is neither. So what went wrong? That year begat *The Limits to Growth*, a book from the Club of Rome, which called itself a "project on the predicament of mankind." It sold 12 million copies, staggered *The New York Times* ("one of the most important documents of our age"), and argued that economic growth was doomed by intractable scarcities.[67] Bjorn Lomborg, the Danish academic and "skeptical environmentalist," says the book "helped send the world down a path of worrying obsessively about misguided remedies for minor problems while ignoring much greater concerns," such as subsistence-level poverty, which only economic growth can ameliorate. MIT's models foresaw the collapse of civilization because of "nonrenewable resource depletion" and population growth. "In an age more innocent of and reverential toward computers," Lomborg writes, "the reams of cool printouts gave the book's argument an air of scientific authority and inevitability" that "seemed to banish any possibility of disagreement." Then—as now, regarding climate change—respect for "settled" science was said to require reverential suspension of skepticism about scientific hypotheses. *Time* magazine's 1972 story about *The Limits to Growth* exemplified the media's frisson of hysteria: "The furnaces of Pittsburgh are cold; the assembly lines of Detroit are still. In Los Angeles, a few gaunt survivors of a plague desperately till freeway center strips…Fantastic? No, only grim inevitability if society continues its present dedication to growth and 'progress.'"[68] The modelers examined nineteen commodities and said twelve would be gone long before now—aluminum, copper, gold, lead, mercury, molybdenum, natural gas, oil, silver, tin, tungsten, and zinc. Lomborg notes:

Technological innovations have replaced mercury in batteries, dental fillings, and thermometers, mercury consumption is down 98 percent and its price was down 90 percent by 2000. Since 1970, when gold reserves were estimated at 10,980 tons, 81,410 tons have been mined and estimated reserves are 51,000 tons. Since 1970, when known reserves of copper were 280 million tons, "about 400 million tons have been produced globally, and…reserves are estimated at almost 700 million tons." Aluminum consumption has increased sixteen-fold since 1950, the world has consumed four times the 1950 known reserves, and known reserves could sustain current consumption for 177 years. Potential US gas resources have recently doubled. And so on.

The MIT modelers missed something—human ingenuity in discovering and innovating. This did not just appear after 1972. Aluminum, Lomborg writes, is one of earth's most common metals. But until the 1886 invention of the Hall-Héroult process, it was so difficult and expensive to extract aluminum that "Napoleon III had bars of aluminum exhibited alongside the French crown jewels, and he gave his honored guests aluminum forks and spoons while lesser visitors had to make do with gold utensils."[69]

In 1980, economist Julian Simon made a famous wager in the form of a complex futures contract. He bet with Paul Ehrlich, whose 1968 book *The Population Bomb* predicted that "hundreds of millions of people" would starve to death in the 1970s as population growth swamped agricultural production. Simon's wager was that by 1990, the price of any five commodities that Ehrlich and his advisers picked would be lower than in 1980. Ehrlich's group picked five metals. All were cheaper in 1990. The bet cost Ehrlich $576.07. But that year he was awarded a $345,000 MacArthur Foundation "genius" grant and half of the $240,000 Crafoord Prize for ecological virtue.[70] One of Ehrlich's advisers, John Holdren, became Barack Obama's science adviser.

Mark Twain offered a droll response to those who confidently extrapolate prognostications from prior events. Noting that the Mississippi had several times shortened itself by cutting new channels, becoming straight where it had been serpentine, Twain said it was a lead pipe cinch that at the rate the river was becoming shorter, in 742 years the lower Mississippi would be just a mile and three-quarters long and Cairo, Illinois, and New Orleans would sit cheek by jowl, with a single mayor. Twain was tweaking the intellectuals for their tendency to first discern trends and then postulate that they will continue indefinitely. When the philosopher Michael Oakeshott said that we know no more about where history is going than we know about the future fashions in hats, he inadvertently proved his point: Since he said that, hats have gone out of fashion. Modern life is an ongoing tutorial about why it is reasonable to expect the unexpected.

And about the folly of standing athwart economic dynamism shouting, "Stop!" Besides, government must promote growth to pay for the promises it has made.

The promises, however, become impediments to growth, for two reasons. The weight of the public sector—of the entitlement state—suffocates the energy of the private sector. And the cultural effects of economic growth are inimical to its continuation.

Government, Burke said, exists to deal with wants. Modern government, however, exists in part to generate wants, to stimulate appetites for public goods and services that the political class will be rewarded for providing. So government must promote economic growth that will throw off sufficient revenues to pay for an even richer menu of benefits. The problem is that the weight of benevolent, redistributive government can be inimical to the economic growth that such government presupposes. Marx, who thought that capitalism was doomed by its "contradictions," did not foresee this one. Or the one that the Harvard sociologist Daniel Bell postulated: Capitalism produces affluence that is inimical to the virtues capitalism requires—thrift, industriousness, deferral of gratification. Bell's worry resembled that of another Harvard man and virtuoso worrier, John Adams.

In 1819, he wrote to Jefferson: "Will you tell me how to prevent riches from becoming the effects of temperance and industry? Will you tell me how to prevent riches from producing luxury? Will you tell me how to prevent luxury from producing effeminacy, intoxication, extravagance, vice, and folly?"[71] In 1976, this capitalist nation's bicentennial, Bell warned about "the cultural contradictions of capitalism." Capitalism, he said, flourishes because of virtues that its flourishing undermines. Its success requires thrift, industriousness, and deferral of gratifications, but this success produces abundance, expanding leisure, and the emancipation of appetites, all of which weaken capitalism's moral prerequisites.

The cultural contradictions of welfare states are comparable. Such states presuppose economic dynamism sufficient to generate investments, job creation, corporate profits, and individuals' incomes from which come tax revenues needed to fund entitlements. But welfare states produce in citizens an entitlement mentality and a low pain threshold. That mentality inflames appetites for more entitlements, broadly construed to include all government benefits and protections that contribute to welfare understood as material well-being, enhanced security, and enlarged leisure. The low pain threshold causes a recoil from the rigors, insecurities, and dislocations inherent in the creative destruction of dynamic capitalism. The recoil takes the form of protectionism, regulations, and other government-imposed inefficiencies that impede the economic growth that the welfare state requires. So welfare states are, paradoxically, both enervating and perversely energizing.

There is a clear and present danger that America's sterling contribution to the Great Enrichment might be petering out because Americans might be entering what will be called the Great Flinch, a reaction against the uncertainties and other stresses inherent in dynamism. This might be happening at the very moment when dynamism is needed more than ever. An aging population is retiring into the embrace of the entitlement state that has made expensive promises about pensions and, even more, medical care. For many Americans, slower growth seems less a menace than a promise—the promise of restfulness, of respite from the accelerated social churning imposed by globalization. "People suppose that the new societies are going to change shape daily," wrote Tocqueville nearly two centuries ago, "but my fear is that they will wind up being too unalterably fixed with the same institutions, prejudices and mores, so that mankind will stop progressing and will dig itself in."[72] The digging in is far advanced in twenty-first-century America.

Ameliorative measures that might forestall or at least moderate the Great Flinch would help workers prepare to move from declining occupations to expanding ones. This, however, requires private individuals and entities to do something that few know how to do, and it requires governments to do something that they rarely know how to do and are disinclined to do. Preparing for a rapidly unfolding future requires the kind of forecasting that requires information that few can acquire. And it requires government not merely to discern the economy's emerging contours, but also to encourage prospective rather than existing interests. So, ameliorative measures for those who are disadvantaged by trade or technology face two impediments. One is the knowledge limits about which Hayek warned (the "fatal conceit"). The other is the institutional inertia inherent in interest-group democracy functioning through the viscosity of the administrative state. Still, it is worth trying, in spite of its large transaction costs. More promising measures, which do not require difficult-to-acquire knowledge, would enable individual risk-taking by removing barriers to enterprise (e.g., rent-seeking occupational licensure) and by subsidizing workers' mobility from stagnant to vibrant regions.

Senator Ben Sasse, the Nebraska Republican, believes that the opioid epidemic in the early twenty-first century is akin to the epidemic of alcoholism early in the twentieth century. Then there was a mass movement from farms to rapidly expanding urban centers, where the new arrivals were without the social capital—the local attachments of families, neighborhoods, churches, clubs—that could prevent an epidemic of loneliness, against which deracinated individuals self-medicate with substance abuse. If economic dislocations, created by new technologies and patterns of trade, tend to create loneliness, this is another reason for government to experiment with technology- and trade-mitigation policies as prophylactic measures to forestall a Great Flinch.

The success of a society often produces a congealing as successful people apply their social skills to the task of reproducing in the rising generation the conditions in which they became comfortable. What the Italian economist Vilfredo Pareto called the "circulation of elites" slows as the elites reproduce themselves through "assortative mating"—people of similar educational and professional backgrounds marrying.[73] There is a determined, skillful transmission of cultural capital to their children in the competition for access to elite educational institutions that impart momentum for success.

Deirdre McCloskey notes that in 1800, at least 80 percent of American workers were on farms; today, thanks to the mechanization of agriculture and hybrid crops, fewer than 2 percent are. But the displaced agricultural workforce was not consigned to unemployment. By 1910, one in twenty workers were working on the railroads. In the late 1940s, of the approximately 66 million in the workforce (43 million men, 17 million women), AT&T employed 350,000 as manual telephone operators, almost all of them women. In the 1950s, hundreds of thousands of jobs operating elevators in hotels, department stores, and office buildings disappeared when elevator passengers were trusted to push buttons by themselves. More recently, 10,000 people lost their jobs when Borders bookstores disappeared, partly because of competition from Amazon. More than 100,000 people who in 2000 worked in video rental stores are working elsewhere because Netflix and other entities killed rentals. In today's America, with about 160 million jobs, about 1.7 million jobs—more than 1 percent of the total—disappear *every month* as companies downsize, fail, merge, or decide that this or that job is dispensable. So about 10 percent of jobs vanish in a year. Says McCloskey, "In just a few years at such rates—if disemployment were truly permanent—a third of the labor force would be standing on street corners, and the fraction still would be rising."[74]

Various public policies could drastically slow the employment churning that is caused by innovations. But who wants to live in a stagnant society? Invoking John Rawls' idea of a "veil of ignorance," McCloskey says that people should ask which kind of society they would rather be born into—without knowing where within the society they will end up.[75] Do people want to live in a society where jobs are protected by policies that suppress economic dynamism—meaning growth—and government decides who gets subsidies and other protections? Or in a society in which workers are expected, and helped, to adapt to a constant stream of uncertainties—and opportunities?

In creating a commercial republic replete with a saving multiplicity of factions, the Founders hoped that potentially disruptive passions might be tamed by being diverted from factional politics into commerce. They hoped that dangerous energies would be sublimated in the creation and acquisition of wealth. But what was to prevent acquisitive people from coming to regard government as just another arena in which they could strive for material well-being through political advantages? Nothing did prevent that, because the nation abandoned the Constitution's underlying ideas of limited government. And because some new ideas emerged to encourage the conception of government as deliverer of material well-being. In October 1932, the Democratic Party's presidential nominee said, "I have…described the spirit of my program as a 'new deal,' which is plain English for a changed concept of the duty and responsibility of Government toward economic life."[76] The "changed concept" of government put America on the straight path to the present.

In the first quarter of the twenty-first century, American government is increasing like what Andrew Jackson warned against in the second quarter of the nineteenth century. In his prescient 1832 message explaining his veto of the bill to re-charter the Bank of the United States, Jackson began by acknowledging that such a bank would be "in many respects convenient for the government and useful to the people."[77] But near the end of his 8,086-word attack he described the bank as a government intrusion in the allocation of economic benefits, the granting of "monopolies and exclusive privileges" that would presage "a fearful commotion":

It is to be regretted that the rich and powerful too often bend the acts of government to their selfish purposes. Distinctions in society will always exist under every just government. Equality of talents, of education, or of wealth can not be produced by human institutions. In the full enjoyment of the gifts of Heaven and the fruits of superior industry, economy, and virtue, every man is equally entitled to protection by law; but when the laws undertake to add to these natural and just advantages artificial distinctions, to grant titles, gratuities, and exclusive privileges, to make the rich richer and the potent more powerful, the humble members of society—the farmers, mechanics, and laborers— who have neither the time nor the means of securing like favors to themselves, have a right to complain of the injustice of their government. There are no necessary evils in government. Its evils exist only in its abuses. If it would confine itself to equal protection, and, as Heaven does its rains, shower its favors alike on the high and the low, the rich and the poor, it would be an unqualified blessing.[78]

What Jackson knew, Madison did, too. In Federalist 62 he tried to warn posterity about "instability" born of government's incontinent interventions in society:

Another effect of public instability is the unreasonable advantage it gives to the sagacious, the enterprising, and the moneyed few, over the industrious and uninformed mass of the people. Every new regulation concerning commerce or revenue, or in any manner affecting the value of the different species of property, presents a new harvest to those who watch the change, and can trace its consequences; a harvest reared not by themselves but by the toils and cares of the great body of their fellow citizens. This is a state of things in which it may be said with some truth that laws are made for the *few* not for the *many*.[79]

This is much more urgently true today, in the vast shadow cast by the administrative state, than it was when Madison wrote. Note well his deft and prescient choice of words. Regulation inherently confers advantages on those who have the education and time to "watch" and the skill, or perhaps the hired representation, to "trace" what goes on in government's labyrinthine interior. Today, what Jackson denounced and Madison feared is called rent-seeking and explains modern Washington, including the fact that five of the nation's ten most affluent counties are in the Washington area. The libertarian theorist David Boaz says, "When you lay out a picnic, you get ants. When you hand out more wealth through government, you get lobbyists. The federal budget is the biggest picnic in history."[80] Big government incites, by enabling, a flight from entrepreneurship—other than the enterprise of rent-seeking, which is a degenerate diversion of entrepreneurial energies. The more government spending and regulating disposes or influences the disposition of wealth and opportunity, the more opportunities there will be to make money by manipulating the political system. To get a feel for what is ominous about this, take a step, in your imagination, behind a veil of ignorance.

John Rawls, author of *A Theory of Justice*, the most influential twentieth-century work of American political philosophy, proposed a thought experiment. To judge the equity of social arrangements, "Imagine you are a risk-averse person making rules for society behind a veil of ignorance about your own location in the society."[81] Regarding economic practices, the threshold question is: Behind that veil, are you more comfortable endorsing a society largely driven by the spontaneous order of voluntary transactions, or a society in which government, meaning political power, has a large role in the allocation of wealth and opportunity? Remember, you are rationally risk-averse, and you are ignorant of your social position relative to the various constellations of political influence. Remember also that the government's large role is apt to grow ever larger, for this reason: Government interventions to modify market outcomes breed more of the same. As such interventions become common, and then routine, and society becomes more comfortable with them, factions within society become more focused on advancing their interests not by competition in the market but by capturing government's attention and solicitousness. Factions are formed for this purpose.

Gresham's Law (bad money drives out good money) has a political corollary: Competition to capture government favoritism tends to supplant competition as the way to prosper amid the welter of market uncertainties. Besides, you have no choice: When the halls of Congress and the offices of regulatory agencies become the cockpits where more and more social and economic outcomes are determined, more and more factions will compete there. And few will have the option of being absent from this arena. Unilateral disarmament in the lobbying arms race is not a realistic choice. So life becomes more saturated by politics as government grows ineluctably. And government becomes regressive, transferring wealth upward to those who can exploit the system. Too often in today's political economy—today's *very* political economy—the rich get richer not just or even primarily because they are gifted participants in market processes of wealth creation. Instead, they get rich because they are nimble at using their mastery of mechanisms for influencing political processes.

AN EXAMPLE OF CONSERVATIVE ECONOMIC THINKING: THE CASE FOR PROGRESSIVE TAXATION, STILL UNEASY AFTER ALL THESE YEARS

This adds new urgency to a perennial question. Daniel Patrick Moynihan said that democracies always must decide how much government they want and how much economic growth. His point was that there is tension between the goal of growing the nation's wealth by allowing the market to direct resources to the most productive uses and the goal of redistributing incomes in accordance with this or that political conception of equity. From Moynihan's question, subsidiary questions flow, such as: What do we want that only government can do or give? Or that government can do or give much better than other institutions can? What price, in taxes or otherwise diminished freedom or slowed economic growth, are we willing to pay for these things? Conservatism can bring to this discussion two things that are often missing from it. One is realism about the inevitable costs and benefits of the trade-offs that are inescapable. The other is candor about the ethical premises that too often go unarticulated or unexamined. So this is a suitable point for a case study of conservative reasoning. The subject is progressive taxation and how the policy of progressive taxation intersects with society's commitment to equality.

"Taxes," Oliver Wendell Holmes said, in words now carved in stone on the Constitution Avenue side of Washington's Internal Revenue Service building, "are what we pay for civilized society." This is true to the extent that civilization is the result of government rather than government being the result of civilization. Woodrow Wilson, who was nimble at infusing the mundane with moral grandeur, said that paying taxes is a "glorious privilege."[82] Perhaps. But the history of American taxation shows that the privilege has been inextricably bound up with war.

The Civil War briefly gave the nation its first income tax. It was signed into law on July 1, 1862, by President Abraham Lincoln. Karl Marx described Lincoln as "the single-minded son of the working class," but, a few years earlier, as a prosperous lawyer with railroads as clients, Lincoln had an income of about $2,000 a year, placing him in at least the top 2 percent of American earners. The first iteration of an American income tax was probably never paid by more than 1 percent of the American people, but one of them was pleased by the experience. Mark Twain said that his 1864 tax bill of $36.82 (plus a $3.12 fine for filing late) made him feel "important" because it meant the government was paying attention to him. This tax was repealed after the war, partly because manufacturers and other protectionists assumed, correctly, that abolishing this stream of federal revenue would strengthen support for high tariffs as an alternative source of revenue. Nevertheless, the Civil War income tax was, as Steven R.

Weisman says, "a momentous piece of legislation, rivaling, in its way, the abolition of slavery, the Homestead Act, the establishment of a national currency and federal bank regulation."[83] The income tax compelled public debate about the allocation of gains and sacrifices in providing for the national state. What is remarkable is how little debate there was about the principle of progressivity: From the start, rich people would be taxed at a higher rate than others. When the income tax was revived more than four decades later, this principle was generally accepted as uncontroversial.

In the early years of the twentieth century, a few states tentatively tried taxation of income, sometimes with unfortunate results. According to Weisman, "Virginia enacted a tax in 1909, but many citizens refused to pay it. After some tax agents sent to rural areas were never heard from again, Virginia repealed the tax, having collected less than $100,000."[84] Two forces revived the national income tax. One was the desire to lower tariffs, which were indirect, semi-hidden sales taxes that crimped the consumption of Americans with modest incomes. Lowering tariffs would, however, jeopardize a major source of federal revenue. The other force propelling the nation toward an income tax was the desire to lower the boom on demon rum: Prohibition would threaten alcohol taxes, another major source of federal revenue. These two pressures presaged ratification of the Sixteenth Amendment.

Rear-guard resistance to the income tax relied on flimsy arguments. *The New York Times* fretted that income taxation would hurt the poor by reducing the ability of the rich to contribute to charities. The *Albany Evening Journal* said the income tax would divide the nation between those who do and those who do not "contribute to the support of the national government," which was silly because all consumers were supporting the government through tariffs and excise taxes. In 1913, 95 percent of federal revenues came from the purchase of commodities subject to tariffs or excise taxes paid disproportionately by persons of modest means.[85]

Nevertheless, the national income tax arrived in 1913, the first year of Woodrow Wilson's presidency, when the glorious privilege of paying it was indeed for the privileged few: The average worker's income was $500 a year. The tax fell only on incomes over $4,000, so it was paid only by the top 3 percent of earners. The incomes of the president and federal judges were exempt because this was somehow thought to be required by the separation of powers. In 1913, the top rate was 7 percent. In 1917, America went to war, and the top rate went to 77 percent. The Second World War democratized the income tax. In 1939, 3.9 million Americans paid it; by 1945, 42.6 million did. The Cold War and, even more important, the welfare state would entrench the income tax as a democratic experience. But by the second decade of the twenty-first century, more than 75 percent of earners paid more in payroll taxes than in income taxes. The top 1 percent of earners paid 39 percent of the income taxes, the top 5 percent paid 60 percent, the top 10 percent paid 70 percent. And the bottom 50 percent of earners paid a paltry 3 percent. Sixty percent of households paid either no income tax or less than 5 percent of their income in taxes.[86] This is what is called a situation of moral hazard, where incentives are for perverse behavior: A large and growing majority have no incentive to restrain the growth of a government they are not paying for through the principal sources of its revenues. This is a hazard directly related to progressivity.

Jefferson, in an 1816 letter, argued that what we have come to call progressive taxation would violate natural justice: "To take from one, because it is thought that his industry and that of his fathers has acquired too much, in order to spare to others, who, or whose fathers have not exercised equal industry or skill, is to violate arbitrarily the first principle of association, the guarantee to every one of a free exercise of his industry, and the fruits acquired by it."[87] With his phrase "the first principle of association" Jefferson, who had a bust of Locke at Monticello, was harkening back to Locke's reasoning from the state of nature: *This* is why we come together in political association in the first place. All men are created equal as rational pursuers of happiness as they define it, and are equally entitled to the enjoyment of the fruits of their striving. Lincoln thought that economic inequality could and should be a spur to industry: "That some should be rich, shows that others may become rich, and hence is just encouragement to industry and enterprise." And in the next sentence of his March 21, 1864, letter to the Workingmen's Association he implicitly cautioned against what today is known as redistribution: "Let not him who is houseless pull down the house of another; but let him labor diligently and build one for himself, thus by example assuring that his own shall be safe from violence when built."[88]

Nevertheless, of the ten principal demands in the Communist Manifesto, a "progressive or graduated income tax" now is, like another demand, "free education for all children in public schools," normal in developed nations. But the case for progressive taxation of income is just as "uneasy" today as it was when, in a famous 1952 essay, two professors at the University of Chicago Law School, Walter J. Blum and Harry Kalven, Jr., so described it. Arguments for progression are invariably linked to arguments for greater equality of social outcomes. But egalitarian aspirations live in tension with the disincentivizing effects of progression.[89]

Few would disagree with the proposition that there are some extremes of inequality that are intolerably *unlovely*. That word puts off, for the moment, the use of the more problematic word *unjust*, which propels the argument into deep and choppy philosophic waters. Inequality can be unlovely in and of itself. It also can be unlovely because it arises from unjust social arrangements. It is, however, not logically entailed that social arrangements that produce inequalities, even unlovely ones, are for that reason unjust. The degree to which inequality is troubling does depend somewhat on the degree to which the process by which the rich have become so is considered an equitable process—one based on merit and self-reliance rather than political influence and rent-seeking. Once existing inequalities are deemed unacceptable because they are somehow inequitable, the question becomes: Does equity demand, and does the ethic of redistribution mandate, only the elimination of extreme privation? Or is the proper objective the achievement of some ideal narrowing of the gap between the top and the bottom of the income or wealth distributions? If so, how is the ideal determined? And how, and how much, should this determination depend on empirical questions about the disincentive effects that progressive taxation must have? To the extent that one believes (in the 1960 words of Senator John F. Kennedy) that "a rising tide lifts all boats"—that economic growth is very broadly beneficial to most members of most social strata—then to that extent the case for progressive taxation depends on a demonstration that such taxation, or a particular degree of progression, does not do more harm to economic growth than economic growth would do in distributive good.[90]

So the argument for progressive taxation must pivot from a moral assessment of social conditions to a moral assertion about the equities of individuals' sacrifices. The assertion is that money has declining marginal utility. That is, $1,000 subtracted from a wealthy person's income diminishes that person's happiness less than $1,000 subtracted from a person with a modest income would diminish that person's happiness. One problem, however, is this, as formulated by Blum and Kalven: "The ostensibly scientific form of sacrifice theory, which purports to deal with the way people actually react to money, frequently conceals a normative judgment either about the way that people ought to value money or about the social value of typical expenditures at different levels of income." This brings us back to the actual centrality of an aesthetic judgment ("unlovely"). It is an aesthetic judgment chock-full of moral judgments. And these judgments rub up against this fact: "Presumably, it is one of the virtues of a free society that, within the widest limits, men are free to maximize their satisfactions according to their own hierarchy of preferences."[91]

Is this still a foundational presumption of American society? It certainly is not shared by those who argue as follows: An individual's preferences are so socially conditioned, so colored by inherited class assumptions, so derivative from advertising and other external and imposed stimuli and promptings, that these preferences need not really be considered the individual's at all. Hence they need to be only lightly respected, if at all. This argument is just one facet of the social and political relevance of one of the great preoccupations and debates of the last two centuries, the debate about the extent to which individuals are responsible for their differences.

A proportionate levy on income will tax each income at the same rate regardless of how many dollars the taxpayer earns: If taxpayer A earns twenty times more than taxpayer B earns, taxpayer A pays twenty times more dollars. Under a progressive tax, taxpayer A pays more than twenty times more dollars. Whatever else is to be said for or against a proportionate tax, it is simple. Progressive taxation is never simple. The foundational assumption that justifies progression—the faith that, at any moment in society's ongoing evolution, equity can be known and fine-tuned by government—also justifies, indeed mandates, incessant tinkering with the tax code. This certainly has been the American experience. This is how the nation got a tax code as baroque as the current one, a code that, since the heralded simplification of 1986—which left it quite complex—has been re-complicated by more changes than the number of days that have passed since then.

Majority rule is a good principle for groups to use in making decisions. But as Blum and Kalven said, "It is the very nature of majority rule that the majority can vote distinctive burdens for the minority."[92] And some of the burdens targeted at a minority can rebound against the entire community if, by impairing economic incentives, they suppress economic growth. Progression, by reducing the prospective rewards of risk-taking investments, always makes such investments less attractive. Progression also encourages consumption by discouraging saving. It does this by reducing the real rate of return on savings. Progressive taxation is aimed at those who have the most money, and the more money people have, the more apt they are to save some of it. As Blum and Kalven said, the more the burden of taxation is shifted to the wealthy, the more substantial will be the diminution of saving, and therefore the diminution of the potential for capital formation. The challenge for advocates of progression is to strike a balance between the equity pursued and the damage done to growth by that pursuit.

Clearly a 100 percent marginal tax rate would have *some* depressing effect on investment, and hence on productivity, and hence on society's general level of satisfaction. At any rate, it would do this unless you believe, as socialists do, or used to, that the state, having drained what used to be the reservoirs of investment capital, can step in and do the investing with at least as much skill as that of private investors deploying their own money. That belief, however, requires another belief: That government, which everywhere and always is political in every fiber of its being, will nevertheless be a consummate investor, because in allocating capital to productive uses it will not allow its decisions to be tainted by political considerations.

It is difficult to justify progressive taxation by arguing that there is a strong correlation between the amount of income one earns and the amount that one benefits from government. And as Blum and Kalven noted, "the principle of progression requires not merely that the benefits increase with income but that they increase more rapidly than income."[93] It is difficult to argue this, unless you argue as follows: All striving occurs in a social context, so all success is conditioned by its context. Hence individualism is a chimera, because each individual's achievement, like each individual, is a derivative of society. So the achievements need not be regarded as really belonging to the individual. This justifies, or even entails, a collectivist agenda: Society is entitled to socialize—i.e., conscript—whatever portion of the individual's acquisitions that government calculates is its share. This computation will inevitably be quite complex. A manufacturer may make a lot of money, but in what sense did *he* really make it? The materials he used came to his factory on public roads. His products were fabricated by workers who were educated in public schools, as was he. His finished products were shipped on those roads or perhaps flown away on air cargo planes operating out of public airports. His factory is protected by public police and fire departments. And so on. With each invocation of another facet of the social context, the sense of individual achievement supposedly becomes more attenuated.

But does it really? Not according to this foundational American belief: Government—including all those public goods such as roads, airports, schools, fire and police departments—is instituted to facilitate *individual* striving, aka the pursuit of happiness. The fact that collective choices, resulting in public goods, facilitate this striving does not compel the conclusion that the collectivity is entitled to take as much of the results of the striving as the collectivity decides that it made possible. Were this conclusion valid, government, representing the collectivity, would be judge and jury in its own case and would make a generous estimate of its contributions and hence of its entitlements.

Today, arguments about progressive income taxation are only arguments about the degree of progressivity. This indicates that many people are more distressed by inequalities of income than of wealth. By itself, a progressive income tax can make inequalities of wealth more durable, as Blum and Kalven noted: The income tax alone can do nothing to mitigate existing inequalities in wealth, and, moreover, it retards the accumulation of new fortunes. The progressive income tax alone, no matter how steep the progression, tends to preserve and magnify the advantages of inherited wealth. This is one reason why the egalitarian's work is never done. Redistributive taxation seems to *require* redistributive wealth-transfer taxes. But, then, from the redistributors' point of view, why not? They have a sturdy, two-fold confidence—in their moral vision of the correct distribution of social rewards and in their ability to engineer this condition, which will require constant fine-tuning by them.

To say that the case for progressive taxation is "uneasy" is not to suggest that it is wrong to question the market's allocation of wealth. Rather, it is to say three other things. First, markets—the consensual transactions of millions of people making billions of daily decisions—do deserve initial deference. Second, inequalities of income and wealth, which arise from unequal distributions of the attitudes and aptitudes essential to adding value to the economy, are not prima facie disturbing. Third, to the extent that resulting inequalities are disturbing, progressive taxation is a blunt and ineffective remedy. This is so because, as Blum and Kalven wrote, the most important source of intractable inequality of opportunity in America is what is called "cultural inheritance." In the more than half a century since they wrote, abundant research and bitter experience have confirmed their judgment that much of the transmission of culture "occurs through the family, and no system of public education and training can completely neutralize this form of inheritance."[94] Since 1952, when the percentage of American children born out of wedlock was about 4 percent, we have seen that percentage rise to 40 percent. The causes of this are unclear; the consequences are calamitous, particularly regarding opportunities for upward mobility. The cures for family disintegration are as unknown as are its causes. What is certain is this: Progressive taxation is a flimsy lever with which to try to reshape a society, many of whose problems are driven by family disintegration.

Blum and Kalven proposed a thought experiment to clarify the weak link between distress about inequality and support for progressive taxation. Suppose, they said, that society's wealth trebled overnight without any change in the relative distribution among individuals. Would the unchanged inequality at much higher levels of affluence decrease concern about inequality? Their answer was: Surely not. The issue of inequality has become *more* salient as affluence has increased, which suggests two conclusions: People are less dissatisfied by what they lack than by what others have. And when government engages in redistribution in order to maximize the happiness of citizens who become more envious as they become more comfortable, government is apt to become increasingly frenzied and futile.

ENVY, POSITIONAL STRIVING, AND ANDREW CARNEGIE'S SIXTEEN CENTS

Besides, envy is not something that should be encouraged by being rewarded. The sociologist and philosopher Robert Nisbet was correct: "Of the seven deadly sins, of all the states of the human mind indeed, envy is the basest and ugliest. It is also the most corrosive of spiritual and moral fiber in the bearer and the most destructive of the social fabric....Envy is a compound of covetousness, felt impotence, and nihilistic resentment of anything and everything that is honored in a culture." Envy is "the tax which all distinction must pay," according to Emerson. It is, according to Samuel Johnson, the vice closest to "pure and unmixed evil" because, inevitably, it motivates "lessening others though we gain nothing to ourselves." Envy is the common denominator of the many flavors of populism and, paradoxically, envy intensifies as equality of social conditions increases. "When inequality is the general rule in society," wrote Tocqueville, "the greatest inequalities attract no attention. When everything is more or less level, the slightest variation is noticed. Hence the more equal men are, the more insatiable will be their longing for equality."[95] This longing is the fertilizer of envy.

The fact that envy has increased as society has become more wealthy made sense to Fred Hirsch, a British economist who in his 1976 book *Social Limits to Growth* distinguished between the "material economy" and the "positional economy." The former is the economy as we normally think and speak about it—the aggregate production of goods and services. The latter, which is increasingly important, concerns goods, services, and jobs that are (*inherently*) minority enjoyments. As affluence has satisfied more and more basic material needs, more income, aspiration, and energy have been devoted to "positional competition" for such things as a "choice" suburban home, an "exclusive" vacation spot, an "elite" education, a "superior" job. As affluence increases, competition moves more and more from the material sector to the "positional" sector, where one person's gain is necessarily a loss for many other persons. Unlike the demand for radial tires and laundry detergents, supplies of which can be expanded indefinitely, each demand for a positional good can be satisfied only by frustrating the similar demands of many other people. Because affluence sharply increases competition for positional goods, a society's economic success actually increases frustrations and tensions. The nagging sense that affluent people are more harried than ever is sometimes explained in terms of consumption of material goods: The supply of such goods increases while the time to consume stays constant—or decreases because of the time devoted to the work that is necessary to fund acquisition. But an additional explanation concerns the time and income needed for "positional competition."[96]

Materially, economic growth has been a leveling force. Cars and air conditioners and other goods that are luxuries for one generation become necessities for the next generation. The richest American cannot purchase better antibiotics than the average American can. No billionaire in 2000 could have purchased a technological marvel like the smartphones carried today in the pockets of millions of middle-class teenagers. Now, however, affluent consumers face increasing frustrations because the *collective* advance of the middle class is inherently impossible regarding "positional goods." Tension, not satisfaction, results when the middle class, observing the top strata of society, acquires an appetite for "elite" education, "superior" jobs, and beachfront properties. Positions of status and leadership, like beachfront acreage, cannot be expanded indefinitely to become majority enjoyments. The intractable problem of the "positional economy" is social congestion: The desires of the middle class have expanded beyond middle-class opportunities. The dominant political aspiration of the modern age is equality, but the reality of the "positional economy" is that, in an important way, the affluent society *must* become steadily *less* egalitarian. The pursuit of positional goods becomes steadily more important, and such goods are inherently restricted to a minority.

The complexity of positional striving is vividly illustrated in higher education. Economic growth has made possible a vast expansion of what is called "educational opportunity." But one reason there are so many bored or sullen students is that for many of them college is not an "opportunity." Rather, it is what Hirsh called a "defensive necessity." The sullen student pursues a degree only because it will raise his or her income above what it would be if others got degrees and he or she did not. This grim scramble for position is an aspect of modern society's mania for "credentials," like the current pursuit of meaningless master's degrees. As Hirsch said, there is a sense in which "more education for all leaves everyone in the same place....it is a case of everyone in the crowd standing on tiptoe and no one getting a better view." And the number of persons who are, or—just as important—who think they are, educationally equipped for "superior" jobs increases faster than the number of such jobs.[97]

A society that values individualism, enterprise, and a market economy is neither surprised nor scandalized when the unequal distribution of marketable skills and inclinations produces large disparities in the distribution of wealth. Long experience with government's attempts to use progressive taxation to influence the distribution of income suggests the weakness of that instrument and the primacy of social and cultural forces in determining the distribution of wealth. Consider two things that might conduce to a smaller gap between the most and least affluent households. A stock market crash would devalue the portfolios of the wealthy. And curtailing access to college and postgraduate education would limit the disparities in the marketable skills that increasingly account for income disparities. To suggest such "solutions" is, however, to come face-to-face with the fact that the problem of increasing inequalities of wealth is not a problem we will pay whatever price is necessary to remedy. And it might not be a problem at all. In an increasingly knowledge-based economy, education disparities drive income disparities, which are incentives for the rising generation to take education seriously as a decisive shaper of individuals' destinies. The market is saying, insistently: "Stay in school." In today's global economy, with highly mobile capital and an abundance of cheap labor, the long-term prosperity of an advanced nation is a function of a high rate of savings—the deferral of gratification that makes possible high rates of investment in capital, research, and education. All these forms of social capital are good for society as a whole and are encouraged by high rewards for those who accept the discipline involved. This is why promoting more equal distribution of wealth might not be essential to, or even compatible with, promoting a more equitable society. And this, in turn, is why increasingly unequal social rewards can lead to a more truly egalitarian society, one that offers upward mobility to all who accept its rewarding discipline.

Government uses redistribution to correct social, meaning market, outcomes that offend it or some of its powerful constituencies. But government rarely explains, or perhaps even rarely recognizes, the reasoning by which it decides why particular outcomes of consensual market activities are incorrect. When taxes are levied not merely in order to efficiently fund government but to impose this or that notion of distributive justice, remember this: Taxes are *always* coerced contributions to government, which is *always* the first, and often the principal, beneficiary of taxes. Furthermore, in any complex modern society, any ambitious redistributionist agenda faces an epistemic barrier: The diffusion and division of knowledge about actions and their consequences is such that the project of redistributing wealth must give rise to government agencies guessing about consequences, and wielding vast discretion in doing so, with unhealthy consequences for the rule of law. The first function, and often the final achievement, of any redistributionist ideology is to legitimate the existence and activities of these agencies of redistribution.

In modern democracies, where majorities rule and the poor are far from a majority, the poor are not the principal beneficiaries of a redistributionist state. At first, perhaps, the middle class is. But any attempt to impose upon society a politically determined, government-approved allocation of wealth—and with it, of opportunity—will, over time, favor the wealthy because a redistributionist state *inevitably* distributes upward. This means that such government is inherently regressive; it tends to distribute power and money to the strong—including, first and foremost, itself. Government becomes big by having big ambitions for supplementing, and even supplanting, markets as society's primary allocator of wealth and opportunity. Therefore ameliorative government becomes a magnet for factions muscular enough, in money or numbers or both, to bend government to their advantage. When government embraces redistribution, it summons into existence factions eager to get in on the action. Government constantly expands under the unending, intensifying pressures to correct what it and its many client groups disapprove: the distribution of wealth produced by consensual market activities. But as government, prompted by its own preferences or those of clients, presumes to dictate the correct distribution of social rewards, politics becomes a maelstrom of infinite appetites in competition for finite resources. The result is that social strife, not solidarity, is generated by government's distributional activities that are intended to promote harmony, or are advertised as so intended.

An oft-repeated story about redistribution might be apocryphal, but is nevertheless instructive: A socialist came to Andrew Carnegie's office to argue that the wealth of the rich should be redistributed to the less fortunate. Carnegie directed an aide to bring him an estimate of his, Carnegie's, net worth, and of the Earth's population. He divided the former by the latter, then told the aide to give the socialist his share of Carnegie's wealth: sixteen cents. Although redistributive government is a fact—67 percent of the federal budget consists of transfer payments—redistributive fiscal policies have been minor factors in the egalitarian gains of modern society. The major factors have been economic and social changes, such as agriculture shrinking from the largest sector of the economy to less than 2 percent of employment. Many changes have made human capital—education, information, skills—more important than land and physical capital in the productive process. Government did, however, play a large role in this by making primary and secondary education compulsory and free, by multiplying the number of colleges, universities, and other postsecondary education options, and by expanding scholarship programs that democratized access to these options. By making private contributions to colleges and universities tax deductible, government encouraged the transformation of old wealth produced by land and physical capital into human capital—skills—possessed by children from outside the upper classes of old wealth. Cumulatively, these acts constituted, as Robert Fogel had said, one of the largest programs of redistribution of wealth in history. The wealth was redistributed not by giving wealth directly to individuals but by equipping individuals for strivings that add value to the economy.

Of the three economic conditions that are important causes of social distress—poverty, insecurity, and inequality—the latter is surely the least important. The first stunts opportunity. The second casts a pall over daily life and prevents people from transcending present-mindedness. The third is not inherently injurious to anyone. The philosopher Harry G. Frankfurt argues that economic inequality is not *inherently* objectionable as a matter of moral reasoning: "To the extent that it truly is undesirable, it is on account of its almost irresistible tendency to generate unacceptable inequalities of other kinds." These can include access to elite education, political influence, and other nontrivial matters. But Frankfurt's alternative to economic egalitarianism is the "doctrine of sufficiency": The moral imperative should be that everyone has *enough*. The pursuit of increased economic equality might, but need not, serve the ethic of sufficiency. And Frankfurt says this pursuit might distract people from understanding, and finding satisfaction with, "what is needed for the kind of life a person would most sensibly and appropriately seek." This should have nothing to do with "the quantity of money that other people happen to have" because "doing worse than others does not entail doing badly." Furthermore, an obsession with the quantity and quality of others' resources "contributes to the moral disorientation and shallowness of our time."[98] And to the failure to recognize that egalitarian effects can have calamitous causes. And that modern life has some astonishingly egalitarian aspects.

Stanford's Walter Scheidel, whose scholarship encompasses classics, history, and human biology, has a wonderfully startling insight that is pertinent to the debate about economic inequality. Tight labor markets shrink such inequality by causing employers to bid up the price of scarce labor. Therefore epidemics can be helpful to the egalitarian cause. Wars, too. The tendency in stable, peaceful, and prosperous societies is for elites to become entrenched and adept at using their entrenchment to augment their advantages. Many of the most potent solutions to this problem are unpleasant. They are disruptions that cause the crumbling of the cake of custom, and of much else. Wars, revolutions, and plagues have egalitarian consequences by fracturing society's crust, opening fissures through which those who had been held down can rise. Scheidel says that mass-mobilization wars have given the masses leverage and have required the confiscation, through high taxation, of much wealth from the comfortable. Revolutions often target categories of people who are considered impediments to the strivings of those in the lower orders, e.g., "landlords" and "the bourgeoisie." The Black Death, too, was particularly useful. By killing between 25 and 45 percent of Europeans in the middle of the fourteenth century, the bubonic plague radically changed the ratio of the value of land to that of labor, to the advantage of the latter. The well-off, who owned land, were not amused. Scheidel notes that in England, the Chronicle of the Priory of Rochester noted unhappily that "the humble turned up their noses at employment, and could scarcely be persuaded to serve the eminent for triple wages." The king decreed wage controls, but the canon of Leicester dourly noted that "the workers were so above themselves and so bloody-minded that they took no notice of the king's command." They benefited from the robust attack on inequality waged by the rats that carried the fleas whose intestines carried the bacteria strain and produced the Black Death.[99]

Fortunately, six centuries later, capitalism provided a nicer path to egalitarian results. Capitalism depends on what it makes possible: *mass* consumption. Hence capitalism's principal beneficiaries are not the wealthy, for whom positional goods, which must be scarcities, are particularly important. Joseph Schumpeter illustrated this seventy-five years ago: "Electric lighting is no great boon to anyone who has money enough to buy a sufficient number of candles and to pay servants to attend to them. It is the cheap cloth, the cheap cotton and rayon fabric, boots, motor cars and so on that are the typical achievement of capitalist production, and not as a rule improvements that would mean much to the rich man. Queen Elizabeth owned silk stockings. The capitalist achievement does not typically consist in providing more silk stockings for queens but in bringing them within the reach of factory girls in return for steadily decreasing amounts of effort."[100] Similarly, Schumpeter said that the invention of nylon reduced the social distance, as measured by consumption, between the duchess who wore silk and the shop clerk who wore cotton. Time was, the upper crust rode in carriages, the lower orders walked. No such dramatic difference distinguishes the driver of a Mercedes from the driver of a Chevrolet. So "conspicuous consumption" has lost some of its saliency as a signal of status.

It is important to recognize that the consumption gap between the wealthy and the middle class is less dramatic than the income and wealth gaps. John Cochrane notes: "Rich people mostly give away or reinvest their wealth. It's hard to see just how this is a problem.... Look at Versailles. Nobody, not even Bill Gates, lives like Marie Antoinette.

And nobody in the US lives like her peasants." Some Standard and Poor's economists have written, "As income inequality increased before the [2008] crisis, less affluent households took on more and more debt to keep up with—or in this case, catch up with—the Joneses." And economist Joseph Stiglitz argues that income inequality is a problem because it causes the problem of "a well-documented lifestyle effect—people outside the top one percent increasingly live beyond their means," which Stiglitz calls "trickle-down behaviorism." Cochrane is unconvinced: "Aha! Our vegetable picker in Fresno hears that the number of hedge fund managers in Greenwich with private jets has doubled. So, he goes out and buys a pickup truck he can't afford." Do we therefore need confiscatory wealth taxation in order to encourage thrift among the lower classes? Not so fast. The Standard and Poor's economists also say that inequality is a problem because rich people save too much and poor people do not save much, so by redistributing money from the rich to the poor, overall consumption can be stimulated, avoiding "secular stagnation." This, too, makes Cochrane grumpy: "I see. Now the problem is too much saving, not too much consumption. We need to forcibly transfer wealth from the rich to the poor in order to overcome our deep problem of national thriftiness."[101]

There seems to be a pattern of egalitarians deciding on the result they want—expansion of redistributionist government—and then defining problems to justify this. This sometimes requires severe intellectual contortions, as when they locate the root of the evil of inequality in what they take to be the baneful nexus between money and politics. Their argument is that money, in the form of campaign contributions, determines electoral outcomes (a dubious empirical claim) and that if we purify politics by removing or regulating private money that can be given for the supposed purpose of corrupting politics, the wealthy will no longer be able to buy the political influence that translates into successful rent-seeking. At this point, the Grumpy Economist becomes the Incredulous Economist: "If the central problem is rent-seeking, abuse of the power of the state to deliver economic goods to the wealthy and politically powerful, how in the world is *more government* the answer?"[102] America's problem, Cochrane believes, is not that wealth is the primary determinant of political power but that political power is much too often the determinant of wealth. So the way to reduce the role of money in politics is to reduce the role of politics in the distribution of money, thereby lowering the stakes of politics and the incentive for investing in it.

Talking about income inequality is a way to avoid talking about all the ways the supposed cure for this—more ambitiously assertive government—has been failing to deliver brisk economic growth, competent education, adequate infrastructure, etc. "Restarting a centuries-old fight about 'inequality' and 'tax the rich,' class envy resurrected from a Huey Long speech in the 1930s," says Cochrane, "is like throwing a puppy into a third-grade math class that isn't going well. You know you will make it to the bell."[103]

BEING RICHER THAN ROCKEFELLER

Some historians estimate that on September 29, 1916, a surge in the price of John D. Rockefeller's shares of the Standard Oil Company of New Jersey made him America's first billionaire. Others say he never reached this milestone and that Henry Ford was the first. Never mind. If Rockefeller was the first, his billion was worth $23 billion in today's dollars. Don Boudreaux, an economist at George Mason University's Mercatus Center, asks if you would accept this bargain: You can be as rich as Rockefeller was in 1916 if you will consent to live in 1916. Boudreaux says that if you had Rockefeller's riches back then, you could have had a palatial home on Fifth Avenue, another overlooking the Pacific, and even a private island if you wished. Of course, going to and from the coasts in your private but un-air-conditioned railroad car would be time-consuming and less than pleasant. And communicating with someone on the other coast would be a protracted chore. Commercial radio did not arrive until 1920, and 1916 phonographs would lacerate 2017 sensibilities, as would 1916's silent movies. If in 1916 you wanted Thai curry, chicken vindaloo, or Vietnamese pho, you could go to the phone hanging on your wall and ask the operator (direct dialing began in the 1920s) to connect you to restaurants serving those dishes. The fact that there were no such restaurants in your community would not bother you because in 1916 you had never heard of those dishes, so you would not know what you were missing. If in 1916 you suffered from depression, bipolar disorder, influenza, a sexually transmitted disease, erectile dysfunction, or innumerable other ailments treatable in 2017, you also would not know that you were missing antibiotics and the rest of modern pharmacology. And don't even think about getting a 1916 toothache. You could afford state-of-the-art 1916 dentures—and probably would need them. Your arthritic hips and knees? Hobble along until you cannot hobble any more, then buy a wheelchair. Birth control in 1916 will be primitive, unreliable, and not conducive to pleasure. You could enjoy a smattering of early jazz, but rock-and-roll is almost four decades distant, and Netflix and Google are even farther over the horizon. Your pastimes would be limited, but you could measure the passage of time on the finest Swiss watch. It, however, would be less accurate than today's Timex or smartphone.[104]

So, as a 1916 billionaire, you would be materially worse off than a 2017 middle-class American. An unhealthy 1916 billionaire would be much worse off than an unhealthy 2017 American. Intellectually, your 1916 range of cultural choices would be paltry compared with today's. And your moral tranquility might be disturbed by the contrast between your billionaire's life and that of the normal American. In 1916, life expectancy at birth was 54.5 years (today, 78.8), and fewer than 5 percent of Americans were sixty-five or older. One in ten babies died in the first year of life (today, 1 in 168). A large majority of births were not in hospitals (today, fewer than 1 percent).

Only about 14 percent of people ages fourteen to seventeen were in high school, an estimated 18 percent age twenty-five and older had completed high school, and nearly 75 percent of women working in factories had left school before eighth grade. There were four renters for every homeowner, partly because mortgages (usually for just five to seven years) required down payments of 40 to 50 percent of the purchase price. Less than one-third of homes had electric lights. Small electric motors—the first Hoover vacuum cleaner appeared in 1915—were not yet lightening housework. Iceboxes, which were the norm until after World War II, were all that 1916 had.[105]

Such facts from the first quarter of the twentieth century should serve as inoculations against America's recurring bouts of social hypochondria. In the first quarter of the twenty-first century, however, another American affliction is political consensus. Yes, consensus. America today is more distant in time from the March 1933 beginning of the New Deal than that beginning was from the April 1865 end of the Civil War. Both episodes involved the nation's understanding of equality: The war affirmed equality of natural rights, the New Deal addressed unequal social conditions. The New Deal's redefinition of American politics and of the purposes of government supposedly still defines the parties' differences. But in spite of all the discord and vituperation between the parties, the political class today seems more united by class interest than it is divided by doctrines.

Until well into the twentieth century, writes Michael Barone, Republicans were "the national, activist, even busybody party," while Democrats, professing Jeffersonian defense of localisms, respected regional mores, "from segregation in the South to the saloon in the North."[106] In the 1920s and 1930s, some Republicans—Robert La Follette, George Norris, Fiorello La Guardia—were among the strongest congressional advocates of government policies of nationalization and redistribution. It was a Republican administration—Dwight Eisenhower's—that undertook the simultaneous construction of two of the most ambitious modern public works, the St. Lawrence

Seaway and the Interstate Highway System. At their post–Civil War apogee, nineteenth-century Republicans had been the party of activist government, using protectionism to pick commercial winners, gifts of land to subsidize railroads and other forms of corporate welfare, and promising wondrous benefits from government's deft interventions in economic life. Which is to say, the Republican Party, like the Republic, got to the present by a serpentine path.

This much is indisputable: The Republican Party was the great "nationalizing" force and the architect of modern energetic government. America's Founders learned (from John Locke, among others) that government exists for the modest purpose of protecting liberty, understood primarily as freedom from government. But the Republican Party's commitment to minimalist government could not survive the first Republican presidency. As the Civil War changed from a war to restore the Union as it had been to a crusade for "a new birth of freedom," the federal government came to be regarded differently. It was seen less as a threat to freedom and more as a provider and enlarger of freedom. The proximate cause of this changed perception was the Emancipation Proclamation, which was made possible by the Union victory at Antietam. In a sense, John Locke died at Antietam.

Before the Civil War, the federal government had been barely visible to most Americans. By the end of the war the federal civilian bureaucracy, 53,000 strong, was the nation's largest employer, and the Republican Party was going to use it, vigorously. The war inaugurated a Republican era. Reconstruction in the South, and government-driven economic development in the North and West, reflected a redefinition of American freedom as something served by, not threatened by, government power. As Eric Foner writes in his history of Reconstruction, the Emancipation Proclamation clothed federal power with moral purpose, and a new class put that power to the service of what that class considered moral—its interest in economic growth.[107]

The war stimulated industry, from railroads to meatpacking to clothing, and after the war the Republican Party became the instrument of a commercial class demanding activist government to keep the growth going. Republican administrations provided tariffs, a national paper currency, and a national banking system, public debt, encouragement of immigration by the Homestead Act, the Land Grant College Act to spread scientific agricultural and other remunerative knowledge, land grants and bond issues for railroads and other "internal improvements," and wars against Native Americans who were reluctant to recognize the romance of railroading and ranching on their lands. The nineteenth century might have been a century of "individualism" but it also was a century of tariffs, subsidies, and monopoly grants to canals and railroad companies. Ten percent of the public domain was given in land grants to finance the transcontinental railroads. The Union Pacific alone was given 4,845,977 acres of Nebraska—one-tenth of the state—including every other section along its right of way for twenty-four miles on each side of the track.

By the end of the 1880s there was intense pressure to reduce tariffs, then the largest source of federal revenue. And because America was by then an industrial power, it was importing primarily raw materials, which were subject to lower tariffs than finished goods. Thus revenues were falling. Furthermore, federal land sales, another source of revenue, were declining. But spending was increasing, especially for the navy, which by 1905 received 20 percent of the federal budget. Congress, acquiring a taste for redistributing income, substantially increased pensions for veterans, a lobby then almost as potent as the elderly are today.

The post–Civil War Republican Party normalized vast government interventions in the nation's economic life. Franklin Roosevelt took this to another level, making interest-group politics systematic and routine. New Deal policies were calculated not merely to please or placate existing constituencies but to *create* many constituencies—labor, retirees, farmers, union members—who would be dependent on the government whose programs summoned them to dependency. Before the 1930s, the adjective "liberal" denoted policies of individualism and individual rights; since Roosevelt, it has primarily pertained to the politics of group interests. Roosevelt's wager was that by assiduously using legislation and regulations to multiply federally favored groups, and by rhetorically pitting those favored by government against the unfavored, he could create a permanent majority coalition.

In 1913, with the ratification of the Sixteenth Amendment and enactment of the income tax, the foundation of the modern state—the mechanism for raising vast streams of revenue—had been put in place. The mere existence of this mechanism altered America's political culture by quickening the itch of the political class to provide benefits to client groups who were convinced that they would be net winners from income transfers. This, in time, hastened the growth of the politics of envy, clothed in the language of "fairness." Today, such politics is practiced by a political class offering an ever-expanding menu of popular benefits that ostensibly will be paid for by unpopular minorities ("the rich," "corporations"). The New Deal's rupture with nineteenth-century liberalism was its abandonment of the premise that society, as sharply distinguished from government, produces most of the elements of happiness, and that most of government's functions are to maintain a framework of order in which people *pursue* happiness. What made the New Deal truly new was the notion that government has a duty to *provide* people with some, and more and more, of the tangible elements of happiness. About this, FDR was, as we have seen, clear-eyed and candid in his October 6, 1932, radio address. There he explained that his phrase "new deal" was simply "plain English for a changed concept of the duty and responsibility of Government toward economic life."[108] So, the final responsibility would be removed from private life to the public sector. Thus was the "well-being" of the citizen defined exclusively with reference to material conditions, without reference to how the citizenry's character might be affected by this new relationship to a caring and, inevitably, controlling government.

In his second inaugural address, FDR spoke of government's responsibilities toward the "one-third of a nation ill-housed, ill-clad, ill-nourished."[109] Seven years later, in his 1944 State of the Union message, he upped the ante: Government had a "duty" to drive the standard of living ever higher, and "we cannot be content, no matter how high that general standard of living may be, if some fraction of our people—whether it be one-third or one-fifth or one-tenth—is ill-fed, ill-housed, and insecure."[110] The insertion of insecurity onto the list of intolerable conditions is telling, and problematic, for two reasons. First, it expands the list of intolerable conditions beyond the citizen's material circumstances to the citizen's mental or emotional condition, thereby opening a vast, potentially limitless new array of government "duties" and "responsibilities." Second, this new entitlement to a particular mental or emotional state, that of feeling secure, is in tension with the constant social churning of a dynamic free society.

Roosevelt's ambitious agenda was an incitement to permanent discontent on the part of citizens and government. It bestowed on government a roving commission to tweak the public's material and mental states. In that 1944 message, he called for a "second Bill of Rights" to pull the nation up from what Roosevelt considered the cramped mission of merely insuring "equality in the pursuit of happiness." From the idea that the government is negligent if even one-tenth (or, presumably, one-fiftieth) of the country is ill-housed, etc., "no matter how high" the general standard of living is, it is a short step to the stance that *whether* an individual is ill-housed, etc., depends on how that individual's housing, etc., ranks *relative to* the general standard of living.[111]

The presidential election of 1936 had raised the curtain on a new politics, the pursuit of power in the context of the regulatory, administrative state. Roosevelt cultivated the support of groups his policies had created as self-conscious groups. These included farmers attached to the federal government by the Agricultural Adjustment Act of 1933 and the Farm Security Administration of 1935, union members empowered by the Wagner Act of 1935, and the elderly entitled by the Social Security Act of 1935. So, fifty years later, President Ronald Reagan, whose politically formative years were during the New Deal, and who had been an ardent supporter of FDR, spoke at the Illinois State Fair, where he made this boast: "No area of the budget, including defense, has grown as fast as our support of agriculture."[112] The farmers' applause interrupted his eleven-minute speech fifteen times. Confession is, as Mark Twain said, good for the soul but bad for the reputation, which perhaps explains why the Republican Party does not confess that it has largely come to terms with New Deal–style politics in the context of a regulatory state and an entitlement society. And with permanent deficit spending.

For this nation's first two centuries, deficit spending was largely for investments—building infrastructure, winning wars—that benefited future generations. So government borrowing appropriately shared the burden with those generations. Now, however, there is continuous borrowing because there are unending deficits, even when the economy is growing briskly and there is full employment. The borrowing and deficits burden future generations in order to fund current consumption of government goods and services. As Christopher DeMuth says, we have gone from investing in the future to borrowing from the future. This is because the promises we have made to ourselves through the entitlement state cannot, as a political matter, be funded by taxation sufficient to fund the government that the political class has been pleased to create and that the public has been pleased to have created. And there is approximately no constituency for additional kinds of taxes—consumption or value added taxes—to fund the entitlement state architecture. It is unreasonable to expect there to be, given that, in today's decadent democracy, there are no ethics to restrain the off-loading of burdens onto the unborn. Infantilism—the refusal to will the means for the ends that one wills—has become the national norm.

Modern conservatism began in Edmund Burke's splendid recoil

from the French Revolution, not only from the terror but also from the Revolution's assault on privacy in the name of civic claims. Conservatism has always been defined by its insistence on limits to the claims the collectivity—the public sector—could make on the individual. Contemporary American conservatism was born in reaction to the New Deal and subsequent excessive enlargements of the state. Today, this conservatism is a persuasion without a party, a waif in a cold climate. However, over the last fifty years America's politics have shifted in one way disadvantageous to progressives. Watergate and Vietnam caused an erosion of confidence in the motives of government. The internationalization of economic life has weakened the power of governments to control economic forces. The mobility of money and businesses inhibits governments because wealth can flee from currencies threatened by inflation, or from jurisdictions where growth is slow because government is meddlesome. Furthermore, recurrent recessions and slow growth have increased individuals' anxieties and decreased social solidarity, thereby weakening society's support for collective actions through government. Perhaps there is a paradox lurking here. If government does what conservatives wish it would do, if it retrenches and does less to impede growth, it might experience a rebirth of prestige and be poised to advance the progressives' agenda. This is a risk conservatives should cheerfully run.

Lincoln's vision, and the essence of the early Republican Party's free labor doctrine, was that "the prudent, penniless beginner in the world labors for wages awhile, saves a surplus with which to buy tools or land for himself, then labors on his own account another while, and at length hires another new beginner to help him."[113] Lincoln insisted that in America "there is no such thing as a freeman being fatally fixed for life, in the condition of a hired laborer."[114] The essence of America's aspiration, however imperfectly realized, is that no one should be "fatally fixed for life." Hence the constant need to refresh the nation's commitment to a life of constant social churning by forces beyond the control of politics and of government with its bias toward the status quo.

People often lament the "impersonal" economic forces that shape the lives of individuals and communities. But personal forces, meaning political forces, are rarely preferable. Often they are more bitterly resented, *because* they are seen and felt to be personal. Also, before too heartily celebrating the organic life of small communities, one should revisit an American literary genre that gave us Sinclair Lewis' depiction of Gopher Prairie, Minnesota, and Sherwood Anderson's Winesburg, Ohio. Before deploring the disruptive effects of new technologies, consider the fact that one of the best things that ever happened to African-Americans was the mechanization of agriculture that destroyed so many of their jobs. Time was, in places like rural Mississippi, African-Americans lived in stable, traditional, organic communities of a sort often admired by intellectuals who praised them from far away. African-Americans led lives of poverty, disease, and oppression, experiencing the grim security of peonage. Then came machines that picked cotton more efficiently than stooped-over people could, so lots of African-Americans stood up, packed up, got on the Illinois Central, got off at Chicago's Twelfth Street station, and went to the vibrant South Side where life was not a day at the beach but was better than rural Mississippi. Destruction of a "way of life" by "impersonal" economic forces can be a fine thing.

In any case, Americans have no alternative to embracing economic dynamism, with its frictions and casualties and uncertainties. Otherwise they must live with the certainty of stagnation and of a zero-sum politics of distributional conflicts driven by government as the allocator of wealth and opportunity. Americans must choose to live somewhere on the continuum between stasis and the whirl and fluidity of modern life—people, ideas, and capital flowing hither and yon. This is inherently unsettling; it tests and disrupts settled ideas and arrangements. Theodore Roosevelt said the mission of public officials is "to look ahead and plan out the right kind of civilization."

This, from the man who peered into the future and spotted an imminent "timber famine" caused by railroads' needs for wood rail ties, a famine that never arrived. Decades later, another New Yorker, urban planner Robert Moses, spoke of "the clean-cut, surgical removal of all of our old slums," some of which, of course, remain, as do human casualties from the surgery. Ross Perot, a billionaire businessman, ran for president in 1992 saying that he had been unintentionally training for this job because "I've spent the last forty years designing, engineering, testing, and implementing complex systems." Today, the idea of empowering the political class to design and engineer society has lost its allure. The Bible, Virginia Postrel reminds us, teaches that no sooner had God created man and woman than He seemed to lose control of events.[115] To the conservative sensibility, much of the pleasure of life derives from the fact that in an open society, events, and the future, are splendidly beyond control.

CHAPTER 6

CULTURE AND OPPORTUNITY

THE SCISSORS THAT SHREDDED OLD CONVICTIONS

The central conservative truth is that it is culture, not politics, that determines the success of a society. The central liberal truth is that politics can change a culture and save it from itself.

Daniel Patrick Moynihan[1]

There had been an unusual spring snowstorm on March 30, 1964, the day protracted debate and attendant maneuverings began as the US Senate took up the Civil Rights Act. The temperature in Washington was one hundred degrees when the Senate finally voted for the cloture that led to the July 2 passing of this legislation that, among other things, forbade racial discrimination in "public accommodations"—places of business open to the public. Also on July 2, 940 miles away in Kansas City, Missouri, Eugene Young, a thirteen-year-old African-American, had been turned away from the barbershop at the Muehlebach Hotel, which had refused service to African-Americans since it opened in 1915. That afternoon, at a White House ceremony, President Lyndon Johnson signed the bill into law. At eight a.m. the next day, Young returned to the Muehlebach, and for two dollars received a haircut from Lloyd Soper, who said: "I didn't mind cutting that little boy's hair."[2]

Getting Eugene Young that haircut was difficult. It took a century of struggle, culminating in months of legislative maneuverings. But getting that boy into that barber's chair was much the easiest part of America's long coming-to-terms with its racial problem. In 1964, Americans had not begun to fathom how entangled racial problems were, and remain, with problems of class, a subject that makes Americans deeply uneasy. A decade earlier, the US Supreme Court had begun confronting the problems of class, without quite realizing that it was doing so.

The Muehlebach Hotel is sixty-two miles east of what then was Monroe Elementary School in Topeka, Kansas. In 1951, Oliver Brown, whose wife, Leola, had attended Monroe, decided that his daughter Linda, nine, should not have to. Monroe, a school for black children in Topeka's segregated school system, was separate from, but not equal to, schools for white children. Linda's name is associated with the Supreme Court case *Brown v. Board of Education*, which propelled progress toward the 1964 Civil Rights Act and the dismantling of racial segregation by law. The fact that the board of education being sued for its segregation policies was in Kansas is indicative of the fact that segregation was widely practiced, and even more widely approved. In Montgomery, Alabama, it was illegal for a white person to play checkers in public with a black person. Congress was running a segregated school system in the nation's capital. In 1948, President Harry Truman could not persuade Congress to make lynching a federal crime. When *Brown* was first argued in 1952, the Supreme Court was composed entirely of Democratic—of Roosevelt and Truman—appointees. If the court's composition had not been unexpectedly changed in 1953 by the addition of a Republican nominee, the legal basis of segregation—the doctrine that "separate but equal" public facilities are constitutional—probably would have been affirmed in 1954. No Republican nominee had served on the court since Owen Roberts, a Hoover nominee, resigned in 1945. But eight months into Dwight Eisenhower's presidency, there occurred the most fateful heart attack in American history. It killed Chief Justice Fred Vinson, a Kentuckian who believed the "separate but equal" doctrine, enunciated in the 1896 *Plessy v. Ferguson* decision, should remain. If he had survived, the *Plessy* precedent probably would have, too.

In *Brown*, the court held that assigning white and black children to separate schools on the basis of race violates the Fourteenth Amendment's guarantee of equal protection of the laws. Unfortunately, the court's ruling was insufficiently radical. The court waxed sociological, citing such data as the preference of some black children for white dolls, which might have been related to feelings of inferiority caused by school segregation. And the court cited studies—studies more problematic than the court assumed—concerning the effects of segregation on children's abilities to learn. By resting the desegregation ruling on theories of early childhood development, the court's rationale limited the anti-discrimination principle of the ruling to primary and secondary education. As Robert Bork said, making the ruling contingent on sociological findings "cheapened a great moment in constitutional law."[3] The proper, more radical rationale for the *Brown* outcome was simply that the government's use of racial classifications in making decisions is incompatible with the Constitution's guarantee of equal protection of the laws. Had the court said this plainly in 1954—had the justices been content to apply not sociology but this sweeping legal principle—much subsequent court-produced mischief might have been avoided. Instead, before a generation had passed, the court was ordering busing—excluding, on the basis of race, children from neighborhood schools, and transporting them to more distant schools, to which they were assigned because of their race.

The *Brown* decision presaged the 1964 Civil Rights Act, in which Congress mandated non-discrimination in much of public life, proscribing discrimination by government and by individuals in employment and public accommodations. Or so Congress thought. Just four years later the court was saying otherwise. The 1964 act defined school "desegregation" as "the assignment of students to public schools…without regard to their race." But in 1968 the court held that compliance with *Brown* involved more than ending segregation, which hitherto had been understood as the government-compelled separation of the races by the law. The court said that where almost all white or almost all black schools—so-called "de facto segregation"— still existed, government-ordered racial discrimination was required.

The phrase "de facto segregation" is an Orwellian oxymoron. Segregation, properly understood, is *de jure*—by law—or it is not segregation. Nevertheless, soon there was compulsory busing, which became one of the most costly failures—costly in money, ill will, educational distortion, and flight from public schools—in the history of American social policy. One tragedy of racial policy since *Brown* is that the 1964 Civil Rights Act was twisted, against legislative intent, by people whose idealism made them serene in their cynicism. Racial discrimination is any action based on race. The 1964 act forbade discrimination in employment. Yet the court has held that the spirit of the act requires what the letter of the act forbids—that employers often must take race into account for various "affirmative action" purposes. *Brown* begat the Civil Rights Act of 1964, which propelled the nation toward a painful, still ongoing reckoning with this fact: Dismantling the laws that enforced inequality did not bring the nation close to a general enjoyment of equal opportunity. Rather, the path to the present ran through a tragedy of social regression and through economic and educational developments that would produce new forms of social stratification and new impediments to social mobility.

LIFTING WEIGHTS

The American creed is that all individuals are created equal in the possession of freedom—the capacity for human agency—and in the right to exercise it. Government is instituted to give citizens equal protection of their enjoyment of liberty. An open and democratic society is one in which people are equally free to become socially and politically unequal. It is indisputable that equality of rights will breed inequality of conditions. People with equal rights will have unequal aptitudes, abilities, situations, and random instances of advantages and disadvantages.

For generations conservatives have been recoiling from what they correctly consider many unwise, unjust, and counterproductive government policies redistributing wealth. In doing so, however, conservatives have clung to a distinction that is increasingly difficult to draw: They have said that they favor equality of opportunity, not equality of condition. This is facile because opportunities are conditioned by conditions. Chapter 4 argued that conservatives' reflexive rhetoric in praise of judicial "restraint" enabled the progressive agenda and disabled conservatism from standing for a political end, liberty, rather than a political process, majority rule. This chapter argues that conservatives have allowed their intelligence to be anesthetized by lazy recourse to the tired formulation "equality of opportunity, not of outcomes." Equality of outcomes is, as conservatives rightly argue, neither possible nor desirable. Equality of opportunity is, however, far more complex and elusive than conservatives can comfortably acknowledge.

In his long, circuitous train trip from his home in Springfield to Washington for his inauguration, Abraham Lincoln paused in Philadelphia where, at Independence Hall, he was prompted to give what he said was "wholly an unprepared speech." In it he said that the Declaration of Independence's affirmation of equality "gave promise that in due time the weights would be lifted from the shoulders of all men, and that all should have an equal chance."[4] Before we in the twenty-first century can understand what it would mean for all to have an equal chance, conservatives, especially, must think more clearly than many of them have done about what Lincoln called "weights" on individuals' shoulders.

Lyndon Johnson, the greatest presidential benefactor of African-Americans since Lincoln, advanced the nation's thinking on June 4, 1965, at Howard University in Washington, D.C. There he delivered the most consequential speech on race ever given by an American president, and perhaps the most important ever given by a white American. Johnson's crucial contention was that "freedom is not enough." He declared: "You do not wipe away the scars of centuries by saying: Now you are free to go where you want, and do as your desire, and choose the leaders you please. You do not take a person who, for years, has been hobbled by chains and liberate him, and bring him up to the starting line of a race and then say, 'you are free to compete with all the others,' and still justly believe that you have been completely fair. Thus it is not enough just to open the gates of opportunity. All our citizens must have the ability to walk through those gates."[5] The subsequent pursuit of even incomplete fairness—there can be no other kind—has been generally noble and in many ways successful. It also has been an arduous tutorial in the truth of Michael Oakeshott's axiom that attempting the impossible is inherently corrupting.

It would have been helpful—wholesomely disconcerting and embarrassing—if Johnson had given an example of how the federal government itself had closed to African-Americans "the gates of opportunity." Created in 1934, the Federal Housing Administration invented and enforced "redlining," explicitly steering new mortgages away from black buyers to maintain the racial homogeneity of neighborhoods. A 1946 FHA manual said: "Incompatible racial groups should not be permitted to live in the same communities." And: "Properties shall continue to be occupied by the same social and racial classes." And: "Appraisers are instructed to predict the probability of the location being invaded by . . . incompatible racial and social groups." *Invaded.* During World War II, when a developer sought FHA guarantees for proposed housing on the last of the farmland still within the sprawling city of Detroit, the FHA initially refused because the development would be contiguous with a black neighborhood. The developer proposed a solution: I will build a wall. It would be between his development and the incompatibles. He did; you can see it today. Mollified, the FHA guaranteed mortgages on the white side. Almost half of all postwar suburban homes built in the United States had FHA mortgage guarantees. From 1934 through 1962, whites received 98 percent of those guarantees.[6]

Johnson was neither the first progressive nor the first president to employ the rhetorical trope about life as a race. In 1909, Herbert Croly said it was government's duty to do what it can to make possible for all "an equal start in the race."[7] The next year, Theodore Roosevelt said: "I know perfectly well that men in a race run at unequal rates of speed. I don't want the prize to go to the man who is not fast enough to win it on his merits, but I want them to start fair."[8] Barack Obama, in his 2013 State of the Union address, advocated universal pre-K education as a means of making "sure none of our children start the race of life already behind."[9] But the many problems with the "race of life" metaphor begin with the fact that a footrace is a simple and zero-sum event. It is, unlike life, simple because it is about a physical skill— the ability of the contestants' muscles to propel them forward. It is a zero-sum event because all contestants know, and do not resent, the fact that one person will win and the rest will not. In an individual's life, however, successes are many and various, and most successes do not subtract from the successes or happiness of others. So "the race of life" is much more complex—and satisfying—than a track meet. And to assign government the open-ended task of enabling everyone to have a "fair" opportunity to "win" is to ensure that government's size, intrusiveness, and frustration will expand in tandem. By now, the "race of life" phrase has become foggy language that obscures much and clarifies nothing. Nevertheless, Johnson's 1965 speech, to the writing of which Daniel Patrick Moynihan contributed, was a serious attempt to come to grips with the many complexities of the concept of equal opportunity.

The problem that Johnson addressed at Howard University had

been addressed almost a century earlier by Frederick Douglass. Contemplating the "sudden derangement" of the lives of African-Americans in the South in the aftermath of the Civil War, he said that the ex-slave was "free from the individual master but a slave of society. He had neither money, property, nor friends. He was free from the old plantation, but he had nothing but the dusty road under his feet.... He was turned loose naked, hungry, and destitute to the open sky."[10] And then things got worse. Jim Crow laws created a caste system enforced by extra-judicial violence. The sharecroppers' system that had replaced slavery had itself been virtual slavery enforced by terror. It was peonage: In 1965, Martin Luther King, Jr., met Alabama sharecroppers who, having been paid all their lives in plantation scrip, had never seen US currency. In the sharecropper society of enveloping despair, there often was no money for weddings and no formal divorces because there were no possessions to divide. All the coming weaknesses of the urban underclass were present: out-of-wedlock childbearing, female-headed households, violent crime, substance abuse (mostly home-brew whiskey, but other drugs, too). And then, one hundred years after Appomattox, there were signs that matters might take a turn for the worse.

In the mid-1960s, Moynihan noticed something that was especially ominous because it was so counterintuitive. It came to be called "Moynihan's scissors." Two lines on a graph had crossed, resembling a scissors' blades. The descending line depicted the decline in the minority—then overwhelmingly African-American—male unemployment rate. The ascending line depicted the simultaneous rise of new welfare cases. The disappearance of the correlation between improvements in employment and decreased welfare dependency was not just bewildering, it was frightening. It shattered policymakers' serene and long-held faith in social salvation through better economic incentives and fewer barriers, legal and other, to individual initiative.

We now know what was happening. In the 1960s, as the civil

rights movement and legislation dismantled barriers to opportunity, there was a stunning acceleration of a social development that would cripple the ability of many people, especially young people, to take advantage of expanded opportunities. It was social regression driven by the explosive growth of the number of children growing up in single-parent, overwhelmingly female-headed, families. This meant, among other things, a continually renewed cohort of adolescent males—an inherently turbulent tribe—from homes without fathers. This produced chaotic neighborhoods and schools where the task of maintaining elementary discipline eclipsed that of teaching. Policymakers were confronted with the disconcerting possibility that the decisive factors in social amelioration are no longer economic but cultural—habits, mores, customs, dispositions. This was dismaying for two reasons. First, in the 1960s Americans in general, and economists even more than most Americans, believed that they had at last mastered the management of the modern industrial economy. Economic "fine-tuning," a favorite phrase of the time, supposedly would henceforth smooth out business cycles and guarantee brisk and steady growth. Second, it is easier for government to remove barriers and alter incentives than to manipulate—"fine-tune," if you will— family structure. A dawning appreciation of the crucial importance of family structure refuted the assumption that the condition of the poor *must* improve as macroeconomic conditions improve.

In January 1964, President Johnson, just two months in office, proclaimed in his first State of the Union address: "This administration today, here and now, declares unconditional war on poverty in America."[11] What meaning were listeners supposed to attach to the word "unconditional"? In an actual war, this would mean that there would be no limits to the material mobilizations and excisions from freedom (conscription, censorship, etc.) that the government might deem exigent. Regarding poverty, however, the language of "unconditional war" betokened an ominous misconception: It was that poverty persisted only because of a weakness of governmental will—only because government had not been sufficiently rigorous in marshalling material resources and undertaking necessary behavior modifications that it knew how to administer.

Johnson's language indicated that the war on poverty was to be, as actual wars are, mostly about bringing to bear material resources. The war on poverty's premise was that Ernest Hemingway was right: In his short story "The Snows of Kilimanjaro," the character Julian, based on F. Scott Fitzgerald, says, "The very rich are different from you and me," eliciting the reply, "Yes, they have more money."[12] The war on poverty assumed that the poor and the not poor were alike in all essentials other than material possessions and resources. If this assumption were correct, the war on poverty would have been won by something government does constantly and often well: distributing money. But this assumption was to be shredded by Moynihan's scissors.

The social policies put in place in those years were shaped by people who themselves were shaped by the searing experience of material deprivation in the 1930s, especially unemployment. And the premise of those policies was that long-term poverty exists in our wealthy nation only because we have not done what clever and warm-hearted people can do—use government to equitably and rationally distribute our material abundance. The assumption was that poverty could be cured by government fiat, by a redistribution of goods and services that government can orchestrate: money, housing, schools, transportation, jobs. In 1966, Sargent Shriver, a good and intelligent man, was in charge of President Johnson's war on poverty. While testifying to Congress, Shriver was asked how long it would take to end poverty in America. He answered crisply: ten years. That was not a foolish answer—if the premise of social policy until then was still correct. If, that is, poverty was material poverty, to be cured by material measures. Then came Moynihan's scissors, which meant that in a portion of the nation, government had to deal with an impacted poverty that was, and is, immune to even powerful and protracted economic growth.

This portion should have been defined and addressed as posing a problem of class, much as the problems of Europe's urban industrial working class had been defined and addressed. It was not so defined because of this fact: Although a majority of America's poor were white, a disproportionate portion were not. And the fact of race was entangled with the most toxic and destructive idea that was ever in general circulation and broad acceptance in America. This rule simplified the administration of slavery and, later, Jim Crow laws. It also enabled racial thinking with a minimum of thought— no troublesome distinctions about degrees of racial identity. The idea was—and such is the durability of folly, still is—the "one-drop rule." Also known as the "one black ancestor rule," it holds that anyone with any ancestor from sub-Saharan Africa is considered black.

Booker T. Washington, Frederick Douglass, Jesse Owens, Roy Campanella, and, of course, Barack Obama each had a white parent. Martin Luther King, Jr. (who had an Irish grandmother and some Indian ancestry), W. E. B. Du Bois, and Malcolm X had some Caucasian ancestry. The NAACP estimates that 70 percent of those who identify themselves as African-American are of mixed racial heritage. It is impossible to know how American history might have been different if the one-drop rule had never thoroughly infected American thinking. Perhaps the "peculiar institution" of slavery required, for its administration, this peculiar rule. If so, trying to imagine American history without the one-drop rule requires imagining American history without slavery. Be that as it may, the one-drop rule gave an artificial clarity and bogus precision to all race talk. This was talk that might have benefited from a large element of blurriness.

Instead, there has developed a destructive set of behaviors among some adolescent African-American males that is a perverse assertion of racial identity. The African-American sociologist Elijah Anderson says lack of confidence in the police and criminal justice system produces a defensive demeanor of aggression. This demeanor expresses a proclivity for violent self-help in a menacing environment. A readiness to resort to violence is communicated by "facial expression, gait and verbal expressions—all of which are geared mainly to deterring aggression" and to discouraging strangers "from even thinking about testing their manhood." Inner city youths are apt to acquire faux families in the form of gangs and construct identities based precariously on possessions—sneakers, jackets, jewelry. The taking and defense of these items is a part of a tense and sometimes lethal ritual. It has, Anderson says, a "zero-sum quality" because raising oneself requires putting someone down. Hence the low threshold of violence among people who feel they have no way of gaining or keeping status other than through physical displays. The street is the alternative source of self-esteem because work experiences are so often unsatisfactory, partly because of demeanors and behaviors acquired in the streets. A prickly sensitivity about "respect" causes many black youths to resent entry-level jobs as demeaning. For such a person, work becomes a horizontal experience of movement from one such job to another. And the young person's "oppositional culture" is reinforced by the lure of the underground economy of drugs. Furthermore, Anderson says, some young people develop "an elaborate ideology in order to justify their criminal adaption" to their situation, an ideology "portraying 'getting by' without working as virtuous."[13] And, in an especially cruel outcome, the criminal justice system becomes the source of a welcomed embrace. In Scott Turow's novel *The Laws of Our Fathers*, a judge broods about the endless parade of young black defendants before her bench, each an "atom waiting to be part of a molecule":

I've been struck by how often a simple, childish desire for attention accounts for the presence of many of these young people. Most of these kids grow up feeling utterly disregarded—by fathers who departed, by mothers who are overwhelmed, by teachers with unmanageable classrooms, by a world in which they learn, from the TV set and the rap of the street, they do not count for much. Crime gathers for them, if only momentarily, an impressive audience: the judge who sentences, the lawyer who visits, the cops who hunt them—even the victim who, for an endless terrified moment on the street, could not discount them.[14]

The one-drop rule was, in a sense, self-fulfilling. It identified a category of Americans without ambiguity and concentrated attention on the utter uniqueness of the African-American experience. That experience must have *something* to do with African-Americans' especially intense susceptibility to the society-wide phenomenon of family disintegration. The problem, again, is behavior. The problem is not material poverty but rather a poverty of intangible social capital—a poverty of inner resources, of the habits, mores, values, customs, and dispositions necessary for an individual to thrive in a complex, urban, industrial society. These missing attributes range from industriousness to sexual continence, from the ability to defer gratification to the determination to abstain from substance abuse. This is a depressing diagnosis because government does not know how to replenish such intangible social capital, once it has been dissipated.

Any list of the government's most substantial successes in the twentieth century is apt to be long on material achievements—the Tennessee Valley Authority, the Manhattan and Apollo projects, the Interstate Highway System. Other successes include the civil rights acts, but with those, the government was not required to impart aptitudes to people; rather government removed impediments to the exercise of aptitudes by people. There would be other successes on the list, but most would be like these, programs that delivered clearly defined durable goods. Similarly, the great successes of nineteenth-century governance were in causing canals and railroads to be built and in distributing a natural bounty, land. But government becomes discouraged, and discouraging, when it tries to deal with concepts more complicated than dams and highways, when it tries to deliver "meaningful jobs" for adults, "head starts" for children, and "model cities" for all. Yet increasingly government is asked to deliver such complicated commodities. That is why, if power is the ability to achieve intended effects, government is decreasingly powerful. This thought only seems perverse if you equate size with power, which admittedly would make sense if government were a machine. But as President William Howard Taft wearily exclaimed to no one in particular when a zealous aide began lecturing him about the "machinery" of government, "The young man really thinks it's a machine!"[15]

It is actually a jumble of fractious, rivalrous power centers through which it sometimes accomplishes marvelous things. Consider two of the most successful government programs of the previous century: Social Security and the GI Bill. Social Security largely eliminated poverty in the elderly portion of the population. But this attack on poverty was not complicated. It involved nothing more arcane than mailing checks to a stable, easily identified population group. The government is good at delivering transfer payments. It is not so adept at delivering services, still less at delivering planned changes in attitudes and behavior. There is, however, one counter-example that is rich in lessons that were not learned by the authors of the Niagara of social policies that came two decades after it.

The GI Bill was partly intended as a prophylactic measure against prospective discontents: The rise of European fascism had been fueled by the grievances of demobilized servicemen from the First World War. It is not correct to say that hitherto American veterans had been neglected. Far from it. In 1865, one-fifth of Mississippi's state budget went for artificial limbs to replace limbs left in places like Shiloh and Cold Harbor. And in the 1890s more than 40 percent of the federal budget went to one entitlement: pensions for Civil War veterans. However, veterans of the First World War had not been well cared for, and that mistake would not be repeated.

The GI Bill's primary purpose was to jump-start the social project that the war had interrupted, the completion of the New Deal program of social amelioration. This purpose was different, and better, in important ways than the purposes of some social policies in the 1960s. The GI Bill, which subsidized education and home buying for veterans, employed liberal means to achieve profoundly conservative consequences.[16] It encouraged a middle-class form of striving to replace the working-class path to upward mobility. In 1940 only one in nine Americans was a high school graduate, there were fewer than 1.5 million college students, and only one in twenty Americans had a college degree. By the spring of 1947, the 1.6 million veterans enrolled in college were 49 percent of all registered students. Sixty percent of the veterans enrolled in science and engineering programs, including many among the 400 whose dormitory at the University of Illinois was the ice rink. That university had been expecting at most 11,000 students, but 15,000 enrolled. By the time the national program ended in 1956, 2.2 million veterans had gone to college, 3.5 million to technical schools, and 700,000 had received off-campus agricultural instruction. By 1990, there were 14 million Americans in college, and one in five Americans had a degree. The GI Bill contributed mightily to making college a middle-class expectation. And in modern America, expectations mutate into entitlements.

In 1940, two-thirds of Americans were renters. By 1949, 60 percent of Americans were homeowners, partly because of subsidized loans for veterans. A veteran of the Navy Seabees, Bill Levitt, bought broad swaths of Long Island farmland and marketed a basic house for $7,990, a bargain at a time when the average family income was about $2,500. A veteran interviewed for a PBS program on the GI Bill remembered: "No money down. I can afford that. And I get four rooms, and there's a washing machine. In those days people didn't have washing machines in their houses. They went to the corner to a launderette. But Levitt houses came with a washing machine! Oh, it was unbelievable!"[17] Levitt himself saw a political dimension to Levittown: "No man who owns a house and lot can be a Communist. He has too much to do."[18] He had a point: Would the Winter Palace have been stormed if more people in Leningrad had had leaves to rake and lawns to mow?

The total cost of the GI Bill was $14.5 billion, which was serious money back then. However, the bill was not akin to today's entitlements. Its benefits were contingent on the recipients' having rendered a social service of the most serious sort—military service. And the bill was congruent with the broad social strategy described by Michael Barone in *Our Country*, his history of American politics from FDR to Reagan. It was a strategy of honoring "those who worked their way up in society" and of placing "society's stamp of approval on their affluence and success." It was a strategy "which aimed not at servicing a lower class but at building a middle class."[19] With the GI Bill, social policy sent strong cues to young Americans, telling them to stay in school, grind out good grades, defer marriage past the teenage years, defer children until the family income had begun to rise.

At the end of the war, American confidence was at an apogee, in part because American society then was characterized by cultural homogeneity, buttressed by bourgeois judgmentalism. Social policy reflected a broad consensus about the proper behavior for facilitating socially useful aspirations. Twenty years later, however, liberalism, as it then still preferred to be known, became bifurcated between economic and lifestyle liberals. The latter despised as "repressive" all social policies that promoted behavior deemed worthy by "bourgeois values." Lifestyle liberals sought to de-moralize policy. By the late 1960s, liberalism's tone and content were deeply influenced by liberalism's political base in the so-called "caring professions." They served "clients" in the urban population who had been disorganized by behaviors, particularly involving drugs and sex, that were insuperable impediments to aspirations for greater equality of income.

America's social pathologies have multiplied during a burst of wealth creation without precedent in world history. America's poverty problem is not one of material scarcities but of abundant bad behavior. Data demonstrate that there are three simple behavioral rules for avoiding poverty: finish high school, produce no child before marrying or before age twenty. Only 8 percent of families who conform to all three rules are poor; 79 percent of those who do not conform are poor. And recent social learning includes this: The trajectory of a child's life is largely determined in the earliest years. "The human personality emerges early; if it is to be shaped," James Q. Wilson wrote, "it must be shaped early."[20] And by far the best predictor of a child's flourishing is the fervent devotion of two parents. Beyond the earliest years, the presence of two parents is also crucial to the success of primary and secondary education, as was disconcertingly learned half a century ago, when family disintegration was beginning to accelerate.

"GUESS WHAT COLEMAN'S FOUND":
THE PROBLEM OF ESCAPE VELOCITY

It was, appropriately, at a 1966 gathering at the Harvard Faculty Club that Daniel Patrick Moynihan was greeted by his friend Seymour Martin Lipset, the political scientist, with news that was a harbinger of trouble for the academic consensus about social policy: "Hello, Pat, guess what Coleman's found: Schools make no difference, families make a difference."[21] Actually, James Coleman did not, of course, quite say that, but what he did find was dramatic enough to unsettle conventional thinking. When the baby boom generation began moving through the public school system like a pig through a python, policymakers of all philosophic stripes were agreed: Cognitive outputs would correlate with financial inputs, so the best predictor of a school's performance is the amount of money spent on it. Postwar education policy was focused where the public education lobby wanted it focused, on such matters as teachers' salaries, per-pupil spending, and pupil-teacher ratios.

However, in the 1960s one benefit from social scientists being ascendant in Washington was a hunger for data. By 1966, an ambitious government study conducted by sociologist James Coleman had come to a conclusion so "seismic"—Moynihan's characterization—that President Johnson's administration considered not releasing it, and did release it on the Friday of the Fourth of July weekend, hoping the report would receive minimal attention. The conclusion was: "Schools are remarkably similar in the way they relate to the achievement of their pupils when the socioeconomic background of the students is taken into account."[22] That is, the crucial predictor of a school's performance is the quality of the families from which the children come. Granted, some schools are heroic exceptions to this rule. Nevertheless, it is the rule.

In 1989, a researcher reported in confirmation of Coleman that "variations in school expenditures are not systematically related to variations in student performance."[23] And later: "Researchers have tried to identify inputs that are reliably associated with student achievement and school performance. The bottom line is, they have not found any."[24] Paul Barton of the Educational Testing Service estimated that about 90 percent of the differences among schools in average proficiency can be explained by five factors: number of days absent from school, number of hours spent watching television, number of pages read for homework, quantity and quality of reading material in the home, and the presence of two parents in the home. That fifth factor is supremely important, not least because it is apt decisively to influence the other four. The importance of these findings for American education is in the 9/91 factor: Between birth and their nineteenth birthdays, American children spend 9 percent of their time in school, 91 percent elsewhere. The fate of American education is being shaped not by legislative acts but by the fact that, increasingly, "elsewhere" is not an intact family. Until the government finds a way to make Barton's five variables change, positively and quickly, the government's various announced goals about graduation rates and math and science achievements are airy puffs of legislative cotton candy.

Pause for a moment to dwell on why "school comes too late for many children." Schools are supposed to do what parents cannot do as well, such as teach algebra. Schools cannot, however, supplant families as transmitters of the social capital—habits, manners, mores—necessary for thriving. How are teachers supposed to do the work of the families from which seven-year-old children come to school not knowing numbers, shapes, or colors because they come from a home culture of silence, where no one, while making dinner, says, "Here are three round green grapes."

Consider what has been learned about the life-shaping importance of verbal interactions between parents and their very young infants, and the differences between those interactions in poor and middle-class households. The most important preparation for learning in school is learning at home in the years before school, beginning immediately at birth and continuing through age three. And the most important influence on early learning is being talked to by parents or other caregivers. In what has been called "the early catastrophe," the life trajectories of poor and middle-class children begin to diverge radically during those years, in large measure because of the number of words to which they are exposed and the differences between the positive and negative reinforcements conveyed by the words. In terms of aptitude for learning, at age one a child from a poor family is already apt to be significantly behind a one-year-old from a middle-class family. Children raised in poverty are apt to hear 600 words per hour. Working-class children hear 1,200, and children of professional-class parents hear 2,100. The issue is not the substance of the chatter ("I am going to load the dishwasher with these dirty plates"; "Do you see that large yellow truck?") but the torrent of verbal stimuli as the child's brain is developing. By age three, children from poor homes have heard, on average, 30 million fewer words spoken at home than children in professional-class homes. It is not altogether clear why more affluent and educated parents talk to their children more, although fatigue might be a factor in the relative silence of poor homes. And people tend to parent as they were parented, so those who have reached or remained in the middle class are apt to have been raised in homes with verbal cultures.

Furthermore, it is unclear how policymakers can make use of the data about the importance of language. Parents can be encouraged to talk and read to their children, but the parents most in need of such encouragement might be the least apt to receive or respond to it. The depressing truth is that inequality has deeper, more complex origins than we have thought. And America's foundational promise of equality of opportunity is far more problematic and elusive than we, particularly we conservatives, have thought. Equality of opportunity remains more aspirational than actual, and the challenge of rectifying this is becoming more daunting because of the increase in "assortative mating"—the tendency of the educated and upwardly mobile to marry one another—which deepens the "cognitive stratification" of society.

Physicists refer to the "escape velocity" of particles circling in an orbit. Some particles spin, or outside intervention causes them to spin, free from the prison of orbit, onto their own long trajectory. Society's challenge is to give poor children sufficient outward velocity from the orbit that imprisons them. The propensity of a child to flourish is established very early. The crucial variable is the child's expectation that the world will be consistently interested, supportive, and encouraging. The absence of a propensity to flourish can be "read" in the behavioral language of even a nine-month-old. Doctors can read that language in such simple activities as elementary play with blocks. The grim message of some play is that the babies expect to fail for the rest of their lives. Handed two blocks, a baby who is at ease in the world—a baby probably already accustomed to the praise of interested adults—will manipulate the blocks vigorously, dropping one to see who retrieves it, and looking bright-eyed at any observing adult, expecting praise. A baby who expects to fail will have a more limited repertory of play, limited by the realization that no one will care. Poor children sense and acquire the helplessness of their parents—or, more likely, of a single parent.

Progressivism's ascent in the first three-quarters of the twentieth century reflected the new belief that government could and should confer capacities on individuals who were ill-equipped to cope with the complexities of modern life. Progressivism's decline in the final quarter of the century reflected doubts about whether government has this competence to deliver capacities—and doubts about whether a tutelary government that is good at such delivery would be good for the nation's character. One count in conservatism's indictment of progressivism is that it takes too much for granted. According to conservatism, progressivism does not understand how its programs threaten those habits—thrift, industriousness, deferral of gratification—that make free societies succeed. Conservatives worry that the severest cost of solicitous government is not monetary but moral. This cost is measured in the diminution of personal responsibility and of private forms of social provision. This worry has a distinguished pedigree. Tocqueville warned of a soft despotism that "makes the exercise of free choice less useful and rarer, restricts the activity of free will within a narrower compass, and little by little robs each citizen of the proper use of his own faculties." The foremost victims of this robbery are the children of the poor. Today, as when Charles Dickens' Mr. Jarndyce in *Bleak House* said it, "The children of the very poor are not brought up, but dragged up."

Three decades ago, I was shown an almost silent video that was as searing as it was short. At first glance, the scene the video captures is sweet: a mother feeding her infant from a bowl. Ten minutes later, at its end, you understand: The mother does not know how to mother. The video is from a steady camera focused on a twenty-two-year-old woman and her six-month-old baby. The mother feeds the baby, which sits on her knee, with a spoon. The spoon moves steadily; the baby makes no sound and neither does the mother. The only noise, every minute or so, is the soft sound of the baby vomiting. This occurs each time the baby turns with its hands extended, reaching for contact with the mother's warmth. The mother reflexively—not unkindly, but stiffly—holds the baby away. Then the baby regurgitates the food swallowed since the last such rebuff. Vomiting is the baby's tactic for at least prolonging the attention of feeding.

Pediatricians serving some disadvantaged children see many babies with bald spots on the back of their heads, evidence that the babies are left for long stretches on the backs. A child-care—actually, a non-care—product is a pillow made to hold a bottle next to an infant so the infant can take nourishment without an adult in attendance. It is perhaps natural to think that parenting is a natural talent, a spontaneously acquired skill. It is not. It is learned, as language is, early, and largely by parental example. As the woman in the video fed her baby, she gave to it the sort of verbal stimulation she probably got from her mother: none. Depressed, unstimulating, or unavailable mothers produce in babies "maternal deprivation syndrome," which suppresses their infants' development. A mother reared in poverty is apt to have a barren "inner world" of imagination and emotional energy, a consequence of her own impoverished early experiences. And such a mother nowadays may be the only nurturing adult in an infant's life. A study of turn-of-the-twentieth-century Massachusetts showed that 90 percent of households included three or more adults—two parents plus perhaps a grandmother, a bachelor uncle, a maiden aunt. Today many homes have but one adult, and infants are handed around to various caretakers. This can be disorienting and developmentally damaging early in life.

Until the 1940s, it was widely believed that it did not matter who raised babies, if basic competence was assured. A good orphanage would suffice. Subsequent studies, however, documented the bewilderment, withdrawal, and depression of infants who begin but do not adequately complete bonding with their mothers. In too many homes today, says one clinical psychiatrist, "the lights are on but no one is home." People are there, but not there. Inattentive parents are producing children who are like that: They seem normal but they are not what they should be, and will not become what they could have been, given better early nurturing. Verbal stimulation of middle-class infants produces in their babble the sounds of the phonetic alphabet much earlier than those sounds occur in the babble of lower-class children. Will children reared in poverty catch up in school? Probably not. They are not just behind; they are, in a sense, crippled. Animals reared in nonstimulative isolation have been shown to have less brain weight than those reared amid the stimulation of company. Those reared in a stimulative environment have a higher ratio of differentiated (specialized functioning) to undifferentiated brain cells. The chilling possibility is that an infant can fail to develop some early brain functions as a consequence of social deprivation. There is a critical period early in the developmental process of every infant: The merry-go-round goes around only once, and the infant does or does not get the brass ring of the full enjoyment of the potential that was his or her birthright.

This should shock American sensibilities because it refutes the assumption that equality of opportunity is a fact as long as there are no obvious formal, legal, institutional impediments to it. Hence the vast—and increasingly misplaced—faith in schools as the great equalizers of opportunity for upward mobility in a meritocratic society. Studies of early childhood development indicate that school comes too late for many children. Before they cross their first schoolyard, severe damage has been done to their life chances. Even superb schools often cannot correct the consequences of early deprivation, and superb schools are not frequently found in the neighborhoods where children who are damaged by their social environment receive those damages. At least 15 percent of IQ points are experientially rather than genetically based, and the preschool experiences of some children can cost them a significant portion of those points. Studies of "failure to thrive" babies and their mothers suggest a strategy for combating the syndrome. Very early intervention, involving close and protracted supervision of young mothers, can "jump-start" their mothering skills. There are, however, too many single mothers who need this long, labor-intensive, and therefore expensive attention. An America in which a majority of mothers under thirty are not living with the fathers of their children is simply not going to be able to supply a social policy that can compensate for the defects of fragmented families.

In fact, it is arguable that the most molecular word in political discourse, the noun that denotes something on which all else depends and builds, is neither "justice" nor "freedom" nor "equality." It is "family." Without the nurturing and disciplining done in intact families, individuals are apt to be ill-equipped to exercise the freedom to become unequal, and therefore are handicapped in the pursuit of justice for themselves and others.

THE COSTS OF DESTIGMATIZING DEPENDENCY

When shattered family structure is not the negative determinant of life chances, America has made remarkably swift progress in reducing the malignant power of race to distort the quest for more equality of opportunity. Attitudes have undergone sweeping changes that have been precursors to behavioral changes. This has not been good news for those who have a professional and political stake in bad news.

The Depression deepened Americans' feelings of dependency, but when the postwar boom and the democratization of access to higher education increased Americans' confidence in their social competence, the civil rights movement gave progressives renewed relevance by giving government a new mission. The mission was to improve the behavior, and by doing so to improve the character, of Americans regarding race. This was a resounding success and progressivism's finest service to the nation. Then, however, the mission was redefined to give progressivism the unending—indeed unendable—purpose of orchestrating identity politics.

The premise of such politics is that identities, and rights, should derive from group membership, and special rights are owed to grievance groups composed of America's myriad and ever-multiplying victims. A corollary of this theory is "categorical representation," the idea that the interests of particular groups can be understood and articulated only by members of those groups. Such thinking has produced racial gerrymandering and other facets of a racial spoils system, a detour on the road to more genuine equality of opportunity. Progressives steeped in identity politics are not convinced that people can be readily reached by reason. Rather, progressives regard people as defined by, and enclosed in, their race, ethnicity, class, or gender. This leads to a contraction of the ambit of the democratic politics of persuasion. The vacated social space is filled by the brokering of identity-group interests in the name of a spurious equality of opportunity.

The creation of "minority-majority" congressional districts expresses the ideology of identity politics: You *are* whatever your racial or ethnic group is. But that ideology, promulgated by political entrepreneurs with a stake in the racial and ethnic spoils system, is false regarding the facts of human differences, and bad as an aspiration and an exhortation. Furthermore, such congressional districts are bad for civic health because they reduce the incentive for politicians to form coalitions by reaching across racial lines. Such gerrymandering is the quintessential "outcome-based" racial policy. And it is a provocative political entitlement. The purpose of drawing lines to create districts in which minorities constitute a majority of the voters is to assist, virtually to the point of ensuring, the election of minorities to offices to which they are entitled by virtue of their race or ethnicity. The result is "political apartheid," to use Justice O'Connor's phrase from the 1993 ruling invalidating a North Carolina districting scheme that produced a 160-mile-long district that straggled down Interstate 85 and for most of its length was no wider than the highway.[25] Other racially concocted districts have shapes like roadkill—like raccoons that have had run-ins with eighteen-wheelers. All such districts rest on the assumption that people of a particular race will and should think and act alike. This assumption undergirds the doctrine of categorical representation.

Although racial gerrymandering is another example of cures that exacerbate diseases, the most important news about America's race problem is that there is so much good news. To appreciate how far and fast America was transformed in the twentieth century, consider some events that occurred during the lives of grandparents of Americans now living. The 1893 World's Columbian Exposition, which is generally known as the Chicago World's Fair, named as its poet laureate a well-named Mississippian, James D. Lynch, whose most well-known poem celebrated the Ku Klux Klan. On the exposition's designated "Colored People's Day," 2,500 watermelons were distributed to attendees. That same year, at the Paris, Texas, fairgrounds, a black seventeen-year-old accused of a crime was burned in front of a crowd of perhaps 15,000, which had been assembled with the assistance of railroad companies that scheduled special trains to accommodate those eager to enjoy the spectacle. A year earlier, a mob had seized from the Texarkana jail a black man accused of raping a white woman. He was skinned before being burned alive. In 1894, a black man accused of raping a white St. Louis woman was hanged from a bridge over the Meramec River. There were one hundred witnesses. The coroner ruled the death a suicide.[26]

America then was often barbaric. It is not anymore. The velocity of moral change has matched the velocity of change in material conditions, and both kinds of change influence how we think about enlarging equality of opportunity.

We are surrounded by products, from computers to smartphones (computers in our pockets) to pharmacological marvels that were unimaginable fifty years ago. One hundred years ago, a three-minute telephone call from New York to California cost ninety hours of the average worker's labor; today it costs ninety seconds. As Deidre McCloskey writes, "Andrew Carnegie despite his wealth could not buy a cure for the pneumonia that killed his mother." And Lewis Thomas, dean of the Yale and New York University medical schools, who was known as "the father of modern immunology," estimated that "until the 1920s going to a doctor lowered your odds of survival."[27] But the most remarkable change in American circumstances has had nothing to do with applied science in technology and medicine. Rather, it has to do with American attitudes, which have proven to be amazingly impermanent and improvable.

In 1955, Adlai Stevenson, who was considered by advanced thinkers to be an advanced thinker, delivered the commencement address to those he called the "gallant girls" of Smith College. He said they had "a unique opportunity to influence us, man and boy." He urged them "to restore valid, meaningful purpose to life in your home" and to address the "crisis in the humble role of housewife." He said they could do all this "in the living room with a baby in your lap, or in the kitchen with a can opener in your hands" and "maybe you can even practice your saving arts on that unsuspecting man while he's watching television."[28] Any speaker talking like that even just fifteen years later would have been hanged from a branch of one of the campus' stately elms by an enraged regiment of women. Fifteen years can be a long time in modern America. Watch a southeastern conference football game—say, Alabama against Mississippi—and watch an African-American referee imposing penalties and generally bossing everyone around. For Americans of a generation now passing from the scene, a generation that remembers when this was unimaginable, it is a reminder of this: Because America is a creedal nation, when Americans become convinced that certain practices and the attitudes that sustain them are discordant with the creed, they change both.

The American problem of enhancing equal opportunity necessarily begins with race, but hardly ends with it. Today, the problem involves the long reverberations from what began in 1964.

Standing on—yes, on—the presidential limousine, Lyndon Johnson, campaigning in Providence, Rhode Island, in September 1964, bellowed through a bullhorn: "We're in favor of a lot of things and we're against mighty few."[29] This was a synopsis of what he had said four months earlier at the University of Michigan. There Johnson had proposed legislating into existence a Great Society. It would "rebuild the entire urban United States" while fending off "boredom and restlessness," slaking "the hunger for community," and enhancing "the meaning of our lives" by assembling "the best thought and the broadest knowledge."[30] In 1964, 76 percent of Americans trusted government to do the right thing "just about always or most of the time." Today, fewer than 20 percent do. The former number is one reason Johnson did so much; the latter is one consequence of his doing so.

In 1964, Johnson won a landslide victory that also reshaped Congress. After voters rebuked FDR in 1938 for attempting to "pack" the Supreme Court, Republicans and Southern Democrats prevented any liberal legislating majority in Congress until 1965. That year, however, when 68 senators and 295 representatives were Democrats, Johnson was unfettered. As a result, he remains, regarding government's role, the most consequential twentieth-century president. Nicholas Eberstadt rightly says LBJ, more than FDR, "profoundly recast the common understanding of the ends of governance." When Johnson became president in 1963, Social Security was America's only nationwide social program. His programs, and those they subsequently legitimated, put the nation on the path to the present, in which changed social norms—dependency on government has been destigmatized—have changed America's national character.

Between 1959 and 1966—before the war on poverty was implemented—the percentage of Americans living in poverty, as the government measured this, plunged by about one-third, from 22.4 to 14.7, just slightly higher than in 2018 (12.7 percent). But, Nicholas Eberstadt cautions, the poverty rate is "incorrigibly misleading" because government transfer payments have made income levels and consumption levels diverge significantly. Medicare, Medicaid, food stamps, disability payments, heating assistance, and other entitlements have, Eberstadt says, made income "a poor predictor of spending power for lower-income groups." Stark material deprivation is now rare: "By 2011... average per capita housing space for people in poverty was higher than the US average for 1980.... [Many] appliances were more common in officially impoverished homes in 2011 than in the typical American home of 1980.... DVD players, personal computers, and home Internet access are now typical in them—amenities not even the richest US households could avail themselves of at the start of the War on Poverty."[31]

The nation urgently needs a sensible measurement of the poverty rate. This requires taking cognizance of non-cash government benefits (for food, housing, health care, and other matters), counting the effect of the Earned Income Tax Credit, revising the Consumer Price Index to achieve a more accurate measurement of inflation, and a more realistic treatment of households composed of cohabiting couples. A more realistic measure of poverty as actual deprivation would give a better picture of well-being and might cut the poverty rate by two-thirds. This would, of course, be resisted by those in the interlocking and overlapping networks of anti-poverty institutions and programs, people who have a stake in measurements that maximize the estimate of the number of people in poverty. These anti-poverty officials are the reason Moynihan said that if one-third of the money that flows to, but not always through, such institutions and programs were given directly to poor people, no one would be in poverty. But the institutionalization of anti-poverty policy has been, Eberstadt says carefully, "attended" by the dramatic spread of a "tangle of pathologies." Moynihan coined this phrase in his 1965 report calling attention to family disintegration among African-Americans. This tangle, which now ensnares all races and ethnicities, includes welfare dependency and "flight from work."[32]

Thirty-five percent of Americans—about 47 percent of blacks and 48 percent of Hispanics—live in households receiving means-tested benefits. And, says Eberstadt, "the proportion of men 20 and older who are employed has dramatically and almost steadily dropped since the start of the War on Poverty, falling from 80.6 percent in January 1964 to 67.6 percent 50 years later." Work, which requires independence and self-reliance, is essential to the culture of freedom. So, ominous developments have coincided with Great Society policies: For every adult man ages twenty to sixty-four who is between jobs and looking for work, more than three are neither working nor seeking work, a trend that began with the Great Society. And what Eberstadt calls "the earthquake that shook family structure in the era of expansive antipoverty policies" has seen out-of-wedlock births increase from 7.7 percent in 1965 to more than 40 percent in 2012, including 72 percent of black babies. LBJ's bifurcated legacy includes the triumphant Civil Rights Act of 1964 and Voting Rights Act of 1965—and the tragic aftermath of many of his other works. Eberstadt asks: Is it "simply a coincidence" that male flight from work, and family breakdown, have coincided with Great Society policies, and that dependence on government is more widespread and perhaps more habitual than ever?[33] Barry Goldwater's insistent 1964 question is increasingly pertinent: "What's happening to this country of ours?"[34]

Half a century on, the nation's mood is tinged with sadness stemming from well-founded fear that America's new, post–Great Society government is subverting America's old character. This government's agenda is a menu of temptations intended to change the nation's social norms by making Americans comfortable with dependency. And with the degradation of democracy by the practice of financing dependency by piling up public debt that forces unconsenting future generations to finance current consumption. America's national character had to be changed if progressives were going to implement their agenda. To understand how far this has advanced, and how difficult it will be to reverse the inculcation of dependency, consider the data Eberstadt has gathered:

Beginning two decades after the death of Franklin Roosevelt—who would find today's government unrecognizable—government became a geyser of entitlements. In 2010, government at all levels transferred more than $2.2 trillion in money, goods, and services to recipients—$7,500 per individual, about $30,000 per family of four. Before 1960, only in two Depression years, 1931 and 1935, did federal transfer payments exceed other federal expenditures. During most of FDR's twelve presidential years, income transfers were a third or less of federal spending. But between 1960 and 2010, entitlements exploded from 28 percent to 67 percent of federal spending. By 2010, more than 34 percent of households were receiving *means-tested* benefits. Republicans were more than merely complicit, says Eberstadt: "The growth of entitlement spending over the past half century has been distinctly greater under Republican administrations than Democratic ones. Between 1960 and 2010, to be sure, the growth of entitlement spending was exponential—but in any given calendar year, it was on the whole over 8 percent higher if the president happened to be a Republican rather than a Democrat.... The Richard Nixon, Gerald Ford and George W. Bush administrations presided over especially lavish expansions of the entitlement state."[35]

As evidence of the moral costs of this, Eberstadt cites the fact that means-tested entitlement recipience has not merely been destigmatized, it has been celebrated as a basic civil right. Hence the stunning growth of supposed disabilities. The normalization and then celebration of dependency help explain the "unprecedented exit from gainful work by adult men." Since 1948, male labor force participation has plummeted from 89 percent to 73 percent. Today, 27 percent of adult men do not consider themselves part of the workforce: "A large part of the jobs problem for American men today is that of not wanting one." Which is why "labor force participation ratios for men in the prime of life are demonstrably *lower* in America than in Europe." One reason work now is seen as neither a duty nor a necessity is the gaming—let us not mince words: the defrauding—of disability entitlement programs. In 1960, an average of 455,000 workers were receiving disability payments; in 2011, 8.6 million were. This was more than four times the number of persons receiving basic welfare benefits under Temporary Assistance for Needy Families. Nearly half of the 8.6 million were "disabled" because of "mood disorders" or ailments of the "musculoskeletal system and the connective tissue." It is, says Eberstadt, essentially impossible to disprove a person's claim to be suffering from sadness or back pain.[36]

"In 1960," Eberstadt says, "roughly 134 Americans were engaged in gainful employment for every officially disabled worker; by December 2010 there were just over 16." This, in spite of the fact that public health was much improved, and automation and the growth of the service/information economy had made work less physically demanding. Eberstadt says collecting disability is an increasingly important American "profession." For every hundred industrial workers in December 2010, there were seventy-three no-longer-workers receiving disability payments. Between January 2010 and December 2011, the US economy created 1.73 million nonfarm jobs—but almost half as many (790,000) workers became disability recipients. This trend is not a product of the Great Recession of 2008–2009: In the fifteen years ending in December 2011, the United States added 8.8 million nonfarm private sector jobs—and 4.1 million workers went on the disability rolls. The radiating corruption of this entitlement involves the collaboration of doctors and health care professionals who certify dubious disability claims. The judicial system, too, is compromised in the process of setting disability standards that enable all this. America's ethos once was what Eberstadt calls "optimistic Puritanism," combining an affinity for personal enterprise with a horror of dependency.[37] No longer.

What Eberstadt calls the "quiet catastrophe" is particularly dismaying because it is so quiet, without social turmoil or even debate. It is this: A smaller percentage of American males in the prime working years (ages twenty-five to fifty-four) are working than were working near the end of the Great Depression in 1940, when the unemployment rate was still above 14 percent. The work rate for adult men has plunged 13 percentage points in a half century. This is a "work deficit" of "Great Depression-scale underutilization" of male potential workers. Since 1948, the proportion of men twenty and older without paid work has more than doubled, to almost 32 percent. This "eerie and radical transformation"—men creating an "alternative lifestyle to the age-old male quest for a paying job"— is largely voluntary. Men who have *chosen* to not seek work are two and a half times more numerous than men that government statistics count as unemployed because they are seeking jobs. What Eberstadt calls a "normative sea change" has made it a "viable option" for "sturdy men," who are neither working nor looking for work, to choose "to sit on the economic sidelines, living off the toil or bounty of others." Only about 15 percent of men twenty-five to fifty-four who worked not at all in 2014 said they were unemployed because they could not find work.[38]

For fifty years, the number of men in that age cohort who are neither working nor looking for work has grown nearly four times faster than the number who are working or seeking work. And the pace of this has been "almost totally uninfluenced by the business cycle." The "economically inactive" have eclipsed the unemployed, as government statistics measure them, as "the main category of men without jobs." Those statistical categories were created before government policy and social attitudes made it possible to be economically inactive. Eberstadt does not say that government assistance causes this, but obviously it finances it. To some extent, however, this is a distinction without a difference. Largely because of government benefits and support by other family members, nonworking men twenty-five to fifty-four have household expenditures a third *higher* than the average of those in the bottom income quintile. Hence, Eberstadt says, they "appear to be better off than tens of millions of other Americans today, including the millions of single mothers who are either working or seeking work." The US economy is not less robust, and its welfare provisions not more generous, than those of the twenty-two other affluent nations of the Organization for Economic Co-operation and Development (OECD). Yet America ranks twenty-second, ahead of only Italy, in twenty-five-to-fifty-four male labor force participation. This, Eberstadt says, is the "unwelcome 'American Exceptionalism.'"[39]

In 1965, even high school dropouts were more likely to be in the workforce than is the twenty-five- to fifty-four-year-old male today. And, Eberstadt notes, "the collapse of work for modern America's men happened *despite* considerable upgrades in educational attainment." The collapse has coincided with a retreat from marriage ("the proportion of never-married men was over three times higher in 2015 than 1965"), which suggests a broader infantilization. As does the use to which the voluntarily idle put their time: watching TV and movies 5.5 hours daily, two hours more than men who are counted as unemployed because they are seeking work. Noting that the 1996 welfare reform "brought millions of single mothers off welfare and into the workforce," Eberstadt suggests that policy innovations that alter incentives can reverse the "social emasculation" of millions of idle men.[40] Perhaps. Reversing social regression is, however, more difficult than causing it.

America's welfare state transfers more than 14 percent of GDP to recipients, with more than a third of Americans taking "need-based" payments. In our wealthy society, the government officially treats an unprecedented portion of the population as "needy." Transfers of benefits to individuals through social welfare programs has increased from less than one federal dollar in four (24 percent) in 1963 to almost three out of five (59 percent) in 2013. Since the mid-1960s, entitlement payments have been, Eberstadt says, America's "fastest growing source of personal income," growing twice as fast as all other real per capita personal income. By 2018, a majority of Americans received payments. This is not primarily because of Social Security and Medicare transfers to an aging population. Rather, the growth is overwhelmingly in means-tested entitlements. More than twice as many households receive "anti-poverty" payments than receive Social Security or Medicare. Between 1983 and 2012, the population increased almost 83 million—and people accepting means-tested benefits increased 67 million. So, for every hundred-person increase in the population there was an eighty-person increase in recipients of means-tested payments. Food stamp recipients increased from 19 million to 51 million—more than the combined populations of twenty-four states.[41]

What has changed? Not the portion of the population below the poverty line. Rather, poverty programs have become untethered from the official designation of poverty: In 2012, more than half the recipients were not classified as poor, but they accepted being treated as needy. Expanding dependency requires erasing Americans' traditional distinction between the deserving and the undeserving poor. This distinction was rooted in this nation's exceptional sense that poverty is not an unalterable accident of birth, and the distinction is related to traditions of generosity arising from immigrant and settler experiences. Eberstadt argues that the entitlement state is extinguishing this sense and those traditions.[42]

America, he says, "arrived late to the 20th century's entitlement party." The welfare state's European pedigree traces from post-1945 Britain, back through Sweden's interwar "social democracy," to Bismarck's late-nineteenth-century social insurance. European welfare states reflected European beliefs about poverty: Rigid class structures rooted in a feudal past meant meager opportunities for upward mobility based on merit. People were thought to be stuck in neediness through no fault of their own, and welfare states would reconcile people to intractable social structures. Eberstadt notes that the structure of US government spending "has been completely overturned within living memory," resulting in the "remolding of daily life for ordinary Americans under the shadow of the entitlement state." In two generations, the American family budget has been recast: In

1963, entitlement transfers were less than one dollar out of every fifteen dollars; today they are more than one dollar out of every six dollars.[43]

Causation works both ways between the rapid increase in family disintegration and the fact that, Eberstadt says, for many women, children, and even working-age men "the entitlement state is now the breadwinner of the household." Eberstadt believes that the entitlement state poses "character challenges" because it powerfully promotes certain habits, including habits of mind. To repeat, these include corruption. Moynihan warned that "the issue of welfare is not what it costs those who provide it, but what it costs those who receive it." As a growing portion of the population succumbs to the entitlement state's ever-expanding menu of temptations, the costs, Eberstadt concludes, include a transformation of the nation's "political culture, sensibilities, and tradition," the weakening of America's distinctive "conceptions of self-reliance, personal responsibility, and self-advancement," and a "rending of the national fabric." As a result, "America today does not look exceptional at all."[44]

The now normal practice of running enormous deficits in all economic conditions is additional evidence that American democracy is fully susceptible to the descent of democracy into looting. It is looting future generations. There is nothing novel about groups (including entire generations) maximizing their interests by voting themselves benefits to be paid for by borrowing—by transferring wealth from future generations to present ones. That temptation has always been inherent in democracy. Why, then, have large peacetime deficits become normal only recently? One reason, said James Q. Wilson, is the declining moral force of the idea of self-restraint. An unwillingness to defer consumption in order to facilitate future benefits has become a willingness, even an eagerness, of voters to "beggar their children."

From 1789 until the 1960s, debates about new government activities were usually about whether it was proper for government to do this or that, such as run Social Security or Medicare systems.

Since the 1960s, debate has been solely about how to pay for such things—or how to avoid paying for them by fobbing off the costs on future citizens. The rise of conservatism has not reversed this; it has not even slowed it. This political practice is symptomatic of a cultural change, the supplanting of the ethic of self-control by the ethic of self-absorption. As economists Glenn Hubbard and Tim Kane explain, the US political system "cannot govern the entitlement state" that "exists largely to provide material benefits to individuals." Piling up unsustainable entitlement promises—particularly, enactment of Medicare in 1965 and the enrichment of Social Security benefits in 1972—has been improvident for the nation but rational for the political class. The promised expenditures, far in excess of revenue, will come due "beyond the horizon of political consequences." "Our politicians," say Hubbard and Kane, "are acting rationally," but "politically rational behavior is now fiscally perverse." Both parties are responding to powerful electoral incentives to neither raise taxes nor cut spending. So, the perils of the entitlement state are (in Hubbard's and Kane's words) "safely beyond the politicians' career horizons."[45]

IS "INDIVIDUAL ACHIEVEMENT" AN OXYMORON?

As the braided problems of race and dependency demonstrate, it is exasperatingly difficult to clarify what might constitute equality of opportunity for individuals who are socially situated in vastly different familial and other settings. For progressives, this difficulty becomes an opportunity to argue the following: Because everyone is socially situated, equality of opportunity for individuals to strive and achieve is unattainable. Therefore the sensible, equitable way to maximize equality of opportunity is to minimize the degree to which achievements should be ascribed to individuals. Instead, we should think of everyone's achievements as more or less society's achievements. So individuals should be taught that equality of opportunity means as much equality as possible in reaping the rewards of society's success. Because government is the organizer of society, and because society is the shaper of the individual, government is the enabler of striving and thus is the proper arbiter of the equitable distribution of the social product, wealth.

For example, one progressive theorist, Edwin C. Hettinger, has attacked the idea of intellectual property rights by attacking the very idea of individual achievement: "Invention, writing, and thought in general do not operate in a vacuum: intellectual creation is not creation *ex nihilo*. Given this vital dependence of a person's thoughts on the ideas of those who came before her, intellectual products are fundamentally social products. Thus even if one assumes that the value of these products is entirely the result of human labor, this value is not entirely attributable to *any particular laborer* (or small group of laborers)."[46]

Something quite sinister is being done here. The banal fact that no person lives or thinks or works in a "vacuum"—the fact that everyone is situated in a society—becomes the basis for asserting a "vital dependence" of the individual on society. This, in turn, is said to justify declaring that there can be no suitable individual property right to intellectual work. The products of such work are, because of the individual's immersion in society, properly regarded as inherently socialized. So individualism is attenuated to the point of disappearance, and society can claim ownership to whatever portion it feels entitled to of what individuals produce.

In the Soviet Union, "society" claimed ownership of the individual: People wishing to emigrate were denied permission on the ground that they would be taking away education that had been provided by the state. Because the education could not be left behind, the individual could not be allowed to disassociate from society. In effect, the individual could not be distinguished from society. This is where the attack on individualism leads. It begins with the assertion that the conception of democracy "exaggerates the part played by human choice."[47] So wrote

Professor Woodrow Wilson in 1889. One can sympathize with the exasperation that caused Margaret Thatcher to exclaim, "There is no such thing as society."[48] There is such a thing, of course, but its existence should not be seen as an excuse for dissolving the individual into a broth of dependencies or regarding the idea of individual achievement as a sociologically unsophisticated oxymoron. This dissolution, and this disparagement of the idea of individual achievement, remains part of the pulse of progressivism. During the 2012 presidential election there occurred one of those remarkably rare moments when campaign rhetoric actually clarified a large issue. It happened when Barack Obama, speaking without a written text, spoke from his heart and revealed his mind:

> Look, if you've been successful, you didn't get there on your own. You didn't get there on your own. I'm always struck by people who think, well, it must be because I was just so smart. There are a lot of smart people out there. It must be because I worked harder than everybody else. Let me tell you something— there are a whole bunch of hardworking people out there. If you were successful, somebody along the line gave you some help. There was a great teacher somewhere in your life. Somebody helped to create this unbelievable American system that we have that allowed you to thrive. Somebody invested in roads and bridges. *If you've got a business—you didn't build that. Somebody else made that happen.* The Internet didn't get invented on its own. Government research created the Internet so that all the companies could make money off the Internet. The point is, is that when we succeed, we succeed because of our individual initiative, but also because we do things together. There are some things, just like fighting fires, we don't do on our own. I mean, imagine if everybody had their own fire service. That would be a hard way to organize fighting fires.[49] (emphasis added)

The italicized words ignited a heated debate, and Obama aides insisted that their meaning was distorted by taking them "out of context." But Obama was merely reprising something said a few months earlier by Elizabeth Warren, a former member of his administration who was campaigning to become a US senator from Massachusetts. She said: "There is nobody in this country who got rich on his own. Nobody. You built a factory out there—good for you. But I want to be clear. You moved your goods to market on the roads the rest of us paid for. You hired workers the rest of us paid to educate. You were safe in your factory because of police forces and fire forces that the rest of us paid for…. You built a factory and it turned into something terrific or a great idea—God bless, keep a big hunk of it. But part of the underlying social contract is you take a hunk of that and pay forward for the next kid who comes along."[50]

Warren, who was then a member of Harvard's faculty, was being with her statement, as Obama was with his, a pyromaniac in a field of straw men (as William F. Buckley characterized his friend John Kenneth Galbraith, a Harvard economist). Warren, like Obama, was energetically refuting propositions no one asserts. Everyone knows that all striving occurs in a social context and all attainments are, to some extent, enabled and conditioned by contexts that are shaped by government. What made Warren's riff interesting, and Obama's echo of it important, is that both spoke in order to advance the progressive project of diluting the concept of individualism. Dilution is a prerequisite for advancement of a collectivist political agenda. The more that individualism can be portrayed as a chimera, the more that any individual's achievements can be considered as derivative from society, the less the achievements warrant respect. And the more society is entitled to conscript—that is, to socialize—whatever portion of the individual's wealth that it considers its fair share. Society may, as an optional act of political grace, allow the individual to keep the remainder of what society thinks is misleadingly called the individual's possession. Note that "society" necessarily means society's collective expression: the government. Note also that government will not be a disinterested judge of what is its proper share of others' wealth.

The collectivist agenda is antithetical to America's premise, which is: Government—including such public goods as roads, schools and police—is instituted to facilitate *individual* striving, aka the pursuit of happiness. Of course individuals often collaborate, often through government, to make collective choices that facilitate individual striving. This does not, however, compel the conclusion that the collectivity (Warren's "the rest of us") is entitled to take as much of the results of striving as it judges itself entitled to.

Warren's and Obama's statements were footnotes to progressivism's comprehensive disparagement of individualism and individual autonomy. Progressivism assiduously defends the autonomy of the individual in making lifestyle choices. Remember, however, that in one of progressivism's symptomatic texts, *The Affluent Society*, John Kenneth Galbraith asserted—he offered no empirical evidence—that corporations' marketing powers are so potent that corporations can manufacture demands for whatever goods and services they want to supply. If corporations can nullify consumer sovereignty and vitiate the law of supply and demand, this, too, licenses "society," meaning government, to supplant the private sector as the distributor of resources. If the mass of Americans are a malleable, hence vulnerable, herd, then the herd needs paternal supervision by a protective herder.

Warren and Obama asserted something unremarkable—that the individual depends on cooperative behavior by others. But they obscured this point: It is conservatism, not progressivism, that takes society seriously. Conservatism understands society not as a manifestation of government but as the spontaneous order of cooperating individuals in consensual, contractual market relations. Progressivism preaches confident social engineering by the regulatory state. Conservatism urges government humility in the face of society's extraordinary—and creative—complexity. American society, understood as hundreds of millions of people making billions of decisions daily, is a marvel of spontaneous cooperation. Sensible government facilitates this cooperative order by providing public goods (roads, schools, police, etc.)—and by getting out of the way of spontaneous creativity. *This* is a dynamic, prosperous society's "underlying social contract."

Many contemporary ethicists, however, believe that inequalities of wealth that are produced by exceptional individual productivity arising from exceptional natural aptitudes do not deserve society's deference or protection. Economist Arthur Okun argued that "society should aim to ameliorate, and certainly not to compound, the flaws of the universe."[51] But is the unequal distribution of abilities a "flaw" in "the universe," aka reality? A flaw is a defect, a detraction from perfection. But what, then, would be a perfect universe: Absolute equality not just of conditions but of abilities?

Surely before one can reasonably—or, more to the point, responsibly—declare that there is a duty to "ameliorate" some social condition, one should attempt to calculate the consequences of trying to do so. To ameliorate is to make better, so Okun was trying to win his argument by semantic fiat rather than evidence: He was assuming that what he prefers would make things better. But would it? This is, to a large extent, an empirical question, unless one stipulates, as self-evidently true, that all inequalities deriving from the unequal distribution of capacities are unjust, regardless of their social consequences. What would be the results of Okun's egalitarian policies? What if tolerating extraordinary rewards accruing to those with extraordinary natural gifts will make an entire society more affluent? Henry Sidgwick, the nineteenth-century English philosopher and economist, has been validated by subsequent experience: "I object to socialism not because it would divide the produce of industry badly, but because it would have so much less to divide."[52]

People who receive great natural gifts from the lottery of life might not in any obvious way "deserve" them. But, then, someone born with a heart defect or a susceptibility to arthritis does not in any meaningful sense "deserve" those flaws. There are two arguments for leaving people free to exercise, and reap the results of, their (perhaps superior) capabilities. One is utilitarian: This freedom is conducive to *social* abundance, and the greatest happiness for the greatest number. See Sidgwick, above. Or heed John Stuart Mill on industry and frugality, from which society, as well as industrious and frugal individuals, profits: "Industry and frugality cannot exist, where there is not a preponderant probability that those who labor and spare [sic] will be permitted to enjoy."[53] The second reason for respecting the right to the free exercise of inherited capacities is the argument for individual freedom: There should be a presumption in favor of protecting the right of the individual to develop and exercise his or her capacities, and to enjoy the fruits thereof, and a presumption against conscripting the individual into subordination in order to serve politically determined notions of equity.

The more that science establishes genetic bases for differences of aptitudes and even of attitudes and desires, the more pressure there will be for government actions to remedy the unfairness of life's lottery. Many of these pressures, however, will be opportunistic—old agendas seeking, through science, new momentum for respect. And it is not obvious why political power should be put in the service of ironing out differences that are, strictly speaking, natural. Nevertheless, the science of genetics is joining the social sciences in complicating our understanding of what equality of opportunity means. For example, as the acquisition and manipulation of information becomes more important to individuals' prosperity, life becomes more regressive. This is because the benefits of information accrue disproportionately to those who are already favored by natural aptitudes and aptitudes acquired through education and other socialization. It is, however, not necessarily unfortunate when a society experiences considerable cognitive stratification. After all, we actually do want the gifted and accomplished to ascend to positions that give scope to their talents. As Robert Frost said, "I'm against a homogenized society because I

341

want the cream to rise."[54] What is unfortunate is when the transmission of cognitive aptitudes and skills becomes so much a matter of the transmission of family advantages that a child's prospects can be largely predicted by information about his or her parents.

Americans have long fancied that ours is a middle-class society without other significant, calcified class distinctions, a society open to upward mobility. Americans have been reluctant, and hence slow, to recognize what the sociologist Richard Sennett called the "hidden injuries of class."[55] This reluctance is, however, receding, for at least two reasons. One is apparent to the middle class as it looks down with alarm; the other is apparent to the middle class as it looks up with envy and resentment. After more than half a century of attempts at ameliorative social policies, it is undeniable that there exists an underclass trapped by the intergenerational transmission of poverty. Furthermore, the middle class believes, and is not mistaken, that as society becomes more technocratic and complex, and more given to rewarding cognitive elites, those elites become more adept at entrenching themselves by passing their advantages on to their children.

As modern society has moved—somewhat—away from assigning status and opportunity on the basis of kinship, patronage, or class, it has sought quantitative measurements to enable society to be one of, in Napoleon's phrase, "careers open to talents."[56] But even as a meritocratic society seeks to assign rewards on the basis of impersonal and objective standards, kinship, patronage, and especially class creep back in on little cat's feet. As the sociologist Daniel Bell warned nearly fifty years ago, "There can never be a pure meritocracy because high-status parents will invariably seek to pass on their positions, either through the use of influence or simply by the cultural advantages their children inevitably possess. Thus after one generation a meritocracy simply becomes an enclaved class."[57] The cultural advantages are so potent that the resort to crass influence becomes of diminishing importance.

To the extent that a meritocratic society measures and rewards intelligence, and to the extent that differences in intelligence result from genetic inheritances, to that extent a society of truly equal opportunity is a receding chimera. Meritocracy, in theory, seems at first to be the translation of the conditions of modernity into the spirit of democracy. In practice, however, meritocratic aspirations are apt to result in a hierarchal society that seems especially ruthless because it is produced by impersonal, supposedly scientific processes. It is a society in which social standing is supposedly the result of objective credentialing. So, those who do not flourish are apt to feel a special bitterness: They are denied the consolations of concluding that the competition was inherently unfair.

In *A Theory of Justice*, John Rawls argued that "inequalities of birth and natural endowment are undeserved."[58] Therefore, he said, social benefits accruing to persons because of such endowments are justified if, but only if, the prospering of the fortunate also improves the lot of those who are less lucky. This moral imperative sweeps broadly because Rawls had a capacious conception of what counts as a "natural" endowment. He included not just intelligence, physical beauty, and innate aptitudes for, say, music or mathematics, but also advantages resulting from a more nurturing family setting. The Rawlsean imperative requires a government that relentlessly pursues a "fair" distribution of social rewards. This, of course, guarantees an exhausting politics of constant distributional conflict. And how would government equalize the influence of the factions that try to use democratic measures—persuasion; mass mobilization—to influence government decision-making? If some political participants are more skillful and articulate than others, what is to be done?

One should avoid promiscuously bandying accusations of incipient "totalitarianism." It is, however, clear that any government true to the Rawlsean imperative would have to intensely monitor and closely micromanage not only economic transactions but even social interactions. And the family, the primary transmitter of social capital, would have to be considered an inherent rival of, and impediment to, a determinedly egalitarian government. This is why apparently anodyne bromides about "leveling the playing field" can license much mischief. Government should tread lightly when it ventures into the fraught debate about how, if at all, the transmission of family advantages should be regulated or impeded.

Besides, although cognitive stratification and other causes of income inequality make America in some ways less egalitarian, do not ignore some hugely egalitarian aspects of modernity. Anyone can have as much access to the Internet as Bill Gates has; Jeff Bezos and you have the same access to one of the twentieth century's greatest blessings, antibiotics. The devices and medicines that have vast leveling effects on the distribution of well-being have been produced by cognitive elites whose capabilities are not resented by the multitudes who benefit from the results of those capabilities. This is so in spite of the fact that as the acquisition and manipulation of information becomes more important to individuals' prosperity, life becomes more regressive: The benefits of information accrue disproportionately to those who are already favored by natural aptitudes and by other characteristics acquired through education and socialization.

Two centuries ago, the great source of wealth in America was land. It was so plentiful that eventually, with the Homestead Act of 1862, it was essentially given away. A century ago, the distinctive source of wealth was heavy fixed capital: Think of Andrew Carnegie's steel mills, Cornelius Vanderbilt's New York Central railroad, and then Henry Ford's River Rouge assembly plant. Today's distinctive source of wealth is what is called human capital—knowledge, information, cognitive skills. Although these are widely distributed by nature and augmented by universal free public education, there are limits to how much education—even if competently conducted, which it not always is—can do to equalize the ability of individuals to thrive in a competitive society.

In a society where material well-being has become more or less universal, or at least where severe material deprivation has become rare, competition for cultural advantages has intensified. This is only partly because many such advantages, such as education at elite institutions, have considerable cash value over a lifetime of earning. As societies become wealthier, and basic needs are supplied and insecurities are assuaged, monetary measurements become less useful as measures of individual welfare. Today, Christopher DeMuth notes, government's principal activity consists of transferring income from workers to nonworkers for the subsidization of two things that were virtually unknown just a few generations ago: nonwork (retirement, extended schooling, extended disability payments) and ambitious medical care (replaceable body parts, exotic diagnostic and pharmacological technologies). The Cato Institute's Brink Lindsey is correct that "the triumph over scarcity shifted the primary focus of liberal egalitarianism from lack of material resources to lack of cultural acceptance."[59] In 1943, the behavioral scientist Abraham Maslow introduced the idea that human beings have a "hierarchy of needs." At the base of "Maslow's pyramid" are physiological imperatives—needs for food, shelter, nourishment, safety, and sex. In advanced societies, people have advanced needs. These include what Maslow called "belonging needs," such as acceptance and affiliations. Then come "esteem needs," such as self-respect and social status. And at the pyramid's apex is the need for what Maslow called "self-actualization," meaning a sense of fulfillment. In developed societies where the satisfaction of physiological needs is taken for granted, the "higher" needs become political subjects, and the satisfaction of such needs becomes a political agenda. Politics follows society's ascent up the pyramid.

As broad considerations of economic class have lost political importance, considerations of ethnicity, sex, culture, and religion have become more salient. This is why welfare-state answers to the basic questions about material distributive justice have not calmed our politics. Quite different concerns, even more passionately fought over, have broadened the range of political argument. Americans have always been torn between two desires: for absence of restraint and for a sense of community. As the nation's social pyramid becomes steeper, those closer to the base than to the apex feel increasingly at the mercy of governing and media elites who do not seem to be elites of character as well as of achievement. People measure fine character, in part, by shared values. In most societies, most of the time, the most basic values are not much thought about. If questioned, they elicit what sociologists have called "of course" statements, which express the community's "world-taken-for-granted." A dubious achievement of the culture shaped by today's elites has been to diminish the "world-taken-for-granted." Questions that touch the quick of our existence, such as the nature of a well-lived life and the meaning of sex, recently did, but no longer do, elicit "of course" answers.

In this context of cultural disorientation, government tried to engineer outcomes less tangible and more complicated than physical infrastructure. It decided it could deliver more ambitious forms of assistance. As the journalist Max Ways once wrote: "At the time when St. Francis impulsively gave his fine clothes to a beggar, nobody seems to have been very interested in what happened to the beggar. Was he rehabilitated? Did he open a small business? Or was he to be found next day, naked again, in an Assisi gutter, having traded the clothes for a flagon of Orvieto? These were not the sorts of questions that engaged the medieval mind. The twentieth century has developed a more ambitious definition of what it means to help somebody."[60]

As Moynihan said in this chapter's epigraph, politics can change culture, on which a society's success depends. But although politics can save culture from itself, it also can damage the culture. It has done so by destigmatizing dependency for the purpose of universalizing it. In this cultural context, there might even be a cultural contradiction in education, which is supposed to equip individuals for lives of confident independence. The more educated a nation becomes, the wealthier it is apt to become, and the wealthier it becomes, the more benefits its government can dispense to the citizenry. The wealthier the citizens become, the more they pay in taxes, and the more benefits they expect from government. So, although prosperity makes people confident and assertive, and gives them the means to be self-sufficient, it is not conducive to small government or to self-sufficiency. So perhaps democratic life undermines the prerequisites of democracy. It produces first a toleration of dependency, then a hunger for it, and finally an insistence that dependency is a fundamental right.

As dependency on government for various entitlements has grown, so has another kind of dependency. A perverse form of entrepreneurship is spawned as economic interests maneuver to become dependent on government-provided opportunities. As people become more deft at doing so, government becomes an engine of unearned inequality. This is especially a peril in successful societies. Mancur Olson warned that the longer a successful society is stable, the more numerous are the successful factions—*not* the poor, or the unemployed, or the new entrepreneurial risk-takers who are trying to gain a foothold against established competitors—who become deft at gaming the political system for advantages.[61] These include domestic protectionism in the form of occupational licensure; or regulations that are more burdensome to newer and smaller entrants into a market than to large, wealthy corporations; or international protection in the form of tariffs and import quotas. More and more factions figure out how to prosper by achieving distributional advantages through politics. And society slowly succumbs to energy-sapping sclerosis. Prevention of this requires a political ethic that stigmatizes rent-seeking, and an engaged judiciary that is not too timid to declare some of these practices to be unconstitutional because they violate enumerated rights to due process and equal protection of the laws, and such unenumerated rights as the right to apply one's talents to earning a living.

"MOST THINGS ARE NEVER MEANT"

Conservatism's foundational instruction is that we should be cognizant of, comfortable with, and respectful of, complexity. "The nature of man," said Burke, "is intricate; the objects of society are of the greatest possible complexity; and therefore no simple disposition or direction of power can be suitable either to man's nature or the quality of his affairs."[62] This is why (in a maxim formulated by a scientist and systems analyst, Jay W. Forrester, and frequently cited by Moynihan) this is true: "With a high degree of confidence we can say that the intuitive solution to the problems of complex social systems will be wrong most of the time."[63] Hence Moynihan's complaint when a witness before a congressional committee gave testimony that had "all the clarity of logic but none of the fuzziness and grit and dirt and detail of reality."[64] Moynihan served in government during the vaulting ambitions associated with John Kennedy's New Frontier and, even more, Lyndon Johnson's Great Society. Looking back in disappointment, Moynihan recalled that the 1964 election seemed to promise the "direct transmission of social science into governmental policy."[65] Social science knew, or thought it did, how to "manage" the economy to maximize employment, and it assumed that employment was a reliable predictor of healthy family structures. If macroeconomic trends are not the decisive influence, what is? The answer is: Many things that were jettisoned as American society embarked upon a great adventure of liberation, pursuing what can be called the Shelley ecstasy:

> *The painted veil is… torn aside;*
> *The loathsome mask has fallen, the man remains*
> *Sceptreless, free, uncircumscribed, but man*
> *Equal, unclassed, tribeless, and nationless,*
> *Exempt from awe, worship, degree, the king*
> *Over himself…*[66]

Today's culture is a reason for thinking that perhaps people should be a bit more circumscribed by manners and mores, and would be improved by a pinch of awe about something other than their own splendor. America's normally sunny disposition has become clouded by anxieties about the uses to which freedom is being put. Libertarian conservatives and social conservatives occasionally are at daggers drawn, but libertarians need social conservatives. Social conservatives are concerned with society's moral ecology, and with the families, schools, churches, and other mediating institutions that nurture it. These are prerequisites for liberty being put to worthy uses—for, that is, what the Constitution's preamble calls the "blessings" of liberty. Remember Walter Lippmann proclaiming in 1914 progressivism's determination to "put intention where custom has reigned."[67] Today's America has ample evidence that when you shed customs, you get accelerating social regression. Customs are normative; they affirm some behaviors and stigmatize others. When norms come to be considered optional or, worse, repressive, liberty degenerates into license, which is not a blessing.

"Most things are never meant." That is the first line of the last stanza of Philip Larkin's melancholy, almost despairing poem "Going, Going" (1972), in which he says goodbye to all that England had been before modernity overwhelmed it: "England gone/The shadows, the meadows, the lanes,/The guildhalls, the carved choirs."[68] The poem is, as it says, perhaps the poet feeling "age, simply." He was forty-nine; he died at sixty-three. There is, however, a more cheerful implication of the great truth that "most things are never meant." It is a central insight of conservatism that most social arrangements, from families to communities to commercial systems, are not meant. They are not the results of conscious intentions, of premeditation, of design. Rather, they are the results of swarms of independent variables that defy subordination to supervision. The uncheerful aspect of this is that when unintended arrangements, such as families, are unintentionally weakened to the point of disintegration, no one knows how to put them back together. What made the desolation of the South Bronx in the 1970s and 1980s so shocking was not that it was a slum but that in living memory it had not been. As Moynihan said, "In the 1930s, the Bronx was known as 'the city without a slum'" and was "the one place in the whole of the nation where commercial housing was built during the Great Depression." Then came social regression, "an Armageddonic collapse that I do not believe has its equal in the history of urbanization."[69] Reversing social regression by using public policies that create, or re-create, a healthy culture is a challenge at home akin to "nation building" abroad. It is not theoretically impossible; it is, however, beyond our current abilities.

Meanwhile, we need government to swear a version of the Hippocratic oath: "Do no harm." Government needs to get back to basics. The political class, defined broadly to include persons actively engaged in electoral politics and policy-making along with those who report and comment on civic life, is more united by a class characteristic than it is divided by philosophic differences. The characteristic is a tendency to overestimate the importance of public policies, from which the political class derives its sense of importance. This is especially so regarding economic and social inequalities. These, the political class tends to believe, are largely the result of public policies and are therefore susceptible to decisive amelioration by better government actions. In the argument about which is primary, nature or nurture, the former receives an emphatic affirmation from the Founders' philosophy. Beneath the myriad patinas of culture, there is a fixed human nature that neither improves nor regresses. What does change for the better is the capacity of certain portions of humanity to improve the legal, institutional, and social structures for coping with the constants of human nature.

Founding this republic largely on interests rather than virtues was prudent because interests, unlike virtues, are always with us. They are spontaneous; everyone has them. To imagine not having them is to imagine being something otherworldly. Virtues are difficult to acquire, which is why virtuousness is much rarer than interestedness. This is why prudent people seeking to fashion a firm founding for a polity under popular sovereignty will not count primarily on virtue.

Nevertheless, a function of law is to use incentives to point people toward worthy ways of living, thereby strengthening what the polity considers essential virtues. The assertion that virtues need no help from the law is an empirical claim, perhaps correct, perhaps mistaken, but in any case arguable. The assertion that there are *no* essential virtues, or none that is a proper concern of the law, is as absurd as would be the idea of a polity with no notion of the public good. In an open, pluralistic society, government concerns itself with a minimum of what can be called moral essentials. The family is one because much else depends on it. Government can at least avoid encouraging or enabling dissolute habits. It has done much harm by destigmatizing and encouraging dependency.

Good character and the social settings that influence it are crucial to equality of opportunity and are not beyond the influence of public policy in a free society. James Q. Wilson's definition of good character includes two qualities. One is empathy, meaning regard for the needs, rights, and feelings of others. The second is self-control, meaning the ability to act with reference to the more distant consequences of current behavior. Character is shaped by public forces—by general opinion, neighborhood expectations, artistic conventions, elite understandings, "in short, by the ethos of the times."[70] Public policy primarily reflects that ethos, but can shape it a bit, and perhaps even, as Wilson's colleague Moynihan said, "save it from itself."

CHAPTER 7

THE AIMS OF EDUCATION

TALENTS FOR PRAISING AND FOR PESSIMISM

> However, it is sometimes necessary to repeat what all know. All mapmakers should place the Mississippi in the same location, and avoid originality. It may be boring, but one has to know where he is. We cannot have the Mississippi flowing toward the Rockies for a change.
>
> Saul Bellow, *Mr. Sammler's Planet*[1]

We are a young nation," George Washington wrote when the nation was seven years old, in 1783, "and have a character to establish."[2] The nation is now nearly 250 years old and it needs to re-establish its character and to take care that the first words of the Constitution's Preamble—"We the People"—actually denote something real.

The Declaration of Independence began briskly but also problematically: "When in the course of human events, it becomes necessary for one people to..." In what sense were the residents of the thirteen colonies "one people"? They were of many faiths. They spoke several languages: Benjamin Franklin, sensitive to Pennsylvania peculiarities, suggested that Congress publish laws in German, and in the 1850s Abraham Lincoln would invest in several German-language newspapers to further the reach of his campaign. The residents of what suddenly, on July 4, 1776, had ceased being colonies, had powerful local attachments: Even eighty-five years later, Robert E. Lee, a career officer in the US Army, would resign from it rather than draw his sword against "my country," Virginia.[3]

In the second Federalist Paper, John Jay described Americans as "one united people, a people descended from the same ancestors, speaking the same language, professing the same religion, attached to the same principles of government, very similar in their manners and customs."[4] That was more or less true. Never mind that, in an era when religious differences were taken very seriously indeed, Catholics, Quakers, and various Protestant sects would have vigorously disputed the idea that they all professed the same religion. In the aftermath of independence, New York's 1777 constitution banned Catholics from holding public office, and Massachusetts Catholics were not allowed to hold public office unless they renounced papal authority. Maryland Catholics had full civil rights, but Jews did not, and Delaware required an oath swearing belief in the doctrine of the Trinity.

Nevertheless, Jay had a point: Americans, having largely descended from Northern European stock and having been fused in the furnace of "a long and bloody war," were a more or less united people.[5] But as Edward C. Banfield wrote two centuries later, "the harsh fact is that American society—any society—is not a band of brothers but a set of competitors."[6] And as Jay's collaborator in *The Federalist*, James Madison, noted with asperity in Federalist 37, people are not altogether nice competitors, being human and therefore full of "discordant opinions," "mutual jealousies," and other "infirmities and depravities." And "if, in a few scattered instances a brighter aspect is presented, they serve only as exceptions to admonish us of the general truth; and by their lustre to darken the gloom of the adverse prospect to which they are contrasted."[7] So what is to be done to make competitors, if not into brothers and sisters, at least into congenial fellow citizens? Tocqueville's sojourn in turbulent, regionally divided

Jacksonian America convinced him that "in order that society should exist…it is required that all the minds of the citizens should be rallied and held together by certain predominant ideas."[8] Seven decades later, at the peak of pre–World War I immigration, Theodore Roosevelt worried that the nation might be becoming "a polyglot boarding house," a transitory association of strangers.[9] Or something akin to Theseus' ship.

In the Greek legend, the sailor Theseus sailed his wooden ship for years, replacing planks one at a time as wear and tear required, until none of the original planks remained. At that point, was it still the same ship? Human beings do not feel that their identity is attenuated or otherwise problematic just because, as the years pass, the cells in their bodies are gradually replaced by others. But what about a nation's identity? This was a question of existential urgency in March 1861, expressed in the rolling cadences of the last paragraph of Lincoln's first inaugural address: "I am loath to close. We are not enemies, but friends. We must not be enemies. Though passion may have strained it must not break our bonds of affection. The mystic chords of memory, stretching from every battlefield and patriot grave to every living heart and hearthstone all over this broad land, will yet swell the chorus of the Union, when again touched, as surely they will be, by the better angels of our nature."[10] At that moment of desperation, with seven states having already voted to secede, national memory was a vital instrument of governance.

But the memory of a nation needs attending to; it does not nurture and transmit itself. It must be transmitted; it must be taught. Fifty years ago, Ronald Knox, Catholic chaplain at Oxford, noted that in this century, for perhaps the first time in human history, this is true: "You do not believe what your grandfathers believed, and have no reason to hope that your grandsons will believe what you do."[11] No community can passively accept that proposition unless it is reconciled to passing away, or—much the same—being transformed beyond recognition in every generation.

Democracy requires a *demos*. Government of, by, and for the people requires a people, understood as a collectivity defined by more than mere proximity. It must be defined by a moral ecology, a shared identity that is built—consciously *made*—by education and civic liturgies that nourish shared memories. Ralph Waldo Emerson complained in 1836 that "our age is retrospective." It "builds the sepulchres of the fathers," thereby limiting itself: "Why should not we also enjoy an original relation to the universe?"[12] Here is why: An original relation would require us to deny the fact that we are situated creatures, that we are rooted in the moral setting in which we have been placed as citizens. Today's America is insufficiently retrospective. Emerson lamented that college education often was a ship "made of rotten timber, of rotten, honeycombed, traditional timber without so much as an inch of new plank in the hull."[13] But education should be more laden with traditional intellectual timber than brimming with new ideas. After all, most new knowledge is false.

As Princeton's president, Woodrow Wilson wrote often and well about the university as society's "seat of vital memory," an "organ of recollection" for the transmission of the best traditions. He regarded education as a conserving enterprise, a way of making young people artificially "old" by steeping them in seasoned ideas. "We seek to set them securely forward at the point at which the mind of the race has definitely arrived, and save them the trouble of attempting the journey over again," Wilson said. "We are in danger of losing our identity and becoming infantile in every generation.... We stand dismayed to find ourselves growing no older, always as young as the information of our most numerous voters.... The past is discredited among them, because they played no part in choosing it."[14] Hence American society needs to take seriously the unending political task of recapturing the past through the cultivation of memories. Nations are naturally forgetful, and democracy makes them more so. Democracy's insistent message is that all arrangements rest on opinion, so democracies are disposed to focus on the fluidity of the present. The capital of the American democracy, Washington, is a city of frequent comings and goings and many short leases, and is so busy trying to design the future it has little energy left over for learning about, or from, its past.

A utopian tendency, or at least a penchant for perfectionism, was present at the creation of Western political philosophy. In his *Republic*, Plato held out the hope that the more perfectly future generations are educated, the more perfect life would be. America's Founders aimed not for perfection but for the humble attribute of happiness. It is well to distinguish, as the Founders did, between freedom and liberty. A hawk is free, as is a salmon, in that they may go and do as they are inclined. Liberty, however, is reserved to human beings, who are thinking creatures who can choose how they shall be inclined. Reasoning about the proper use of freedom is liberty in practice. Regarding individual behavior, the Founders were moral realists in the sense that they thought moral truths to be objective realities. They believed that such truths could be apprehended by ordinary minds that are neither clouded by superstition nor addled by passion, and that the surest route to happiness was to live in conformity with these truths. If, Locke asked, the mind is a "white paper void of all characters, without any ideas," how then is it "furnished"? "To this I answer, in a word, from experience."[15] From Locke's question and his epistemology came America's one-word answer: Education.

In a 1790 essay "On the Education of Youth in America," Noah Webster said, "As soon as [a child] opens his lips...he should lisp the praise of liberty."[16] Forty-eight years later, Lincoln, in his address to the Young Men's Lyceum of Springfield, Illinois, said, "Let reverence for the laws, be breathed by every American mother, to the lisping babe, that prattles on her lap."[17] Nothing is more American than the belief that the Republic's safety depends on beginning early with education's potent mission. In its short life after the Revolution, the Continental Congress was, because of limitations imposed by the Articles of Confederation, largely condemned to futility. But it had one great accomplishment, the Northwest Ordinance, which included a federal subsidy for primary and secondary education. The subsidy was the requirement that a portion of each township be reserved for the maintenance of public schools. Horace Mann was an impressionable innocent abroad when he became, as many later progressives would be, smitten by things German. Prussia's approach to primary and secondary education intensified his very American confidence in education's improving powers: "Men are cast-iron; but children are wax."[18] Presumably, then, adults will be durable ("cast-iron") versions of whatever the education system made of them when they were young and malleable.

THE VIRTUE OF SOCIAL INERTIA

Politics, properly understood, is a vast field of study and reflection: It concerns how we ought to live in our social, collective capacities. Therefore it is always true that everything of importance, from literature to recreation, is in some sense pertinent to politics. It is, however, a non sequitur to conclude that politics is, always and everywhere, of paramount importance, and hence everything, including education, should be refracted through the prism of politics. The point of politics is the promotion of human flourishing. The excitement of political philosophy, from Plato to the present, and the excitement of politics in every age, is in the clash of different convictions about what flourishing is and how best to achieve it. The American polity is grounded in the belief that freedom is the foundational value, and that freedom consists of protected spheres for free choosing by individuals. The problem, however, is this: Individuals can choose to satisfy their appetites, but their appetites can constrain their freedom to choose. If freedom is, among other things, freedom from the bondage of appetites and passions—from what Yuval Levin calls "inner anarchy"—then the American project depends on pre- or extra-political arrangements for disciplined living.[19] Therefore, although the right to freedom exists prior to government, it depends for its enjoyment on institutions of civil society and government. Hence statecraft is, inescapably, soulcraft, because education is, too.

The fundamental function of liberal education still should be the transmission of the basic truths of the arts and sciences in order to enable students to become critical and independent thinkers. If, however, you believe, as many progressives do, that history's trajectory is knowable, and that it is known by an identifiable clerisy, then you are also apt to believe that the means of facilitating history's unfolding are known or knowable. If so, the purpose of higher education is to produce students who can take their place in history's vanguard, enabling it to reach its foreordained destination more quickly and smoothly than it otherwise would. Hence John Dewey, the foremost theorist of progressive education, said that "every teacher" should be considered "a social servant set apart for the maintenance of proper social order and the securing of the right social growth." The devil is in Dewey's adjectives, "proper" and "right." If you postulate that teachers are custodians of correct politics, it is then natural to define education as Dewey did, as "a regulation of the process of coming to share in the social consciousness."[20] Once the cultivation of one proper and right consciousness is declared the government's task, and to be administered through public education, a particular uniformity of thought becomes prescriptive.

Primary and secondary education should, however, have the more mundane and useful aim of equipping everyone with the literacy, numeracy, and civic and historical information needed for remunerative work and responsible citizenship. And K through twelve education should prepare some—perhaps a majority, perhaps not—for higher education, which should have among its many objectives three that are paramount. It should teach students how to praise, by teaching them the standards by which we decide that a few things are, and most things are not, especially praiseworthy. It should give students a lively sense of historical contingencies. And it should help students develop a talent for pessimism.

A cardinal tenet of conservatism is that social inertia is and ought to be strong. It discourages and, if necessary, defeats the political grandiosity of those who would attempt to engineer the future by rupturing connections with the past. The American Republic is a woven figure that should be disinclined to unravel the threads that connect it to its antecedents. There was a time when education— including and especially what is too complacently called higher education—was considered primarily an exercise in transmission. Its essential purpose was to pass from the past to the future the creative residue of the centuries—what Matthew Arnold called "the best that has been thought and said in the world."[21] The modern revolution in higher education has been its embrace of a contrary mission of liberation. This is the mission of emancipating young people from ideas and norms formed in, and by, an imperfect past. This is to be accomplished, in part, by inoculating students with historicism, which is the principle that every principle is the product of a historical context and is no more durable or valuable than the context was or is.

One result of this inoculation is a constantly renewed cohort of young people for whom tolerance is the sovereign virtue because all other things that are considered virtues are products of contingent conditions and therefore lack solid philosophic foundations. But this tolerance tends to become a fierce intolerance of attempts to assert that there are such foundations. The result is an educated class inarticulate about, because unconvinced of, the foundational premises of the limited government essential for an open society.

Aristotle said the aim of education is to get the student to like and dislike what he or she ought to like and dislike. John Henry Newman said the aim of education is not simply to satisfy curiosity but to arouse the right kind of curiosity. Education, he believed, is the thread on which received knowledge, jewels of the great tradition, can be strung. A university should be, not entirely but for most students, primarily a place that keeps young people from getting lost rather than a place where they find things hitherto undiscovered in the human experience. This entails a curriculum rich in required courses. Granted, this restricts a student's freedom, if freedom is defined merely as an absence of restraints imposed by others. But true freedom is impossible without comprehension of, and submission to, things that are *known*. The most direct path to such comprehension is through the body of knowledge that is civilization's patrimony. What we are losing today is the understanding that education consists largely of arguing from, not with, this patrimony.

At some point, "pluralism" in the curriculum of the university becomes an abdication of responsibility. The attempt to make universities all things to all people ignores the fact that not all good things are good for all people. Modern societies flinch from this fact because much flows from it. Universities are, of course, elitist: a society is judged, in part, by the caliber of elites it produces. A serious university is inherently hierarchical and authoritarian: The few who are qualified to be students go there to benefit from supervision by a few people who know more than students do, especially about what is good for students. To those who say that this is antidemocratic, the correct response is that the idea of democracy is irrelevant to the idea of a university's purpose. Democracy is a political, not a social, concept. It pertains to constitutional arrangements, to the source of sovereignty, not to a "life-style" or a society without hierarchies. It is the opposite of the truth to say that because a democracy is a politically egalitarian *regime*, a democracy presupposes an egalitarian society. It is democratic sentimentality to expect the political process rather than the social system to produce a leadership class. It is a mystification of voting to hope that the casting of ballots will generate rather than just elevate excellence. Generating excellence is the task of many institutions, including universities, that best serve an egalitarian political system when they furnish standards, and elites that measure up to them, for all sectors of society.

However, a specter is haunting our democratic order. It is the possibility, which looks increasingly like a probability, that the democratic ethos encourages ideas and habits of mind that are subversive of the intellectual and moral prerequisites of a stable and durable regime of liberty. The American regime is founded on the principle that human beings are rights-bearing creatures. But if that is all they are, we had better batten down the hatches. Individuals bristling with rights, but with a weak understanding of the manners and morals of community living, are going to produce an irritable and unneighborly community. The primary political problem of the quarter of a millennium since the Enlightenment has been the tension between self-assertion and self-control. Education is the business of enlarging, strengthening, furnishing, and refurbishing minds for the purpose of improving them, partly by enlarging their capacity for self-control.

Although Lincoln estimated that he spent less than a year in school, he had a thirst for learning that guaranteed a lifelong receptivity to information and an aptitude for reasoning. Lincoln was a miracle of self-creation. Miracles are not, however, to be counted on; society must take auxiliary precautions. Religion gives individuals injunctions and other motivations to control themselves. But as the religious impulse recedes, other sources of self-control must be found. Education has been assigned a large and, it seems, ever expanding role in maintaining social equilibrium by buttressing self-control. And in fertilizing the soil of patriotism, which presupposes a purpose beyond, a purpose sometimes higher than, that of the individual. So, patriotism involves transcending, or circumscribing, the value of individual autonomy.

Although the word "education" is not in the Constitution, the importance of education is implied by the political philosophy that produced the Constitution. The very idea of American citizenship is demanding in a way unique to this nation. It requires continual intellectual exertion by members of the relatively small cohort that steadily participates in the nation's civic debates. America is, at bottom, about individual freedom, and one cannot love American freedom deeply or defend it successfully without understanding its grounding in the Founders' philosophy. The constitutional scholar Walter Berns noted that other nations do not have locutions comparable to our "un-American." Few say that this or that person or principle is "un-French" or "un-Danish."[22] Americans are exceptional because they are a creedal people. They are "a people" because they are creedal.

In 1938, when the world had become a cockpit of fighting faiths, the US House of Representatives created the House Un-American Activities Committee (HUAC), which in 1969 changed its name to the Committee on Internal Security, and ceased operations in 1975. Although HUAC did some good (e.g., it brought to light Alger Hiss' treachery), the mischief it did when wielded for unconstrained investigations by demagogic members suggests that elected officials should not be empowered to designate un-American "activities." Nevertheless, there are such, because there are un-American principles. Berns argued that "in the traditional or Spartan sense, patriots are citizens who love their country simply because it is their country." Such patriotism is "a sentiment or state of mind, an awareness of sharing an identity with others."[23] This is, of course, a component of American patriotism. There is, however, something more, something exceptional about American patriotism, something complex and demanding because it involves assent to a creed that says rights are natural to, meaning inherent in, our humanity. A rights-centered society, must, however, take seriously the fact that duties are not natural. They must be taught. Self-interest is common and steady; virtue is rare and unpredictable. A society devoted to guaranteeing a broad scope for self-interested behavior must be leavened by virtue. So measures must be taken to make virtue less rare and more predictable. Among those measures, Americans have always considered education crucial.

John Adams, the most dour of the Founders, expressed typical American optimism about one thing: "The virtues and powers to which men may be trained by early education and constant discipline, are truly sublime and astonishing." But Adams also said something that reveals why education and equality are American values in tension: "Education makes a greater difference between man and man, than nature has between man and brute."[24] If so, the more resources that are invested in education, the more stratified society will become. If education is going to create and widen disparities between citizens, it must take care to inculcate some commonalities. Otherwise, links of shared values and understandings will become dangerously attenuated.

In Locke's imagined state of nature, human beings are, he said, of the same "species and rank" and have "all the same advantages of nature," meaning the same "faculties." Therefore they should "be equal one amongst another without subordination."[25] Elsewhere, in his *Conduct of the Understanding*, Locke acknowledged that there is "great variety in men's understandings" and "amongst men of equal education there is great inequality of parts." This inequality inheres in "their very natures."[26] As regards understanding, "there is a greater distance between some men and others…than between some men and some beasts." All persons have the "seeds" of rationality, but many are "of low and mean education" and are never mentally elevated "above the spade and the plow." So, "in his own subdued way, Locke is as much of an 'elitist' as Plato or Aristotle."[27] But his way was subdued because it allowed for education to enable everyone to reach the threshold of rationality requisite for participation as equals in society's governance.

Benjamin Rush, the eighteenth-century Philadelphia physician and friend of many of the Constitution's Framers, said: "Human nature is the same in all ages and countries, and all the difference we perceive in its characters in respect to virtue and vice, knowledge and ignorance, may be accounted for from climate, country, degrees of civilization, form of government, or accidental causes." Education would be among the accidental, as opposed to natural, causes. Rush held that man "cannot alter his nature; he can only cultivate it."

But there is more than the mind to cultivate—more than the mind, that is, at birth, the blank slate postulated by Lockean epistemology. There also is a natural moral sense or aptitude. "State a moral case to a ploughman and a professor," wrote Jefferson, and "the former will decide it as well, and often better than the latter, because he has not been led astray by artificial rules." The opposite of artificial rules are those that are natural, meaning innate. Here Jefferson supplies a more robust conception of human equality than that derived from Locke's epistemology. People are born equal, not just by being born as equally blank slates, but also in their equal endowment with "rules" that constitute a moral sense. As Gordon Wood says, "Once men came to believe that they could control their environment and educate the vulgar and lowly to become something other than what the traditional monarchical society had presumed they were destined to be, then they began to expand their sense of moral responsibility for the vice and ignorance they saw in others and to experience feelings of common humanity with them."[28]

HISTORY DEPRIVATION

So, at the dawn of this Republic's voyage on the choppy seas of democracy, education was counted on to provide a ballast of moral responsibility. "The object of government," wrote Madison in Federalist 62, is "the happiness of the people."[29] He and his fellow Founders conceived of happiness as Aristotle did, as a durable state of worthy satisfaction with life. To be worthy, satisfaction must flow from the vigorous employment of the faculties that make us human: individual reasoning and social participation. Happiness, therefore, is an *activity*. From philosophy and literature, from Aristotle to George Eliot, we learn that the ethical life is lived by persons of good character, and that such character is acquired slowly, and more or less arduously, by the disciplines of imitation and habituation. And by the study of history, which provides a record of human experiences with imitation and habituation. In his brief biography of Frederick Douglass, Timothy Sandefur notes that "history-deprivation" was one of the instruments of control that made American slavery especially thorough and brutal. "History," Sandefur says, "is a shared tradition about one's origins and the glorification of the achievements of ancestors, which gives one a sense of purpose and a role in the progress of the world. History can generate pride and solidarity among a people." Which is, of course, why history-deprivation was inflicted on slaves. "Lacking a conception of their part in the progress of a nation or a people," Sandefur says, "enslaved people were encouraged to regard themselves not as dynamic and full of potential, but as static and fixed in the landscape. If the slave could be deprived of a past, he could not imagine a future."[30] America is doing to itself absentmindedly what was done to slaves malevolently.

Contemporary America does this by indulging in the pleasure known as presentism, which is the practice of judging the past by the standards of the present. This amalgam of ignorance and arrogance invariably leads the complacent people doing the judging to flatter themselves as much more discerning, sensitive, and generally better than, say, George Washington, who did not free his slaves, or Abraham Lincoln, who never allied himself with abolitionists. It is peculiar. Practitioners of identity politics insist that their contemporaries be understood, and empathized with, entirely as situated products of their race, ethnicity, gender, or class. But these practitioners cannot make the imaginative leap of placing themselves in the historical situations of earlier generations that grappled, as all generations do, with reconciling universal moral principles with the inertia of institutions and mores in the society they had inherited from earlier generations. Presentism is an intellectual failure to which progressives are especially susceptible because, believing in the upward unfolding of history, they are confident that they are the pinnacle—so far—of human understanding. But by validating each generation's vanity, presentism stunts the historical imagination that enables us to take pleasure as well as instruction from our place in continuum with our distinguished predecessors. People who flatter themselves by engaging in presentism should remember that they are tomorrow's past. By condescending to the past, they make themselves hostages to the condescension of the future.

To study history is to immerse oneself in human particularities. To do philosophy is, among other things, to attempt to pierce the veil of particularities and reach commonalities. It is, however, a prejudgment to assume that there are such commonalities to be reached. The only people we ever encounter are formed by particular, and different, histories and regimes. Can we assume or demonstrate that beneath the veneer of culture there is something constant and universal? What if human beings are only this veneer—culture—straight through? What if when we know history we know all that there is to know about human beings? What if historicity is everything, and man is therefore *essentially* nothing other than malleability, with some ability— and not much ability—to direct his own transformation? What if even the supposedly most elemental passions are not universal? If so, then philosophy is a waste of time, and history is anthropology on a grand scale, supplanting philosophy's search for natural standards for assessing human endeavors.

Many American historians, especially, have asserted a professional duty to "desacralize" their subject, stripping away what they consider a long refusal to acknowledge disagreeable facts about the nation's past, facts that supposedly have been obscured by mists of sentiment about spurious heroism and faux nobility in the service of ideals. "Once, not very long ago," historian David Harlan wrote in his study of what he considers "the degradation" of American history, "history was one of our primary forms of moral reflection." Americans criticized their society "just as they criticized their friends: on the assumption that they shared a common set of moral references." American writers and historians engaged in a "centuries long, transgenerational conversation" as they endeavored to help us "locate ourselves in time" and to "gather the strands of American history and weave them into a fabric of possibilities." They helped us to "place ourselves in time" because "there is a distinctive set of moral and political values hidden away at the base of American history."[31]

Of late, however, "history as moral reflection" has given way to "history as cultural unmasking." The "redemptive power of the past" evaporates when historical actors come to be seen not as socially situated selves but as socially saturated selves. Hence "the very idea of a single authentic self, with a stable and clearly defined cluster of character traits, has come to seem hopelessly anachronistic." So people became increasingly inclined to believe, with Jay Gatsby, that identity is and ought to be unstable and kaleidoscopic, "an unbroken series of successful gestures."[32]

What else can identity be, if the conventional wisdom is correct that there is no knowledge of, only opinion about, morality, and that human beings have no nature other than their capacity to acquire culture? We must, however, be careful about what we think we are, lest we become this. Human nature is not infinitely plastic; we cannot be socialized to accept anything. We do not recoil from Auschwitz only because our culture has so disposed us. The fact that much about America nowadays, from random violence to family disintegration to scabrous entertainment, is shocking is evidence for, not against, the moral sense. This sense is what is shocked.

Studies have produced powerful empirical evidence of a moral sense that is a component of a universal human nature. This moral sense is the most plausible explanation of much of our behavior. The political challenge is to encourage the flourishing of a culture that nurtures rather than weakens the promptings of the moral sense. Inside every person there is (in Konrad Lorenz's phrase) a "parliament of instincts."[33] The moral sense, James Q. Wilson wrote, is among the calmer passions; it needs help against its wilder rivals. We have selfish interests, but also the capacity—and inclination—to judge disinterestedly, even of our own actions. Wilson asked: Could mankind survive if parents had to have the skill, perseverance, and good luck to teach every rule of right conduct the same way they teach multiplication tables? Right conduct is so important that the tendency to engage in it must be rapidly acquired. This suggests that children are biologically disposed to imitate behavior and learn the underlying rules by observation. Children are intuitive moralists, equipped by nature for making distinctions and rendering judgments. Instincts founded in nature are developed in the family, strengthened by daily habits—particularly in work—and reinforced by fears of punishment and social ostracism. We acquire virtues as we acquire crafts, by the practice of them.

Above all, the family transforms a child's natural sociability into a moral sense. Most of the things likely to produce enduring happiness—education, employment, stable families—require us to forgo immediate pleasures. Today, unfortunately, instant gratification is promised, and delivered, by torrents of entertainments, which are provided by the well-named method of "streaming." Furthermore, the rising generation is being taught—yes, taught—that all that can be known for sure is what is instantaneous, and hence it cannot be highly valued because it is only of our instant.

The educated, temperate portion of the American public is right to wonder about the temperateness of many educators. It is reasonable to wonder whether many of them remain faithful to the educator's traditional mission. That mission is the conservation, enlargement, and transmission of the ideas, understandings, and virtues on which a society such as ours—a society based on persuasion and consent—depends. A particular cluster of ideas, and a concomitant sensibility, has gained currency in academic circles. What happens on campuses does not stay there, so if the ideas are not identified, understood, and refuted, they will seep like slow, cumulative toxins into the larger society, with large and lasting consequences in our politics, our governance, and our traditions of civility.

For a while, these ideas advanced under a battle flag that has now been furled because the battle has been largely won, the banner of "postmodernism." That is a faith with many factions, but it had a founding prophet. Friedrich Nietzsche proclaimed the core tenet of postmodernism when he said: There are not facts, but only interpretations. There are, however, facts, and being oblivious of them can be embarrassing. During the campus convulsions of the late 1960s, when rebellion against any authority was considered obedience to every virtue, the film *To Die in Madrid*, a documentary about the Spanish Civil War, was shown at a small liberal arts college famous for, and vain about, its dedication to all things progressive. When the film's narrator intoned, "The rebels advanced on Madrid," the students, who adored rebels and were innocent of information, cheered. This college had been so busy turning undergraduates into vessels of progressivism and apostles of social improvement that it had not found time for the mundane task of teaching them facts, such as: The rebels in Spain were Franco's fascists.

At a moment when the phrase "higher education" prompts the question "Higher than what?" it is well to remember the poet Robert Frost's advice: "Don't join too many gangs. Join few if any. Join the United States and join the family—but not much in between unless a college."[34] That advice, like the man who proffered it, is quintessentially American. It is especially American in its general injunction in favor of individualism and against excessive joining—against defining oneself too much by group affiliations. But it also is very American in its inclusion of an institution of higher education, along with family and nation, in a trinity of essential allegiances. America's universities are entrusted with a task central to the nation's identity and success. The task is to transmit the best of the West—the culture of our civilization—to successive generations who will lead America, which is the most successful expression of that civilization. Because there is a high idea-content to American citizenship, being an American is complicated. We are not made up of randomly aggregated moral and intellectual materials. Rather, we are made up of moral and intellectual resources that have been winnowed by time and should be husbanded by universities. We define our polity by decisions about what schools should do, about what the rising generation should read and learn. This is why America's primary and secondary schools have always been cockpits of religious and ethnic conflicts. And what is now occurring on campuses is an episode in the unending American drama of adjusting the tension between the rights of the individual and the rights of the community.

Individuals have a broad right to study and teach what they wish—up to a point. That point is set, in part, by the community's right to perpetuate itself. Lincoln said: A house divided against itself cannot stand. It is equally true that a society unaware of itself—with no consensus about its premises and purposes—cannot long endure. In Lincoln's day, a collision of two clear and diametrically opposed premises nearly proved fatal to America. Today, there is a potentially fatal idea in circulation. It is the idea that this pluralistic society should not want to have, should not be allowed to have, any core culture passed on from generation to generation.

To those who say we are threatened by a suffocating "hegemony" of Western civilization's classic works, the correct response is: If only that were the problem. The danger is not cultural hegemony but cultural amnesia, and the concomitant balkanization of the life of the mind. This begins with the assertion that any syllabus composed of traditional classics of Western civilization will "underrepresent" certain groups—racial, sexual, ethnic, or class-based. Are the great works of Western civilization primarily products of social elites? Of course they are, for many reasons, including the fact that these works come to us from centuries where literacy itself was an elite attainment. But it is a non sequitur to argue that therefore these works perpetuate an oppressiveness that allegedly is the essence of Western civilization.

Some people who fancy themselves intellectually emancipated— who think themselves liberated from what they call a stultifying cultural inheritance—actually reside in what G. K. Chesterton called "the clean, well-lit prison of one idea."[35] Today's imprisoning idea is philosophically primitive and empirically insupportable. It is that any humanities text merely "reflects" its social context, and thus should be read as a political document, a symptom of the "power relations" when and where it was produced. Too often the meaning of the word "reflects" disappears in a mist of imprecision. Usually the assertion that a text "reflects" its context is either trivially true or flagrantly false. It is trivially true if it means only that the text, like its author, stands in some relation to the setting in which the author wrote. But it is false if it means that any text should be construed politically, with politics understood crudely as mere relations of domination and subordination in the author's era. Such thinking causes the study of literature to become a subdivision of political history, and to be studied as sociology. This reduction of the arts to social sciences is reverse alchemy—turning gold into lead.

This is the result of the imprisoning idea that the nature of everything, from intellectual works to political acts, is determined by race, gender, and class. *Any* single idea purporting to be a universal explanation—a comprehensive simplifier of social complexities—requires its adherents to be simple. It makes them simpleminded. Today's dubious idea also makes its adherents condescending—and worse. It is condescending and deeply anti-democratic when intellectuals consign blacks, or women, or ethnics, or the working class, or whomever to confining categories, asserting that they can be fully understood as mere "reflections" of their race, gender, or class, and that members of those groups should be presumed to have the "consciousness" supposedly characteristic of those groups.

The root of such mischief is the assertion that everything is "political." If the word "political" is used to describe any choice or judgment involving what is or should be valued, then indeed everything is "political." But this then becomes a classification that does not classify. One cannot say this too emphatically: Not all judgments about what is valuable are political judgments. It is not a political judgment that certain works have contributed mightily to the making of our civilization and hence must be known if we are to know ourselves. It is not a political judgment that certain books have demonstrated the power, down the generations, to instruct us in history, irony, wit, tragedy, pathos, and delight. Education is an apprenticeship in those civilized—and civilizing—things, and not all texts are equal as teachers.

Civilization's enemies attack civilization's foundational idea, the proposition that human nature is not infinitely plastic and therefore that people cannot be socialized to accept or do whatever those in charge of socialization desire. These enemies believe that human beings have no common nature, no shared moral sense that is a component of a universal human nature. Rather, they say, all we have in common is a capacity to acquire an infinite variety of cultures. The cult of cultural diversity in higher education contains an aggressive ideology concerning the meaning of culture, the aims of education, and the merits of the United States. Multiculturalism is a fact: Americans have various racial and ethnic backgrounds and experiences. But multiculturalism as a policy is not primarily a response to this fact. Rather, it is an ideology, the core tenet of which is this: Because all standards for judging cultures are themselves culture-bound, it is wrong to "privilege" Western culture and right to tailor university curricula to rectify the failure to extend proper "recognition" and "validation" to other cultures. Multiculturalism attacks individualism by defining people as mere manifestations of groups (racial, ethnic, sexual) rather than as self-defining participants in a free society. And one way to make racial, ethnic, or sexual identity primary is to destroy alternative sources of individuality and social cohesion, such as a shared history, a common culture, and unifying values and virtues. This explains the multiculturalists' attempts to politicize and purge higher education curriculums. And once universities are reduced to therapeutic institutions working to heal victimized groups and reform the victimizing society, our trickle-down culture produces similar distortions in primary and secondary education.

The proper legacy of Western thought is a mind capable of comprehending and valuing other cultures while avoiding the nihilism that says all cultures are incommensurable and hence all of equal merit. Sensible people rejoice at any chance to study another culture's Rousseau or Cervantes or Dickens. But education is too serious a matter to become a game of let's pretend, a ritual of pretending that enduring works of the humanities are evenly distributed throughout the world's cultures. We want to be able to imaginatively enter, and to empathize with, other cultures. We must, however, live in our own, which is being injured by some academic developments that impede understanding.

We see on campuses the baneful habit of joining what Robert Frost would have considered too many gangs—and the wrong sort of gangs. We see the spread of intellectual gerrymandering, carving up curricula into protected enclaves for racial, gender, and ethnic factions. Often this is done on the insulting assumption that members of these groups have only watery and derivative identities, which stem from membership in victim groups. The premise of this analysis is that Western civilization has a disreputable record consisting primarily of oppression and exploitation—that Western civilization has been prolific only at producing victims. This idea leads, in turn, to the patronizing notion that members of a victim group are disadvantaged unless taught by members of their own group, and unless they study works by members of their group. Otherwise (so the theory goes) members of the group will lack self-esteem, which is presumed to be a precondition for, not a result of, achievement. Such thinking promotes envy, resentment, suspicion, aggression, self-absorption, self-pity, and, ultimately, separatism.

It is a non sequitur to say that because America is becoming more diverse, university curricula must be balkanized. Actually, America's increasing diversity increases the importance of universities as transmitters of the cultural legacy that defines and preserves national unity. Some policies advanced today in the name of "diversity" might better be designated as instruments of fragmentation. Some policies instituted in the name of "multiculturalism" are not celebrations of the pluralism from which American unity is woven, they are capitulations: They involve withdrawal from the challenge of finding, and teaching, a common ground on which Americans can stand together. Instead, people increasingly stand on little patches of fenced-off turf for irritable groups.

Many of today's balkanizing policies are motivated by a desire to show "sensitivity" to the feelings of particular groups. Sensitivity is admirable, but remember: The four most important words in political discourse are "up to a point." Armies, police, taxation, even freedom and equality are good only up to a point. In the context of today's campus disputes, "sensitivity," too, is good only up to a point. What is not good is the notion that "sensitivity" about one's own opinions generates for oneself an entitlement not to be disagreed with or otherwise offended. Or that the only way to prove one's "sensitivity" is by subscribing to a particular political agenda.

Some critics complain that a traditional curriculum built around the canon of great works of the Western mind necessarily reinforces authority and encourages docile acceptance of existing arrangements. But these critics, some of whom fancy themselves radicals, could take lessons in real radicalism from the many writers of those classic works. Virtually every subsequent radicalism was anticipated in Plato's inquiries. No person more radical than Machiavelli ever put pen to paper—Machiavelli, whose *The Prince* became the handbook for modern masterless men and women who are obedient only to rules they write for themselves. Four years after *The Prince* was written, Martin Luther nailed his 95 Theses to a church door, asserting the primacy of private judgment—conscience. There is a golden thread of magnificent radicalism connecting this German theologian to his namesake, the black American minister, a thread connecting Luther's

95 Theses and Dr. King's "Letter from Birmingham Jail." Europe's late-twentieth-century revolutions against tyranny were fueled by the words of two American presidents, the third and sixteenth, Jefferson and Lincoln.

There is today a warm-hearted idea that every academic activity must contribute to the reforming of society by assuaging this or that group's grievances. This idea leads to fracturing the community into antagonistic groups; to the drowning of individuality in group-thinking; to the competitive cultivation of group grievances; to the subordination of education to political indoctrination. Too much educational energy is being invested in the pursuit of social goals that are peripheral to education's main mission. A university cannot be a democracy, all sail and no anchor, blown about by gusts of opinion and fashion. It must be anchored in the convictions of intellectual leaders who are confident of their authority because they know they stand on the shoulders of giants, the great thinkers of whose legacy today's teachers are custodians and transmitters.

Arguments about university curricula should not be narrowly, crudely political. They are, however, in an important sense, consti-tutional arguments: They concern how the American mind shall be constituted. And in a democracy, mind is what matters most because everything rests on opinion. This is why democracies are in permanent danger, and why it is prudent to keep one's capacity for pessimism awake. One should not be paralyzed by fatalism, but one should be alert to the perpetual danger threatening a democracy's mind with amnesia. The moral of the human story is that things go wrong more often than they go right because there are so many more ways to go wrong than there are to go right. Truths increase arithmetically, but errors increase exponentially. Most new ideas are false; hence most "improvements" make matters worse. This is why wise people are wary of intellectual fads and are respectful of the received greatness that in academic context is called, and frequently disparaged as, the canon.

No academic fad in recent decades has been as consequential as the dogmatic skepticism that postmodernism labeled "deconstruction." Novelist Walker Percy defined a "deconstructionist" as someone, usually an academic, who claims that the meaning of all communication is radically indeterminate but who leaves a message on his wife's answering machine requesting pepperoni pizza for dinner.[36] The indeterminists launch a non sequitur from a truism. The truism is that because our knowledge of facts is conditioned in complex ways by the contexts in which facts are defined and encountered, the acquisition of knowledge is not simple, immediate, and infallible. The non sequitur is: Therefore all assertions are equally indeterminate and respectable, and all ascriptions of truth are arbitrary, hence there are no standards of intellectual conscientiousness. So whoever has power shall decree the truth. Postmodernism was erected on the rickety scaffolding of what is less a paradox than an absurdity, the assertion that it is a fact that there are no facts. Unfortunately, the fact that something is absurd does not mean it is inconsequential. Indeed, much of modern history is a sad story of absurdities that became cloaked in power.

Postmodernism is preoccupied with power because it has no content other than the assertion that the content of any proposition, book, or mind is arbitrary. All content is the result of race or ethnicity or sex or class, and deserves no more or less respect than any other content of any other proposition, book, or mind. Sensible people might suspect that this is a caricature of the postmodernist idea. As evidence to the contrary, consider a pamphlet issued in 1989 by the American Council of Learned Societies. The pamphlet boldly asserted that "the most powerful modern philosophies and theories" are "demonstrating" that "claims of disinterest, objectivity and universality are not to be trusted and themselves tend to reflect local historical conditions."[37] But how can anything be "demonstrated" when disinterestedness and objectivity are untrustworthy?

The crux of postmodernism is the postulate—asserted, not "demonstrated"—that any supposedly disinterested deliberation actually is merely self-interest disguised. And, postmodernists say, it is a duty to "unmask" the "power struggles" that are the reality beneath every pretense of reasoned persuasion. These ideas subvert civilization by denying that truth is found by conscientious attempts to portray accurately a reality that exists independently of our perceptions, attitudes, or other attributes such as race, ethnicity, sex, or class. Once a foundation of realism is denied, the foundation of a society based on persuasion crumbles. All arguments necessarily become *ad hominem*. They become arguments about the characteristics of the person presenting a thought, not about the thought. Once a society abandons its belief in facts and truths, and its belief in standards for distinguishing facts and truths from fictions and falsehoods; once intellectuals behave as though "We are all Nietzscheans now, and there are no facts, only interpretations"; once this occurs, then it seems arbitrary, elitist, and "judgmental" to assert that some books are intellectually superior to others, that some theories are truer than others, and that some cultures are superior to others. If there are no standards rooted in reason, if there are only preferences and appetites arising from group "solidarity" and interests, then there can be no education as it has traditionally been understood.

Until recently it was believed that the study of literary classics gave the reader insights into human nature and the human condition. Nowadays, however, many intellectuals consider it arrogant folly to speak of "classics" or, for that matter, of human nature. Being "subversive" is a postmodernist's aspiration, so to subvert the "privileging" of classics, they are referred to as "texts." The works of, say, Walt Whitman or Walt Disney are all, and equally, texts, and merely texts. Infusing academic life with such sandbox politics and frivolity subverts the function of, and dissipates the social support for, colleges and universities. And when the relationship of such institutions to the surrounding and sustaining society becomes problematic, those institutions swiftly learn a painful lesson about the perishable nature of prestige.

I once stood with a friend, an Oxford don, looking out from his study window at the university's "dreaming spires." He was worried about the decreasing public support for the university. "This is the prettiest view in Oxford. Hence the prettiest view in the south of England. Hence the prettiest view in Europe. Hence the prettiest view in the world. And yet the time may come when young people and scholars will no longer beat a path to our many doors. Remember, three centuries ago everyone wanted to go to the University of Padua." Who in a future shaped by the postmodern sensibility will want to attend any college or university steeped in the idea that "there are not facts, but only interpretations"? What society will devote scarce resources to the support of institutions that regard intellectual life as merely sublimated—barely sublimated—power struggles over competing political agendas of racial, ethnic, or sexual groups asserting solidarity against one another?

We are witnessing, on campuses and throughout society, the displacement of learning—a culture of reason and persuasion—by politics of a peculiar and unwholesome kind, "identity politics." Its premise is that the individual is decisively shaped, and irrevocably defined, not by conscious choices but by accidents; that people are defined not by convictions arrived at by reasoning and persuasion, but by accidents of birth and socialization. The theory is that we *are* whatever our group is, with its circumscribed mental makeup. Although this theory is incompatible with the premises of American democracy, many intellectuals are receptive to the idea that all politics is, or should be, "identity politics," and that all intellectual life is really politics. The idea is that intellectual life may be unconscious politics, but it is politics nonetheless—a struggle for power—and should become conscious of itself. We are told it is simple honesty to get the struggle aboveboard, front and center, by calling every intellectual distinction and dispute what it is: a political move in a power game.

Often nowadays we hear a question posed that is not really a question. It is an oblique assertion of what the ostensible questioner considers a self-evident truth. The question is: Should we not all honor one another's differences? But in what sense should "honor" accrue to accidents of birth? Given that they are accidents, what precisely is there to honor? Surely respect is owed to *individuals* because of their humanity, not because of any membership in any group. Surely honor should flow to *individuals* because of their attainments of intellectual and moral excellence, not merely because of any membership in any group.

If identity politics is valid, then the idea that education should make the educated a member of a larger intellectual culture is invalid. If the premise of identity politics is true, then the idea on which America rests is false. If the premise of identity politics is true, then there is in no meaningful sense a universal human nature, and there are no general standards of intellectual discourse, and no ethic of ennobling disputation, no process of civil persuasion toward friendly consent, no source of legitimacy other than power, and we all live immersed in our tribes, warily watching other tribes across the chasms of our "differences." No sensible person wants to live in such a society.

Today, therefore, sensible people should be worried. Identity politics tends toward a ruthlessness that comes from the dark belief that there can be no other kind of politics—no politics of ideas and persuasion. When groups assume that they are locked in their mutually unintelligible differences, the postmodern sensibility produces premodern tribalism. A society steeped in the postmodern sensibility will have an uneasy conscience about teaching certain great truths, values, or works because it will wonder: Who are we— who is anyone—to say that anything is greater than anything else? And a postmodernist community cannot long remain a community. It will lose the confidence necessary for the transmission of precious things—tested ideas and celebrated virtues—held in common.

Virtues, however, cannot be celebrated when talk about them is displaced by talk about "values." In this regard, we have come a long way, in the wrong direction, since the Marquis de Lafayette returned to America for a hero's tour in 1824. His extended visit catalyzed the young republic's unease about what it sensed was a decline from the pinnacle achieved by the Revolutionary generation that by then had largely passed from the scene. The nation then was feeling its oats economically, but was feeling queasy about whether its character was as strong as its economy. It worried that the process by which it was becoming rich—the banking, industrialization, speculation, and urbanization of early capitalism—was leading it away from the sturdy virtues of a yeoman's republic. The anxiety of that day was, however, not voiced in talk about values. Americans talked then as the Founders had talked: of virtues.

You may well wonder: values, virtues, what's the difference? Today, talk about "values" is so incessant that it is difficult to recognize that it is a new and regrettable departure from our traditional vocabulary of moral aspirations. Once upon a time, the word "value" was used most often as a verb, meaning "to esteem," as in "I value your friendship." It also was a singular noun, such as in "inflation hurts the value of the currency." However, in today's political discourse, value is used most as a plural noun denoting beliefs and attitudes of individuals and societies. This is evidence of the de-moralization of society. De-moralization advances when the categories virtue and vice are "transcended" and we are left with the thin gruel of values talk as we slide beyond talk about good and evil.

How very democratic values talk is. Unlike virtues, everyone has values; everyone has as many as they choose. Hitler had scads of values. George Washington had virtues. Who among those who knew him—surely not the Marquis de Lafayette—would have spoken of George Washington's "values"? Values talk, however, alas, suits today's zeitgeist. It is the talk of a non-judgmental age. Ours is an age judgmental only about the sin of being judgmental. Today, it is a mark of broadmindedness to say, "Oh, one person's values are as good as another's." It is, of course, nonsense to say, "One person's virtues are as good as another's." Values are an equal-opportunity business; they are mere choices. In contrast, virtues are habits, difficult to develop and therefore not equally accessible to all. Speaking of virtues rather than values is elitist, offensive to democracy's egalitarian, leveling ethos, which is precisely why talk of virtues should be revived and talk of values should be devalued.

PREVENTIVE VIRTUES

Alexis de Tocqueville, who toured America not long after Lafayette did, noted that although much is gained by replacing aristocratic with democratic institutions and suppositions, something valuable is often lost—the ability to recognize, and the hunger to honor, hierarchies of achievement and character. Therefore, democracy requires the cultivation of preventive virtues that counter certain unhealthy tendencies in democracies. People, particularly young people, need to be taught how to praise. They need to learn, especially in school, to look up—to the elevated and the heroic in thoughts and deeds, in history, politics, literature, science, and faith. After all, some of the glittering minority of men and women who became heroes often were pulled up to greatness by visions of nobility found in history and literature. The proper purpose of education in American democracy is not to serve as a values cafeteria, where young people are invited, and therefore encouraged, to pick whatever strikes their fancies. Rather, the purpose of education, and especially higher education, for young citizens of a democracy is to help them identify a rarity—excellence—in various realms, and to study what virtues bring it about and make it excellent.

Denying that great individuals are great history-makers is a democratic impulse in the historians' craft—"history from the bottom up" or "history with the politics left out." "Elitist" history that stresses great individuals and events—political, military, diplomatic, intellectual—supposedly insults common people. The supposed corrective is "affirmative-action history," which allots more attention to ordinary activities of the many than to the extraordinary activities of the few. This involves painting mankind's story without the bright primary colors of personal greatness. Which has two bad consequences. Pastel history teaches that mastery of events is a chimera, so why bother with politics? And it makes the idea of "leadership" suspect, so who cares about the character and caliber of leaders?

Ours is an age in which children are taught not to discover the good but to manufacture "values," not so they can lead noble lives but so they can devise pleasant "lifestyles." It is an age in which the aim of life is not autonomy in the sense of a life regulated by exacting standards but rather "authenticity" in following strong feelings. It is an age of the egalitarian distribution of esteem, so indiscriminateness is a moral imperative. And this extends to the whole wide world. In 1991, Florida's legislature enacted a law requiring public schools to teach that no "culture is intrinsically superior or inferior to another." The word "intrinsically" seems intended to make the assertion foggy. This entire law must have been especially mystifying to the many Floridians who are refugees from communist Cuba and know from firsthand experience that the law is rubbish.[38]

It is probably said by every generation that the problem with the younger generation is that it has not read the minutes of the last meeting. Today, however, the rising generations have not been instructed at school in the Founders' premises. Perhaps this helps to explain the ravenous appetite, in the relative small portion of the public that reads such things, for biographies of the Founders. The Founders' premises have few adherents in higher education, which in our homogenized intellectual culture sets the tone and agenda for all education. Today, students are not taught that, as the Founders believed, a hierarchy of moral and political choices can be established by reason. Instead, the social sciences teach that the world is a bazaar of cultures, no one of which is demonstrably superior to another. Some cultures place high value on tolerance, but relativism teaches that a preference for tolerance is as arbitrary as any other preference. Intellectual openness—to experience, to arguments—used to be an instrumental virtue valued because it made possible the quest, through reason, for knowledge of the objectively good. Now openness is not instrumental for important ends, it *is* an end. It is the only universal value because reason has been declared powerless to discern the good. There is, however, vanity beneath this supposed intellectual humility: Openness makes the absence of principle look principled. The American mind is being closed in the name of openness—closed to the idea of reasoned discrimination between ways of living.

The sociology of virtue would be a fertile field for research, if more sociologists believed in virtue. Jefferson, who wrote the distilled essence of the American creed, was a sociologist of virtue. He is sometimes caricatured as a person who was optimistic to the point of simplemindedness. He did, indeed, have the confidence of a natural aristocrat, and the expansive intellectual expectation of progress that characterized the eighteenth-century Enlightenment of which he was an exemplar. But consider what he actually said about the problems of governance, and about the myriad lurking threats to the goodness of America. Democracy, he said, depends on the nurturing of certain virtues in its citizens. On those virtues, personal independence depends. But those virtues, and hence the strength of character that we recognize as true independence in individuals, depends, he thought, on a very particular kind of social order. It depends on a rural society that produces sturdy yeomen. Hence his warning against piling up people in cities. He did not allow his enjoyment of Paris to crimp his theorizing that cities are, inherently and everywhere, "pestilential."[39] He exhorted Americans to let Europe have the cities—and hence the workshops, as well. Jefferson lived with his customary flair and zest in the Paris of the 1780s, a city fermenting with cultural and political upheaval. And having seen urban crowds abroad and at home, he still said, "I am not among those who fear the people."[40] But cut the people off from connection with the land, from a life of rural husbandry, and Jefferson's trust became as attenuated as he said the people's virtue must then become. He believed that human nature presented political problems but that those problems could be ameliorated by nature itself—by the education in hardihood and independence that comes from a life engaged in labor on the land.

The contrast between Jefferson's political philosophy and the philosophies of the ancients is stark. The words "civic," "citizen," and "city" have a common root. Classical political philosophy taught that man could only become civilized—made suitable for life in the city, and for citizenship—by the close proximity to, and involvement with, other people that is required by life in a polity compact enough to be walked across in a day. Compactness was a necessary condition for the flourishing of a political community. So said most political philosophers prior to America's Founders. Jefferson's and America's break with this classical tradition was complete. He wanted space not only between the citizen and the government, but also between citizens. Hence the alacrity with which he leaped at the opportunity to make the Louisiana Purchase for Americans' suddenly very "extensive Republic."[41] From the beginning, American virtue was linked with space, meaning room enough for Americans to develop the virtues that undergird personal independence.

Classical political philosophy taught that the fulfillment of human life depended on active engagement in the civil, political life of the country. Jefferson lived such a life, but he did not live it contentedly or even happily, and he did not recommend it. To him, political engagement was a duty to be done, but not a career to be sought, still less a pleasure to be relished. He delighted in shaking the dust of Washington from his shoes. Government, he thought, should not be at the center of American life, or at the center of the life of any American who could honorably avoid it. In 1813, speaking after what he called "an intimacy of forty years with the public councils and characters," he said: "An honest man can feel no pleasure in the exercise of power over his fellow citizens."[42] In American political thought, and especially in Jefferson's thought, it is work, which takes place in the private sphere of life, not politics in the public sphere, that is the primary source of American dignity. In this regard, Lincoln was squarely in the Jeffersonian tradition. Lincoln came (in the words of his campaign song) "out of the wilderness, down in Illinois" when people still spoke of "the Illinois frontier."[43] Lincoln came from where people were grappling with nature, subduing it, fulfilling their (and the nation's) manifest destiny in work.

American literature reflects—and reinforces—this national yearning for private space in which to work out one's personal destiny. James Fenimore Cooper in the forest, Herman Melville at sea, Mark Twain on the Mississippi, Henry David Thoreau by his pond: All expressed an American—a Jeffersonian—faith in virtue developed without dependence on political engagement, or even on "society." Few people in contemporary America have even an inkling of what that cowboy from Manhattan, Teddy Roosevelt, called "the Iron desolation" of the Great Plains. What Willa Cather, the novelist from Red Cloud, Nebraska, called "the inconceivable silence of the plains" is indeed inconceivable to most modern Americans who are enveloped by the cacophony of metropolitan living.[44] For this reason, America needs to become again what it once was: more Lockean and less Hobbesian.

Locke, so important to America's Founders, tempered his philosophic individualism by stressing shareable norms that come to us from nature and common experience, and which require us to take into account things other than our own desires. Locke's intellectual precursor, Thomas Hobbes, had portrayed human beings almost as not possessing true personhood—as not rational, responsible, or free beyond a few elemental calculations. Hobbes said people are subject to irresistible stimuli and hence are as determined as physical objects, like billiard balls struck by a cue or other balls. Human rights, as Hobbes understood them, arise from, and are defined by, irresistible urges, such as fear and the desire for security from violent death. People who become comfortable with such a characterization of human beings will lose their ability to take responsibility for their self-creation through moral choices. And a society morally anesthetized by the reduction of persons to bundles of impulses, and by the definition of rights in terms of powerful desires, should not be surprised by the coarsening of the culture. Hobbes famously said that life in the state of nature is completely presocial ("solitary"). But a society that describes, as Hobbes did, a world void of natural norms will become barely social. The void at its center will be filled entirely by individual's interests and drives. Man, said the philosopher and novelist Iris Murdoch, is a creature who makes pictures of himself—and comes to resemble the pictures. Hobbes' de-moralized and demoralizing picture of mankind can be self-fulfilling, and is becoming so on campuses.

Leave aside the pandemic infantilization of students, faculty, and administrators as colleges and universities descend into perpetual hysteria about "microaggressions" that "trigger" stampedes to "safe spaces" where students, traumatized by encounters with—or rumors of—uncongenial ideas recover their emotional equilibrium with the help of coloring books and videos of frolicking puppies. But dwell upon this: Through eight centuries of ecclesiastical and political interferences, the West evolved its great research universities, and now, in a generation, some of them are frittering away their prestige and forfeiting their reputations for seriousness. And notice the truth of this mordant definition: "College: Those magical seven years between high school and your first warehouse job."[45] Students study many fewer hours a week than they did two generations ago, a fact masked by grade inflation for young adults who as children all won participation trophies for just showing up for soccer practice. Graduation rates at hundreds of public colleges and universities are under 25 percent, and barely more than half of those who matriculate graduate in even six years. According to the Federal Reserve and Bureau of Labor Statistics, 40 percent of recent graduates have jobs that do not require a college degree—which is perhaps a good thing, considering that often their degrees do not denote serious encounters with demanding curricula.

New technologies have exacerbated certain disturbances in the intellectual atmosphere. In 2005, Lynne Truss presciently warned that we were slouching into "an age of social autism" with a "Universal Eff-Off Reflex." Before video streaming brought us binge-watching, she foresaw people entertaining themselves into inanition with portable technologies that enable "limitless self-absorption" and make people solipsistic and unmannerly. Truss foresaw an age of "hair-trigger sensitivity" and "lazy moral relativism combined with aggressive social insolence."[46] This was twelve years before some Wellesley College professors said that inviting controversial, meaning conservative, speakers to campus injures students by forcing them to "invest time and energy in rebutting the speakers' arguments."[47]

The consequences of growing intolerance are enumerated by Tom Nichols, who says that our devices and social media are producing people who confuse "Internet grazing" with research and equate this faux research with higher education. Today, students demand to run institutions that the students insist should treat them as fragile children. "It is," Nichols writes, "a new Declaration of Independence: no longer do we hold these truths to be self-evident, we hold all truths to be self-evident, even the ones that aren't true. All things are knowable and every opinion on any subject is as good as any other." In today's therapeutic culture, which seems designed to validate every opinion and feeling, there will rarely be disagreement without anger between thin-skinned people who cannot distinguish the phrase "you're wrong" from "you're stupid." Equating "critical thinking" with "relentless criticism" results in worse than the indiscriminate rejection of this or that actual expert. This equation produces what Nichols calls "a Google-fueled, Wikipedia-based, blog-sodden" disdain for even the ideal of expertise. This ideal is an affront in a culture that "cannot endure even the slightest hint of inequality of any kind." Unfortunately, Nichols notes, "specialization is necessarily exclusive."

And aren't we glad: "When you take an elevator to the top floor of a tall building, the certificate in the elevator does not say 'good luck up there'; it says that a civic authority, relying on engineers educated and examined by other engineers, have looked at that box and know, with as much certainty as anyone can, that you'll be safe."[48]

The "spreading epidemic of misinformation" gives rise to a corollary to Gresham's Law ("bad money drives out good"): "Misinformation pushes aside knowledge." Everyone with a smartphone has in his or her pocket, Nichols says, more information "than ever existed in the entire Library of Alexandria." This can, however, produce a self-deluding veneer of erudition and a sense of cheap success. Nichols recounts an old joke about a British Foreign Office official who retired after forty years: "Every morning I went to the Prime Minister and assured him there would be no world war today. And I am pleased to note that in a career of 40 years, I was only wrong twice."[49] This official deserved an A grade, like everyone else.

It would help if people would put their electronic devices away from the center of their existences and pick up a book. Johannes Gutenberg's invention of printing with moveable type was the necessary precursor of mass literacy, and hence was, as Senator Ben Sasse says, "arguably the most radical leveling event in history."[50] Democratizing access to information was a necessary solvent of hierarchies based on privileged access to knowledge, and a necessary precondition for social mobility. There have been times when reading was regarded with suspicion. Some among the ancient Greeks regarded the rise of reading as cultural decline: They considered oral dialogue, which involves the constant posing of clarifying questions, more conducive to truth. But the transition from an oral to a print culture has generally been a transition from a tribal society to a society of self-consciously separated individuals. In Europe, that transition alarmed ruling elites, for whom the "crisis of literacy" was the fact that there was too much literacy: Readers had, inconveniently, minds of their own. Reading is inherently private; hence the reader is potentially beyond state supervision or crowd psychology. This suggests why there are perils in the transition from a print to an electronic culture. Time was, books were the primary means of knowing things. Now many people learn most things visually, from the graphic presentation of immediately, effortlessly accessible pictures. People grow accustomed to the narcotic effect of their own passive reception of today's sensory blitzkrieg of surfaces. They recoil from the more demanding nature of active engagement with books—with the nuances encoded in the limitless permutations of alphabetic signs on pages. Besides, reading requires two things that are increasingly scarce, and to which increasing numbers of Americans seem allergic: solitude and silence.

"BUT IF NOT"

Reading books that are part of a community's shared experience is one way of assuring the reality of a community. In 1872, Theodore Roosevelt, Sr., took his family to Europe for an extended tour, during which his son Teddy did what fourteen-year-olds often do: He had a growth spurt. His parents had to buy him a new suit because his wrists and ankles protruded comically from the suit he had brought from New York. He and his family called his outgrown clothes "my 'Smike suit,' because it left my wrists and ankles as bare as those of poor Smike himself."[51] Smike was one of the forty urchins badly treated by Wackford Squeers at Dotheboys Hall, the Yorkshire school that Charles Dickens described so darkly in *Nicholas Nickleby*. For fourteen-year-old Teddy and his family, this secondary character from a Dickens novel—a novel published thirty-three years before the Roosevelts' European tour—was familiar enough to provide cultural references. Smike was part of the shared vocabulary, the casual discourse of this family.

In 1910, Teddy Roosevelt had for two years been a former president, and was not happy. The political mores of that day required would-be presidential candidates to manifest diffidence, if not reluctance, about seeking office. During a trip to Boston, TR stayed at the home of a supporter, and when journalists asked the supporter if TR would be a candidate in 1912, he answered simply, "Barkis is willin'." Barkis was the stagecoach driver in *David Copperfield*, who relentlessly courted Clara Peggotty, Copperfield's childhood nurse. Dickens' readers remembered Barkis for his reiteration of the phrase "Barkis is willin'." Eleven decades later, we are unlikely to encounter the easy, unaffected insertion of such literary references into conversations.[52]

In June 1940, a British officer in the desperate circumstances of Dunkirk beach flashed to London a three-word message: "But if not." What meaning, if any, would we today find in such an opaque—to us—message? Far from seeming opaque in 1940, it was instantly recognized, as its sender assumed it would be, as a Biblical quotation. It is from the Book of Daniel, from the passage in which Nebuchadnezzar commands Shadrach, Meshach, and Abednego to either worship the golden image or be thrust into the fiery furnace. The three threatened men respond defiantly: "Our God whom we serve is able to deliver us from the burning fiery furnace, and he will deliver us out of thine hand, O king. But if not, be it known unto thee, O king, that we will not serve thy gods, nor worship the golden image…"[53] A British officer, with his back to the English Channel and his face to the Wehrmacht, expressed heroic defiance with elegant economy. He distilled his situation and his moral stance into three one-syllable words. In the cacophony of war, in the deadly confusion of an evacuation under attack, he deftly plucked from the then-common culture an almost universally familiar fragment of a passage from a book. With the fragment he connected himself, and his interlocutors, with a resonant story from the Western canon.

Today, the very few Americans who know about it probably look back upon the "five-foot shelf" phenomenon with bemused condescension. Charles W. Eliot, who had been president of Harvard for forty years when he retired in 1909, once told a group of working men that although not everyone could go to Harvard, anyone could read like "a Harvard man." What was required, Eliot said, was a five-foot shelf of those books that define our common culture. P. F. Collier and Son publishing company obliged by publishing fifty-one volumes as Harvard Classics, selling 350,000 sets in twenty years.[54] Today, it would be rash to assume that Harvard itself acquaints its students with such a canon.

The shared stock of literary and historical knowledge is not as plentiful as it used to be. When in 1840 and 1841 Dickens was publishing *The Old Curiosity Shop* serially in newspapers, some of his ardent readers in New York went to the docks when transatlantic ships arrived with English newspapers, anxiously shouting up to the crew members on deck, "Did little Nell die?" Times and sensibilities change, and years later Oscar Wilde said that anyone who could read of the death of Little Nell without laughing must have a heart of stone. But without regretting the passing of the hunger for Dickensian melodrama, one should very much regret the passing of the passionate reading public.

It is simply impossible to imagine a book—any book on any subject—having the impact that Harriet Beecher Stowe's *Uncle Tom's Cabin* had when published in 1852. This novel sold 300,000 copies in the United States in the first year of its publication. Relative to population, this is comparable to selling four million copies in a year today. And the literate portion of the population was much smaller then. Within a decade Stowe's novel sold more than two million copies in the United States. It is to this day the best-selling book of all time in proportion to population. Lincoln may or may not have said to Stowe when she visited the White House, "So you're the little woman who started this big war."[55] But because opinion drives events in a democracy, her book was indeed a precipitant of the war. She put pen to paper and changed the world.

Karl Marx, her contemporary, might have had trouble shoe-horning her achievement into his philosophy of history. His grave in London's Highgate Cemetery bears these of his words: "The philosophers have only interpreted the world, in various ways. The point, however, is to change it."[56] Marx misinterpreted the world in various ways, and changed it for the worse, because interpretations have consequences. Marx devalued humanity's intellectual history by arguing that human consciousness is not just conditioned by, it is controlled by, a society's system of production. As H. Stuart Hughes observed, Marx and Marxists became fond of "obstetrical metaphors" about the present being pregnant with the future, which must be mid-wived by this or that force or political party. Such biological categories encouraged thinking about social change as a non-volitional process with a progressive inner logic. Soon after Marx, Freud stressed the irrational, or non-rational, instinctive side of life. Marx focused on the limited freedom of human consciousness circumscribed by social arrangements. Freud saw freedom limited by inner "drives." Marx, Freud, and other intellectuals were convinced that they had pierced the veil of appearances, unmasked illusions, and found a substratum that supposedly is the real basis of things, thereby solving the problem of observing and analyzing society.[57]

There was, however, an anti-intellectual aspect to what such think-ers were thinking. They all said, in one way or another, that ideas were derivative from, or reflections of, other things. In one way or another, this made the idea of human agency problematic, which in turn com-plicated the study of history and the valuing of self-government. The motivated individual is supposedly the crux of historical study. But in what sense is the individual the master of his motives, and therefore really a history-maker? If Marx was right, classes, not individuals, are history's motors. And when Darwinian categories infused social thinking, the idea of consciousness became entangled with the ideas of environmental and hereditary causation. One result was "scientific fatalism," a retreat not necessarily from the idea of progress, but from the seventeenth- and eighteenth-century Enlightenment idea that progress could be produced by largely uncircumscribed choices, consciously made for clear motives on the basis of objectively verifiable social ideas.[58] The Enlightenment idea was that humanity could understand and manipulate the social world because humanity made it. This idea was challenged by a new intellectual field, the sociology of knowledge. Interest in the social conditioning of thought—the thought of individuals, classes, or entire societies—was a consequence of the new insistence on the historicity of *everything*.

Humanity has been plied and belabored by various historicisms purporting to prove what has happened had to happen, that history is a dry story of the ineluctable working of vast impersonal forces unfolding according to iron laws of social evolution. In his preface to *Kapital*, Karl Marx said that "the economic law of motion in modern society"—the "natural laws of capitalist production"—are "working with iron necessity towards inevitable results."[59] This theory of history was of a piece with his theory that human nature was not a permanent essence (*wesen*) but something constantly created by the unfolding of teleological History in accordance with those "iron" laws. If Marx was right, the task of understanding the past becomes difficult, perhaps insuperably so. Besides, why bother? If the ancient Greeks and Romans, or the people of the Middle Ages, had natures that were not natural, but were "reflections" of the relations of classes to their social systems, understanding them is not pertinent to our situation. If there is no human nature and therefore no constant categories—if it is not consciousness that determines existence, but existence that determines consciousness—then the understanding of previous eras is difficult, moral judgments about them are pointless, and they are not relevant to the ongoing human story.

When such thinking spreads, so does the danger that life will be swallowed by the politics of consciousness. If people are taught that they are mere corks bobbing on a tide of irresistible causality, they will be tempted by passivity and tormented by the fact that their consciousness is not really theirs. Surely there is a connection between the various theories about human agency being attenuated or chimerical and the emergence of a cowering, timid generation of students embracing a cult of fragility and demanding to be made "safe" from almost everything. Furthermore, to deny the autonomy of culture, explaining it as an "epiphenomenon," a "reflection" of other forces, is to drain culture of dignity. The reduction of the study of literature to sociology, and of sociology to mere ideological assertion, has a central tenet: Writers are captives of the conditioning of their class, sex, race. All literature on which canonical status is conferred merely represents the disguised or unexamined assumptions and interests of the dominant class, sex, race. Critics armed with what has been called the "hermeneutics of suspicion" radically devalue authors and elevate the ideologists—the critics themselves— as indispensable decoders of literature, all of which is, by definition, irreducibly political.

Shakespeare's *Tempest* reflects the imperialist rape of the Third World. Emily Dickinson's poetic references to peas and flower buds are encoded messages of feminist rage, exulting clitoral masturbation to protest the prison of patriarchal sex roles. Jane Austen's supposed serenity masks boiling fury about male domination, expressed in the nastiness of minor characters who are "really" not minor. In *Wuthering Heights*, Emily Brontë, a subtle subversive, has Catherine bitten by a male bulldog. The supplanting of aesthetic by political responses to literature makes literature primarily interesting as a mere index of who had power and whom the powerful victimized. The left's agenda liberates literature from aesthetic standards, all of which are defined as merely sublimated assertions of power by society's dominant group. It follows that all critics and authors from particular victim groups should be held only to the political standards of their group. Administration of these standards, and of the resulting racial and sexual spoils system in the academy, "requires" group politics: Under the spreading chestnut tree, I tenure you and you tenure me.

As aesthetic judgments are politicized, political judgments are aestheticized: The striking of poses and the enjoyment of catharsis are central in the theater of victimization in academic life. All of this, although infantile, is not trivial. By "deconstructing," or politically decoding, or otherwise attacking the meaning of literary works, critics strip literature of its authority. Criticism displaces literature and critics displace authors as bestowers of meaning. In the writing of history, too, there is a stilted style that makes the writer the center of attention. It does so by—to use a verb much favored in academia—privileging a strange vocabulary. To select at random just one from uncountable possible examples, when an American historian says that Franco's Spain was "as savagely hierarchizing" as Hitler's Germany, she is writing in a manner that no one outside the academy writes. When, in her ostentatiously mannered way, she says that Catholicism "problematized" the ideological rapprochement between Francoism and Nazism, or when she says that liberalism, constitutionalism, and democracy are concepts that must be "interrogated" in specific contexts, her vocabulary aggressively signals her membership in a closed clerisy with its private argot.[60] If one believes that all literature, properly "contextualized," is to be seen through the lens of politics; if one believes that because history is opaque, it should be discussed in opaque jargon; if one believes that things that are judged to be true, good, and beautiful are, anytime and everywhere, judged by standards that are mere matters of opinion and beyond rational defense; if one believes these things, they have consequences for our understanding of what education should, or can, be.

Many educators in the humanities—not in, say, engineering: the bridges and dams would collapse—have embraced epistemological skepticism, even epistemological nihilism, believing that the past is inaccessible because it is impossible to be objective about it, or about anything else. If our understanding of the present, too, is a "cultural construct," merely a reflection of contemporary social forces and dominances, then our understanding of the past must be even more attenuated. The postmodernists' revolution in historiography has been to insist that the past, too, is "constructed." Actually, the past deserves respect, not because it is a record of successes that reproaches our imperfect present, but because it is a record of attempts to do what we are trying to do: respond reasonably to the more or less intractable circumstances of the human condition.

Unfortunately, the new historians resemble literary critics who displace authors in order to explain what the particular authors were "really" doing when they wrote, whether the authors knew it or not. The new history elevates the historian to the role—half priest, half artist—of explaining history's meaning to those who obdurately persist in thinking that politics matter greatly. If political events are mere "epiphenomena," then politics loses its history-shaping grandeur, and ordinary people lose the dignity that attaches to participation in the human pageant. If, as the new historians insist, social "structures" and impersonal "forces" make both individuals and history, then individuality and freedom are discounted. When historians deny that a preeminent few have had disproportionate impacts on the destinies of the many, these historians also deny people's ability to rise above determinism and modify their lives' trajectories. Thus does the new historians' anti-elitism breed fatalism about the very possibility of leadership. This style of history abolishes man as a political animal who uses reason and responds to rhetoric to seek fulfillment in civic life. If you discount the importance of individuals and their utterances—their choices, and the rhetoric that justifies and elicits support for them—you discount the importance, and perhaps even the possibility, of democracy, a regime of persuasion.

Two converging and reinforcing intellectual tendencies have had demoralizing and de-moralizing effects on the way we understand history. This matters because the way we think about the past conditions how we act—or do not act—to shape the future. The first tendency has blurred the picture of human beings as responsible, consequential actors in history. The second tendency involves painting mankind's story without the bright primary colors of personal greatness. Some say that people should outgrow the desire for, or belief in, heroes because only an unhappy nation needs heroes. But only an unusually fortunate nation can do without them. No democracy, least of all a diverse, continental democracy, should want to do without those rare figures who capture and condense in their careers a moment, a movement, an idea. The idea of heroes makes democracies uneasy. Democracies want to disperse credit for achievement and to believe that virtue and vision well up spontaneously and broadly from the common people. Still, even unenthralled democracies should have heroes. One of today's most unattractive aspects is the absence of sympathy, affection, and respect for the people who struggled with the problems of the recent past. And there is something awfully small about someone who cannot admit that anyone else was exceptionally large. As has been said, if no man is a hero to his valet, that is not because no men are heroes, but because all valets are valets.

Ordinary people think that extraordinary princes and presidents, heroes and villains have been event-making individuals. But in the hands of the new history, such individuals dissolve into mere manifestations of "deeper" forces. It is perverse that such writing of history flourishes after a century so shaped by event-makers—Hitler, Stalin, Mao, Churchill, Roosevelt, de Gaulle, Reagan. But implausibility is a price the new historians gladly pay for the ideological correctness that, not coincidentally, enhances their status as decipherers of things that supposedly are beyond the ken of persons outside the clerisy. If, as the new historians insist, social "structures" and impersonal "forces" make history, then it is not surprising that students turn away from history taught without the drama of autonomous individuals moved by reason and conviction and the rhetoric that appeals to the better angels of their natures. Rhetoric is systematic eloquence that, at its best, does not induce irrationality; rather, it leavens reason, fusing passion to persuasion. And it influences how history is made.

A nation needs, and the American nation has had, many heroes. It also has had villains, and examining the history of its villainy, in the light of the national principles that define villainy, is constructive. So there should be an unblinking focus on the nation's failures to live up to its commitments. In this regard, and at this time, it is necessary, particularly after America's serial disappointments with projects of nation-building abroad, to distinguish between nation-building and state-building. As Francis Fukuyama says, state-building requires the creation of institutions—agencies, militaries, bureaucracies—as tangible as the buildings that house them. Nation-building requires the creation of a national identity, which is the stuff of intangibles such as traditions, memories, and cultural patrimonies such as literature, poetry, music, and architecture. State-building is necessarily done from the commanding heights of society; nation-building is often largely a matter of ferment from a society's loam. A sense of national identity is a prerequisite for social cohesion, and a sense of national identity becomes both more urgent and more elusive because of forces loosed by modernity—such as geographic and social mobility, attenuated familial and community attachments, diluted religious identities, occupational mobility, and different levels of education. The same is true of personal identity. As Fukuyama says, "In agrarian societies, a person's important life choices—where to live, what to do for a living, what religion to practice, whom to marry—were mostly determined by the surrounding tribe, village, or caste. Individuals consequently did not spend a lot of time sitting around asking themselves, 'Who am I, really?'"[61] Hence, in modern urbanized societies, national identities become components of personal identities, more than they did in agrarian societies.

To some extent—the extent varies widely by nations' histories— national identity is something deliberately cultivated. Ernest Renan, an early student of nationalism, said that this cultivation can require historical amnesia, or even the deliberate promotion of misunderstanding. State-building always involves unlovely things, including violence. As Fukuyama says, the United States was not built on a hitherto unpopulated continent. The state, whose identity "is based on principles of equality, individual rights, and democracy," was built in part by the violent displacement of indigenous inhabitants.[62] Nation-building, which never ends, neither requires nor should it encourage amnesia regarding the oppressiveness, lawlessness, and violence attendant on state-building. This is especially so in the United States, where the process of state-building should be judged against the severe principles that define this creedal nation's identity. The gross departures from those principles—slavery, semi-genocide against Native Americans, imperialism—were not just grotesque behaviors, they were particularly appalling because they were apostasies. America not only knew better than to do what it did, it was simultaneously proclaiming better as it did what it did. Therefore, giving unsparing attention to America's lapses from its principles serves to imbue those principles with fresh relevance and vitality.

SAVORING CONTINGENCY AND A TALENT FOR PESSIMISM

Edna St. Vincent Millay was right about what to read but wrong about what to think about it:

> Read history: so learn your place in Time;
> And go to sleep: all this was done before.[63]

Actually, one reason to read history is to know how little has generally been known about what was coming next. Which is to say, reading history is a cure for historicism. Nothing is as distinctively modern, and as demoralizing, as the sense that change is autonomous. Thus nothing is such fun as a demonstration that a solitary figure can make a difference, that history is a realm of surprise, not of necessity. Hence the exhilaration of well-taught history, which is an education in contingency.

Suppose the car had hit the pedestrian slightly harder. What car? The one on Fifth Avenue the evening of December 13, 1931, when an

English politician on a lecture tour momentarily forgot the American rules of the road and looked the wrong way when stepping into the street. Winston Churchill might have died. Then, perhaps in 1940 or 1941, a prime minister less resolute and inspiriting than Churchill might have chosen to come to terms with Germany before Hitler attacked the Soviet Union. Imagine the hegemony of a National Socialist Germany stretching across the Eurasian landmass from Korea to Calais. Or suppose Robert E. Lee had occupied Cemetery Hill on the first night at Gettysburg, which he might have done if Stonewall Jackson had not been accidentally killed two months earlier by friendly fire from confused Confederate soldiers at Chancellorsville. The dynamic of the first three days of July 1863, in south central Pennsylvania would have been different. Lee might have prevailed there, and this might now be two nations. Actually, there might be lots of nations in the territory that was the Confederacy, because those fractious people would have improvidently established a weak central government and the right of secession. Or suppose the northeast wind blowing across New York Harbor had not suddenly turned into a southwest wind on the night of August 29, 1776, and that a thick fog had not rolled in the next day. There might never have been an independent United States for Lee to try to dismember. Those climatic changes facilitated the evacuation whereby George Washington and 10,000 soldiers—about half the entire Continental Army—escaped capture by the British after the Battle of Long Island.

The study of history should be an immersion in the realities of contingencies. This immersion should lead to a talent for pessimism: Things can, and frequently do, go wrong. Pessimism can be, but need not be, a consequence of nihilism. Pessimism can be conjoined with, but is not necessarily, a theory of social decline. Pessimism does not entail fatalism. On the contrary, it is a form of activism, of perpetual wariness, born of historically informed realism. Pessimism, far from promoting passivity, should be a constant spur to political engagement. And pessimism, far from being a recipe for unhappiness, is an inoculation against innumerable optimisms that expose adherents to dashed hopes, bewilderment, disillusionment, and inertia.

When grounded in philosophy, pessimism is much more than a mere frame of mind. This has been demonstrated by the philosopher Joshua Foa Dienstag, who has traced pessimism's long pedigree in Western political philosophy. "In the twentieth century," he writes, "pessimism has been the philosophy that dares not speak its name," such has been the "imperialism of optimism." Pessimism's "animating principle" is "that time is an unshakable burden for human beings because it leads to the ultimate destruction of all things." He argues that the widespread refusal to take pessimism seriously as an important thread in the fabric of intellectual history "reflects the continuing grip that ideas of progress retain on contemporary consciousness."[64] This does not mean that philosophic pessimism involves a denial of the fact of progress. Pessimism as a foundation of political wariness should, however, point to certain prudential conclusions about institutions.

The "sudden ubiquity of mechanical clocks in the fourteenth century" presaged a modern consciousness of linear time and an emancipation from a sense of imprisonment in cyclical history. Thus the idea of linearity, combined with the simultaneous quickening of intellectuals' appreciation of the cumulative nature of scientific inquiry, prepared humanity to embrace the idea of progress. Because modern philosophies of pessimism are, Dienstag says, critiques of the idea of progress, "pessimism, like progress, is a modern idea." A depiction of the human condition that severs a linear understanding of history from the idea of progress is, as Dienstag says, "discomfiting" to human beings. They, unlike other animals, have a sense of time, and hence an awareness of death. No one lasts, and it is implausible that any social arrangements will last. The human capacity to reason gives us the power to manipulate aspects of the world, and this power has achieved wonderful ameliorative effects. But human beings, always in the grip of unfulfilled desires and destined for death, must come to terms with limitations. Optimists, disposed to expect continuous improvement, are set up for disappointment. As Dienstag says, "*The Pessimist expects nothing*." Free from what one pessimist has called the "idolatry of tomorrow," a pessimist has an "openness to the music of chance" which can give the pessimist a kind of "equanimity." And a pessimist experiences "the vitalization of life that comes through the embrace of uncertainty."[65] Whirl is king? Excellent.

Nietzsche thought that the pessimistic atheist, no longer seeking a "justification" of the world's ills, "now takes delight in a world disorder without God, a world of chance." For Nietzsche, as construed by Dienstag, "pessimism promotes an unblinkered examination of the world, and of the self, without built-in moral assumptions. From this perspective, it is actually optimism, relying on such assumptions, that inhibits truly free inquiry." Such pessimism, says Dienstag, "looks toward the future, not with the expectation that better things are foreordained, but with a hope founded only on taking joy in the constant process of transformation and destruction that mark out the human condition." We are fated to live in a condition of radical insecurity but also radical possibility. So, "pessimism envisions a democracy of moments" for individuals who can neither escape time nor be imprisoned by it.[66] Pessimism is an immunization from the passivity bred by the sense that we are objects of events. Pessimism clarifies where satisfactions can be found in the real zone of sovereignty that individuals have.

Such pessimism informs the conservative sensibility by eschewing "both progress and circularity as guiding temporal frames." Pessimism "simply does not view philosophy as a technique for sweeping darkness from the universe and replacing it with light. Its goal, instead, is to teach us how to live with what we cannot eradicate, the limitations of death and time with which the universe saddles us." Dienstag closes with Albert Camus' judgment in *The Myth of Sisyphus*: "We must imagine Sisyphus happy." Happy because he attained the dignity of attempting. As Camus says in his essay, "The important thing...is not to be cured, but to live with one's ailments."[67] The ailments of the human condition are chronic, so they must be constantly countered by prophylactic political and cultural institutions and measures. Otherwise, social regression is not just possible but probable.

There has been stupendous progress, moral as well as material, in our time. It has been noted that until about 1900, most people lived half their lives with toothaches, but few people born after 1960 know what a toothache is. In some ways, moral progress has been as striking: Try explaining segregated buses to someone born after 1970. One reason politics has lost some of the sizzle of olden days is that many injustices have not merely been corrected, they have been relegated to the realm of unintelligible bygones. But beware belief in a ratchet of history that clicks only in the direction of improvement.

Western political philosophy began with Plato's search for ways to prevent history from being a story of cycles, with virtue decaying into tyranny. One admirable aspect of modernity is a preoccupation with history as linear, as a narrative infused with the drama of possibilities. History, properly taught, infuses people with a prerequisite for democratic life—an insouciant disrespect for bogus inevitabilities. Tomorrow the present will be history, the study of which is one long warning: Nothing is inevitable but change, and the permutations of possible disagreeable outcomes are infinite. So, prudence calls for auxiliary precautions, the beginning of which should be the restoration of education as a process of learning to praise, and to excavate from history knowledge of the praiseworthy, and of the cautionary, in the human story.

Marx drew an unsentimental picture of our species enmeshed in history's dialectic. Darwin drew an unsentimental picture of the childhood of our species. Freud drew an unsentimental picture of childhood. Each influenced thinking about the nature and meaning of politics and the political vocation. Some people worry that genetics will, too. They argue that individual autonomy is an illusion that will be steadily dispelled by the deciphering of supposedly controlling genetic codes, understood as the chemical engine of existence. If such scientific materialism reduces the self to chemistry, what then becomes of the aspiration of liberal societies—self-government by consent. If humanity is irreducibly embedded in the necessities of nature, then who, exactly, is doing the consenting? And what is the value, the moral imperative, of consent?

The foundational premise of modernity, and of liberal democratic societies, is that individuals are self-constituting creatures who manufacture themselves in the ongoing process of making free choices, assembling their purposes from a vast cafeteria of possibilities. One of the greatest novels written in the most modern nation is about a person as a work of art. It is the cautionary story of Jay Gatsby's self-creation. This nation's answer to determinists of all stripes has always been that education can enable self-constituting individuals to freely choose the praiseworthy. It is a favorite jest of philosophers: "Of course I believe in free will—what choice do I have?" The more educated a person is about fine things and noble behavior, the more a person is equipped for the pleasures of intelligent praising, the more he or she is equipped for intelligent pessimism, a prerequisite for the defense of liberty.

CHAPTER 8

GOING ABROAD

A CREEDAL NATION IN A WORLD ON
PROBATION

> Man isn't all one, after all—it takes so much of
> him to be American, to be French, etc.
>
> Henry James[1]

I n 1910, a twenty-five-year-old Missourian working on his family farm behind a horse-drawn plow, put in his pocket a copy of Alfred Tennyson's poem "Locksley Hall," which anticipated a world without wars, a world subdued by law:

> *Till the war-drum throbb'd no longer, and the battle-flags were furl'd*
> *In the Parliament of man, the Federation of the world.*
> *There the common sense of most shall hold a fretful realm in awe,*
> *And the kindly earth shall slumber, lapt in universal law.*[2]

The Missourian carried the poem with him as an artillery captain when the war-drums throbbed in France. And he carried it on April 12, 1945, when the death of Franklin Roosevelt elevated him to the presidency, thirteen days before the opening of the San Francisco Conference at which the United Nations was organized.[3] The UN has been less a parliament of man than an assemblage of regimes, less a federation for a kindly world than a cockpit for competition among nations. But then the Stele of the Vultures, the world's oldest known historical document, is a carved limestone slab telling, in the Sumerian language, the story of a battle in what is now Iraq about twenty-five centuries ago. So, humanity's oldest document is about war. And in the eleven decades since Harry Truman put that poem in his pocket, war has been much with us. Humanity has never been without it. Yet nine years after farmer Truman plowed that field, and one year after Captain Truman had commanded the US Army's 129th Field Artillery Regiment in France, an American was determined to put an end to war. But Woodrow Wilson was sleepless in Paris.

The president was awake all one night in 1919 because, he told his doctor the next morning, "my mind was so full of the Japanese-Chinese controversy." An American president was attending a conference to end a war that began in Belgium and raged mostly within 220 miles of the English Channel. Yet Wilson's sleep was troubled by Sino-Japanese relations. According to historian Margaret MacMillan, Wilson was worried about "what Japan was getting in China, right down to the composition of the railway police in Shantung. (They were to be Chinese with, where necessary, Japanese instructors.)"[4] Where "necessary"? America's president was struggling to measure the necessity of the Japanese component of the Chinese railway police. Such granular preoccupations were enough to give a man a stroke. And might have done so.

While sailing to Paris, Wilson told his young secretary of the navy, thirty-seven-year-old Franklin Roosevelt, that the United States "is the only nation that all feel is disinterested and all trust."[5] The idea of a disinterested nation must have been grimly amusing to the leaders of Europe's blood-soaked continent. Because Wilson, unlike his French, British, and Italian counterparts at the Versailles peace conference, was a head of state, he was given a chair a few inches taller than those for France's Georges Clemenceau, Britain's David Lloyd George, and Italy's Vittorio Orlando. Not that Wilson needed that slight physical augmentation of his moral self-confidence. Potential pupils for this former professor came to Paris from far and wide. Or tried to come. MacMillan writes that "the Koreans from Siberia set out on foot in February 1919 and by the time the main part of the Peace Conference ended in June had reached only the Arctic port of Archangel." However, some pupils were already in Paris when the conference convened—such as a twenty-nine-year-old Vietnamese working in a hotel kitchen: Ho Chi Minh. Many advocates of subjugated peoples and nascent nations came to Paris, drawn by the magnetism of the central Wilsonian principle: self-determination. What exactly Wilson meant by that was a mystery to, among others, Wilson's secretary of state, Robert Lansing, who wondered: "When the President talks of 'self-determination' what unit has he in mind? Does he mean a race, a territorial area, or a community?"[6]

Ethnicity makes the world go round. And bleed. This is a nasty surprise, not least to all the advanced thinkers who convinced themselves that modernity would mean the eclipse of ethnicity, among other sources of strife. What Daniel Patrick Moynihan called the "liberal expectancy" was that ethnic attachments would weaken, even disappear.[7] Such attachments are (or so the theory said) anachronistic, primitive, transitional echoes of mankind's infancy. Equally mistaken was the Marxist prediction that all preindustrial components of identity—cultural, religious, racial—would be superseded by components of social class. This did not happen: The breaking of nations by ethnic fragmentation dominates world polities today. Many an ethnic group thinks it is a "self" entitled to "self-determination."

The nineteenth century was a century of consolidations. The United States bound a continent together by steel rails and a strong central government. Germany unified, as did Italy. Americans, however, injected into the discourse of diplomacy the idea that "self-determination" is a universal "right." Before the First World War ended, Woodrow Wilson told a cheering session of Congress that "self-determination" is "an imperative principle of action." But self-determination by what sort of entities? Wilson said, "National aspirations must be respected; peoples may now be dominated and governed only by their own consent."[8] He was sowing dragon's teeth. He seemed to assume that the nouns "nations" and "peoples" are synonyms, or that these entities are coterminous. But in many cases they were not, and still are not.

Six of Wilson's Fourteen Points concerned self-determination. There was to be, for example, "autonomous development" of the "peoples of Austria-Hungary" and also of "other nationalities...under Turkish rule."[9] "Peoples." "Nationalities." And ethnicities, which are not the same thing as nationalities. The fact of ethnicity still disrupts the game of nations. The world would be calmer if history had caused ethnic groups to coincide neatly with national boundaries. But the distribution of peoples does not always fit political borders, particularly when those borders have been drawn by diplomats confident of their ability to tidy up the world and make it rational. Rationalism in politics is risky; when combined, as in Wilson's statecraft, with moralism, it is explosive.

Secretary Lansing said Wilson "is a phrase-maker par excellence," but warned that "certain phrases" of Wilson's "have not been thought out." While Wilson was enunciating this "imperative" principle, a German corporal, recovering from a gas attack, was planning a political career. And on September 26, 1938, the former corporal said, "[At] last, nearly twenty years after the declarations of President Wilson, the right of self-determination for these three and a half million [Germans] must be enforced."[10] So spoke Hitler as Czechoslovakia was dismembered. A nation was sacrificed for the "self-determination" of a "people"—Sudeten Germans.

Lansing had seen such trouble coming. The "undigested" phrase "self-determination" is, he had said, "simply loaded with dynamite...It will, I fear, cost thousands of lives...What a calamity that the phrase was ever uttered!"[11] Undeterred, FDR and Churchill affirmed in their Atlantic Charter of August 1941 the rights of "peoples." And the UN Charter endorses self-determination of "peoples." In 1915, Walter

Lippmann wrote, "When you consider what a mystery the East Side of New York is to the West Side, the business of arranging the world to the satisfaction of the people in it may be seen in something like its true proportions."[12] But just two years later Lippmann, just twenty-eight years old, was an earnest arranger working for the Inquiry, a small, secret group serving Wilson. From the New York offices of the American Geographical Society, the Inquiry planned a rearrangement of the world that would, the rearrangers expected, make the twentieth century rational. Ronald Steel, Lippmann's biographer, writes:

> The Inquiry, working from maps and piles of statistics, attacked the question of frontiers by drawing up charts showing the concentration of national groups within Europe. Lippmann then coordinated these charts and lists with national political movements to determine how these ethnic entities could be granted self-determination without triggering new European rivalries. Then he correlated this blueprint with the secret treaties—deciding which territorial changes were acceptable and which defied justice and logic. Once the Inquiry team…had matched the aspirations of the ethnic groups with the geography and economics of each region, Lippmann organized the conclusions into…[13]

Enough. Has there ever been quite such a spectacle of naïveté and hubris? Soon Wilson was off to the Versailles peace conference, from which a member of his delegation sent home a letter containing one of the twentieth century's most telling vignettes: "We went into the next room where the floor was clear and Wilson spread out a big map (made in our office) on the floor and got down on his hands and knees to show us what had been done; most of us were also on our hands and knees. I was in the front row and felt someone pushing me and looked around angrily to find that it was Orlando, on his hands and knees crawling like a bear toward the map."[14] What were they working on? Perhaps that soon-to-be-born state of Yugoslavia, which lasted until ethnic conflicts dismembered it in 1992. Harold Nicolson, a British diplomat at the conference, wrote to his wife, "But, darling, it is appalling, those three ignorant and irresponsible men [Wilson, Lloyd George, Clemenceau] cutting Asia Minor to bits as if they were dividing a cake."[15] Thus was rationality imposed upon the Middle East. With steady hands those men would redraw maps, relying on ethnic data. But the principle of ethnicity got out of hand. Again, Moynihan: "Fascism, Italian, then German, was much about 'blood.' The Second World War was as much a pogrom as anything else, and far the greatest incidence of violence since has been ethnic in nature and origin."[16]

There was a vast carelessness—an earnest carelessness—in the Versailles conference's rearranging of the world. MacMillan, who is Lloyd George's great-granddaughter, says that in 1916, he mused: "Who are the Slovaks? I can't seem to place them." Three years later, he was helping place them in a new—and perishable—nation, Czechoslovakia. Not until 1918 did Lloyd George discover that New Zealand is east of Australia. When, in Paris, he dramatically spoke of the Turks retreating eastward toward Mecca, Lord Curzon sternly corrected him: the retreat, said Curzon, was toward Ankara, not Mecca. Lloyd George breezily replied: "Lord Curzon is good enough to admonish me on a triviality." Arthur Balfour, a laconic aristocrat who rarely seemed deeply stirred by anything, was angered by the spectacle of "all-powerful, all-ignorant men sitting there and partitioning continents." Harold Nicolson told his diary: "How fallible one feels here! A map—a pencil—tracing paper. Yet my courage fails at the thought of the people whom our errant lines enclose or exclude, the happiness of several thousands of people."[17]

Several thousands? Many millions, actually. The maps were large, the pencils busy. Turkey was on the conference's agenda but was not auspicious clay for the experts to mold. Its recent rulers had included one who went mad and another who was so fearful of enemies that, when he desired a cigarette, he had a eunuch take the first puff. In polyglot Turkey, for the dockworkers in Salonika to function, they had to speak half a dozen languages. Never mind. Those experts in Paris, crawling on their hands and knees around those big maps, would fix Turkey in due time. When French officials invited Wilson to tour the scarred moonscape of the Flanders battlefields, he angrily refused to go, saying that the French were trying to arouse his emotions. Pure reason, he thought, must prevail. Yet Wilson perhaps included in his Fourteen Points the restoration of Polish independence because at a White House party in 1916 he had been stirred by the pianist Paderewski's rendition of Chopin.

Speaking to Lloyd George's mistress, Frances Stevenson, over a luncheon plate of chicken, Clemenceau said: "I have come to the conclusion that force is right. Why is this chicken here? Because it was not strong enough to resist those who wanted to kill it. And a very good thing too!"[18] What shaped Clemenceau's dark realism was life on a continent that included such countries as Albania, in parts of which one man in five died in blood feuds. A story, perhaps apocryphal but certainly plausible, is that when Wilson asked Clemenceau if he did not believe that all men are brothers, Clemenceau exclaimed: "Yes, all men are brothers—Cain and Abel! Cain and Abel!" Clemenceau certainly did say to Wilson, "We [Europeans], too, came into the world with the noble instincts and the lofty aspirations which you express so often and so eloquently. We have become what we are because we have been shaped by the rough hand of the world in which we have to live and we have survived only because we are a tough bunch."[19]

Most of the political calamities through which the world has staggered since 1919 have resulted from the distinctively modern belief that things—including nations and human nature—are much more malleable than they actually are. It is the belief that nations are like Tinkertoys: They can be taken apart and rearranged at will. It is the belief that human beings are material that can be sculpted by the tools of political artists. In the one hundred years since 1919, many more than 100 million people have perished in violence intended to force the world into new configurations. The violence has served ambitious attempts at social engineering—attempts to create racial purity or a classless society or the New Soviet Man.

When Lenin and Wilson died ten days apart in 1924, the structure of twentieth-century conflict was in place. Twenty-eight years later, on June 2, 1952, in Fulton, Missouri, where six years earlier, at Westminster College, Winston Churchill had fired the opening rhetorical shot of the Cold War with his "iron curtain" speech ("From Stettin in the Baltic to Trieste in the Adriatic an iron curtain has descended across the Continent"), a politically engaged Hollywood actor gave the commencement address at William Woods College. He told the graduates: "America is less a place than an idea…the idea of the dignity of man, the idea that deep within the heart of each one of us is something so God-like and precious that no individual or group has a right to impose his or its will upon the people."[20] Twenty-eight years after that, the speaker, Ronald Reagan, would be elected president and proceed to put in place the policies that led to the end of the Cold War without military shots being fired. The idea that America "is an idea," and that the idea is about principles of universal validity, has always had foreign policy consequences.

"Sometimes people call me an idealist," Wilson said. "Well, that is why I know I am an American. America is the only idealistic nation in the world."[21] Wilson had a piece of a point. He would, however, have been more accurate if he had said that America is the only nation whose relations with the rest of the world are shaped by the universalism of its creed. As Walter Berns wrote, because American patriotism is inextricably entwined with those principles, "ours is not a parochial patriotism."[22] This must, and should, have a profound continuous effect on the conduct of American foreign policy. When Henry James wrote, in a letter to his fellow novelist William Dean Howell, "Man isn't at all one, after all—it takes so much of him to be American, to be French, etc." he was affirming a truism: Humanity never has had, and likely never will have, a common culture.[23] Therefore, national differences must be acknowledged and prudently accommodated. This does not, however, refute the American premise that humanity is one in this sense: In just societies, under legitimate governments, all persons have certain rights that are respected. The question, which is of particular urgency for the conduct of US foreign policy, is how should this premise condition the intercourse of the United States with other Nations? This intercourse has always had and should always have an indelible color of idealism. Conservatism should embrace this, but should leaven it with an unsentimental, almost bleak realism.

Reflection about foreign policy, as about all other spheres of politics, should begin with this basic question: What is the essential, unchanging nature of human beings? Conservatism's answer is: Human beings are desirous and competitive, hence they often are anxious, and hence they were given to conflict. Man is indeed "born unto trouble, as the sparks fly upward."[24]

In foreign policy, as elsewhere, one of conservatism's functions is to say some things that people do not want to hear, such as this: War, which always has been part of the human story, always will be. More than ninety years ago, and more than that many wars ago, the United States took the lead in another effort to make war a thing of the past. On August 27, 1928, representatives of fifteen nations met in Paris to sign the Kellogg-Briand Pact, thereby renouncing the use of war as an instrument of national policy. Today Kellogg-Briand seems like something written on water in ink of smoke. But it is wrong to regard the pact banning war as just another example of the feather-headedness typical of an American nation that was then also struggling to enforce a ban on alcohol. The pact was more than a pale flame of idealism in the closing dusk of American innocence. It expressed an aspect of the American temper that still exists. Specifically, Americans are temperamental optimists about the power of understanding to defuse conflicts. It is, however, when we achieve real understanding of the world that we understand that it is and ever will be a dangerous place, full of conflicts. Neither cameras nor commerce nor even more intimidating weapons will change that.

SEVERAL GRAND ILLUSIONS

In September 1862, two men worked their way across some dark and bloody ground in northern Maryland. They were armed with devices of profound importance for the future of war, and hence of politics: cameras. They had been sent by Mathew Brady, at whose Manhattan studio there soon opened an exhibit called "The Dead of Antietam." *The New York Times* reported: "The dead of the battle-field come up to us very rarely, even in dreams...Mr. Brady has done something to bring home to us the terrible reality and earnestness of war. If he has not brought bodies and laid them in dooryards and along the streets, he has done something very like it."[25] But the civilian world would not soon look war in the face. In World War I, no photo of a corpse appeared in a British, French, or German newspaper. It was not until 1943 that *Life* magazine created controversy, and a new era in journalism (and, in time, in the conflicts between nations), when it published a photograph, which had been held back for many months, of three dead Americans on a New Guinea beach. By the time of Vietnam, graphic journalism was ascendant in a wired world, as was the hope that the impact of such journalism would give war such disturbing immediacy that the world would flinch from violence. The twentieth century was, however, replete with bitter surprises for optimists, such as the editors of the renowned eleventh edition of the *Encyclopaedia Britannica*, published in 1910–11. Its entry on "torture" said that "the whole subject is one of only historical interest as far as Europe is concerned."[26]

In 1910, forty remarkably peaceful years after the Franco-Prussian War, Norman Angell, a British economist, wrote and paid for the publication of a book that would become one of the first international best-sellers. His cost-benefit analysis in *The Grand Illusion* was that nations could no longer benefit from war, so there would never be another one. Wishes are potent fathers of thoughts, so Angell's thought caught on. In 1913, the president of Stanford University said, "The great war of Europe, ever threatening…never will come…The bankers will not find the money for such a fight, the industries will not maintain it."[27] This was a version of a theory put into disappointing practice by President Jefferson, who tried to use a trade embargo to bring the dogs of war to heel. Republics, he and others hoped, would have a distinctive diplomacy based not on the sword but on the ledger book. The assumption was that when goods are free to cross borders, armies will not cross them because commercial interests will guarantee a concert of interests in tranquility. Commerce, once considered not conducive to virtue, came to be considered indispensable to modern virtue. But the ledger book proved to be no match for human atavism.

In 1914, Rupert Brooke spoke for many when he thanked God for the outbreak of war, rejoicing in it as an awakening from "a world grown old and cold and weary." He relished war as a cleansing, invigorating experience for young men "as swimmers into cleanness leaping."[28] However, the nations that turned wearily to the Second World War had read *All Quiet on the Western Front* (1929) and seen the movie of it. They had read Dos Passos' *Three Soldiers*, Hemingway's *A Farewell to Arms*, Robert Graves' *Good-bye to All That*, and other literary works conveying the taste of ashes from the last war. Airplanes were supposed to make war obsolete by encouraging travel and hence (non sequitur alert) understanding. Broadcasting—radio, then television, then satellite distribution of content—supposedly would make everyone agreeably cosmopolitan. An American media guru has said that because of the Internet, future children "are not going to know what nationalism is."[29]

The study of medicine begins, in a sense, with the study of

death. The study of modern politics should begin with the study of Hitler. Serious interest in Hitler is related to this fact: His regime was founded at least in part in the heart as well as on the neck of a great civilized nation. The regime was run, as all large states are, by civil servants whose principal attributes were what normally are called virtues—patriotism, a sense of duty, regularity. Men who would never cheat at cards or condone adultery by a fellow civil servant condoned hitherto unimagined evils. As Thomas the Cynic says in Ignazio Silone's *The School for Dictators*: "No dictator has ever had trouble finding civil servants."[30] Hitler was the founder of a secular religion, and was tireless in performing priestly functions at events like the Nuremberg rallies, with holy relics like the "Blood Flag" from the attempted Munich Putsch of 1923. His rise to power was a meeting of the man and the moment, but his perverse genius was in seeing an aching emptiness in people that his passion could fill. And if you accept the notion that freedom is just the absence of restraints, then Hitler was a radically free man, a man operating on society from outside, unrestrained by any scruples or ties of affection. He is evidence against the theory that only vast, impersonal forces, and not individuals, can shake the world.

Hitler, who was not German, was like Stalin, who was not Russian, and Napoleon, who was not French. Hitler was a complete outsider, outside all restraints grounded in principles or affections. He had a megalomaniac's estimate of the importance of his undertakings: When planning to invade England he said: "Eight hours of night in favorable weather would decide the fate of the universe."[31] He fused megalomania with demented superstitions. When he sent Foreign Minister Joachim von Ribbentrop to Moscow in August 1939 to sign the nonaggression pact with the Soviet Union, he sent along his personal photographer with instructions to obtain close-ups of Stalin's earlobes because Hitler wondered whether Stalin had Jewish blood and wanted to see if his earlobes were "ingrown and Jewish, or separate and Aryan."[32]

Attempts to explain Hitler began with the idea that he was unfathomable, a lunatic "*Teppichfresser*" (carpet chewer). The comforting theory was that no theory can explain Hitler because he was inexplicable, a monster, a phenomenon without precedent or portent. In 1996, however, Daniel Goldhagen's book *Hitler's Willing Executioners: Ordinary Germans and the Holocaust* argued that the explanation for the genocide was acculturation—centuries of German conditioning by the single idea of "eliminationist antisemitism."[33] Goldhagen's cognitive determinism reduced Hitler to a mere catalyst who unleashed a sick society's cultural latency. This drew a rejoinder from Christopher Browning, author of *Ordinary Men* (1992), a study of middle-aged German conscripts who became consenting participants in mass-murder police battalions in Poland. Browning noted that protracted socialization—centuries of conditioning—could not explain the Khmer Rouge's murder of millions of Cambodians, or the slaughter of millions of Chinese during Mao's Cultural Revolution. As the philosopher John Doris has written, "It takes a lot of people to kill…six million…human beings, and there just aren't enough monsters to go around. Unfortunately, it does not take a monster to do monstrous things."[34]

Corporal Hitler was decorated for bravery at the recommendation of a Jewish officer, but was never promoted because another officer said "we could discover no leadership qualities in him."[35] Until he was thirty he never gave a speech or joined a party, and when he did join one its membership was so small it could meet in a beer hall. Thirteen years later, Hitler led this party's conquest of Europe's most modern state. His first public office was Germany's chancellorship. He was an anti-democratic populist. Some politicians sail with the wind. Others tack into the wind. Hitler raised the wind and blew the masses about like so much dust. Like four other leaders of the war in the European theater—Stalin, FDR, Churchill, and de Gaulle—Hitler neither knew nor cared much about economics. Which helps to explain why they were leaders: They did not believe in the reality of *homo economicus*—economic man, a creature moved primarily by calculations about material matters.

There is much truth in, but something vital missing from, Modris Eksteins' understanding of Nazism: "It was not the substance—there was no substance to the frantic neurotic tirades—that allowed the party to survive and later to grow. It was the style and the mood. It was above all the theater, the vulgar 'art,' the *grand guignol* productions of the beer halls and the street. It was the provocation, the excitement, the *frisson* that Nazism was able to provide, in the brawling, the sweating, the singing, the saluting. Nazism, whether one wore brass knuckles and carried a rubber hose or simply played along vicariously, beating up communists and Jews in one's mind, was action. Nazism was involvement. Nazism was not a party; Nazism was an event."[36] William James, who died in 1910, would have understood. "Man lives by habits indeed," wrote James, "but what he lives for is thrills and excitement. The only relief from habit's tediousness is periodical excitement."[37] And the only participatory excitement more available to the masses than immersion in a mass movement on the march through city streets is marching off to war.

Mankind's modern political history might be the story of a grim paradox: The attempts, from Locke through the American Founding, to make politics safe might have made it dangerous. Attempts to drain politics of what made it volatile might have made it susceptible to new forms of destabilizing discontents. The homogenization of humanity by the many forces of modernity might have bred a troubling backlash of assertive particularities. Humanity retains a hankering for membership in tribes or nations or tribal nations. The desire for collective identity, meaning, and excitement is a desire to escape from the "iron cage" that Max Weber foresaw imprisoning modern people in a disenchanted world: "With the progress of science and technology, man has stopped believing in magic powers, in spirits and demons; he has lost his sense of prophecy and, above all, his sense of the sacred. Reality has become dreary, flat and utilitarian, leaving a great void in the souls of men which they seek to fill by furious activity and through various devices and substitutes."[38] As nature abhors a vacuum, some souls abhor the absence of a struggle—*kampf,* in German—into which they can immerse themselves.

The sociologist Robert Nisbet understood this. "Among the forces that have shaped human behavior, boredom is one of the most insistent and universal." Wars, famines, pestilences, and economic convulsions are easier to quantify, which is an important reason why they get more attention from historians and social scientists. Aristotle defined man as a language-using creature, but Nisbet stressed a different attribute: "Man is apparently unique in his capacity of boredom." Perhaps this is because humans' central nervous systems evolved to enhance the survival of beings who needed to be vigilant and aggressive. If so, it is not surprising that people are susceptible to the monotony and tedium of orderly, peaceful societies and the repetitive routines of work. Nisbet notes that although America's Civil War was ghastly in its slaughter, primitive medicine, and epidemic diseases, "there was no end to the lines of young men fleeing the deadly monotony of farm and village for enlistment under one banner or the other." Many of the men mustered out of the German army in 1919 did not miss the mud and lice and rats of the trenches, but were nostalgic about the brotherhood and sense of a great endeavor. Given the continuing attractions of political and religious excitements, the world could benefit from what Nisbet called a "sociology of boredom."[39]

Boredom can be dispelled by intellectual intoxication, by the excitement of embracing a comprehensive, universally valid explanation of *everything.* The largest and most lethal eruptions of irrationality have occurred in the name of reason. The Soviet Union made mincemeat of scores of millions of lives in the name of a "scientific socialism" that purported to explain the economic motor of history's trajectory. The National Socialists went on a rampage of military expansion and industrialized murder in the name of elaborate racial theories that purported to explain what they supposed to be the biological dynamics of history. The mountains of corpses from the Gulag and the Final Solution (this locution reeked of calm reasoning: the project addressed a problem to be solved) were monuments to the extravagant aspirations entertained by people whose smatterings of education sufficed only to make them susceptible to the radicalism of persons with one big idea. Armies in the service of these two ideas collided at Stalingrad, Kursk, and elsewhere, causing the death of National Socialism and delaying for almost half a century the death of "scientific socialism."

Yet in the debris-strewn wake of all this, there persists a strain of invincible innocence in the American approach to the world. When Serbians took hostages from UN personnel in Bosnia and chained them to military targets as human shields, US Secretary of State Warren Christopher was puzzled: "It's really not part of any reasonable struggle that might be going on there."[40] The United States is a commercial republic where the modes of reasoning used by business people and lawyers, like Warren Christopher, are considered normal and sufficient. Business people, however, like economists, think in terms of rational behavior models. In international relations, cost-benefit analyses are difficult, and even where they are possible they are often rendered irrelevant by animal spirits, national atavisms, and ideological frenzies. Lawyers regard a negotiated outcome as the normal form of conflict resolution, and winning is measured in adjustments at the margins of disputes. Relations between adversarial nations are rarely if ever so mild. A capitalist country, where one person's gain usually profits another, is apt to underestimate the extent to which the game of nations can be a zero-sum game in which one nation's gain is another's symmetrical loss.

It was possible to hope, and many intelligent people did hope, that as weapons became worse, the world would, of necessity, become tamer. In a sense, it has. Since history's most destructive war ended with an atomic thunderclap, there has been no global war, no war between great powers. But war evolves and persists. Observers of the battle of Ravenna in 1512, the first battle decided by an artillery barrage, considered it mass destruction when one cannonball claimed thirty-three casualties. A year later, at Novara, also in Italy, cannon killed 700 in three minutes. When, in 1784, General Henry Shrapnel developed the first exploding artillery shell containing subprojectiles, "mass destruction" became routine. At least it was massive compared to the killing of Homeric warfare, killing with edged weapons and muscle power, before war was dominated by the chemical energy of explosives. On April 5, 1585, a Dutch ship named *Hope*, packed to the gunnels with explosives, was set adrift to collide with a pontoon bridge packed with Spanish troops. The Spaniards thought it was just a fire ship. It was a time bomb. It may have caused 2,000 casualties when it exploded with the loudest man-made noise up to that point. It certainly produced the largest number of casualties inflicted by a single weapon up to that time. By 1864, under General William Tecumseh Sherman, total war meant industrialism, conscription, and tactics that blurred the distinction between combatants and non-combatants by attacking the farms, factories, and transportation on which modern armies depend. By the 1940s, the fury of total war had grown exponentially because of three additional ingredients: the modern state's uses of bureaucracy, propaganda, and especially forced-draft science.

In 1918, Ernest Rutherford, a physicist, missed a meeting of experts advising the British government on anti-submarine warfare. When criticized, he replied: "I have been engaged in experiments which suggest that the atom can be artificially disintegrated. If this is true, it is of far greater importance than a war."[41] In an astonishing few years, while the mass of men were preoccupied with unstable currencies, societies, and politicians, a few dozen scientists demonstrated the annihilating instability of matter itself. Einstein had postulated the equivalence of matter and energy; other scientists proved this by transforming matter into energy. The scientists who built the bomb were understandably fond of Einstein's aphorism that the world has more to fear from bad politics than from bad physics. It is, however, important to note that science usually is the subservient partner in a marriage between science and the modern state. This relationship was tidily summarized in an incident in the New Mexico desert the morning the atomic age dawned. A scientist lamented that the unexpected violence of the explosion had destroyed his measuring instruments. A general soothed him: "If the instruments couldn't stand it, the bang must have been a pretty big one. And that, after all, is what we wanted to know."[42]

The atomic age, which began in secret in that desert at dawn July 16, 1945, announced itself twenty-one days later when the *Enola Gay*'s bomb bay door opened. The bomb's fuse—incorporating the lens David Greenglass had sketched for the Rosenbergs' spy ring—unleashed neutrons that turned twenty-two pounds of uranium into an explosion that occurred in one-tenth of a millionth of a second. The flight of the *Enola Gay* began, in a sense, in 1932 in Cambridge, England, in Cavendish Laboratory, when James Chadwick discovered the neutron, the key to penetrating the atom's nucleus and unlocking energy from matter. As the *Enola Gay* approached Japan, the copilot was writing a letter to his parents. He wrote this sentence: "There will be a short intermission while we bomb our target." Next, he wrote this in a wild hand: "My God."[43]

The government committee that had kept the secret of the bomb project (neither Admiral Chester Nimitz nor General Douglas Mac-Arthur, the naval and army commanders in the Pacific theater, knew about the bomb until July) said it should be considered not just as a weapon but "in terms of a new relationship to the universe."[44] It would be extravagant to say the new technology of mass destruction has had such a transforming effect, spiritually or practically. Why should it have had? Conventional munitions on the ground at Verdun killed many more people than nuclear weapons have. The same was true at the Somme, seventeen years before the neutron was discovered.

AMERICA'S PUBLIC PHILOSOPHY AND FOREIGN POLICY

The first nation to possess nuclear weapons, and the only nation to have used them, is unique in other ways that are much more fundamentally important to its conduct in foreign policy. Technology is secondary to political philosophy. The United States, unique in the clarity of its founding moment and purposes, would inevitably be unique in its approach to international relations. Joseph Addison's 1713 play *Cato*, which was notably popular in the American colonies—George Washington saw it many times—expresses an Enlightenment aspiration:

> *A Roman soul is bent on higher views:*
> *To civilize the rude, unpolished world,*
> *And lay it under the restraint of laws;*
> *To make man mild and sociable to man;*
> *To cultivate the wild licentious savage*
> *With wisdom, discipline, and liberal arts—*
> *The embellishments of life; virtues like these*
> *Make human nature shine, reform the soul,*
> *And break our fierce barbarians into men.*[45]

Addison was exhorting the British to have "a Roman soul." The British who colonized North America did not have to look far beyond their front doors—the American frontier was well east of the Allegheny Mountains—to find "a rude unpolished world" replete with "wild licentious" savages. Addison, however, was connecting Britain's imperial impulse with the Enlightenment's mission of bringing universal values to the four corners of the world. And when the United States became an independent power, it had elements of *Cato* in its temperament. It fell to the man who in 1825 would become the sixth president to try to express the limits of those elements. In 1821, on the nation's forty-sixth Independence Day, John Quincy Adams, then secretary of state, delivered one of the most lucid and measured statements of America's stance toward the world:

> Wherever the standard of freedom and independence has been or shall be unfurled, there will her heart, her benedictions and her prayers be. But she goes not abroad in search of monsters to destroy. She is the well-wisher to the freedom and independence of all. She is the champion and vindicator only of her own. She will recommend the general cause, by the countenance of her voice, and the benignant sympathy of her example. She well knows that by once enlisting under other banners than her own, were they even the banners of foreign independence, she would involve herself, beyond the power of extrication, in all the wars of interest and intrigue, of individual avarice, envy, and ambition, which assume the colors and usurp the standard of freedom. The fundamental maxims of her policy would insensibly change from liberty to force.[46]

This is a policy most twenty-first-century Americans would like to be able to live by, a policy they wish they could have in a world that they wish made it prudent. In 1821, it was the proper policy for a nation with only modest military capabilities, a nation protected by the existence of two weak and placid neighbors and two broad oceans traversed only by wind-powered ships, a nation preoccupied with the unfinished business of western expansion. Two centuries on, however, the challenge of American statecraft is, and for at least eight decades has been, to make prudent departures from Adams' ideal. Prudence, however, often has been scarce.

Any new republic, wrote Machiavelli, must decide whether to expand her dominion by power, like Rome, or to be like Venice, located "in some strong place" that protects it as it goes about its business, which for Venice was business. During America's first century, geography enabled it to be Venetian—in a strong place, practicing commerce. But even then there was an itch to be Roman, too—but with a difference. America would seek, in Jefferson's words, an "empire of liberty," but without becoming imperial.[47] In October 1915, however, *The New Republic*, which then was the house organ of American progressivism, was feeling left out of the world's drama: "That calm moral grandeur in which we revelled a year ago, when it seemed as if we were destined to be the arbiter of nations, is no more.... Instead of the thankfulness that we are providentially escaping the storm, one finds on every hand the sense that we are missing something."[48] In 1915, Europe was engulfed in war, and the United States was a bystander. Progressivism, of which *The New Republic* was an exponent, was brimful of confidence of the sort that characterized the first great progressive, Theodore Roosevelt, who liked nothing less than being a bystander.

The first of TR's many intellectual passions was Darwin, whose influence grew not only in natural science but in social thought, including the social sciences and politics. That influence was ubiquitous. It immediately disturbed humanity's peace of mind. It was neither the first nor the last such disturbance by an idea, but it was the most profoundly unsettling. Not, however, to TR, who found it inspiring. Nature, as deciphered by Darwin, is constant competition resulting in the survival of the fittest. In the late nineteenth century, it seemed natural to have an analogous understanding of politics in nations and between nations: The natural dynamic of human societies is the conquest of territories by, and the rise to dominance of, the fittest races. And for progressives at the turn of the twentieth century, the complexity of the world, like the complexity of rapidly urbanizing and industrializing American society, was a reason not for caution but for ambition, for rolling up government's sleeves and getting on with big projects.

"More and more, the increasing interdependence and complexity of international, political and economic relations render it incumbent on all civilized and orderly powers to insist on the proper policing of the world." So wrote the former police commissioner of New York City, TR.[49] In June 1896, probably before Roosevelt had heard of San Juan Hill, the *Washington Post* wrote: "A new consciousness seems to have come upon us—the consciousness of strength—and with it a new appetite, the yearning to show our strength.... Ambition, interest, land hunger, pride, the mere joy of fighting, whatever it may be, we are animated by a new sensation. We are face to face with a strange destiny. The taste of Empire is in the mouth of the people even as the taste of blood in the jungle. It means an Imperial policy, the Republic, renascent, taking her place with the armed nations." Albert J. Beveridge, historian (biographer of John Marshall and Abraham Lincoln) and US senator from Indiana, was a progressive leader who wanted to export progress to retrograde peoples and nations: "God has not been preparing the English-speaking and Teutonic peoples for nothing but vain and idle self-contemplation and self-admiration. No! He has made us the master-organizers of the world." God, of whose intentions the Hoosier senator was confident, selected "the American people as His chosen nation to finally lead in the regeneration of the world."[50]

When former president Grover Cleveland spoke of "the fatal un-American idea of imperialism," he placed himself among those whom Theodore Roosevelt dismissed as "men of a bygone age."[51] While the Boer War was raging in South Africa, Mark Twain, then sixty-five and an opponent of the war, found himself back stage at the Waldorf-Astoria hotel, where he was to introduce a speech by an Englishman who ardently supported the war. When twenty-six-year-old Winston Churchill asked Twain to autograph a Twain book that Churchill had brought to the event, Twain inscribed it: "To do good is noble; to teach others to do good is nobler, and no trouble."[52] Theodore Roosevelt was on Churchill's side. Roosevelt was an assertive individualist who considered the individualism of others an impediment to the social cohesion required for national greatness. Preaching what he called "warrior republicanism," he envisioned virtue emerging from the subordination of individuals to—the immersion of them in—the nation's strenuous collective exertions.[53] William Graham Sumner, the Yale social scientist and classic liberal, detested the Spanish-American War because he thought that by making the United States resemble empire-building European nations, the war refuted American exceptionalism. Theodore Roosevelt read in *McClure's* magazine Rudyard Kipling's poem urging America to "take up the White Man's burden," starting with the Filipinos, whom Kipling described as

Your new-caught sullen peoples,
Half devil and half child.

"Rather poor poetry," wrote TR, by then New York's governor, "but good sense from the expansion standpoint." By the time, several decades later, the United States had set down the burden of guerilla war in the Philippines, Kipling's words had been shown to be better poetry than foreign policy.[54]

America has fought eight significant wars since the battleship *Maine* blew up (by accident, it now seems probable) in Havana harbor in 1898. This explosion showered sparks on the dry tinder of American nationalism and detonated the "splendid little war" that made a president of the Rough Rider of San Juan Hill.[55] One of George H. W. Bush's first gestures as president was to put TR's portrait in the Cabinet Room, in the place where Bush's predecessor had put a portrait of Coolidge. Victory over Spain led to fourteen years of counterinsurgency combat in the Philippines. There also was an intervention in China during the Boxer Rebellion, and Black Jack Pershing's Mexican Expedition. All told, some Americans have been involved in combat in more than half of the 121 years since the *Maine*'s keel settled into Havana's harbor mud.

Woodrow Wilson's detestation of Theodore Roosevelt would have been reciprocated even if Wilson had not selected as his secretary of state a moralizing pacifist, William Jennings Bryan. After doing so, Wilson got busy, turning his improving impulse toward Mexico, where a general, Victoriano Huerta, who was in the pay of British oil interests, had set himself up as dictator. Wilson announced that he would "require Huerta's retirement" by "such means as may be necessary." Referring to Mexico as a "distracted republic," Wilson ordered the US Navy to seize the city of Veracruz to prevent a German merchant ship from landing supplies for Huerta.[56] Wilson then offered to intervene on behalf of a revolutionary named Carranza against Huerta, if Carranza would promise to be a gentlemanly revolutionary. Carranza disdained Wilson's offer and overthrew Huerta on his own. Then a Carranza subordinate persuaded Wilson's agents that he, the subordinate, was a tamed and decorous revolutionary who deserved Wilson's support against Carranza. The subordinate was Pancho Villa. The honeymoon was brief. Carranza drove Villa into his native northern Mexico where, in January 1916, Villa, in an attempt to provoke Wilson, rode over into New Mexico and killed nineteen Americans. So, Wilson sent an expedition into Mexico. Before his presidency ended, he had also intervened with troops in Haiti, the Dominican Republic, Cuba, and the Soviet Union. No wonder the nation voted in 1920 to replace Wilson with a president promising "normalcy."[57] As we shall see, several decades later there was another occasion for consideration of what it means for America to be a normal nation. On the road to that horizon, however, the nation would do some hard learning.

BEFORE AND AFTER THE PROFESSORS' WAR

Flying over Nebraska in the summer of 1943, an Englishman was struck by the "normality—hundreds of miles of it and not a sight or sound to remind me that this was a country at war." Then his lunch tray arrived, and inscribed on the pat of butter was an injunction: "Remember Pearl Harbor."[58] The fact that butter was available was striking; even more so was the fact that perhaps people needed to be reminded how the war began. Five years after Pearl Harbor, Senator Arthur Vandenberg, the Michigan Republican who helped wean his party from isolationism, said the attack "drove most of us to the irresistible conclusion that world peace is indivisible. We learned that the oceans are no longer moats around our ramparts. We learned that mass destruction is a progressive science which defies both time and space."[59] The era of (in Walter Lippmann's phrase) "effortless security" was over.[60] "Progressive science" meant the end of security, as traditionally understood, forever. And we now must hope that in an age of constant regional conflicts, peace can be divisible.

Four days after Pearl Harbor, Hitler declared war on the United States and, immediately, photographs of FDR replaced those of Mussolini in many store windows on Mulberry Street in Manhattan's Little Italy. The attack punctuated a dreary dozen years. An eighteen-year-old in 1941 had been six when the stock market collapsed. Suddenly eighteen-year-olds had jobs, some of them dangerous. It is, however, still the case that in terms of the number of fatalities as a proportion of the population, the most lethal war in American history occurred in the seventeenth century: King Philip's War of 1675–76. Today, without the mass mobilization required for protracted global conflicts, military service has become the experience of a small minority. World War II's fatalities included 691 Harvard graduates. In Vietnam, the Harvard classes from 1962 through 1972 lost just twelve members. During the forty-three days of Desert Storm in 1991, violence in America killed many more than the 148 US troops killed by hostile action. The United States became a great power through late participation in wars that cost other and earlier participants in those wars much more.

In World War I, the United States suffered 116,516 war-related deaths, totaling one-tenth of 1 percent of its population. Great Britain lost one-thirtieth of 1 percent of its population between seven a.m. and seven p.m. on July 1, 1916, at the Somme, where a four-month battle cost Britain 100,000 dead. In the four years of war, Britain lost three-quarters of 1 percent of its population. France lost 5 percent. In World War II, US war-related deaths totaled one-quarter of 1 percent, and the United States suffered four civilian deaths from home-front bombing. (A Japanese balloon bomb launched from a submarine blew up an Oregon picnic.) The USSR lost at least 8 percent of its population. During World War II, more than seven million soldiers took part in the Battle of Moscow, which lasted six months and churned over territory the size of France. The Soviet Union lost more soldiers in this battle—926,000—than the United Kingdom lost in World War I, more than the combined British and American deaths in World War II. Four million men fought at Stalingrad in 1943, two million at Kursk in 1943, three and a half million in the Battle for Berlin in 1945. Two thirds of the estimated 26 million Soviet military and civilian dead have no known graves.[61] NATO was created in 1949 to counter the Soviet Union, but in nearly fifty-three years the only invasion of a NATO member's territory occurred in the South Atlantic, when Argentina attacked the Falkland Islands. The Korean War, which began in 1950, severely strained the American public's tradition of deference toward the foreign policy elite. This self-renewing group served the executive branch and believed, not without reason, in itself and was trusted by a deferential public. The Korean War undermined public support of President Truman and made Secretary Dean Acheson, symbol of the traditional foreign policy elite, a subject of bitter controversy. The war was ended by a president whose single memorable election promise was "I will go to Korea," which meant: I will end the war.[62]

One lesson of this long story is that an internationalist foreign policy has been possible only when Americans have subordinated their natural isolationism—meaning their disposition to think as little as possible about the rest of the world—to their tradition of deference to the foreign policy elite. Vietnam, however, destroyed that tradition. Vietnam was less a presidential war than a professors' war. It was too clever by half, with carefully calibrated violence—remember the "escalation ladder"?—sending "signals" to an uncomprehending enemy. David Halberstam used the title of his best-seller about Vietnam, *The Best and the Brightest*, to express the self-image of the professors, soldier-scholars, systems analysts, and others who presided over the escalation in Vietnam. More interesting than the Halberstam book is the fact that the phrase "the best and the brightest" has entered the nation's political lexicon as a piece of all-purpose sarcasm to express disdain not just for the "Kennedy-Johnson intellectuals" who Halberstam detested, but for elites in general.[63] Since then, the very idea of a foreign policy elite has been suspect.

In the United States, the general suspicion of elites ended deference toward an unnatural internationalism, and contributed to the rebirth of the nation's natural isolationism. Human beings, in Tuscany or Tennessee, are "natural" isolationists in that they sensibly do not want their sons or treasure conscripted and won't put up with it unless their government is persuasive or coercive. The United States for many years thought it had started fresh, that it was immaculately conceived, born without sin, and protected by God's oceans from unregenerate nations. America could dispense with the world because the world had served its purpose, which was to be prologue to America.

This attitude was caricatured, but captured, too, by a novelist from the American heartland: "Main Street is the climax of civilization. That this Ford car might stand in front of the Bon Ton Store, Hannibal invaded Rome and Erasmus wrote in Oxford cloisters. What Ole Jensen the grocer says to Ezra Stowbody the banker is the new law for London, Prague, and the unprofitable isles of the sea..."[64] Sinclair Lewis published *Main Street* in 1920, the last sad year of government by one of Princeton's "best and brightest," Professor Wilson. For twenty years after that, Americans reverted to the trait that James Bryce had detected in his 1888 *The American Commonwealth*: "The only one principle to which people have learnt to cling in foreign policy is that the less they have of it the better."[65] This is why, after the brief intoxication of involvement in World War I, and the long hangover of disappointment with the aftermath, America attempted a twenty-year holiday from history. On September 1, 1939, the day Germany attacked Poland, eighteen nations had armies larger than America's, which had only forty tanks on that day, when George C. Marshall became army chief of staff. Less than four months before Pearl Harbor, Congress came within one vote of virtually disbanding the army: The House voted 203–202 to extend conscription. The way World War II began for the United States, and the successful mobilization of economic muscle to win it, left the nation brimming with confidence. Events would take care of that.

Hell, said Hobbes, is truth seen too late. American foreign policy since the beginning of the Vietnam War has repeatedly been hellish. Campaigning in 1960 to become President Dwight Eisenhower's successor, Senator John Kennedy described Ike's remarkably peaceful and generally prosperous tenure as "eight years of drugged and fitful sleep."[66] Under Kennedy, the next few years—the Bay of Pigs, the Cuban Missile Crisis, increased US involvement in Vietnam—would be more stimulating. They also would make lethargy, or at least a lack of dash and élan, attractive. In November 1963, the Kennedy Administration was complicit in the coup that accomplished regime change (and murdered President Diem), sealing the US immersion in Vietnam's agony. In April 1965, President Lyndon Johnson, who had entered Washington politics when the city was dominated by the New Dealer who produced the Tennessee Valley Authority, promised to transform South Vietnam's Mekong River into a marvel that would "provide food and water and power on a scale to dwarf even our own TVA."[67] There were two problems with this promise. The TVA was not built in the middle of a raging civil war. And war in Vietnam was not about food or water or electric power. It was about nationalism and sharply different ideas of what Vietnam's regime should be. "This nation," said President Lyndon Johnson of the United States, "is mighty enough, its society is healthy enough, its people are strong enough, to pursue our goals in the rest of the world while still building a Great Society here at home."[68] Our productivity could and would overwhelm problems. So, when the military contemplated building a physical barrier between North Vietnam and South Vietnam, it purchased "five million steel fence posts and enough barbed wire to circle the globe twice."[69]

Johnson's vice president, Hubert Humphrey, a leader of postwar liberalism first as mayor of Minneapolis and then as a US senator, found Vietnam exhilarating: "We ought to be excited about this challenge, because here's where we can put to work some of the ideas about…nation building, of new concepts of education, development of local government, the improvement of health standards of people and really the achievement and fulfillment of full social justice."[70] In *The Quiet American*, Graham Greene's Vietnam novel, a character says of the title character, "I never knew a man who had better motives for all the trouble he caused."[71]

Vietnam became a heartbreaking story—comic, were it not staggeringly tragic—of earnestness foundering on mutual incomprehension. In 1954, when North and South Vietnam were being sorted out, refugees from the North were greeted in the South by Americans who gave them gifts, including, Max Boot writes, large, cellophane-wrapped blocks of American cheese. The Vietnamese received this politely but soon there were complaints: The cellophane-wrapped soap did not foam properly. Informed that it was cheese, they sold it to street merchants, who sold it back to the Americans. McNamara, on a 1964 visit to Saigon, tried to say, in Vietnamese, to a crowd "Vietnam ten thousand years," but, Boot writes, "his pronunciation was so atrocious that it sounded to many listeners as if he had said, 'Ruptured duck wants to lie down.'" Also in 1964, General William Westmoreland, the senior military officer in Vietnam, received a young Harvard professor, to whom Westmoreland said that Americans were much better liked than the French had been in Vietnam because "when the

French wanted a woman they simply grabbed her off the streets and went to bed with her," but "when an American soldier wants a woman he pays for her." The professor, Henry Kissinger, wrote in his diary, "I thought at first he was kidding but then I found out he was absolutely serious."[72] As was the predicament of the United States, having embarked with the likes of Westmoreland on a long, waist-deep wade into the morass of another nation's history and culture.

Military expertise supposedly would enable the United States to economize violence by administering finely calibrated—"flexible" and "graduated"—force. By adjusting the bombing intensity up and down, the United States would communicate the nuances of our intentions, and would adjust, as with a rheostat, incentives for North Vietnam to behave better. When in 1966 McNamara was asked if an increase in US troop levels constituted an escalation of the war, McNamara replied in language suitable to a laboratory experiment: "Not at all. It is merely an incremental adjustment to meet a new stimulus level." The United States used prodigious quantities of ordnance to communicate with North Vietnam—to "get our point across," in McNamara's words. Even before the Tet offensive began on January 30, 1968, US bomb tonnage dropped in the theater exceeded that dropped in the European and Pacific theaters in all of World War II. In 1967, Daniel Patrick Moynihan said the Vietnam War "most surely must be judged our doing." By "our" he meant progressives, and particularly progressive intellectuals suffused with confidence about their ability to control a world that they thought would be, abroad as well as at home, malleable in their skillful hands.[73]

The philosopher Michael Oakeshott warned that "the conjunction of dreaming and ruling generates tyranny."[74] Or, in foreign policy, it generates overreaching. Karl Marlantes, who was a decorated combat Marine in Vietnam before writing one of the great novels about that war, *Matterhorn*, regrets that "the prudence we learned from our involvement in Indochina has been widely derided as 'Vietnam syndrome.'" He says: "If by Vietnam syndrome we mean the belief that the U.S. should never again engage in (a) military interventions in foreign civil wars without clear objectives and a clear exit strategy, (b) 'nation building' in countries about whose history and culture we are ignorant, and (c) sacrificing our children when our lives, way of life, or 'government of, by, and for the people' are not directly threatened, then we should never get over the Vietnam syndrome. It's not an illness; it's a vaccination."[75]

The vaccination soon wore off. The December 1989 invasion of Panama, ordered by President George H. W. Bush, a month after the fall of the Berlin Wall, was for the United States the dawn of the post–Cold War world, the use of force to enforce international etiquette, without reference to a threat, existential or otherwise, to the United States. It was back to the future, an echo of Woodrow Wilson's vow "to teach the South American republics to elect good men," an application of Wilson's faith that "when properly directed, there is no people not fitted for self-government."[76] This was an impulse indulged after 9/11. In October 2001, Secretary of Defense Donald Rumsfeld said of terrorists and the nations that supported them, "We have two choices. Either we change the way we live, or we must change the way they live. We choose the latter."[77] Changing the way people live turned out to be a very comprehensive and open-ended undertaking.

In 1946, at the Nuremberg trials of the major Nazi war criminals, the tribunal declared: "To initiate a war of aggression…is the supreme international crime differing only from other war crimes in that it contains within itself the accumulated evil of the whole."[78] On June 1, 2002, at the United States Military Academy at West Point, President George W. Bush announced a war of aggression as US policy. Modern technology had, he said, come into the hands of people whose pre-modern and anti-modern beliefs rendered them impervious to the sort of prudential reasoning on which deterrence depends. So, he said, "We must take the battle to the enemy, disrupt his plans, and confront the worst threats before they emerge." Hence he endorsed what his administration would call "anticipatory self-defense": "In the world we have entered, the only path to safety is the path of action."[79]

In 1949, with membership in NATO, which committed the United States to go to war if other nations were attacked, something fundamental changed. As Daniel Patrick Moynihan said, "Foreign policy began to anticipate, rather than merely react to, conflicts."[80] NATO's primary function—muscular anticipation of a threat to Western Europe by conventional Soviet forces—was a resounding success. But the business of anticipating conflicts has been less so. Three weeks before the March 20, 2003, invasion of Iraq, President Bush said, "Human cultures can be vastly different, yet the human heart desires the same good things, everywhere on Earth…freedom and democracy will always and everywhere have greater appeal than the slogans of hatred and the tactics of terror."[81] This statement is either demonstrably false or it is unfalsifiable. That is, either it is refuted by the blood-soaked history of many fanaticisms, political and religious, including the history currently being written, or it necessarily means that wherever freedom and democracy are not preferred, "the human heart" is not being expressed, or heard, or heeded.

The assumption that "the human heart" is the same everywhere, and hence that everyone is more or less alike, give or take a few cultural differences, can lead to interesting misjudgments. Patrick Hurley, Franklin Roosevelt's personal representative in China in 1944, reported that Mao Zedong was an agrarian populist: "The only difference between Chinese Communists and Oklahoma Republicans is that Oklahoma Republicans aren't armed." Woodrow Wilson's first secretary of state, William Jennings Bryan, thought Pancho Villa was an "idealist" because he neither smoked nor drank. He did, however, have a short fuse, as Barbara Tuchman related: "On one occasion, angered by the yells of a drunken soldier while he was being interviewed by an American journalist, Villa casually pulled his pistol and killed the man from the window without interrupting the conversation."[82]

The "human heart theory" of foreign policy died in Iraq. In April 2004, as the Iraq war entered its second year, Bush said, "I also have this belief, strong belief, that freedom is not this country's gift to the world; freedom is the Almighty's gift to every man and woman in this world. And as the greatest power on the face of the Earth, we have an obligation to help the spread of freedom."[83] This was a justification for the invasion that was quite independent of the prudential justification—the theory that something specific, the "survival" of American liberty, depended on something particular, this invasion. In his January 20, 2005, second inaugural address, Bush said, "The survival of liberty in our land increasingly depends on the success of liberty in other lands."[84] Note the word "survival," which makes the spread of liberty a matter of existential urgency for the United States. Bush began with the idea that American liberty is made insecure by all deprivations of liberty elsewhere: "The defense of freedom requires the advance of freedom."[85] Bush was a short step from Woodrow Wilson's insatiable hunger for world improvement. Wilson said: "I will not cry 'peace' so long as there is sin and wrong in the world."[86] Bush could have learned a saving moderation from an unlikely source, Robespierre: "The most extravagant idea that can be born in the head of a political thinker is to believe that it suffices for people to enter, weapons in hand, among a foreign people and expect to have its laws and constitution embraced. No one loves armed missionaries."[87]

America invaded Iraq to disarm a rogue regime thought to be accumulating weapons of mass destruction. When no such weapons were found, the appropriate reaction would have been dismay and indignation about intelligence failures. Instead, Washington's reaction was Wilsonian. Never mind the weapons of mass destruction; a sufficient justification for the war was Iraq's noncompliance with various UN resolutions. So a conservative American administration said that war was justified by the need—the opportunity—to strengthen the UN, aka the "international community," as the arbiter of international behavior. It was then counted as realism in Washington to say that creating a new Iraqi regime might require perhaps two years. Washington did not remember that it took about 110, from 1865 to 1975, to bring about, in effect, regime change—a change of Jim Crow institutions and mores—in the American South. Would a Middle Eastern nation prove more plastic to Washington's touch than Mississippi was? Would two years suffice for America to teach Iraq to elect good men?

One of the animating theories that were involved to justify the Iraq invasion was espoused by, among others, Condoleezza Rice, President Bush's national security advisor. The theory was that democratic institutions do not always need to spring from a hospitable culture; they also can help to create such a culture. Certainly they *can*. They did, she correctly said, in America. Benjamin Rush, the Philadelphia physician, had spoken of first establishing government institutions and then preparing "the principles, morals, and manners of our citizens, for those forms of government."[88] Iraq, however, was different in ways that advocates of the war were too ideologically blinkered to see.

It is perhaps unfair to say that America's nation-builders went about their work incompetently. That suggests that there is, somewhere, a reservoir of nation-building competence. But many misadventures in Iraq, Afghanistan, and elsewhere would have been more forgivable if they had not been driven by an ideology. They came from the Jeffersonian poetry of democratic universalism. If everyone yearns for freedom, and freedom is understood identically everywhere, how hard can building a democratic nation be? Why would many US forces, or much time and treasure, be needed? If a natural— almost spontaneous—moral consensus, not power, is going to be the regulator of people and of relations among nations, then of course international politics will be undemanding.

An English skeptic once said he wanted to carve on all the churches of England three cautionary words: "Important If True."[89] Those words were germane in July 2003 when, with the invasion of Iraq just four months old, British Prime Minister Tony Blair told a joint session of the US Congress: It is a "myth" that "our attachment to freedom is a product of our culture," and he added: "Ours are not Western values. They are the universal values of the human spirit and anywhere anytime ordinary people are given the chance to choose, the choice is the same. Freedom, not tyranny. Democracy, not dictatorship. The rule of law, not the rule of the secret police." That assertion is important. But is it true? Everyone everywhere does not share "our attachment to freedom." Freedom is not defined the same way everywhere, let alone valued the same way relative to other political goods such as equality, security, social cohesion, and piety. Did Blair really believe that our attachment to freedom is not the product of complex and protracted acculturation by institutions and social mores that have evolved over centuries—the centuries that it took to prepare the stony social ground for seeds of democracy? When Blair said that freedom as we understand it, and democracy and the rule of law as we administer them, are "the universal values of the human spirit," he was not speaking as America's Founders did when they spoke of "self-evident" truths.[90] The Founders meant truths obvious not to everyone everywhere but to minds unclouded by superstition and other ignorance—minds like theirs. Blair seemed to think: Boston, Baghdad, Manchester, Mecca—what's the difference?

At the beginning of the Iraq misadventure, Bush also said something that is important—if true. Actually, it is even more important if it is not true. He denounced "cultural condescension"—the belief that some cultures lack the requisite aptitudes for democracy. He said: "Time after time, observers have questioned whether this country or that people or this group are ready for democracy, as if freedom were a prize you win for meeting our own Western standards of progress."[91] Multiculturalists probably purred with pleasure about the president's delicate avoidance of gauche chauvinism about "Western standards of progress." His idea—that there is no necessary connection between Western political traditions and the success of democracy—is important. But is it true? His hypothesis was tested in Iraq, where an old baseball joke was pertinent. At spring training, a manager says, "Our team is just two players away from being a championship team. Unfortunately, the two players are Babe Ruth and Lou Gehrig." Iraq was just three people away from democratic success. Unfortunately, the three were George Washington, James Madison, and John Marshall.

Iraq lacked a Washington, a universally revered hero emblematic of national unity and identity. Iraq lacked a Madison, a genius of constitutional architecture, a profound student of what the president called "Western standards of progress," and a subtle analyst of the problem of factions and their centrifugal, disintegrative possibilities. Iraq lacked a Marshall, someone who could so persuasively construe the text of a constitution that the prestige of a court, and of law itself, ensures national compliance. Iraq lacked a Washington, a Madison, a Marshall—and it lacked the astonishingly rich social and cultural soil from which such people can sprout. From America's social soil in the eighteenth century sprang all the members of the Constitutional Convention and of all the state legislatures that created all the conventions that ratified the Constitution. So, Iraq in its quest for democracy lacked only what America in 1776 had: an existing democratic culture.

It is a historical truism that the Declaration of Independence was less the creator of independence than the affirmation that Americans had already become independent. In the decades before 1776 they had become a distinct people, a *demos*, a nation held together by the glue of shared memories, common strivings, and shared ideals. In his 1982 Westminster address to the British parliament, Ronald Reagan said the US aim was "to foster the infrastructure of democracy," including a free press, political parties, labor unions, and other means of achieving peaceful resolution of domestic conflicts. Then Reagan used the phrase that George W. Bush would several times appropriate: Reagan said it would be "cultural condescension" to say that "any people prefer dictatorship to democracy."[92]

People are, however, rarely confronted with such a binary choice.

Rather, they are faced with moving from a messy present to an opaque future in which they might be required to do unaccustomed things and accept discomfiting outcomes—tolerate religious and political pluralism, compromise deeply held social convictions, abandon cherished national aspirations. So, people tiptoeing toward, or sidling crabwise into, an open society rarely have tidy preferences or clear expectations. Rather, they have a concrete present to weigh against a hypothetical future. In February 2004, Condoleezza Rice said: "We reject the cultural condescension which alleges that Arabs or Muslims are somehow not interested in freedom, or aren't ready for freedom's responsibilities."[93] But being "interested" in a demanding social system and being ready for it are very different. In December 2004, President Bush said: "It is cultural condescension to claim that some peoples or some cultures or some religions are destined to despotism and unsuited for self-government."[94] Perhaps it is necessary—perhaps it is, in the best sense, politic—for a president to talk that way. But being "destined" or "unsuited" for something is not an informative description. The truth is that life in an open society—a society that is democratic in governance so that it can remain open—requires talents and aptitudes that do not appear spontaneously, and are not distributed democratically, meaning evenly, across the globe.

The question is: What should the United States do to encourage, in the words of President John F. Kennedy's inaugural address, "the survival and the success of liberty"?[95] What can US foreign policy do to expand the recognition and enjoyment of the natural rights essential for human flourishing and therefore conducive to peace among nations? In moral reasoning, "ought" implies "can": There is no duty to do the impossible. The last fifty years have been a painful tutorial in the limits of the possible. This has been instruction in the relevance to foreign policy of Friedrich Hayek's idea of the fatal conceit, the dangerous belief that we can know, and can control, more than we actually can. The good news from the twentieth century is that because human nature is real, human beings are not as malleable as is presupposed by the authors of the worst political practices.

Extravagant political aspirations breed dangerous political practices: Hitler's Holocaust, Stalin's Gulag Archipelago, Mao's Culture Revolution. And they breed weird aspirations like this: Leon Trotsky concluded his 1924 book *Literature and Revolution* with the prophecy that under communism "man will become immeasurably stronger, wiser and subtler; his body will become more harmonized, his movements more rhythmic, his voice more musical. The forms of life will become dynamically dramatic. The average human type will rise to the heights of an Aristotle, a Goethe, or a Marx."[96] It is important to take seriously the fact that a man of undoubted intelligence and substantial political talents could think like this. There are many more forms of political intoxication than Americans' relatively tame political experience encompasses. In Tom Stoppard's play *Travesties*, set in 1917, a character is told that a "social revolution" has erupted in Russia. He asks, "A social revolution? Unaccompanied women smoking in the Opera, that sort of thing?" He is told, "Not precisely that, sir."[97] The distinctive radicalism of twentieth-century revolutions was incomprehensible to people who, being sensible, did not understand the new totality of revolutionary aspirations—the aim to take control of consciousness itself.

The twentieth century's two most dreadful inventions were nuclear weapons and totalitarianism. In the physics and politics of these, a crucial concept is "critical mass." In physics, it can be the key to huge explosions. In politics, the cardinal tenet of totalitarianism is that the masses must not be allowed to amass on their own, spontaneously. Totalitarianism is a mortar and pestle, grinding society to dust, atomizing individuals and assembling them only into compounds controlled by the state. The twentieth-century's art, literature, and morals reflected pervasive anxiety about impermanence: everything from empires to atoms had been shattered. Yet amidst all the disorienting flux, totalitarianism suggested the possibility of an awful permanence. Armed with modern communications and other technologies of social control, totalitarians tried to immunize themselves against internal change that would challenge the state's total sovereignty over society. Imagine, said Orwell, a boot in your face—forever. His nightmare is the totalitarians' dream, the terrifying promise of permanence.

The totalitarian pretense was the claim to have broken history, and all human spontaneity, to the political party's will. Plato, who sought ways to prevent cycles of civic virtue from decaying into tyranny, had comprehensive prescriptions for education, poetry, rhetoric. Modernity has meant preoccupation with history as linear, not cyclical. That is, history as a narrative infused with the drama of the possibility of progress. The last two centuries have given birth to various historicisms, theories stipulating that history is a series of inevitabilities independent of individuals' political wills and choices. The totalitarian impulse arises from the claim that a particular party has a monopoly on understanding history's dynamic and therefore has a right to unbridled administration of its insight, however brutal this administration might be for those who contest its monopoly of interpretation. Paradoxically, in the twentieth century, when history accelerated giddily, the great political invention, totalitarianism, promised regimes that would perpetuate themselves forever. The world has been haunted by the specter of permanence, the permanent boot in the face.

In 1951, Hannah Arendt, a refugee from Hitler's Europe, published *The Origins of Totalitarianism*. Her thesis was that induced ideological intoxication, combined with modern instruments of social control, such as bureaucracy and mass media, might make totalitarianism an unassailable tyranny, immune to all dynamics of change from within. Terrorism—the end of legality; random violence—is but one totalitarian instrument. Another is gray bureaucracy controlling all cultural institutions. Totalitarianism aims at the conscription of the citizen's consciousness—state ownership not merely of industries but of minds. So, totalitarianism requires control of the flow of information, which means the central scripting of all public argument, which means no real public argument. Intermediary institutions standing between the individual and the state—schools, churches, clubs, labor unions, even families—must be pulverized or permeated by the state. The totalitarian aim is the atomization of society into a dust of individuals, a dust blown around by gusts of ideology emitted by the tutelary party. The totalitarian enterprise is the extirpation of all autonomous institutions and hence of autonomous impulses in society. Instead of Marx's withering away of the state, there is the withering away of society through the unlimited penetration of life by the state—by politics.

But in 1956, in the streets of Budapest, Arendt's profoundly pessimistic theory was slain by a luminous fact. For twelve days, Hungary flung its unconquered consciousness in the face of the totalitarian state. There was no civil war because the nation was not divided: Ideological indoctrination had left the public utterly unmarked. In Budapest, tanks prevailed, but Arendt rejoiced in the refutation of her hypothesis. In an epilogue to the 1958 edition of her book, she wrote: "The voices from Eastern Europe, speaking so plainly and simply of freedom and truth, sounded like an ultimate affirmation that human nature is unchangeable, that nihilism will be futile, that even in the absence of all teaching and in the presence of overwhelming indoctrination, a yearning for freedom and truth will rise out of man's heart and mind forever." Arendt saw in this a spontaneity that was "an ultimate affirmation that human nature is unchangeable," that no state succeeds in "interrupting all channels of communication," and that "the ability of people to distinguish between truth and lies on the elementary factual level remains unimpaired; oppression, therefore, is felt for what it is and freedom is demanded."[98]

Human nature is real and unchangeable; national characters, however, are real but, over a long time, changeable. History is, to a significant extent, a story of hostilities between groups—tribes, clans, cities, nations. They are hostile because they have different characters. Hence the idea of national character, which became of intense practical interest during and after World War II, when policy-makers turned to scholars in the hope of finding predictive guidance for dealing first with Germans and Japanese, then with Russians. The idea of national character should rescue us from having our intelligence bewitched by anesthetizing language about the "community of nations." Nothing can be properly called a "community" if it jumbles together entities as different as Saudi Arabia and New Zealand, Japan and Sudan, Italy and Iran, Norway and North Korea. The phrase "community of nations" may seem harmless, if hackneyed, but it is a symptom of a blinding sentimentality. Different nations involve different notions of justice. A "community" consists of people held together by a broad, deep consensus about justice under a common sovereignty.

The stubborn persistence of nations and nationalisms is a redundant refutation of Marx's core contention: economic determinism. Marx's belief in the sovereignty of economic forces over ethnicity and other cultural factors is just another failed prophecy from "scientific socialism." Because Marxism was so boastful about its predictive powers, Marxists suffered traumas when events refuted it, as in August 1914 when Reichstag deputies representing working-class parties, supposedly the most "progressive" in Europe, voted to finance Germany's war effort. This nationalist behavior stunned those who believed, as Marx did, that the proletariat has no fatherland. When Stalin, who was Lenin's commissar for nationalities, said, "Marxism replaces any kind of nationalism," he was echoing Lenin, who said socialism "abolishes" and "merges" nations.[99] Lenin had correctly represented Marx: "There is not a single Marxist who, without making a total break with the foundations of Marxism and Socialism, could deny that the interests of Socialism are above the interests of the right of nations to self-determination."[100] Marx said in *The Communist*

Manifesto that the acids of international capitalism would dissolve "every trace of national character."[101]

A steady aim of US engagement with the world should be to create incentives for the slow, incremental modification of certain nations' characters to bring them more into conformity with the universalism of the American creed. Pressure can come from the United States by the constant support—rhetorical, financial, diplomatic—of people in those countries who are asserting natural rights that have been denied recognition. This can prudently increase internal pressures on repressive regimes. And this places the United States where it belongs, in the vanguard of the most powerful force in the modern world, the demand for recognition of dignity.

Human beings differ from other animals in having a sense of their dignity, and a desire for its recognition by others. This, a manifestation of what Plato called the soul's "spirited" part, is as important to politics as the soul's reasoning part. Francis Fukuyama credits Hegel as the first to understand that "the primary motor of human history is not modern natural science or the ever expanding horizon of desire that powers it, but rather a totally non-economic drive, the *struggle for recognition.*" Fukuyama's "end of history" hypothesis was this: With the end of the Soviet Union and the exhaustion of socialism's intellectual confidence as a fighting faith, mankind's ideological evolution might have reached its terminus. This would be so if liberal democratic societies satisfied citizens' material needs—and their desires for recognition. If they did, history, for all its violence, irrationality, and detours, would be revealed to be, after all, not "a blind concatenation of events" but rather *fundamentally* directional, universal, and coherent, vindicating the idea of progress.[102]

Most of the twentieth century had been hard on this hypothesis. The century, Fukuyama says, had "made all of us into deep historical pessimists."[103] The century had begun full of confidence that science would transform nature from mankind's adversary into its servant. Evil was supposedly a manifestation of backwardness, which was well on its way to being banished by universal free public education and the application of science to society. The cumulative nature of scientific discovery seemed to refute the age-old belief that history is cyclical, an endless repetition. Science certainly nourished hopes for social progress. And Machiavelli had provided the foundation for modern political confidence—meaning modern politics—by asserting that mankind, properly led by political people who are properly emancipated from moral strictures inappropriate to politics, could subdue *fortuna*, meaning history's contingencies. So the twentieth century ended with Americans hoping that foreign policy could recede from the center of the nation's consciousness.

A NORMAL COUNTRY?

After the collapse of the Soviet Union sealed the US victory in the Cold War, Jeane Kirkpatrick, who as Ronald Reagan's UN ambassador was an architect of that victory, wrote an essay in which she welcomed a new era in which the United States could become (this was the essay's title) "a normal country in a normal time."[104] During the Cold War— what John Kennedy in his inaugural address called "a long twilight struggle"—foreign policy had taken on, Kirkpatrick said, "an unnatural importance."[105] Unnatural, that is, in that there seemed to be no limits to what implicated US national interests important enough to require at least the threat of military force. She said: "There is no mystical American 'mission' or purpose to be found independently of the U.S. Constitution.... There is no inherent or historical 'imperative' for the U.S. government to seek to achieve any other goal—however great— except as it is mandated by the Constitution or adopted by the people through elected officials." Kirkpatrick was expressing understandable relief, tinged with fatigue, after more than four decades of Cold War tensions. Her wishes, however, gave rise to a thought that was not quite right. Kirkpatrick correctly said that "a good society is defined not by its foreign policy but by its internal qualities."[106] But what is normality for this nation regarding the rest of the world? Kirkpatrick was correct that "America's purposes are mainly domestic."[107] Mainly. But not entirely. Here is the rub:

The Declaration of Independence is the continuing "conscience of the Constitution," and hence of the American regime. Intelligent people of good will can and do debate what this means for America's engagement with the world. But surely it means something. From the nation's beginning, with varying intensity and involving varying specifics, most Americans have felt that the nation does have some sort of mission. It is independent of the Constitution in that this document allocates powers; it does not direct the purposes to which the powers shall be put, beyond those mentioned in the Preamble, only one of which ("provide for the common defense") is germane to foreign policy. But the national mission is not independent of the Constitution's conscience. The Declaration's declaration that rights, being natural, are universal must in *some* way inform this nation's foreign policy.

While he was president, the author of the Declaration wrote, "We feel that we are acting under obligations not confined to the limits of our society. It is impossible not to be sensible that we are acting for all of mankind."[108] Two centuries later, Henry Kissinger, no Jeffersonian, argued that Americans' belief that their principles are universal implies that governments with other principles are "less than fully legitimate" and that much of the world "lives under a kind of unsatisfactory, probationary arrangement."[109] American universalism, combined with America's geography and geology—America's location between two broad oceans; its endowments of natural resources— made Americans "uncomfortable with the prospect of foreign policy as a permanent endeavor for contingent aims." Until the Second World War, Americans could and frequently did "treat foreign policy" as an "optional activity." Optional and hence intermittent. And eventually, they hoped, unnecessary.

The belief that American principles *should* be universal begets the belief that America's ambitious purpose in the world should be to shape the world in such a way that America will no longer have to have ambitious purposes. American's Lockean belief in humanity's natural sociability has disposed America to believe that peace among nations is natural and spontaneous, or would be if other nations would clear their minds of the superstitions that prevent them from recognizing the universal validity and demonstrable utility of our self-evident truths. Small wonder that in 1890, at the dawn of the decade that would end with a burst of American imperialism, the US army was only the world's fourteenth largest, behind Bulgaria's.[110]

Twenty years after the Spanish-American War and the acquisition of the Philippines in 1898, the United States had a president, Woodrow Wilson, who proclaimed the First World War to be "the culminating and final war for human liberty," and who traveled to Paris to get on with the business of implementing universal principles *right now.* This could be done because America's principles "are also the principles and policies of forward looking men and women everywhere, of every modern nation, of every enlightened community." All that would be required would be to codify everyone else's commitment to modernity and enlightenment. A quarter of a century later, when Franklin Roosevelt, a Wilson protégé, was president, he reportedly assured his former ambassador to the Soviet Union, William C. Bullitt, that he had a "hunch" that Joseph Stalin was not going to be a postwar problem: "I think if I give him everything that I possibly can and ask nothing from him in return, *noblesse oblige,* he won't try to annex anything and will work for a world of democracy and peace."[111] FDR did not have the tragic sense of life that is a facet of the talent for pessimism that in turn is a facet of the conservative sensibility.

Kissinger, brooding about the long peace between the 1815 Congress of Vienna and the cataclysm of 1914, wondered whether the century of calm "might have contributed to disaster. For in the long interval of peace the sense of the tragic was lost."[112] But, then, those Americans who think human nature inclines humanity toward common objectives really have no tragic sense to lose. "Any society," Kissinger wrote as a thirty-four-year-old academic, "faces a point in its development where it must ask itself if it has exhausted all the possibilities of innovation inherent in its structure. When this point is reached, it has passed its zenith. From then on, it must decline, rapidly or slowly, but nonetheless inevitably."[113] This was the European Kissinger, a historicist comfortable with theories of inevitability and with the Hegelian ideas of possibilities dictated and limited by social structures. Two decades later, Kissinger worked for a leader who was susceptible to similar thoughts.

On one occasion, President Richard Nixon mused about thoughts he occasionally had when seeing the tall columns that flank the entrance to the National Archives building on Constitution Avenue: "I think of what happened to Greece and to Rome and, as you see, what is left—only the pillars. What has happened, of course, is that great civilizations of the past, as they have become wealthy, as they have lost their will to live, to improve, they then have become subject to the decadence which eventually destroys a civilization. The United States is now reaching that period."[114] This was unlike anything ever said publicly by an American president. Of course, the Western intellectual tradition is replete with philosophers, historians, and others who have wondered whether history is cyclical, driven by seeds of social decline that were sown by the processes of social ascent. The thoughts stirred in Nixon by the National Archives' pillars were spoken by the highest elected official of a nation founded on, and still steeped in, the Enlightenment belief in humanity's ability to make informed and rational—enlightened—choices that can master impersonal forces.

Historical pessimism of the sort that Nixon and Kissinger entertained must have a profound influence on a foreign policy agenda. Kissinger would later deplore Woodrow Wilson's susceptibility to "the irrepressible American conviction that understanding between peoples is normal, that tension is an aberration, and that trust can be generated by the strenuous demonstration of good will."[115] Daniel Patrick Moynihan had Kissinger in mind when he acidly described those who would completely purge US foreign policy of Wilsonian aspects as "men who know too much to believe anything in particular and opt instead for accommodations of reasonableness and urbanity that drain our world position of moral purpose."[116] That moral purpose is, strictly speaking, congenital: from birth. It is encoded in America's national DNA. It is admirable. And it is problematic.

In 1989, at the United Nations, Mikhail Gorbachev said, impertinently: "Two great revolutions, the French revolution of 1789 and the Russian Revolution of 1917, exerted a powerful impact on the very nature of history...those two revolutions shaped the way of thinking that is still prevalent..."[117] *Two* great revolutions? Trust a historicist to miss one of the largest lessons of history. It is that the American Revolution unleashed the most potent force surging through the last two centuries, the passion for freedom grounded in respect for natural rights. The man who would bring Gorbachev into the liquidation of the Cold War understood this force, if not its provenance. "You can call it mysticism if you want to," said Ronald Reagan amiably but mystically, "but I have always believed that there was some Divine plan that placed this great continent between two oceans, to be sought out by those who were possessed of an abiding love of freedom and a special kind of courage."[118]

Once you postulate divine guidance of the planet's drifting tectonic plates, it is only natural to assume a continuing divine interest in the nation that dominates its continent. The American Revolution was, at bottom, about the right of a distinctive people, conscious of itself as a single people, to govern itself in its distinctive manner, in nationhood. Here was a great eighteenth-century insight: Popular sovereignty is inextricably entwined with nationality. The nation-state has been a great instrument of emancipation. It has freed people from the idea that their self-government is subject to extra-national restraints, such as the divine right of kings, or imperial prerogatives, or traditional privileges of particular social classes. Certainly Americans will not passively watch their nation's distinctive ideas of justice be subordinated to any other standards. Most Americans are not merely patriots; they are nationalists, too. They do not merely love their country; they correctly believe that its political arrangements, its universal truths, and the understanding of the human condition that those arrangements reflect are superior to other nations' arrangements. They believe, but usually are too polite to say, that American arrangements are not suited to everybody right now. These superior American arrangements are suited to culturally superior people—those up to the demands made by self-government.

Lincoln correctly said that ours is a nation founded on permanent truths "applicable to all men and all times."[119] So the permanent puzzle for the nation's foreign policy is: How are these truths "applicable"? The answer is: By implacable but delicate insistence that fidelity to these truths demands US fidelity to the painstaking process of preparing the social soil of other nations to receive and express those truths in institutions and practices. Among the most frequently quoted lines of English language poetry are from William Butler Yeats' "The Second Coming":

The best lack all conviction, while the worst
Are full of passionate intensity.[120]

The world has suffered much from nations with dangerous convictions that fuel missionary impulses to conquer the backward and recalcitrant, and to coerce them into obedience and virtue. Hence, the peculiar delicacy required of those who formulate and conduct the foreign policy of the United States, a nation whose identity is inseparable from its conviction—its *correct* conviction—that it is the pioneer and bearer of certain universal truths.

Nothing would be more gratifying than for America to lose much of its exceptionalism because its premises have become universally embraced, as Jefferson hoped would happen and as he tentatively expected. In a letter written on June 24, 1826, eleven days before his death on the fiftieth anniversary of the Declaration of Independence, he said of that document: "May it be to the world, what I believe it will be, (to some parts sooner, to others later, but finally to all,) the signal of arousing men to burst the chains, under which monkish ignorance and superstition had persuaded them to bind themselves, and to assume the blessings and security of self-government.... All eyes are opened, or are opening, to the rights of man."[121]

Today, however, the immediate danger is an American apostasy, a slow, shambling slouch away from its exceptional premises, in foreign as well as domestic policies. Americans should not regret the fact that their nation's foreign policy will always have a meliorist dimension. It flows from two premises. First, America has a mission to make the world better because the American model of a pluralistic commercial republic is a universally valid aspiration. And exporting the model is in the national interest because spreading bourgeois civilization, with its preoccupations with pluralism and prosperity, is a way to tranquilize an often murderous world.

What Bismarck said in the nineteenth century is even more true in the twenty-first: "We live in a wondrous time, in which the strong is weak because of his moral scruples and the weak grows strong because of his audacity."[122] As the Second World War approached and then began, it almost seemed as though the civilized were too civilized to protect their civilization. In his 1946 memoir *Not So Wild a Dream*, perhaps the best nonfiction book to come out of the war, Eric Sevareid, the broadcast journalist, told of a small episode during the 1939–40 "phony war," before Germany lunged west in May 1940. During a night that Sevareid spent with French forces near the Rhine, a young corporal who had been working with a spade was killed by a German sniper across the river:

Just one man, one soldier out of millions of soldiers who presumably were expected to die. The lieutenant in charge was close to tears as he described the terrible tragedy—how the boy had fallen, what he had told them to write to his parents before he died. The other men in the pillbox scarcely spoke all evening, but stared at the floor, thinking of the frightful thing that had just happened. It was awful; it was murder....It was not that the French were not brave....They were not *afraid* of death; they were *unprepared for* death. It was not true that they did not think their country worth fighting for; they wished to avoid defeat, but they had no particular wish to win a war. Their last experience had taught them that there is no such thing as a true victory for civilized men who have no desire to conquer others. Their tragedy was that they had reached a high point of human progress too soon; they were living before their time. They were the last people on earth who should have had Germany for a neighbor.[123]

But is it actually progress if one is paralyzed by a challenge from barbarism? A nation living before its time may not live to see its time. Just a generation earlier, these two contiguous nations had suffered hitherto unimaginable slaughters during the first industrial war. In 1939, one of those nations flinched from another war, the one for which the other nation had prepared. The cultural divide between France and Germany then was much wider than the Rhine. Nations can pick neither their neighbors nor the time in which they live. In today's world of ballistic missiles, cyber threats, and democratized air travel that facilitates small bands of terrorists, every nation is every other nation's neighbor, and there are clashes between civilizations that are more unalike, and more mutually unintelligible, than France and Germany were in 1939.

"This nation," said Woodrow Wilson of the United States, "was created to be the mediator of people, because it draws its blood from every civilized stock in the world and is ready by sympathy and understanding to understand the peoples of the world."[124] Again, we encounter the cheerful progressive premise: Conflicts arise from misunderstandings and hence can be prevented or ended by the dissemination of clarifications. Machiavelli knew better. He became a permanent torment to the Western mind by saying something that, once said, forced us to face a permanent difficulty. He said that the question of how people should live—which human goals should be exalted—will never result in a single, universally satisfying answer. As Isaiah Berlin wrote, Machiavelli still disturbs our peace by "the planting of a permanent question mark" over society; by, that is, his coldly matter-of-fact recognition that, in Berlin's words, "ends equally ultimate, equally sacred, may contradict each other, that entire systems of value may come into collision without possibility of rational arbitration."[125] So people must either be prepared for perpetual fighting against divergent views or they must find paths to accommodations.

Progressivism holds out the hope that human material is malleable, that the present is endlessly manipulable, and that the future is predictable. From this flows the recurring belief—it recurs soon after events refute it—that peace is the natural relation between nations and that war is an aberration explainable by the bad character of rulers and by benighted traditions and institutions. For two centuries progressives have been explaining the obsolescence of war—their explanations often hard to hear over the roar of cannon—in terms of the spread of democracy. Or the disappearance of religious and ethnic and nationalistic fervor. Or the pacifying power of commerce. Or the increase of travel. Or the communications revolution. But, as Yale classicist and historian Donald Kagan notes, "Over the past two centuries the only thing more common than predictions about the end of war has been war itself." Kagan says that "statistically, war has been more common than peace, and extended periods of peace have been rare in a world divided into multiple states." Given what Kagan calls war's "ubiquity and perpetuity," the first duty of political leadership is to act on the axiom that "peace does not keep itself."[126] Leaders must act also on the probability, for which there is accumulating evidence, that nations that are respectful of natural rights domestically will be disposed to peace in dealing with other nations. This is only a probability. But life is, at almost every turn, a wager on inconclusive evidence. To think otherwise is to embrace what could be a truly fatal conceit.

CHAPTER 9

WELCOMING WHIRL

CONSERVATISM WITHOUT THEISM

Whirl is King, having driven out Zeus.

Aristophanes[1]

As Huck Finn and Jim floated down the Mississippi River on their raft, they occasionally indulged in theological—more precisely, Deistic—ruminations. "We had the sky up there," Huck recalled, "all speckled with stars, and we used to lay on our backs and look up at them, and discuss about whether they was made, or only just happened."[2] This question has been asked since the dawn of human curiosity, which means since the emergence of beings who were recognizably human. But perhaps the most pertinent answer to this question today is another question: Without divine revelations, what difference does the answer—"was made" or "just happened"—really make?

Those whose answer concerning the stars—and everything else—is "was made" are theists. The "just happened" contingent consists of those who think that invoking transcendence as an explanation for everything that exists is neither necessary nor persuasive. To ask why the dispute between the "was made" and the "just happened" schools matters is not to doubt or disparage the history-shaping saliency of religions. They infuse individuals' lives and animate nations and other collectivities. Those who dismiss religion as fossilized philosophy neglect the obvious fact that religions often do what philosophy rarely does: They set in motion cascading events. After all, the most consequential life in human history was lived twenty-one centuries ago in the eastern portion of the Roman empire by a person who never traveled a hundred miles from his birthplace, never held public office, never wrote a book, and died at the hands of the state in his early thirties. The second-most potent life was that of Muhammad. He was born in the second half of the sixth century and died in the first half of the seventh century without ever having ruled a state, but his effects are not merely still radiating, they are increasingly important as the twenty-first century lurches on. Religions have shaped world politics and culture more broadly and lastingly than any political philosophy has done. This lesson of humanity's experience is clear: Intangibles, such as religious faith, have historic heft. "A flame rescued from dry wood has no weight in its luminous flight yet lifts the heavy lid of night."[3] So wrote the poet who became Pope John Paul II, whose large role in ending the Cold War was a riposte to a materialist's—Stalin's—dismissive question, "How many divisions does the pope have?"[4]

For the purpose of this book, however, the question is not whether religion does or should matter, but rather whether religious faith is, or ever has been, necessarily integral to American conservatism or a prerequisite for a conservative sensibility. The argument of this chapter is that not only can conservatives be thoroughly secular, but that a secular understanding of cosmology and of humanity's place in the cosmos accords with a distinctively conservative sensibility. Philosophy is downstream from sensibility, which cannot be disentangled from philosophy because sensibility disposes a person to see the world and experience life in particular ways.

Huck Finn's creator, Mark Twain, said: "What God lacks is convictions—stability of character. He ought to be a Presbyterian or a Catholic or something—not try to be everything."[5] Ah, there's the rub. "To attempt to be religious without practicing a specific religion," wrote George Santayana, "is as possible as attempting to speak without a specific language."[6] Of course, many people do attempt that, tarting up any yearning for "meaning" or any hope for eternity as a religious episode, so almost anyone who is occasionally "spiritual" can consider himself or herself episodically religious. But go beyond speaking about religion in general, go beyond Huck's brand of natural theology to particular religions involving divine revelations, and religion becomes subject to interpretations. It becomes more than an explanation (of, for example, Huck's stars) but less than a source of universally acknowledged moral imperatives.

If God is uninterested in humanity's undertakings or prayers, He is uninteresting and need not impinge upon humanity's political or ethical thinking. Religion becomes politically relevant and problematic when divine revelation enters the picture, with God taking an active interest in, and intervening in, human affairs, and supplying strictures about how people should behave. People will differ about what all of this means, and these differences are not easily splittable. Virginia Woolf wrote in a letter, "I read the book of Job last night— I don't think God comes well out of it."[7] Woolf was channeling her inner Huck, the empiricist. Let us leave it to theologically grounded persons to decide whether, or how, the progressive doctrine of a changing human nature can be squared with the teachings of various religions. This much, however, is clear: A nation such as ours, steeped in and shaped by Biblical religion, cannot comfortably accommodate a politics that takes its bearings from the proposition that human nature is a malleable product of social forces, and that improving human nature, perhaps unto perfection, is a proper purpose of politics. Biblical religion is concerned with asserting and defending the dignity of the individual. Biblical religion teaches that individual dignity is linked to individual responsibility and moral agency. Therefore, Biblical religion should be wary of the consequences of government untethered from the limited (and limiting) purpose of securing natural rights.

Some keen observers of America could see this long before the advent of modern progressivism. Alexis de Tocqueville wrote *Democracy in America* just two generations after the American founding—two generations after Madison identified tyranny of the majority as the distinctive political evil that democracy could produce. Tocqueville had a different answer to the question of what kind of despotism democratic nations should fear most. His warning is justly famous and more pertinent now than ever. This despotism, he said, would be "milder" than traditional despotisms, but

> it would degrade men without tormenting them.... That power is absolute, minute, regular, provident, and mild. It would be like the authority of a parent, if, like that authority, its object was to prepare men for manhood; but it seeks, on the contrary, to keep them in perpetual childhood.... For their happiness such a government willingly labors, but it chooses to be the sole agent and the only arbiter of that happiness; it provides for their security, foresees and supplies their necessities, facilitates their pleasures, manages their principal concerns, directs their industry, regulates the descent of property, and subdivides their inheritances: what remains, but to spare them all the care of thinking and all the trouble of living?
>
> Thus, it every day renders the exercise of the free agency of man less useful and less frequent; it circumscribes the will within a narrower range, and gradually robs a man of all the uses of himself.... Each nation is reduced to being nothing better than a flock of timid and industrious animals, of which the government is the shepherd.[8]

Each of us must decide to what extent Tocqueville's foreboding is being fulfilled. People of faith, however, should ask this: Does the tendency of modern politics to take on more and more tasks in order to ameliorate the human condition tend to mute religion's message about reconciling us to that condition? And people of faith should worry about whether religious institutions can flourish in the shade cast by government that presumes to supply every human need and satisfy every appetite. Secularists must confront the other side of the same question: Can our limited government and free society long endure if the work of civil society, which often is the work of our religious institutions, is taken up instead by the government? To the extent that the politics of modernity reduces the role of religion in society, it threatens society's vitality, prosperity, and happiness. Irving Kristol understood this. Although not an observant Jew, he described himself as "theotropic," by which he meant oriented to the divine. He explained why in these words:

> A society needs more than sensible men and women if it is to prosper: It needs the energies of the creative imagination as expressed in religion and the arts. It is crucial to the lives of all of our citizens, as it is to all human beings at all times, that they encounter a world that possesses a transcendent meaning, a world in which the human experience makes sense. Nothing is more dehumanizing, more certain to generate a crisis, than to experience one's life as a meaningless event in a meaningless world.[9]

We may be approaching what is, for our nation, unexplored and perhaps perilous social territory. Europe is now experiencing a widespread waning of the religious impulse, and the results are not attractive. It seems that when a majority of people internalize the big-bang theory of the origin of the universe and ask, "Is that all there is?," when they decide that the universe is merely the result of a cosmic sneeze with no transcendent meaning, when they conclude that therefore life should be filled to overflowing with distractions and comforts and entertainments to assuage boredom, then they may become susceptible to the excitements of politics that promise ersatz meaning and spurious salvation from the human condition without the comfort of belief in transcendence.

We know from the bitter experience of twentieth-century fanaticisms the political consequences of felt meaninglessness. Human nature abhors a vacuum, and a vacuum of meaning has been filled by secular fighting faiths, such as fascism and communism. Fascism gave its adherents a meaningful life of racial destiny. Communism taught its adherents to derive meaning from their participation in the eschatological drama of History's unfolding destiny. The excruciating political paradox of modernity is that secularism advanced in part as revulsion against the bloody history of religious strife, but there is no precedent for bloodshed on the scale produced in the twentieth century by secular political faiths. In this regard, America has been exceptional—exceptionally fortunate. It has, however, not simply been lucky. Luck, a wise man once said, is the residue of design. Regarding religion, America's luck has been the residue of philosophy, including political philosophy.

Two hundred fifty years ago, Americans were a religious people. The Founders were markedly less so.

The Massachusetts constitution, whose principal drafter was John Adams, was completed in 1780. It declared that "the happiness of a people, and the good order and preservation of civil government, essentially depend upon piety, religion and morality; and as these cannot be generally diffused through a community, but by the institution of the public worship of GOD, and of public instructions in piety, religion and morality." Therefore, the people "have a right to invest their legislature with the power to authorize and require" provision for "the public worship of GOD, and for the support and maintenance of public protestant teachers of piety, religion and morality, in all cases where such provision shall not be made voluntarily." And the legislature may require "attendance upon the instructions of the public teachers." The Massachusetts constitution added that "no subordination of any one sect or denomination to another shall ever be established by law."[10] Unless, of course, the sect or denomination was other than a Protestant variant of Christianity. The sharpest religious conflict in the pre-Revolutionary and Founding eras was between Christian factions—especially between Protestants and Catholics—and was colored by political considerations important to a new and understandably insecure republic. The Puritans and other early immigrants to America brought with them memories of European religious strife, particularly that which had roiled England since the Reformation. "Prior to the Revolutionary War," writes Edward J. Larson, "Catholics were persecuted in every colony."[11] Nowhere could they vote or hold public office, not even in Maryland, which was founded to be welcoming to Catholics. Not even in Rhode Island, whose famous tolerance extended to atheists but not to Catholics. Massachusetts made it a capital offense for a priest to proselytize or say Mass.

The Founders, however, were not like this. As a group they did not seethe with strong feelings about religious differences, other than the feeling that differences must be accommodated. The fact that two American colonies, Pennsylvania and Rhode Island, were conceived as experiments in religious liberty is perhaps more important than that eleven colonies were not. The eleven eventually took up the challenge of reaching conformity with the two. The two were founded, more or less explicitly, on the principle of religious freedom—the toleration of what the First Amendment came to call the "free exercise" of religion.

America's political arrangements are affirmations of the political thinking that aimed at the subordination of religion to the political order, which meant, in the American context, the primacy of democracy. The Founders, like Locke before them, wished to tame and domesticate religious passions of the sort that had convulsed Europe. The Founders aimed to do so not by establishing religion but by establishing a commercial republic. They aimed to submerge people's turbulent energies in self-interested pursuit of material goals. Hence religion was to be perfectly free as long as it was perfectly private—mere belief. It must, however, bend to the political will (law) as regards conduct. Thus Jefferson held that "operations of the mind" are not subject to legal coercion, but that "acts of the body" are.[12] It matters not, said Jefferson, if one's neighbor believes in one god or twenty gods or no god; the believing neither picks one's pockets nor breaks one's legs.

Jefferson's distinction rests on Locke's principle—Jefferson considered Locke one of the three greatest men who had ever lived— that religion can be useful or can be disruptive, but its truth cannot be established by reason. Hence Americans would not "establish" religion. Rather, by guaranteeing free exercise of religions, they would make religions private. The Framers of the Constitution included in it "a guarantee to every state" of a republican form of government (Article IV, Section 4) because they considered that the truth about the best form of government was known. This was a closed question for proponents of an open society. But the First Congress, which included the most important Framer, Madison, quickly added the First Amendment to forbid the "establishment of religion" because he and Congress thought that religious truth was unknowable and so must forever remain an open question.

Some of the Founders read David Hume, a contemporary of theirs until his death in the eventful year 1776. Most of them would have subscribed to his belief that "Generally speaking, the errors of religion are dangerous; those of philosophy only ridiculous."[13] This is so because disputes about religious claims, especially claims derived from supposed revelations, cannot be settled by reason. Many of the Founders read John Locke, who addressed a problem that had begun to be understood as a problem seventeen centuries before he wrote. When Jesus enjoined his followers to "render therefore unto Caesar the things which are Caesar's; and unto God the things that are God's," Western political thought began to develop the distinction between private and public spheres, and between private and public virtues, with the former given primacy.[14] Although the separation of church and state was a long time coming, it was implicit in, and eventually understood to be entailed by, what Walter Berns called "Locke's formula for unity." This formula was that "religion would have no state, and the state would have no religion." Confessional states, those concerned with controlling consciences, are gone from the West. Madison insisted that America has achieved "a perfect separation between ecclesiastical and civil matters."[15] A separation that is "perfect" means a perfectly—completely—secular state.

This was foreshadowed by the language of the first paragraph of the Declaration of Independence. It says that Americans are a people entitled to independence by "the Laws of Nature and of Nature's God." It is not altogether clear what was meant by "Nature's God" but this is a reasonable surmise: What was not meant was the God of the Bible. "Nature's God," Berns noted, "issues no commandments, no one can fall from his grace, and, therefore, no one has reason to pray to him asking for his forgiveness; he makes no promises." He endows us with rights, including the right to worship other gods or no god, and then he absconds, never again to intervene in the human story. Domestic tranquility, so elusive in a Europe of confessional states, would be insured in America—or, at any rate, not threatened in America—by a secular regime. So, the Constitution, the Preamble of which enumerates domestic tranquility among the Constitution's objectives, leaves religion "unendowed." Again, Berns: "I mean by this that, whereas (for a telling example) it grants Congress the power 'to promote the Progress of Science and the useful Arts,' it nowhere gives it the power to promote religious belief."[16] State governments, from the outset and for a long time, promoted religion by mandating or tolerating public school curriculums permeated with it. The various twentieth-century Supreme Court decisions that ended this were intensely controversial, but clearly congruent with the Framers' intentions.

Those intentions have been aggressively misconstrued in our times by people with religious axes to grind. Not since the medieval church baptized, as it were, Aristotle as some sort of early—*very* early—

church father has there been an intellectual hijacking as audacious as the attempt to present America's most important Founders as devout Christians. The argument is that they were kindred spirits with today's evangelicals and that they founded a "Christian nation." This thoroughly irritates Brooke Allen, an author and critic, who robustly argues that Franklin, Washington, Adams, Jefferson, Madison, and Hamilton subscribed, in different ways, to the watery and undemanding Enlightenment faith called deism. This doctrine appealed to rationalists by being explanatory but not inciting; it made the universe intelligible without arousing dangerous zeal.

Eighteenth-century deists believed there was a God but, tellingly, they frequently preferred synonyms for him—"Almighty Being" or "Divine Author" (Washington) or "a superior agent" (Jefferson). If this agent merely set the universe in motion like a clockmaker, the agent is, as an eighteenth-century aphorist described him, the "God who winds our sundials."[17] But this God is not very interesting if all he ever does, or did, was wind up the universe and then turn his back on it. We can be grateful that he did the winding; we can wish that in the beginning, before disappearing, he had made provisions so that the passage of time would not include some of the things that have come to pass (e.g., World War I and pediatric oncology wards). But be that as it may, the Sundial Winder has no claim on our continuing interest because he has no continuing interest in us. Providence might reward and punish, perhaps in the hereafter, but does not intervene in human affairs. Deists rejected the incarnation, hence the divinity of Jesus. "Christian deist" is an oxymoron. It has been well said that the deist God is like a rich aunt in Australia—benevolent, distant, and infrequently heard from. Deism seeks to explain the existence and nature of the universe. But so does the big bang theory, which is not a religion. If a religion is supposed to console and enjoin as well as explain, deism hardly counts as a religion.

The Founders spoke of religion often, but usually in terms of temporal needs, individual or social, rather than timeless truths.

Many thought that religion was necessary, regardless of its veracity: If churches are, on balance, useful, that is perhaps a sufficient reason for them. When Benjamin Franklin was given some books written to refute deism, the deists' arguments "appeared to me much stronger than the refutations. In short I soon became a thorough Deist." Revelation "had indeed no weight with me." He believed in a creator and the immortality of the soul, but considered these "the essentials of every religion."[18] What Brooke Allen calls George Washington's "famous gift of silence" was particularly employed regarding religion, but his behavior spoke. He would not kneel to pray, and when his pastor rebuked him for setting a bad example by leaving services before communion, Washington mended his ways in his austere manner: He stayed away from church on communion Sundays. He acknowledged Christianity's "benign influence" on society, but no ministers were present and no prayers were uttered as he died a Stoic's death.[19]

John Adams declared that "philosophy looks with an impartial eye on all terrestrial religions," and told a correspondent that if they had been on Mount Sinai with Moses and had been told the doctrine of the Trinity, "we might not have had courage to deny it, but we could not have believed it."[20] As he said, the longer he lived, the shorter grew his creed, and in the end his creed was Unitarianism. Jefferson, writing as a laconic utilitarian, urged his nephew to inquire into the truthfulness of Christianity without fear of consequences: "If it ends in a belief that there is no god, you will find incitements to virtue in the comforts and pleasantness you feel in its exercise, and the love of others which it will procure you."[21]

Madison, always commonsensical, briskly explained—essentially, explained away—religion as an innate appetite: "The mind prefers at once the idea of a self-existing cause to that of an infinite series of cause & effect." When the First Congress hired a chaplain, Madison said that "it was not with my approbation." When, during the War of 1812, congressmen urged President Madison to proclaim a day of fasting and prayer for the nation's success, he refused, saying that people so inclined could and would pray. In 1781, the Articles of Confederation acknowledged "the Great Governor of the World," but six years later the Constitution made no mention of God. When Hamilton was asked why, he supposedly quipped, "We forgot." Ten years after the convention, the Senate *unanimously* ratified a treaty with Islamic Tripoli that declared the US government "is not in any sense founded on the Christian religion."[22] Regardless of the reasons why this stipulation was deemed expedient, the stipulation was and is accurate. The regime is founded on precepts, many of which are congruent with, or buttressed by, Christian doctrine, which taught the universal equality of individuals capable of moral choices informed by faith. "Critique of religion" Marx wrote, "is the prerequisite of every critique."[23] He believed this because religion was the bedrock impediment to the modern political project, as Marx understood it. This project is to rescue humanity from contradictions and imperfections that produce individual and societal failures. Religion, however, and especially Christianity, with its doctrine of original sin, teaches that inadequacy is an irremediable constant of the human condition.

As noted in Chapter 1, there is another argument, independent of this or that statement by this or that Founder, for why the United States is a thoroughly secular polity. The Constitution mandates the establishment of a political truth by guaranteeing each state the same form of government ("republican"). It does so because the Founders thought the most important political truths are knowable. But because they thought religious truths are unknowable, they proscribed the establishment of religion, while respecting religion's instrumental value.

Two days after President Jefferson wrote his public letter endorsing a "wall of separation" between church and state, he attended, as he occasionally did, religious services in the House of Representatives, where the speaker's chair served as a pulpit.[24] During Jefferson's administration, Sunday services were held every week in government buildings. Ministers included Anglicans, Presbyterians, Baptists,

Quakers, Swedenborgians, a Roman Catholic bishop, a Unitarian, and a female evangelist. Jefferson was an observant yet unbelieving Anglican/Episcopalian throughout his public life. This was a statesmanlike accommodation of the public's strong preference, which then as now was for religion to have ample space in the public square.

Christianity, particularly its post-Reformation ferments, fostered attitudes and aptitudes associated with popular government. Protestantism's emphasis on the individual's direct, unmediated relationship with God, and the primacy of individual conscience and choice, subverted conventions of hierarchical societies in which deference was expected from the many toward the few. But beyond that, America's Founding owes much more to John Locke than to Jesus. New Jersey's Luther Martin said few of his fellow delegates to the Constitutional Convention were "so unfashionable as to [think] that a belief in the existence of a Deity and of a state of future rewards and punishments would be some security for the good conduct of our leaders."[25] Heaven and Hell are all very well, but the convention was looking for auxiliary precautions. It found them in the Madisonian architecture of federal institutions, and in the multiplicity of factions produced by the sociology of "extensive Republics."[26]

In 1786, the year before the convention constructed the regime, Jefferson, in the preamble to Virginia's statute for religious freedom, proclaimed that "our civil rights have no dependence on our religious opinions, any more than our opinions in physics or geometry."[27] Thomas Paine could be, simultaneously, the colonies' most influential writer of political advocacy and also the author of this: "Of all the systems of religion that ever were invented, there is none more derogatory to the Almighty, more unedifying to man, more repugnant to reason, and more contradictory in itself than this thing called Christianity."[28] Many of Paine's readers could compartmentalize their assessment of him, relishing his political ideas while deploring his thoughts about "invented" religions. And others simply did not care that much about religion.

Since the Founding, America's religious enthusiasms have waxed and waned, confounding Jefferson's prediction, made in 1822, four years before his death, that "there is not a young man now living in the United States who will not die an Unitarian."[29] In 1908, William Jennings Bryan, the Democrats' presidential nominee, said his Republican opponent, William Howard Taft, was unfit because, being a Unitarian, he did not believe in the virgin birth of Jesus. The electorate yawned and chose Taft. In 1953, the year before the words "under God" were added to the Pledge of Allegiance, President Dwight Eisenhower proclaimed the Fourth of July a national day of prayer. On that day, he fished in the morning, golfed in the afternoon, and played bridge in the evening. Were there prayers in the interstices of these recreations? Perhaps when the president faced a particularly daunting putt. When George Washington swore the first presidential oath of office, he did not conclude with the words "so help me God." After reciting the constitutionally prescribed presidential oath, and his brief—1,428 words—inaugural address, Washington immediately walked across the street from Manhattan's Federal Hall for a two-hour service at St. Paul's Chapel.[30] This conformity to expectations of public piety was probably as perfunctory as it was obligatory.

On September 22, 1881, following the death of President James Garfield, Vice President Chester Arthur—who as president would sign the law giving federal workers Christmas day off—took the presidential oath of office, which he ended with the words "so help me God." He seems to have been the first president to do so. Several versions of these words were used, intermittently, at the installation of other presidents; Herbert Hoover was the last president not to use them. America's public piety is more frequently avowed than constraining—so much so that it has invited raillery. In 1958, during Eisenhower's second term, Peter De Vries, whose novels are splendid satires of America in the second half of the twentieth century, created the Reverend Mackerel of the People's Liberal Church in a posh Connecticut suburb. The reverend spoke from a pulpit made of a "slab of marble set on four legs of four delicately differing fruitwoods, to symbolize the four Gospels, and their failure to harmonize." He offered this prayer during a flood: "Let us hope that a kind Providence will put a speedy end to the acts of God under which we have been laboring."[31] In the years immediately after the 1962 Supreme Court decision forbidding organized prayers in public schools, some polls indicated that more Americans favored such prayers in schools than regularly prayed in churches. Today, many people who insist on the importance of piety in the lives of individuals and society are not particular concerning what people should be pious about. They are like the British ethicist who said: "I am fully convinced that the highest life can only be lived on a foundation of Christian belief—or some substitute for it."[32]

In 1952, William O. Douglas, one of the most progressive justices ever to sit on the Supreme Court, wrote: "We are a religious people whose institutions presuppose a Supreme Being."[33] If by that Douglas meant that the natural rights tradition logically requires belief in God, he was simply mistaken. And as recently as 1984 the Supreme Court repeated Douglas' words.[34] The first part of this is more or less true (and less true than it once was) but of no relevance to constitutional law. The second part is of uncertain meaning. It is, however, certainly false: Are the institutions senseless, imprudent, or doomed if there is no Supreme Being? The nation's first president was more circumspect. George Washington had a way of taking an indirect path to his point, as when he said in his first inaugural address, "No people can be bound to acknowledge and adore the invisible hand which conducts the affairs of men, more than those of the United States."[35] And in his Farewell Address, Washington said: "Let us with caution indulge the supposition that morality can be maintained without religion. Whatever may be conceded to the influence of refined education on minds of peculiar structure, reason and experience both forbid us to expect that national morality can prevail in exclusion of religious principle."[36]

The third president, whose relationship to religion was cool and attenuated, sounded a theme similar to Washington's. Jefferson wondered whether American liberties could be secure without "a conviction in the minds of the people that these liberties are a gift from God."[37] Jefferson was suggesting an empirical postulate—that, absent a certain "conviction" about the origin of natural rights, those rights will not receive sufficient respect. Less than a month before his inauguration, president-elect Eisenhower said, "Our form of government has no sense unless it is founded in a deeply felt religious faith, and I don't care what it is."[38] By having "no sense," Eisenhower might have meant that, absent a general acceptance of some character-forming and behavior-shaping theisms, our form of government will not be stable or durable. That, too, is an empirical assertion, and one that an increasingly secular America is testing.

The "bulk of mankind," Locke thought, requires religious instruction, not because human reason is inherently insufficient to reveal how one should live, but because most people are incapable of the "long and sometimes intricate deductions" to reach that wisdom. "Such trains of reasonings the greatest part of mankind have neither leisure to weigh; nor, for want of education and use, skill to judge of." Thus "you may as soon hope to have all the day-labourers and tradesmen, the spinsters and dairy maids perfect mathematicians, as to have them perfect in ethics this way."[39]

Many Americans—perhaps a majority—agree that democracy, or at least our democracy, which is based on a belief in natural rights, presupposes a religious faith. People who believe this cite, as Eisenhower did, the Declaration of Independence and its proposition that all of us are endowed by our Creator with certain unalienable rights. However, two separate and related questions are pertinent to any consideration of the role of religion in American politics. One is an empirical question: Is it a fact that the success of self-government requires a religious *demos*—religious people governing themselves by religious norms? The other is a question of logic: Does belief in America's distinctive democracy—a government with clear limits defined by the natural rights of the governed—require religious belief? Regarding the empirical question: Religion has been, and can still be, supremely important and helpful to the flourishing of American democracy. But what is the *evidence* that it is necessary for good citizenship? Regarding the question of our government's logic, the idea of natural rights does not require a religious foundation, and the Founders did not uniformly think that it did. It is, however, perhaps the case that natural rights are especially firmly grounded when they are grounded in religious doctrine.

So, religion is helpful and important, but is not essential. This formulation, which is hardly a departure from the American tradition, is neither hypocritical nor self-contradictory precisely because of the character of the American tradition. This is a tradition that has always marked out a division of labor between the institutions of politics and those of civil society, including those of religion, which play a role in sustaining our limited government by shaping self-sufficient citizens. Hence citizens who want limited government should be friendly to the cause of American religion, even if they are not believers themselves. The division of labor between society and government in America and the character of America's political community grounded in the concept of natural rights are in dispute today. Understanding those disputes can help us better grasp the place of religion in the republic's life.

Religion has been central to the American polity precisely because religion has not been central to American politics. Religion has played a large role in nurturing the virtues that republican government presupposes, particularly micro self-government—the individual's governance of his or her self. The nation assigns to politics and public policy the secondary and subsidiary role of encouraging, or at least not stunting, the infrastructure of institutions that have the primary responsibility for nurturing civic and other virtues. American religion therefore coexists comfortably with, but is not itself a component of, American government. Religion's independence of politics has been part of its strength. There is a fascinating paradox at work in our nation's history: America, the first and most relentlessly modern nation, is, to the consternation of social scientists, also the most religious modern nation. One reason for this is that we have disentangled religion from public institutions.

The modern world got rolling when Martin Luther, appearing at an inquiry into his thinking, reportedly declared: "*Hier steh' ich, ich kann nicht anders.*" Here I stand, I can do no other.[40] This was a peculiar avowal of freedom—"I have no choice"—but it foreshadowed societies based on recognition of "unalienable" rights. Luther's words announced the ascendance of private judgment—of conscience. He thought the state legitimately could be, and probably must be, powerful and sometimes ruthless. By his reckoning, the state should be cloaked in less dignity than it was when church and state were melded. The state, he thought, is responsible only for order and is barely relevant to the serious business of life, which is the afterlife—salvation. Christianity's assessment of man, at once high and severe, is just about right for political philosophy: Man can be magnificent, but he is magnificent rarely, and never spontaneously—never without help from nurturing institutions. Luther had a haunting sense of humanity's utter fallenness, and of humanity's total dependence on God's grace for even the slightest amelioration of the consequences of sin. This insulated Luther from the political temptation to believe in the perfectibility of man through the improvement of social arrangements. In the endless argument about which dominates, nature or nurture, Luther knew: nature. His quest for purity in religious experience—an anticipation of the modern quest for "authenticity"—led him to minimize the institutional help that is necessary to assist mankind's quest for religious satisfaction and social fulfillment. But the radical individualism implicit in his thought was tempered by his celebration of the family as society's molecular unit.

Luther's career was made possible by another German's career,

Johannes Gutenberg's. Luther's was the first great life bound up with mass communication—printing with moveable type. He was the most prolific serious writer in history. One edition of his works exceeds 100 volumes; more than 2,500 of his letters survive. When people could read scripture, priests were challenged in their role as mediators between people and God. Luther's doctrine of salvation by faith alone rather than by good works expressed the doctrine that salvation derives from God's gift of unmerited grace. This doctrine challenged the role of priests as deliverers of grace through sacraments. Luther was no democrat, but with seven words—"each and all of us are priests"—he asserted an idea of equality that evolved into an underpinning of popular sovereignty.[41]

But are we sovereign over ourselves? If so, in what sense? Political philosophy cannot proceed far without addressing the problem of free will. This is the problem of understanding the extent to which our behavior might be, or perhaps must be, determined by forces outside ourselves. By, that is, what Lucretius, an early worrier about this, called the "everlasting sequence of cause and effect."[42] In his bill for the establishment of religious freedom in Virginia, Jefferson said, "Almighty God hath created the mind free, and manifested his supreme will that free it shall remain by making it altogether insusceptible of restraint: that all attempts to influence it by temporal punishments, or burthens, or by civil incapacitations, tend only to beget habits of hypocrisy and meanness."[43] Jefferson was, however, concerned with a premodern, or at least a pre–nineteenth century, understanding of what might count as a free mind. Jefferson rightly said that once a person has made up his or her mind on a subject, punishments or civil incapacitations can deter a person from expressing his or her thoughts but cannot prevent the thoughts. A more modern worry is that it is not clear how sovereign a person is in "making up"—in furnishing—his or her mind.

All consciousnesses are immersed in their times. This is not, however, to say that we are "in" our times in the same way that fish are in water—that we are oblivious of what surrounds us. Not all individuals are, however, equally interested in, or aware of, their social surroundings. Not all individuals are equally equipped by their native intellectual abilities or by education to comprehend and critique their social contexts. In most societies most of the time, a disposition to comprehend and critique is characteristic of only a small minority. Social inertia is disrupted by minorities who are able to step, at least partially, out of their times, and whose thinking is conditioned by an awareness of their own social conditioning. We accept the reality that we are conditioned by factors beyond our control, and that this does not nullify the concept of free will. From the fact that our thinking, remembering, and aspiring is the result of neurons firing in the brain, it does not follow that our brains' activities are as automatic, or autonomous, as the breathing of our lungs, the blinking of our eyelids, or the beating of our hearts.

It is one thing to acknowledge that there is *some* determinism at work in our lives, that there are causes beyond our control that have effects on our thinking and behavior. It is quite different to suppose that the fact of *some* determinism validates fatalism—the belief that our thoughts and decisions are not in any meaningful sense really "ours." Surely the crucial question is: Can we choose to have choices? That is, can we will into existence an array of alternative thoughts and behaviors?

The prophet of modern masterless man, Niccoló Machiavelli, stands where the ancients end and the moderns begin. The ancients took their political bearings from their understanding of the best of which people were capable. They sought to increase the likelihood of the emergence of fine and noble leaders, and fine and noble attributes among the led. Machiavelli, however, took his bearings from people as they were. He defined the political project as making the best of this flawed material. He was no democrat, but he is among democracy's precursors because he reoriented politics toward accommodation of strong and predictable forces arising from a great constant: the human nature common to all people in all social stations. Martin Luther, Machiavelli's contemporary, was no democrat, in theory or temperament. But he was one of democracy's potent precursors. Without fully intending to do so, he celebrated individualism at the expense of tradition and hierarchy—paving the way for a democratic ethos that he could not have imagined.

The advent of modernity in political philosophy coincided with parallel developments in a closely related field of philosophy— epistemology, the philosophy of knowledge, which concerns how we know things. Here René Descartes played a role comparable to Machiavelli's role in reorienting political thought. Descartes sought a ground of certainty, a ground beyond religious revelation. He found it in cognition itself: *Cogito ergo sum*—I think, therefore I am. The senses would supply the foundations for whatever certainties humanity can achieve. It was in Hobbes' political philosophy that epistemology became decisive. Hobbes' experience of religious strife in seventeenth-century England taught him that all human beings fear violent death. On this powerful, simple desire for physical security he erected a philosophy of despotism: In exchange for such security, people would willingly surrender the precarious sovereignty they possessed in the state of nature.

However, Hobbes' thoroughly secular philosophy contained the seeds of democracy in four ways. First, Hobbes said that all human beings are *equally* under the sway of this strong imperative. Second, all human beings can, without the assistance of a priestly clerisy, comprehend the basic passions that move the world. Third, to the extent that the world of politics is driven by strong and steady passions and interests, to that extent there can be a science of politics. A science of politics based on what all human beings have in common— knowledge supplied by the senses—is a political science deriving its data from the *demos*, the people. Fourth, because people do not agree about religious truth, and because they fight over their disagreements, social tranquility is served by regarding religion as a voluntary matter for private judgment, not state-supported and state-enforced orthodoxy.

These converging and mingling streams of epistemology and political philosophy helped to produce the US Constitution. It includes no editorial exhortations or admonitions comparable to those in the Northwest Ordinance, which affirmed the importance of religion to the governance of a republic. When some New England divines complained to President Washington because "some explicit acknowledgment of THE TRUE ONLY GOD, AND JESUS CHRIST whom he has sent" had not been "inserted somewhere" in the Constitution, Washington replied laconically that "the path of true piety is so plain as to require but little political direction." Gordon Wood asserts that "most leading Founders were not deeply or passionately religious, and few of them led much of a spiritual life," and Washington "seems never to have purchased a Bible." Yet religious forms were respected, even by Jefferson, who was baptized and married in his parish and served on his local vestry. Yet, during the 1800 presidential campaign, the *Connecticut Courant* published what Wood calls "a typical Federalist outburst" warning about the consequences of electing the religiously suspect Jefferson: "Murder, robbery, rape, adultery, and incest will be openly taught and practiced."[44]

With that unfulfilled forecast of apocalyptic secularism in mind, a brief autobiographic snippet by the author of this book seems apposite. My father's father was a Lutheran minister who served a number of churches in northern Maryland, eastern Ohio, and western Pennsylvania. As a boy, my father would listen outside pastor Will's study as he and some thoughtful parishioners would wrestle with the problem of reconciling the doctrine of grace with the belief in free will. Perhaps this formative experience had something to do with my father growing up to be an atheist—for philosophic reasons, not because he had seen quite enough of the inside of churches—and a professor of philosophy. I grew up in a completely secular home where the subject of religion simply did not arise. I, like my father, am an amiable, low-voltage atheist. And like my father, my model of amiability is David Hume. A story that Hume often told about himself is that one day as he was walking along an Edinburgh bog he slipped into it and, seeking help in extracting himself, he called out to some nearby fishwives. They, however, recognized him as "the wicked unbeliever" and refused to help him unless he solemnly recited the Lord's Prayer. He did this, and they rescued him. They were pleased, and he was not discommoded by gratifying them.[45] Thus are social frictions relating to religion lubricated by mildness.

Having no religious affiliation is not, however, the same as having no affinity. I began in journalism, after a brief sojourn in academia, as the first Washington editor of William F. Buckley's *National Review* magazine. Buckley was a devout Catholic who believed that a real conservative need not be religious but could not be hostile to religion. Some atheists (and some theists) might think such an attitude is impossible, but as we have seen, our nation's Founders surely thought, and proved, otherwise. The Founders created a distinctly modern regime, one respectful of rights that exist before government and are natural because, as Locke said, they are not creations of the regime that exists to secure them. Locke's theory of knowledge, which was that all knowledge and every individual's inner life come from external prompts, sped the displacement of the soul by the mind as the basis of individual identity and agency.

When John Adams said that asserting the divinity of Jesus was "awful blasphemy," he was, strictly speaking, saying that the assertion was an affront to God, although it is not clear how, or how often, Adams thought about God.[46] Adams did believe that religion was indispensable in a republic: "We have no government armed with power capable of contending with human passions unbridled by morality and religion. Avarice, ambition, revenge, or gallantry, would break the strongest cords of our Constitution as a whale goes through a net. Our Constitution was made only for a moral and religious people. It is wholly inadequate to the government of any other."[47]

Adams, however, insisted that a republic "is only to be supported by pure religion or austere morals."[48] Note the "or," which implies that an acquired morality can be independent of, and an alternative to, religion in sustaining republics.

In the middle of the twentieth century, however, the revival of conservatism was partly propelled by some prominent thinkers who insisted on the indispensability of theism. Whittaker Chambers, in his characteristically extreme recoil from his characteristically extreme commitment to the materialism of Communism, said that a man without mysticism is a monster. A person capable of saying this is capable of monstrous thoughts and, perhaps, monstrous deeds. Chambers was, so to speak, excommunicating atheists, agnostics, and skeptics— any person without a theism—from the human community. He thereby sided with those who are always with us, those who reduce others to a status less than human. By making religiosity a defining attribute of men who are not monsters, Chambers, like others of the same mentality before and since, planted the predicate for committing monstrosities against those who they see as not fully human. The fact that Chambers continues to occupy a place in what many American conservatives consider the pantheon of their persuasion must make conservatism at least problematic, and often off-putting, to temperate theists as well as the non-mystics—meaning non-theists— whom Chambers execrated. Such conservatives are courting political difficulties. Between 2007 and 2017, the non-religious portion of the American population rose from 16 percent to 29 percent. This portion now outnumbers the combined congregations of all the mainline Protestant churches.

Another luminary of mid-twentieth-century conservatism, Russell Kirk, said, "Until human beings are tied together by some common faith, and share certain moral principles, they prey upon one another."[49] To which three responses are required. First, religion can be socially useful without being true. Second, human beings can share many ethical principles without sharing the same faith, or having any faith. Third, people who share a faith or moral principles frequently have preyed upon one another, and on others. It is false, and politically ruinous, for conservatives to assert that conservatism requires a shared religion or even ubiquitous religiosity. The assertion that particular virtues depend, or that virtue generally depends, on religion is an empirical claim, and demonstrably false. There are many virtuous unbelievers, and many virtues with no religious provenance, and many religious people who are not virtuous.

In *The Conservative Mind*, one of postwar conservatism's canonical texts, Kirk asserted that a defining attribute of a conservative is the belief that "revelation, reason and an assurance beyond the senses tell us that the Author of our being exists." So all those who are lacking this "assurance beyond the senses" are ineligible to join, or must be excommunicated from, conservatism. So, too, are those who are blind "to the effulgence of the burning bush" and deaf "to the thunder above Sinai." Kirk's stark dichotomy is between believers and "restless, shallow, self-intoxicated" atheists. Defined in such gaseous terms, conservatism can sink, and with Kirk it did sink, into a romantic longing for aristocracy, about which Kirk gushed: "To be bred in a place of estimation; to see nothing low and sordid from one's infancy...." Good grief. (Kirk, living in rural Michigan, had met few actual aristocrats.) For Kirk, it was a short step from asserting that "the foundation of social tranquility is reverence" to revering social hierarchies. And to a recoil against urbanity, as in Kirk's dismissal of Alexander Hamilton: "For he was eminently a city-man, and veneration withers upon the pavements. 'It is hard to learn to love the new gas station,' writes Walter Lippmann, 'that stands where the wild honeysuckle grew.'" It is hard to convince Americans to embrace a conservatism that presumes an alienation from life amidst the pavement of their modern, urban society. Kirk did not try to disguise his detestation of "the enormous smoky cavern of modern American life."[50] But a conservatism that is restricted to the devout, and that is inhospitable to those who like and feel at home in modern America, is a persuasion that will never persuade an American majority.

Kirk and Chambers were extending an old and, truth be told, tiresome argument that at least was fresh when Locke said, "Those who deny the existence of the Deity are not to be tolerated at all. Promises, covenants and oaths, which are the bonds of human society, can have no hold upon or sanctity for an atheist." This, too, is an empirical claim the truth of which is not dependent upon a Deity actually existing. Locke is saying only that fear of divine punishment, which can be a groundless fear, is all that guarantees "the bonds of human society."[51] And even this claim is empirically false: There are multitudes of conscientious promise keepers who are not faithful; conscientiousness is not coterminous with faithfulness. And there are multitudes of people who subscribe to theisms but are not exemplary respecters of the bonds of society.

The fact that the religious impulse is so ubiquitous as to seem intrinsic to humankind may be of practical importance. It is, however, not of *any* importance in establishing the truth of any religion, any theism, or any theory of transcendence. Granted, many people do reason that the fact that so many people seem designed to yearn for God is evidence of the existence of that for which they yearn. But it is not such evidence. Furthermore, it is arguable that the more the religious impulse is found to be intrinsic—that is, to be, so to speak, part of the wiring of most human beings as the species has evolved—the more religion seems to be merely an adaptive phenomenon. However, in an increasingly secular society, in what Max Weber called the "disenchanted world," religious faith decreasingly infuses life. It organizes neither space (towers of commerce, not the spires of cathedrals, are at the center of the modern city) nor time (schools, even religious ones, have spring breaks, not Easter breaks). Given the number of fighting faiths that have taken political form, and the number of casualties claimed by these secular faiths, it is wise to worry about the political consequences of what Matthew Arnold called "the melancholy, long,

withdrawing roar" of faith leaving the culture, and leaving it susceptible to feverish quests for redemption through political action.

Would, however, the world be worse—because of a decrease in
individuals' happiness and virtue, or because of collective pathologies
arising in the vacuum left by withdrawing religion—if the world
were entirely secular? This is possible. Religion valuably informs,
affirms, and motivates many aspects of many people's lives, from
social institutions such as family formation through marriage, to art
and sustaining rituals. Many human beings have needs, or at least
anxieties and desires, that religion serves or assuages. Perhaps a sense
of incompleteness is natural, as is a desire for collective amelioration
of that sense. Certainly throughout history almost every society has
had at its core some idea of the transcendent. Perhaps those religious
people are correct who assert that all religions are in some sense
true, in that they are durable responses to important constants in the
human condition. Perhaps secularists are mistaken, and themselves
are incomplete, in not sharing an aching need for completion, or in
not embracing religion as a reasonable, or at least a practical, response
to this need. Perhaps it would serve the greatest happiness for the
greatest number if people were encouraged to embrace theisms.
But then, by this utilitarian calculus, a case could be made for a
pharmacological approach to the delivery of happiness. At least a case
can be made for such a "brave new world"—Aldous Huxley made it,
darkly, in his dystopian novel with that title—if one is indifferent to
the quality of the happiness pursued.

Jefferson was a utilitarian when he undertook to separate the
"diamonds" of rational Christianity from the "dunghill" of revelation;
he was attempting to reduce this religion to a branch of ethics.[52] This
project produced Jefferson's truncated and expurgated version of the
Bible. The immaculate conception and divinity of Jesus, his miracles
and resurrection, the trinity—all were discarded as "artificial scaffolding" obscuring a rather agreeable ethical system.[53] Jefferson remained
a materialist, which involved for him quite enough of a puzzle. In a

March 1820 letter to John Adams, he wrote that, like his hero Locke, he preferred to live with "one incomprehensibility rather than two." He accepted that the cerebrum possesses "the faculty of thinking," and therefore he accepted "the single incomprehensibility of matter endowed with thought." He saw no need to embrace a second, involving two dubious propositions: "first that of an existence called spirit, of which we have neither evidence nor idea, and then, secondly, how that spirit, which has neither extension nor solidity, can put material organs in motion."[54]

Jefferson the utilitarian regarding religion was also an empiricist: The senses provide all the fodder that the intellect has to work with. And the logic of empiricism propelled him to a severe—or, better, pure—individualism, wherein every person must, and has a right to, conduct his life according to his reason as it works with the data provided by experience. This individualism took Jefferson beyond Locke regarding toleration. "Locke," wrote Jefferson, "denies toleration to those who entertain opinions contrary to those moral rules necessary for the preservation of society," such as atheists. It was, he wrote, "a great thing" for Locke "to go so far," but "where he stopped short we may go on."[55]

Tocqueville thought that religion, true or false, was a social necessity, especially in a democracy: "How is it possible that society should escape destruction if the moral tie be not strengthened in proportion as the political tie is relaxed? And what can be done with a people which is its own master, if it be not submissive to the Divinity?"[56] Tocqueville's assumption is that the "political tie" that binds is necessarily weaker—more "relaxed"—in a democracy than under a monarchical, aristocratic, or other authoritarian regime. This, however, has not proven to be the case. With the help of party allegiances, which were not anticipated by the Founders, and the regular emersion in politics by participation in frequent elections, the political tie has proven to be stronger than Tocqueville anticipated.

The act of associating in religious communities helps to develop what Tocqueville called "the art of association" and the "habits of the heart" that augment the stock of social capital that contributes to social cohesion. "It turns out," says Britain's Rabbi Lord Sacks, "that Western freedom, the thing that was born in England in the revolution of the 1640s and in America in 1775, is not the default setting of the human condition."[57] Rather, it is the result of a culture deeply conditioned by the Judeo-Christian tradition of individual autonomy and dignity. This culture is susceptible to decay: Individualism can beget hedonism and atheism with consequent loss of social cohesion and energy. This is not, however, an argument that establishes the social necessity of religion. Whether or not religion is true is, of course, an important question. But so is this: Is a moral sense independent of religion constitutive of human nature? Again, most things likely to produce lasting happiness—education, employment, stable families—require us to forego immediate pleasures. Religion can help with this. It is not, however, indispensable.

"Religion," wrote Tocqueville, reflecting on his American sojourn, "is considered as the guardian of mores, and mores are regarded as the guarantee of the laws and pledge for the maintenance of freedom itself": "Despotism may be able to do without faith, but freedom cannot.... What can be done with a people master of itself if it is not subject to God?"[58] Nearly two centuries after Tocqueville wrote that, it is clear that in an increasingly secular America the moral ties between citizens are loosening and the self-mastery of the populace is weakening. Perhaps America will demonstrate the utility of religions, the veracity of which cannot be demonstrated. But one difference, and perhaps the most important difference, between the modern age and all previous eras is this: It is no longer considered extraordinary to believe that one can understand the world without reference to a transcendent power that shapes human destinies. The mood of modernity is impatience with reasoning that must be explained or defended by appeals to some authority beyond reason.

COSMOLOGY AND THE CONSERVATIVE SENSIBILITY

Theism is an optional component of conservatism. Cosmology, however, can nurture a conservative sensibility, beginning with this fact: Already 99.9 (and about fifty-eight more 9s) percent of the universe is outside the Earth's atmosphere, and the universe is expanding lickety-split. Into what? No one knows, but never mind. Hold a penny at arm's length and you block from your field of vision three galaxies, including billions of stars and other things, that are 350 million light-years away. And these three galaxies are right next door to us in our wee corner of the universe, although of course the universe cannot be said to have corners. There is a lot more space than there is stuff in space: If there were only three bees in America, the air would be more crowded with bees than space is with stars. What, you may wonder, has any of this to do with conservatism? The answer is: It fuels the capacity for wonder and for finding beauty and exhilaration in the unplanned complexity of the whirl that has driven out Zeus.

It is astonishing that we do not live in a state of perpetual astonishment. Conservatism should embrace and cultivate a cheerful, even exuberant acceptance of the unplanned and the undersigned, in the cosmos and in society. In the cosmos, because it is a great given that we must accept. In society, because of the fecundity of spontaneous order in an open society. Second only to Einstein's famous question, Did God have a choice in the creation of the world?, is this one: How did matter, which is what we are, become conscious, then curious? The Scottish physicist James Clerk Maxwell (1831–79), an early authority on Saturn's rings, had, as a cosmologist should have, a poetic bent:

At quite uncertain times and places,
The atoms left their heavenly path,
And by fortuitous embraces,
Engendered all that being hath.[59]

A contemporary of Maxwell was born in 1838, the great-grandson of the second president, grandson of the sixth. Henry Adams watched with mingled awe and dismay the swift transformation of an agrarian republic into an industrial society, and eventually he "found himself lying in the Gallery of Machines at the Great Exposition of 1900, his historical neck broken by the sudden eruption of forces totally new":

> The year 1900 was not the first to upset schoolmasters. Copernicus and Galileo had broken many professorial necks about 1600; Columbus had stood the world on its head towards 1500; but the nearest approach to the revolution of 1900 was that of 310, when Constantine set up the Cross.... To Adams the dynamo became a symbol of infinity...he began to feel the 40-foot dynamos as a moral force, much as the early Christians felt the Cross. The planet itself seemed less impressive, in its old-fashioned, deliberate, annual or daily revolution, than this huge wheel, revolving within arm's length at some vertiginous speed...before the end, one began to pray to it; inherited instinct taught the natural expression of man before silent and infinite force.[60]

No doubt all this, which was said about "mere" electricity, today seems quaint and overwrought. We, after all, have discovered the neutron and the force it can unleash. Modern people, unlike Adams, have a slight sense of awe about the world around them. But before condescending to Adams, modern people should consider that, in a sense, they take more things on faith than did a thirteenth-century peasant tilling the fields in the shadow of Chartres. When the peasant wanted light, he built a fire from wood that he had gathered. Modern people flip switches, trusting that someone, somewhere, has done something that will let there be light. How many switch-flippers can say what really happens in the flux of electrons when a generator generates? The most advanced form of travel for the peasant was a sailing ship or a wagon; their mechanisms were visible and understandable. In a normal year, more than 75 million passengers pass through Chicago's O'Hare airport, obedient to disembodied voices, electronically amplified, telling them that it is time to get into cylindrical membranes of aluminum that will be hurled by strange engines through the upper atmosphere. The passengers will not understand, and will be quite content not to understand, how any of this works. Yet they think the fourteenth century was an age of faith.

The marvels of applied science are not nearly as astonishing as what science continues to reveal by deciphering what has been around for about 13.5 billion years—the universe—and predates us by most of these years. The human species has been around for about 250,000 years, approximately .0015 percent of the history of all earthly life. The planet, like the rest of the universe, got along swimmingly without us until, as it were, just the other day. This makes our arrival look awfully like a cosmic afterthought, an accident rather than the culmination of a plan. Astronomers are gathering and studying light that has taken 10 billion years to reach their instruments. This light helps them to understand what Martin Rees, Astronomer Royal of Britain, with British understatement, calls the universe's "inclement" conditions: "violent explosions, jets of particles at 99.99 percent of the speed of light, flashes that disgorge in a few seconds far more light than the Sun emits in its 10-billion-year history." And speaking of the sun, which means everything to us: Although it is a small thing in the cosmic scheme of things, it is so big that, Rees says, "it would take as many human bodies to make up the Sun's mass as there are atoms in each of us."[61] It has taken just a bit more than a billion years for natural selection to proceed from the first multicellular organisms to us, and those billion years are 20 percent of the entire story of life on Earth. In just five billion years, the sun will be extinguished, and we with it.

"It is not to be conceived," wrote Isaac Newton, "that mere mechanical causes could give birth to so many regular motions.... This most beautiful system of the sun, planets and comets could only proceed from the counsel and dominion of an intelligent and powerful Being."[62] Since Newton's day, however, new instruments of astronomy have revealed that there are many highly irregular goings-on in the universe, the beauty of which is real but terrifyingly inhospitable. Yes, Earth is so finely tuned as to be hospitable to human and other life. This leads many people to conclude that a Fine Tuner had us in mind: If the Earth's atmosphere were slightly thicker or slightly thinner, not enough or too much of the sun's radiation would arrive to sustain life. But this planetary friendliness can be understood as a happy accident of the evolution of this cooling cinder, Earth. And although this planet is friendly to human life, it has always been less than friendly for many lives. Searing heat, punishing cold, tornados, hurricanes, earthquakes, volcanoes, tsunamis, wild animals, poisonous snakes and spiders and plants, infestations of food-destroying and disease-carrying insects, diseases galore, and the proclivity of humans to prey upon and war against one another—all these are ingredients of life as experienced beneath the biophilic atmospheric layer that envelops Earth. Surely the Fine Tuner could have left out some of these ingredients—could have tuned the world to work a bit differently— had He been feeling a bit more friendly.

Life is, presumably, either a cosmic fluke or a cosmic imperative. But because *everything* is a reverberation from the big bang—every atom of the material in us, and in everything else, is nuclear waste from that explosion—what, really, is the difference between fluke and imperative? Our universe is biophilic, meaning friendly to life, only because molecules of water and atoms of carbon, which are necessary for life, would not have resulted from a big bang if there had been even a slightly different recipe for the cosmic soup that existed after the explosion, a recipe that was cooked in the universe's first one-hundredth of a second, when the temperature was a hundred thousand million degrees centigrade. The fact that a biophilic universe is like Goldilocks' porridge—not too hot, not too cold, just right—is an invitation for natural theology to say this: The distillation of the post–big bang residue into particles and then into atoms and then, about a billion years ago, into the first multicellular organisms that led to us—all this involves a precision of such stupendous improbability that there must have been a Designer. This, however, requires a problematic premise— that no hugely consequential accident is really an accident.

Besides, natural theology must reckon with the fact that this is not going to end well. The antecedent of the pronoun "this" is: everything. The universe, currently expanding, will either continue to do so, ending in intolerable cold, or it will collapse backward, ending in incinerating heat. What does natural theology make of these destinations for what the Designer set in motion? Astronomy's and cosmology's withering rejoinder to zealotry is: "What's the use?" Recently two University of Michigan astronomers reported that if the laws of physics as currently understood continue to operate, then in 10,000 trillion trillion trillion trillion trillion trillion trillion trillion years the universe, which is pretty much everything, will run down. Carbon-based life, including us, will long since have disappeared, and the entire cosmos will be a thin soup of diffuse particles.

Early astronomy might have displaced our planet from the place of honor in the cosmos, but at least Newton said that the universe is intelligible, even tidy. Early in the twentieth century, however, a minor Swiss civil servant, who traveled home in a streetcar from his job in the Bern patent office, wondered: What would the city's clock tower look like if observed from a streetcar racing away from the tower at the speed of light? The clock, he decided, would appear stopped because light could not catch up to the streetcar, but his own watch would tick normally. "A storm broke loose in my mind," Albert Einstein later remembered.[63] He produced five papers in 1905, and for physicists the world has never seemed the same. For laypeople, it has never felt the same. Hitherto, space and time were assumed to be absolutes. They still can be for our everyday business because we and the objects we deal with do not move at the speed of light. But since

Einstein's postulate of relativity, measurements of space and time are thought to be relative to speed.

In the 1920s, while people were enjoying being told that space is warped and that it pushes things down (this is the real "force" of gravity), Einstein became an international celebrity of a sort not seen before or since. Selfridges department store in London pasted six pages of an Einstein paper on a plate glass window for passersby to read. Charlie Chaplin said to him, "The people applaud me because everyone understands me, and they applaud you because no one understands you."[64] The precision of modern scientific instruments makes possible the confirmation of implications of Einstein's theories—e.g., the universe had a beginning (the big bang) and its expansion is accelerating; time slows in a large gravitational field and beats slower the faster one moves; the sun bends starlight from across the sky, and there are black holes so dense that they swallow light. Does all this bewilder you? The late Richard Feynman, winner of the Nobel Prize in Physics, said, "I think I can safely say that nobody understands quantum mechanics."[65]

Einstein's theism, such as it was, was expressed in his aphorism that God does not play dice with the universe. He meant that there are elegant, eventually discoverable laws, not mere randomness, at work. Saying "I'm not an atheist," he explained: "We are in the position of a little child entering a huge library filled with books in many different languages. The child knows someone must have written those books. It does not know how. It does not understand the languages in which they are written. The child dimly suspects a mysterious order in the arrangement of the books but doesn't know what it is."[66] Einstein postulated that fixed "space" and "time" are illusory, and that "energy" and "matter" are fungible, and the public accepted this. What choice did it have? And what did accepting it mean or entail? An interesting subject for intellectual history is whether Einstein's theory of relativity somehow contributed to the subversion of other absolutes, including religious and political ones.

In 1927, in *The Future of an Illusion*, Sigmund Freud confidently said, "The more people gain access to the treasures of our knowledge, the more widespread will be the falling away from religious belief."[67] This idea that religion is just a rung on humanity's ladder up from ignorance is challenged by those, and they are legion, who find in some new knowledge—of cosmology, biology, and much else—sustenance for theism. The 1965 discovery that the universe is permeated with background radiation confirmed the theory that a big bang set what are now distant galaxies flying apart. A famous aphorism holds that the most incomprehensible thing about the universe is that it is comprehensible. It is becoming ever more so because of advances in mathematics and particle physics, and in telescopes that, operating above the filter of Earth's atmosphere, "see" the past by capturing for analysis light emitted from events that occurred perhaps—we cannot be sure how fast the universe is expanding—12 billion years ago.

Astronomy is history. It is the history of what has happened in the 13 billion or so years since the big bang, which lasted a trillionth of a trillionth of a trillionth of a second, inflating a microscopic speck into everything that is. As astronomy unfolds the history of all this, mankind is being put in its place. But where is that? Martin Rees said we must put aside "particle chauvinism": All the atoms that make up us can be truly said to be stardust, or residues from the fuel that makes the stars shine.[68]

So, perhaps the supposedly crucial question—is life a cosmic fluke or a cosmic imperative?—is not much of a question. Human life exists at the back of beyond in an overwhelmingly hostile universe. So cosmology gets pressed into the service of natural theology, which rests on probability—or, more precisely, on the stupendous improbability of the emergence from chaos of complexity and then consciousness. Natural theology says: A watch implies a watchmaker, and what has happened in the universe—the distillation of the post–big bang cosmic soup into particles, then atoms, then wonderful us, reveals or implies a creator with a precise design. We know, however, that biological evolution has been beset by lots of accidents—climate changes, asteroid impacts, epidemics, etc. As Rees said, if Earth's history were to be rerun, the biosphere almost certainly would end up quite different. And without us.

The estimated number of stars is 10 followed by 22 zeros—so far. When the Hubble telescope took a picture of a speck of space less than 1/150th the size of a full moon, it peered into the location of more than 5,000 galaxies. From this fact it is possible to make a rough estimate that the visible universe contains more than 150 billion galaxies, each with billions of stars. It is not yet known what initiated life on Earth, but whatever it was, it probably has been in some way replicated somewhere else in the still expanding universe. Is there a plausible reason for thinking otherwise? As to whether there are other planets with life like Earth's, Rees said the chance of there being two similar ecologies is less than the chance of two randomly typing monkeys producing the same Shakespearean play.

As fascinating and disconcerting as are the questions raised by what astronomy and cosmology are learning, perhaps more disorienting and revolutionary are discoveries about what is within us. Not all revolutions are heralded by rhetorical drumrolls like "When in the course of human events" and "A specter is haunting Europe." And not all revolutions are explicitly political; some are revolutions in thinking or sensibility that have political reverberations. On April 25, 1953, such a revolution was announced by a bland sentence in a British science journal, *Nature*: "We wish to suggest a structure for the salt of deoxyribose nucleic acid (D.N.A.)."[69] The world that was shaken by this deceptively downbeat announcement from Francis Crick and James Watson was the narrow one inhabited by a few scientists who were competing with the intensity of athletes in a race to discover the structure of the chemical that controls heredity in all living things. History is, however, the history of ideas, perceptions, assumptions, values—the history of mind. And the wider world continues to be changed by the aftershocks of the intellectual earthquake that had its epicenter in a laboratory at Cambridge University in England. Each of us has 10 thousand trillion cells, give or take. Each cell contains a strand of DNA that, uncoiled, would extend about six feet. If an individual's DNA were spliced into a single strand, it would extend 20 million kilometers, enough to wrap around the equator approximately 500 times. This is just one measure of the unfathomable strangeness of us.

The myriad and rapidly multiplying benefits from DNA research include advancements in medicine and agriculture that have improved, and saved, the lives of hundreds of millions. But from this still-new science has come a challenge to something ancient: mankind's estimate of itself. Nineteenth-century biology, and especially the theory of evolution, seemed strongly to suggest that mankind is not the apex of nature's pyramid, but rather is a bead on a string—perhaps an early bead on a potentially very long string. Twentieth-century biology posed a political problem: It seemed to make dubious the concept around which liberal societies are organized, the concept of the self. The supreme value of liberal democratic societies is self-expression, including the political manifestation of this in self-government. But how, in the aftermath of the scientific and social revolution that Crick and Watson set in motion, are we to understand the self? A nineteenth-century poet famously insisted, "I am the master of my fate: I am the captain of my soul."[70] But what does such mastery mean if many things—if perhaps most things, including some of the most important things—are somehow foreordained by the genetic code?

Darwin, Marx, and Freud suggested that various kinds of change—biological, personal, social—are driven by autonomous processes. Now DNA suggests new circumscriptions of autonomy. Expanding knowledge of how DNA works makes possible willful interventions in the chemical engine of existence. Such interventions can reassert human autonomy, but perhaps at a cost to human dignity. Can our understanding of human autonomy, and hence of moral agency, be enhanced by thinking of the self as something reducible to chemistry? Or by affirming a radical materialism? In 1980, the US Supreme Court ruled that a living microorganism—a product of human artifice; a genetically engineered product with industrial uses—was patentable matter. This was just a technical ruling, a matter of statutory interpretation (of patent law). The court, however, held this: The fact that the manufactured product was alive was irrelevant to its patentability because it was a "composition of matter," just like a better mousetrap. But what if we decide that human beings, too, are just "compositions of matter"? What if thinking that this is the case makes us behave in certain ways?

Liberal democratic societies assume that individuals are in some sense self-constituting creatures, producing themselves by their free and educated choices, assembling their purposes from a vast and potentially limitless buffet of possibilities. But what if this process of self-assertion, this exercise of autonomy, takes place in the context of an assumption that human beings are, like everything else, mere "compositions of matter," neither more nor less? Then what is this "self" that is doing the asserting? Again, one of the greatest novels of the first modern nation is about Jay Gatsby's creation of his self. This did not turn out well, which was his fault. Or was it? How do we assign fault, or make sense of praise or blame, among "compositions of matter"?

Christianity was a source of three ideas central to the American founding. One is the idea of humanity's irremediable imperfectability. The second is that original sin does not vitiate individual dignity. The third is that there are universal moral truths. All this poses a challenge for societies that are increasingly secular and given increasingly to believing in the social or genetic influences on consciousness: How do we define and defend the integrity of the self? This matters for self-government because since the second half of the nineteenth century the unitary understanding of the human personality—the idea of personhood—has come to seem problematic. Yet, strangely—

or perhaps understandably—as the idea of the self has become more attenuated there has been increased emphasis on self-assertion and self-expression. As the self has become a hazier concept, there has been a more urgent desire to celebrate the assertion and expression of this elusive thing.

The human brain has a hundred billion neurons, and 1,000 connections between each of them, so there are hundreds of trillions of possible connections. This means that the number of possible permutations is larger than the number of stars in the universe—not in the galaxy, in the universe. This lump of matter in the skull is the seat of the self. The brain is responsible for perception, motor control, cognition, and emotion. Hence the brain is an organ of behavior. Actually, it is *the* organ. A stomachache can make a person cranky or sad, but those are mental conditions, not stomach conditions. More and more, brain imaging can, in some still very limited sense, show how some brain functions underlie human behavior. Neuroscience deepens our understanding of the human experience and has the potential to make the human experience better. It is, however, healthy to have—in the back of one's brain, so to speak—an anxiety about whether, or in what sense, the improved experience will still be understood in the way that human experience has hitherto been thought of as distinctly human.

A fundamental philosophic debate is between those who say, "I have a body," and those who say, "I am a body." There are many more of the former than of the latter, partly, no doubt, because humanity's self-esteem is served by—or is dependent upon—the idea that there is more to us than flesh and blood and sinew. Probably for as long as there have been human beings, they have been comfortable thinking of themselves as creatures composed of flesh and blood and also something grander. Now, however, neurobiology is making problematic the idea that we are both bodies and quite distinct minds or spirits. The idea of "the ghost in the machine" may be yielding to the idea that we are just machines.[71] Are we, however, merely the sum of the chemical reactions bubbling within us? Happily, the more we know, the less we know. The more we know about the brain, the more we are awed by how much there is to know, not only about the brain but about the totality of creation that has culminated (we are the culmination…aren't we?) in something as intricate as we are. But the more that is learned about our intricacies, the more attenuated our sense of personhood becomes. Brain "mapping" is not just a way of discovering what particular parts of the brain do in response to external events; it is a way of discovering how the brain's parts engage in "conversation" with one another, and how they can change over time. Much brain activity—much thinking—is not the result of external stimuli. So, is the brain conversing with—acting upon—itself? This internal conversation is at the core of who—and what—we are. New technologies, such as functional magnetic resonance imaging (fMRI), enable scientists to watch the brain in action, monitoring neural activity as it thinks. In fifty years, fMRI images probably will seem as crude as Magellan's maps. We will understand thought processes with instantaneous cellular resolution, and hence the essence of what brains do and what disrupts them.

Habits enable us to function because neurons are "conversing" with networks involving thousands of other cells. But ethicists—and courts, and poets—will be warily watching what is learned about the neural basis of choices, habits, love, and other important things. Again, do we *have* bodies or *are* we bodies? What will become of the field of psychology as explorations of brain anatomy advance our understanding of how the brain's architecture influences, or even determines, behavior? "The devil made me do it" is, in a secular age, no longer an exculpation. But what about "My brain circuitry made me do it"? Someday debates about free will might revolve around what we are really saying when we say that we are responsible for our actions because we each have "ownership" of the three pounds of matter that is our brain. The idea that we have in our skulls "thinking matter"—indeed, that we *are* thinking matter—seems powerfully counterintuitive. But that is because our intuitions have been conditioned by our language, which insists that the mind and the body are distinct. This distinction is further complicated by the theological legacy of language about the immaterial soul that survives the body.

The subject of the supposed mind-body dichotomy is not just, or even primarily, for philosophers to clarify. Neuroscientists, especially, but also psychologists, anthropologists, and even theologians have long since become central to the debate. In the 1950s, the Oxford philosopher Gilbert Ryle argued that there is no "ghost in the machine." That idea no longer seems radical. What remain to be sorted out are questions such as these: Is what we speak of, if we do still speak of it, as the "soul" different from what we speak of as the "self," as in "self-control," and if so, how is it different? If the soul or the self, or both, are "embodied" or "contained" or "generated" in the bit of the body called the brain, what problems does this pose for our understanding of identity?[72] Given that the working of the brain can be measured, injured, stimulated, and even manipulated—chemically, electrically, by psychiatric analysis, and by many promptings from the social environment, from advertising to political rhetoric, what does this mean for our understanding of moral agency? The concept of human dignity is indissolubly linked to the fact of human agency, which is linked to each person taking responsibility for his or her life. Humanity's dignity derives from the fact that it is not completely determined by external promptings from its social context. It is, ultimately, undetermined because it can make choices of a sort lower animals do not make—moral choices. To understand this is to understand Hitler's unsurpassable radicalism.

Yale historian Timothy Snyder argues that the origins of Hitler's most radical act, the Holocaust, have been hidden in plain sight, in his speeches and *Mein Kampf*. Snyder convincingly portrays Hitler as much more interesting and troubling than a madman: Hitler implemented the logic of a coherent worldview. His life was a single-minded response to an idea so radical that it rejected not only the entire tradition of political philosophy but even the idea, the possi-bility, of philosophy. Hitler supplanted philosophy with zoology. "In Hitler's world," Snyder writes, "the law of the jungle was the only law." The immutable structure of life casts the various human races as separate species. Only races are real; other supposed human differ-ences are superficial and ephemeral. The races are locked in mutual and unassuageable enmity because life is, always and everywhere, a constant struggle over scarcities—of land, food, and other necessities. Hitler thought, however, that one group poisoned the planet with another idea. To Hitler, says Snyder, "It was the Jew who told humans that they were above other animals, and had the capacity to decide their future for themselves." To Hitler, "Ethics as such was the error; the only morality was fidelity to race." Hitler, who did not become a German citizen until eleven months before becoming Germany's chancellor, was not a nationalist but a racialist. Hitler, in Snyder's analysis, insisted that "the highest goal of human beings" is not "the preservation of any given state or government, but the preservation of their kind." And "all world-historical events are nothing more than the expression of the self-preservation drive of the races."[73] The moral of this dreadful story is that no idea can have worse consequences than Hitler's idea that human beings lack the capacity for moral agency. If they lack it, they are like lower animals. They might be cleverer than other animals in calculating their interests, but they are no more capable than other animals of making meaningful choices about what their interests *should* be and how they *should* be pursued.

A character in a John Updike novel says, "Life, that's what we seek in one another, even with the DNA molecule cracked and our vitality arraigned before us as a tiny Tinkertoy."[74] But the mystery of our vitality is surely not "arrayed before us." Cracking the genetic code has not, at least not yet, removed the mystery from the fact that matter can become conscious of itself. Or from the fact that human beings have the kind of consciousness that enables them—actually, in some as yet inexplicable way it *causes* them—to wonder this about themselves:

Given what we are, how ought we to behave? The neural basis of mind does not nullify the role of reason, and hence of free choice, which is the basis of self-governance, by individuals and polities. Yes, our brains are material things from which come thoughts and actions. Yes, promptings from our physical surroundings influence how our brains function. Yes, the mind is not an emanation of the brain, it *is* the brain. This, however, does not make each of us, in the words of another Updike character, "just a soft machine."[75] And none of this means that our reasoning is beyond our control, or that we are, at bottom, beyond the control of our reasoning.

The Lisbon earthquake of 1755 shook people's confidence in the idea of progress and of a divinely ordained orderliness of the universe. That earthquake was an intellectually improving event, as had been Galileo's 1610 discovery of the moons around Jupiter. The earthquake shook intellectual complacency about the benign orderliness of things. Galileo's discovery delivered the deflating news that Earth is not the center of the universe, so this planet's passengers are not situated in a place of cosmic preeminence. Eventually, God was written out of the human story, replaced by a process that was depicted as having as its motor a constant churning of random changes. This meant not only the erasure of Jefferson's Creator who endowed all persons equally with certain natural rights, but also, in some interpretations, the evaporation of the idea of a settled, durable human nature.

Already science has sown enough uncertainty about the integrity and responsibility of the self to disturb legal reasoning. James Q. Wilson noted how "abuse excuse" threatens the legal system and society's moral equilibrium.[76] Genetics and neuroscience seem to suggest that self-control is more attenuated—perhaps to the vanishing point—than our legal and ethical traditions assume. The part of the brain that stimulates anger and aggression is larger in men than in women, and the part that restrains anger is smaller in men than in women. "Men," Wilson writes, "by no choice of their own, are far more prone to violence and far less capable of self-restraint than women."[77] That does not, however, absolve violent men of blame. As Wilson says, biology and environment interact. The social environment includes moral assumptions, sometimes codified in law, concerning expectations about our duty to desire what we ought to desire. It is scientifically sensible to say that all behavior is in some sense caused. But a society that thinks scientific determination renders personal responsibility a chimera must consider it absurd not only to condemn depravity but also to praise nobility. Moral derangement, and vast political consequences, can flow from exaggerated notions of what science teaches, or can teach, about the biological and environmental roots of behavior.

"JE N'AI PAS EU BESOIN DE CETTE HYPOTHÈSE"

A remarkable intersection of politics and science was set in motion on what might have been the most momentous day in human history. On February 12, 1809, the day Lincoln was born, so was Charles Darwin. Lincoln, whose life's mission was to reconnect the nation with the Founders' thinking, became the most brave, eloquent, and consequential proponent of the idea that human dignity inheres in the capacity of individuals to shape their lives' trajectories by exercising their natural rights to make moral choices. Darwin, however, unleashed an idea that seemed to challenge humanity's understanding of its dignity. His intellectual bravery took him to a difficult conclusion: The human race is continuous with the primordial slime from which it emerged. But Darwin, like Lincoln, presented a deeply satisfying picture of the way the world works, a picture that omits transcendence but that is congenial to what should be the conservative sensibility. Darwin's idea of natural selection, when misapplied as social doctrine (Yale sociologist William Graham Sumner: "A drunkard in the gutter is just where he ought to be"), was abused, for a while, to question the equal worth of individuals and the equal capacities of races. But Darwin's most lasting disruption was to religious thinking.[78]

Some theists ask, what is more difficult to believe—what is more improbable—that there is something providential in the human story or that primordial slime evolved randomly into, among other marvelous things, Lincoln? Tom Stoppard said that it may be slightly less improbable that a deity intended us, and planned our wayward path to existence, than that green slime began to change and gave rise, in time, to Shakespeare's sonnets. Stoppard is a playwright, so perhaps he is sympathetic to an explanation that features a Playwright who purposely causes characters to come and go on the cosmic stage. Other creators of fictional worlds react differently. "What baffles me," wrote novelist Peter De Vries, "is the comfort people find in the idea that somebody dealt this mess. Blind and meaningless chance seems to me so much more congenial—or at least less horrible. Prove to me that there is a God and I will really begin to despair."[79]

In a poem celebrating his long marriage, Richard Wilbur said that his and his wife's long love

... has the quality of something made,
Like a good fiddle, like the rose's scent,
Like a rose window or the firmament[80]

There is a human impulse, so powerful and ubiquitous as to be properly termed natural, to postulate intentionality—mind—behind anything beautiful, including and especially the firmament. We want to think that beauty is somehow enhanced by having elements that denote a designer, having the quality of something that "was made," as Huck Finn said. Darwin, however, had the courage to say goodbye to all that.

"Descended from the apes!" exclaimed the wife of the Church of England's bishop of Worchester. "Let us hope that it is not true, but if it is, let us pray that it will not become generally known."[81] But with remarkable speed, the theory became widely known, and although it was not nearly as widely accepted, at least not at first, it immediately disturbed humanity's peace of mind. It was neither the first nor last such disturbance by an idea, but it was the most profoundly unsettling. Darwin had an evidence-driven epiphany when he encountered the different but closely related species of finches on the Galapagos Islands. Darwin surmised, and subsequent scientists confirmed, that somehow the finches' different beaks were adaptive, evolving through natural selection as changing climactic conditions changed the birds' food supplies. Darwin was puzzled by the data and developed a theory to explain it. He brought science to bear on the project of putting humanity in its place. According to him, that place is on a continuum between man and lesser assemblages of protoplasm. Which raised this question: Just how much lesser are other creatures? And Darwin raised the possibility that, given the continuum, humanity might not be nature's final word.

Darwin's rejection of a premeditated design helped to validate an analogous political philosophy. Darwin believed that the existence of order in nature does not require us to postulate a divine Orderer. Similarly, the existence of a social order does not presuppose a government giving comprehensive and minute direction to the social order. Granted, government is necessary for maintaining society. So, government cannot be expelled from our understanding of society in the way that Darwin expelled God from our understanding of nature. But Darwinism opened minds to the fecundity of undirected, organic social cooperation of the sort that does most of the creating and allocating of wealth and opportunity in open societies. This is the largely spontaneous order celebrated by various thinkers from Edmund Burke to Karl Popper and Friedrich Hayek, the order produced by lightly governed individuals consenting to arrangements of their devising.

Darwinian postulates, when wielded by thinkers less subtle and judicious than Darwin, could become, or could seem to validate, a worldview that simultaneously encourages both fatalism and optimism. Fatalism because it postulated an autonomous process in which randomness can play a large role, and in which human agency is diminished, if not largely nullified. But also optimism because this process is said to produce progress. To such optimists, progress must be whatever is churned out by the processes of history, be they natural or social. Against the evidence of "design & beneficence," Darwin saw "too much misery."[82] Too much misery that seemed gratuitous, as with cats that delight in torturing mice. Or that wasp, which we shall meet anon.

It is possible for people to be religious and to believe in evolution. Many do. It is not, however, as simple as some think. And Darwin himself did not manage this mental accommodation. David Quammen in his perfectly titled book *The Reluctant Mr. Darwin* describes Darwin in 1838, already at age twenty-nine wrestling with the question of how humanity was related to natural selection:

"It wasn't just a matter of mockingbirds, rabbits, and skinks. It was the whole natural world. 'But Man—wonderful Man,' he wrote, trying out ideas on this most dangerous point, 'is an exception.' Then again, he added, man is clearly a mammal. He is not a deity. He possesses some of the same instincts and feelings as animals. Three lines below the first statement about man, Darwin negated it, concluding firmly that, no, 'he is no exception.' From that terrible insight, despite pressures and implications, Charles Darwin would never retreat." Nor would he take refuge in the intellectual fudge that has come to be called "intelligent design." When Darwin read a book postulating that "an Overruling Intelligence" surely directed the process of evolution, he was having none of it. Quammen says that Darwin recognized that natural selection was meaningless if some transcendent Intelligence "overruled the haphazardness of the variations, directing them toward foreordained purposes. In the margins of his copy [of Alfred Wallace's article], Darwin scratched 'No!!!' "[83]

Religion's intellectual sheet-anchor in the nineteenth century was natural theology, which taught that if you seek proof of God's existence and kindliness, look around at nature's marvelous combination of complexity and predictability. Darwin's theory of natural selection cut the anchor rope. There is, he argued, an explanation of nature's awesome orderliness that did not need to postulate a divinity's intentions. The Marquis de Laplace, the French mathematician and astronomer, presented a copy of his *Mecanique Celeste* to Napoleon who, after reading it, pointedly noted to Laplace, "You have written a large book about the universe without once mentioning the author of the universe." Laplace replied, *"Je n'ai pas besoin de cette hypothèse"*— "I have no need of that hypothesis."[84] Darwin's theory displaced the hypothesis that anchored natural theology, the theory that God's existence was written in nature's complexity and comprehensibility. Darwin did not set out to displace the postulated God who gave the world a design and a destination. But Darwin did displace Him.

Before Darwin, many people believed that no living thing could become extinct because extinction would suggest that there had been imperfection in God's original plan. Darwin himself said it is not illogical for religious people to try to accommodate theology and biology by postulating that God is the Great Initiator who set in motion natural selection in the hope or expectation—but not the certainty—that it would result in a world agreeable to His purposes. If, however, natural selection is to be natural rather than supernatural, God cannot have been certain about the outcome: God's involvement in natural selection ends the instant it begins. But this is just another flavor of deism, and like all the others it is too watery to summon anything as robust as religious *faith* that compels sometimes arduous and uncomfortable behaviors.

William James defined religious faith as "the belief that there is an unseen order, and that our supreme good lies in harmoniously adjusting ourselves thereto."[85] Just so. Reasonable atheism asserts the absence of convincing evidence—evidence that can be seen, sifted, tested—of such an order. Therefore, atheists—those without a theism—embark on the project of finding other reasons for adjusting, and adjusting to, moral rules and social norms that enable us to live in harmony with our natures and with others. Virtues are acquired human qualities that enable the individual who possesses them to achieve certain good outcomes, and the absence of which impedes such achievement. Qualities are acquired by habituation—by emulation, instruction, and, especially, immersion in social practices. This, then, is the crux of the conservative project: to advocate those practices—political, economic, and cultural—that are conducive to flourishing, understood as living virtuously.

The philosopher Tim Crane, writing about "religion from an atheist's point of view," sensibly distinguishes between attempts to find meaning *in* life and attempts to find the meaning *of* life as a whole. The former can be achieved by quotidian things and moments, from a baby's smile to professional successes. The latter requires, or so billions of people think, religion, meaning belief in transcendence. This requires belief in some supernatural agency. Atheism is the disbelief in this. Agnosticism is the milder judgment that, as yet, not enough is known to speak with certainty about the existence of God. The philosopher Bertrand Russell was asked what he would say if his atheism turned out to be mistaken and he found himself standing in front of the throne of God. Russell answered that he would say to God, "I'm terribly sorry, but you didn't give us enough evidence."[86]

Christianity, especially, rests audaciously on confidence about evidence—on a series of assertions of historical facts, one of which is supreme. As Saint Paul said, "If Christ be not risen, then is our preaching vain, and your faith is also vain." Religion involves more than a cosmology. Because religion involves the moral imperative of adjusting to its claims, there is a clear answer to the question with which this chapter began: What difference does it make if the stars "just happened" or "was made"? It makes a big difference for this reason: Not every moral code enjoining certain behavior is religious, but every religion has such a code. As Crane notes, the first of the

Ten Commandments is the only one that is cosmological in that it concerns God's existence. The other nine are about how we should behave, in worship and toward one another. This is why Durkheim was correct to say that one does not just believe in a religion, one belongs to it and lives it.[87]

There is such a thing as a religious temperament. It involves the will to believe in order to assuage an ache. It rejects, it recoils from, the sense that contingency is everywhere and everything, that there is nothing *beyond* it. As Alfred North Whitehead wrote, "Religion is the vision of something which stands beyond, behind and within the passing flux of immediate things."[88] There is, however, a conservative sensibility that finds flux exhilarating, that is delighted rather than depressed by the idea that there is no beyond and that everything is contingent. A secular conservative sensibility, even a secular conservative aesthetic, finds beauty in the Darwinian view of the world, a beauty that is a close analogue to the conservative vision of a just society respectful of, and dependent on, spontaneous order. Darwin's view has a lineage that traces to Lucretius' *On the Nature of Things*, written nineteen centuries before Darwin introduced into the modern consciousness the idea that the world is propelled by creative contingencies and randomness. Historian Stephen Greenblatt presents an almost ecstatic sense of the liberation that comes from embracing this poetic—*On the Nature of Things* is a poem—idea:

The stuff of the universe, Lucretius proposed, is an infinite number of atoms moving randomly through space, like dust motes in a sunbeam, colliding, hooking together, forming complex structures, breaking apart again, in a ceaseless process of creation and destruction. There is no escape from this process. When you look up at the night sky and, feeling unaccountably moved, marvel at the numberless stars, you are not seeing the handiwork of the gods or a crystalline sphere detached from our transient world. You are seeing the same material world of which you are a part and from whose elements you are made. There is no master plan, no divine architect, no intelligent design. All things, including the species to which you belong, have evolved over vast stretches of time. The evolution is random, though in the case of living organisms it involves a principle of natural selection. That is, species that are suited to survive and to reproduce successfully endure, at least for a time; those that are not so well suited die off quickly. But nothing—from our own species to the planet on which we live to the sun that lights our days—lasts forever. Only the atoms are immortal.[89]

The philosophic tradition that traces to Lucretius but flowered as the Renaissance ignited modernity is, as Greenblatt says, "incompatible with the cult of the gods and the cult of the state." The vision of a world of atoms and void and constant motion is "a world not rendered insignificant but made more beautiful by its transience, its erotic energy, and its ceaseless change." The turn away from supernatural beings and immaterial causes, and toward the understanding that "humans are made of the same stuff as everything else and are part of the natural order"[90]—this turning away is a great emancipation from all restraints on inquiry. Inquiry, which is the engagement of an active mind with an endlessly interesting world, ranks high in the hierarchy of pleasures. There is such a hierarchy, and one purpose of philosophy is to define and defend it. Achieving the higher pleasures is a path to happiness, and enabling the pursuit of happiness is a stated purpose of the first modern nation.

For Darwin, inquiring was happiness, but his inquiry forced him to face the fact that aspects of creation appalled him. In 1860, he confided in a letter to a friend: "I had no intention to write atheistically" but "I cannot persuade myself that a beneficent & omnipotent God would have designedly created the Ichneumonidae with the express intention of their feeding within the living bodies of caterpillars."[91] What appalled him had fascinated entomologist William Kirby

(1759–1850): The ichneumon wasp inserts an egg in a caterpillar, and the larva hatched from the egg, Kirby said, "gnaws the inside of the caterpillar, and though at last it has devoured almost every part of it except the skin and intestines, carefully all this time avoids injuring the vital organs, as if aware that its own existence depends on that of the insect on which it preys!"[92]

Darwin's dismay about aspects of reality was profound. Nevertheless, at the conclusion of *The Origin of Species*, Darwin wrote one of the most stirring sentences in English letters: "There is grandeur in this view of life, with its several powers, having been originally breathed into a few forms or into one; and that, whilst this planet has gone cycling on according to the fixed law of gravity, from so simple a beginning endless forms most beautiful and most wonderful have been, and are being evolved."[93] Darwin, a cleric's son, knew his King James Version of the Bible: "And the Lord God formed man of the dust of the ground, and breathed into his nostrils the breath of life; and man became a living soul."[94] Darwin chose to echo the evocative word "breathed." He did not, however, choose to intimate what Scripture stipulates.

Gertrude Himmelfarb, a scholar of both the American enlightenment that nourished the deism of many Founders and of Victorian culture, wrote: "Before-Darwin a bold spirit could be tempted to think of God as merely the custodian of the laws of nature. After-Darwin it took no great courage to think of the laws of nature as the custodians of the universe."[95] This was deism without the deity, which was not much of a change. Darwin's life of steady intellectual heroism is a shining chapter in the human story and a rebuke to anyone who would assert that religious faith is indispensable to a life nobly lived. Darwin demonstrated that the *absence* of faith can be a source of virtue.

So did Shakespeare. Imagine if Shakespeare could be brought back to contemplate what humanity has been taught by Einstein. Einstein could tell Shakespeare this: "When Falstaff slams a flagon of mead down on a table, the table, like the flagon—and like Falstaff, actually—is mostly space and electricity. Furthermore, matter—table, flagon, Falstaff—is a form of energy. Now, Mr. Shakespeare, what was all that about man and dust?"

Let the man who used words better than anyone else ever has have the last word here.

What a piece of work is a man! how noble in reason! how infinite in faculty! in form and moving how express and admirable! in action how like an angel! in apprehension how like a god! the beauty of the world! the paragon of animals! And yet, to me, what is this quintessence of dust? man delights not me: no, nor woman neither, though by your smiling you seem to say so.[96]

This was not Shakespeare's only mention of man and dust:

To-morrow, and to-morrow, and to-morrow,
Creeps in this petty pace from day to day
To the last syllable of recorded time,
And all our yesterdays have lighted fools
The way to dusty death. Out, out, brief candle!
Life's but a walking shadow, a poor player
That struts and frets his hour upon the stage
And then is heard no more: it is a tale
Told by an idiot, full of sound and fury,
Signifying nothing.[97]

Shakespeare was expressing, with almost furious candor, his basic sense of the human condition. He was, as the critic Kenneth Clark said, the first "supremely great poet to have been without a religious belief, even without the humanist's belief in man." Clark asked: "Who else has felt so strongly the absolute meaninglessness of human life." Nevertheless, Shakespeare wrote. He wrote with a passion that would have been not just incongruous but impossible for someone who really felt the meaninglessness of everything. Surely it would be more accurate to say that Shakespeare believed that the meaning of life does not derive from any source beyond itself. Shakespeare's greatness is indeed related to the fact that he presented the multifaceted human condition without reference to transcendence but also without immobilizing despair. The nobility, humor, and pathos presented in his plays and poems testify to his fervent belief that somehow the way we behave matters, even if—or perhaps it matters especially because—we live beneath a blank sky. "I feel," said Clark of Shakespeare, "that the human mind has gained a new greatness by outstaring this emptiness."[98]

Here the conservative sensibility protests: Why speak of emptiness when our world is still filled with the astonishments, including the worlds Shakespeare created and peopled? Given the beauty that art can conjure into existence, and the ethical excellence and political nobility that man, "this quintessence of dust," can attain, what difference does it make if the sky is blank? Besides, as Huck and Jim saw there on their raft, the sky is not blank. It is flecked with stars that twinkle prettily whether they "was made" or "just happened."

CHAPTER 10

BORNE BACK

THE QUEST FOR A USEABLE PAST

> In the old days, in blizzardy weather, we used to
> tie a string of lariats from house to barn so as to
> make it from shelter to responsibility and back
> again. With personal, family and cultural chores
> to do, I think we had better rig up such a line
> between past and present.
>
> Wallace Stegner[1]

We who came to social consciousness in the 1950s acquired, with every breath, the sense of America's vigor, the "glittering in the veins" and the "crush of strength" that the poet Wallace Stevens sensed one night in 1954 on the Connecticut Turnpike.[2] It is truly said that ignorance of history makes us libel our own times. America has not done badly in the struggle to achieve that elusive balance of freedom and security that characterizes a society in which the strong may freely strive and the weak need not feel fear. Most Americans live lives as soft as soufflés, insulated from terrors—of nature, of disease, of criminality—that were daily accompaniments of all generations until recent ones. There are, however, dangerous currents to beat on against, currents carrying us away from what should be America's normative and useable past.

In the first paragraph of the first Federalist Paper, Alexander Hamilton wrote that Americans would, by their "conduct and example," answer the question of "whether societies of men are really capable or not, of establishing good government from reflection and choice, or whether they are forever destined to depend, for their political constitutions, on accident and force."[3] In the last paragraph of the eighty-fifth and final Federalist Paper Hamilton quotes the "solid and ingenious" David Hume: "To balance a large state or society whether monarchical or republican, on general laws, is a work of so great difficulty, that no human genius, however comprehensive, is able by the mere dint of reason and reflection, to effect it." Hume meant that no *single* genius could do so, and that even when "the judgments of many" are united in the work, reason and reflection will not suffice: "Experience must guide their labour: Time must bring it to perfection: And the feeling of inconveniences must correct the mistakes which they *inevitably* fall into, in their first trials and experiments." Time and inconveniences continue to shape Americans' governance by "reason and reflection," and ever will.[4] So there will always be laurels to be won by those who practice statecraft.

Speaking in 1825 at the dedication of the Bunker Hill monument, Daniel Webster said: "We can win no laurels in a war for independence. Earlier and worthier hands have gathered them all. Nor are there places for us by the side of Solon, and Alfred, and other founders of states. Our fathers have filled them. But there remains to us the great duty of defense and preservation."[5] Thirty-five years later, this duty would prove to be at least as testing as the challenges of establishing America's independence and founding its government. Indeed, just thirteen years after Webster spoke, the man who would preside over the preservation of the union in its gravest crisis spoke to the Young Men's Lyceum of Springfield, Illinois. He expressed a kind of regret that the great "race of ancestors" had created a "political edifice of liberty and equal rights" and that the task of Abraham Lincoln's generation was only "to transmit these." Even in 1838, however, he discerned how the task of transmission might require Herculean exertions from heroic leadership because "the silent artillery of time" is constantly doing its destructive work.[6] So steps must be constantly taken to spike that artillery by repairing the edifice the Founders bequeathed to us.

The truly conservative sensibility is always alert to the fact that time is, as Cervantes said, the "devourer and destroyer of all things."[7] J. Robert Oppenheimer, the physicist who directed the Manhattan Project that developed the atomic bomb, studied Sanskrit so he could read the *Bhagavad Gita*. When at 5:29 and 45 seconds on the morning of July 16, 1945, at Alamogordo, New Mexico, he witnessed the first atomic explosion, he remembered a line from the Hindu classic: "Now I am become death, the destroyer of worlds."[8] But this line does not appear in most English translations of the *Bhagavad Gita*. The Sanskrit word Oppenheimer translated as "death" is usually translated as "time." For example, the Penguin Classics edition renders the line as: "I am all-powerful Time, which destroys all things."[9] Time, unlike a nuclear explosion, does damage slowly. But it can do it thoroughly. Thus for Lincoln the fragility of America's political arrangement was a constant preoccupation. Referring to slavery, he warned that "a house divided against itself cannot stand."[10] And at Gettysburg he interpreted the Civil War as a test of whether a nation dedicated to the proposition that "all men are created equal" can "long endure." But, then, worries about the dangers of social decay and the perishable nature of all institutions are as old as Plato's *Republic*, which means they are as old as Western political philosophy. It is very American to worry about whether the kind of government created by the Founders might "perish from the Earth."[11] It also is prudent.

This is a chastening axiom: All rising is by a winding staircase. But the axiom is perhaps insufficiently chastening: One can descend a winding staircase. The Whig theory of history, according to Irving Kristol, who was skeptical of it but scrupulous in defining it, is that history "is the record of the struggle between Freedom and Authority,

Reason and Prejudice, Left and Right, with the victory of the former assured by the growing preponderance among mankind of rational opinions and rational conduct."[12] So the Whig theory is not only content about the past and cheerful about the future, it is flattering to the present. Kristol's friend, Daniel Patrick Moynihan, was no Whig. "The lively sense that liberals have of the possibility of progress," Moynihan said, "is matched by a conservative sense of the possibility of decline. Both concerns need attending."[13] It is, however, the possibility of decline that most needs attention because people flinch from it as powerfully as they are drawn to promises of progress.

Many thoughtful Americans worry that the Republic peaked a little early, and has been trundling downhill since Bunker Hill. One Founder fixed upon posterity a preemptively disapproving squint. George Washington said: "The foundation of our empire was not laid in the gloomy age of ignorance and superstition, but an epocha when the rights of mankind were better understood and more clearly defined, than at any former period.... At this auspicious period, the United States came into existence as a nation, and if their citizens should not be completely free and happy, the fault will be entirely their own."[14] Seventy years later, in 1852, a gloomy Ralph Waldo Emerson was haunted by the portrait of Washington hanging in his dining room: "I cannot keep my eyes off of it...the heavy, leaden eyes turn on you, as the eyes of an ox in a pasture. And the mouth has a gravity and depth of quiet, as if this man had absorbed all the serenity of America, and left none for his restless, rickety, hysterical countrymen."[15] Leaving aside the question of whether Washington's grave and quiet mouth expressed character or the tortures of wooden false teeth, we know what Emerson meant. This book is, among other things, a summons to pessimism. What is needed now, and what it is especially incumbent on conservatives to provide, is intelligent pessimism that is more than a mere mood. It should be a mentality grounded in a philosophic tradition that has a distinguished pedigree, and that is validated by abundant historical evidence for this proposition: Nothing lasts.

In a 1911 letter to the Italian philosopher Benedetto Croce (1866–1952), Georges Sorel (1847–1922), the French philosopher who advocated revolutionary syndicalism, said that "movements toward greatness" are "always *an effort*, and movements toward decadence always *natural*."[16] The Founders bequeathed to posterity a republic that throve under a limited government that provided social space for the creativity of society's spontaneous order. The abandonment of the Founders' ideas is having several large consequences. Current discontents are fueling a boiling distrust of government and corrosive distrust of Americans regarding one another. For the last fifty years, especially, the government's ambitiousness and solicitousness have varied inversely with the government's prestige. It is time for second thoughts—or, in many cases, first thoughts—about the price we are paying for what has been lost. Interest in the problem of—perhaps the inevitability of—the decay of political regimes is as old as Western political philosophy: So, the preoccupation with decay had a distinguished pedigree long before Edward Gibbon, on October 15, 1764, in Rome, "sat musing amidst the ruins of the Capitol, while the barefooted friars were singing vespers in the Temple of Jupiter." It was then "that the idea of writing the decline and fall of the city first started to my mind." He wrote "the last lines of the last page" of *The History of the Decline and Fall of the Roman Empire* on June 27, 1787.[17] On that day, in Philadelphia, the Constitutional Convention debated the institutional architecture for limited government that would resist the degenerations to which other republics had succumbed.

"Because the civilization of ancient Rome perished in consequence of the invasion of the Barbarians," Tocqueville wrote, "we are perhaps too apt to think that civilization cannot perish in any other manner. If the light by which we are guided is ever extinguished, it will dwindle by degrees and expire of itself."[18] Human beings are unique among living creatures in that they are capable of being dissatisfied with themselves. For American conservatives, dissatisfaction is a retrospective frame of mind. Conservatism's task is to urgently warn about what is perishable: Everything. Lincoln's anxiety was about the perishable nature of national memory, particularly America's memory of its Founding. It would, he said, inevitably "grow more and more dim by the lapse of time." At the close of the Revolutionary War, its "living history was to be found in every family." But that history, the memories of participants "are gone," destroyed by "time." Lincoln spoke when some Americans from the Revolutionary era were still alive. Mrs. Alexander Hamilton, final survivor of the Founders' circle, died in Washington in 1854 in her ninety-seventh year, having lived the entire life of the Republic. So had the slave interviewed in Virginia during the Civil War's 1862 Peninsula Campaign, who recalled hearing cannonading at the Battle of Yorktown eighty-one years earlier. But even in 1838, memories of the Founding era were few and flickering, so Lincoln toiled to supply new supports for the American project, supports "hewn from the solid quarry of sober reason."[19] His public life was devoted to reconnecting the country with the principles of the Founding. This is conservatism's core purpose today.

CONSERVATISM'S RADICAL WORRY

Politics is usually driven by competing worries. Today, conservatives are more radically worried than are progressives concerning conditions in America's government and culture. Conservatives worry about the relationships they think they discern between government and culture. Progressives still express their worries in an essentially 1930s vocabulary of distributive justice, understood in economic, meaning material, terms. This assumes a reassuringly mundane politics of splittable differences—how much concrete to pour, how many crops to subsidize by how much, which factions shall get what. Conservatives worry in a more contemporary vocabulary, questioning the power and ambitions of the post–New Deal state, and finding a causal connection between those ambitions and the fraying of the culture. Many of today's conservatives believe, or say they do (their actions in office often say otherwise), that the nation needs to rethink the proper scope and actual competence of government.

In 1893, three years after the Census Bureau declared the closing of the frontier, Woodrow Wilson pondered the changes that were challenging the old American faith that freedom is, in large measure, a function of space—that freedom consists partly of not being able to see the smoke from your neighbor's cabin or to hear the sound of his ax. In 1893, Wilson wrote, "Slowly we shall grow old, compact our people, study the delicate adjustments of an intricate society."[20] In classical political theory, compactness was a precondition for a successful republic—a small population compacted in a small polity that might be free of factions. The audacity of the American experiment was and still is its attempt to have a republic that is big, but in which life nevertheless is conducive to the virtues requisite for self-government, the virtues of self-reliance and self-restraint. However, in the more than twelve decades since Wilson brooded about the emergence of "an intricate society," our big country has acquired a big government that seems to foster dependence, and which inflames incontinent appetites, including appetites for government provision of illimitable wants.

Liberalism as originally understood—limited government supervising market societies; government respectful of individual autonomy and individuals' voluntary transactions—is thin gruel for those with an appetite for red meat politics. As Isaiah Berlin wrote, "A liberal sermon which recommends machinery designed to prevent people from doing each other too much harm, giving each human group sufficient room to realize its own idiosyncratic, unique, particular ends without too much interference with the ends of others, is not a passionate battle-cry to inspire men to sacrifice and martyrdom and heroic feats."[21] Passions sometimes have their places in political life, but should not be the routine features of normal political processes. Sacrifice, martyrdom, and heroism can be necessary, but usually are so only when things have gone badly awry. A political order that requires such things constantly or even frequently is failing to provide good order. Americans who think their government is now failing at that task are not wrong. What they require is leadership that tells them that they and their political appetites are large parts of the problem.

Locke and Montesquieu were important to the American Founding, but our national wagon really got rolling because Americans came to believe what Huckleberry Finn said: "All kings is mostly rapscallions."[22] Thoughts like that came easily to, say, a farmer who had just broken his plow on a Connecticut rock, and who would rather buy a new one than pay taxes to a distant monarch. We have come a long way from sod huts and muddy boots to an economy that produces billions of dollars' worth of soap. And we may be learning what Mark Twain meant: "Soap and education are not as sudden as a massacre, but they are more deadly in the long run."[23] The easing of the physical strain of Americans' existence has proceeded apace with a general loosening of social restraints. As recently as 1944, the library of the US Naval Academy would not issue the novel *Forever Amber*—it was considered quite racy—to anyone of the rank midshipman or lower. American hedonism has come a long way, fast. And there are many persons who think America's modern history is summed up by a Thurber cartoon that shows a woman perched on the arm of a sofa, talking animatedly to a circle of enthralled men. Behind her, a disgruntled woman says to another: "She built up her personality, but she's undermined her character."[24] Many thoughtful people today think the Republic has more personality and less character than is healthy, and that it is afflicted with a weakness, decadence, that may be the fatal flaw of developed free nations. The theory is as follows.

The material success of capitalism—to which we owe the marble in our lives—has been made by hardships of life in the mud of Connecticut and Nebraska and the Oregon Trail. But abundance both produces and requires a constant increase in consumption, and in appetites. This dynamic generates a culture of self-indulgence. Such a culture is incompatible with self-government, which is, after all, about governing the self. That is why the concluding stanza of "America the Beautiful" is a kind of prayer: "Confirm thy soul in self-control..."[25] There is tension between the economic dynamic that inflames appetites and the need for discipline—political as well as economic—in a free society. Some people say this is the "cultural contradiction" of capitalism. Others call it the "cultural consequence" of capitalism. Be that as it may, in its third century, the Republic's most pressing task is to demonstrate that political habits of restraint and moderation are compatible with an economic and cultural ambience that celebrates, and often provides, instant gratification of immoderate appetites. It is a national triumph, of sorts, that this problem of abundance confronts the descendants of the generations that walked through the mud to Oregon.

We characterize various eras and epochs, from the Founding era to the Roaring Twenties to the complacent Fifties to the convulsive Sixties, in order to slice history into discrete episodes. They are, however, parts of a seamless flow of events, each one birthed by previous ones and pregnant with others. Today Americans wonder how it came to pass that a tiny collection of thirteen loosely related communities could produce the generation of American founders who, at Philadelphia in 1776 and 1789, accomplished history's most stunning feat of political creation, which was to become a continental democracy. The answer is not, or at least not primarily, that an accident of history blessed the colonies with an extraordinary number of wise and decent men. A better explanation is that there was then a habit of deference to excellence in public life. After all, the remarkable thing is not just that the Founding Fathers existed, separately, but that the political process brought them together in Philadelphia.

Since then, however, there have been changes in the theory and, hence, the practice of American democracy. The changes began with the "Jacksonian revolution" in democratic thinking. In his first message to Congress in 1829, President Andrew Jackson said: "The duties of all public offices are, or at least admit of being, made so plain and simple that men of intelligence may readily qualify themselves for their performance."[26] The duties of public office are, however, "plain and simple" only if government problems are only problems of administrative technique. But such a mild conception of politics is blind to the political virtues of judgment, prudence, and courage. The devaluing of the political vocation has been followed in our time by a related degradation of government. Today, government exists to be "responsive." Politicians exist to respond like simple mechanisms to impulses recorded from demanding constituencies. This plain and simple task requires no uncommon virtues. To be vigorously servile to all demands, a politician should be "a person of the people," prepared to serve democracy by representing its common denominators, including (perhaps especially) the lowest. Today's servile government possesses, at most, utility, never dignity. Not surprisingly, the public evidently thinks it would be unreasonable to expect dignified politicians, and, besides, that dignity is irrelevant to the politician's low function. Half a century ago, Governor George Wallace, the Alabama Democrat who was an early voice of the populism that has flourished in our time, said: "Hell, we got too much dignity in government now."[27] That is not a contemporary complaint.

How did America come to its present condition? By a protracted apostasy from principles that, by limiting the scope of government, protected the stature of politics. Our nation had a founding moment, which means it is founded on more than inertia. Our nation emerged not from forces obscured by the mists of the past but from a clear, public act of choosing—an affirmation. Of the correctness of their choice, the Founders were breathtakingly confident. Think about this: The First Amendment forbids the establishment of religion because the Founders thought that religious truth was unknowable and so must remain an open question. But the Constitution guarantees the establishment of a republican form of government in all the states because the Founders considered the best form of government a closed question in our open society.

One measure of a political philosophy's seriousness is what it requires of its adherents. Conservatives today are required to tell people that they should be formed by respect for the Constitution. They should be formed for a life of choosing not to choose all that government can offer because those offerings come at a cost to the virtues of independence and moderation. Which brings us back to what may be the cultural contradiction of conservatism: Conservatism depends on eliciting from citizens public-spirited self-denial. But that is not easily elicited in a commercial republic of the sort that conservatism celebrates, where individualism enjoys maximum scope for private pursuits. Public-spirited self-denial can only be elicited by a conservatism standing for more than the sum of the demands of the groups in its coalition. It can only be elicited by respect for the Constitution and, hence, for the virtues of self-reliance and self-restraint that our polity presupposes. As today's conservatives struggle to develop a constitutional vocabulary for infusing self-government with self-restraint, they should remember this: The Republican Party, the former and perhaps future vessel of conservatism, first became a national factor because of one man's refusal to accept popular sovereignty as a complete expression of the formative project of American politics. The party's intellectual pedigree traces directly to Lincoln's denial that Kansans could choose to have slaves.

Lincoln's noble insistence was that a great continental nation could be, indeed had to be, a single moral community. Conservatism's task today is to demonstrate that the dignity of constitutional government depends on restraints of a sort that do not come easily to conservatives or any other Americans. And these restraints will not come automatically or spontaneously from institutional arrangements—from federalism or the separation of powers or judicial review. The restraints requisite for limited government, and hence requisite for the virtues that republican government presupposes, will come only from thoughtful reverence for the nation's founding, a reverence that not only honors the memory of the Founders but is conscientious in understanding their principles.

The search for restraint is an American constant. It is a search in which progressivism is not helpful. Liberalism entered Western political thought with a breezy faith that the good life would flourish when the last king had been strangled in the entrails of the last priest. Today, we know it is not that simple. The good life is menaced by forces of disorder, and big government has become one of those forces. As Alexander Bickel said, "The future will not be ruled; it can only possibly be persuaded."[28] The foundation of a democratic society is opinion, so conservatism's task is rhetorical. It is to be persuasive about enlarging whatever remains of Americans' reverence for the Founders and their premises. It is ominous that today the word "rhetoric" carries almost entirely negative connotations. It once denoted a means of persuading others by offering reasons for beliefs. Now it means deceptive, duplicitous, or plainly false spoken words. "I don't like eloquence," said one of Dashiell Hammett's hardboiled anti-heroes in 1924. "If it isn't effective enough to pierce your hide, it's tiresome; and if it is effective enough, then it muddles your thoughts."[29] There you have it—rhetoric is obfuscation.

Leadership in a democracy is, however, the ability to persuade a majority to consent to things they are not disposed to desire. It is to get a majority to accept short-term pains in the expectation of long-term gains. So, the mission of contemporary conservatism is at once melancholy, daunting, and, because it is so challenging, exhilarating. It is to convince people that governmental promises have been made to them that the government—that American society, actually—cannot afford to keep and to persuade them that the kind of supposedly ameliorative government that has been created on their behalf, and at their behest, is both unattractive and unsustainable. It is unattractive because it is the plaything of avaricious factions. It is unsustainable because it has a powerful and permanent incentive to disguise, by deferring the costs of, the goods and services to which it has told people they are entitled.

Conservatism has the paradoxical burden of telling people that attempts to conserve some of today's settled arrangements and familiar expectations are going to be futile, costly, and potentially ruinous. Conservatism, which often in history has been devoted to the defense of the existing order, must now accept the task of reconciling people to the disruption and churning that accompanies economic and cultural dynamism. The political class has prospered by hiding from the public the cost of the public's appetites. By making vast deficit spending not an occasional counter-cyclical recourse but a constant governing strategy, it has made big government deceptively cheap, giving today's public a dollar's worth of goods and services and charging them only about 80 cents. By doing so, government deepens America's infantilization. It is characteristic of children to will an end without willing the means to this end. This is now a national characteristic.

But what, then, about compassionate politics? Compassion is a passion, and passions are, the Founders agreed, problems to be coped with. Compassion is not, strictly speaking, a virtue. As a passion, it is disconnected from reason and often at odds with it. Hence compassion is an unreliable guide to justice, which must be defined by reason. Compassion may be put to the service of virtue; it may prompt virtuous action. But this is a contingent, not a necessary, relation. And when compassion is elevated to a principle of political philosophy, it is incompatible with a conservatism of limited government. President George W. Bush, who called himself a "compassionate conservative," said: "When somebody hurts, government has got to move."[30] That is less a compassionate thought than a flaunting of sentiment to avoid thinking about government's limited capacities and unlimited confidence. Compassion does indeed involve the desire to prevent or ameliorate pain or distress. Because there never is a shortage of those things, compassion is steady work. So, as a political imperative, compassion as an animating force of government can mean expanding government without end. Hence the contradiction between compassionate conservatism and constitutionalism.

What ruins individuals and nations are overdeveloped appetites, which we stimulate by the illusion that mankind has escaped the constraints of scarcity. Government has nourished this illusion. It has tried to be all things to all people, or at least as many things to as many people as possible, in order to spur consumption of governmental goods and services, and to satisfy the most voracious interest groups. Progressives fault government as "unresponsive." Actually, government today has a hair-trigger responsiveness to intense, organized interests. Conservatives claim that government is too strong and overbearing. Actually, government is fat but pathetically weak. It does not have the strength to say "no" to determined petitioners.

Until the late 1970s, conservatives argued, as Barry Goldwater did, that many government programs, although popular, must be opposed because they take an intolerable toll on the freedom and character of the people. But the "Reagan Revolution" rested on the premise that Goldwaterite opposition to government programs was politically futile. So conservatives would attack taxes rather than the programs they support. This was conservatives' accommodation to the fact that scores of millions of Americans are ideologically, meaning rhetorically, conservative, but are behaviorally liberal. So conservatives would "starve the beast," limiting government growth by depriving government of revenues. This was worse than futile because it taught the beast to feed on borrowing.

Modern government—spending more than it taxes, subsidizing and regulating and conferring countless other blessings—is a mighty engine for the stimulation of consumption. Every government benefit creates a constituency for expansion of the benefit, so the servile state inflames more appetites than it slakes. It has fostered a perverse entrepreneurship, the manipulation of government—public power—for private purposes. It has eroded society's disciplining sense of the true cost of things. This has accelerated what Moynihan called "the leakage of reality from American life."[31] The era of the servile state began during the last American experience of real scarcity. It began in 1933, when the governor of the then most populous state became president and altered the relationship between the citizen and the federal government. Today citizens receive more than ever from government, and government receives less respect than ever from them.

And one suspects that the citizens do not respect themselves as citizens. They must know, in moments of clarity, that they are in the grip of cognitive dissonance. They hold, with equal fervor, flatly incompatible convictions. They talk as Jefferson did in his first inaugural address: "wise and frugal Government, which shall restrain men from injuring one another, shall leave them otherwise free to regulate their own pursuits of industry and improvement, and shall not take from the mouth of labor the bread it has earned. This is the sum of good government, and this is necessary to close the circle of our felicities."[32] But Americans who talk like Jeffersonians vote for modern-day Hamiltonians, for those who will protect, and steadily endorse, a government that is omnipresent and omniprovident. The point of elections is to ensure that government has what Madison in Federalist 51 called a "dependence on the people."[33] The preoccupation of modern government, however, is to make more and more people, in more and more ways, dependent on the government. Tocqueville anticipated with foreboding that Americans would come to terms with comfortable dependency: "They console themselves for being under schoolmasters by thinking that they have chosen them themselves.... Under this system the citizens quit their state of dependence just long enough to choose their masters and then fall back into it."[34] In today's context, conservatives need a sobering immersion in the realism of James Madison.

Irving Kristol's 1944 description of E. M. Forster's "moral realism" also describes the Madisonian and the conservative sensibility:

"Though dissatisfied, of course, with the ways of men, it foresees no new virtues, but, at best, a healthier distribution of the old. It is non-eschatological, skeptical of proposed revisions of man's nature, interested in human beings as it finds them, content with the possibilities and limitations that are always with us."[35] Notice the combination of dissatisfaction and contentment. The ability to hold those attributes in some sort of equilibrium is a mark of a mature mind. A conservative sensibility knows that the possibilities of politics, although limited, are not negligible. And it knows that although all the virtues are already known, a healthier distribution of them is a worthy and demanding project. The Founders bequeathed to us a political order founded on realism about human attributes, beginning with this truth: In human beings, interestedness is a given, but virtue must be acquired. Contemporary conservatism is resoundingly right when it argues that government itself has become inimical to the virtues essential for responsible self-government. Government has become inimical because it fosters both dependency and uncivic aggressiveness in attempting to bend public institutions to private factional advantage.

Do conservatives have the steely resolve required to tell the country the hard truth about how radically it has gone wrong in its thinking about, and expectations of, government? Today, conservatism senses, and is struggling to act on, the fact that human beings are biological facts, but citizens suited to self-government are social artifacts. Conservatism is not yet, however, sufficiently clear-sighted about how our constitutional order is supposed to contribute to the creation of such artifacts. And conservatism is not alert to the way its own tenets can complicate the creation of virtuous citizens. Let us be clear about what conservatism is not saying about citizens as social artifacts. Conservatives are implacably hostile to the idea that human nature has a history. The hostility is implacable because that idea is subversive of government based on respect for natural rights. If human nature has a history, then there really is no such thing as human nature, understood as something the essence of which is unchanging. The idea that human nature has a history—that human beings have only a malleable nature shaped by their time and place—has animated modern tyrannies. It has done so because people susceptible to that idea are also susceptible to the idea that self-government is a chimera—an impossibility— because the self is a fiction or, at best, a mere reflection of the individual's social setting. To say that human nature is plastic is to open the way to governments that regard the creation of new, improved forms of humanity as the highest government project. Such governments are apt to unleash "consciousness-raisers" who use political power to extirpate "false consciousness." Such people insist that, until proper consciousness is made universal, any consent necessarily arises from false consciousness and, hence, is not worth seeking or respecting.

Conservatives acknowledge that individuals are not entirely autonomous and unconditioned, but warn that people who believe there is no human nature *must* believe that *no* rights are natural rights. If there is no human nature, then rights are just appetites cloaked in "rights talk" in order to acquire momentum for respect. Conservatism seeks equilibrium, arguing that nature has political claims and that nurturing has a political role. Nature's political claims rise from this fact: The idea of human nature involves the idea of essential human qualities that are conducive to excellence and happiness. And the task of political nurturing takes its bearings from that idea of excellence. Wise conservatives take that task seriously. The Founders understood that popular government would be an exercise in continuing education; self-government must be a formative experience, for better or worse. They thought that popular government, properly constituted, would be good for our souls. Today, however, conservatives correctly argue that our government has become a deforming force, corrupting the country's character. They say government has become a bland Leviathan, confirming Tocqueville's warning that government can "degrade men without tormenting them."[36]

In his second inaugural address, Ronald Reagan said our "system has never failed us, but for a time, we failed the system. We asked things of government that government was not equipped to give."[37] Perhaps, however, the system failed us by allowing us, even prompting us, to become, over time, a people with unreasonable expectations and importuning desires. The more educated a nation becomes, the wealthier it is apt to become. The wealthier it becomes, the more benefits its government can dispense. The wealthier citizens become, the more they pay in taxes and the more benefits they expect from government. So, although prosperity makes people confident and assertive and gives them the means to be self-sufficient, it is not conducive to small government. Government grows because of the bargaining process among interest groups, none of which has an incentive to opt for unilateral disarmament in the scramble for benefits from government action. Jonathan Rauch believes that both liberals and conservatives have become unreasonably dyspeptic about government because they are all "governmentalists," in the sense that they define themselves—their passions, their stances toward life—"in relation to government": "Liberals hunt for a governmental solution for every problem; conservatives hunt for a governmental cause for every problem."[38]

Societies of all sorts are always replete with problems, and governments, even the best of them, are always characterized by inefficiencies and transaction costs in trying to cope with problems. This is because governments—especially the best of them, democracies—are not supposed to be efficient. They are supposed to be more or less prudent, more often than not, and generally just and safe. These are modest goals and attributes that do not cause pulses to race. But surely the American nation could stand to have a steadier, slower pulse rate than it recently has had.

Today, saturation journalism, reporting and commenting on the politicization of almost everything, has society, or at least a conspicuous and articulate portion of it, at a constant boil. But politics matters, now more than ever, because the problem of confining politics to a proper sphere is a political problem and arguably the most important project for politics. Addressing a labor audience during the first of his four Senate campaigns, Daniel Patrick Moynihan said with a mixture of weariness and exasperation, "Look, there's this particular fringe, and their one fundamental problem is they simply never accepted the New Deal." Moynihan added: "Didn't Franklin Roosevelt settle this issue once and for all? I mean, do we really *have* to go over it *again*?"[39] To his plaintive question, the answer was, and is: Yes and no. Roosevelt—with the subsequent help of the man whose political apprenticeship was as a New Deal functionary, Lyndon Johnson—did indeed extinguish the argument that the federal government's powers are, as Madison insisted, "few and defined."[40] But Americans are less than pleased with the performance and trajectory of this government.

In 1964, Americans emphatically rejected the candidacy of Barry Goldwater, who carried just six states while warning voters: "A government that is big enough to give you all you want is big enough to take it all away."[41] In that year, 77 percent of Americans said that they trusted the federal government to do the right thing "just about always" or "most of the time." In 2017, a Pew Research Center poll found that just 20 percent felt that way. It is, surely, not a mere coincidence that this hemorrhaging of trust coincided with "the leaking of reality" from American life. The decline of trust occurred during a half century in which the government became markedly bigger as it expanded its attempts to ameliorate society's imperfections with ever more ambitious programs of distributive justice. On January 19, 1997, the day before the inauguration of President Bill Clinton for a second term and a year after he had proclaimed in a State of the Union address that "the era of big government is over," a *Washington Post* report of an interview with Clinton carried this headline: "Clinton Sees End of Fight over Government's Role."[42] That ending certainly would be momentous news: An argument at least as old as Plato's *Republic* was coming to an end. Of course the argument was not, is not, and never will end. It is a hardy perennial, varying in intensity, and just now it is notably intense. This is why Moynihan was so fond of using William Butler Yeats to remind his fellow Democrats and progressives not to exaggerate the power of politics to transform life:

> *Parnell came down the road, he said to a cheering man:*
> *Ireland shall get her freedom*
> *and you will still break stone.*[43]

Which is to say: Regimes are important, but not all-important. "This," said Moynihan, "is the knowledge life gives us, and it is indispensable to politics. And yet how alien to it."[44] Alien because politics often offers intoxicating promises of sweeping transformations, and because, especially in democracies, politics tends to be an ongoing auction whereby parties bid for the allegiances of majorities.

Political intoxication is a constant susceptibility in a nation that vibrated like a tuning fork when struck by *The Adventures of Huckleberry Finn*. Huck's story still resonates in America's heart because it is about freedom understood in a distinctively American way, as the absence of social restraints, and obedience to the promptings of a pure heart. Mark Twain, like Tocqueville, feared the invisible shackles of social conformity almost as much as he feared oppressive institutions. And Huck? He did not even take to new clothes, which made him "feel all cramped up." And he took to the river when he found out "how dismal regular and decent the widow was" who was bent on "civilizing" him.[45] Twain's novel about this shrewd boy is for grown-ups but it has a childish notion at its core. The notion is that (in today's jargon) "authenticity" and "self-realization" are achieved outside of, or against, society, not through it. Huck is an "alienated" fourteen-year-old. The American idea of freedom is Huck going down the Mississippi or Thoreau going up the Merrimack. To be free is to be footloose in a pathless wilderness, unbounded by geography or history, utterly unconstrained by social bonds. But why must we speak of "bonds" in a way that suggests ropes biting into wrists? Human beings are social animals whose capacities, including the capacity for virtue, can be realized only in a social setting, not isolated on a raft borne ceaselessly past communities where individuals acquire only burdens and bad consciences and cramping clothes.

By 1990, one century after the US Census Bureau declared the frontier closed, half of all Americans lived in metropolitan areas—thirty-nine of them—with populations of one million or more. We had passed a milestone on a journey from what we were once proud of being to what we never wanted to be. The superintendent of the 1890 Census reported, "The unsettled areas have been so broken by isolated bodies of settlement that there can hardly be said to be a frontier line."[46] Time was, geography was America's destiny. The abundance of Western lands explained the nation's development, moral as well as material. It shaped our democratic values of egalitarianism, individualism, pleasure in physical mobility, confidence in social mobility, and faith in the possibility of rebirth through a fresh start out yonder, over the next mountain range. In short, it nourished optimism. But it was a peculiar optimism because it made the idea of progress problematic: If the "unspoiled"—by population—frontier was so fine, what was progress supposed to be?

Frederick Jackson Turner's thesis was that the pedigree of our values, character, and institutions ran not east across the Atlantic but west across the Alleghenies and then the wide Missouri. His thesis implied American exceptionalism, a uniqueness and exemption from many of the world's woes and vices. It also implied, however, that Americanism was unexportable. But in the 1890s American energy leaped outward in "the splendid little war" with Spain that presaged America's entry into world history. Turner's theory called into question the Jeffersonian tradition, whose namesake said that government could be virtuous only "as long as there shall be vacant lands."[47] So what would become of us now, our saving spaces being exhausted? Turner said, "In the spirit of the pioneer's 'house raising'"—voluntary cooperation in the private realm—"lies the salvation of the Republic."[48] What would become of an America in which pioneering was a thing of the past?

Prior to the American Founding, the pedigree of republican institutions had been traced back to ancient ideas. But if American republicanism is actually grounded on the ground, in the vastness of the American land, the "geographical" understanding of American history makes the American future problematic. Early in the twentieth century, many thoughtful Americans—Herbert Croly for one; Walter Lippmann for another—thought individualism was no longer an answer to American problems, but rather had become a problem. This problem, they thought, had two facets. One was the weakness of government, so the challenge was to strengthen the state in order to enable it to tame the surging energies of industrialism. The problem was to weaken individualism so that a spirit of community could flourish. For these ends, the state has been expanding for more than a century.

Conservatives' task is to build a society that nurtures individuals to self-sufficiency, including independence from politics. Now more than ever conservatives need to be focused on this nurturing because the related forces of urbanization and statism are exerting a powerful pull toward an enervating dependency. It is a dependency on large economic entities, and on government, for security. Ultimately, it is dependency on—and addiction to—security as the highest aim of life. This addiction produces, over time, a timid, fearful debased people erecting barriers against a competitive world and aggressively asserting an entitlement mentality, including an entitlement to government protection against uncertainty. This entitlement exacts a steep moral cost. Government that acknowledges such an entitlement becomes a bland Leviathan, administering a soft, kindly, but ultimately corrupting statism of benighted benevolence.

The city of Washington that Jefferson fled in 1809 has, in our time, become an agency of dependency. So a sensible first step would be to restore the wrecked equilibrium of our federal system. From Jefferson's era until well into this century, political debate in Washington about what Washington should do about this or that usually began with examination of the question of whether Washington should do anything—whether the federal government was constitutionally entitled to act. Some people will say that the constitutional question is firmly closed. They will say that for many decades now the Constitution has been consistently construed to emancipate the federal government from any serious circumscription of its latitude for action. That is true. By construing the Constitution in a way that enables and encourages the federal government to act everywhere, we have taught Americans to think that it is natural and right for the federal government to take custody of every problem, to organize the provision of every need, and to satisfy every want.

This author knows a stark fact when he sees one; he can face facts of constitutional construction even when he regrets them. So what now needs to be developed is not a constitutional but a prudential inhibition on the central government. After all, it is not as though the federal government today has surpluses of energy, intelligence, and money, or is conspicuously successful at its undertakings. So it would be an act of fidelity to the Founders to revive the idea of states' rights—and states' responsibilities. Some people wince when you hear the phrase "states' rights." But consider a story.

Shelby Foote, in his history of the Civil War, recounts an episode concerning a Virginian, General George Thomas, who served in the Union Army. Immediately after the bloody assault on Missionary Ridge in the battle of Chattanooga, Thomas discerned an attractive spot for a military cemetery and put a detail to work on the project. The chaplain in charge asked Thomas if the dead were to be buried in plots assigned to the states their units represented, as was done at Gettysburg, where Lincoln had briefly spoken at a cemetery dedication a few weeks earlier. General Thomas lowered his head in thought, then shook it decisively. Making a tumbling gesture with both hands, he said, "No, no; mix 'em up. I'm tired of states' rights."[49]

Americans old enough to remember America's great domestic conflicts over race relations in the 1940s, 1950s, and 1960s may well say, as Thomas did, that they want to hear no more about states' rights. But it is well to remember that an idea should not be discredited merely by the fact that it has been put to ignoble uses. It is also well to remember that in 1800, when the nation still had not spilled westward over the Alleghenies, Jefferson wrote: "Our country is too large to have all its affairs directed by a single government."[50] So let us send more political power back to the state and local levels. Even more important, let us move politics as much as possible to the periphery of American life, where Jefferson wanted it. To do so we will have to reverse powerful tendencies in modern history, tendencies that tend to recur. The mind of the West has long been haunted by the fear that history is, or will be if we are not careful, cyclical. The fear is that powerful forces, even the very logic of social development, propels societies into cycles of decay and—if society is resourceful and lucky—regeneration. Decay is more probable than regeneration. Although America's Founders were firm believers that history could be linear, they knew that progress was not inevitable. Just as there can be a "cultural contradiction of capitalism," there can be a political contradiction of democracy: The very responsiveness of democratic government to the popular will can corrupt the popular will. The more that government tries to satisfy the appetites of particular groups, the more group appetites are inflamed, and the more groups organize to make their demands felt. So the very virtues that democracy presupposes—individualism, self-restraint, and self-reliance—are subverted, over time, by the very responsiveness of democratic government.

We have not been properly mindful of warnings about the tendency of government to swell. Or about the tendency of the central government in a federal system to absorb other governments' responsibilities. Or about the tendency of politics to permeate life

and constrict the private sphere of life. These tendencies are, however, only tendencies, not inevitabilities. Americans are a relentlessly
forward-looking people, but they can yet learn to live looking back to
the Founders for guidance.

After the Founders passed from the scene, in Nathaniel Hawthorne's
day, the voices of various "realists" gravely warned that because
society's problems were more daunting than ever, old principles must
yield to new realities. Hawthorne, however, kept his head. It was time,
he said, to consult "those respectable old blockheads who still...kept
a death-grip on one or two ideas which had not come into vogue
since yesterday morning."[51] All of America's yesterdays recede with
the speed of the nation's pell-mell plunge into the future. The nation's
oldest tradition is its eager embrace of the new, so a young man from
St. Louis, unenthralled by this feature of democratic culture, went to
England in search of a more palpable past. T. S. Eliot spoke not only
of the pastness of the past, but of its presence. A useable past will not
be present, however, unless conservatives make it so. Their challenge is
to make the Founders constantly consulted as the nation approaches
its quarter-millennium mark. Thoughtful Americans who revisit the
great arguments of their nation's political tradition will be rewarded
by a richer sense of their home. The man from St. Louis understood
at least this:

> We shall not cease from exploration
> And the end of all our exploring
> Will be to arrive where we started
> And know the place for the first time.[52]

Americans cannot regain what they do not recognize that they have
lost, which is the Founders' exhilarating sense that social possibilities
can continue to expand into the openness and ferment of the natural
rights Republic that came close to being extinguished on a field near
Princeton.

In 1913, three years after Woodrow Wilson left the president's room in Nassau Hall, and while he was occupying the White House Oval Room, as it was then called, a seventeen-year-old from the upper Middle West arrived at Princeton. In 1925, F. Scott Fitzgerald would publish *The Great Gatsby*, which is a snapshot of the 1920s, but much more than that. It is suffused with melancholy and regret. These are discordant with the supposed American penchant for optimism and cheerful ignorance of life's tragic dimensions. Among the most famous paragraphs in American literature, those that conclude the novel convey chagrin. Standing on a lawn on the shore of Long Island Sound, looking across the water toward East Egg, the novel's narrator, Nick Carraway, imagined Dutch sailors seeing the "fresh, green breast of the new world" at a moment when "man must have held his breath in the presence of this continent…face to face for the last time in history with something commensurate to his capacity for wonder":

And as I sat there brooding on the old, unknown world, I thought of Gatsby's wonder when he first picked out the green light at the end of Daisy's dock. He had come a long way to this blue lawn, and his dream must have seemed so close that he could hardly fail to grasp it. He did not know that it was already behind him, somewhere back in that vast obscurity beyond the city, where the dark fields of the republic rolled on under the night.

Gatsby believed in the green light, the orgiastic future that year by year recedes before us. It eluded us then, but that's no matter—tomorrow we will run faster, stretch out our arms farther…. And one fine morning—

So we beat on, boats against the current, borne back ceaselessly into the past.[53]

What was this "last and greatest of all human dreams"?[54] Fitzgerald's answer is implicit in two words: The pure "presence" of this continent that the first European visitors experienced as "fresh," when it had been green with now long-vanished trees. The dream was of a fresh start of a sort hitherto unimaginable—of an uncircumscribed future that Americans would be uniquely free to shape by choices not constrained by the viscosity of history. So the last and greatest dream was nothing less than perfect freedom, a state of nature on a continent that seemed to be a blank canvas on which to work.

It is tempting, and not quite wrong, to think of America's Founding as a transitory enchanted moment. Yes, of course, we know—historians, intent on "unmasking this" and "desacralize" that, delight in telling us so—that the Revolutionary War was America's first civil war, with all the savagery that usually attends protracted fratricide. The military battles during the eight years from Lexington and Concord, Trenton and Princeton, through Yorktown were remarkably few and relatively small: Just twenty-three soldiers on the American side and 156 on the British side died at Yorktown. Away from the battlefields, however, there was a maelstrom of violence, frequently opportunistic and often sadistic. Nevertheless, the American Founding was a luminous moment, a hinge on which world history turned, because of the ideas it affirmed and then translated into constitutional institutions and processes.

The fact that the nation had a uniquely inspiriting creation has become dispiriting. The past has become a reproach, judging the present for its departure from the Founders' blended patrimony of philosophy and prudence. So the question now is: Can we get back, not to the conditions in which we started, but to the premises with which we started? Note Fitzgerald's plural pronoun in the paragraph above: It is "we" who beat on, in boats—plural. Fitzgerald's summation pertains, surely, not just to the individual characters in his novel but to our national project. We cannot escape the challenge of living by the exacting principles of our Founding, so we should beat on, boats against many modern currents, borne back ceaselessly toward a still-useable past.

Acknowledgments

Without Sarah Walton, the organizer of my office and my energies, this book could not have come about. Jessica Cruzan and Elayne Allen, the most recent in a long line of my assistants, continued their high standards of diligence and accuracy in helping the preparation of this book. In turning a manuscript into a book, Paul Whitlatch and the other superb professionals at Hachette did what Joe DiMaggio did, making the difficult look easy. One suspects that they have done this before.

What I have written is the distilled wisdom, as I understand this, that I have acquired from half a century in Washington, my home, which I love. So I should acknowledge the enjoyment that I have had there. As readers of this book will detect from my numerous references to him, having Daniel Patrick Moynihan as a friend was an instructive privilege. He served his country brilliantly and exuberantly, having a good time all the way, demonstrating that debating about the proper trajectory of our splendid nation is a high calling and tremendous fun. To him and the many good men and women of American governance, I gratefully acknowledge the pleasure of their company and the value of their example.

SELECT BIBLIOGRAPHY

Ackerman, Kenneth. 2016. *Trotsky in New York, 1917: A Radical on the Eve of Revolution.* Berkeley: Counter Point.

Adams, Henry. 2008. *The Education of Henry Adams.* Blacksburg: Wilder Publications.

Adams, John. 1789. "From John Adams to George Washington, 17 May 1789." National Archives Founders Online. May 17. https://founders.archives.gov/documents/Adams/99-02-02-0564.

———. 1776. "From John Adams to Mercy Otis Warren, 16 April 1776." National Archives Founders Online April 16. https://founders.archives.gov/documents/Adams/06-04-02-0044.

———. 1775. "John Adams to Abigail Adams, 29 October 1775." National Archives Founders Online October 29. https://founders.archives.gov/documents/Adams/04-01-02-0209.

———. 1856. *The Works of John Adams.* Boston: Little, Brown and Company.

Addison, Joseph. 1856. *The Works of the Right Honourable Joseph Addison: Poems on Several Occasions.* London: Henry G. Bohn.

Allen, Brooke. 2006. *Moral Minority: Our Skeptical Founding Fathers.* Chicago: Ivan R. Dee.

Anderson, Bernard, and Isabel Sawhill. 1980. *Youth Employment and Public Policy.* Englewood Cliffs: Prentice-Hall.

Andrews, Robert, ed. 1997. *Famous Lines: A Columbia Dictionary of Familiar Quotations.* New York: Columbia University Press.

Bagehot, Walter. 1916. *Physics and Politics.* New York: D. Appleton and Company.

Bailey, Andrew, ed. 2011. *First Philosophy, Second Edition: Fundamental Problems and Readings in Philosophy.* Toronto: Broadview Press.

Balkin, Jack M. 2011. *Living Originalism.* Cambridge: The Belknap Press of Harvard University Press.

Banfield, Edward C. 1991. *Here the People Rule: Selected Essays.* Washington, DC: The AEI Press.

Barnes, Albert. 1853. *Notes on the Book of Job.* New York: Leavitt & Allen.

Barnett, Randy E. 2009. "Is the Constitution Libertarian?" Georgetown University Law Center. https://scholarship.law.georgetown.edu/cgi/viewcontent.cgi?article=1839&context=facpub.

———. 2016. *Our Republican Constitution: Securing the Liberty and Sovereignty of We the People.* HarperCollins.

———. 1998. *The Structure of Liberty: Justice and the Rule of Law.* Oxford: Oxford University Press.

Barone, Michael. 1990. *Our Country: The Shaping of America from Roosevelt to Reagan*. New York: The Free Press.

———. 2010. "The Enduring Character of Democrats and Republicans in Times of Political Change." *The American*. October 16. http://www.aei.org/publication/the-enduring-character-of-democrats-and-republicans-in-times-of-political-change/.

Bates, Katharine. 1893. "America the Beautiful." Hymnary.org. https://hymnary.org/text/o_beautiful_for_spacious_skies.

Bell, Daniel. 1972. "On Meritocracy and Equality." *National Affairs* 29–68. https://www.nationalaffairs.com/storage/app/uploads/public/58e/1a4/b60/58e1a4b603517781616817.pdf.

———. 1980. *Sociological Journeys: Essays 1960-1980*. London: Pearson Education.

Bellow, Saul. 1971. *Mr. Sammler's Planet*. New York: Fawcett Crest.

Berlin, Isaiah. 2013. *Against the Current: Essays in the History of Ideas*. Princeton: Princeton University Press.

———. 2013. *The Crooked Timber of Humanity*. Princeton: Princeton University Press.

Berns, Walter. 2001. *Making Patriots*. Chicago: The University of Chicago Press.

Bernstein, David. 2014. "Flashback: Barack Obama on the 'Biggest Problems We're Facing.'" *Washington Post*, November 21. https://www.washingtonpost.com/news/volokh-conspiracy/wp/2014/11/21/flashback-barack-obama-on-the-biggest-problems-were-facing/?utm_term=.ea3e40a1f2c3.

Bernstein, David E. 2011. *Rehabilitating Lochner: Defending Individual Rights Against Progressive Reform*. Chicago: The University of Chicago Press.

2003. *Bhagavad Gita*. London: Penguin Books.

Bickel, Alexander. 1975. *The Morality of Consent*. New Haven: Yale University Press.

Bickel, Alexander M. 1986. *The Least Dangerous Branch: The Supreme Court at the Bar of Politics*. New Haven: Yale University Press.

Blackstone, William. 1827. *Commentaries on the Laws of England, Volume 2*. New York: E. Duyckinck, et al.

Blair, Tony. 2011. *A Journey: My Political Life*. Canada: Vintage Canada.

———. 2004. *Tony Blair in His Own Words*. Politico's Publishing.

Blake, Aaron. 2016. "The Final Trump-Clinton Debate Transcript." *Washington Post*. October 19. https://www.washingtonpost.com/news/the-fix/wp/2016/10/19/the-final-trump-clinton-debate-transcript-annotated/?utm_term=.454453576604.

Bluhm, William. 1978. *Theories of the Political System: Classics of Political Thought and Modern Political Analysis*. Prentice-Hall.

Blum, John. 1962. *Woodrow Wilson and the Politics of Morality*. Boston: Little, Brown and Company.

Blum, Walter J., and Harry Kalven Jr. 1952. "The Uneasy Case for Progressive Taxation." *The University of Chicago Law Review* 19 (3): 417–520. https://chicagounbound.uchicago.edu/cgi/viewcontent.cgi?article=2722&context=uclrev.

Boaz, David. 2015. *The Libertarian Mind*. New York: Simon & Schuster.

Boller, Paul. 2004. *Presidential Campaigns: From George Washington to George W. Bush*. Oxford: Oxford University Press.

Boorstin, Daniel J. 1953. *The Genius of American Politics*. Chicago: University of Chicago Press.

Boot, Max. 2018. *The Road Not Taken*. New York: Liveright Publishing Corporation.

———. 2002. *The Savage Wars of Peace: Small Wars and the Rise of American Power*. New York: Basic Books.

Bork, Robert. 1991. *The Tempting of America: The Political Seduction of the Law*. New York: Simon & Schuster.

Boudreaux, Don. 2016. "Most Ordinary Americans in 2016 Are Richer Than Was John D. Rockefeller in 1916." Cafe Hayek. February 20. https://cafehayek.com/2016/02/40405.html.

Bradford, William. 1912. *History of Plymouth Plantation, 1620–1647*. Boston: Houghton Mifflin Company.

1862. "Brady's Photographs." *The New York Times*. October 20. https://www.nytimes.com/1862/10/20/archives/bradys-photographs-pictures-of-the-dead-at-antietam.html.

Brandeis, Louis D. 1978. *Letters of Louis D. Brandeis: Volume V, 1921–1941: Elder Statesman*. New York: State University of New York Press.

Brands, H. W. 2003. *Woodrow Wilson*. New York: Times Books.

Breyer, Stephen. 2010. *Making Our Democracy Work: A Judge's View*. New York: Vintage Books.

Brinkley, Alan, and Davis Dyer. 2004. *The American Presidency*. Boston: Houghton Mifflin Company.

Brodie, Bernard, and Fawn Brodie. 1973. *From Crossbow to H-Bomb*. Bloomington: Indiana University Press.

Brooke, Rupert. 2018. *1914 and Other Poems*. Boston: Squid Ink Classics.

Buchanan, Patrick. 2007. *Day of Reckoning: How Hubris, Ideology, and Greed Are Tearing America Apart*. New York: Thomas Dunne Books.

Buchanan, Patrick J. 2008. *Churchill, Hitler, and "The Unnecessary War": How Britain Lost Its Empire and the West Lost the World*. New York: Crown Publishers.

———. 2007. "The Good Neocon." *The American Conservative*. May 7. https://www.theamericanconservative.com/articles/the-good-neocon/.

Bullock, Allan. 1993. *Hitler and Stalin: Parallel Lives*. New York: First Vintage Books Edition.

Burke, Edmund. 1903. *The Works of Edmund Burke, Volume 3*. London: George Bell and Sons.

———. 1839. *The Works of Edmund Burke, Volume 4*. Boston: Freeman and Bolles Printers.

Bush, George W. 2002. "Commencement Address at the United States Military Academy in West Point." The American Presidency Project. June 1. http://www.presidency.ucsb.edu/ws/index.php?pid=62730.

———. 2005. "Inaugural Address." The American Presidency Project. January 20. http://www.presidency.ucsb.edu/ws/index.php?pid=58745.

———. 2003. "Remarks at the American Enterprise Institute Dinner." The American Presidency Project. February 26. http://www.presidency.ucsb.edu/ws/index.php?pid=62953.

———. 2004. "Remarks in Halifax, Canada." The American Presidency Project. December 1. http://www.presidency.ucsb.edu/ws/?pid=72844.

———. 2003. "Remarks on Labor Day in Richfield, Ohio." The American Presidency Project. September 1. http://www.presidency.ucsb.edu/ws/?pid=63752.

———. 2003. "Remarks on the 20th Anniversary of the National Endowment for Democracy." The American Presidency Project. November 6. http://www.presidency.ucsb.edu/ws/index.php?pid=844.

———. 2005. "Remarks on the War on Terror." The American Presidency Project. March 8. http://www.presidency.ucsb.edu/ws/index.php?pid=64430.

———. 2004. "The President's News Conference." The American Presidency Project. April 13. http://www.presidency.ucsb.edu/ws/index.php?pid=62604.

Carter, Jimmy. 1977. "Address to the Nation on Energy." The American Presidency Project. April 18. http://www.presidency.ucsb.edu/ws/?pid=7369.

Cather, Willa. 2016. *The First Willa Cather MEGAPACK*. Wildside Press.

Ceaser, James. 2008. "The Presidential Nomination Mess." *Claremont Review of Books*. Vol. VIII, Number 4. Fall. https://protect-us.mimecast.com/s/bC6YCgJDQJCqLAkQTNmar3?domain=claremont.org.

Cervantes, Miguel de. 1895. *The Ingenious Gentleman Don Quixote of La Mancha*. London: Adam and Charles Black.

Chernow, Ron. 2010. *Washington: A Life*. New York: Penguin Books.

Clark, Kenneth. 1987. *Civilisation: A Personal View*. Penguin Books.

Clarke, Desmond, and Catherine Wilson. 2011. *The Oxford Handbook of Philosophy in Early Modern Europe*. Oxford: Oxford University Press.

Cleva, Gregory. 1989. *Henry Kissinger and the American Approach to Foreign Policy*. Lewisburg: Bucknell University Press.

Cloward, Richard, and Frances Piven. 1979. "The Welfare Vaudevillian." *The Nation*, September 22: 236–239.

Cochrane, John. 2017. "Russ Roberts on Economic Humility." The Grumpy Economist. March 3. https://johnhcochrane.blogspot.com/2017/03/russ-roberts-on-economic-humility.html.

———. 2014. "Why and How We Care about Inequality." The Grumpy Economist. September 29. https://johnhcochrane.blogspot.com/2014/09/why-and-how-we-care-about-inequality.html.

Cohen, Ronen, ed. 2015. *Identities in Crisis in Iran: Politics, Culture, and Religion*. Lanham: Lexington Books.

Cohens v. Virginia. 1821. 19 U.S. 264 (Supreme Court of the United States, March 4).

Coleman, James. 1966. "Equality of Educational Opportunity." Education Resources Information Center. https://files.eric.ed.gov/fulltext/ED012275.pdf.

1877. *Collections of the Massachusetts Historical Society*. Boston.

Combs, James, and Dan Nimmo. 1996. *The Comedy of Democracy*. Westport: Praeger.

Committee on the Judiciary. 2010. "The Nomination of Elena Kagan to be an Associate Justice of the Supreme Court of the United States." https://www.judiciary.senate.gov/meetings/the-nomination-of-elena-kagan-to-be-an-associate-justice-of-the-supreme-court-of-the-united-states.

1790. *The Congressional Register, Vol. II*. New York: Hodge, Allen, and Campbell.

Conquest, Robert. 1986. *The Harvest of Sorrow: Soviet Collectivization and the Terror-Famine*. New York: Oxford University Press.

Cooke, Jacob E., ed. 1964. *The Federalist*. Middletown: Wesleyan University Press.

Coolidge, Calvin. 1926. "Address at the Celebration of the 150th Anniversary of the Declaration of Independence in Philadelphia, Pennsylvania." The American Presidency Project. July 5. http://www.presidency.ucsb.edu/ws/?pid=408.

———. 2001. *The Price of Freedom: Speeches and Addresses*. Amsterdam: Fredonia Books.

Cooper, Charles J. 2015. "Confronting the Administrative State." *National Affairs* 96–108. https://www.nationalaffairs.com/publications/detail/confronting-the-administrative-state.

Corwin, Edward S. 1957. *The President: Office and Powers*. New York: New York University Press.

Cost, Jay, and Randy Barnett. 2015. "Fix the Filibuster." *The Weekly Standard*, November 2. https://www.weeklystandard.com/jay-cost-and-randy-e-barnett/fix-the-filibuster.

Cowen, Tyler. 2017. *The Complacent Class: The Self-Defeating Quest for the American Dream*. New York: St. Martin's Press.

Crane, Tim. 2017. *The Meaning of Belief: Religion from an Atheist's Point of View*. Cambridge: Harvard University Press.

Croly, Herbert. 1914. *Progressive Democracy*. New York: The Macmillan Company.

———. 1911. *The Promise of American Life*. New York: The Macmillan Company.

2017. "Cultural Climate Change." The Office of Rabbi Sacks. July 20. http://rabbisacks.org/cultural-climate-change/.

Darwin, Charles. 1993. *The Correspondence of Charles Darwin, Volume 8*. Cambridge: Cambridge University Press.

————. 2008. *The Origin of Species*. New York: A Bantam Book.

Dean, John. 2004. *Warren G. Harding: The American Presidents Series: The 29th President, 1921–1923*. New York: Times Books.

de Gaulle, Charles. 1998. *The Complete War Memoirs of Charles de Gaulle*. New York: Carroll & Graf Publishers.

DeMuth, Christopher. 2018. "Repairing Our Fractured Politics." Hudson Institute. January 11. https://www.hudson.org/research/14106-repairing-our-fractured-politics.

————. 2013. "The Bucks Start Here." Claremont Review of Books, August 26. https://www.claremont.org/crb/article/the-bucks-start-here/.

————. 2012. "The Regulatory State." *National Affairs* 70–91. https://www.nationalaffairs.com/publications/detail/the-regulatory-state.

Department of Transportation v. Association of American Railroads. 2015. 575 U.S. __ (Supreme Court of the United States, March 9).

De Vries, Peter. 2005. *The Blood of the Lamb*. Chicago: University of Chicago Press.

————. 1984. *The Mackerel Plaza: A Novel*. Oxford: Oxford University Press.

Dewey, John. 1897. *My Pedagogic Creed*. New York: E. L. Kellogg & Co.

————. 1935. "The Future of Liberalism." *The Journal of Philosophy* 32 (9): 225–230.

Diamond, Martin. 1976. "The American Idea of Equality: The View from the Founding." *The Review of Politics* 38 (3): 313–331.

Diggins, John. 1989. *The Proud Decades: America in War and in Peace, 1941–1960*. New York: W. W. Norton & Company.

Diggins, John P. 2007. *Ronald Reagan: Fate, Freedom, and the Making of History*. New York: W. W. Norton & Company.

Dinwiddy, J. R. 1992. *Radicalism and Reform in Britain, 1780–1850*. London: The Hambledon Press.

Drehle, David Von. 2003. *Triangle: The Fire that Changed America*. New York: Atlantic Monthly Press.

Duggan, Mike. 2017. Mayor Mike Duggan Keynote Address. May 31. https://www.youtube.com/watch?v=PrPAcQaYISg.

Eberstadt, Nicholas. 2012. *A Nation of Takers: America's Entitlement Epidemic*. West Conshohocken, Pa.: Templeton Press.

————. 2015. "American Exceptionalism and the Entitlement State." *National Affairs* 25–38. https://www.nationalaffairs.com/publications/detail/american-exceptionalism-and-the-entitlement-state.

————. 2016. *Men Without Work: America's Invisible Crisis*. West Conshohocken, Pa.: Templeton Press.

————. 2014. "The Great Society at Fifty." *The Weekly Standard*. May 19. https://www.weeklystandard.com/nicholas-eberstadt/the-great-society-at-fifty.

Ehrenberg, John. 1999. *Civil Society: The Critical History of an Idea*. New York: New York University Press.

Eisenhower, Dwight. 1952. "Religion." Eisenhower Foundation. December 22. https://www.dwightdeisenhower.com/193/Religion.

Eksteins, Modris. 2012. *Rites of Spring: The Great War and the Birth of the Modern Age*. Vintage Canada Edition.

Eliot, T. S. n.d. "Little Gidding." Columbia University. http://www.columbia.edu/itc/history/winter/w3206/edit/tseliotlittlegidding.html.

2011. "Elizabeth Warren on Fair Taxation." YouTube. September 30. https://www.youtube.com/watch?v=60fQCDqXfq0.

Ellis, Geoffrey. 2003. *The Napoleonic Empire*. New York: Palgrave Macmillan.

Ellis, Joseph J. 2015. *The Quartet: Orchestrating the Second American Revolution, 1783–1789*. New York: Alfred A. Knopf.

Emerson, Jason. 2009. *Lincoln the Inventor*. Carbondale: Southern Illinois University Press.

Emerson, Ralph Waldo. 1959. *Emerson: A Modern Anthology*. Boston: Houghton Mifflin Company.

———. 1983. *Essays and Lectures*. New York: The Library of America.

———. 1972. *The Early Lectures of Ralph Waldo Emerson, Volume III*. Cambridge: The Belknap Press.

———. 1900. *The Early Poems of Ralph Waldo Emerson*. New York: A. L. Burt.

2014. "English Translation of Magna Carta." British Library. July 28. https://www.bl.uk/magna-carta/articles/magna-carta-english-translation.

1971. "Environmental Housing and Life Styles." Education Resources Information Center. https://files.eric.ed.gov/fulltext/ED097480.pdf.

Epstein, Richard A. 2003. "Beware of Legal Transitions: A Presumptive Vote for the Reliance Interest." *Journal of Contemporary Legal Issues* 69–91. https://chicagounbound.uchicago.edu/cgi/viewcontent.cgi?referer=https://www.google.com/&httpsredir=1&article=2395&context=journal_articles.

Erler, Edward. 2013. *The American Polity: Essays on the Theory and Practice of Constitutional Government*. New York: Routledge.

Fadiman, Clifton, ed. 1997. *The Little, Brown Book of Anecdotes*. Boston: Little, Brown and Company.

Fadiman, Clifton, and Andre Bernard. 2000. *Bartlett's Book of Anecdotes*. Boston: Little, Brown and Company.

Farnsworth, Ward. 2016. *Farnsworth's Classical English Metaphor*. Jaffrey: David R. Godine.

Feldman, Noah. 2010. *Scorpions: The Battles and Triumphs of FDR's Great Supreme Court Justices*. New York: Grand Central Publishing.

———. 2017. *The Three Lives of James Madison: Genius, Partisan, President*. New York: Random House.

Fest, Joachim. 1974. *Hitler*. Orlando: Harcourt, Inc.

Feynman, Richard. 1988. *The Character of Physical Law*. Cambridge: The MIT Press.

Fischer, David. 2005. *Liberty and Freedom: A Visual History of America's Founding Ideas*. Oxford: Oxford University Press.

Fisher, Matthew. 2015. "Searching for Explanations: How the Internet Inflates Estimates of Internal Knowledge." *Journal of Experimental Psychology* 674–687. https://www.apa.org/pubs/journals/releases/xge-0000070.pdf.

Fitzgerald, F. Scott. 2004. *The Great Gatsby*. New York: Scribner.

Fletcher v. Peck. 1810. 10 U.S. 87 (Supreme Court of the United States, March 16).

Fogel, Robert. 2000. *The Fourth Great Awakening and the Future of Egalitarianism*. Chicago: University of Chicago Press.

Foner, Eric. 2015. *A Short History of Reconstruction*. New York: HarperCollins.

Forman, Samuel. 1922. *Our Republic: A Brief History of the American People*. New York: The Century Co.

Foss, Sam Walter. 1895. *Whiffs from Wild Meadows*. Boston: Lothrop, Lee & Shepard Co.

Frady, Marshall. 1975. *Wallace: The Classic Portrait of Alabama Governor George Wallace*. New York: Random House.

Frankfurt, Harry. 2015. *On Inequality*. Princeton: Princeton University Press.

Franklin, Benjamin. 2015. *The Autobiography of Benjamin Franklin*. South Kingstown: Millennium Publications.

Freedman, Diane, ed. 1995. *Millay at 100: A Critical Reappraisal.* Carbondale: Southern Illinois University Press.

Freud, Sigmund. 2012. *The Future of an Illusion.* Buffalo: Broadview Press.

Frost, Robert. 1979. *The Poetry of Robert Frost: The Collected Poems.* New York: Henry Holt and Company.

Fukuyama, Francis. 2014. *Political Order and Political Decay: From the Industrial Revolution to the Globalization of Democracy.* New York: Farrar, Straus and Giroux.

———. 2006. *The End of History and the Last Man.* New York: Free Press.

———. 2011. *The Origins of Political Order: From Prehuman Times to the French Revolution.* New York: Farrar, Straus and Giroux.

Galbraith, John Kenneth. 1998. *The Affluent Society.* Boston: Houghton Mifflin Company.

———. 2007. *The New Industrial State.* Princeton: Princeton University Press.

Gibbon, Edward. 1905. *The History of the Decline and Fall of the Roman Empire.* New York: Harper & Brothers Publishers.

Gitlow v. New York. 1925. 268 U.S. 652 (Supreme Court of the United States, June 7).

Goldfarb, Zachary A. 2013. "Obama Administration Pushes Banks to Make Home Loans to People with Weaker Credit." *Washington Post,* April 2. https://www.washingtonpost.com/business/economy/obama-administration-pushes-banks-to-make-home-loans-to-people-with-weaker-credit/2013/04/02/a8b4370c-9aef-11e2-a941-a19bce7af755_story.html?utm_term=.e60a8a2aca57.

Goldhagen, Daniel. 1997. *Hitler's Willing Executioners: Ordinary Germans and the Holocaust.* New York: First Vintage Books Edition.

Goldwater, Barry. 1988. *Goldwater.* New York: Doubleday.

Gorbachev, Mikhail. 1988. "Text of Gorbachev's Speech to the United Nations." AP News. December 8. https://www.apnews.com/1abea48aacda1a9dd520c380a8bc6be6.

Gordon, John Steele. 2014. "The Little Miracle Spurring Inequality." *Wall Street Journal.* June 2. https://www.wsj.com/articles/john-steele-gordon-the-little-miracle-spurring-inequality-1401751381.

Gottlieb, Anthony. 2016. *The Dream of Reason: A History of Western Philosophy from the Greeks to the Renaissance.* New York: W. W. Norton & Company.

Graham, Helen. 2005. *The Spanish Civil War: A Very Short Introduction.* Oxford: Oxford University Press.

Green, Mark. 1982. *Winning Back America.* New York: Bantam Books.

Greenblatt, Stephen. 2011. *The Swerve: How the World Became Modern.* New York: W. W. Norton & Company.

Greene, Graham. 1996. *The Quiet American.* New York: Penguin Group.

Greenhouse, Steven. 1995. "Conflict in the Balkans." *The New York Times.* May 31. https://www.nytimes.com/1995/05/31/world/conflict-balkans-europe-us-nato-demand-quick-release-hostages.html.

Gregg, Gary. 1997. *The Presidential Republic: Executive Representation and Deliberative Democracy.* Lanham: Rowman & Littlefield Publishers.

Gutierrez-Brizuela v. Lynch. 2016. 14-9585 (United States 10th Circuit Court of Appeals, August 23).

Hakim, Joy. 2006. *War, Peace, and All that Jazz: 1918–1945.* Oxford: Oxford University Press.

Halberstam, David. 1992. *The Best and the Brightest.* New York: Ballantine Books.

Hale, William Bayard. 1912. *Woodrow Wilson: The Story of His Life.* Garden City: Doubleday, Page & Company.

Hamilton, Alexander. 1791. "Alexander Hamilton's Final Version of the Report on the Subject of Manufactures, [5 December 1791]." National Archives Founders Online. December 5. https://founders.archives.gov/documents/Hamilton/01-10-02-0001-0007.

———. 1786. "Annapolis Convention. Address of the Annapolis Convention, [14 September 1786]." National Archives Founders Online. September 14. https://founders.archives.gov/documents/Hamilton/01-03-02-0556.

———. 1775. "The Farmer Refuted, &c., [23 February] 1775." National Archives Founders Online. February 23. https://founders.archives.gov/documents/Hamilton/01-01-02-0057.

Hamilton, John. 1879. *Life of Alexander Hamilton: A History of the Republic, Volume VII.* Boston: Houghton, Osgood and Company.

Hamilton, Neil. 2010. *Presidents: A Biographical Dictionary.* New York: Facts on File.

Hammett, Dashiell. 1992. *The Continental Op.* New York: Random House.

Handlin, Oscar, and Mary Handlin. 1966. *The Popular Sources of Political Authority: Documents on the Massachusetts Constitution of 1780.* Cambridge: Belknap Press of Harvard University Press.

Hanushek, Eric A. 1989. "The Impact of Differential Expenditures on School Performance." *Educational Researcher* 18 (4): 45–62.

Harlan, David. 1997. *The Degradation of American History.* Chicago: The University of Chicago Press.

Harrison, Antony. 209. *The Cultural Production of Matthew Arnold.* Athens: Ohio University Press.

Hartz, Louis. 1991. *The Liberal Tradition in America.* New York: Harcourt Books.

Hawley, Joshua. 2008. *Theodore Roosevelt: Preacher of Righteousness.* New Haven: Yale University Press.

Hawthorne, Nathaniel. 1894. *The Blithedale Romance.* Boston: Houghton, Mifflin and Company.

Hayek, Friedrich. 1988. *The Fatal Conceit: The Errors of Socialism.* New York: Routledge.

———. 1945. "The Use of Knowledge in Society." *The American Economic Review* 519–530.

Hayek, Friedrich A. 2011. *The Constitution of Liberty: The Definitive Edition.* Chicago: The University of Chicago Press.

———. 1974. "The Pretence of Knowledge." The Nobel Prize. December 11. https://www.nobelprize.org/prizes/economics/1974/hayek/lecture/.

———. 2007. *The Road to Serfdom: Text and Documents—The Definitive Edition.* Chicago: The University of Chicago Press.

Hayward, Steven. 2004. "Reagan Casts Big Shadow with Achievements." American Enterprise Institute. June 12. http://www.aei.org/publication/reagan-casts-big-shadow-with-achievements/.

———. 2001. *The Age of Reagan: The Fall of the Old Liberal Order, 1964–1980.* New York: Three Rivers Press.

Hayward, Steven F. 2017. *Patriotism Is Not Enough.* New York: Encounter Books.

Healy, Gene. 2009. *The Cult of the Presidency: America's Dangerous Devotion to Executive Power.* Washington, DC: Cato Institute.

Hegel, Georg. 2003. *Hegel: Elements of the Philosophy of Right.* Cambridge: Cambridge University Press.

Heidler, David S., and Jeanne T. Heidler. 2015. *Washington's Circle: The Creation of the President.* New York: Random House.

Hemingway, Ernest. 1961. *The Snows of Kilimanjaro and Other Stories.* New York: Scribner.

Henley, William Ernest. 1893. *A Book of Verses.* London: David Nutt.

Himmelfarb, Gertrude. 2001. *One Nation, Two Cultures.* New York: Vintage Books.

———. 2006. *The Moral Imagination: From Edmund Burke to Lionel Trilling.* Chicago: Ivan R. Dee.

———. 1995. *Victorian Minds: A Study of Intellectuals in Crisis and Ideologies in Transition.* Chicago: Ivan R. Dee.

Hirsch, Fred. 1976. *Social Limits to Growth.* Cambridge: Harvard University Press.

Hobbes, Thomas. 2017. *Leviathan.* Dumfries & Galloway: Anodos Books.

Hodgson, Godfrey. 2005. *America in Our Time: From World War II to Nixon—What Happened and Why.* Princeton: Princeton University Press.

———. 2000. *The Gentleman from New York.* Boston: Houghton Mifflin Company.

Holmes, Oliver Wendell. 1920. *Collected Legal Papers.* New York: Harcourt, Brace and Company.

———. 2009. *The Path of the Law.* The Floating Press.

Holmes, Oliver Wendell, and Felix Frankfurter. 1996. *Holmes and Frankfurter: Their Correspondence, 1912–1934.* Hanover: University Press of New England.

Holmes, Oliver Wendell, and Harold J. Laski. 1953. *Holmes-Laski Letters: The Correspondence of Mr. Justice Holmes and Harold J. Laski.* Vol. II. Cambridge: Harvard University Press.

———. 1953. *Holmes-Laski Letters: The Correspondence of Mr. Justice Holmes and Harold J. Laski.* Vol. I. Cambridge: Harvard University Press.

Holowchak, M. Andrew, ed. 2014. *Thomas Jefferson and Philosophy: Essays on the Philosophical Cast of Jefferson's Writings.* Lanham: Lexington Books.

Holzer, Henry. 2012. *The Supreme Court Opinions of Clarence Thomas, 1991–2011.* Jefferson: McFarland & Company.

1991. "House of Representatives." Government Publishing Office. March 14. https://www.gpo.gov/fdsys/pkg/GPO-CRECB-1991-pt5/pdf/GPO-CRECB-1991-pt5-2-2.pdf.

Hubbard, Glenn, and Tim Kane. 2018. "Regaining America's Balance." *National Affairs* 27–39. https://www.nationalaffairs.com/publications/detail/regaining-americas-balance.

Hughes, H. Stuart. 2017. *Consciousness and Society.* New York: Routledge.

Hume, David. 1817. *A Treatise of Human Nature.* London: Thomas & Joseph Allman.

Hutchinson, John, and Anthony D. Smith. 1994. *Nationalism.* Oxford: Oxford University Press.

Jackson, Andrew. 1832. "Veto Message." The Avalon Project. July 10. http://avalon.law.yale.edu/19th_century/ajveto01.asp.

Jackson, Robert H. 1953. "The Task of Maintaining Our Liberties: The Role of the Judiciary." *ABA Journal* 961–965.

James, Henry. 1980. *Letters, Volume 3.* Cambridge: The Belknap Press.

James, William. 1912. *Memories and Studies.* New York: Longmans, Green and Co.

———. 1911. *The Varieties of Religious Experience.* New York: Longmans, Green and Co.

Jefferson, Thomas. 1801. "First Inaugural Address." The Avalon Project. March 4. http://avalon.law.yale.edu/19th_century/jefinau1.asp.

———. 1800. "From Thomas Jefferson to Benjamin Rush, 23 September 1800." National Archives Founders Online. September 23. https://founders.archives.gov/documents/Jefferson/01-32-02-0102.

———. 1787. "From Thomas Jefferson to James Madison, 20 December 1787." National Archives Founders Online. December 20. https://founders.archives.gov/documents/Jefferson/01-12-02-0454.

———. 1802. "From Thomas Jefferson to Joseph Priestley, 19 June 1802." National Archives Founders Online. June 19. https://founders.archives.gov/documents/Jefferson/01-37-02-0515.

———. 1829. *Memoir, Correspondence, and Miscellanies: From the Papers of Thomas Jefferson.* Charlottesville: F. Carr, and Co.

———. 1900. *The Jeffersonian Cyclopedia: A Comprehensive Collection of the Views of Thomas Jefferson*. New York: Funk & Wagnalls Company.

———. 1884. *The Works of Thomas Jefferson: Published by Order of Congress from the Original Manuscripts Deposited in the Department of State*. Vol. 7. New York: Townsend.

———. 2011. *The Writings of Thomas Jefferson, Volume 8*. Cambridge: Cambridge University Press.

———. 1893. *The Writings of Thomas Jefferson, Volume II*. New York: G. P. Putnam's Sons.

———. 1898. *The Writings of Thomas Jefferson: 1807–1815, Volume IX*. New York: G. P. Putnam's Sons.

———. 1899. *The Writings of Thomas Jefferson: 1816–1826, Volume X*. New York: G. P. Putnam's Sons.

———. 1813. "Thomas Jefferson to John Adams." *The Founders' Constitution*. October 28. http://press-pubs.uchicago.edu/founders/documents/v1ch15s61.html.

———. 1813. "Thomas Jefferson to John Adams, 12 October 1813." National Archives Founders Online. October 12. https://founders.archives.gov/documents/Jefferson/03-06-02-0431.

———. 1826. "Thomas Jefferson to Roger Weightman." Library of Congress. June 24. https://www.loc.gov/exhibits/jefferson/214.html.

———. 1904. *Thomas Jefferson: The Declaration of Independence and Letters, Addresses, Excerpts and Aphorisms*. St. Louis.

———. 2011. *Thomas Jefferson: Writings*. New York: The Library of America.

Johnson, Lyndon. 1965. "Address at Johns Hopkins University: 'Peace Without Conquest.'" The American Presidency Project. April 7. http://www.presidency.ucsb.edu/ws/?pid=26877.

———. 1964. "Annual Message to the Congress on the State of the Union." The American Presidency Project. January 8. http://www.presidency.ucsb.edu/ws/?pid=26787.

———. 1966. "Annual Message to the Congress on the State of the Union." The American Presidency Project. January 12. http://www.presidency.ucsb.edu/ws/index.php?pid=28015.

———. 1965. "Commencement Address at Howard University." The American Presidency Project. June 4. http://www.presidency.ucsb.edu/ws/?pid=27021.

———. 1964. "Remarks Before the National Convention Upon Accepting the Nomination." The American Presidency Project. August 27. http://www.presidency.ucsb.edu/ws/index.php?pid=26467.

Johnson, Lyndon B. 1964. "Remarks at the University of Michigan." The American Presidency Project. May 22. http://www.presidency.ucsb.edu/ws/?pid=26262.

Jones, Gareth. 2016. *Karl Marx: Greatness and Illusion*. Cambridge: Belknap Press of Harvard University Press.

Jones, Richard. 2013. *The Black Book: Wittgenstein and Race*. Lanham: University Press of America.

Judis, John. 2004. *The Folly of Empire: What George W. Bush Could Learn from Theodore Roosevelt and Woodrow Wilson*. New York: Scribner.

Kagan, Donald. 1996. *On the Origins of War: And the Preservation of Peace*. New York: Anchor Books.

Kaku, Michio. 2005. *Einstein's Cosmos: How Albert Einstein's Vision Transformed Our Understanding of Space and Time*. New York: W. W. Norton & Company.

Kass, Leon. 2017. *Leading a Worthy Life: Finding Meaning in Modern Times*. New York: Encounter Books.

Keller, Morton. 2007. *America's Three Regimes: A New Political History*. New York: Oxford University Press.

Kennedy, John F. 1960. "Address of Senator John F. Kennedy Accepting the Democratic

Party Nomination for the Presidency of the United States—Memorial Coliseum, Los Angeles." The American Presidency Project. July 15. http://www.presidency.ucsb.edu/ws/index.php?pid=25966.

———. 1962. "Annual Message to the Congress on the State of the Union." The American Presidency Project. January 11. http://www.presidency.ucsb.edu/ws/?pid=9082.

———. 1962. "Commencement Address at Yale University." The American Presidency Project. June 11. http://www.presidency.ucsb.edu/ws/?pid=29661.

———. 1961. "Inaugural Address." The American Presidency Project. January 20. http://www.presidency.ucsb.edu/ws/index.php?pid=8032.

———. 1960. "Remarks of Senator John F. Kennedy, Municipal Auditorium, Canton, Ohio." The American Presidency Project. September 27. http://www.presidency.ucsb.edu/ws/?pid=74231.

Kesler, Charles R., and John B. Kienker. 2012. *Life, Liberty, and the Pursuit of Happiness: Ten Years of the Claremont Review of Books*. Lanham, Md.: Rowman & Littlefield Publishers.

Kirby, William, and William Spence. 1828. *An Introduction to Entomology*. London: Longman, Rees, Orme, Brown, and Green.

Kirk, Russell. 2014. *The Essential Russell Kirk: Selected Essays*. Wilmington: Intercollegiate Studies Insitute.

Kissinger, Henry. 2014. *World Order*. New York: Penguin Books.

Knox, Ronald. 2000. *The Belief of Catholics*. San Francisco: Ignatius Press.

Koestler, Arthur. 1967. *The Ghost in the Machine*. London: Hutchinson & Co.

Kosar, Kevin. 2015. "How to Strengthen Congress." *National Affairs* 48–61. https://www.nationalaffairs.com/publications/detail/how-to-strengthen-congress.

Krames, Jeffrey. 2003. *The Rumsfeld Way*. New York: McGraw-Hill.

Krauthammer, Charles. 2008. "The Audacity of Vanity." *Washington Post*, July 18. http://www.washingtonpost.com/wp-dyn/content/article/2008/07/17/AR2008071701839.html.

Kristol, Irving. 1995. *Neoconservatism: The Autobiography of an Idea*. New York: The Free Press.

———. 2013. *The Neoconservative Persuasion*. Philadelphia: Basic Books.

———. 1952. "The Rise of Totalitarian Democracy, by J. L. Talmon." *Commentary Magazine*. September 1. https://www.commentarymagazine.com/articles/the-rise-of-totalitarian-democracy-by-j-l-talmon/.

Larkin, Philip. 2015. *High Windows*. London: Faber & Faber.

Larson, Edward J. 2014. *The Return of George Washington: Uniting the States, 1783–1789*. New York: HarperCollins.

Lawson, Gary. 1994. "The Rise and Rise of the Administrative State." *Harvard Law Review* 107 (6): 1231–1254.

Lee, Mike. 2016. *Our Lost Consitution*. New York: Penguin Random House.

Lefever, Ernest. 1999. *America's Imperial Burden: Is the Past Prologue?* Boulder, Co.: Westview Press.

Lehman, David, ed. 2006. *The Oxford Book of American Poetry*. Oxford: Oxford University Press.

Leonard, Thomas. 2016. *Illiberal Reformers: Race, Eugenics, and the American Economics in the Progressive Era*. Princeton: Princeton University Press.

Leuchtenburg, William E. 1995. *The Supreme Court Reborn: The Constitutional Revolution in the Age of Roosevelt*. New York: Oxford University Press.

Levin, Yuval. 2016. "Edmund Burke's Economics of Flourishing." American Enterprise Institute. http://www.aei.org/spotlight/human-flourishing-burke/.

———. 2014. *The Great Debate: Edmund Burke, Thomas Paine, and the Birth of Right and Left*. New York: Basic Books.

Levine, George, et al. 1989. "Speaking for the Humanities." American Council of Learned Societies. http://archives.acls.org/op/7_Speaking_for_Humanities.htm.

Lewis, Sinclair. 1920. *Main Street*. New York: P. F. Collier & Son.

Lincoln, Abraham. 1989. *Abraham Lincoln: Speeches and Writings Vol. 2 1859–1865*. New York: The Library of America.

———. 1863. "Address at the Dedication of the National Cemetery at Gettysburg, Pennsylvania." The American Presidency Project. November 19. http://www.presidency.ucsb.edu/ws/?pid=73959.

———. 1861. "First Annual Message." The American Presidency Project. December 3. http://www.presidency.ucsb.edu/ws/?pid=29502.

———. 1861. "Fragment on the Constitution and the Union." Collected Works of Abraham Lincoln. January. https://quod.lib.umich.edu/l/lincoln/lincoln4/1:264.1?rgn=div2;view=fulltext.

———. 1991. *Great Speeches*. Mineola: Dover Publications.

———. 1861. "Inaugural Address." The American Presidency Project. March 4. http://www.presidency.ucsb.edu/ws/index.php?pid=25818.

———. 1914. *Lincoln Addresses and Letters*. New York: American Book Company.

———. 1989. *Lincoln: Speeches and Writings: 1859–1865*. New York: The Library of America.

———. 1989. *Speeches and Writings 1832–1858: Speeches, Letters, and Miscellaneous Writings: The Lincoln-Douglas Debates, Volume 1*. New York: The Library of America.

———. 1865. *The Writings of Abraham Lincoln: Volume 7*. New York: P. F. Collier & Son.

Lindsey, Brink. 2008. *The Age of Abundance: How Prosperity Transformed America's Politics and Culture*. New York: HarperCollins.

Lippmann, Walter. 1914. *Drift and Mastery: An Attempt to Diagnose the Current Unrest*. New York: Mitchell Kennerley.

———. 1915. *The Stakes of Diplomacy*. New York: Henry Holt and Company.

Lipset, Seymour Martin. 1997. *American Exceptionalism: A Double-Edged Sword*. New York: W. W. Norton & Company.

Lochner v. New York. 1905. 198 U.S. 45 (Supreme Court of the United States, April 16).

Locke, John. 1753. *An Essay Concerning Human Understanding*. London.

———. 1689. "Second Treatise." *The Founders' Constitution*. http://press-pubs.uchicago.edu/founders/documents/v1ch17s5.html.

———. 1801. *The Conduct of the Understanding*. London: William Baynes.

———. 1821. *Two Treatises on Government*. London: Whitmore & Fenn.

Lomborg, Bjorn. 2012. "Environmental Alarmism, Then and Now." *Foreign Affairs*. July. https://www.foreignaffairs.com/articles/2012-07-01/environmental-alarmism-then-and-now.

Lorenz, Konrad. 2005. *On Aggression*. London: Taylor and Francis.

2010. "Louisiana Caskets." Institute for Justice. https://ij.org/case/saint-joseph-abbey-et-al-v-castille-et-al/.

2004. "Louisiana Florists." Institute for Justice. https://ij.org/case/meadows-v-odom/.

Lukacs, John. 2004. *A New Republic: A History of the United States in the Twentieth Century*. New Haven: Yale University Press.

Lynch v. Donnelly. 1984. 465 U.S. 668 (Supreme Court of the United States, March 4).

MacMillan, Margaret. 2003. *Paris 1919: Six Months That Changed the World*. New York: Random House Trade Paperback.

Madison, James. 1795. "Political Observations, 20 April 1795." National Archives Founders Online. April 20. https://founders.archives.gov/documents/Madison/01-15-02-0423.

———. 1789. "Rights." *The Founders' Constitution*. June 8. http://press-pubs.uchicago.edu/founders/documents/v1ch14s50.html.

———. 1901. *The Writings of James Madison: 1783–1787*. New York: G.P. Putnam's Sons.

Magnet, Myron. 2018. "The Founders' Grandson, Part II." *City Journal*, Winter. https://www.city-journal.org/html/founders-grandson-part-ii-15651.html.

Mann, Mary Tyler Peabody. 1865. *Life of Horace Mann*. Boston: Walker, Fuller and Company.

Mansfield, Harvey C. 1991. *America's Constitutional Soul*. Johns Hopkins University Press.

Marbury v. Madison. 1803. 5 U.S. 137 (Supreme Court of the United States, February 23).

Marlantes, Karl. 2017. "The Bloody Pivot." *The Wall Street Journal*. June 2. https://www.wsj.com/articles/the-bloody-pivot-1496437497.

Marx, Karl. 1982. *Critique of Hegel's "Philosophy of Right."* Cambridge: Cambridge University Press.

Marx, Karl, and Friedrich Engels. 2012. *Das Kapital*. Aristeus Books.

———. 2018. *The Communist Manifesto*. Minneapolis: Lerner Publishing Group.

Maxwell, James Clerk. n.d. "Molecular Evolution." Poetry Foundation. https://www.poetryfoundation.org/poems/45777/molecular-evolution.

McClay, Wilfred M. 2018. "How to Think about Patriotism." *National Affairs* 105–115.

McClintock, Tom. 2017. "How and Why the Senate Must Reform the Filibuster." Imprimis. https://imprimis.hillsdale.edu/wp-content/uploads/2017/01/Imprimis-Senate-Filibuster-Jan-2017.pdf.

McCloskey, Deirdre. 2017. *Bourgeois Equality: How Ideas, Not Capital or Institutions, Enriched the World*. Chicago: University of Chicago Press.

———. 2007. *The Bourgeois Virtues: Ethics for an Age of Commerce*. Chicago: The University of Chicago Press.

———. 2017. "The Myth of Technological Unemployment." *Reason*. August. https://reason.com/archives/2017/07/11/the-myth-of-technological-unem.

McConnell, Michael W. 1995. "Originalism and the Desegregation Decisions." *Virginia Law Review* 81 (4): 947–1140. https://chicagounbound.uchicago.edu/cgi/viewcontent.cgi?article=12624&context=journal_articles.

———. 1995. "The Originalist Justification for Brown: A Reply to Professor Klarman." *Virginia Law Review* 81 (7): 1937–1955. https://chicagounbound.uchicago.edu/cgi/viewcontent.cgi?article=12613&context=journal_articles.

McCullough, David. 2005. *1776*. New York: Simon & Schuster.

McDowell, Gary, and Sharon Noble. 1997. *Reason and Republicanism: Thomas Jefferson's Legacy of Liberty*. Lanham, Md.: Rowman & Littlefield Publishers.

McPherson, James. 2003. *Battle Cry of Freedom: The Civil War Era*. Oxford: Oxford University Press.

McSmith, Andy. 2010. *No Such Thing as Society: A History of Britain in the 1980s*. London: Constable & Robinson.

Meinig, Donald. 1993. *The Shaping of America: A Geographical Perspective on 500 Years of History*. New Haven: Yale University Press.

Meyer, Karl. 2012. *Pax Ethnica: Where and How Diversity Succeeds*. New York: PublicAffairs.

Meyers, Marvin. 1960. *The Jacksonian Persuasion: Politics and Belief.* Stanford: Stanford University Press.

Mill, John Stuart. 1899. *Principles of Political Economy*. New York: The Colonial Press.

Miller, Jeffrey. 1996. *Discovering Molecular Genetics*. Cold Spring Harbor, N.Y.: Cold Spring Harbor Laboratory Press.

Miller, John. 1986. *Norman Angell and the Futility of War: Peace and the Public Mind*. New York: Palgrave Macmillan.

Miller, Marion Mills, ed. 1913. *Great Debates in American History, Vol. II*. New York: Current Literature Publishing Company.

———. *Great Debates in American History, Vol. VI.* New York: Current Literature Publishing Company.

Miller, Perry. 1984. *Errand into the Wilderness.* Cambridge: The Belknap Press of Harvard University Press.

Minersville School District v. Gobitis. 1940. 310 U.S. 586 (Supreme Court of the United States, June 3).

Morison, Samuel. 2001. *The Rising Sun in the Pacific.* Urbana: University of Illinois Press.

Moynihan, Daniel. 1973. *Coping.* New York: Random House.

———. 1980. *Counting Our Blessings: Reflections on the Future of America.* Boston: Atlantic Monthly Press.

———. 1978. "Imperial Government." *Commentary Magazine*, June 1. https://www.commentarymagazine.com/articles/imperial-government/.

———. 1998. *Secrecy: The American Experience.* New Haven: Yale University Press.

2011. "Nashville Limos." Institute for Justice. https://ij.org/case/nashville-limos/.

Nau, Henry. 2015. *Conservative Internationalism: Armed Diplomacy under Jefferson, Polk, Truman and Reagan.* Princeton: Princeton University Press.

Nelson, Craig. 2006. *Thomas Paine: Enlightenment, Revolution, and the Birth of Modern Nations.* New York: Penguin Books.

New York (state). 1825. *The Speeches of the Different Governors to the Legislature of the State of New York.* Albany: J. B. Van Steenberg.

Newman, Roger K., ed. 2009. *The Yale Biographical Dictionary of American Law.* New Haven: Yale University Press.

Nichols, Tom. 2017. *The Death of Expertise: The Campaign against Established Knowledge and Why it Matters.* Oxford: Oxford University Press.

Nisbet, Robert. 1982. *Prejudices: A Philosophical Dictionary.* Cambridge: Harvard University Press.

Niskanen, William A. 2008. *Reflections of a Political Economist: Selected Articles on Government Policies and Political Processes.* Washington, DC: Cato Institute.

Nixon, Richard. 1969. "Inaugural Address." The American Presidency Project. January 20. http://www.presidency.ucsb.edu/ws/?pid=1941.

———. 1971. "Remarks to Midwestern News Media Executives Attending a Briefing on Domestic Policy in Kansas City, Missouri." The American Presidency Project. July 6. http://www.presidency.ucsb.edu/ws/index.php?pid=3069.

Novak, Michael, ed. 2000. *A Free Society Reader: Principles for the New Millennium.* Lanham, Md.: Lexington Books.

Obama, Barack. 2013. "Address Before a Joint Session of Congress on the State of the Union." The American Presidency Project. February 12. http://www.presidency.ucsb.edu/ws/index.php?pid=102826.

———. 2012. "Remarks by the President at a Campaign Event in Roanoke, Virginia." The White House. July 13. https://obamawhitehouse.archives.gov/the-press-office/2012/07/13/remarks-president-campaign-event-roanoke-virginia.

Okun, Arthur. 2015. *Equality and Efficiency: The Big Tradeoff.* Washington, DC: The Brookings Institution.

Olcott, Charles. 1916. *William McKinley: Volume II.* Boston: Houghton Mifflin Company.

Olson, Mancur. 1982. *The Rise and Decline of Nations: Economic Growth, Stagflation, and Social Rigidities.* New Haven, CT: Yale University Press.

Oshisanya, Oshitokunbo. 2016. *An Almanac of Contemporary and Comparative Judicial Restatements .* Ikoyi: Almanac Foundation.

Paine, Thomas. 1984. *Paine: Collected Writings.* New York: The Library of America.

———. 1818. *The Age of Reason, Volume II.* London: R. Carlile.

Passell, Peter, Marc Roberts, and Leonard Ross. 1972. "The Limits to Growth." *The New York Times.* April 2. https://www.nytimes.com/1972/04/02/archives/the-limits-to-growth-a-report-for-the-club-of-romes-project-on-the.html.

Paul II, Pope John. 1982. *Collected Poems.* New York: Random House.

Paul, Ellen Frankel, Fred D. Miller, and Jeffrey Paul. 2012. *Natural Rights Individualism and Progressivism in American Political Philosophy.* Cambridge: Cambridge University Press.

Paul, Joel Richard. 2018. *Without Precedent: Chief Justice John Marshall and His Times.* New York: Riverhead Books.

Perez v. Brownell. 1958. 356 U.S. 44 (Supreme Court of the United States, March 30).

Pestritto, Ronald J. 2005. *Woodrow Wilson and the Roots of Modern Liberalism.* Lanham, Md.: Rowman & Littlefield Publishers.

Polanyi, Karl. 2001. *The Great Transformation: The Political and Economic Origins of Our Time.* Boston: Beacon Press.

Polish National Alliance v. Labor Board. 1944. 322 U.S. 643 (Supreme Court of the United States, June 5).

Postrel, Virginia. 1999. *The Future and Its Enemies: The Growing Conflict over Creativity, Enterprise, and Progress.* New York: Touchstone.

Powers v. Harris. 2004. 03-6014 (United States 10th Circuit Court of Appeals, August 23).

Quammen, David. 2007. *The Reluctant Mr. Darwin: An Intimate Portrait of Charles Darwin and the Making of His Theory of Evolution.* New York: W. W. Norton & Company.

Rasmussen, Dennis. 2017. *The Infidel and the Professor: David Hume, Adam Smith, and the Friendship that Shaped Modern Thought.* Princeton: Princeton University Press.

Ratcliffe, Susan, ed. 2011. *Concise Oxford Dictionary of Quotations.* New York: Oxford University Press.

Rauch, Jonathan. 1999. *Government's End: Why Washington Stopped Working.* New York: PublicAffairs.

Rawls, John. 2003. *A Theory of Justice.* Cambridge: The Belknap Press.

Reagan, Ronald. 1982. "Address to Members of the British Parliament." The American Presidency Project. June 8. http://www.presidency.ucsb.edu/ws/index.php?pid=42614.

———. 1985. "Inaugural Address." The American Presidency Project. January 21. http://www.presidency.ucsb.edu/ws/index.php?pid=38688.

———. 2016. *The Last Best Hope: The Greatest Speeches of Ronald Reagan.* West Palm Beach: Humanix Books.

n.d. "Records of the Federal Convention of 1787." *The Founders' Constitution.* http://press-pubs.uchicago.edu/founders/documents/a2_1_1s4.html.

Rees, Martin. 2001. *Our Cosmic Habitat.* Princeton: Princeton University Press.

Rice, Condoleezza. 2004. "National Security Advisor Dr. Condoleezza Rice Discusses War on Terror at Reagan Library and Museum." The American Presidency Project. February 28. http://www.presidency.ucsb.edu/ws/index.php?pid=80779.

Ridley, Matt. 2015. *The Evolution of Everything: How New Ideas Emerge.* New York: HarperCollins.

Risen, Clay. 2014. *The Bill of the Century: The Epic Battle for the Civil Rights Act.* New York: Bloomsbury Press.

Roberts, Peri, and Peter Sutch. 2012. *Introduction to Political Thought.* Edinburgh: Edinburgh University Press.

Robertson, Connie, ed. 1998. *The Wordsworth Dictionary of Quotations.* Hertfordshire: Wordsworth Editions Ltd.

Robinson v. Crown Cork and Seal Company. 2010. 06-0714 (Supreme Court of Texas, October 22).

Roland, Charles. 1995. *Reflections on Lee: A Historian's Assessment.* Baton Rouge: Louisiana State University Press.

Roosevelt, Franklin. 1938. "Annual Message to Congress." The American Presidency Project. January 3. http://www.presidency.ucsb.edu/ws/index.php?pid=15517.

———. 1932. "Campaign Address on Progressive Government at the Commonwealth Club in San Francisco, California." The American Presidency Project. September 23. http://www.presidency.ucsb.edu/ws/index.php?pid=88391.

———. 1933. "Inaugural Address." The American Presidency Project. March 4. http://www.presidency.ucsb.edu/ws/index.php?pid=14473.

———. 1937. "Inaugural Address." The American Presidency Project. January 20. http://www.presidency.ucsb.edu/ws/?pid=15349.

———. 1932. "Radio Address to the Business and Professional Men's League Throughout the Nation." The American Presidency Project. October 6. http://www.presidency.ucsb.edu/ws/index.php?pid=88394.

———. 1944. "State of the Union Message to Congress." The American Presidency Project. January 11. http://www.presidency.ucsb.edu/ws/index.php?pid=16518.

Roosevelt, Theodore. 1910. "The Radical Movement Under Conservative Direction." Theodore Roosevelt. December 13. http://theodore-roosevelt.com/images/research/txtspeeches/792.pdf.

———. 2009. *The Strenuous Life: Essays and Addresses.* Mineola: Dover Publications.

———. 1897. *The Works of Theodore Roosevelt: American Ideals.* New York: P. F. Collier & Son.

———. 1922. *Theodore Roosevelt: An Autobiography.* New York: Charles Scribner's Sons.

Rousseau, Jean-Jacques. 2016. *The Social Contract.* Sovereign Classics.

Rovere, Richard H. 1963. *The Goldwater Caper.* New York: Harcourt, Brace & World, Inc.

Rustow, Dankwart, and Salvator Attanasio. 1980. *Freedom and Domination: A Historical Critique of Civilization.* Princeton: Princeton University Press.

Ryle, Gilbert. 2000. *The Concept of the Mind.* Chicago: University of Chicago Press.

Sandefur, Timothy. 2018. *Frederick Douglass: Self-Made Man.* Washington, DC: Cato Institute.

Sandler, Stanley. 2003. *The Korean War: No Victors, No Vanquished.* London: UCL Press.

Sasse, Ben. 2015. "Senator Ben Sasse's Maiden Speech." US Senator for Nebraska Ben Sasse. November 5. https://www.sasse.senate.gov/public/index.cfm/2015/11/senator-ben-sasse-s-maiden-speech.

———. 2017. *The Vanishing American Adult: Our Coming-of-Age Crisis—and How to Rebuild a Culture of Self-Reliance.* New York: St. Martin's Press.

Scalia, Antonin. 2017. *Scalia Speaks: Reflections on Law, Faith, and Life Well Lived.* New York: Crown Forum.

Scheidel, Walter. 2017. *The Great Leveler: Violence and the History of Inequality from the Stone Age to the Twenty-First Century.* Princeton: Princeton University Press.

Schmitt, Gary J., Joseph M. Bessette, and Andrew E. Busch. 2017. *The Imperial Presidency and the Constitution.* Lanham, Md.: Rowman & Littlefield.

Schudson, Michael. 1999. *The Good Citizen: A History of American Civic Life.* Cambridge: Harvard University Press.

Schumpeter, Joseph. 2003. *Capitalism, Socialism and Democracy.* London: Taylor & Francis.

Scott, James, ed. 1918. *President Wilson's Foreign Policy: Messages, Addresses, Papers.* New York: Oxford University Press.

Sennett, Richard, and Jonathan Cobb. 1993. *The Hidden Injuries of Class*. New York: W. W. Norton & Company.

Shakespeare, William. n.d. "The Tragedy of Hamlet, Prince of Denmark." *The Complete Works of William Shakespeare*. http://shakespeare.mit.edu/hamlet/full.html.

———. n.d. "The Tragedy of Macbeth." *The Complete Works of William Shakespeare*. http://shakespeare.mit.edu/macbeth/full.html.

Shaw v. Reno. 1993. 509 U.S. 630 (Supreme Court of the United States, June 27).

Shelley, Percy Bysshe. 1907. *The Poetical Works of Percy Bysshe Shelley*. London: Macmillan and Co.

Sidgwick, Henry. 1887. *The Principles of Political Economy*. London: Macmillan and Co.

Siegel, Fred. 2013. *The Revolt Against the Masses: How Liberalism Has Undermined the Middle Class*. New York: Encounter Books.

Silverglate, Harvey. 2011. *Three Felonies a Day: How the Feds Target the Innocent*. New York: Encounter Books.

Smith, Adam. 1850. *An Inquiry Into the Nature and Causes of the Wealth of Nations, Volume 1*. Edinburgh: Adam and Charles Black.

———. 1809. *The Theory of Moral Sentiments*. Glasgow: R. Chapman.

Smith, Jean Edward. 2008. *FDR*. New York: Random House Trade Paperback.

———. 1998. *John Marshall: Definer of a Nation*. New York: First Owl Books.

Somin, Ilya. 2016. *Democracy and Political Ignorance: Why Smaller Government Is Smarter*. Stanford: Stanford University Press.

Souter, David H. 2010. "Text of Justice David Souter's Speech." *The Harvard Gazette*. May 27. https://news.harvard.edu/gazette/story/2010/05/text-of-justice-david-souters-speech/.

Spalding, Matthew. 2009. *We Still Hold These Truths: Rediscovering Our Principles, Reclaiming Our Future*. Wilmington: Intercollegiate Studies Institute.

Spark, Muriel. 1998. *The Girls of Slender Means*. New York: New Directions Publishing.

2014. "Speech Acts." *Stanford Encyclopedia of Philosophy*. October 2. https://plato.stanford.edu/entries/speech-acts/.

Steel, Ronald. 2017. *Walter Lippmann and the American Century*. London: Routledge.

Stegner, Wallace. 1969. *The Sound of Mountain Water*. New York: Doubleday.

Stelzer, Irwin, ed. 2004. *The Neocon Reader*. New York: Grove Press.

Stevens, Richard. 1976. *American Political Thought: The Philosophic Dimension of American Statesmanship*. Kendall Hunt Publishing Company.

Stevenson, Adlai. 1955. *Commencement Address by Adlai Stevenson*. https://www.equityalliancemn.org/uploads/7/4/4/0/74401303/commencemnet_address_by_adliai_stevenson_smith_college.pdf.

Stigler, George J. 1965. "The Intellectual and the Marketplace." *The Kansas Journal of Sociology* 1 (2): 69–77.

Stoppard, Tom. 1975. *Travesties*. New York: Grove Press.

Sumner, William Graham. 2007. *What Social Classes Owe Each Other*. Auburn: Ludwig von Mises Institute.

Swainson, Bill, ed. 2000. *Encarta Book of Quotations*. New York: St. Martin's Press.

Tennyson, Alfred. 1869. *Locksley Hall*. Boston: Ticknor and Fields.

Thomas, Karen, dir. 1997. *The G.I. Bill: The Law That Changed America*. Aired on PBS.

Thompson, Derek. 2016. "America in 1915: Long Hours, Crowded Houses, Death by Trolley." *The Atlantic*. February 11. https://www.theatlantic.com/business/archive/2016/02/america-in-1915/462360/?utm_source=nl__link8_021216.

Thurber, James. 1942. "She Built Up Her Personality but She's Undermined." *Fine Art*

America. March 28. https://fineartamerica.com/featured/she-built-up-her-personality-but-shes-undermined-james-thurber.html.

Tierney, John. 1990. "Betting on the Planet." *The New York Times*. December 2. https://www.nytimes.com/1990/12/02/magazine/betting-on-the-planet.html.

Tocqueville, Alexis de. 2002. *Democracy in America*. Chicago: University of Chicago Press.

———. 1862. *Democracy in America*. London: Longman, Green, Longman and Roberts.

———. 1855. *Democracy in America*. New York: A. S. Barnes & Co.

———. 2002. *Democracy in America*. Translated by Henry Reeve. Washington, DC: Regnery Publishing.

———. 1862. *Democracy in America, Volume 2*. Cambridge: Sever and Francis.

Trevelyan, George M. 1905. *The American Revolution*, Vol. 3. New York: Longmans, Green, and Co., 113.

Trilling, Lionel. 2008. *The Liberal Imagination*. New York: New York Review Books.

Trop v. Dulles. 1958. 356 U.S. 86 (Supreme Court of the United States, March 30).

Tropman, John, Milan Dluhy, Roger Lind, Wayne Vasey, and Tom Croxton. 1978. *Strategic Perspectives on Social Policy*. New York: Pergamon Press.

Trotsky, Leon. 2005. *Literature and Revolution*. Chicago: Haymarket Books.

Truss, Lynne. 2005. *Talk to the Hand: The Utter Bloody Rudeness of the World Today, or Six Good Reasons to Stay Home and Bolt the Door*. New York: Gotham Books.

Tulis, Jeffrey, and Nicole Mellow. 2018. *Legacies of Losing in American Politics*. Chicago: University of Chicago Press.

Turner, Frederick Jackson. 1998. *Rereading Frederick Jackson Turner: "The Significance of the Frontier in American History" and Other Essays*. New Haven: Yale University Press.

Turner, Jonathan, and Alexandra Maryanski. 2016. *On the Origin of Societies by Natural Selection*. New York: Routledge.

Turow, Scott. 1996. *The Laws of Our Fathers*. New York: Farrar, Straus and Giroux.

Twain, Mark. 1885. *Adventures of Huckleberry Finn*. New York: Charles L. Webster and Company.

———. 1971. *Mark Twain's Notebook*. New York: Scholarly Press.

———. 1922. *The Writings of Mark Twain, Volume 7*. New York: Gabriel Wells.

———. 1917. *What Is Man?* New York: Harper & Brothers Publishers.

1946. "Two Hundred and Seventeenth Day." The Avalon Project. September 30. http://avalon.law.yale.edu/imt/09-30-46.asp.

Udehn, Lars. 1996. *The Limits of Public Choice: A Sociological Critique of the Economic Theory of Politics*. New York: Routledge.

United States v. Lopez. 1995. 514 U.S. 549 (Supreme Court of the United States, April 25).

Updike, John. 1996. *A Month of Sundays*. Ballantine Books.

———. 1990. *Rabbit at Rest*. New York: Random House Trade Paperback.

Wallison, Peter. 2016. "Decentralization, Deference, and the Administrative State." *National Affairs* 69–82. https://www.nationalaffairs.com/publications/detail/decentralization-deference-and-the-administrative-state.

Warner, Charles Dudley. 1902. *A Library of the World's Best Literature*. Volume 1. New York: J. A. Hill & Co.

Washington, George. 1783. "Circular to the States." *The Founders' Constitution*. June 8. http://press-pubs.uchicago.edu/founders/documents/v1ch7s5.html.

———. 1789. "Inaugural Address." The American Presidency Project. April 30. http://www.presidency.ucsb.edu/ws/index.php?pid=25800.

———. 1787. "Letter of the President of the Federal Convention, Dated September 17, 1787, to the President of Congress, Transmitting the Constitution." The Avalon Project. September 17. http://avalon.law.yale.edu/18th_century/translet.asp.

———. 1939. *The Writings of George Washington.* Edited by John C. Fitzpatrick. Best Books.

———. 1796. "Washington's Farewell Address 1796." The Avalon Project. http://avalon.law.yale.edu/18th_century/washing.asp.

Webster, Daniel. 1903. *The Writings and Speeches of Daniel Webster.* Boston: Little, Brown & Company.

Weeks, Albert. 2002. *Stalin's Other War: Soviet Grand Strategy, 1939–1941.* Lanham: Rowman & Littlefield Publishers.

Weisman, Steven R., ed. 2010. *Daniel Patrick Moynihan: A Portrait in Letters of an American Visionary.* New York: PublicAffairs.

2017. "Wellesley Statement from CERE Faculty." FIRE. March 20. https://www.thefire.org/subject-facstaffdiscuss-statement-cere-faculty-re-laura-kipnis-freedom-project-visit-aftermath/.

Wenzi, Terence. 2014. *A Conscious Endeavor: A Judeo-Christian Reflection on the Distribution of Wealth.* Eugene, Or.: Wipf and Stock.

West Virginia State Board of Education v. Barnette. 1943. 319 U.S. 624 (Supreme Court of the United States, June 14).

White, Theodore. 2010. *The Making of the President 1964.* New York: HarperCollins Publishers.

Whitehead, Alfred North. 1978. *Process and Reality: An Essay in Cosmology.* New York: The Free Press.

Wickard v. Filburn. 1942. 317 U.S. 111 (Supreme Court of the United States, November 8).

Wilbur, Richard. 2004. *Collected Poems: 1943–2004.* Orlando: Harcourt.

Will, George F. 1992. "Bedeviled by Ethnicity." *Newsweek.* August 23. https://www.newsweek.com/bedeviled-ethnicity-198122.

———. 1992. "Labels Do Matter." *Newsweek.* July 26. https://www.newsweek.com/labels-do-matter-200410.

———. 2008. *One Man's America: The Pleasures and Provocations of Our Singular Nation.* New York: Crown Forum.

———. 1992. *Suddenly: The American Idea Abroad and at Home, 1986–1990.* New York: Free Press.

———. 1995. *The Leveling Wind: Politics, the Culture, and Other News.* New York: Penguin Books.

———. 1986. *The Morning After.* New York: Free Press.

———. 1978. *The Pursuit of Happiness and Other Sobering Thoughts.* New York: Harper & Row.

———. 1983. *The Pursuit of Virtue and Other Tory Notions.* New York: Simon & Schuster.

———. 1997. *The Woven Figure: Conservatism and America's Fabric.* New York: Scribner.

———. 2002. *With a Happy Eye, But…: America and the World, 1997–2002.* New York: Free Press.

Wilson, James Q. 1979. "American Politics, Then & Now." *Commentary.* February.

———. 2010. *American Politics, Then & Now: And Other Essays.* Washington, DC: The AEI Press.

———. 1997. *Moral Judgment: Does the Abuse Excuse Threaten Our Legal System?* New York: Basic Books.

———. 1995. *On Character: Essays.* Washington, DC: The AEI Press.

———. 1998. *Two Nations.* Washington, DC: The AEI Press.

Wilson, Woodrow. 1918. "Address to Congress on International Order." The American Presidency Project. February 11. http://www.presidency.ucsb.edu/ws/index.php?pid=110448.

———. 2011. *Constitutional Government in the United States.* New Orleans: Quid Pro Books.

———. 1913. *The New Freedom: A Call for the Emancipation of the Generous Energies of a People.* Garden City: Doubleday, Page & Company.

———. 1970. *The Papers of Woodrow Wilson, Volume 9.* Princeton: Princeton University Press.

———. 1925. *The Public Papers of Woodrow Wilson.* New York: Harper and Brothers.

———. 2005. *Woodrow Wilson: The Essential Political Writings.* Lanham, Md.: Lexington Books.

Winchester, Simon. 2014. *The Men Who United the States: America's Explorers, Inventors, Eccentrics, and Mavericks, and the Creation of One Nation, Indivisible.* New York: Harper Perennial.

Wister, Owen. 1902. *The Virginian.* New York: The Macmillan Company.

Wood, Gordon S. 2009. *Empire of Liberty: A History of the Early Republic, 1789-1815.* Oxford: Oxford University Press.

———. 2017. *Friends Divided: John Adams and Thomas Jefferson.* New York: Penguin Press.

———. 2011. *The Radicalism of the American Revolution.* New York: Vintage Books.

Woolf, Virginia. 1924. *Mr. Bennett and Mrs. Brown.* London: Hogarth Press.

Yarbrough, Jean M. 2012. *Theodore Roosevelt and the American Political Tradition.* Lawrence: University Press of Kansas.

Yeats, William Butler. 2008. *Collected Poems of W. B. Yeats.* New York: Collier Books.

———. n.d. "The Second Coming." Poetry Foundation. https://www.poetryfoundation.org/poems/43290/the-second-coming.

Zorach v. Clauson. 1952. 343 U.S. 306 (Supreme Court of the United States, April 27).

Zwonitzer, Mark. 2016. *The Statesman and the Storyteller: John Hay, Mark Twain, and the Rise of American Imperialism.* Chapel Hill, N.C.: Algonquin Books.

NOTES

EPIGRAPH

1   Lincoln, *Speeches and Writings 1832–1858*, 35–36.

PREFACE

1   Rees, *Our Cosmic Habitat*, ix.

INTRODUCTION

1   Chernow, *Washington: A Life*, 282.
2   Trevelyan, *The American Revolution, Volume III*, 113.
3   de Gaulle, *The Complete War Memoirs of Charles de Gaulle*, 10.
4   Hale, *Woodrow Wilson: The Story of His Life*, 153.
5   Feldman, *Scorpions*, 179.
6   Ibid., 180.
7   *Minersville v. Gobitis*, 310 U.S. 586 (1940).
8   Ibid.
9   Feldman, *Scorpions*, 184.
10   *West Virginia State Board of Education v. Barnette*, 319 U.S. 624 (1943).
11   Gottlieb, *The Dream of Reason*, xi.
12   McClay, "How to Think about Patriotism," *National Affairs*, 107.
13   Lipset, *American Exceptionalism*, 18.
14   Whitehead, *Process and Reality*, 39.
15   Trilling, *The Liberal Imagination*, xv–xvi.
16   Goldwater, *Goldwater*, 119.
17   Ibid., 154.
18   Meyers, *The Jacksonian Persuasion*, vii–viii.

19   Wister, *The Virginian*, 29.
20   Rovere, *The Goldwater Caper*, 10.
21   Barone, "The Enduring Character of Democrats and Republicans in Times of Political Change," 2010.

CHAPTER 1: THE FOUNDERS' EPISTEMOLOGICAL ASSERTION

1   Hamilton, "The Farmer Refuted, &c., [23 February] 1775," 1775.
2   Lincoln, *Speeches and Writings 1832–1858*, 82–83.
3   Coolidge, "Address at the Celebration of the 150th Anniversary of the Declaration of Independence," 1926.
4   Ibid.
5   Hamilton, "The Farmer Refuted, &c., [23 February] 1775," 1775.
6   Collections of the Massachusetts Historical Society, 436–437.
7   Handlin, *The Popular Sources of Political Authority*, 330, 327.
8   Hobbes, *Leviathan*, 69.
9   Handlin, *The Popular Sources of Political Authority*, 440–441.
10   Miller, *Errand into the Wilderness*, 2.
11   Paul, *Natural Rights Individualism and Progressivism in American Political Philosophy*, 98.
12   Ibid., 104.
13   Hobbes, *Leviathan*, 69.
14   Locke, *An Essay Concerning Human Understanding*, 218–219.
15   Bluhm, *Theories of the Political System*, 219.
16   Paul, *Natural Rights Individualism and Progressivism in American Political Philosophy*, 3–5, 9.
17   Wood, *Friends Divided*, 5, 121–122.
18   Hegel, *Hegel: Elements of the Philosophy of Right*, 21.
19   Hamilton, "The Farmer Refuted, &c., [23 February] 1775," 1775.
20   Cooke, *The Federalist,* 578.
21   Paine, *Paine: Collected Writings*, 6.
22   Hume, *A Treatise of Human Nature*, 106.
23   Hobbes, *Leviathan*, 37.
24   Paul, *Natural Rights Individualism and Progressivism in American Political Philosophy*, 114–115.
25   Ibid., 112.
26   Hamilton, "The Farmer Refuted, &c., [23 February] 1775," 1775.
27   Hayward, *Patriotism Is Not Enough*, 78, 104–109.
28   Barnett, *The Structure of Liberty*, 15.
29   Roberts, *Introduction to Political Thought*, 48.
30   Wood, *The Radicalism of the American Revolution*, 4–5.
31   Ibid., 5.
32   Ibid., 11, 23, 27, 44, 51, 61, 66.

33   Ibid., 123, 171, 189.

34   Burke, *The Works of Edmund Burke*, 444.

35   Cooke, *The Federalist*, 56–65, 347–353.

36   Mansfield, *America's Constitutional Soul*, 16.

37   Rustow, *Freedom and Domination*, 519.

38   Cooke, *The Federalist*, 347–353.

39   Lincoln, *Great Speeches*, 60–61.

40   Jefferson, "First Inaugural Address," 1801.

41   Diamond, "The American Idea of Equality," 316.

42   Ibid., 315.

43   Ibid., 316.

44   Ibid., 316, 318.

45   Ibid., 318–319.

46   Ibid., 320–321.

47   Ibid., 321.

48   Ibid., 323, 326.

49   Ibid., 329–330.

50   Cooke, *The Federalist*, 347–353.

51   Jefferson, "Thomas Jefferson to John Adams," 1813.

52   Hamilton, *Presidents*, 34.

53   Lee, *Our Lost Constitution*, 19.

54   Cooke, *The Federalist*, 28, 378.

55   Paine, *Paine: Collected Writings*, 52, 551.

56   Hartz, *The Liberal Tradition in America*, 140.

57   Kesler, *Life, Liberty, and the Pursuit of Happiness*, 82.

CHAPTER 2: THE PROGRESSIVES' REVISION

1   Wilson, *The New Freedom*, 51.

2   Drehle, *Triangle*, 1, 3, 127, 195, 214.

3   Will, "Labels Do Matter," 1992.

4   McDowell, *Reason and Republicanism*, 211.

5   Roosevelt, "Annual Message to Congress," 1938.

6   McPherson, *A Political Education*, 301.

7   Johnson, "Remarks at the University of Michigan," 1964.

8   Lippmann, *Drift and Mastery*, 267, 318.

9   Bagehot, *Physics and Politics*, 53.

10   Hayward, *Patriotism Is Not Enough*, 89.

11   Merriam, *A History of American Political Theories*, 305.

12   Fukuyama, *The End of History and the Last Man*, 65.

13   Merriam, *A History of American Political Theories*, 306–307.

14   Paul, *Natural Rights Individualism and Progressivism in American Political Philosophy*, vii.

15   Merriam, *A History of American Political Theories*, 311.
16   Cooke, *The Federalist*, 3.
17   Merriam, *A History of American Political Theories*, 311–313, 315–316, 322.
18   Beard, *An Economic Interpretation of the Constitution of the United States*, 161–162.
19   Mansfield, *America's Constitutional Soul*, 7.
20   Paul, *Natural Rights Individualism and Progressivism in American Political Philosophy*, 202.
21   Croly, *The Promise of American Life*, 53, 169, 275–279, 399.
22   Ibid., 276, 282–283, 287.
23   Ibid., 170, 278–279.
24   Croly, *Progressive Democracy*, 123, 231, 256.
25   Ibid., 124, 208–209.
26   Ibid., 210–211.
27   Ibid., 227.
28   Roosevelt, "Inaugural Address," 1933.
29   Croly, *The Promise of American Life*, 413.
30   Lippmann, *Drift and Mastery*, 267.
31   Zwonitzer, *The Statesman and the Storyteller*, 170.
32   Holmes, *Holmes and Frankfurter*, 19.
33   Holmes, *Holmes-Laski Letters*, Vol. II, 1035.
34   Farnsworth, *Farnsworth's Classical English Metaphor*, 7.
35   Holmes, *Collected Legal Papers*, 314.
36   Holmes, *Holmes-Laski Letters*, Vol. II, 1146.
37   Twain, *What is Man?*, 138.
38   Holmes, *The Path of the Law*, 27.
39   Siegel, *The Revolt Against the Masses*, 53.
40   Leonard, *Illiberal Reformers*, 13, 22, 40, 69, 109, 127.
41   Ibid., 73–74.
42   Ibid., 73, 142, 157.
43   Ibid., 110, 115.
44   Ibid., 119.
45   Zwonitzer, *The Statesman and the Storyteller*, 224–225.
46   Paul, *Natural Rights Individualism and Progressivism in American Political Philosophy*, 247–248.
47   Roosevelt, *The Works of Theodore Roosevelt*, 307.
48   Paul, *Natural Rights Individualism and Progressivism in American Political Philosophy*, 241, 246, 250.
49   Dewey, "The Future of Liberalism," 225–227.
50   Jones, *Karl Marx*, 563.
51   Marx, *Das Kapital*, 2.
52   Burke, *The Works of Edmund Burke*, Volume 3, 340.
53   Levin, *The Great Debate*, 67.
54   Dewey, "The Future of Liberalism," 227–228.

55 Locke, *An Essay Concerning Human Understanding*, 67.

56 Rousseau, *The Social Contract*, 7–8.

57 Paul, *Natural Rights Individualism and Progressivism in American Political Philosophy*, 194–195.

58 Will, *The Woven Figure*, 310.

59 Roosevelt, *The Strenuous Life*, 4.

60 Foss, *Whiffs from Wild Meadows*, 260.

61 Jefferson, *The Works of Thomas Jefferson*, 377.

62 Yarbrough, *Theodore Roosevelt and the American Political Tradition*, 99, 109, 114.

63 Turner, *Rereading Frederick Jackson Turner: "The Significance of the Frontier in American History" and Other Essays*, 74–75.

64 Yarbrough, *Theodore Roosevelt and the American Political Tradition*, vii.

65 Cooke, *The Federalist*, 349.

66 Yarbrough, *Theodore Roosevelt and the American Political Tradition*, 6–7.

67 Ibid., 11, 19.

68 Ibid., 23.

69 Roosevelt, *Theodore Roosevelt*, 357.

70 Ibid., 357.

71 Paul, *Natural Rights Individualism and Progressivism in American Political Philosophy*, 322–323.

72 Bickel, *The Morality of Consent*, 121–122.

73 Hawley, *Theodore Roosevelt: Preacher of Righteousness*, 51.

74 Ibid., 138.

75 Hawley, *Theodore Roosevelt*, 51, 138, 148.

76 Woolf, *Mr. Bennett and Mrs. Brown*, 4.

77 Wilson, *Woodrow Wilson*, 107–108, 112, 119.

78 Ibid., 40.

79 Paul, *Natural Rights Individualism and Progressivism in American Political Philosophy*, 346–347.

80 Ibid., 328.

81 Brands, *Woodrow Wilson*, 25.

82 Hayward, *Patriotism Is Not Enough*, 194.

83 Lukacs, *A New Republic*, 319.

84 Tocqueville, *Democracy in America*, 67.

85 Keller, *America's Three Regimes*, 107.

86 Cooke, *The Federalist*, 471.

87 Pestritto, *Woodrow Wilson and the Roots of Modern Liberalism*, 3.

88 Cooke, *The Federalist*, 58.

89 Pestritto, *Woodrow Wilson and the Roots of Modern Liberalism*, 6, 56.

90 Ibid., 122.

91 Ibid., 58.

92 Lincoln, *Abraham Lincoln: Speeches and Writings Vol. 2 1859–1865*, 213.

93 Ibid., 19.

94 Pestritto, *Woodrow Wilson and the Roots of Modern Liberalism*, 6, 68.

95   Ibid., 6.
96   Udehn, *The Limits of Public Choice*, 48.
97   Pestritto, *Woodrow Wilson and the Roots of Modern Liberalism*, 60.
98   Wilson, *Woodrow Wilson*, 7.
99   Pestritto, *Woodrow Wilson and the Roots of Modern Liberalism*, 8, 15.
100 Ibid., 16.
101 Ibid., 34.
102 Ackerman, *Trotsky in New York*, 1917, 157.
103 Emerson, *The Early Poems of Ralph Waldo Emerson*, 116.
104 Lincoln, *Lincoln Addresses and Letters*, 206.
105 Olcott, *William McKinley: Volume II*, 96.
106 Pestritto, *Woodrow Wilson and the Roots of Modern Liberalism*, 36.
107 Ibid., 38, 40.
108 Ibid., 35.
109 Ibid., 9.
110 Ibid., 101.
111 Ibid., 102–103.
112 Holmes, *Holmes-Laski Letters, Vol. I*, 249.
113 Pestritto, *Woodrow Wilson and the Roots of Modern Liberalism*, 34, 107.
114 Ibid., 55, 70, 74.
115 Ibid., 75, 119–120.
116 Ibid., 77, 118.
117 Ibid., 79, 113, 116.
118 Ibid., 80–81.
119 Ibid., 82–83.
120 Ibid., 85, 122, 124.
121 Ibid., 133, 136–137, 139.
122 Ibid., 157, 165, 168–169.
123 Ibid., 180, 206.
124 Ibid., 182, 207–208, 231.
125 Ibid., 212–213.
126 Ibid., 214, 229.
127 Ibid., 243.
128 Hobbes, *Leviathan*, 123.
129 Pestritto, *Woodrow Wilson and the Roots of Modern Liberalism*, 230, 232–233.
130 Ibid., 239.
131 Ibid., 254, 259, 262.
132 Ibid., 255.
133 Ibid., 256.
134 Roosevelt, "Radio Address to the Business and Professional Men's League Throughout the Nation," 1932.
135 Roosevelt, "Annual Message to Congress," 1938.
136 Roosevelt, "State of the Union Message to Congress," 1944.
137 Ibid.

138 Johnson, "Remarks Before the National Convention Upon Accepting the Nomination," 1964.

139 Kesler, *Life, Liberty, and the Pursuit of Happiness*, 49.

140 Johnson, "Commencement Address at Howard University," 1965.

141 Roosevelt, "Campaign Address on Progressive Government at the Commonwealth Club in San Francisco, California," 1932.

142 Ibid.

143 Ibid.

144 Ibid.

145 Ibid.

146 Roosevelt, "Inaugural Address," 1933.

147 Spark, *The Girls of Slender Means*, 17–18.

148 Fogel, *The Fourth Great Awakening and the Future of Egalitarianism*.

CHAPTER 3: PROGRESSIVISM'S INSTITUTIONAL CONSEQUENCES

1 Scalia, *Scalia Speaks*, 157.

2 Cooke, *The Federalist*, 60.

3 Hayward, *Patriotism Is Not Enough*, 77.

4 Heidler, *Washington's Circle*, 79.

5 Keller, *America's Three Regimes*, 54.

6 Feldman, *The Three Lives of James Madison*, 354.

7 Adams, "From John Adams to George Washington, 17 May 1789," 1789.

8 Brinkley, *The American Presidency*, 10.

9 Heidler, *Washington's Circle*, 66, 70–71.

10 Cooke, *The Federalist*, 452.

11 "Records of the Federal Convention of 1787," 1787.

12 Gregg, *The Presidential Republic*, 20.

13 Schmitt, *The Imperial Presidency and the Constitution*, 129.

14 Healy, *The Cult of the Presidency*, 1–2, 281-282.

15 Ibid., 76.

16 Ibid., 79, 124.

17 Krauthammer, "The Audacity of Vanity," 2008.

18 Healy, *The Cult of the Presidency*, 132–133.

19 Lukacs, *A New Republic*, 6.

20 Keller, *America's Three Regimes*, 152.

21 Will, *The Pursuit of Virtue and Other Tory Notions*, 297.

22 Healy, *The Cult of the Presidency*, 86.

23 Cooke, *The Federalist*, 461.

24 Erler, *The American Polity*, 55.

25 Schudson, *The Good Citizen*, 6, 115, 145.

26 Ibid., 182, 185, 189.

27 Ceaser, "The Presidential Nomination Mess."

28   Madison, "Political Observations, 20 April 1795," 1795.

29   Miller, *Great Debates in American History*, Vol. II, 19.

30   Keller, *America's Three Regimes*, 89, 108.

31   Ibid., 124.

32   Moynihan, "Imperial Government," 1978.

33   Ibid.

34   Corwin, *The President*, 18.

35   Wilson, "American Politics, Then & Now."

36   Roosevelt, "Inaugural Address," 1933.

37   Bernstein, "Flashback: Barack Obama on the 'Biggest Problems We're Facing,'" 2014.

38   Paul, *Natural Rights Individualism and Progressivism in American Political Philosophy*, 79.

39   Coolidge, *The Price of Freedom*, 200.

40   Lawson, "The Rise and Rise of the Administrative State," 1994.

41   Lee, *Our Lost Constitution*, 63–65.

42   Wallison, "Decentralization, Deference, and the Administrative State," 2016.

43   Cooke, *The Federalist*, 324.

44   *Marbury v. Madison*, 5 U.S. 137 (1803).

45   Ibid., 66.

46   Ibid., 67.

47   Ibid., 70.

48   Ibid.

49   Lee, *Our Lost Constitution*, 71, 75.

50   Cooke, *The Federalist*, 421.

51   Lee, *Our Lost Constitution*, 69–70.

52   Silverglate, *Three Felonies a Day*, xlx.

53   Lee, *Our Lost Constitution*, 82.

54   Will, *The Leveling Wind*, 72.

55   Keller, *America's Three Regimes*, 232.

56   DeMuth, "The Bucks Start Here," 2013.

57   Ibid.

58   Ibid.

59   Goldfarb, "Obama Administration Pushes Banks to Make Home Loans to People with Weaker Credit," 2013.

60   DeMuth, "The Bucks Start Here," 2013.

61   Ibid.

62   Ibid.

63   DeMuth, "The Regulatory State," 2012.

64   *Department of Transportation v. Association of American Railroads*, 575 U.S. __ (2015).

65   Wilson, *Woodrow Wilson*, 242.

66   Cooper, "Confronting the Administrative State," 2015.

67   Ibid.

68   Sasse, "Senator Ben Sasse's Maiden Speech," 2015.

69   Kosar, "How to Strengthen Congress," 2015.

70   McClintock, "How and Why the Senate Must Reform the Filibuster," 2017.

71   Cost, "Fix the Filibuster," 2015

72   Kennedy, "Annual Message to the Congress on the State of the Union," 1962.

73   Kosar, "How to Strengthen Congress," 2015.

74   Niskanen, *Reflections of a Political Economist*, 131–132, 134.

75   Cooke, *The Federalist*, 313.

76   DeMuth, "Repairing Our Fractured Politics," 2018.

77   Cooke, *The Federalist*, 349.

78   *Gutierrez-Brizuela v. Lynch*, 14-9585 (2016).

CHAPTER 4: THE JUDICIAL SUPERVISION OF DEMOCRACY

1   Jackson, "The Task of Maintaining Our Liberties," 1953.

2   Kass, *Leading a Worthy Life*, 383.

3   Keller, *America's Three Regimes*, 38.

4   Holzer, *The Supreme Court Opinions of Clarence Thomas, 1991–2011*, 4.

5   Sandefur, *The Conscience of the Constitution*, 2.

6   Ibid., 6–7.

7   *West Virginia State Board of Education v. Barnette*, 319 U.S. 624 (1943).

8   Smith, *John Marshall*, 171.

9   "English Translation of Magna Carta," 2014.

10   Sandefur, *The Conscience of the Constitution*, 13.

11   Washington, "Letter of the President of the Federal Convention," 1787.

12   Feldman, *The Three Lives of James Madison*, 75.

13   Paul, *Without Precedent*, 26–27.

14   Cooke, *The Federalist*, 313.

15   Ellis, *The Quartet*, 150–151.

16   *Perez v. Brownell*, 456 U.S. 44 (1958).

17   Cooke, *The Federalist*, 526–527.

18   Madison, "Rights," 1789.

19   Cooke, *The Federalist*, 251.

20   Boorstin, *The Genius of American Politics*, 1–2.

21   Barnett, *Our Republican Constitution*, 23, 34.

22   Ibid., 21, 23.

23   Ibid., 19, 21.

24   Barnett, "Is the Constitution Libertarian?" 2009.

25   Barnett, *Our Republican Constitution*, 160–161.

26   "The Nomination of Elena Kagan," 2010.

27   *The Congressional Register*, Vol. II, 197.

28   Sandefur, *The Conscience of the Constitution*, 14–15, 163.

29   Magnet, "The Founders' Grandson, Part II," 2018.

30   Hayward, *Patriotism Is Not Enough*, 145, 168.
31   Lincoln, "Fragment on the Constitution and the Union," 1861.
32   *Fletcher v. Peck*, 10 U.S. 87 (1810).
33   *Lochner v. New York*, 198 U.S. 45 (1905).
34   Bernstein, *Rehabilitating Lochner*, 29.
35   Ibid., 29–33.
36   Ibid., 12, 34.
37   Ibid., 35–36.
38   Ibid., 36.
39   Ibid., 56–57.
40   Ibid., 96.
41   Ibid., 78–79.
42   Ibid., 36, 85, 92.
43   Ibid., 122.
44   Ibid., 36.
45   Bork, *The Tempting of America*, 49.
46   Sandefur, *The Conscience of the Constitution*, 84.
47   Wood, *Empire of Liberty*, 491–492.
48   Ibid., 492–493.
49   *Trop v. Dulles*, 356 U.S. 86 (1958).
50   "Speech Acts," 2014.
51   Bailey, *First Philosophy*, 625.
52   Balkin, *Living Originalism*, 4, 7, 11–14, 16, 257.
53   Ibid., 28.
54   McConnell, "Originalism and the Desegregation Decisions," 1995.
55   McConnell, "The Originalist Justification for Brown," 1995.
56   Souter, "Text of Justice David Souter's Speech," 2010.
57   Ibid.
58   Ibid.
59   Ibid.
60   Ibid.
61   Ibid.
62   Ibid.
63   Ibid.
64   Ibid.
65   Ibid.
66   Ibid.
67   Paul, *Natural Rights Individualism and Progressivism in American Political Philosophy*, 272.
68   "The Final Trump-Clinton Debate Transcript," 2016.
69   Lincoln, "Inaugural Address," 1861.
70   Bork, *The Tempting of America*, 190.
71   *Wickard v. Filburn*, 317 U.S. 111 (1942).
72   Ibid.

73   *United States v. Lopez*, 514 U.S. 549 (1995).

74   Ibid.

75   Ibid.

76   Leuchtenburg, *The Supreme Court Reborn*, 220, 236.

77   Holzcr, *The Supreme Court Opinions of Clarence Thomas, 1991–2011*, 43, 46.

78   *Polish National Alliance v. Labor Board*, 322 U.S. 643 (1944).

79   Cooke, *The Federalist*, 523.

80   Bickel, *The Least Dangerous Branch*, 16, 18.

81   Burke, *The Works of Edmund Burke, Volume 3*, 112.

82   Cooke, *The Federalist*, 396.

83   Somin, *Democracy and Political Ignorance*, 17.

84   Ibid., 19–20, 56, 220.

85   Blair, *A Journey*, 70.

86   Fisher, "Searching for Explanations," 2015.

87   Somin, *Democracy and Political Ignorance*, 143.

88   *Gitlow v. New York*, 268 U.S. 652 (1925).

89   McCloskey, *The Bourgeois Virtues*, 395, 397.

90   Mansfield, *America's Constitutional Soul*, 156.

91   Jackson, "The Task of Maintaining Our Liberties," 1953.

92   *The Yale Biographical Dictionary of American Law*, 42–43.

93   Hayward, *Patriotism Is Not Enough*, 167.

94   Sandefur, *The Conscience of the Constitution*, 5.

95   Ibid., 6.

96   Ibid., 33, 57, 116, 121.

97   Breyer, *Making Our Democracy Work*, 79.

98   *Robinson v. Crown Cork and Seal Company*, 06-0714 (2010).

99   *Marbury v. Madison*, 5 U.S. 137 (1803).

100   *Robinson v. Crown Cork and Seal Company*, 06-0714 (2010).

101   Ibid.

102   Cooke, *The Federalist*, 353.

103   Epstein, "Beware of Legal Transitions," 2003.

104   "Nashville Limos," 2011.

105   "Louisiana Florists," 2004.

106   "Louisiana Caskets," 2010.

107   *Powers v. Harris*, 03-6014 (2004).

108   Keller, *America's Three Regimes*, 96.

109   Brandeis, *Letters of Louis D. Brandeis*, 344–345.

110   Jackson, "The Task of Maintaining Our Liberties," 1953.

CHAPTER 5: POLITICAL ECONOMY

1   Hayek, *The Fatal Conceit*, 76.

2   Emerson, *Lincoln the Inventor*, 14.

3   New York (state), *The Speeches of the Different Governors to the Legislature of the State of New York*, 154, 237.

4   Hamilton, "Annapolis Convention. Address of the Annapolis Convention, [14 September 1786]," 1786.

5   *Cohens v. Virginia*, 19 U.S. 264 (1821).

6   Meinig, *The Shaping of America*, 399.

7   McPherson, *Battle Cry of Freedom*, 11–12.

8   Wilson, *Constitutional Government in the United States*, 26.

9   Gordon, "The Little Miracle Spurring Inequality," 2014.

10   Winchester, *The Men Who United the States*, xvi–xix.

11   Ibid., xxiv, 255, 258.

12   Green, *Winning Back America*, 81.

13   Bradford, *History of Plymouth Plantation, 1620–1647*, 299–301.

14   Fukuyama, *The Origins of Political Order*, 65.

15   Will, *Suddenly*, 12.

16   Fogel, *The Fourth Great Awakening and the Future of Egalitarianism*, 11, 58–59, 166.

17   Lindsey, *The Age of Abundance*, 32–34.

18   McCloskey, *Bourgeois Equality*, xiv–xv, xxiii.

19   McCloskey, *The Bourgeois Virtues*, 4.

20   McCloskey, *Bourgeois Equality*, 202–203, 205.

21   Blackstone, *Commentaries on the Laws of England*, Volume 2, 261.

22   Fukuyama, *The End of History and the Last Man*, 265.

23   McCloskey, *Bourgeois Equality*, 203, 207.

24   Smith, *The Theory of Moral Sentiments*, 29.

25   McCloskey, *The Bourgeois Virtues*, 410.

26   Tulis, *Legacies of Losing in American Politics*, 34, 147–148.

27   Gottlieb, *The Dream of Reason*, 266.

28   Cooke, *The Federalist*, 419.

29   Locke, "Second Treatise," 1689.

30   Tocqueville, *Democracy in America*, 231.

31   Keller, *America's Three Regimes*, 25.

32   McCloskey, *Bourgeois Equality*, 49.

33   Jefferson, *Thomas Jefferson*, 124.

34   Hamilton, "Alexander Hamilton's Final Version of the Report on the Subject of Manufactures," 1791.

35   Cooke, *The Federalist*, 471.

36   Zwonitzer, *The Statesman and the Storyteller*, 122.

37   Feldman, *The Three Lives of James Madison*, 344.

38   Hamilton, *Life of Alexander Hamilton*, 584.

39   Tocqueville, *Democracy in America*, 331–333.

40   Stevens, *American Political Thought*, 76.

41   Madison, *The Writings of James Madison*, 365.

42   Polanyi, *The Great Transformation*, 147.

43 Kennedy, "Commencement Address at Yale University," 1962.
44 Nixon, "Inaugural Address," 1969.
45 Smith, *An Inquiry Into the Nature and Causes of the Wealth of Nations*, 311.
46 Hayek, "The Use of Knowledge in Society," 1945.
47 Ibid.
48 Smith, *An Inquiry Into the Nature and Causes of the Wealth of Nations*, 241.
49 Hayek, *The Constitution of Liberty*, 78.
50 Ridley, *The Evolution of Everything*, 110.
51 Hayek, "The Pretence of Knowledge," 1974.
52 Ibid.
53 Ibid.
54 Ibid.
55 Hayek, *The Fatal Conceit*, 76–77.
56 Smith, *The Theory of Moral Sentiments*, 318.
57 Hayek, *The Road to Serfdom*, 91.
58 Cochrane, "Russ Roberts on Economic Humility," 2017.
59 Gordon, *The Rise and Fall of American Growth*, 1, 37, 57–58, 287, 321.
60 Lukacs, *A New Republic*, 373.
61 Diggins, *The Proud Decades*, 349.
62 Galbraith, *The Affluent Society*, 8, 191.
63 Galbraith, *The New Industrial State*, 36.
64 Will, *One Man's America*, 35.
65 Stigler, "The Intellectual and the Marketplace," 1965.
66 Carter, "Address to the Nation on Energy," 1977.
67 Passell, "The Limits to Growth," 1972.
68 Lomborg, "Environmental Alarmism, Then and Now," 2012.
69 Ibid.
70 Tierney, "Betting on the Planet," 1990.
71 Adams, *The Works of John Adams*, 386.
72 Cowen, *The Complacent Class*, 168.
73 Ibid., 105, 149.
74 McCloskey, "The Myth of Technological Unemployment," 2017.
75 McCloskey, *The Bourgeois Virtues*, 263.
76 Roosevelt, "Radio Address to the Business and Professional Men's League Throughout the Nation," 1932.
77 Jackson, "Veto Message," 1832.
78 Ibid.
79 Cooke, *The Federalist*, 421.
80 Boaz, *The Libertarian Mind*, 241.
81 McCloskey, *The Bourgeois Virtues*, 263.
82 Weisman, *The Great Tax Wars*, 2–3.
83 Ibid., 11, 57, 102.
84 Ibid., 253.
85 Ibid., 34, 258–259, 345.

86 Ibid., 281, 354.
87 Paul, *Natural Rights Individualism and Progressivism in American Political Philosophy*, 133.
88 Lincoln, *The Writings of Abraham Lincoln*, 106, 110.
89 Blum, "The Uneasy Case for Progressive Taxation," 1952.
90 Kennedy, "Remarks of Senator John F. Kennedy," 1960.
91 Blum, "The Uneasy Case for Progressive Taxation," 1952.
92 Ibid.
93 Ibid.
94 Ibid.
95 Nisbet, *Prejudices*, 107–109.
96 Hirsch, *Social Limits to Growth*, 18, 20, 26, 48, 52.
97 Ibid., 49, 51.
98 Frankfurt, *On Inequality*, x, 7, 10–11, 14, 69.
99 Scheidel, *The Great Leveler*, 298–300.
100 Schumpeter, *Capitalism, Socialism and Democracy*, 67.
101 Cochrane, "Why and How We Care about Inequality," 2014.
102 Ibid.
103 Ibid.
104 Boudreaux, "Most Ordinary Americans in 2016 Are Richer Than Was John D. Rockefeller in 1916," 2016.
105 Thompson, "America in 1915," 2016.
106 Barone, *Our Nation*, 28.
107 Foner, *A Short History of Reconstruction*, 10.
108 Roosevelt, "Radio Address to the Business and Professional Men's League Throughout the Nation," 1932.
109 Roosevelt, "Inaugural Address," 1937.
110 Roosevelt, "State of the Union Message to Congress," 1944.
111 Ibid.
112 Will, *Suddenly*, 159.
113 Lincoln, "First Annual Message," 1861.
114 McPherson, *Battle Cry of Freedom*, 28.
115 Postrel, *The Future and Its Enemies*, 16, 51, 79, 91, 147.

CHAPTER 6: CULTURE AND OPPORTUNITY

1 Weisman, *Daniel Patrick Moynihan*, 3.
2 Risen, *The Bill of the Century*, 1, 189, 227–238.
3 Bork, *The Tempting of America*, 76.
4 Miller, *Great Debates in American History*, Vol. VI, 13.
5 Johnson, "Commencement Address at Howard University," 1965.
6 Duggan, "Mayor Mike Duggan Keynote Address," 2017.
7 Croly, *The Promise of American Life*, 181.

8   Roosevelt, "The Radical Movement Under Conservative Direction," 1910.

9   Obama, "Address Before a Joint Session of Congress on the State of the Union," 2013.

10   Berns, *Making Patriots*, 120.

11   Johnson, "Annual Message to the Congress on the State of the Union," 1964.

12   Hemingway, "The Snows of Kilimanjaro," 23.

13   Anderson, *Youth Employment and Public Policy*, 64–87.

14   Turow, *The Laws of Our Fathers*, 66, 247.

15   Will, *The Pursuit of Happiness and Other Sobering Thoughts*, 197.

16   Thomas, dir. *The G.I. Bill: The Law That Changed America* (video).

17   Ibid.

18   Will, *With a Happy Eye, But…*, 252–253.

19   Barone, *Our Country*, 201.

20   Wilson, *Two Nations*, 19.

21   Hodgson, *America in Our Time*, 448–449.

22   Coleman, "Equality of Educational Opportunity," 1966.

23   Hanushek, "The Impact of Differential Expenditures on School Performance," 1989.

24   "House of Representatives," 1991.

25   *Shaw v. Reno*, 509 U.S. 630 (1993).

26   Sandefur, *Frederick Douglass*, 101, 103, 108.

27   McCloskey, *Bourgeois Dignity*, 54, 57.

28   Stevenson, "Commencement Address by Adlai Stevenson," 1955.

29   Hayward, "Reagan Casts Big Shadow with Achievements," 2004.

30   Johnson, "Remarks at the University of Michigan," 1964.

31   Eberstadt, "The Great Society at Fifty," 2014.

32   Ibid.

33   Ibid.

34   White, *The Making of the President*, 365.

35   Eberstadt, *A Nation of Takers*, 8–9, 23.

36   Ibid., 43, 47–48, 56–57.

37   Ibid., 24, 53.

38   Eberstadt, *Men Without Work*, 3, 18, 27, 35, 38, 80.

39   Ibid., 41, 127, 180–181.

40   Ibid., 68, 152–154.

41   Eberstadt, "American Exceptionalism and the Entitlement State," 2015.

42   Ibid.

43   Ibid.

44   Ibid.

45   Hubbard, "Regaining America's Balance," 2013.

46   Paul, *Natural Rights Individualism and Progressivism in American Political Philosophy*, 288.

47   Wilson, *Woodrow Wilson*, 40.

48   McSmith, *No Such Thing as Society*.

49   Obama, "Remarks by the President at a Campaign Event in Roanoke, Virginia," 2012.

50   "Elizabeth Warren on Fair Taxation," 2011.

51   Okun, *Equality and Efficiency*, 42.

52   Sidgwick, *The Principles of Political Economy*, 517.

53   Mill, *Principles of Political Economy*, 212.

54   Robertson, *The Wordsworth Dictionary of Quotations*, 133.

55   Sennett, *The Hidden Injuries of Class*.

56   Ellis, *The Napoleonic Empire*, 30.

57   Bell, "On Meritocracy and Equality," 1972.

58   Rawls, *A Theory of Justice*, 86.

59   Lindsey, *The Age of Abundance*, 61, 65, 67, 78, 235.

60   "Environmental Housing and Life Styles," 1971.

61   Olson, *The Rise and Decline of Nations*.

62   Hutchinson, *Nationalism*, 104.

63   Tropman, *Strategic Perspectives on Social Policy*, 342.

64   Cloward, "The Welfare Vaudevillian," 1979.

65   Hodgson, *The Gentleman from New York*, 87.

66   Shelley, *The Poetical Works of Percy Bysshe Shelley*, 283.

67   Lippmann, *Drift and Mastery*, 267.

68   Larkin, *High Windows*.

69   Moynihan, *Came the Revolution*, 262–263.

70   Wilson, *On Character*, 1.

CHAPTER 7: THE AIMS OF EDUCATION

1   Bellow, *Mr. Sammler's Planet*, 208.

2   Washington, *The Writings of George Washington*, 11–13.

3   Roland, *Reflections on Lee*, 20.

4   Cooke, *The Federalist*, 9.

5   Ibid., 9.

6   Banfield, *Here the People Rule*, 9.

7   Cooke, *The Federalist*, 238–239.

8   Tocqueville, *Democracy in America* (Henry Reeve), 397.

9   Lukacs, *A New Republic*, 135–136.

10   Lincoln, "Inaugural Address," 1861.

11   Knox, *The Belief of Catholics*, 6.

12   Emerson, *Essays and Lectures*, 7.

13   Emerson, *The Early Lectures of Ralph Waldo Emerson*, Volume III, 288.

14   Wilson, *The Public Papers of Woodrow Wilson*, 274–276, 451.

15   Locke, *An Essay Concerning Human Understanding*, 67.

16   Scalia, *Scalia Speaks*, 66.

17   Lincoln, *Speeches and Writings, 1832–1858*, 32.

18   Mann, *Life of Horace Mann*, 83.
19   Levin, "Edmund Burke's Economics of Flourishing," 2016.
20   Dewey, *My Pedagogic Creed*, 16, 18.
21   Harrison, *The Cultural Production of Matthew Arnold*, 100.
22   Berns, *Making Patriots*, 3.
23   Ibid., 10–11.
24   Adams, "John Adams to Abigail Adams, 29 October 1775," 1775.
25   Locke, *Two Treatises on Government*, 189.
26   Locke, *The Conduct of the Understanding*, 8.
27   Paul, *Natural Rights Individualism and Progressivism in American Political Philosophy*, 5, 9.
28   Wood, *The Radicalism of the American Revolution*, 216, 236–237, 240.
29   Cooke, *The Federalist*, 419.
30   Sandefur, *Frederick Douglass*, 5.
31   Harlan, *The Degradation of American History*, xv–xix, 3.
32   Ibid., xix, xxi.
33   Lorenz, *On Aggression*.
34   Frost, *The Poetry of Robert Frost*, 325.
35   Will, *The Woven Figure*, 325.
36   Ibid., 144.
37   Levine, "Speaking for the Humanities," 1989.
38   Berns, *Making Patriots*, 79.
39   Jefferson, "From Thomas Jefferson to Benjamin Rush, 23 September 1800," 1800.
40   Jefferson, *Memoir, Correspondence, and Miscellanies*, 37.
41   Holowchak, *Thomas Jefferson and Philosophy*, 46.
42   Jefferson, *The Writings of Thomas Jefferson*, 376.
43   Boller, *Presidential Campaigns*, 112.
44   Cather, *The First Willa Cather MEGAPACK*, 377.
45   Nichols, *The Death of Expertise*, 73.
46   Truss, *Talk to the Hand*, 36, 85, 123, 164.
47   "Wellesley Statement from CERE Faculty," 2017.
48   Nichols, *The Death of Expertise*, x, 3–4, 25, 30, 35–36, 99, 118.
49   Ibid., 9, 14, 106, 203.
50   Sasse, *The Vanishing American Adult*, 212.
51   Roosevelt, *Theodore Roosevelt*, 20.
52   Will, *With a Happy Eye But…*, 184.
53   Will, *The Morning After*, 392.
54   Sasse, *The Vanishing American Adult*, 220.
55   Will, *With a Happy Eye But…*, 189.
56   Dinwiddy, *Radicalism and Reform in Britain*, 421.
57   Hughes, *Consciousness and Society*, 4, 74.
58   Ibid., 39.
59   Marx, *Das Kapital*, xvii, xix.

60 Graham, *The Spanish Civil War*, 12, 84, 86.
61 Fukuyama, *Political Order and Political Decay*, 185–187.
62 Ibid., 196–197.
63 Freedman, *Millay at 100*, 120.
64 Dienstag, *Pessimism*, 5, 118, 168, 202.
65 Ibid., 12, 17–18, 21, 40, 42, 79.
66 Ibid., 41, 79, 187, 195.
67 Ibid., 221, 270–272.

CHAPTER 8: GOING ABROAD

1   James, *Letters, Volume 3*, 282.
2   Tennyson, *Locksley Hall*, 53.
3   Nau, *Conservative Internationalism*, 164.
4   MacMillan, *Paris 1919*, 338.
5   Smith, *FDR*, 170.
6   MacMillan, *Paris 1919*, xxviii, 11.
7   Will, *One Man's America*, 32.
8   Wilson, "Address to Congress on International Order," 1918.
9   Wilson, *Woodrow Wilson*, 262–263.
10 Will, *The Leveling Wind*, 357.
11 Will, *With a Happy Eye But…*, 84.
12 Lippmann, *The Stakes of Diplomacy*, 9–10.
13 Steel, *Walter Lippmann and the American Century*, 133–134.
14 Buchanan, *Churchill, Hitler, and "The Unnecessary War,"* 109.
15 Meyer, *Pax Ethnica*, 24.
16 Will, "Bedeviled by Ethnicity," 1992.
17 MacMillan, *Paris 1919*, 42, 132, 435.
18 Ibid., 23–24.
19 Stelzer, *The Neocon Reader*, 132.
20 Nau, *Conservative Internationalism*, 172.
21 Lukacs, *A New Republic*, 319.
22 Berns, *Making Patriots*, 8.
23 James, *Letters, Volume 3*, 282.
24 Barnes, *Notes on the Book of Job*, 84.
25 "Brady's Photographs," 1862.
26 Fukuyama, *The End of History and the Last Man*, 4.
27 Miller, *Norman Angell and the Futility of War*, 9.
28 Brooke, *1914 and Other Poems*, 69.
29 Cohen, *Identities in Crisis in Iran*, 147.
30 Will, *The Pursuit of Happiness and Other Sobering Thoughts*, 23.
31 Will, *Suddenly*, 3.
32 Bullock, *Hitler and Stalin*, 633.

33   Goldhagen, *Hitler's Willing Executioners*, 23.

34   McCloskey, *The Bourgeois Virtues*, 283.

35   Fest, *Hitler*, 69.

36   Eksteins, *Rites of Spring*, 312.

37   James, *Memories and Studies*, 303.

38   Bell, *Sociological Journeys*, 327.

39   Nisbet, *Prejudices*, 22–23, 27.

40   Greenhouse, "Conflict in the Balkans," 1995.

41   Brodie, *From Crossbow to H-Bomb*, 234.

42   Will, *The Pursuit of Happiness and Other Sobering Thoughts*, 229.

43   Hakim, *War, Peace and All that Jazz*, 187.

44   Wenzi, *A Conscious Endeavor*, 146.

45   Addison, *The Works of the Right Honourable Joseph Addison*, 180.

46   Warner, *A Library of the World's Best Literature*, 141.

47   Wood, *Empire of Liberty*, 357.

48   Lukacs, *A New Republic*, 221.

49   Zwonitzer, *The Statesman and the Storyteller*, 481.

50   Lukacs, *A New Republic*, 204, 210, 213.

51   Keller, *America's Three Regimes*, 176.

52   Zwonitzer, *The Statesman and the Storyteller*, 413–414.

53   Hawley, *Theodore Roosevelt*, 138.

54   Zwonitzer, *The Statesman and the Storyteller*, 375.

55   Lukacs, *A New Republic*, 203.

56   Blum, *Woodrow Wilson and the Politics of Morality*, 89–90.

57   Dean, *Warren G. Harding*, 100.

58   Fischer, *Liberty and Freedom*, 517.

59   Morison, *The Rising Sun in the Pacific*, 210.

60   Steel, *Walter Lippmann and the American Century*, 409.

61   Stahel, *The Battle for Moscow*, 309.

62   Sandler, *The Korean War*, 233.

63   Halberstam, *The Best and the Brightest*, 667.

64   Lewis, *Main Street*.

65   Judis, *The Folly of Empire*, 11.

66   Kennedy, "Address of Senator John F. Kennedy Accepting the Democratic Party Nomination for the Presidency of the United States," 1960.

67   Johnson, "Address at Johns Hopkins University," 1965.

68   Johnson, "Annual Message to the Congress on the State of the Union," 1966.

69   Hayward, *The Age of Reagan*, 114.

70   Ibid., 108.

71   Greene, *The Quiet American*, 60.

72   Boot, *The Road Not Taken*, 223, 429–430.

73   Hayward, *The Age of Reagan*, 41, 71, 111, 154.

74   Himmelfarb, *The Moral Imagination*, 188.

75   Marlantes, "The Bloody Pivot," 2017.

76   Boot, *The Savage Wars of Peace*, xxii; Scott, *President Wilson's Foreign Policy*, 389.

77   Krames, *The Rumsfeld Way*, 117.

78   "Two Hundred and Seventeenth Day," 1946.

79   Bush, "Commencement Address at the United States Military Academy in West Point," 2002.

80   Moynihan, *Secrecy*, 179.

81   Bush, "Remarks at the American Enterprise Institute Dinner," 2003.

82   Will, *The Morning After*, 300, 383.

83   Bush, "The President's New Conference," 2004.

84   Bush, "Inaugural Address," 2005.

85   Bush, "Remarks on the War on Terror," 2005.

86   Wilson, *The Public Papers of Woodrow Wilson*, 294.

87   Nelson, *Thomas Paine*, 215–216.

88   Keller, *America's Three Regimes*, 36.

89   Fadiman, *Bartlett's Book of Anecdotes*, 321.

90   Blair, *Tony Blair in His Own Words*, 249.

91   Bush, "Remarks on the 20th Anniversary of the National Endowment for Democracy," 2003.

92   Reagan, "Address to Members of the British Parliament," 1982.

93   Rice, "National Security Advisor Dr. Condoleezza Rice Discusses War on Terror at Reagan Library and Museum," 2004.

94   Bush, "Remarks in Halifax, Canada," 2004.

95   Kennedy, "Inaugural Address," 1961.

96   Trotsky, *Literature and Revolution*, 207.

97   Stoppard, *Travesties*, 12.

98   Will, *With a Happy Eye But…*, 83.

99   Will, *Suddenly*, 73.

100   Conquest, *The Harvest of Sorrow*, 33.

101   Marx, *The Communist Manifesto*.

102   Fukuyama, *The End of History and the Last Man*, 51, 135.

103   Ibid., 3.

104   Buchanan, *Day of Reckoning*, 132.

105   Kennedy, "Inaugural Address," 1961; Buchanan, *Day of Reckoning*, 132.

106   Buchanan, *Day of Reckoning*, 132.

107   Buchanan, "The Good Neocon," 2007.

108   Jefferson, "From Thomas Jefferson to Joseph Priestley, 19 June 1802," 1802.

109   Kissinger, *World Order*, 236–237, 279.

110   Ibid., 245.

111   Ibid., 257–258, 271.

112   Kagan, *On The Origins of War*, 567.

113   Cleva, *Henry Kissinger and the American Approach to Foreign Policy*, 97.

114   Nixon, "Remarks to Midwestern News Media Executives Attending a Briefing on Domestic Policy in Kansas City, Missouri," 1971.

115   Diggins, *Ronald Reagan*, 412.
116   Hayward, *The Age of Reagan: The Fall of the Old Liberal Order*, 442.
117   Gorbachev, "Text of Gorbachev's Speech to the United Nations," 1988.
118   Reagan, *The Last Best Hope*, 20.
119   Lincoln, *Lincoln: Speeches and Writings, 1859–1865*, 6.
120   Yeats, "The Second Coming."
121   Jefferson, "Thomas Jefferson to Roger Weightman," 1826.
122   Lefever, *America's Imperial Burden*, 132.
123   Sevareid, *Not So Wild a Dream*, 115, 124–125.
124   Judis, *The Folly of Empire*, 114.
125   Berlin, *Against the Current*, 94.
126   Kagan, *On the Origins of War*, 1, 566–567, 570.

CHAPTER 9: WELCOMING WHIRL

1   Combs, *The Comedy of Democracy*, 84.
2   Twain, *Adventures of Huckleberry Finn*, 159.
3   Paul II, *Collected Poems*, 39.
4   Weeks, *Stalin's Other War*, 32.
5   Twain, *Mark Twain's Notebook*, 344.
6   Will, *With a Happy Eye But…*, 102.
7   Ratcliffe, *Concise Oxford Dictionary of Quotations*, 406.
8   Tocqueville, *Democracy in America* (Henry Reeve), 626–628.
9   Kristol, *Neoconservatism*, 134.
10   Handlin, *The Popular Sources of Political Authority*, 442–443.
11   Larson, *The Return of George Washington*, 116.
12   Jefferson, *The Writings of Thomas Jefferson, Volume 8*, 400.
13   Himmelfarb, *The Moral Imagination*, 239.
14   Matthew 22:21 KJV.
15   Berns, *Making Patriots*, 30, 33.
16   Ibid., 32, 43.
17   Jones, *The Black Book*, 61.
18   Franklin, *The Autobiography of Benjamin Franklin*, 39–40, 54.
19   Allen, *Moral Minority*, 27.
20   Adams, *The Works of John Adams*, 67, 85.
21   Allen, *Moral Minority*, 77.
22   Ibid., xii, 105, 116, 138, 142.
23   Marx, *Critique of Hegel's "Philosophy of Right,"* 131.
24   Allen, *Moral Minority*, 72.
25   Keller, *America's Three Regimes*, 40.
26   Cooke, *The Federalist*, 62.
27   Allen, *Moral Minority*, 91.
28   Paine, *The Age of Reason, Volume II*, 86.

29   Jefferson, *The Writings of Thomas Jefferson: 1816–1826*, 220.

30   Heidler, *Washington's Circle*, 34–35.

31   De Vries, *The Mackerel Plaza*, 7, 28.

32   Will, *The Morning After*, 175.

33   *Zorach v. Clauson*, 343 U.S. 306 (1952).

34   *Lynch v. Donnelly*, 465 U.S. 668 (1984).

35   Washington, "Inaugural Address," 1789.

36   Washington, "Washington's Farewell Address 1796," 1796.

37   Oshisanya, *An Almanac of Contemporary and Comparative Judicial Restatements*, 1052.

38   Eisenhower, "Religion," 1952.

39   Paul, *Natural Rights Individualism and Progressivism in American Political Philosophy*, 34–35.

40   Andrews, *Famous Lines*, 251.

41   Ehrenberg, *Civil Society*, 65.

42   Gottlieb, *The Dream of Reason*, 304.

43   Jefferson, *The Jeffersonian Cyclopedia*, 976.

44   Wood, *Empire of Liberty*, 577–587.

45   Rasmussen, *The Infidel and the Professor*, 152.

46   Adams, *The Works of John Adams*, 415.

47   Spalding, *We Still Hold These Truths*, 139.

48   Adams, "From John Adams to Mercy Otis Warren, 16 April 1776," 1776.

49   Kirk, *The Essential Russell Kirk*, 52.

50   Kirk, *The Conservative Mind*, 29–32, 62, 66, 80, 184.

51   Clarke, *The Oxford Handbook of Philosophy in Early Modern Europe*, 583.

52   Jefferson, "Thomas Jefferson to John Adams, 12 October 1813," 1813.

53   Jefferson, *The Works of Thomas Jefferson*, 210.

54   Jefferson, *The Jeffersonian Cyclopedia*, 545.

55   Jefferson, *The Writings of Thomas Jefferson, Volume II*, 103.

56   Tocqueville, *Democracy in America*, 364.

57   Sacks, "Cultural Climate Change," 2017.

58   Himmelfarb, *One Nation, Two Cultures*, 87.

59   Maxwell, "Molecular Evolution."

60   Adams, *The Education of Henry Adams*, 236–238.

61   Rees, *Our Cosmic Habitat*, xx, 60.

62   Gottlieb, *The Dream of Reason*, 205.

63   Kaku, *Einstein's Cosmos*, 61.

64   Ibid., 127.

65   Feynman, *The Character of Physical Law*, 129.

66   Kaku, *Einstein's Cosmos*, 129.

67   Freud, *The Future of an Illusion*, 99.

68   Rees, *Our Cosmic Habitat*, 75.

69   Miller, *Discovering Molecular Genetics*, 6.

70   Henley, *A Book of Verses*, 57.

71 Koestler, *The Ghost in the Machine.*
72 Ryle, *The Concept of the Mind.*
73 Snyder, *Black Earth*, 1, 4–6.
74 Updike, *A Month of Sundays*, 28.
75 Updike, *Rabbit at Rest*, 273.
76 Wilson, *Moral Judgment*, 23.
77 Wilson, *American Politics, Then & Now*, 186.
78 Sumner, *What Social Classes Owe Each Other*, 114.
79 De Vries, *The Blood of the Lamb*, 207–208.
80 Wilbur, *Collected Poems*, 30.
81 Turner, *On the Origin of Societies by Natural Selection*, 1.
82 Darwin, *The Correspondence of Charles Darwin, Volume 8*, 224.
83 Quammen, *The Reluctant Mr. Darwin*, 38, 207, 217.
84 Fadiman, *The Little, Brown Book of Anecdotes*, 343.
85 James, *The Varieties of Religious Experience*, 53.
86 Crane, *The Meaning of Belief*, 8–9, 12, 65.
87 Ibid., 11, 21.
88 Ibid., 78.
89 Greenblatt, *The Swerve*, 5–6.
90 Ibid., 7, 10.
91 Darwin, *The Correspondence of Charles Darwin*, 224.
92 Kirby, *An Introduction to Entomology*, 344.
93 Darwin, *The Origin of the Species*, 478.
94 Genesis 2:7 KJV.
95 Himmelfarb, *Victorian Minds*, 206.
96 Shakespeare, *The Tragedy of Hamlet, Prince of Denmark.*
97 Shakespeare, *The Tragedy of Macbeth.*
98 Clark, *Civilisation*, 123.

CHAPTER 10: BORNE BACK

1 Stegner, *The Sound of Mountain Water*, 201.
2 Lehman, *The Oxford Book of American Poetry*, 270–271.
3 Cooke, *The Federalist*, 3.
4 Ibid., 594.
5 Webster, *The Writings and Speeches of Daniel Webster*, 253–254.
6 Lincoln, *Speeches and Writings 1832-1858*, 28, 36.
7 Cervantes, *The Ingenious Gentleman Don Quixote of La Mancha*, 113.
8 Rhodes, *The Making of the Atomic Bomb*, 662–676.
9 *The Bhagavad Gita*, 55.
10 Lincoln, *Great Speeches*, 25.
11 Lincoln, "Address at the Dedication of the National Cemetery at Gettysburg, Pennsylvania, 1863."

12 Kristol, "The Rise of Totalitarian Democracy, by J. L. Talmon," 1952.
13 Moynihan, *Counting Our Blessings*.
14 Washington, "Circular to the States," 1783.
15 Emerson, *Emerson*, 291.
16 Hughes, *Consciousness and Society*, 171.
17 Gibbon, *The History of the Decline and Fall of the Roman Empire*, 150, 190.
18 Tocqueville, *Democracy in America*, Volume 2, 54.
19 Lincoln, *Speeches and Writings 1832–1858*, 35–36.
20 Wilson, *The Papers of Woodrow Wilson, Volume 9*, 266.
21 Berlin, *The Crooked Timber of Humanity*, 50.
22 Twain, *Adventures of Huckleberry Finn*, 199.
23 Twain, *The Writings of Mark Twain, Volume 7*, 322.
24 Thurber, "She Built Up Her Personality but She's Undermined," 1942.
25 Bates, "America the Beautiful," 1893.
26 Forman, *Our Republic*, 270.
27 Frady, *Wallace*, 11.
28 Bickel, *The Least Dangerous Branch*, 98.
29 Hammett, *The Continental Op*.
30 Bush, "Remarks on Labor Day in Richfield, Ohio," 2003.
31 Will, *Suddenly*, 167.
32 Jefferson, "First Inaugural Address," 1801.
33 Cooke, *The Federalist*, 349.
34 Novak, *A Free Society Reader*, 328–329.
35 Kristol, *The Neoconservative Persuasion*, 23.
36 Tocqueville, *Democracy in America*, 53.
37 Reagan, "Inaugural Address," 1985.
38 Rauch, *Government's End*, 269.
39 Will, *The Woven Figure*, 20.
40 Cooke, *The Federalist*, 313.
41 Swainson, *Encarta Book of Quotations*, 384.
42 Will, *The Woven Figure*, 256–257.
43 Yeats, *Collected Poems of W. B. Yeats*, 344.
44 Moynihan, *Coping*, 31.
45 Twain, *Adventures of Huckleberry Finn*, 9, 17–18.
46 Will, *The Leveling Wind*, 57.
47 Jefferson, "From Thomas Jefferson to James Madison, 20 December 1787," 1787.
48 Turner, *Rereading Frederick Jackson Turner*, 9.
49 Will, *The Leveling Wind*, 78.
50 Jefferson, *Memoir, Correspondence, and Miscellanies*, 437.
51 Hawthorne, *The Blithedale Romance*, 164.
52 Eliot, "Little Gidding."
53 Fitzgerald, *The Great Gatsby*, 180.
54 Ibid., 180.

INDEX